The Shaping
of the American Past

5**TH EDITION**

The Shaping
of the American
Past

VOLUME 1

To 1877

Robert Kelley
University of California, Santa Barbara

PRENTICE HALL, Englewood Cliffs, New Jersey 07632

Library of Congress Cataloging-in-Publication Data

Kelley, Robert Lloyd
    The shaping of the American past / Robert Kelley. -- 5th ed.
        p.   cm.
    Also issued in combined ed.
    Includes bibliographical references.
    ISBN 0-13-808361-4 (v. 1). -- ISBN 0-13-808379-7 (v. 2)
    1. United States--History.   I. Title.
    E178.1.K27   1990
    973--dc20   89-23052
                                                                CIP

Editorial/production supervision: Virginia L. McCarthy
Interior and cover design by Linda J. Den Heyer Rosa
Picture research by Anita Duncan, Judy Ball, Barbara
    Cushing Schultz, and Madge Kelley
Cover art: Bostonians reading
    news of the Stamp Act in August
    1765, colored engraving, 19th
    century. The Granger Collection.
Acquisition editor: Stephen Dalphin
Manufacturing buyer: Ed O'Dougherty

Acknowledgments of Excerpts

p. 93, from *Colony to Country, 1750–1820*, by Ralph
Ketcham (New York: Macmillan, 1974).
p. 91, by permission of Stanford University Press.
p. 171–72, by permission of University of Chicago Press.
p. 342, copyright © 1982 by The University of Alabama
Press.

© 1990, 1986, 1982, 1978, 1975 by Prentice-Hall, Inc.
A Division of Simon & Schuster
Englewood Cliffs, N.J. 07632

Printed in the United States of America
10 9 8 7 6 5 4 3 2 1

ISBN 0-13-808361-4

Prentice-Hall International (UK) Limited, *London*
Prentice-Hall of Australia Pty. Limited, *Sydney*
Prentice-Hall Canada Inc., *Toronto*
Prentice-Hall Hispanoamericana, S.A., *Mexico*
Prentice-Hall of India Private Limited, *New Delhi*
Prentice-Hall of Japan, Inc., *Tokyo*
Simon & Schuster Asia Pte. Ltd., *Singapore*
Editora Prentice-Hall do Brasil, Ltda., *Rio de Janeiro*

to Madge

Contents

3 *The Beginnings: New England* 35

4 *The Beginnings: The Middle Colonies* 50

5 *The New People: American Life and Thought in the Eighteenth Century* 66

6 The New People Seize Independence 87

7 Forming the Nation 110

8   The New Nation: The Federalist Era   127

9   The Age of Jefferson: Expansion and War   143

10   The Nationalist Era   160

11 *The Great Transformation 1815–1850: Physical and Human Dimensions*   179

12 *The Age of Jackson: A Republican Culture*   196

13   *The Age of Jackson Center Stage: The National Debate*   217

14   *Surge to the Pacific*   240

15 *Abolitionism: The Building Storm* 263

16 *The Shifting Balance: The North and the South at Midcentury* 280

17 *Disruption Begins: Bleeding Kansas* 299

18 *The Nation Splits Apart*   316

19 *The Civil War*   334

20 *Reconstruction*   359

Preliminary Remarks to the Fifth Edition

Those who write the particular kind of book which has traditionally been called a "textbook" have a special task, one few other scholars undertake: telling the whole of a particular story, in this case the story of America and its people; saying to their readers *this* is what it is important to know about this vast country, if we are to understand it and how it has come to be what it is in the 1990s. Few scholarly tasks are more important, despite its risks, or are more intellectually exciting. Trying to catch the totality of this story, in print, seeking to sketch out its entire framework and meaning, is a challenge of enduring attraction for those who like to look at the whole of things, paint large canvases on large themes, find the basic, foundational patterns, and try to explain them.

Writing a work of this kind takes a long time; typically, the first edition of *The Shaping of the American Past* was six years in the writing. What is hoped for is that the book that eventually results will have sufficient literary appeal and explanatory power to survive beyond the perilous first edition and become a work with a continuing life and presence of its own. It is, therefore, an especially lifting moment to be writing the introductory words for a fifth edition of *The Shaping of the American Past*. That since 1975 it has been in regular use in hundreds of institutions in this country and abroad, that many thousands of people have learned about America and the Americans from reading it, has been for me a continuing source of deep encouragement.*

* The names "American" and "America" bear remark. As we will later see, the people of what would become the United States of America did not choose the name for

Every year a considerable flood of new books and articles in American history appears, many of which, like every other academic, I draw upon in the teaching of my courses, while others are read and noted for the next edition. The result is that when the time for the fifth edition's writing arrived, I had selected certain key topics, presented in about fifty books of quite recent publication—most in the past five years, as listed in the chapter bibliographies—for fresh treatment, or deepening, or even entirely new presentation. In over a year's steady work I have written some 65,000 words of new narrative and analysis (making room for it by tightening and shortening elsewhere). In most cases in this edition,

themselves. Rather, it was the English in the home country who began applying the term "American" to the people of the thirteen British North American colonies long before the Revolution, in the 1740s, to set them off from those living in England itself. (They did not like sharing the name "British" with despised colonials.) The colonists thereafter seized on the term for the same purpose, and to the world at large it simply became their name from then on. During the Revolutionary uproar the British commonly referred to the thirteen colonies, collectively, as "America," and so the nation they later founded was universally named.

In our own times other peoples living in North, Central, and South America have condemned the usage as an arrogant "taking" of a name that could well apply to them, but in fact this was not how it originated. In the 1740s, of course, the rest of the peoples of the Americas were still members of the French, British, Spanish, and Portuguese empires; they would not become self-governing peoples, with names of their own, until the nineteenth century, by which time the people of the United States had been called Americans for upwards of a century.

xviii Preliminary Remarks to the Fifth Edition

my material has been at depth in a relatively few locations, rather than in the form of widely scattered shorter entries (details later).

My aim in writing *The Shaping of the American Past* has been to prepare a work of history, rather than simply the stereotypical textbook. That is, my goal—whether realized or not, only the reader of the following pages can judge—has been to write a narrative which carries the reader along by its interest and inner momentum, develops main themes and follows them from the book's opening to its conclusion, and avoids the merely encyclopedic. My purpose, too, has been to write as if I were speaking directly, face to face, to my readers, talking to them through the word processor.

In form, each broad group of chapters in *The Shaping of the American Past* scans the entire spectrum of national life in its period, carrying forward through the generations an account that brings together all of its major dimensions: ideas, public life and government, economics, social trends and relationships, the quality of American life, the westward movement and the rise of urbanization, America's relations with the outside world, and, of course, the great crises through which the American people have struggled. Seeing how all of this flows together has always absorbed me; how great organizing patterns in the story may be seen which appear early and persist through the centuries.

It is, of course, impossible to relate everything that has occurred in the American past. Necessarily, authors must select, with the result that each history has its own particular centers of emphasis. This work focuses, first of all, on America's *public* life, its *politics and public policy*. As Thucydides, one of the ancient Greek founders of history, has told us, explaining these things should lie at the center of history. I have therefore been keenly interested in paying close attention to the national public argument on the issues facing the American people over the generations; describing the kinds of peoples who followed the banners of the major political parties and why they did so; and explaining how the governing system Americans have built for making public decisions works both institutionally and in its inner dynamics. The narrative regularly traces the context, the key players, the way they defined the issues and imaged each other, and especially the differing things that, within the larger consensus, Democrats and Republicans (and their predecessors) have believed in and their deepest public values.

This last point is crucial: following the continuing argument Americans have engaged in, in the arenas of local and national politics, over what their country means and should be. It is this core debate that fuels the constant, urgent national discussions and full-scale controversies, sometimes erupting into violence and even civil war, as to how, specifically, the United States should deal with its problems, what policies it should adopt in each instance. These arguments in the United States are given special force by the fact that at its birth it proclaimed to the world in the Declaration of Independence that it was coming into being to embody certain crucial human values, among them the assertion that "all men are created equal," that their Creator has endowed them "with certain unalienable Rights, that among these are Life, Liberty, and the pursuit of Happiness." Throughout their history as a nation, Americans have struggled to find policies that express most faithfully what their country has said it stands for and represents in the world.

This brings us, of course, to the national ideology of *republicanism*, a term not to be confused with the name of a particular political party, and to the term that took its place in the twentieth century, *democracy*. In the fifth edition as in the prior two editions, throughout the narrative, right into the years of Nixon, Carter, and Reagan, I pay close attention to what people believed these concepts meant, and how they sought to give them expression in the kind of America, and world, they sought to build.

Taking American values seriously has meant, of course, exploring a story of deep paradox, for human nature is driven by angers and fears and hatreds and selfishness as well as by high visions and a readiness to sacrifice for them. The historian records a Declaration of Independence that proclaims the equality of all humankind, and then a national history filled with tragic and, too frequently, savage violations of that enduring ideal. Watched with fascination by the rest of the world, the United States has had something to prove, and it has often failed badly in doing so. The cry "hypocrisy" is regularly cast at those who proclaim their dedication to high values, and America has often heard that cry. Thus, as we shall see, it has been more or less continuously in a turmoil of self-doubt as to how well it has carried out what Americans have conceived of as their national trust.

I must confess that exploring American public life has always absorbed me—doubtless this is why my narrative focuses there—but at the same time it is a simple fact that nowhere else do all the strands that make up American life come together so openly and interconnectedly, and revealingly, as in its politics. From its beginnings the United States was the world's first mass democracy, with millions of its people participating directly in running their country, from small communities to the national capital. Uniquely in the world, politics was a *folk* activity in America, not a monopoly of a titled elite. Indeed, more than anything else its distinctively *political* culture was what marked America out from every other nation or empire in the world.

And this quality endures. Nowhere else must heads of state do what the American president must do when running for office: travel all over the nation, month after month, to be in touch with millions of ordinary people. Nowhere else are the powers of government so bewilderingly broken up into many competing and localized elements to keep them close to the people; nowhere else is government so endlessly and remorselessly harassed in the courts, its records so thrown open to public scrutiny, its very laws, made in the fifty states, subject to overturn in referenda, while floods of other laws are made directly by the people themselves, through the initiative process. It is a system that usually bewilders foreign observers, who ask, however does it keep going?

Thus, in our national politics is to be found America's national theater. The lights are almost never out; something is always on the boards. In the play Americans reveal themselves as a people, proclaim their visions, animosities, and fears. And when we explore the political culture more closely, looking to see who it is who lines up on either side within the two major parties, we see the very ethnocultural structure of American life displayed. We note the "tribes" on both sides, staring across the line at their enemies, such as Yankees and Southerners; Protestants and Catholics; whites and blacks; the Irish and the English; beer and whisky drinkers and teetotalling prohibitionists; feminists and traditionalists; the native born and the ethnic immigrant; and the deeply pious (in our own time, for example, the "Moral Majority") who believe government should listen to the teachings of the churches and control private behavior as against those who argue passionately for personal liberty, and for a complete separation between church and state—which usually translates into angry controversies, given the era, over saloons, theatres, movies and television, sexual behavior, the ways of the young, and free-swinging life styles. In this continuing struggle we see a deep and enduring confrontation: that between the "core

culture" and the minority outgroups. It is a confrontation that goes far to explain much of American history, and it is paid close attention to herein.

Life is a web without seam, so that in exploring the ethnocultural patterns within the community to see how they shape American politics we are at the same time moving over into the arena of social history, or the life of the people at large. This is the second focus of attention in *The Shaping of the American Past*: the American people themselves. One reviewer, in fact, has termed this book a work of both the "new political history" and of the "new social history." In pursuing this great subject the narrative ranges far beyond politics and public policy to explore ways of life: the relations between men and women and how these relations have evolved (so central a realm in each nation's life); the lives of working people and farmers; how the economy they have built functions; incomes and life expectancy; sexual behavior (and policy) and birthrates; what it has meant to be young in America; and what it has meant to be a member of an ethnic and racial minority. There is much herein on Native American history, into recent decades; certainly on African-American history, on Catholics and Jews and Mexican-Americans, on Asians and Italians—and a great deal on the white South, one of the book's major sub-themes. I have also returned with particular care, throughout the narrative, to regular explorations of the history of women in America.

At the same time, readers of this book will find themselves following me in explorations of what people have believed, in each era, concerning the transcendent, non-national questions: Who is God, what is our relationship to that being, what shall we believe about the purpose of life, about the natural world, about human nature itself? So, too, they will read of how the life of the mind was pursued, in differing periods of American history, how it took form in colleges and universities, and how these institutions have in their turn shaped the larger culture. That is to say, intellectual history must also be explored to get at the inner life of the American people, through time, and it forms the book's third principal focus.

Another of my concerns in *The Shaping of the American Past* is to impart a sense of how historians actually "do history," from time to time identifying for readers key areas of scholarly disagreement so that the fundamental problem of interpretation, inescapable in history writing, is not obscured. History is not a package of cold facts and explanations, set permanently in type. To explore this and other characteristics of the historical enterprise, there continues to be included a special introduction entitled "The Historian's Task."

What is new in the fifth edition of this book? To give a brief but not exhaustive overview I have done the following: examined ways of life and thought in the early Spanish empire at some length, including the crucial argument over the nature of the Indians (were they human beings?) and the ways in which slavery came to the New World (Chapter 1); given that theme more discussion when examining the English southern colonies (Chapter 2); discussed the nature of the English migration (Chapter 5); written a much-extended narrative on the actual course of the fighting during the Revolution, that powerful, dramatic, explosive story of enormous importance for all that follows (Chapter 6); spent considerable time with the fascinating new generation of Henry Clay, Daniel Webster, and John Calhoun that seized national leadership in the era of the War of 1812 (Chapter 9); and in Chapter 10 undertook my first major foray into developing one of the fifth edition's much expanded new themes, the role and nature of the Supreme Court in American life and policymaking, focusing here on the "mighty case," *Gibbons* v. *Ogden*, and its epochal impact on the long-range nature of the American national economy.

There is splendid new work on the Mexican War, and I was able this time to examine much more closely the American mind concerning that conflict, and follow the debate on who was responsible (Chapter 14). In Chapters 15 and 17 I could draw on Don Fehrenbacher's brilliant book on the Supreme Court and slavery, culminating in the *Dred Scott* case, to give the reader more in-depth understanding of how that Court reasons and behaves, and how the Constitution works. Chapters 18 and 19 dig deeper into the Southern mind, about which we have learned much recently, both before and during the Civil War, and follows more closely the question of Southern nationalism, the course of the war itself—readers will learn new things about tactics—and why (and in what mood) the South lost. In the chapter on Reconstruction (20), I have followed Eric Foner's recent magisterial study to pursue the new class relationship that had to be constructed between white persons and the freed slaves, as well as crucial issues in the Northern mind.

In the next four chapters (21, 22, 23, and 24), which concentrate on the Gilded Age, the fifth edition touches on the work ethic; it takes a considerably

more careful look at the money and banking system in these years, with particular pains to explain how it works—the "gold standard" particularly; it does the same with the tariff argument in President Cleveland's time, an argument that is now increasingly relevant, once again, with the Reagan-era debates over keeping out foreign competition; goes over to visit the Supreme Court again, in a discussion of its reaction to the "new American state" symbolized by the Interstate Commerce Commission; and takes time to examine up close, in vignette fashion, what happened in Hawaii in these decades and why it became part of America. In the chapters on the Progressive Era (26 and 27), I have followed closely the career of Robert LaFollette so as to illuminate what was called "insurgency," and the new politics of "The People" against the interests; examined the burgeoning national passion for efficiency and the conservation crusade; based on Elliot Brownlee's recently-published researches, have presented what is now an almost entirely fresh understanding of the historic income tax argument, and banking and currency, under Woodrow Wilson; and given an essentially new treatment of Wilson and Mexico, derived from Lloyd Gardner's work, which veers off considerably from the standard version.

In the New Deal chapter (31) the narrative continues the theme of coming to fresh grips with banking and currency, and it also draws on surprising new information on the extraordinarily central role of the Hoover-created Reconstruction Finance Corporation in the New Deal generally, as well as the fresh new picture of poverty in America we have been given by James Patterson. John Dower has brought us into sobering fresh contact with the peculiarly savage war between America and Japan (Chapter 32); in the Cold War the narrative takes a closer look at the crucial year of 1947 and the Marshall Plan; and presents a considerably more developed explanation of the remarkably far-sighted peace policy adopted toward Japan, as well as Eisenhower's role in bringing peace to Korea and the beginning of the CIA wars, the "new foreign policy," under that president (Chapter 33).

In the 1970s, the present edition examines at length the historic abortion decision, *Roe* v. *Wade* (Chapter 36); in the Vietnam chapter it discusses the "passionless" war, with its basis in faith in technology (Chapter 37); and the new material in the fifth edition concludes with an exploring of Reagan's second term, especially the spending-fueled boom, misuses of power through the CIA, as in the Iran-

contra scandal and the Reagan administration's obsession with secrecy, and the historic breakthrough in arms reduction agreements following the rise of Mikhail Gorbachev.

My thanks go to the professors who have used this book in their classrooms in its earlier editions and have given me advice as to improving it. Larry Madaras, Howard Community College, Carol Bresnahan Menning, University of Toledo, Ralph R. Menning, University of Montana, James T. Moore, North Harris Community College, and Joseph A. Stout, Jr., Oklahoma State University, reviewed the manuscript for this fifth edition and made helpful suggestions. I wish also to thank the students who, while learning from the book, have said that they have enjoyed reading it, and have been intrigued by its approach. Searching out the nature and meaning of the American past has been a rich learning experience for me for many years. It has been a rare privilege, in this book's several editions, to be able to share the results of that search with so many younger and older students, in practically every state of the Union and overseas.

As always, I am grateful to the staff at Prentice Hall: my long-time editor and friend, Steve Dalphin, Executive Editor, his assistant Sandra Johnson, and particularly Virginia McCarthy, who as production editor in the college division guided the manuscript with care and insight through the publishing process.

My wife, Madge Louise Kelley, has helped me in this edition even more than in the past, for the end-paper maps included in the single-volume combined edition are hers. Once more she has read everything I wrote for the present edition and given me her unfailingly prescient advice. It has been my gift, too, to have her special companionship, in this as in all other parts of our life together, and her wise advice and counsel.

Robert Kelley
Mission Canyon Heights
Santa Barbara, California

Introduction: The Historian's Task

What is the *value* of history? Why has humanity studied its history for literally thousands of years? Tribes that lack a system of writing commonly have a Rememberer whose task it is to commit to memory (by learning it from an older Rememberer in the tribe) all the important things that have happened to that people. He tells the young who they are, what their tribe has suffered through, what things they have learned, who their gods are, and the values given to them that they must follow. History, in this sense, was probably one of the earliest distinctively human activities to emerge when *Homo sapiens* made its appearance many thousands of years ago. Language and recorded memory appear to have been born together.

This is so because human beings have a sense of time—a sense that things happen in sequence, the appearance of each laying the basis for what follows. Thus, we early sensed that we cannot understand ourselves or the world surrounding us without seeing how things have evolved, over time, into what they are. This applies to the history of civilizations; it applies to the history of a town or an industry; it applies to individual lives. No one can be understood simply as he or she stands before us, having taken some intelligence test or shown us what they like or are afraid of. Rather, we instinctively ask, Where did you come from? What has happened to you? What do you do? Why? We are historians of each other in our daily lives.

All of us are imbedded in a culture, in a larger society, that has itself evolved out of the dim past into what it is now. It shapes us, just as we, during the brief span of our individual lives, shape it. The value of history, therefore, comes from its giving to us that same strong basis for understanding the culture that rears us and makes us what we are, that we acquire when we learn about the background of someone we want to be close to and work with.

The value of history lies in more practical directions as well, as we have been discovering in recent years. The nation at large is engaged in rediscovering its *local* history. Americans are tired of being mobile; the "new" is not so exciting. They want a sense of roots, and they are turning to historians to ask, How did this community evolve? Where are the marks of its past, its earlier peoples and eras, as seen in particular buildings or neighborhoods that should be restored and preserved? In city after city "old towns" are appearing, their discovery guided by painstaking research into the surviving records and artifacts.

The dimension of time: This is the historian's unique commodity. And in a country that is no longer heading into the future in such a pell-mell rush but wants to know how it came to where it is, the historian is becoming an ever more valuable person. The historical profession is no longer concerned just with teaching students in class about the past; it is also solving problems in the surrounding public scene. We are, in short, entering the era of "public history" and the "public historian."

In fact, public history as a professional field is now flourishing vigorously. Many hundreds of public historians are busily at work in such fields as historic preservation, interpretation, and museums (called "cultural resources management"); as historians in private corporations or in government agencies (examples: the Wells Fargo Bank, the Salt River Project in Arizona, and such federal departments as State, Energy, and the military, even in the Senate and the House); as researchers helping attorneys prepare cases, or as expert witnesses in court (called "litigation support"); and as contract historians using oral history and archival research methods in a wide variety of consulting situations for private or public clients (examples: in environmental impact studies, histories of firms, of land use, of water rights, or families and institutions). Increasingly, the historical method is being brought into the public process, so that in policy-making decisions, whether private or public, people may consider how in fact the problems they are dealing with have evolved into their present form, as aside from myths and hazy memories and unchallenged "stories." It is common now for historians in government and private organizations to be important resource persons in the policy-making stream. They are asked, How did this happen? What lies behind that program of ours? Why did we make a particular decision, and what are the key documents that explain it? How has this plot of land been used in the past, so that we may know whether earlier operations on it have put toxic wastes in the soil?

In the classroom, of course, academic historians have long focused their efforts on studying and explaining public policy issues in the past, often so that the present generation may understand current issues more deeply. As each generation has faced new problems, historical research has looked in new directions to explain them. When a depression occurs, economic history has flourished and many books on this topic have appeared. When civil rights became a great national problem, historians began searching in the past for the background to this issue and started writing books on black history and race relations. Now that we are concerned with changing the role of women, histories of women in our past, and of the family, have begun appearing from the book publishers. When Americans awakened to the fact that they were a world power, diplomatic history became an active field of study (which it remains today). So we have known for a long time that the value of history is in good part the help it gives us as we attempt to understand the present. On this point, we must note the recent emergence of an active subdiscipline, within history, that is called "policy history." It focuses explicitly and consciously on understanding and explaining the public process in past times, that is, what governments do and say.

History, however, is not read simply because it is "relevant." It has purposes that reach deep into the human condition. History is valuable to the educated mind because it takes us out of the present. By steeping ourselves in the history of an older time or of different peoples, we broaden the horizons of our minds. We develop a greater sensitivity to human possibilities, are humbled by the knowledge that our present culture is not the only way, or perhaps even the best way, that human beings have lived. This helps us begin to lose the present-mindedness that makes for superficial thought. In other words, we become less provincial, less inclined to think that the whole world, all of human life, is somehow exactly like—or should be like—what we see in front of us in our daily lives. In this sense, as the English historian and statesman Thomas Babington Macaulay observed, history is like foreign travel.

History serves, in short, not only specific purposes (how was the TVA built?—for we might want to build another one), but also the large purposes of giving us fundamental understandings of humanity and society: What motivates people in politics? What have our failures been, and our successes? What is it that holds us together as a people? Is life just a repetitive round, or is it evolutionary? Can we anticipate goodness or evil in humankind? In the broadest sense, history is studied because it gives us a frame of reference.

If there are many ways in which history is used, one statement holds true of all historians as they go about their work: They are trying to find out as nearly as they can what the truth is about the past. They are attempting to answer the question of what happened and what it meant.

Thus, the historian searches for the kinds of documents that will bring him or her as close as possible to the events themselves. These are called *primary source* materials, for they are produced by the people who participated in or observed the events. They include letters, diaries, speeches, news articles, testimonies of eyewitnesses, artifacts, and photographs. The historian will also look for all *secondary* sources that will help: books, articles, or reports prepared by someone else who has also studied the primary materials.

This search poses knotty problems: Are the letters genuine? Were the observers close to the event? Were they biased? Do other of their letters give a different picture? How soon after the events did they prepare their account? Are there other observers of the same events, and if so, do the accounts differ? If the document is old, what did the words commonly mean at the time they were written? If it is a secondary work, how thorough was the author's research, how impartial was he or she, and did they ask the right questions?

In short, historians test the evidence they find, using guidelines that their craft has developed over the generations. Above all, they are guided by a judicious skepticism. If the study of history teaches historians nothing else, it teaches that people usually do not fully understand or accurately report what they see. For this reason, the evidence they leave behind does not speak for itself. It usually presents a partial or conflicting story that must be sifted, analyzed, and skeptically yet sympathetically winnowed out. The person who examines historical evidence cannot just passively pile it up; he or she must penetrate it actively and search for the truth.

The problem, of course, is that all evidence is incomplete. We see everything in the past through the eyes of others, but a great deal of information is hidden even from them. Direct observation of a religious ceremony will not reveal much to the onlooker about what the ceremony means to the participants. Direct observation of a speaker will not tell us his motivations—which he may not understand himself.

Historians are hampered, too, by the fact that some activities produce documents while others do not and some societies preserve documents while others do not. A committee hearing produces documents; the dinner party held the evening before in which the committee members discussed the issue does not. The Normandy invasion produced mountains of documents; the Anglo-Saxon invasion of England, so important for all future history, was carried out by an illiterate people and is therefore almost totally beyond the reach of historians.

In short, much that is important about the past never gets written down. Historians have been compared to astronomers who gather light on the mirror of their telescopes and try to decide what the dots and flares tell them about the universe, which they cannot visit personally. Historians too cannot visit the past and must search among its physical traces to elicit the story. In their case, however, many of the heavenly bodies *they* are trying to perceive never report their presence at all!

There is another problem. The American historian Carl Becker reminded us that all perception of historical facts is set in the framework of the perceiver's experience. We cannot avoid our preconceptions; they are the lenses through which we see the world.

Each historian is alive to some aspects of the past, oblivious to others. Just as one person, walking into a crowded meeting, notices those individuals who are important to him or her and remains indifferent to the others, so historians who are by nature inclined to react to one class of evidence, while ignoring others, will assess matters differently from their colleagues. They will "see" some evidence while being blind to other materials—not through conscious bias, but simply because of the way their perceptions work. If a historian is inclined to believe that the profit motive is the key factor in what people do, then he or she will "find" money, vested interest, and wealth-seeking behind events.

In other words, scientific history—reproducing the past exactly as it was—is not the hope of the historian. Not only is the past too huge and complex, not only is the evidence it leaves behind too incomplete, but we are too subjective in our views, guard against this failing as we will.

For that matter, there is a vigorous tradition that the objectivity implied in the ideal of scientific history is not only impossible, but undesirable. It implies blandness, purposelessness, lack of commitment. The British historian Lord Acton insisted that the historian must sit in judgment upon past individuals and their actions, and that the sentences passed must be terrible and harsh. To seek only to "understand" in the light of circumstances—"The Nazis set out to kill off the Jews, and from their point of view did a good job"—is to be guilty of an inhuman and destructive relativism.

Most historians feel, however, that while such terrible events as the massacring of the Jews may be easily condemned, there is a vast range of human activities that is not as easily assessed. The act of preparing oneself to be a historian does not simultaneously endow the scholar with intellect, experience, and knowledge superior to those of the presidents and premiers who actually had the job to do. Making harsh judgments of past individuals may only betray the arrogance of ignorance. An event that seems simple to someone reading about it in a university library may actually have been extremely complex and unmanageable when it took place. One must therefore practice the historical art with appropriate prudence, and try in most cases not to take sides. Suspension of judgment is a valuable historical virtue.

It remains true, however, that complete neutrality is impossible, and that proceeding as though it were possible is a mistake. Carl Becker's view perhaps sums up best the spirit in which most historians work: Basic in their character must be a *concern* about the issues they examine, a deep involvement with the fate of the movements and ideas they describe. There cannot be, and should not be, impartial history in the sense of indifferent history.

These remarks about the subjective aspect of history should not lead to the assumption that the cumulative work of the profession is merely a collection of personal statements. Historians who are true to their craft seek always to base their work on verified facts, and they have succeeded in searching out and validating a steadily mounting quantity of factual historical data. The main point about the problem of the historians' own subjectivity and unconsciousness bias is that they must try to keep these dangers in mind and achieve as much honesty as they can. They are constantly searching for the facts that bear on the question they have asked of the past, and are continually making painful efforts to put the story together as truthfully as they can.

To the extent that history is factual, it is a social science. Historians now draw extensively upon the concepts and methods of the social sciences as they try to understand the past more deeply. From anthropologists we have taken the idea of "culture" as an organizing principle, and have focused on values, life styles, world views, and customs. Psychologists and sociologists have been looked to for theories about behavior, role theory, status and reference groups, and class and mobility.

The application of quantitative methods to historical analysis is flourishing. Here we observe historians making *collective-biography* studies: analyses of large groups of people in the past designed to uncover common and varying characteristics. The methods used include counting the frequency of concepts and words used in speeches and writings (*content analysis*); making extensive population studies (*demography*); and analyzing voting and legislative behavior by the use of statistical methods (*correlation* and *regression*). More complex procedures appear in the use of mathematical models, in what is called the new economic history, to seek answers to such questions as whether slavery was profitable. All of this counting and the use of computers goes under the general term *Cliometrics*—Clio being the ancient muse of history.

There is much controversy about the use of these procedures. In fact, there is a spectrum of opinion and practice ranging from those historians who think of themselves as social scientists and who make rigorous efforts to be scientific in their procedures, to historians who insist that they are humanists, not scientists, and that they deal with essentially unquantifiable entities when studying and recounting the doing of human beings. The gifted historian Richard Hofstadter perhaps said it best when he observed that the fresh perspective provided by the social sciences add to "the speculative richness of history. The more the historian learns from the social sciences, the more variables he is likely to take into account, the more complex his task becomes."

Ultimately, however, most historians believe that their task is not to work out the laws of human behavior (the classic goal of social scientists), but to describe that behavior faithfully in its actual individuality, its actual forms, "warts and all," as Oliver Cromwell told his portraitist to paint him. We take the whole of human life as our concern, and we try to describe its multiplicity, its variety, its stubborn resistance to being shoved into any particular formula. We are essentially pluralists, in that most historians seem, with the philosopher William James, to believe that there is always something left over that does not fit whatever scheme of interpretation is being applied; that life stubbornly and persistently flows out of our ideological containers. Reality is "manyness," and it is best seen in particulars, in actual individuals doing actual things: that is, in narrative.

Therefore, historians do not seek to cast what they describe into a rational system. It is life's unpredictability, the uniqueness of each sequence of events, the capacity life has for presenting us with inexhaustible freshness and uniqueness that history celebrates. This means that our methods cannot be entirely rational. Historians must rely on such qualities as empathy—the capacity to feel oneself into an era, to look at life from inside the other person's situation.

Readers should not be misled by the factual character of the historical account, then, into making false analogies. The historian is not only a scientist with human perspectives, but a creative artist as well. As Sir Lewis Namier has written, historians are like painters, not like photographers. They do not reproduce an exact image of the past, for they are certainly not interested just in its surface appearance. Rather, they analyze the whole, search for its essence, and paint on their canvas what is revealing and important. What matters in history, Sir Lewis observes, "is the great outline and the significant detail, what must be avoided is the deadly morass of irrelevant narrative."

It is in this sense that history is a branch of literature. The greatest practitioners call on the same resources of imaginative insight, grace and clarity of language, sensitivity to human experience, and concern with fundamental questions as do the great writers of fiction. It is, after all, the *human situation* that the historian seeks to describe.

So it is that some of the greatest historians have thought a great deal about the problems of narrative artistry. A brilliant producer of narrative history, Thomas Babington Macaulay, wrote that "history has its foreground and its background; and it is principally in the management of its perspective that one artist differs from another." The selection of detail by which to hint at the whole is extremely important. The portraitist does not depict every pore in the subject's skin, but rather its hue; not the eye entire, but its aspect. History, George Macaulay Trevelyan insisted, is "a tale." It must therefore be as full as life. It must flow; narrative must be its bedrock. The tale must show us past events as if they were fresh, as if we were participants. How is this achieved? By presenting the facts of the past not narrowly, but in their full emotional and intellectual value. This requires that historians have "the largest grasp of intellect, the warmest human sympathy, the highest imaginative powers."

History, then, is at once science and art. This is an ambivalent and precarious condition. Perhaps the perceptive words of the great German historian Johann Gustav Droysen strike closest to the heart of the matter. For all its faults, Droysen remarked, "history is Humanity's knowledge of itself. It is not 'the light and the truth,' but a search therefore. . . ."

About the Author

ROBERT KELLEY

Since he joined the faculty at the University of California, Santa Barbara, in 1955, the focus of Robert Kelley's work has been to search out the larger patterns in the American experience by looking at the whole of it, from its colonial beginnings to the present. He has many times given the year-long freshman survey in United States history at UCSB; his advanced and graduate courses in the history of American politics and public policy, and in intellectual history, explore U.S. life from the Revolution to the near present; and his principal scholarly writings have also examined long spans of that history, on occasion within a comparative framework. As the central project in this long undertaking he has written, and in the light of recent scholarship regularly thinks through again and rewrites, *The Shaping of the American Past*, now in its Fifth Edition.

Professor Kelley is an active participant in the emerging sub-discipline of "policy history," contributing to its theory and content in essays in the *Journal of Policy History* and *The Public Historian*, and most recently in his book *Battling the Inland Sea: American Political Culture, Public Policy, and the Sacramento Valley 1850–1986* (UC Press, Berkeley, Los Angeles, and London, 1989). Currently, he teaches in a new undergraduate major at UC Santa Barbara in the History of Public Policy, and in a doctoral program in the same field, both of which he planned and established.

Dr. Kelley has also been since 1963 a consulting historian and expert witness on the history of water resource policy and management in California. Learning in this work of the power of the historical method in public affairs, in 1975 he conceived the term and concept of "public history" to refer to all the many things historians do in the community at large—from historic preservation planning to litigation support, contract histories, and policy studies—and founded UCSB's graduate program in public historical studies, which now has more than ninety alumni in many professional employments. Public history has since become a national and international movement.

Professor Kelley has been an invited USIA lecturer in various centers and universities in India (September, 1986), and a Fellow of the National Endowment for the Humanities (1975–76), of the Guggenheim Foundation (1982–83), and of the Woodrow Wilson International Center for Scholars (1982–83). In the spring semester of 1979 he and his wife Madge Louise Kelley, a writer, calligrapher, and cartographer, were in residence at Moscow University in the USSR, where he was sixth Fulbright professor of American history. (See his: "Teaching United States History at Moscow State University, 1979," in Lewis Hanke, ed., *Guide to the Study of United States History Outside the U.S., 1945–1980* [White Plains, N.Y., 1985], I, 102–117.)

His published writings include: *The Transatlantic Persuasion: The Liberal-Democratic Mind in the Age of Gladstone* (Knopf, N.Y., 1969; Transaction Publishers, Rutgers, 1989); "Ideology and Political Culture from Jefferson to Nixon," *The American Historical Review* [Bicentennial Essay], 82 (June 1977), 531–62; *The Cultural Pattern in American Politics: The First Century* (Knopf, N.Y., 1979; paperback edition, University Press of America), which has appeared in Spanish as *El Modelo Cultural En La Politica Norteamericana* (Fondo de Cultura Economica, Mexico City, 1985), and in Japanese as *Amerika Seijibunkashi* (Bokutakusha, Tokyo, 1987); "Comparing the Incomparable: Politics and Ideas in the United States and the Soviet Union," *Comparative Studies in Society and History: An International Quarterly* 26 (Oct. 1984), 672–708; "The Interplay of American Political Culture and Public Policy: The Sacramento River as a Case Study," in *Journal of Policy History*, I (Jan., 1989), 1–45; and *Gold vs. Grain: The Hydraulic Mining Controversy in California's Sacramento Valley* (Arthur H. Clark, Glendale, CA, 1959).

The Shaping
of the American Past

1

The Old World and the New World

TIME LINE

Ca. 25,000 B.C.	North Asian peoples begin three migrations into the Americas
Ca. A.D. 1000	Norsemen reach and briefly settle Newfoundland
Ca. 1300	Nahua-speaking peoples conquer and settle the Valley of Mexico
1430	Portuquese begin voyages down western coast of Africa
1492–1504	Voyages of discovery by Cristoforo Colombo; conquest of new peoples begun by Spain
1493–94	Papal bull and Treaty of Tordesillas
1497–98	Giovanni Caboto explores North American coast
1499–1501	Amerigo Vespucci realizes newly discovered lands are a New World
1509–47	Reign of King Henry VIII over England; Protestant Reformation takes place in that country
1519–24	Hernando Cortes invades and conquers Aztec Empire
1520s	European diseases begin bringing death to North American peoples
1524, 1534–35	Voyages of Giovanni da Verrazano and Jacques Cartier establish

	French claim to major segment of North America
1558–1603	Reign of Queen Elizabeth I; Ireland conquered by England after 1565
1584	First English attempt to settle colony of Virginia
1607	Jamestown founded
1603–49	Reigns of Stuart kings James I and Charles I under Charles I (1625–49) Puritan-Anglican friction mounts
1542–49	English Civil War: Puritans behead Charles I
1649–60	Puritan Commonwealth in England under Oliver Cromwell
1660–88	Stuart Restoration, reigns of Charles II and James II: Traditional constitution revived
1688	Glorious Revolution; William and Mary given throne by now-dominant Parliament
1689	Bill of Rights: Parliament supreme in British constitution
1707	England, Wales, and Scotland form United Kingdom
1810	Latin American wars of independence begin

HISTORY IN AN INDIVIDUAL LIFE

ELIZABETH I

She was twenty-five years old, tallish, red-haired, well-educated. And tough. Her mother, Anne Boleyn, had been beheaded at the order of her father, and her own life, which had included a stay in the Tower of London with execution talked of, had often been in danger. Now, seasoned and wary, on November 17, 1558, she became Elizabeth, Queen of England.

What a position for a woman! Before her, only two women had ruled England: her half-sister Mary, who had just died after a short and disastrous reign; and Matilda, an equally unsuccessful monarch centuries before. England was much torn within, having gone through the turmoil of its own Protestant Reformation. Catholic Spain and France threatened to overwhelm the island, intriguing through the Irish and the Scots. Many predicted that Elizabeth, to protect her realm and herself, would soon marry some powerful continental figure and subside into the woman's quiet role.

But marry she did not. Elizabeth remained the Virgin Queen, waving her marriageability tantalizingly in diplomacy while really marrying the English people. She loved them, and they her. She admired her father, Henry VIII, and was determined to be a great prince like him: authoritative, subtle, skilled in picking brilliant men to be her officers of state and in controlling them, and at the same time a power in Europe and the world. Thirty years into her reign the pope said admiringly, "She is a great woman; and were she only Catholic she would be without her match. . . . Just look how well she governs; she is only a woman, only mistress of half an island, and yet she makes herself feared by Spain, by France, by the [Holy Roman] Emperor, by all." An actress in every circumstance, filled with a relish for life, Elizabeth was so remarkable a monarch that her personality and her forty-five-year reign (1558–1603) have fascinated the English people more than those of any other of their sovereigns.

Elizabeth was urged to be the first British monarch to establish a great empire based on the sea, and in truth she was interested in everything having to do with America. In the 1570s she encouraged (and invested her own money in) voyages of exploration to North America, and sent Sir Francis Drake around the world in the *Golden Hind*, an electrifying event to all Europe. Then in 1585 she helped to finance the first attempt to settle the colony named in her honor, Virginia. Meanwhile, Elizabeth encouraged the arts and sciences, which reached a brilliant flowering in her years. She was Edmund Spenser's *Faerie Queene*, and William Shakespeare, that man of prodigious vitality and keen human insight, was a favorite. Elizabeth became identified forever with the awakening of the English, with their bursting outward to all the world in all ways. There was an *energy* in Elizabethan England that seemed to find its origin most of all in the great Queen.

The Context: Vexed and Troubled Englishmen

There were about 4 million of them, living mainly in thousands of villages in the south of England, and they were hungry all the time. It was the year 1600, Elizabeth was still on the throne, and as usual, famine was a constant fear. In England's small cities and in great London, with its 300,000 souls, food could normally be found, but practically everyone lived in the country, just above the subsistence level. Even when food was available, for the ordinary English it was just bread and cheese, with some fish if the villager lived near a river. "We seldome eat to please the palate, or satisfie appetite," a countryman wrote, "onely eate to live, give nature her due."

The low-roofed cottages of the country people were cold, and wood was getting increasingly hard to find. Villagers burned everything they could find, even turf and cow dung. "Start in August," they were warned, "to find firewood for winter," for it was precious and closely guarded. In fact, only during the summer did the English keep consistently warm. They usually went about their homes and work with blue fingers and chapped lips. Bathing was unheard of, and people tried to make sure that the single garment they wore more or less year-round was thick and heavy. When after 1607 the English learned of the new colony in Virginia, with its mild southern climate, thick forests, and unlimited supplies of firewood, it sounded attractive indeed. Even New England looked warm. "Here," wrote a New Englander, "we have plentie of Fire to warme us . . . nay all Europe is not able to afford to make so great Fires as New-England. . . . Here is good living for those that love good Fires."

The English were often sick—deathly sick. Divorces were rare simply because wives and husbands commonly died after a few years, either in childbirth, or of colds which went into pneumonia, or of the bloody flux (dysentery), the pox, measles, tuberculosis, typhoid, venereal disease, bubonic plague—which periodically erupted and swept through the towns and countryside—or of endless other fatal visitations. Farm workers broke bones, died of strangulated hernias from heavy lifting, or were crushed under falling trees. Deformed bodies, crooked legs and feet, snaggle toothed mouths, blind eyes, unsightly skin diseases were common. People knew nothing of the connection between cleanliness and disease. Streets in the towns were choked with filth. Even so fastidious a Londoner as the diarist Samuel Pepys had to be combed for lice every night. How long did the English live? Life expectancy was about thirty years.

For reasons not yet fully understood, the European economy was slowly rising in wealth, so that the standard of living, grim as it was for most people, was rising with this tide. As appears universally to be the rule, with improving conditions came rising expectations. Many in England were no longer content with the kind of lives they and their parents and forebears had always known. Of hardworking, ambitious men who struggled to get ahead and rise out of humble condition, there were many examples. Yeomen farmers (the rural middle class), the gentry, and townspeople acquired more money and began gambling more, buying finer clothes, and building finer houses. Certainly they were drinking more; drunkenness was practically epidemic.

For the great mass of the English people, life was hard. Few owned the land they tilled, and many were being expelled from it to make room for sheep raising. As we will see in the next chapter, alarming economic changes sent thousands wandering the roads and byways. The ancient name Merrie England was now a mockery. Clearly, the future seemed to hold little for most people. In this mood, many of the English watched in growing interest as some of the kingdom's elite launched overseas ventures of colonization, for they were reaching a historic decision: They were being seized by the idea of leaving England to migrate abroad, looking for a better way of life.

The Other "Old World" Beyond the Western Horizon

Perhaps 30,000 years before the English began to be stirred by a migratory urge, the same impulse had moved small bands of North Asian peoples living in the vast watershed of the river Lena in eastern Siberia. Though they knew it not, as these wanderers drifted to the north and east they were heading toward one of the human race's epochal discoveries. Far over their eastern horizon lay two great unpeopled continents covered as far as the eye could see by immense shaggy forests and vast sweeping grasslands, and teeming with game.

The globe was then creaking under the weight of titanic ice sheets so large that the world's oceans, denied the water held in the ice packs, dropped in elevation perhaps 300 feet. Thus, when these bands arrived at the site of the present Bering Strait, a body of water now some 50 miles across that separates Alaska from Siberia, what lay before them was a land bridge, bared by the shrunken seas. Trekking across it, they entered the vast unoccupied continental archipelago on the other side. And so, on some doubtless raw and blustery day of far northern cold and overcast skies, what are now called the Americas were discovered by humankind, and their exploration and settlement begun.

The new arrivals were a hunting and gathering people with coppery skin, dark eyes, wide cheekbones, and straight black hair who shared, probably, a common language. It took them some fifteen thousand years of southward migration to spread a thin film of humanity all the way to the southern tip of the Americas, at Cape Horn. In this long journey they traversed and settled two continents some 16 million square miles in extent—a land area a third larger than all of Africa. At the same time, they evolved into literally thousands of ethnic groups. Each had its own language and occupied its particular territory, perhaps as small as a tiny valley or as wide as a great expanse of plains. Behind the original migrants came two more waves from northeastern Siberia. One arrived between twelve and fourteen thousand years ago to settle the western coastal and mountain region and the interior plains of present-day Canada (and the northwestern United States). The third and last wave, making its appearance perhaps three thousand years later, became the Aleut, Inuit, and Eskimo of the far north.

The world of these many native American peoples was not a fixed and peaceful one, but a scene of movement and conquest. High in what is now called the Valley of Mexico, for example, during the time of the European Middle Ages we observe Nahua-speaking peoples wandering in from the north and west. They found a rich and densely settled agricultural valley, and became its conquerors. By the time of the European fourteenth century, the Nahua were building on islands in Lake Texcoco a capital city for their empire which they called Tenochtitlán, now Mexico City.

Over the next two centuries the empire of the Nahua, or Aztecs, extended far out of the Valley of Mexico. It forced regular payment of tribute from nearby societies of highly skilled farming peoples, among them the Zapotecs, Huastecas, and Otomies. Scholars differ as to how many people lived in the Aztec empire at the opening of the 1500s, but it held at least 10 million and perhaps as many as 25 million souls. Other great civilizations also occupied the two continents, among them the Incas of Peru. We shall here look for a moment at the Nahua to get a sense of life in what by the European sixteenth century was the other of the globe's Old Worlds.

The Nahua Before Conquest

The Nahua of the Aztec empire evolved a complex civilization, despite their lack of a beast of burden (everything had to be carried by human beings) and their failure to develop the concept of the wheel as a machine. Their astronomical calculations and mathematics were sophisticated, their calendar was more accurate than that of the Europeans, and their rich agriculture often made use of irrigation.

In one of the great food discoveries for humankind, the peoples of Mesoamerica—a term referring to southern Mexico and Central America—developed the maize plant, or what North Americans call corn, as their principal crop. Combining it in many dishes with beans, they had a nutritionally complete diet which still remains their staple fare. (The potato was also developed, but in a region to the south of the Aztec empire.) Amazingly creative in food development, the Mesoamerican peoples also had peppers, squash, tomatoes, chocolate, and even cotton. They made paper, had a hieroglyphic form of writing, and evolved exquisite crafts in metalwork, jewelry, pottery, and textiles.

Great temples, pyramids of astonishing size, and elaborate urban architecture were key elements in Aztec life. Their building required the disciplined, organized labor of thousands of workers. Every town, of which there were many, had its market square, and trade was vigorous. Tenochtitlán at the opening of the sixteenth century held perhaps 300,000 people, and tens of thousands of them daily attended the great markets. Though the peoples of Mesoamerica were mainly vegetarians, in market stalls they could also buy the flesh of wild beasts and fowl, and fish and crustaceans. Behind this many-sided daily life lay an intricate system of law and a judiciary; a large governmental bureaucracy and professional army; a powerful monarchy and aristocracy; and a vast priest-hood based in the ritual of human sacrifice, which put thousands of people to death annually on the priests' stone altars, their hearts ripped out with ob-sidian knives while still beating and consigned to holy flames.

Europe Discovers the Wide World

A train of events was underway, however, that would bring a far greater horror than human sacrifice to the Nahua. In the 1400s that part of the human world that we term Western Civilization—essen-tially, the many different peoples of Europe—was preparing to burst out from its physical boundaries into what geographers call the *World Ocean.* Here, in the ensuing centuries, that powerful culture would flow out worldwide to profoundly reshape, di-rectly or indirectly, all the other peoples of the globe.

It was from the far southwestern tip of Europe that this outward-reaching first took place. Since 1430 a small country located there, Portugal, had been sending exploring vessels southward along the Afri-can coast. They were looking for a direct route to Asia, or what Europeans called "the Indies." That fabled region was by their standards fabulously rich and civilized. It produced a lustrously beautiful cloth called silk, and out of the Indies also came the spices that made unrefrigerated meats palatable. In 1488 Bartholomeu Dias rounded the Cape of Good Hope, Africa's southern tip, and in 1498 Vasco da Gama actually reached India.

Meanwhile, a visionary sailor from the northern Italian city of Genoa, Cristoforo Colombo (Chris-topher Columbus), had been seized with a much bolder idea: heading directly westward from Euro-pean waters to the Indies. Long before, westward voyages had in fact been made. In the ninth century, Norsemen had taken over Iceland from earlier Celtic settlers, and about the year A.D. 1000, at a time when the northern climate was relatively mild, had gone farther to establish farming villages on the western Greenland coast. Then, under Leif Ericson, the Norsemen had ranged the coast of Labrador and Newfoundland to settle a tiny village on the lat-ter's north coast.

Soon, however, the Vinland settlement, as they called it, disappeared. As the climate grew

Columbus, taking possession of the new country, confidently called the natives "Indians." To his death he believed he had reached Asia.

colder, the colonies on the Greenland coast also vanished, and the mists and storms west of Iceland again hid the western lands. Indeed, Europeans to the south were unaware of these voyagings, whose existence is known to us primarily through modern discoveries in ancient Viking heroic sagas.

The Greeks had known in antiquity that the world is a sphere, and by Columbus's time this knowledge had revived among educated Europeans. Therefore the idea of a route such as Columbus had in mind was not theoretically inconceivable. The distances, however, were felt to be impossibly huge, for scholars estimated the earth to be about 20,000 to 24,000 miles around (not far off the actual figure of 24,902). Columbus disagreed, for he had a misconception of historic proportions in his head: After poring over ancient writings and making his own calculations, he became convinced that the world is much smaller than was generally believed. In his mind's eye, therefore, he placed Japan in about the location of present-day Cuba. Filled with excitement, in 1484 he asked the king of Portugal to support a westward voyage to the Indies. When the Portuguese refused, he turned to the Spanish. After years of steady pleading, in 1491 Christopher Columbus finally persuaded Queen Isabella. She entitled him Admiral of the Ocean Sea, and sent him on his enterprise westward.

He was heading out into an immense elliptical basin several thousand miles across. Within it, as geographer D. W. Meinig writes,

> the ocean currents move clockwise, accompanied by relatively steady northeasterly trade winds on the south and the much more variable but prevailing westerly winds in the north. Mariners [after Columbus] quickly learned to make use of this natural circulation: southwesterly outbound directly into the American Indies, returning northeasterly, arching parallel with the trend of the North American coast. Therefore this entire continental seaboard and the attenuated [Caribbean] archipelago shielding its tropical seas became a single arena of action for the competition of Atlantic Europe. For more than two centuries events in one sector might ramify into others with important impact thousands of miles away on this western rim.

Columbus was a marvelously skilled sailor, seeming to know by intuition that he needed to sail southward to hook into this immense circling pool of Atlantic winds, ride them westward across the ocean, and return to Spain by getting on the carousel again and letting the eastward-returning winds push

him home by the northern route. Thus, a month after heading westward from the Canary Islands, the moment Columbus had dreamed of for years arrived: At 2 in the morning of October 12, 1492, came the cry *Land! Land!* His expedition had made its way to what is now called the Caribbean Sea, arriving at a small island Columbus promptly named San Salvador.

The Great Surprise: A New World

Columbus clung to his delusion. In this and three subsequent voyages (1493–1504), while Columbus explored the Caribbean basin, to his death in 1506, he insisted passionately that he had found the coast of Asia. He never made contact, of course, with the Great Khan of China, though he tried, and he could bring back almost nothing of real value. Among Europeans, his increasingly far-fetched explanations, which ignored the evidence before him and drew upon fantastic "deductions" from biblical and ancient Greek writings for proofs of his claims, created mounting skepticism.

It was left to another Italian of a more modern cast of mind, Amerigo Vespucci, to break through to the dramatic new truth. Sailing for Portugal, his voyages of exploration (1499–1501) southward from the Caribbean, along a coastline that ran on for thousands of miles and was thickly populated by people who were certainly not Chinese, convinced him that he had found a "Fourth Part of the World." This was an astonishing idea. Ever since the ancient Greeks it had been proclaimed that the world held only Europe, Asia, and Africa, which together formed a World Island. Vespucci, however, was a clear-eyed man of the Renaissance who, unlike Columbus, believed in being guided by what he actually saw with his own eyes—that is, by experience—instead of by dogmas in ancient writings.

Vespucci returned to Europe to publish a sensational book, *The New World* (1502). In it he proclaimed that a vast continent hitherto unknown to Europeans (though by now, of course, an "Old World" to its inhabitants) stretched for thousands of miles south of Columbus's discoveries. Martin Waldseemüller, a German mapmaker, promptly drew a new map of the globe—of which a thousand copies spread rapidly around Europe —depicting the new discovery and naming it

THE NEW WORLD

Columbus bears Christ to the New World. From a Juan de la Cosa map, 1500.

Beginning in the eighth century Viking boats laid terror over most of western Europe; in the middle of the ninth century Norsemen traveled into the western seas to take over Iceland from earlier Celtic settlers. About the year A.D. 1,000, at a time when the northern climate was relatively mild, they went further westward to establish farming villages on the western Greenland coast. Then, under Leif Ericson, they ranged the coast of Labrador and Newfoundland to settle a tiny village

on the latter's north coast for a brief time. Then the Vinland settlement, as they called it, disappeared. As the climate grew colder, so too did those on the Greenland coast, and the mists and storms west of Iceland again hid the western lands.

Almost five centuries later Christopher Columbus began his great adventure, making four voyages to the Caribbean region. To his death he believed he had reached Asia, but Amerigo Vespucci finally realized it to be, and so proclaimed it, a New World. The first European landed on what was later to become United States territory when in 1512 Ponce de León sailed the Florida coast. In 1513 Vasco Nuñez de Balboa crossed the Isthmus of Panama and gazed upon what he called the Pacific Ocean. Soon, in 1524, the king of France was sending Giovanni da Verrazano to explore the North American coast, followed by Jacques Cartier in 1534–35, who sailed far up the St. Lawrence River. Both men had looked in vain for the fabled Northwest Passage to Asia. Almost a century later, in 1610, the Dutch were to send Henry Hudson far into what is now Hudson's Bay in such a quest.

Indeed, only five years after Columbus's first voyages, in 1497 and 1498, the English had sent John Cabot on such a search, subsequently establishing their claim to the North American coast on the basis of his explorations. The only successful effort to reach Asia occurred in 1521, when Ferdinand Magellan pioneered the route around the southern tip of South America, his expedition being the first to circumnavigate the globe.

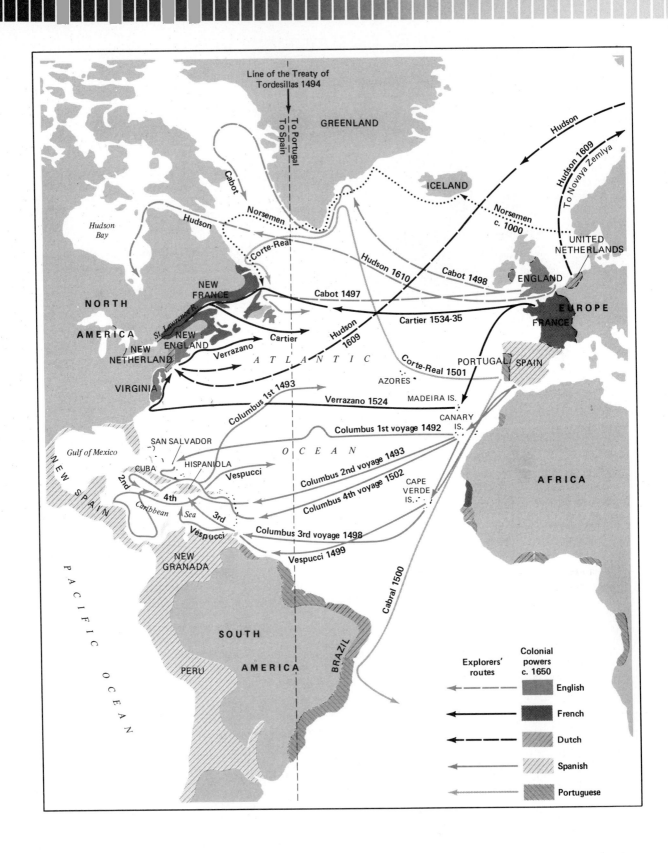

Line of the Treaty of
Tordesillas 1494

To Portugal
To Spain

GREENLAND

Hudson

ICELAND

Hudson 1609

To Novaya Zemlya

Cabot

Norsemen

Norsemen
c. 1000

UNITED
NETHERLANDS

Hudson

Hudson
Bay

Corte-Real

Hudson 1610

Cabot 1498

ENGLAND

NEW
FRANCE

Cabot 1497

EUROPE

NORTH

Cartier 1534-35

FRANCE

St. Lawrence R.

AMERICA

NEW
ENGLAND

Cartier

Hudson
1609

NEW
NETHERLAND

Verrazano

ATLANTIC

Corte-Real 1501

PORTUGAL SPAIN

VIRGINIA

Columbus 1st 1493

Verrazano 1524

AZORES

MADEIRA IS.

CANARY
IS.

Columbus 1st voyage 1492

Gulf of Mexico

OCEAN

SAN SALVADOR

Columbus 2nd voyage 1493

NEW SPAIN

CUBA

HISPANIOLA

Vespucci

Columbus 4th voyage 1502

CAPE
VERDE
IS.

AFRICA

2nd

4th

Caribbean   Sea

3rd

Columbus 3rd voyage 1498

NEW
GRANADA

Vespucci

Vespucci 1499

Cabral 1500

PACIFIC

SOUTH

BRAZIL

PERU

AMERICA

OCEAN

Explorers' routes	Colonial powers c. 1650	
		English
		French
		Dutch
		Spanish
		Portuguese

America in honor of the explorer. After another continent was later revealed to the north, in 1538 Gerardus Mercator published his historic map of the world, which announced for all subsequent generations the existence of a North America and a South America.

For about a century after Columbus's discovery, it was the Spanish almost alone who moved into and created what is now called Latin America. By a bull [edict] of the pope in 1493, and the Treaty of Tordesillas in 1494, Portugal received title to what eventually became Brazil, the rest of the New World being assigned to Spain. For a long time, however, the Portuguese paid attention principally to their African and Asian trade and colonies. Five years after Columbus's first voyages—that is, in 1497 and 1498— the English sent yet a third Italian, Giovanni Caboto (John Cabot) to explore the North American coast from Newfoundland to Chesapeake Bay, and claim it for their king, Henry VII. Jacques Cartier, in 1534–35, sailed far up the St. Lawrence River to lay claim for France to its vast watershed, including the Great Lakes basin. These were isolated ventures, however. America was left to the formidable Spanish, who waxed powerful on the New World's gold and silver and successfully warned all others to stay away.

The Conquerors Arrive

They seemed like gods. To the peoples of the Caribbean islands, Columbus's towering vessels, his astonishing cannon, and the white-skinned men who seemed almost magically to cause their ships to move this way and that were like superhuman creatures and incredible machines come out of nowhere. When the sovereignty of the Spanish crown was proclaimed over the island of Hispaniola, its peaceful peoples, whom Columbus mistakenly named Indians, offered no resistance. Soon they were divided into small territorial groupings called *encomiendas*, which were given to individual Spaniards. These men, in turn, had absolute authority over all who lived on the *encomienda*, and could claim their labor—often, as the angry priest Bartolomé de Las Casas scathingly proclaimed—under slavelike conditions of great cruelty.

The Spanish Empire was not to be an empire of settlement by Spanish families, but one of exploitation, using the labor of the Indians themselves. Few Spanish women went to the New World.

In the frantic search for gold and silver, which erupted almost instantly, it was Indian labor that was mobilized, under the direction of a small Spanish elite. In the Caribbean islands themselves the gold rush produced almost nothing, and after a generation of failure the Spanish began to think of invading the vast mainland now known to lie to the west.

In 1519 Hernando Cortés led a small military force of a few hundred Spanish soldiers ashore at the present Veracruz, on what is now the Mexican coast. Pushing inland, and gathering along the way thousands of local warriors as allies who wanted to throw off Aztec rule, he and his men finally came in sight of Tenochtitlán. They were astonished at its size and magnificence. "We said that it was like the enchantments they tell of in . . . legends," wrote the expedition's chronicler Bernal Díaz del Castillo, ". . . of . . . great towers and . . . buildings rising from the water, and all built of masonry. And some of our soldiers even asked whether the things we saw were not in a dream."

Indeed, almost as if he were in a dream himself, the Aztecs' bewildered emperor, Montezuma II, simply opened the gates of Tenochtitlán to the invaders, whose officers rode like deities on great unknown beasts called horses. The omens Montezuma consulted told him the Spanish were gods, once cast out, whose return to reclaim their rule had been foretold in ancient Toltec myth. Some hard fighting lay ahead for Cortés, but the Aztec empire collapsed swiftly. In 1524 the last Aztec emperor was executed; the Sun God died; and the sacred fires were put out.

The Spanish now finally possessed the fabulous mines of gold and silver for which they had so passionately searched. They possessed, too, millions of new subjects, the Indians, who were now subjects of the faraway king of Spain. As a general rule quietly submissive to the new authorities, the Indians were people of passionate interest to the Roman Catholic Church of Spain. In intimate partnership with the state, the Church set out on a centuries-long missionary pilgrimage to bring the Indians of the Americas to Jesus Christ.

Who Were the Indians?

As soon as they had arrived in the New World, the Spaniards began a great and historic argument:

Were the Indians human beings? How should they be treated? Those who led the conquests or eagerly followed them up for their own profit—that is, the *encomanderos*, to whom the crown gave not only land but also the labor of the Indians who lived on it—were interested only in exploiting the New World's natural resources and its people, not in their welfare. They treated the Indians, therefore, like brutes, and so regarded them.

However, within eight years of Columbus's original discovery, in the year 1500 King Ferdinand and Queen Isabella, the "Catholic Kings," issued a crucial decree of towering historical importance. The Indians of the New World, they ruled, were to be regarded as free human beings. No matter how primitive or uncivilized they were, they were not to be thrust down into slavery. "What a memorable day for the entire world [when the decree was issued]," Rafael Altamira has written, for this was "a principle that had never been proclaimed before in any legislation, let alone practiced in any country."

Why did the kings so rule? Because they and the Roman Catholic Church believed they had before them the divine opportunity of carrying out the greatest act of God since the advent of Christ Himself: converting the pagan peoples across the sea to the true religion, and thereby, as they believed, bringing to the Indians the blessings of eternal life. "[We] desire," they said in 1501, "that the Indians be converted to our holy Catholic faith and that their souls be saved, for this is the greatest good that we can wish for. . . ." Thus, all Spaniards who had Indians laboring for them were to build churches for their instruction and worship and to ensure that they were baptized. That is, not only were the priests sent to the Spanish empire to serve as missionaries, so too were the *encomanderos* themselves, a task they performed only grudgingly.

Thereafter for half a century the argument raged on: If the Indians were human beings, what kind were they? Essentially, the Spanish divided between the "dirty dog" and the "noble savage" schools. Some said that if the Indians were allowed to run free, they would fall back into habits of "idleness, nakedness, dancing, eating spiders and snakes, patronizing witch doctors, drunkenness, improvidence, and gluttony." Left to themselves, many Spaniards insisted, the Indians could never adequately care for themselves; they were not, in other words, "capable." Even a bishop, Francisco Ruiz, said that "they need,

just as a horse or beast does, to be directed and governed by Christians. . . ." Others, however, insisted passionately otherwise. An eminent judge and later priest, Vasco de Quiroga, protested in 1535 that it was tyranny to make the Indians serve Spaniards "like beasts and animals without reason . . . until they are destroyed with work, vexations, and excessive service."

A Great Debate at Valladolid

In 1550 a historic debate took place before the royal Council of the Indies, meeting in Valladolid, Spain. Called by the king himself, it featured a passionately humanitarian and outspoken Dominican priest, Bartolomé de Las Casas. He was a bitter critic of the *encomienda* system, indeed of the entire Spanish Empire itself, as cruel and un-Christian. On the other side was a famous learned scholar, Juan Ginés de Sepúlveda, who for many years had argued that the *encomienda* and even wars against the Indians were just.

Rather than being barbaric or dull-witted or stupid, Las Casas said, the Indians were

> *very talented in learning, and very ready to accept Christian religion, [as well as subtly] skilled in every mechanical art . . . so very beautiful in their skill and artistry . . . in the grace of . . . architecture . . . painting . . . needle-work. . . . In the liberal arts . . . such as grammar and logic, they are remarkably adept. With every kind of music they charm the ears . . . with wonderful sweetness. They write skillfully and quite elegantly.*

They were in truth barbarians, Las Casas said, in that they were not Christians, but they had

> *kingdoms, royal dignities, jurisdiction, and good laws, and there is among them lawful government . . . great cities . . . commerce, buying, selling, lending. . . . [Long] before they had heard the word Spaniard, they had properly organized states, wisely ordered by excellent laws, religion, and custom.*

Now they needed only to be brought to the Catholic faith, and then left alone. There should be no more wars against the Indians! "The Indians are our brothers," Las Casas insisted, "and Christ has given his life for them. Why, then, do we persecute them with such inhuman savagery when they do not deserve such treatment." Elsewhere Las Casas had put his feelings with powerful simplicity: "All mankind is one."

However, no formal ruling was ever made on the Valladolid debate, and things went on as before. In 1553 Las Casas published a heated attack on Spain's rule in the New World, his *Very Brief Account of the Destruction of the Indies*, which was soon translated by Spain's delighted enemies—especially the Protestants—and widely circulated in Europe and even in the Spanish Empire itself. For all time, Las Casas's book established indelibly in Western civilization's mind the "black legend": the image of the Spanish Empire as uniquely bloody, exploitive, cruel, and inhuman.

Nonetheless, the empire did not change its ways. The Spanish continued to expand their rule in the New World by warfare against the Indians, saying such attacks were necessary in order to bring the barbarians to Christ. It is important to note that these were wars of conquest, not of extermination or removal. The Spanish did not drive the Indians out of their territories and settle them (as the English colonists would later do in North America). Rather, they simply moved in as the rulers, who then granted to each other the Indians' lands, including the Indians living on them, whose labor they then exploited.

The New "Mexican" Society

What appeared in the new Spanish Empire in Mesoamerica was not simply a transplanted Spain but a fundamentally distinct and new society that in time would be called "Mexican." It was a profoundly hierarchical society where authority (as in Spain) was held in a few hands. The elite spoke and led, and the masses were silent and followed. A powerful warrior ethic centering on "honor," centuries old in Europe, inspired the daily life of the ruling classes, shaping Mexican life far into the twentieth century.

Formal Spanish institutions and laws (as well as those people who had light skins) were at the top. An enduring Mexican folk culture, tragically wasted and thinned by the great dying (see below) but still full of life, formed the broad human foundation. To the abundant Indian agriculture, the Spanish joined European wheat and barley, vineyards, the use of the wheel in transport, and of the plow to break the soil. Above all, they brought in one towering innovation: beasts of burden to do

the heavy work. Until the Spanish came, all lifting and carrying was done by human beings. Oxen came in with the Spanish, as did horses, burros, and mules.

So too did the herding animals for food and fiber: sheep and cattle. The Spanish, alone among the Europeans, had in the wide grasslands of their homeland learned how to use men on horseback to control large herds of cattle. They transferred this industry directly to Mexico, so much of which was climatically like Spain itself. There, around cattle, they built one of Mexico's core institutions: the ranching economy. Cattle were important not simply for their meat but also for the industrial raw materials that could be derived from their bodies: hides (leather was used to fabricate countless items of daily use) and tallow for candles and lubrication. At the same time, a central feature of the new Mexican identity was the building of mining towns in the many mineral-rich mountain ranges that divided that country.

The Spanish Empire Centered on Cities

Indeed, the Spanish Empire became at its heart an *urban* world. The great masses of the Mexican peoples continued to live in the countryside, but in each region a central municipality governed its surrounding area, setting the tone, directing the economy, and providing centralized authority. It has been said that while the key symbolic figure of the English colonies was the individual pioneer farmer heading out to cut down the trees and break the soil, in the Spanish Empire the central figure was the local royal official sent out into a new frontier area to plan the grids of a new Spanish town that would be its center. A Mediterranean-style town full of red-tile roofs, all gathered around a central plaza with its great church and its government buildings, became the civic hallmark, as well as the typical visual landscape, of Spanish America.

The Creation of a "Mexico"

When the Spanish first arrived, what is now called Mexico was actually a vast heterogeneous territory containing many different ethnic communities, each with their own language and culture. Each one possessed its own intense local loyalties (to a significant degree this is still the case), so that a "Mexico" did not as yet exist.

However, as the twentieth-century Mexican poet Octavio Paz has observed, the Spanish brought in powerful unifying forces: a single language (Castilian) used by those in authority; a single dominant religion in Roman Catholicism; a Mexico-wide ruling class sharing one European cultural heritage; and a single, highly organized imperial ruling government centered in one autocratic monarch, the king of Spain, whose decisions were final. Mexico was so big as well as geographically and culturally diverse that it would always have to strain to keep from flying apart (this would be especially true after it became an independent nation in 1823). Nonetheless, by 1600 Spanish rule, whatever else it had meant, had at least succeeded in creating a strong foundation for what would eventually be a single great nation.

The Long Dying

A human calamity of inconceivable proportions came with the Spanish. Before the horrified eyes of the Spanish, soon after the conquest began, the Indians began dying off in incredible numbers. It was a dying that went on generation after generation. Europe in general blamed the cruelty of Spanish rule for the catastrophe. What in fact happened was that the Spanish had brought Europe's many diseases with them, and the Indians were totally without biological immunities.

In the Americas, somewhere between 50 million and 100 million people were alive in 1500. Suddenly they were faced with smallpox, which swept like a wildfire through densely populated central Mexico in 1522, killing millions. Soon smallpox and other diseases (measles, chicken pox, whooping cough, malaria, yellow fever, and influenza) scythed through the Indian population so murderously that a dying off of about *90 percent* appears to have occurred. By 1650, though the fact seems beyond belief, only a million Indians were left alive in Mexico. On the island of Hispaniola, where there had been at least several million people, the population almost disappeared. (In North America, the Indians were far fewer in numbers than in the original Spanish Empire, they were much more scattered, and the impact of European diseases would be considerably delayed and more

localized, though absolutely devastating when it occurred.)

Though history is crowded with terrible killings, as in the Jewish Holocaust under Hitler and the 20 million Soviet citizens who died in the USSR in World War II, there is really nothing in the past that comes close to this enormous carnage throughout the Americas. For a century and a quarter the Indians of Mexico dwindled in population, then began a slow increase, reaching approximately 2.5 million by 1800. By this time those of Spanish descent had risen to about a million, most of them living in and around Mexico City. Miscegenation (a mixture of races) had long flourished between Spaniard and Indian, since so few Spanish women were in Mexico. It created a great community of peoples called *mestizos* (mixed bloods), or *castas* (half-castes), as they were also called in derogation by the Spanish-descended. By 1800, they numbered about 2 million.

Mexico's millions of deaths sharply reduced the labor supply, yet the shrunken Indian population was still forced to send off its men to such Spanish enterprises as mining, and to pay tribute. Food was therefore always short in the Indian villages, and near-starvation was common. Gravely weakened by this life, it is not surprising that as late as 1784 some 300,000 Indians succumbed to disease in another epidemic.

The Indians were regarded as immature and childlike by the Spanish, denied legal citizenship, and placed under a special legal code. It allowed them to contract only small debts and therefore restricted them to the status of rudimentary farmers, denied them formal education, and forbade them the use of firearms, European dress, or the ownership of cattle. It is no wonder that the festive Indians the Spanish invaders had found in the Aztec Empire had long since become sad, withdrawn, and apparently apathetic—though hiding a rage that would explode against the Spanish in the independence movement after 1810.

The Historic "Place" Where American Slavery Was Born

Though the Indian peoples of Spanish America were legally free, slavery did, nonetheless, come to the Spanish Empire. It came in the guise of a new people, the Africans. Our attention must now be directed, therefore, to a different location in the world. Here

Bartolomé de las Casas, (1474–1566), missionary leader, opposed enslaving Indians. Unfortunately, his concern for the Indians led him to advocate the use of black slaves to replace them.

we will be guided by the work of historical geographers, for whom the concept of *place* plays a central role in explaining why things happen as they do. They believe that what occurs in human affairs is always produced by the interaction of human (cultural and economic) factors with the unique physical dynamics encountered in specific geographic settings. Each such setting has its own particular combination of climate and topography and resources. Furthermore, geographers hold that some of these places, though surprisingly small, have been the brooding places for new and remarkably dynamic ways of living that have been exploded widely over the earth's surface to reshape human history drastically.

In two small groups of unpopulated islands off the coast of Africa—the Cape Verde Islands, which are west of Africa's "bulge," and those around the island of São Tomé in the Gulf of Guinea—there was such a historic place. These islands were taken

over and colonized by the southward-voyaging Portuguese in the latter part of the fifteenth century. As Europeans, they could not live on the coast of Africa itself, for they had no physical immunities to its many diseases. Thus, these empty islands provided convenient off-shore bases from which the Portuguese could trade with the coastal African tribes, getting what they were after: gold (hence the name, the "Gold Coast" of Africa).

At the same time, the Portuguese learned of another highly profitable trade item to be secured from African merchants: *slaves*. These they could sell in various places around the Mediterranean Sea, where slaves (often war captives, and thus not by any means always black) had traditionally been commonly in use in specialized occupations and for domestic service. But suddenly a new, immensely profitable market opened in Europe for sugar, which was normally purchased at great cost from South Asia via Arabian and Turkish traders. When the Portuguese began growing sugar cane in their island colonies off the coast of Africa, they encountered an insatiable appetite for their product in Europe. From the sugar trade the Portuguese gathered in huge profits. Soon, especially on the island of São Tomé, the Portuguese were gathering slaves not to sell in Europe, but to use as gang labor on large sugar plantations. To fuel the sugar boom, something like 50,000 slaves were imported into that island in the year 1550 alone.

Plantation Slavery Appears

Here, then, in a tiny spot on the world's surface, and under the forced draft of high profits, *plantation slavery* as an institution was developed in what became its enduring form, later, in the Western Hemisphere. It had highly distinctive features. Plantation slavery was an economic system based in the work being done by gang labor under an overseer. Thus, it was impersonal, involving few of the feelings that could exist in situations where masters worked closely with slaves in small groups, perhaps as household servants. The slaves were simply bought as a kind of raw material, a commodity, and if they were injured or sickened and died, they were replaced like so many cattle. To procure slaves, a vast trading network was built up, so as to provide a continuing supply. In that network there was an overwhelming emphasis on getting and supplying male slaves only, which prevented the creation of families. Finally, there was a firm link established in plantation labor between color and status, so that only blacks were enslaved. Slaves were regarded as permanently debased, so that when freed, they were not assimilated into the surrounding community.

Westward, across the Atlantic, the Portuguese possessed the immense colony of Brazil. Soon they were carrying the sugar plantation industry that they had evolved on São Tomé across the water to transplant in that huge colonial possession. Primarily via the Cape Verde Islands, the Portuguese were shortly exporting thousands of slaves to Brazil to support an exploding sugar production there, as well as in Spanish America. By the mid-1500s, in short, the Portuguese had become the chief suppliers of an enormous annual flow of African slaves to the Western Hemisphere. In time, African peoples were spread through the whole body of the Portuguese and Spanish empires in the Americas, especially in Brazil. By 1600, well before the British and French colonies emerged in North America, something like 225,000 Africans had been sent across the Atlantic into slavery.

The Slaves

No less than the Europeans, the black slaves brought from Africa varied widely in appearance, stature, skin color, and culture. They came primarily from a narrow band of territory along the West African coast from present-day Senegal to Angola, where many separate nations now exist. Theirs were ancient societies that often had developed powerful states so strong that, except for tiny trading posts here and there, Europeans made no attempt to conquer the vast interior of Africa for hundreds of years after the slave trade began. Slave seekers, as we have seen, *traded* with the Africans, arriving off the coastline and sending in boats; they themselves did not trek into the interior and capture slaves.

In the great African principalities, as in contemporary late medieval Europe, slavery was widespread. In Europe and Africa it was simply an extreme form of servantship applied to captured men and women from outside the nation or faith. Christians in Europe had given up the enslaving of other Christians, but infidels were fair game. The slave in Africa, however, was more than a form of property; he was a human being who could marry, keep his family together,

and progress out of slavery. Only in the New World, and particularly in the English colonies, did the idea evolve of the slave as a subhuman form of chattel, to be bought and sold freely like a piece of real estate.

In their homelands the Africans were primarily villagers who farmed, selling their produce in busy market towns and cities. However, like traditional villagers everywhere in the world, individualism was shunned and disliked. Being part of a village, most of all a *kinship group*, was the central thing in life. Warfare was endemic. Anthropologists tell us that almost universally, primitive peoples fight each other more or less continually. In that situation, everyone has to band together for self-protection; hence, the strong kinship groups.

Furthermore, the climate in equatorial Africa was harsh, fluctuating between droughts and floods. Soils were low in fertility and quickly worked out, and farms often had to be moved about to fresh lands. Therefore, people had to work together simply to survive; they had to help each other, to merge their lives into that of the community. Living apart from it was inconceivable. Everyone existed to give strength and endurance to the community, not for one's own self-development. This was condemned as being selfish. The Lozi had a proverb: "Go the way that many people go; if you go alone you will have reason to lament."

Thus, a kind of seamless web bound everyone together. Even children did not belong just to their parents, but to the entire kinship group: uncles, aunts, grandparents, cousins. For this reason, being carried off to slavery, away from one's own people and put among unknown persons, was a genuine horror, a literally terrifying experience—as it would be, in truth, for any modern person as well.

The English Turn Outward

For almost a century after 1492 the English were too wrapped up in their own domestic troubles to do more than send Giovanni Caboto on a voyage of exploration (1497–98). After he had claimed the North American coast from Newfoundland to Chesapeake Bay and laid claim for England to all the land that he had seen, running to the seas beyond, little more occurred. In the 1530s England plunged into its Protestant Reformation, declaring religious inde-

Native hunters of the New World had to use ingenuity and stealth in a way that fascinated more civilized men.

pendence from the Roman Catholic Church. This set off years of turmoil that did not subside until after Elizabeth became queen in 1558.

As her reign proceeded, the English aristocracy began to dream of overseas ventures. No longer distracted by internal Catholic-Protestant strife, and impelled forward by the vigorous expansion of its business community, England seemed filled with a new confidence. Explorers and traders circled the globe while philosophers, scientists, poets, and dramatists created brilliant, enduring works. New horizons, not only of the world but of the mind as well, beckoned in every direction.

Under Elizabeth, all Ireland was subjugated for the first time, after 1565. Huge areas of Ireland were subsequently granted to English aristocrats as "plantations" on which to settle Protestant English and Scots. Shortly after Elizabeth's death in 1603 there was a vast expansion of "plantations" in Northern Ireland (the province of Ulster). King James I granted almost the whole region to English proprietors, who expelled great numbers of the native Irish and brought in Protestant Scots. In time, flourishing in this part of Ireland, they became the "Scotch-Irish."

The Founding of Virginia

In the 1580s the English began trying to create a colony on the coast of North America named Virginia, for their virgin queen. It took them forty years to succeed. In 1584 Sir Walter Raleigh sent out the first settlers, but they returned home. Another group dispatched in 1587 to Roanoke Island disappeared entirely. The next serious attempt was made in 1606, when the Virginia Company sent a hundred settlers to Virginia; in 1607 this group founded Jamestown. More than a decade of confusion, suffering and death ensued (the southern colonies will be discussed in the next chapter), but by the 1620s the colony was firmly established. In a great surge of migration, the English people now began to create a new country on the eastern coast of North America.

The Nature of the Homeland

What was their new country to be like? To begin with, it was a projection across the Atlantic of the old country. It is important, therefore, to understand the homeland that the British left behind. Like all Europeans in these centuries, they were devoutly religious. During the Europe-wide Protestant Reformation of the sixteenth century, at great cost and suffering they had thrown out Roman Catholicism and created their own form of Protestant Christianity: the Church of England (whose present offshoot in America is the Protestant Episcopal Church). The Church of England was the religious arm of the state, as Parliament was its legislative arm. The two were both headed by the reigning monarch, and still are. Every English person was assumed to belong to the Church of England simply by being born English.

Church and state interpenetrated each other. Bishops sat, and sit today, in the House of Lords, helping to make the laws. The Church of England's Prayer Book still may be changed only by an act of Parliament. Until 1868 every English person, whether or not an Anglican (the name for a member of the Church of England), was supposed to pay tithes to support the church, just as all Americans now pay taxes to support public schools whether or not their children use them. Public education was provided by the church; many legal actions could take place only within its courts; marriage and burial were its prerogatives; and its bishops were appointed, in fact if not in theory, by the prime minister.

Prejudice among Protestants

Until the last hundred years or so, religious belief had always been a matter for war and widespread bloodshed in Western civilization. Life being short, the other world seemed much nearer than it does now, and the state of one's soul was a vital matter. When people thought of hell and the devil, which they did far more then than people do now, they thought of a real place and a real being.

Under Elizabeth the differing Protestant parties began to argue, dividing between those who would take the Church of England even further away from Catholicism toward Calvinism (the Puritans) and those who wished to keep the church along a middle road between Catholicism and Puritanism. Under Charles I these frictions exploded in the great English Civil War (1642–49). Charles I was beheaded, and the Puritan Oliver Cromwell became Lord Protector.

From 1649 to 1660 England tried to get along as a commonwealth without a monarch. At the same time, the religious situation fragmented thoroughly. Protestants veered off in many directions. By 1660, when the Stuart dynasty was restored to the throne in the person of Charles II and England's traditional constitution was reestablished, the unitary character of English religious life had been permanently shattered.

Thereafter the English agreed to disagree on religious matters, allowing the Puritans and others who did not accept the rituals and creed of the Church of England to set up their own churches. Those who did so, however, had to suffer civil disabilities. As Dissenters (they were also called Nonconformists), they would receive religious toleration but would not be allowed the full rights of citizens. Only Anglicans could hold public office, attend Oxford and Cambridge, and the like.

There thus appeared in English life discrimination against Protestants who were not members of the Church of England. At first this meant Congregationalists, Presbyterians, Baptists, and Quakers; later it included Methodists, Unitarians, and all the large and small religious sects that emerged in the following centuries. To be a Dissenter was to be looked down on, for polite and official society was overwhelmingly Anglican. Dissenters had not only their separate chapels but also their separate newspapers, schools, and living areas. They rarely sat in Parliament before the nineteenth century, and not until the 1880s did a Dissenter become a member of the cabinet.

Britain, in sum, was religiously pluralistic after the Restoration of 1660. This alone, if nothing else, finally forced the English to give legal toleration to every Protestant sect; there was no alternative short of endless civil war.

A Businessman's Country

England in the seventeenth century was also becoming, to a degree, a businessman's country. The English economy was developing far more rapidly than that of any other European country save Holland. The entrepreneur, as the economist Joseph Schumpeter pointed out, is the "energizer" of economic life. More than any other single influence, this person is responsible for creating that essential ingredient in economic advance—continual innovation. In England, entrepreneurs had succeeded in breaking out of medieval restrictions before his counterparts elsewhere. As businessmen developed new industries, providing jobs, opportunity, and economic excitement, England moved toward the explosion of the Industrial Revolution, which occurred when steam power was harnessed to machines in the late eighteenth century.

This great economic phenomenon had two sharply contrasting results. In the eighteenth and nineteenth centuries England began to grow wealthy. Populous cities appeared, and liberating changes appeared in the Anglo-American way of life. Higher incomes, greater opportunity for the talented, far greater ease of travel, the appearance in ordinary homes of goods and articles long the privilege of the wealthy—these came with the emergence of individualistic business enterprise. At the same time, however, the new economy tended to create

Predominant Religious Groups in the Seventeenth-Century British Isles

Principal Christian Churches:

Roman Catholic

Presbyterian (Church of Scotland)

Anglican (Church of England)

Minorities:

+ Roman Catholic
○ Puritans
▲ Other Sects

masses of poverty-stricken people working in degraded conditions; stunted children tended the looms and crawled about in the mines; and a few were enabled to enrich themselves at the community's expense.

Throughout the following history runs this central economic paradox: a business community that is extraordinarily creative and at the same time destructive. From almost the beginning of American history to the present, this central contradiction has obsessed American politicians, shaped the two parties—along with other considerations—and divided Americans into bitterly warring camps. One political party in American life has always tended to see the harm that businessmen are doing or threatening; the other has always tended to see the good.

An Aristocratic Country

In the midst of these changes one age-old characteristic of England remained—its aristocracy. The assumption that every person has a "station" in life below certain people and above others, that *inequality* in social standing and *deference* (i.e., holding in awe and respect) toward those above are ineradicable characteristics of life—these were deeply rooted attitudes in the English mind.

Aristocratic societies develop unconscious ways of command; authority comes easily to them, sits proudly on their shoulders. The English ruling classes were conscious of being on top, and they liked being the ones who gave the orders. They regarded the power of government as having been deposited solely in their hands. Accustomed to giving orders, the aristocracy reacted angrily when those below appeared to be giving orders back. Thus, during the prerevolutionary arguments with the colonies, the English aristocracy was enraged because the colonials appeared to be challenging their authority, making demands, and reversing a relationship of superior to inferior. This, to individuals used to running things, was unforgivable.

Ethnic Prejudice

This habit of authority in the English mind was accentuated by the supremacy that England enjoyed within the British Isles. England is far more populous, wealthy, and powerful than the other countries in the British Isles combined (Scotland, Wales, and Ireland), and always has been. Thus England instinctively thought of itself as dominant in the British Isles, much as the United States of America has thought of itself as dominant in the Western Hemisphere. For centuries the English made no secret of that feeling of superiority. It was common for them to look down on the Irish, the Welsh, and the Scots as crude and obstinately backward, as well as troublesome and unable to govern themselves properly. At the least, they were regarded as comic variations from the "proper" English norm.

In 1707 England, Wales, and Scotland joined together in a Union officially called the *United Kingdom* (or, in common usage, *Great Britain*, the ancient name for the largest island in the British Isles). Ireland, long ruled by England, was now subject to the larger, English-dominated United Kingdom, as were the colonies in North America.

The peoples of the United Kingdom did not like each other. Centuries of bloody fighting and mu-

John Locke, great political philosopher whose writings justified for English and Americans limited government controlled by the society at large, and freedom of religion.

tual hatred lay behind them. Scots had long been bitterly conscious of English snobbery toward them, and now, within the new United Kingdom, they were aware that they were second-class citizens. When they migrated to England, as great numbers did to find opportunity in that wealthier country, they faced harsh prejudice. So did the Welsh. The Scots suffered from the stereotype usually applied in other societies to Jews: They were described by the scoffing English as mean, closefisted, self-seeking, shrewd, and concerned only with money. The Welsh were looked upon as a devious, overly subtle, musical, but fundamentally unstable people. The Irish were regarded with contempt by all—English, Scots, and Welsh alike.

This was particularly true of the Catholic Irish, who were the "Negroes" of British life. Exploited for centuries, denied education, land, and opportunity, denied the right to vote and to sit in Parliament, prevented from entering the professions or holding any government post, and devoted to a religion regarded as alien, subversive, medieval, and superstitious, the Catholic Irish seemed to the English and the Scots hardly a species of humanity at all. In the seventeenth century it was not unusual to describe the Irish as wild animals who ate one another.

Britain's Libertarian Constitution

Yet this vigorously aristocratic country possessed a remarkably libertarian constitution for the times, although it was far from being a "democracy" (where the people rule). The English were freer of autocracy than practically anyone else in Europe, and they were proud of it. The reason for this lay partly in England's situation. The country was remote from powerful neighbors and protected from continental attacks by narrow but dangerous seas. Lacking an excuse to maintain standing armies, England's kings were never as powerful as their continental counterparts. Furthermore, Parliament had acquired control over unusual taxation, which gave it power over the monarch in crisis situations. (Kings were given certain taxes they could levy to carry on ordinary government.) While Louis XIV was saying "I am the state" and building an autocracy in seventeenth-century France, the English Parliament was throwing off Charles I and establishing not only its own supremacy but also the basis for the fundamental rights of all English people. Out of the Civil War Parliament acquired practically all the rights underlying the independence and power of Congress today: the power to decide on the qualifications of its members; control of taxation and lawmaking; complete freedom of speech; immunity from arrest while engaged in legislative business; and the right to close scrutiny of the actions of the executive branch.

The Whig Theory of Government

The restoration of the Stuarts in 1660 and the placement on the throne of Charles II led to twenty-five years of quite un-Puritan government. In this period the English people divided over the question of whether the changes of the Civil War had gone far enough or too far. Some lamented the reduction of the king's power, disliked the idea of a strong Parliament, and disliked even more the idea of tolerating all those Dissenters. For obscure reasons, they acquired the name of *Tories*.

Their favorite political philosopher was Thomas Hobbes, an irascible, dogmatic old scholar who had tutored Charles II while he was in exile. Hobbes had long supported the idea that the monarch and not Parliament should have final authority in the land. Men are so selfish, Hobbes maintained, so ready to turn on their neighbors and oppress them or war upon them, that long ago, in the state of nature, they gave up all their self-seeking "rights" to one man to bring the blessings of peace and order. The idea of parliamentary supremacy was nonsense; it was the road to anarchy and disorder. The true road lay in restoring the king's prerogative.

Many disagreed. *Their* favorite philosopher was the young intellectual John Locke, who argued that people were fundamentally good. In that famous state of nature, reasoning individuals (and Locke had great faith in what he felt was the human's divinely given ability to reason) decided that they would create a limited government, retaining final sovereignty in the hands of the whole community. The people's "rights" were fundamental, preexisting the government, and the people were equal to one another in political value. Government existed only to protect lives, individual well-being, and property.

Above all, Locke believed, every person's religious life must be left up to that person's own judgment. Religious experience is between the individual and God. Certainly the state, in Locke's view, had no power to use force in religious matters, for the state is concerned only with the citizen's body and property, not with the person's thoughts.

This moderate man, so reasonable, tolerant, and level in tone, became the philosopher of the people called *Whigs*. In three short years after 1685, the Whigs rose to dominance in English political life. In that year Charles II died and his Catholic brother, James II, took the throne. So quickly did he alienate almost everyone by his autocratic behavior and his favoritism of Catholics that the Whigs were able, in the Glorious Revolution of 1688, to bring over William and Mary from Holland and send James II packing. All this was done under the ruling notion that Parliament was supreme in the state. After William and Mary (a Protestant daughter of James II) accepted the Bill of Rights presented to them by Parliament, they became the new monarchs of England.

The Bill of Rights of 1689, the forerunner and model for the American Bill of Rights, provided as follows:

1. That the making or suspending of law without the consent of Parliament was illegal.
2. That all prerogative courts were illegal.
3. That levying taxes without parliamentary consent was illegal.
4. That everyone has the right to petition the Crown.
5. That the king may not maintain a standing army without Parliament's consent.
6. That it is lawful to keep and bear arms.
7. That all elections of members of Parliament must be free of coercion by the government.
8. That there must be freedom of debate in Parliament.
9. That excessive bail cannot be demanded.
10. That juries must be empaneled and returned in every trial.
11. That Parliament must be frequently convened.

Thus was established the Whig theory of government. It maintained that certain rights were beyond being tampered with by the king and that Parliament was supreme in the constitution. Whigs argued that the people at large were ultimately sovereign, acting through their duly elected representatives. Of course, few actually voted for those representatives, but it was believed that the members of the House of Commons nevertheless represented the whole community, virtually if not actually. Whigs believed that people should be free to think what they wished and worship as they pleased, and that taxation should only be by consent of the governed. These ideas were much cherished by liberal-minded colonials, who proceeded to insist on their being put into effect in the colonies. And in the American Bill of Rights, John Locke is forever enshrined. When the Americans formed their own nation and their own political parties, they consciously looked to the Tories and the Whigs as their models. Jefferson thought himself a Whig, and Alexander Hamilton in many ways fashioned his Federalists on Tory lines.

BIBLIOGRAPHY

Books that were especially valuable to me in thinking about and writing this chapter: A brilliant new interpretation of the American past from the standpoint of historical geography (a scholarly discipline in a state of exciting renaissance), D. W. Meinig's *The Shaping of America: A Geographical Perspective on 500 Years of History*, Vol. I: *Atlantic America, 1492–1800* (New Haven and London, 1986); Lewis Hanke's absorbing *All Mankind Is One: A Study of the Disputation Between Bartolome de Las Casas and Juan Gines de Sepulveda in 1550 on the Intellectual and Religious Capacity of the American Indians* (DeKalb, Illinois: 1974); Carl Bridenbaugh's richly detailed study, *Vexed and Troubled Englishmen 1590–1642* (1968), and Wallace Notesten, *The English People on the Eve of Colonization 1603–1630* (1954); A. L. Rowse, *The England of Elizabeth: The Structure of Society;* Roger Lockyer, *Tudor and Stuart Britain 1471–1714* (1964); Hiram Haydn, ed., *The Portable Elizabethan Reader* (1955).

On the explorations and the peoples and Spanish imperial history of the Americas, I consulted an intriguing recent article by Franklin and Mary Folsom, based on the research of Christy G. Turner II, "Sinodonty and Sundadonty: An Argument with Teeth in It for Man's Arrival in the New World," *Early Man*, summer 1982; Charles C. Cumberland, *Mexico: The Struggle for Modernity* (1968); Octavio Paz's powerful work, *The Labyrinth of Solitude: Life and Thought in Mexico* (1961); Peter Farb, *Man's Rise to Civilization* (1968); Daniel J. Boorstin, *The Discoverers* (1983); Francis Jennings, *The Invasion of America: Indians, Colonialism, and the Cant of Conquest* (1975); and Walter Nugent's splendid demographic study, *Structures of American Social History* (1981).

The basic interpretive view of British politics and culture offered in this chapter has been brought together from a wide variety of sources. It may be explored in the introductory and concluding chapters in Robert Kelley, *The Transatlantic Persuasion: The Liberal-Democratic Mind in the Age of Gladstone* (1969). Valuable here are A. P. Thornton, *The Habit of Authority: Paternalism in British History* (1964); David Beers Quinn, *The Elizabethans and the Irish* (1966); and O. D. Edward, G. Evans, I. Rhys, and H. MacDiarmid, *Celtic Nationalism* (1968). The partial transformation of European culture in its new setting is probed in Howard Mumford Jones's *O Strange New World* (1964). Many works are available on the English Civil War and seventeenth-century political thought, as for example Julian H. Franklin, *John Locke and the Theory of Sovereignty* (1978), and John Philipps Kenyon, *Stuart England* (1978).

2

The Beginnings: The South

TIME LINE

HISTORY IN AN INDIVIDUAL LIFE

POCAHONTAS

Matoaka, daughter of the chief, was a laughing child ten years of age called Pocahontas ("Playful One") when in 1607 the Englishmen arrived to establish Jamestown. Be at peace with the Indians, London had said; cultivate and Christianize them, establish schools, share the country, do not simply take it. For about a decade there were no barriers, Indian and white society flowing into each other and exchanging skills and artifacts. Soon Pocahontas was turning handsprings with the small English boys in the marketplace. In 1608 Captain John Smith was captured by her fierce father, Powhatan, and in a mock execution ceremony that Smith thought real she threw her arms about his head, apparently (to Smith) preventing warriors from dashing out his brains on a great rock.

Meanwhile, the colonists were learning from the Indians, as they had to if they would survive. English wheat (which the English called "corn") did not thrive in Virginia soil, so for their basic food staple they slowly learned to grow "Indian corn." They tried to smoke Indian tobacco, used in Europe as an upper class recreation, but the natural Virginia tobacco was too bitter. Then John Rolfe brought in a mild West Indian type of tobacco and produced, in 1612, a "pleasant, sweet, and strong" leaf. Virginia's economy now focused on this highly profitable product, which was to have such grave consequences: dependence on a single crop for trade, and eventually slavery.

Sporadic fighting between Indian and Englishman had long since begun. To force Powhatan to release hostages, the colonists captured Pocahontas in 1613 and took her to Jamestown, where she was treated with courtesy and converted to Christianity. John Rolfe was soon in love with her, and she with him. Governor Thomas Dale sought to dissuade Rolfe from marriage: "Pocahontas," he said, "is of a different and despised color; of different manners and uneducated; of a hated race, not one of whom has ever looked [to be] above the meanest of the Colonists." But the union took place in 1614, and Powhatan, much pleased, was at peace with the English the rest of his days. All seemed to believe that a lasting bond had been made between the two peoples.

In 1616 husband and wife, with several other Indians, sailed for England. Pocahontas was treated as a princess, was entertained by the Bishop of London "with festivall, state and pompe," and presented to the king and queen. She had a son while there, Thomas, from whom many Virginians in after years descended. However, the Rolfes were hardly on the boat for their return when she sickened and died.

Meanwhile, in Virginia the rush for tobacco lands was sending colonists far out into the Jamestown countryside, where they often took over Indian cornfields. In 1622 the Indians struck back: In a great massacre perhaps a third of the colonists were killed, including John Rolfe. Thereafter, Indians and whites drew apart. A policy of "perpetual enmity" toward the Indians was adopted. There were no more interracial marriages (common in the Spanish empire), no more high-spirited trips to meet the king. The English and the Indians would remain biologically separate peoples.

The Adventure in the New World

The English boats looking for a place to found a colony arrived at the opening of Chesapeake Bay on April 26, 1607, and sent men ashore at Cape Henry. The Chesapeake Indians of the region were angered to find perhaps thirty strangers, oddly dressed, wandering about on their land, and they quickly drove them back to their ships. But this time the newcomers would not go away. The English had arrived in what they called Virginia determined to plant a permanent settlement. Three weeks later they had navigated some 60 miles inland, far enough to be safe from surprise Spanish attacks, to found a village that they called, after their monarch at home, Jamestown. And here the bridgehead of English colonization endured.

There was an odd mixture of motives behind the determination of the English to settle Virginia. Twenty years earlier, when the English had attempted to found their Roanoke Island colony in what are now the outer islands of North Carolina, it was in pursuit of a dream. The wicked Catholic Spanish, autocrats to the core (the English told themselves), had spread death and slavery through what is now Latin America. But northward God had saved a vast region in the New World where English people could establish a free and kindly (and Protestant) regime among the Indians, who seemed to look upon them as gods. There they could teach the Indians how to work fruitfully at farming, crafts, and husbandry. Grateful for their deliverance from the threat of Spanish oppression, the Indians would labor faithfully for their English overlords.

By the time the Roanoke experiment had failed, it was clear that the Indians did not intend to labor in the English style, and that they knew that the English were not gods. Capturing the whole of the New World from the Spanish, with the help of great armies of grateful Indians, had to be forgotten. What remained, however, was a solid realization that Virginia was a potentially fruitful land where English people could go and make valuable products that England could sell to the world. In 1606 the Virginia Company of London was created by a group of wealthy "adventurers" (men ready to risk capital in a large investment abroad), based in a royal charter issued by King James I authorizing them to establish a colony and govern it.

For reasons having something to do with rising trade, the English ruling class was conscious that England's population was rapidly rising, and that it was good policy to create an outlet for "sturdy beggers" in the New World. Shiploads of unemployed English were gathered by the company and dispatched to Virginia to work for seven years in return for the cost of their transportation. After that they were at liberty to enrich themselves in any way they saw fit. Virginia, in short, was begun on very simple terms and for a simple purpose: to employ people and to make money.

Early Virginia

The English who entered Chesapeake Bay had hit upon one of the globe's most extraordinary bodies of water. Almost 200 miles long and up to 30 miles wide, it is in effect a vast saltwater lake fed by many broad tributaries. Protected from the open sea's violent surfs, for the colonials it served as a great highway system offering easy transport within its immense environs. In consequence, settlers would eventually scatter widely around the bay. No significant urban center of population would emerge within the Chesapeake colonies until Baltimore, not long before the American Revolution, began its surge.

The English who disembarked in the Chesapeake Bay found themselves in a setting profoundly unlike that at home. While cool and rainy England lay opposite Labrador, above 50° north latitude, the Chesapeake was more than a thousand miles southward at about 38°. Through much of the year, therefore, it was hot and sweltering. The vast forest which buried the whole of the flat Chesapeake country deep in an unbroken carpet of green was so thick and rank as to be almost junglelike, save where the Indians had cleared it for raising crops. People used to the open and rolling English countryside, with its many villages, could feel almost buried in the Chesapeake country. The trees pressed in on all sides, and the great wide estuary of the James River, like that of the bay's many other tributaries, lay torpid and slow-moving, seeming to shrink the small human habitations which clung to its shores. Homesickness, a deep pining of the soul which at Jamestown was a widely felt affliction—as it would be among generations of migrants to America in the coming centuries—seemed almost by itself to send people into grieving declines, and death.

And the whole enterprise at Jamestown went badly. Troubles with the Indians, for one thing, began almost immediately. King James insisted that the Indians be treated kindly, as co-subjects of the English crown, and there were serious efforts to create a biracial, intermixed society on this basis. But the experiment was doomed. The Chesapeakes of the region, under their principal chief Powhatan, were distrustful. They scorned the English, who seemed perversely unwilling to plant food and support themselves and were therefore dependent upon the Indians for sustenance. Fighting soon began. The English were especially savage in their attacks, possibly because being so reliant upon a people whom they despised made them determined to show their absolute mastery. To punish a haughty village, the English would massacre all the inhabitants. Indeed, to discipline themselves—some Englishmen had a tendency to wander off to live with the relatively affluent Indians, with their abundant food supplies, or to trade with them—the Jamestown authorities hanged, shot, tortured, burned, and flayed their own people. Meanwhile, thousands of settlers died from starvation and disease.

To save the starving Virginia settlement, the Virginia Company soon realized that the colonists had to be given a personal interest in what they were doing. They would not work hard to raise food for the company itself; the power of individual enterprise had to be put to work. In return for a small annual *quitrent*, settlers were allowed to take up sizable tracts of land to farm for themselves. The time of starvation was soon at an end. Then, in 1619 a legislative body was allowed the Virginia settlers, which transformed them from mere employees to citizens of a new country. The tobacco crop successfully introduced by John Rolfe in 1612 fetched such a high price in London that by 1620 a veritable "gold rush" was under way for tobacco land. Virginia had finally found a means of making a living.

Nonetheless, the company seemed a ghastly failure. More than 10,000 colonists had been sent to Virginia, but by the 1620s only 2,000 remained alive. And in 1622 the elusive biracial dream died. The Chesapeakes were increasingly angered by the way the English, in a rage for tobacco land, took up more and more of their cornfields for their purpose. In a sudden stroke aimed at driving the whole settlement out of Virginia, the Indians began a wholesale killing of whites. Almost in relief the English gave up their policy of "restraint" and struck back in force, killing hundreds of Indians in retaliation. Now, the Virginia authorities declared a policy of "perpetual enmity." Henceforth, they simply sent out annual expeditions to kill off the Indians and take their land, telling themselves that this was justified by the killing of 1622. Henceforth, too, they ceased talking of the Indian's admirable qualities, their ingenuity and strength and industry, describing them instead as nothing more than base savages: "sloathfull and idle, vitious . . . slovenly . . . lyers, of small memory, of no constancy or trust . . . sottish . . . less capable than children of six or seaven yeares old, and lesse apt and ingenious."

In 1624, in light of these events and of the Virginia Company's loss of £160,000 in eighteen years, King James transformed Virginia into a royal colony. By this time, ironically, its fundamental problems appeared to be fairly well solved. The death rate was falling, an income was being realized from a staple crop, and a relatively stable form of government, relying in part on a local legislature, had been worked out.

The Great Migration Begins

At the same time, the ancient realm of England was itself alive with unprecedented internal movement. For centuries into the dim past people had lived in their villages from birth to death within sight of the same surrounding fields. For more than a century they had known that there was a New World to the west, over the Atlantic, but they loved their familiar green countryside and had no urge to go to strange lands far beyond dangerous seas. The monarch and some wealthy adventurers had been looking for profit abroad, and to found a colony they had been sweeping up unemployed men in the byways of England. To the ordinary Englishman, however, the colony had seemed to have nothing to do with him.

But by the 1620s everything was coming apart. The long-run impact of gold and silver from the New World had been energizing European trade for decades, and ancient patterns of living had been losing their stability. To make money in the growing market for wool in the increasingly affluent countries of Western Europe, English landowners had begun evicting their tenant farmers and enclosing the traditional common lands to raise sheep. By the 1620s that modern phenomenon, the boom-and-bust cycle, was making its appearance. Personal fortunes, even among simple folk, began gyrating wildly from prosperity to poverty and back again. Thousands were uprooted from their native villages by the enclosure movement and turned out on the roads to look for work. The population as a whole was growing fairly

An illustration of the concept of America held by Europeans in 1671.

rapidly. England seemed full of masterless, penniless, roaming bands of people.

For many of these homeless individuals a psychological event of historic importance was taking place: They were being uprooted. After the first wrench away from their beloved ancestral countryside, other migrations were easier. The idea of long journeys to faraway regions became acceptable. After leaving their villages, however, wanderers had no one to turn to for help. Villages took care only of their own, and spurned strangers, often violently, sending them out on the roads again. Therefore, to a growing proportion of the English people there was only a grim future ahead for them in their homeland.

Now the perils of a voyage across the Atlantic and the dangers to be found in the New World seemed

much more acceptable. Virginia beckoned. Its early troubles were fading, and because of the tobacco boom (which would soon subside considerably, overproduction producing much lower prices), the colony was becoming a place where people could find opportunity. Land-hungry English people, torn from their fields, learned that there was limitless cropland in America practically for the taking. After the 1622 massacre a fence was put across the Jamestown peninsula so that cattle and hogs could wander and multiply, with the result that a meat diet was far more available than in England. New opportunities then opened up in what was called "New England," far to the north, and in Maryland, adjoining Virginia. An emigration fever filled the English air. That epochal event in the whole of North American history, the Great Migration from England, began. Between 1620 and 1642 (when the Civil War began in England, slowing down the migration for a time), 2 percent of the entire population of the kingdom of England, or about 80,000 people, migrated from the homeland, going in many directions (not simply to the colonies).

Tobacco and Labor

The new practice of smoking (which was called "drinking tobacco"), introduced into England in 1565 and popularized by Sir Walter Raleigh, spread like wildfire. As early as 1613 the nation was spending £200,000 a year or more on the weed that was being called "this chopping herbe of hell." King James tried to limit its production—he disliked the idea of founding a great colony in North America just to have it produce a weed to be smoked—but the search for individual profit soon made this impossible. The high prices of the 1620s did not last long, but an enduring market for Virginia tobacco existed. By 1640 the volume of tobacco imported into England was five times larger than in 1620. Tobacco, in fact, was England's most valuable import.

As a crop, however, it produced an intense demand for labor, because each plant requires careful tending. Planters therefore clamored for more and more workers from England. Laborers seemed to die rapidly anyway, not only from disease and bad food, but apparently because they were worked so hard. From the beginning of Southern tobacco agriculture— that is, long before black slaves were used in any numbers—planters anxious to push production in the face of falling market prices got used to forcing their people to labor, it was said, "like slavies." Harsh punishments for poor performance or disobedience were common. Meanwhile, entrepreneurs in the shipping trade spread pamphlets widely in England that glorified life in Virginia, promising profits and opportunities for those who worked out their service periods. They got the English poor to sign indenture papers for work in the colonies (few women were sent, apparently because they were not used in tobacco agriculture; there were always far more men than women). The papers would then be sold to planters when the shipful of immigrants arrived in Virginia. Adding to the speculative excitement was the headright system in Virginia, by which anyone bringing over an immigrant was granted fifty acres of land.

The Founding of Maryland

The colony of Maryland, the first settlement of which was made at St. Mary's in 1634, was the first *proprietary* grant made in North America by the British government. Given in 1632 to George Calvert (Lord Baltimore), it was practically feudal in its legal arrangements. The colony was simply the proprietor's personal possession. The laws were his to make, as were the courts. Like the Virginia Company before him, however, Calvert quickly discovered that he could attract settlers only by granting the right to acquire land and a measure of self-government. It was Calvert's hope, as a Catholic, to make the colony exclusively a refuge for people of his faith, but from the beginning Protestants formed an overwhelming majority.

Maryland was a turbulent colony. Its settlers argued almost constantly with the proprietor over political and other rights. But by skillful management the Calvert family held onto their colony and made a great deal of money from selling its land. From 1691 to 1716 Maryland was a royal colony, but except for that intermission it remained in the hands of the Calverts until the American Revolution. Profiting from the mistakes made in Virginia, it suffered little of that colony's early difficulties of starvation and Indian massacres.

Form of Government

The first legislative assembly in the New World met in Jamestown on July 30, 1619. Soon a bicameral legislature appeared. The royal governor and his coun-

cil, which consisted primarily of the various officers of the government, composed the upper house; the borough representatives formed the lower house, the House of Burgesses.

To provide local government, the royal government established counties throughout Virginia, each administered by a board of commissioners called the county court. Each member of the county board was the justice of the peace for his local region. As in England, the justice of the peace had great power not simply in legal matters, but in administrative ones as well. The wealthier planters eagerly sought the post's power and prestige. Indeed, Virginia's governing institutions were to be dominated by the powerful aristocracy that soon appeared. There were few offices chosen by election, and the elections were rarely held. The masses generally left their "betters" in charge.

The Virginians also divided their counties into parishes. Each parish, through a *vestry* (an elective body) and *churchwardens*, was to maintain by local taxation a worship house of the Church of England and a resident priest. Clerics were difficult to get from England. Frequently a single priest had to take care of a group of parishes. Also, they were often poorly educated and of low social standing. Virginians, indeed, were in their colony to make money, not to save souls like the Puritans of New England. But theirs was a royal colony, and therefore the Church of England was to be established and supported. People could be, and often were, fined for not going to church on Sunday when a priest was present, and the churchwardens were to supervise the private morals of Virginians. A churchwarden's accusation could lead to a trial and sentencing in the courts, for adultery or fornication or habitual drunkenness. Legally and constitutionally, church and state were intermixed, the monarch being the head of both.

Restoration Colonial Policy: New Directions

In 1660, when the Stuarts were restored to the throne, a new era for the Southern colonies began. An increasingly vigorous home government took an ever more direct role in colonial life. There was an amazing burst of colony founding or acquisition. Six of the thirteen colonies that eventually formed the United States of America were acquired during Charles II's twenty-five-year rule: New York, New Jersey, Pennsylvania, Delaware, and the two Carolinas. The English Empire in the New World had become a formidable enterprise.

In 1660 the Restoration government enacted the Navigation Acts. The objective of the acts was simple—to enhance England's power. They required all colonial trade to be carried in English ships, thus building up English maritime strength. They also stipulated that major crops such as tobacco and sugar and a long list of other products be shipped through England before they went to the European continent. Any goods going to the colonies were also to pass through England, except for food products from Ireland and Scotland. Thus, England would become self-sufficient in many products and gather enormous import duties to swell the revenue of the Crown. The Navigation Act of 1660 also stimulated colonial shipbuilding, contributing to the overall economic health of the empire.

After 1700 the Navigation Acts were joined by the Trade Acts, which provided many advantages for colonial products in the English market, and thereafter the system grew relatively popular. But the first reaction in the 1600s was violent protest, for tobacco planters as well as other staple crop producers in the Caribbean and the Chesapeake were suddenly limited to the English market, and their incomes sharply reduced thereby. For many years they suffered depressed prices under the new system.

The new outburst of colonizing under Charles II was led not by business corporations, as in the case of the original charter for Virginia, but by aristocrats. The Dutch colony of New Netherland went to the king's brother, the Duke of York, and was subsequently named after him; Pennsylvania, Delaware, and the Jerseys (East and West, later combined into New Jersey) were given to proprietors; and the Carolinas, not to be separated into North and South until later, were given to a group of eight proprietors in 1663.

The Carolina proprietors spent no money to secure settlers from England. Instead, they counted on local migration from Virginia and the Caribbean to give them experienced colonists without cost. Largely for this reason, the Carolinas developed slowly. Also, North Carolina was hard to get to, for navigation was difficult through the islands that formed the seaward fringe of Albemarle Sound. Tobacco farming was not easy to sustain, for access to markets was limited. As a result, this colony became much more dependent on diversified farming than either Virginia or South Carolina. In consequence, the colony (and later state) had a relatively low proportion of slaves in its population because small farmers raising food could not afford them.

Turmoil in Virginia

By the mid-1600s Virginia had settled down into a well-organized if slowly growing colony. The health of its people was better, but as there was only one large economic activity, the growing of tobacco, there were no cities or the diverse cultural life and economic enterprises associated with them. The population spread widely, in order to find fresh lands (tobacco drained fertility from the soil), but life in Virginia remained plain, monotonous, and bereft of the arts of civilization as seen in England. Both the royal government and Virginians worried about the condition of Virginia. Growing tobacco was hardly enough, in itself, to make a colony proud of its role in English life. But none of the efforts launched to stimulate other economic activities were successful. Indeed, because Virginia lacked schools, newspapers, and learning, and seemed to be a place only for making money in a crude rural setting, its reputation was not an attractive one. The colony was said to be an evil place where men existed without families, labored like animals, drank heavily, and died young.

The mass of Virginia's population did seem to consist of wild young men, often angry, who lived with guns and used them freely. That a powerful upper class was growing rapidly complicated everything. Wealthy Virginians with access to power claimed huge tracts of land by various shady if legal means, so that ordinary men were losing out. It was harder to find good land once a worker was freed from his period of contract servitude. This meant becoming a tenant farmer and paying rents, or moving to the frontier and having trouble with the Indians. Land was so scarce, in fact, that in the 1660s freemen were forced to make themselves available for hire, with the result that they continued working for their former masters. Large planters were at the same time beginning to serve as merchants, for they could sell an entire shipload of their tobacco in London and bring back goods to sell at high prices. In this setting, many small planters were on the verge of sliding back into bankruptcy and servitude. Virginia was no longer a land of opportunity for England's poor.

No wonder the freemen in Virginia were disorderly and in bad humor.

More than anyone else, they confronted and had troubles with the Indians, who were relatively numerous in the sections of Virginia in which poor people had begun congregating. Like all Virginians in the mid-1670s, they were terrified by the ferocious fighting that had erupted in New England in an Indian uprising called King Philip's War. Thousands of New England settlers were massacred by the Wampanoags and Narragansetts. The Indians in Virginia, however, had been decimated by disease and massacres and were relatively peaceful, though occasionally a group of "foreign" Indians would come into the Chesapeake region to kill outlying white farming families. Nevertheless, it was now widely alleged by Virginians that these Indians intended to launch a similar massive assault.

A young aristocrat, Nathaniel Bacon, Jr., suddenly emerged in 1676 to demand of Governor William Berkeley that he be allowed to lead an expedition against the Indians. Berkeley refused, maintaining that it would be wrong to slaughter peaceful Indians. In response, Bacon simply gathered up a force composed mainly of disgruntled and explosive freemen and marched out to lay waste among the friendly Ocaneechees. He then turned on Berkeley himself, sending the governor fleeing across the Chesapeake, and became de facto ruler of Virginia. Traditionally it has been held that this was a democratic uprising and that Bacon proclaimed the legendary Bacon's Laws, establishing many reforms. But this is not so, for Bacon was not a democrat and had no interest in reform. What he did allow was a widespread plundering of estates owned by Berkeley's supporters.

Bacon abruptly died of the "bloody flux" (dysentery), and Bacon's Rebellion, a three-month uprising, died out. Berkeley returned to the main settlements and began executing rebels right and left. Not long afterward a surprisingly large body of troops from London arrived to restore order, and the royal government was again in full control.

The Appearance of Slavery

Heavy ropes bound them together, and a cloud of choking dust rose from their shuffling feet as they marched toward the sea under the oppressive West African sun. For hundreds of miles they had been making their way, thirsty, hungry, exhausted, and in shock. They were simple farmers from serene African countrysides who one terrifying day had been swept up by marauding black slavers and taken from their homes forever. The captives came from quiet, peaceful countries. They were Ibo, Ewe, Biafada, Bakongo, Wolof, and Bambara peoples. Africans who lived in powerful, well-organized countries like the Yoruba, Dahomey, and Ashanti rarely were taken as slaves. Rather, they made war on their less militarized neighbors and delivered them to the slave traders.

It was a grim, traumatizing, heartless ordeal. Captives commonly died from starvation, disease, or simply despair. Their bodies were just cast by the roadside. Those who survived found themselves finally emerging at a shoreline. Here they were thrust into guarded wooden shacks called barracoons where they waited, sometimes for months. Then astonishing great ships with wide sails arrived, sending shoreward strange looking and alarming men with white skin and shockingly ugly faces.

This was a frightening moment, for many believed they had been captured to be eaten, and that now the terrible moment of death had arrived. Instead, they were seized and put through a rough and shaming physical examination, their genitals handled and body cavities explored, followed by searing, shocking pain: Hot branding irons, taken from a fire, were pressed on their bare skins. Shortly after, the captives were taken aboard ship, where the men were put below and chained to the decking, women and children being normally allowed to spend much of the day topside to work for the crew. Then, as before their anguished eyes Africa receded and fell below the horizon, a long and hellish voyage of one to three months began, the vessels heading westward across the Atlantic to the Americas.

The slave trade, as we have seen, began first in the 1500s, bringing workers to the Spanish Empire and to the large Portuguese possession, Brazil. Indeed, Africans have always made up a larger proportion of the Brazilian population than they ever have that of the United States. Until heavy European migration began to arrive in the 1880s, blacks in fact formed a majority of that country's population. An English visitor to Rio de Janeiro in 1829 found a white face to be a rarity. It was common in large parts of the country for slaves to outnumber whites three to one. Brazilian historians today remark that the influence of Africa upon that vast country is second only to that of Portugal.

TO BE SOLD on board the Ship *Bance-Island*, on tuesday the 6th of *May* next, at *Ashley-Ferry*; a choice cargo of about 250 fine healthy NEGROES, juft arrived from the Windward & Rice Coaft. —The utmoft care has already been taken, and fhall be continued, to keep them free from the leaft danger of being infected with the SMALL-POX, no boat having been on board, and all other communication with people from *Charles-Town* prevented.

Auftin, Laurens, & Appleby.

N. B. Full one Half of the above Negroes have had the SMALL-POX in their own Country.

Newspaper advertisements and broadsides announced slave sales.

The English Colonies and Slavery

When the English founded their North American colonies in the 1600s, black people appeared within them almost as soon as the whites. In a famous event in 1619, the first group of black slaves (possibly indentured servants) disembarked at Virginia. During the 1630s, the first colonial laws were enacted formally establishing the institution of slavery. Virginia planters, however, found that for many years into the 1600s it was less costly to use white labor, for slaves were expensive and their death rate was high.

By the 1670s, one disturbing fact was becoming clear to the planters. Running a tobacco colony primarily by the use of white workers was increasingly difficult, and risky. On the one hand the English people were much less ready to leave England than they had been earlier, and white workers were harder to find. On the other, keeping such laborers at their work by making land scarce so they could not live as independent farmers, or by extending their terms of service (which was often done, by various devices), or by keeping them poor, produced a permanently turbulent, potentially explosive lower class.

The alternative was the use of black slaves. It was a step, we must note, that did not require the Virginians actually to create slavery. Though it is an ugly thing to put in this way, black slaves were commonly available as a regular item of trade. Using slaves, then, meant simply keeping them in that condition once purchased, and dispensing with the use of those troublesome white "servants."

Slavery came to Virginia in a major way when planters, in the latter part of the seventeenth century, stopped buying the contracts of white servants from England. By the end of that century possibly half of the Virginia labor force consisted of slaves, and the balance swung swiftly in that direction thereafter. The inflow of white indentured workers from England into Virginia dwindled away, which meant that the later inflow of white freedmen into Virginia life also subsided. Now the threat of an angry laboring class of truculent white men faded. Labor became something attached to skin color. All white men increasingly had something to share, whether rich or poor: their status as free whites, above enslaved blacks. This made for a powerful bond between white people.

Now we see the English colonists finally taking a major role in stimulating the vast movement of peoples from Africa to the New World. Perhaps more people made this crossing, in fact, than from Europe. A conservative estimate is that during the whole course of the slave trade, perhaps 15 million Africans were delivered alive to the New World, from one end of the Americas to the other. The number who perished either in Africa during long slave journeys or on the infamous slave ships might approach that figure. Disease and malnutrition in the slave ships' stinking holds took a frightful toll. The Africans also fought back against their captivity whenever they had a chance, in bloody on-board battles with the crew. On other occasions, captives simply flung themselves en masse into the sea to drown, turning in the water to shout joyously to the ship before disappearing from sight.

However, the Africans sent to the North American colonies were actually a small portion of the total transported across the Atlantic. Fewer than one in twenty ended up either in British North America or in French Louisiana, for a grand total, to the year 1807 (when the slave trade was declared illegal in the United States) of 427,000, from whom essentially all of the 25 million Afro-Americans in the 1980s have descended. Most of the slaves were transported to North America between 1740 and 1807, the peak period being from 1741 to 1760, when about 5,000 a year were brought in.

Using slaves had great attractions to the planters. Living conditions in Virginia were now healthier,
which made investing in slaves a prudent thing to
do. Also, colonists on the North American mainland
made a point of buying women as well as men, so
that their slaves had children, whom planters gained
free of charge. Between 1700 and 1750 Virginia planters imported about 45,000 slaves, but the black population actually increased during those years from perhaps 10,000 to over 100,000. In such a situation
profits could be excellent, for a swelling labor supply
meant swelling sales of tobacco.

As in medieval Europe, the village (in which
most Africans lived) had its skilled labor class, which
was frequently divided into guilds of potters, weavers,
wood-carvers, and metalworkers. Agriculture was a
highly organized communal undertaking since the
land belonged to the whole village. Black slaves
quickly displaced the Indian slaves in the Americas
precisely because they were used to laboring in a
complex agricultural system. In the interior regions
the African economy was largely pastoral, centering
on the raising of goats, sheep, and cattle. Great aggre-
gations of interrelated people formed kinship groups
presided over by a patriarch. This person, in consultation with elders, served as judge, administrator, diplomat, and treasurer.

African society was embedded in a rich cultural
life in which sophisticated sculpturing in bronze,
wood, and ivory played an important part in religious
observance. Complex musical arts, utilizing such instruments as the violin, guitar, flute, zither, harp,
and xylophone, enlivened every aspect of life. Dancing likewise was intimately involved in everyday life.
African literature was primarily oral, but it was rich
in history, professional information, customs, poetry,
and drama.

The Fate of the Afro-American

Slaves were widely used as metalworkers, miners,
builders, and the like. They were primarily put to
work, however, in agriculture, on plantations where
gang labor and disciplined group endeavor were practiced. Until recently historians believed that slaves
were treated more humanely in Latin America than
in English America. Afro-Americans in the Spanish
and Portuguese empires never became mere possessions, losing all civil and personal rights. Marriage
and upward social movement were in law and, often
in practice, open to them.

*The human factories in Africa struggled to keep up
with the demand. In the eighteenth century, between
50,000 and 100,000 Negro slaves crossed the Atlantic
each year. The greatest number, by far, went to the
West Indies and Brazil. At least two million were
shipped to the West Indies, and some five million to
Brazil. As early as 1553, there were twenty thousand
Negroes in Mexico. Some 200,000 slaves were imported before slavery was abolished in Mexico in the
first quarter of the nineteenth century. Hundreds of
thousands of slaves were scattered over the areas of
present-day Panama, Colombia, Ecuador, Chile, Peru,
and Venezuela. In 1810, Venezuela had some 500,000
Negroes in a total population of 900,000. In 1847,
there were 496,000 Negroes in Cuba and only 418,000
whites. In the same year, there were 4,400,000 Negroes
in Brazil's population of 7,360,000. More than
1,000,000 of the Brazilian Negroes . . . were free.
(Lerone Bennett, Jr.,* Before the Mayflower: A History of the Negro in America, 1619–1964 *[1966])*

The question, however, is difficult for historians
to solve because the records are thin and spotty.
Recent research shows that the idyllic picture of a
humane slave system in Latin America must be regarded with considerable skepticism. The actual conditions of life for the slave, whatever the law might
read, were often as unspeakable in Latin America
as anywhere else in the world. Particularly in the
Caribbean islands, slaves were used in enormous numbers and worked in such murderous conditions that
most died in a relatively few years. The king of Spain
reportedly inquired plaintively why the blacks died
so fast. Black uprisings took place frequently in the
West Indies. As early as 1522, one occurred on the
island of Hispaniola, to be followed in succeeding
generations by others in Cuba, Puerto Rico, Marti-
nique, Antigua, Barbados, Jamaica, St. Vincent, and
the Virgin Islands.

Slavery in the Mainland Colonies

English law in the seventeenth century did not recognize slavery, and there was a considerable period
during which the legal status of slaves in the mainland
colonies was in question. For a time the slave was
thought of as a kind of indentured servant, different
from but similar in status to an English person laboring
in the fields under contract. Certainly there appear
to have been free blacks in Virginia and Maryland
not long after the use of slaves began.

Long before 1700, the black person's position
as a slave had been settled. Enslaved men and women
were clearly owned for life, as were their children.

Colonial Settlement by Nationality in the South, 1770

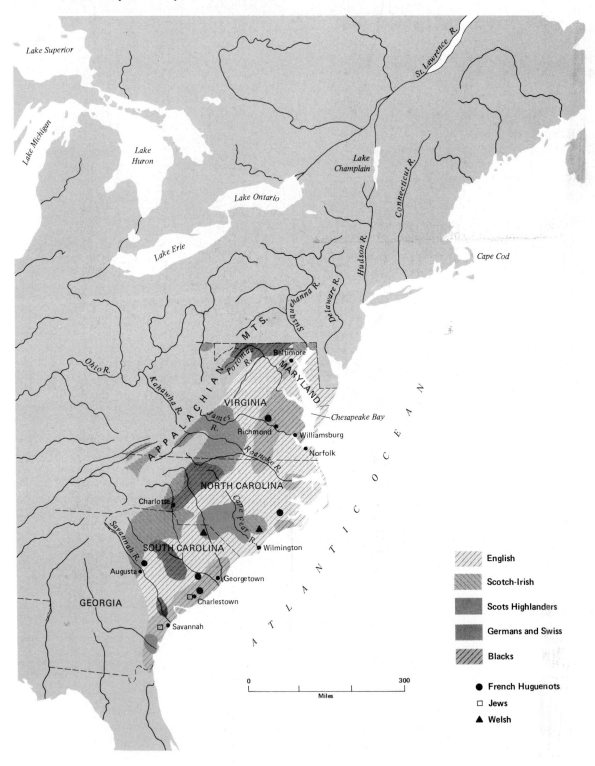

Lake Superior

Lake Michigan

Lake Huron

Lake Ontario

Lake Erie

Lake Champlain

Connecticut R.

St. Lawrence R.

Cape Cod

Hudson R.

Delaware R.

Susquehanna R.

Potomac R.

Ohio R.

Kahawha R.

M T S.

Baltimore

MARYLAND

VIRGINIA

Chesapeake Bay

A P P A L A C H I A N

James R.

Richmond   Williamsburg

Norfolk

Roanoke R.

NORTH CAROLINA

Charlotte

Cape Fear R.

SOUTH CAROLINA   Wilmington

Savannah R.

Augusta   Georgetown

GEORGIA   Charlestown

Savannah

A T L A N T I C   O C E A N

0   300

Miles

| English |
| Scotch-Irish |
| Scots Highlanders |
| Germans and Swiss |
| Blacks |

● French Huguenots

□ Jews

▲ Welsh

A slave auction illustration showing the cruel separation of family members.

They were not yet fully depressed into the legal condition of a mere piece of property with no personal or civil rights, but that status was not far away. Eventually, American slavery became one of the most absolute forms of enslavement known to history. Chattel slavery, where marriages were not recognized in law, where slaves had virtually no appeal to any authority other than their master, existed only in the English-speaking colonies.

The reason for this is found in history rather than in character. The English had developed an institutional structure largely unique in western Europe. It was a system that had tragic results when slavery became a part of it. The economic revolution of the seventeenth century, with its release of the entrepreneur from any government controls, had so thoroughly freed owners of property from constraints that they were able to handle their property entirely as they desired. The *duties* of property to the whole community, long established by custom and law, had given way to the alternative conception of the *rights* of property. That this vastly energized the English economy is without question, but this "progress" also produced deep and lasting social evils.

Southern planters inherited this economic system. They were free to handle their property entirely as they individually desired. They had no Catholic Church looking over their shoulders or, at the least, working with the colonial authorities to lessen abuses and prevent the law from becoming totally harsh and callous. The Anglican Church and the Dissenting sects were weak on the question of slavery because financially they were wholly dependent on their white parishioners. There were no other influences to balance the power of the slaveowner. Supreme on their own plantations, they could be either lenient or tyrannical. When they acted in company with other slaveowners to pass laws, however, any tendency toward individual leniency disappeared. Individuals may have a conscience; groups rarely do. The amorality of mobs and even organized associations has long been recognized as one of their distinguishing characteristics. The self-governing assemblies of white Southerners provide one of the historical sources of pride that Americans take in their history. That self-government without external restraints also enabled them to do things that will forever goad the American conscience is less noted.

BIBLIOGRAPHY

Books that were especially valuable to me in writing this chapter: Edmund S. Morgan's *American Slavery American Freedom: The Ordeal of Colonial Virginia* (1975) has given historians major new insights into the experience of this centrally important colony, especially concerning Bacon's Rebellion and the advent of slavery. Carl Bridenbaugh's *Vexed and Troubled Englishmen, 1590–1642* (1968) is fascinating for its close-up look at why masses of English people suddenly began migrating. The topic of black Americans and slavery has created a library of books. On the aspects here discussed, see Vincent Harding, *There Is a River: The Black Struggle for Freedom in America* (1981); John W.

Blassingame, *The Slave Community: Plantation Life in the Antebellum South* (1979); Winthrop Jordan's *White over Black: American Attitudes toward the Negro, 1550–1812* (1968); and two comparative studies, David Brion Davis, *The Problem of Slavery in Western Culture* (1966), and Carl Degler, *Neither Black nor White* (1971).

The English colonies: how best to understand them? As an element within the British Empire? This is the classic approach, and Charles M. Andrew's magisterial work, *The Colonial Period of American History*, four vols. (1934–38), is a richly detailed place to begin, as is Lawrence H. Gipson's massive 15-volume lifetime work, *The British Empire before the American Revolution* (1936–70).

As to the Southern colonies in particular, we do not have the great volume of historical writing that has concentrated upon New England—American history was in fact written primarily by New Englanders until recent times—but in addition to Morgan's award-winning work cited above, there are a number of valuable studies. Avery Craven's *The Southern Colonies in the Seventeenth Century, 1607–1689* (1949) is a basic, straightforward work long relied upon. The more recent trend has been to look at the colonists themselves, not to the empire, and to see how they lived and evolved into a distinctive people. For a good sampling of this work, see T. H. Breen, ed., *Shaping Southern Society: The Colonial Experience* (1976). Carl Bridenbaugh's *Myths and Realities: Societies of the Colonial South*

(1963) is a fascinating interpretation that has generated historical controversy. John Barth's novel *The Sot-Weed Factor* (1964) is a comic but profound story of tobacco and its various influences on people; Mary Johnston's *To Have and to Hold* (1953) is a historical romance set in colonial Virginia. A fine narrative history in two volumes is Richard Lee Morton's *Colonial Virginia* (1960); students will get from this account a good feeling for what that colony was like to live in. M. Eugene Sirmans explores the other great center of Southern colonial life in *Colonial South Carolina: A Political History, 1663–1763* (1966).

An important newer perspective is to depict black Americans from inside of their life, as in Blassingame's book, above cited, not on the basis of how whites viewed them or talked about them or passed laws concerning them. John Hope Franklin's *From Slavery to Freedom: A History of Negro Americans* (in various editions; the book is regularly revised) is a great work by one of the discipline's most distinguished historians. A shorter, highly readable, and forthright book is Lerone Bennett, Jr.'s *Before the Mayflower: A History of the Negro in America, 1619–1966* (1966). Margaret Shinnie's *Ancient African Kingdoms* (1965) is absorbing and well written, as is Georges Balandier's *Daily Life in the Kingdom of the Kongo* (1968). Gerald Mullin has written the best study of the transplanted Africans in America: *Flight and Rebellion: Slave Resistance in Eighteenth Century Virginia* (1972).

3

The Beginnings: New England

TIME LINE

HISTORY IN AN INDIVIDUAL LIFE

JOHN WINTHROP

It was 1629 and the Puritans of East Anglia were sick at heart. There was a foulness in England, they believed. A wicked and Catholic-leaning monarch, Charles I, was on the throne, persecuting Puritans and spreading "evil doctrine" in the Church of England. The time had come to found a colony in New England where Puritans might erect a holy community to glorify God and serve as an example to Old England. They turned to a quiet, thoughtful man to lead them in their great adventure across the seas and into the wilderness, John Winthrop of Suffolk.

Their choice was understandable. Winthrop was not only a devout, pious Puritan who, now forty years of age, had a strong and closely disciplined character, this grave and sober country gentleman was also an experienced London lawyer. He knew the machinery of government; he was often in the Parliament building and in the walled City of London itself, where the great merchants and bankers thrived. The Massachusetts Bay Company needed such a man. He would give the enterprise weight and standing. "It is come to that Issue as (in all probabilitye) the wellfare of the [colony] . . . dependes upon [my] . . . goeinge,"

he wrote to his wife Margaret, "for divers of the Cheife undertakers (upon whom the reste depende) will not goe without . . . [me]." Winthrop could not turn them down. In its current state England would give a Puritan such as himself little opportunity to influence affairs; abroad there lay, perhaps, a great chance to do God's work. "When a man is to wade throughe a deepe water," he jotted in a note to himself, "there is required tallnesse, as well as Courage, and if he findes it past his depth, and God open a gapp another waye, he may take it."

On April 7, 1630, Winthrop and the first contingent of four hundred colonists left England in their several vessels. After two months of rolling and pitching on the North Atlantic, Governor Winthrop led the colonists ashore and plunged into herculean labors. Shortly a report was being circulated in London that as soon "as Mr. Winthrop was landed, perceiving what misery was like to ensewe through theire Idlenes, he presently fell to worke with his owne hands, and thereby soe encouradged the rest that there was not an Idle person then to be found in the whole Plantation. . . ." A terrible starving time came in the winter, and disease; two hundred of the first thousand settlers died. But Winthrop was absolutely confident, he knew that God's work could not fail, the shipwrights he had had the foresight to bring from England were soon building trading vessels, and the great fisheries that saved New England would before long be in operation. "Oh how it refresheth my heart," he had written Margaret Winthrop, "to thinke that I shall yet againe see thy sweet face in the lande of the livinge, that lovely countenance that I have so much delighted in, and beheld with so great contente!" In the fall of 1631 Margaret and their children arrived from England, and a great feast was held. John Winthrop could look forward to the coming years—he would be governor for most of the eighteen years until his death in 1649—in confidence that he had succeeded. The Massachusetts Bay Colony was planted; it would survive.

Overview

That first Puritan fleet, carrying its four hundred souls, sailed around the tip of Cape Cod bringing with it a great and powerful change for the English empire in North America. Henceforth, there would be two sharply contrasting ways of life occupying polar positions to each other in the English colonies. Virginia was a world where what mattered in the struggle of life was to get a piece of ground, build a fine tobacco farm or plantation, acquire slaves, and become a gentleman of honor and standing. Four hundred miles to the north, where in the 1620s the colonies of New England began to appear, all was different. Here, individual lives and the community at large were built around one central set of obsessions: What do you *believe*? What is your relationship to *God*? Are we, as New Englanders, the saving few in the world, a divinely inspired model for all of humankind? In short, does the community we are forming have *meaning*?

The first settlers who came to Massachusetts Bay to found a believing community were the Pilgrims. Fleeing from the many corruptions of the Old World, they established a tiny village at Plymouth Harbor in 1620. Ten years later there came to Massachusetts Bay from England what Americans have historically called the Great Puritan Migration, followed soon by a large influx bringing a thousand more settlers. Traditionally, we have described this migration in soaring terms as the largest single group to leave Britain, as "unique in the annals of migration." Actually, as historian Bernard Bailyn has recently noted in *The Peopling of British North America: An Introduction* (1986), many tens of thousands of Britons were leaving the British Isles in the decades after 1620, for there was a great outward-spilling milling about, a consuming restlessness in the British Isles. In a single two-year period in the 1630s, at least 10,000 Scots migrated to Ireland! Thus, Bailyn observes, "In the context of the . . . time, the famous Puritan exodus—which, to judge by the weight of subsequent scholarship, must have been a world-historical event—as an organized migration was nothing remarkable."

For Massachusetts Bay, however, it was decisively large enough, rooting deeply in place a community of English Puritans who quickly laid out many settlements, among them Dorchester, Boston, Watertown, Roxbury, Mystic, and Lynn. The great Puritan experiment in living the "true religious faith," the

Massachusetts Bay Colony, was thus fully launched. Some 16,000 additional settlers had arrived by 1642, when the outbreak of the Civil War in England ended the persecution of Puritans there, and emigration dwindled.

By that time religious disagreements had forced dissidents to leave Massachusetts to form Rhode Island, which was chartered in 1644. Others, in search of furs and rich lands, went farther westward to the valley of the Connecticut River. In 1639 several towns adopted the Fundamental Orders of Connecticut as the colony's constitution. In 1662 a royal charter was issued that confirmed Connecticut's independent existence. The first settlements appeared in New Hampshire in 1623. After decades of controversy between ambitious English proprietors and Massachusetts, it became a separate royal colony in 1680. The status of Maine, which had been settled in the 1630s, was similarly troubled until 1691, when it was made part of Massachusetts.

Thus, within a relatively few years, thriving villages and towns all over New England proclaimed that this newest province in the king's domains was flourishing.

What Lay Behind These Events?

Why did the Puritans put their homeland behind them and embark for the wild New World? Because religion was the passion of their lives, and they believed—literally, and with great alarm of soul—that England was being taken over by Satan. They were convinced that it was their divine task to go on an "errand into the wilderness" to establish a pure and holy community as an example for all humankind to study and to follow.

Though the Puritan mentality was obsessed by religion in a way that the modern mind usually finds tedious, New Englanders have powerfully shaped American ways of thinking and it is important for us to take a moment to get inside their consciousness. We must remember, to begin with, that for most people in these years, Satan was a living, breathing, real personage. He and his minions were felt to be continually at work in our daily lives. What the modern mind thinks of as superstition was simple fact to seventeenth-century Europeans. The "other world" was to them vitally alive and always involved in everyday events.

Puritans, then, were not odd and quirky in

their belief in Satan, since practically everyone shared it, but they *were* unusually alarmed about him. Puritans were not, in fact, very comfortable to be around, so obsessed were they by Satan and by God. Quotations from the Bible flowed from them, and they freely condemned other people's ways of living as immoral. Fine clothes and houses and all the other material things of this world were Satan's temptations, Puritans believed, put here to lure us into idolatry. Because most people found the Puritans excessively righteous and preachy, they were not very popular.

For many years they had been arguing that the Protestant Reformation in their country had not gone nearly far enough; that papist (Roman Catholic) corruptions—the work of Satan—were still dangerously at work in the Church of England. Of course, many Protestant goals had been won. The Church of England was now under the English king, not under the Pope in Rome; the Bible had been put into the English language so that ordinary people could read it; and priests no longer stood, in effect, between the worshiper and God. Priests did not dispense forgiveness for sins, that being now a matter between the individual sinner and God, nor did they daily perform the miracle of turning bread and wine into the body and blood of Christ. The Church of England held that no such transformation took place; that if a miracle took place in the Eucharist (communion service), it took place not on the altar but in the soul of the communicant.

Puritans believed, however, that far more needed to be done. The Bible, they insisted, should be made the center of everything, for it was the Word of God. Religious ritual should be simple and brief, and the whole setting inside church buildings should be physically plain and unadorned so as not to get people worshipping material objects. This would allow all attention to be shifted to the sermon, in which the Word of God as found in the Bible would be carefully explained by an educated minister. Education and learning, in fact, were tremendously important to the Puritans, who tended to come from the hard-working, well-schooled, middle classes in England. Year after year, they labored to get a preaching clergy into the Church of England's pulpits. Puritans "would have all in talking, they speak so much of preaching," one of their critics scoffed, "so as all the gates of our senses and ways to man's understanding should be shut up, save the ear alone."

The Anglican Resurgence

By the 1620s the Puritans had moved the Church of England a long way toward their way of doing things, but then a startling reversal occurred. The new king, Charles I, working with those who disagreed with the Puritans—history has come to call them Anglicans—launched a determined counterattack. First, Anglicans revered church buildings as holy places that should be made beautiful, and believed that the worship service should be stately. Elegant robes for the priest, glorious objects of gold and colored glass in use during the worship service, the altar itself treated as a place of almost miraculous significance—all of these, Anglicans insisted, were fitting expressions of reverence toward, and glorification of, God. The prayers of the Prayer Book, and the sacraments, must be the center of all worship—especially communion, for it represented the *Body of Christ.*

Puritans were shocked to see these changes, and even more appalled when hundreds of priests who resisted them were dismissed from their pulpits. Like everyone else, Puritans believed that the Church of England was the driving force, the very center of national life. If it were corrupted, what then? England, everyone agreed, was in a terrible condition. There was whoring, gambling, lying, and thievery; there was rape and murder, cheating, excessive luxury, and selfish greed and individualism. God, the kindly Father who must at the same time chastise, was therefore sending plagues and other disasters to punish his erring children. (That calamities are sent by God to punish us was common belief and would remain so for centuries.) Only when England possessed a fully purified church, Puritans said, would God cease punishing the English for their sins.

Anglicans pointed out that by law the king and his bishops were in charge of the Church and insisted that everyone's duty was to obey them, not to grumble and criticize. All agitation should cease. The Puritans, stiff-necked and determined, reacted angrily to the demand for obedience. Obey the king and his bishops? Not, Puritans replied, if they were going to bring back to the Church of England that "vast, suffocating fog" of Catholic superstition and idolatry that the Protestant Reformation was supposed to have swept away. Meanwhile, across the English Channel on the European continent, powerful armies of Catholic monarchs were sweeping from victory to victory as the Counter-Reformation against Protestantism launched by the Roman Catholic Church, mounted in power. Zealous Puritans now said that what the Anglicans were doing was part of a hidden Roman Catholic plot, working through the king and his followers, to destroy Protestantism in England.

This was not in reality true. However, in this as in so many other situations that we will later explore, what is important, so far as what people do is concerned, is not what actually is the case but what they believe it to be. It is common for fearful people, faced by what to them are terrible dangers, to be seized by delusions about hidden conspiracies. Driven by such beliefs, they feel impelled to do things in response that can have massive and sometimes world-shaking consequences.

The Deeper Argument

Much deeper was the Anglican and Puritan argument over human nature. To Puritans, human beings in their "natural" condition are *totally* depraved, both in their spiritual and reasoning capacities. If any are "saved" (forgiven their sins, and going to heaven), it is entirely because God has willed it so, *not because of anything that individual persons may do on their own.*

Central to all of existence, Puritans said, was the blazing, all-powerful, and awesome majesty of God. Thus, by far the most important of the Ten Commandments were the first four (the "First Table"), which ordered humanity to worship God, to glorify Him, to have no other thing or person in our lives before Him. The dilemma was that human beings were so corrupt, in their natural condition, so stuffed with pride and sensual appetites, that every thought turned them away from God. They chose evil knowingly.

Does everyone, then, go to hell? No. Puritans believed that God, for reasons known only to Him, had decided to save some of humanity from that everlasting torture. He had sent Jesus Christ to save these persons, who are the elect from all eternity. In the course of their lives, after long and prayerful and extremely difficult inward studies, they suddenly learn that they are indeed saved. In that overwhelming moment the old, corrupt person within (i.e.,

In a 1744 Boston edition of John Bunyan's Pilgrim's Progress *the author dreams of the arduous path to salvation.*

Adam, the natural person) dies, and a new person, Christ's own, is born. Thereafter, the person so saved will by divine grace live new and different lives, clearly designed to bear witness to the glory of God.

Their new task is to do God's work, unceasingly, in reshaping, remaking, and saving this world. They must build new Zions and not be swayed by corrupt existing laws and customs. They had a covenant or compact with God, in which salvation is given to them freely and without restriction, but with a clear obligation to live thereafter a devout and unspotted life.

The Anglican Response

Anglicans recoiled from all this. They believed, of course, that we are all sinners, but also that God has made us *reasoning* creatures. Reason, they said, is "the candle of the Lord." Thus, to some degree we have a free will; that is, we do have a role in deciding our personal destinies. Anglicans believed that if we choose to live in God's way, take the sacraments regularly, and by having faith in Christ accept the salvation that a kindly God has offered to all (not just to a few), we are saved.

The important thing was not so much what we believed, but how we treated each other. Certainly we must love God, as the First Table decreed, but equally important were these questions: Are we loving to each other? obedient and dutiful to proper worldly authority? and peaceful? These were what the last six of the Ten Commandments called for ("the Second Table"), and it was here that Anglicans laid their stress.

Given the simplicity of true religion, Anglicans said, why was there a great need for endless sermonizing on complex theological points? How, indeed, could any foolish preacher who stood up and proclaimed his views truly know God's mind? For ordinary people, preaching was probably more confusing than anything else. Theology should be left to the experts. This was why the community should reverently obey when the king and his bishops in their wisdom decided that a particular form of worship should be followed.

Puritanism as a Response to Disorder

Puritans had a powerful social vision. They insisted that godly persons must be self-controlled; that the family must be governed by the father as God rules humanity; that political government must be honest, orderly, impartial, and disciplined.

> The Puritan demand for continuous, organized, methodical activity—to banish idleness—was a reaction to the breakdown of country stability and . . . to the sudden appearance of the mobile urban man. . . . With the intense moral discomfort of the righteous and high-minded, Puritans sought desperately to separate themselves from the chaotic sinfulness that they imagined to surround them. This indeed was the central purpose of their self-discipline and their search for "good company." But they wished also . . . to create a society in which godly order would be the rule and sin not a possible activity. The Puritans sensed in themselves, saints that they assuredly were, men of substance that they often were, the strength and energy to control human wickedness even as they transcended the world of sin and distinguished themselves from its less fortunate members. (Michael Walzer, The Revolution of the Saints: A Study in the Origins of Radical Politics [1965])

It is not surprising, therefore, that Puritans sacrificed freedom of thought in their terrible struggle for control. They disliked unchecked forces, masterlessness, and every influence that was freewheeling, self-centered, and abandoned. Wandering vagabonds were condemned, as were dancing and the maypole. Puritans wanted a productive world of discipline and work. They were fiercely antagonistic to the traditional life of the leisured upper classes, in which status, patronage, corruption, and laziness—not impersonal and binding contracts—were fixed elements. Similarly, they were contemptuous of the "idle poor."

Their task in New England was to fulfill their covenant with God: They would create a Godly Commonwealth, and He would give them His blessing. The Bible, expounded by the ministers, would be the rule in all aspects of daily living. Indeed, in 1635, within five years of their arrival in New England, the Puritans were so zealous that they decided only the "saved" could be church members (in England it took only an honest life, a profession of faith, and an acceptance of church discipline to be a member). This made the Bible Commonwealth even more pious and homogeneous, for only church members could vote in its elections.

After the Civil War and the restoration of the Stuart monarchy, the Puritans in England would finally be forced out of the Church of England and would have to form their own separate religious bodies. From that point on English Puritans would be called Independents (or, in American terms, Congregationalists), for each congregation governed itself independently, chose its own minister, and raised its own funds. Some of the English Puritans followed the Scottish example in organization, worked out in 1560 when John Knox reshaped the Church of Scotland in the presbyterian mold. This arrangement linked congregations together in federal fashion. In New England, however, after the Restoration of 1660 the Congregational Church of the Puritans remained the state church of Massachusetts, supported by common taxation.

The Invasion of America

When John Winthrop's fleet arrived in Massachusetts Bay in 1630, therefore, it was in pursuit of a utopian goal: to found in the New World a pure and undefiled Zion that would serve as an example to the Old World. They were not escaping from England, they were on an "errand into the wilderness." "For wee must Consider," as Governor Win-

Colonial Settlement by Nationality in New England, 1770

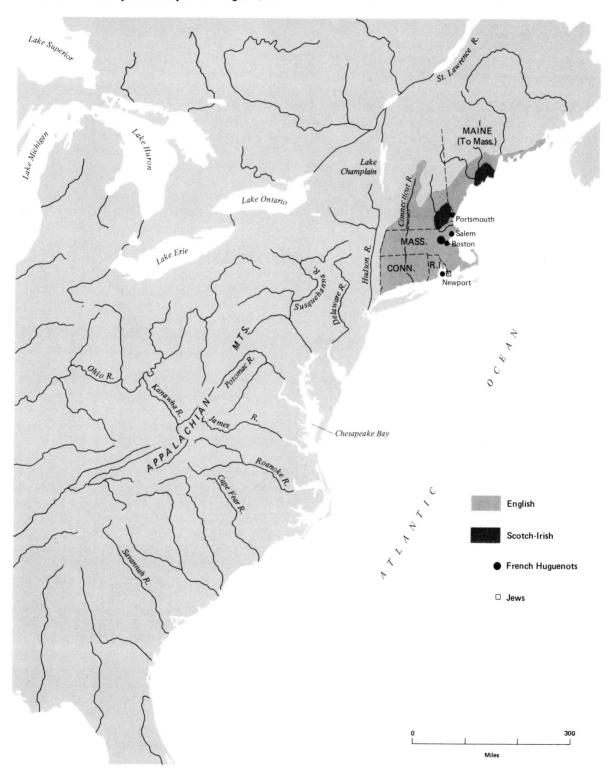

throp said, "that wee shall be as a Citty upon a Hill, the eies of all people are uppon us."

From the point of view of those who already lived in North America, however, this was an invasion. North America was a vast continent occupied for many thousands of years by (according to recent estimates) perhaps 10 million to 12 million native Americans north of the Rio Grande. How could the Puritans make a lasting bridgehead among so numerous a people? For one thing, they had been preceded by European disease bacilli, which had arrived in New England with visiting English fishermen in 1616. Like a great animate scythe, an epidemic had swiftly cut down probably half of the Indians of New England, who had numbered perhaps 25,000. "The bones and skulls," an Englishman wrote, "made such a spectacle . . . it seemed to me a new found Golgotha."

What we would term a tragic human disaster was by the English said to be proof of God's wishes: that the land be made empty for them. And then came a second devastation, smallpox, shortly after the Puritans' arrival, which in the early 1630s killed thousands more Indians. What had happened over the past century in Mexico, where a population of perhaps 25 million had shrunk to less than one-twelfth that number, was occurring around the Puritans as well. Had this not taken place in the Americas, it is possible that the Indians, a powerful people, could have kept the Europeans off their continent. The historian Francis Jennings has written that the "so-called settlement of America was a *resettlement*, a reoccupation of a land made waste by the diseases and demoralization introduced by the newcomers."

The weakened local Indians therefore made room for the Puritans, who in turn stated that since the land was not "occupied" or "settled," it could be rightfully taken. Besides, the English said, they were a "civilized" people and the Indians "inclose noe Land, neither have any setled habytation, nor any tame Cattle to improve the Land by. . . ." So the Puritans simply moved in and established their settlements. Later they made purchases of great tracts from the Indians, but only to establish a "legal" title to the land so that the Dutch of New Amsterdam (later New York City) could not.

There was much talk among the Puritans that they should Christianize the Indian, and small groups of "praying Indians" were eventually formed into villages nearby. But unlike the Spanish, the Puritans did not bring with them great armies of missionaries to spread out among the Indians, but only enough ministers to meet the Puritans' own needs. The authorities of Massachusetts Bay Colony declared that the Indians in their region were subject to the laws of the colony and tried to control their moral behavior. This, however, quickly brought them into conflict with the Pequots, still a strong and aggressive tribe, and led to the Pequot war of 1637, during which the tribe was practically obliterated. Now, for almost forty years, there was peace. As in Virginia, Indians and Puritans remained biologically separate, since Puritans came as families and English men (unlike the Spanish men in their empire) had no need for Indian wives.

Nonetheless, a powerful connection existed between the two peoples. Europeans acquired crops from the Indians that were well suited to North America, such as corn, beans, and squash, and were taught survival techniques in the wilderness. They got improved lands from the Indians because Indian agricultural practices kept the forests cleared of underbrush in order to aid hunting, and created croplands by girdling trees and pulling weeds. Also, the Indian appetite for European cloth and metal goods, especially weapons, created an enormous market for European industry.

On their side, the Indians quickly became dependent, in certain ways, upon the Europeans. They gave up their own crafts to buy European implements and cloth; the many tribes, frequently at war with each other anyway, mounted far more ferocious and destructive campaigns to gain advantages in fur and other markets; and metal weapons, which could only be purchased from Europeans and repaired by them, became essential to Indian life. Alcohol was sought after eagerly, and it induced a widespread demoralization in Indian culture. Soon the Indians were pawns in the rivalries between European powers and in their imperial wars in the New World, which enhanced schism and mutual hatreds among the different Indian nations. The Indians had what the English wanted—land—and so, one way or another, they would be slowly pushed back farther and farther into the interior—or simply killed off, by warfare or disease. Thus, although the English and the Indians did not intermarry, as did the Spanish and the Indians far to the south, they were nonetheless locked in a complex interaction that would persist for centuries. It would never be an equal relationship. The Europeans depended upon the Indians only at the beginning. Thereafter, the balance shifted in the other direction, and the Indians paid an incalculable price: in their lives, in their culture, and in their territory.

The Puritan Village: Communal Utopia

Virginians settled as *individuals* upon the land that they received from the Crown. New Englanders settled as *communities* upon land granted to each village by the General Court (the legislature) of Massachusetts Bay Colony. Individuals got land only from the village, and then only if they were members of that community. That is, they would be looked over first by the members of the village to see if they were godly, if they were true Puritans. Then they would sign the covenant (common agreement) which the founders of the village had drawn up together at its founding. This covenant bound all people living in the town to "fear and reverence . . . Almighty God" and "profess and practice one truth . . . the foundation whereof is everlasting love."

Each *town* (the term refers to a large piece of territory, not just to the village at its core) might be hundreds of thousands of acres in extent. The founding villages, however, turned their backs upon that vast wilderness and formed compact village communities devoted to producing the perfect Christian life. All townspeople accepted the community's moral oversight and discipline. According to the number of persons in each household, their social standing, and the "usefulness in either Church or Commonwealth" of their patriarch—Puritan life was profoundly rooted in male dominance, as echoed in the

Old Testament—the town would grant so much pasture land in the "commons," so many strips of arable farming land, and so much woodland. Everything was done communally. Just as each person's moral life was properly under the oversight of the community, through the church congregation and the minister, so the cattle were grazed under the supervision of a common herdsman and what was planted in the fields was decided upon in common and plowed and harvested in the same way. This was the ancient pattern in "open-field" English villages. (In "closed-field" systems, each man's property was within his own wall, and tilled by himself.) Indeed, economic communalism is the ancient pattern in peasant villages in most of the world.

New England towns were almost entirely self-governing. And no one in them had to pay quit-rents to any overlord for their lands (in contrast with the colonies to the south, where annual quit-rents had to be paid to the Crown or to the proprietors). Land, once granted to individual farmers by the town, was theirs in fee simple: They owned it absolutely. The Puritans were determined never to reproduce in their part of America the ancient curse of tenant farming, which existed as the general rule in England—that is, the rule of manor lords who could raise rents and evict tenants at will. Just as Puritans wanted no bishops over their churches and their religious lives, they wanted no manor lords over their farms and their economic lives.

Several times a week the townspeople would

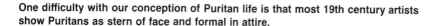

One difficulty with our conception of Puritan life is that most 19th century artists show Puritans as stern of face and formal in attire.

gather in the meeting house, which doubled as the chapel, to hear sermons from their minister. Each congregation was an independent community; there was no religious hierarchy that bound them together with other congregations. This was ultimately to give Congregationalism in New England a great doctrinal vitality, new ideas and movements springing up here and there across the devout countryside. Also, each church was to admit to membership only those who could publicly, and in detail, describe the terrors and the exaltation of having gone through a salvation experience. Congregationalism, in short, was a "church of saints" built around a vision of Christian perfection. Visible holiness, visible faith, a visibly devout way of living: these, it was said, were clearly the marks of God's grace in the saved person. Then, after grave inquiry, the "selectmen" who would govern the town were elected from the community. It was assumed that henceforth these individuals ultimately answered only to God.

The Passion for Unity

Also traditional in the peasant village, wherever located, had been a passion for unity, order, and peace. New England was not founded, as is the myth, as a democracy in the modern sense. People were supposed to talk together and argue things out in the town meeting house, but when decisions were made, all were to "assent unanimously." In practice, Puritans accepted that certain individuals were more substantial and authoritative than others, and the board of selectmen elected from this elite was generally presumed to exercise a divine magistracy that should be obeyed dutifully. Indeed, Puritans generally disliked what we would call democracy, which implies free and open criticism of leaders and the organization of opposition to depose them. This was seen as running against the unity that God desires, and being disobedient to proper authority. The idea of *disunity*, of a kind of "party politics" within the colony or village, was beyond grasping, or accepting, as right. Were they not people of one God? Was there not one truth in all things? *Unanimity*—this was what New Englanders desired and prized. Chaos and anarchy were feared.

What did they think about church and state? On the one hand, they rejected the idea that church and state should be unified in the sense that they should be interwoven. At home, the Church of England shared in the making of laws (its bishops sat,

and sit still, in the House of Lords), and it had a court system that could punish people by fine and imprisonment for moral offenses. The Puritans wanted none of this, and they gave their ministers no such role or powers. However, Puritans were not what were then termed "separatists"—religious radicals who demanded an absolute separation of church and state. Rather, they believed that in a given country there should be only one church, and that a state church supported by public taxes should exist to which all should belong. We must remember, once more, that Puritans believed deeply in unanimity, in the whole community being together.

In 1631, Roger Williams arrived in Boston to be a minister. He was soon preaching that no church (not even New England's Congregational Church) should be supported by general taxation, nor should everyone be required to attend it. Inevitably, he had to leave, and in 1636 he founded his own colony— Rhode Island. Here he created a unique community in which there was complete freedom of conscience and genuine political democracy. Williams believed that only people's actions, not their thoughts, should be supervised by government, and then only if they led to the harm of others. If they wished to gather together and form churches, these should be totally self-supporting and not connected to the state. That is, the gathered worshipers should be "Baptist" churches—and Baptist Protestantism in America has its origins in Roger Williams's Rhode Island.

His colony attracted prickly religious individualists from all over New England. Puritans regarded it with distaste, for Rhode Island seemed an unseemly, radical place that allowed anyone to say anything. Indeed, Puritans shunned anything flighty and unstable. When they settled in a village they remained in it generation after generation. In this respect New England was far more stable than turbulent England, where a notable mobility existed in the people at large. New Englanders were healthier than Englishmen in the homeland, their women lived long and had large families, and sons and their families clustered closely, on their nearby farms, to parents and grandparents.

Massachusetts as a Colony

Having brought their charter with them to Massachusetts Bay Colony, the Puritans were free from any direct say in their government by the English monarch or Parliament. They insisted upon annual election of all officers in the government. After early squabbles, the status of "freemen" was extended to all male members of the Congregational Church (given a property qualification that most could satisfy). Thus, the Massachusetts government was more under popular control than the more aristocratic institutions of Virginia, or of England itself.

The immediate task in New England was to find an economic basis for the new community. The money that emigrating Puritans brought with them sustained Massachusetts through its early years. Meanwhile, a frantic search for furs was under way. By 1640 this search had pushed settlements out to Connecticut, south along Long Island Sound, and north to the Merrimac River. However, the supply of furs in New England was limited. By 1660 the trade had dropped off steeply; by 1675 it was virtually extinct. Worse yet, the outbreak of civil strife in England in 1642 reduced immigration to a trickle, and with it the flow of money from England. Thereafter, Massachusetts entered extremely difficult times.

A lasting source of income was found in the rich fishing waters that lay off the coasts of northern New England and Newfoundland. In this region, where cold Arctic waters mix with the Gulf Stream to produce a great upwelling of nutrients from deep within the sea, a huge fish population provided bountiful fisheries. These productive waters had been worked by the Portuguese and the French for generations, but after 1640 New Englanders moved in so vigorously that within twenty years they dominated the trade. The codfish became Massachusett's symbol, for it provided the basis for a healthy New England economy.

The result was the emergence of a vast, manysided trading system in the Atlantic. Based upon fish, lumber products, rum, wine, tobacco, slaves, and English manufactured goods, it touched England, the Wine Islands (the Azores), West Africa, the Caribbean islands, the Southern colonies, and New England. Through this trade, New England became permanently incriminated in the slave traffic. In 1643

Faneuil Hall, completed in 1742, was given to the city of Boston as a market house by Benjamin Faneuil. It remains in use today in the center of a modern shopping plaza.

the first New England vessel carried a cargo of black slaves to the plantations.

As this great new trading pattern emerged, a new class, the merchants, arose in Massachusetts. The Puritan authorities were not traders, but were usually drawn from the lesser rural gentry in England. They were firmly devoted to the traditional medieval conception that business activities should be regulated so as to benefit the general community, not simply to enrich certain individuals.

Tightening of the Empire

By 1660 New England's merchants were trading freely all over the Atlantic with France, Spain, Holland, and the Caribbean islands. After the Restoration of that year, Charles II's government moved vigorously to pull the New England merchants back into line and to tighten the reins on the empire. In the Navigation Acts, the royal authorities required that most colonial trade be channeled through England. These regulations brought loud complaints, but London was determined.

At the same time, disgruntled New England merchants began trooping to Whitehall, the govern-

ment buildings in London, to complain of the harsh restrictions imposed on them by the Puritan authorities in Boston. They pointed to laws against the residence of "strangers" and to the requirement that one could not vote unless he had gone through the salvation experience and was a member of the church. Few merchants were "saved." They could not bring themselves to sit on a stool in front of a Puritan congregation and pour out their souls. Many, indeed, had converted to Anglicanism, especially since Anglicans were back in power in England.

Moved by these complaints, London began in 1665 the first of a long series of investigations of the troublesome Massachusetts Bay Colony. To the royal authorities, Puritans were hardly attractive people. As tiresome Dissenters and religious zealots, they were implicit allies of those who had beheaded Charles I. In 1684, after twenty years of turbulence, the anti-Puritan forces won, and Massachusetts became a royal colony.

From then on, the governor of Massachusetts was not elected locally from the Puritan gentry, but was almost invariably chosen in London from among English politicians. He administered the colony in company with the powerful upper house of the legislature, the Council, which was composed of the various

Colonial Overseas Trade

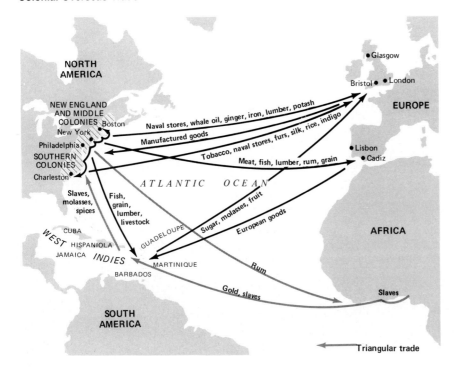

officials of the Massachusetts government, themselves appointed by the governor. They were often chosen from the merchant class, now completely victorious over the Puritans. At the same time, an Anglican church was opened in Boston and all disabilities against Anglicans were removed. The Bible Commonwealth was ended.

The First Great Indian War

By the 1670s the Indians of New England were desperate. Ever since the brief Pequot War of 1637, they had kept their heads low, traded a dwindling supply of furs for guns and European goods (and alcohol), and watched their culture, their standing, and their tribes deteriorating. Meanwhile, the healthy, flourishing Puritans were growing rapidly in numbers: from 25,000 in 1650 to 50,000 in 1675. Several thousand "praying Indians" tried to emulate white ways, but a rising generation of proud younger Indians looked upon them with contempt and burned for revenge against the humiliations their people were suffering.

Metacom, the leader of the Wampanoags (the New Englanders called him King Philip), had for years brooded over his tribe's fate. In 1671 he had been forced to accept a treaty of absolute submission to white authority in all land sales. Soon thereafter, there began gathering around him a movement of resistance to the whites. The moment of crisis was approaching: Either the whites were going to be expelled and the Indians could recapture their pride and dignity and their old lands, or utter defeat would have to be accepted.

When in spring 1675 a praying Indian revealed the Wampanoag's plans, he was put to death. Consequently, three Indians accused of the crime were hanged under New England's laws, following a white man's trial. Now a guerrilla campaign began against isolated New England villages and farms. Militia troops were raised to retaliate; the alarm went out through all New England; and through the summer of that year an elusive Metacom, joined by other tribes, engaged in battle after battle. In time the whole New England frontier was in flames. The fighting continued for months, on into the winter and then to the spring of 1676. By that time, New England settlers were streaming back to towns nearer the coast and the upper Connecticut valley was ravaged. Towns less than twenty miles from Boston were under attack.

An early illustration of the encounter between the colonists and the Indians in King Philip's War, 1675–1676.

But the conflict had become one of simple endurance, and the Indians were running out of munitions, food, and young men to fight. Fleeing westward, they ran into the barrier of the Iroquois, their traditional enemies. Turning back to their ancestral lands, they again came under attack. In the summer of 1676 surrenders began; leaders were executed, or sold into slavery in the West Indies. In August 1676 Metacom was slain.

Several thousand English had died, and possibly twice as many Indians. There were ninety Puritan towns in the colony; fifty-two had been attacked, and twelve destroyed. An even greater ruin had come to the Indian villages themselves. The first of the great Indian wars was over, but it had been a shocking holocaust, easily among the most savage and costly of all such conflicts in American history.

The Dream of Utopia Fades

The world of the Puritans was also undergoing fundamental change. By the latter decades of the seventeenth century the New England dream was fading. The intense Puritanism of the first generation could not be duplicated by the second, who were increasingly less able to become full members of the Congregational Church because they could not truthfully state that they had had a "salvation experience." Therefore, the church itself seemed almost biologically fated to die away. In 1662 with church member-

ship dropping, the Puritans devised, after intense soul-searching and debate, a Half-Way Covenant by which children of individuals who had not been "saved" but who were living blameless lives and who accepted the doctrines of the faith could be baptized. But as these young people grew up in the church, they too would be denied communion or the right to vote in church affairs until they could report being saved. In time even this arrangement had to be set aside. By 1700 all who professed true Christian faith and lived good lives could be baptized and, in some cases, even receive communion. Henceforth, the Congregational churches of New England were no longer just the gathered elect, the "righteous fragment"; they were territorial churches for all those living in the surrounding parish.

This development paralleled the fading of economic communalism. Increasingly, farm families moved out of the villages to live separately on their lands and to till them separately. New arrivals in New England towns were not required to sign the local covenant, and town meetings became more turbulent. Ordinary New Englanders were simply no longer as ready to accept passively the rule of their selectmen. New Englanders were not "saints" any more, and it became increasingly difficult to force people to live up to the moral and religious requirements of earlier times. New England, in contrast with the other colonies, would never lose its special, distinctively Puritan character, but it would no longer be what it had been in its first half century.

BIBLIOGRAPHY

Books that were especially valuable to me in thinking about and writing this chapter: The nature of English Puritanism has recently been freshly explored, and I have learned a great deal from two works: J. Sears McGee's brilliant *The Godly Man in Stuart England: Anglicans, Puritans, and the Two Tables, 1620–1670* (1976); and Patrick Collinson's booklet, *English Puritanism* (1983). I owe much also to John New's keen study, *Anglican and Puritan* (1964), as well as Michael Walzer's *The Revolution of the Saints: A Study in the Origins of Radical Politics* (1965). The surge of fresh scholarship on the New England town and its ways of living is extraordinary: Kenneth A. Lockridge's *A New England Town—The First Hundred Years: Dedham, Massachusetts, 1636–1736* (1970), and Philip J. Greven, Jr.'s *Four Generations: Population, Land, and Family in Colonial Andover, Massachusetts* (1970), have been especially helpful to me.

Francis Jennings, *The Invasion of America: Indians, Colonialism, and the Cant of Conquest* (1975), is a hard-hitting

book, as its title indicates. I have been aided also by both the perspective and the content of Gary B. Nash's *Red, White, and Black: The Peoples of Early America* (1974). More than half a century ago the caustic scholar and social critic Henry L. Mencken described Puritanism as "the fear that someone, somewhere is having a good time." In truth, until the 1930s American history treated the Puritans harshly, as narrow-minded, excessively righteous, preachy folks whose itch was to tell other people how to live their lives. But in the 1930s two extraordinary books revolutionized our view of the Puritans: Samuel Eliot Morison's study of the intellectual life of colonial New England, *The Puritan Pronaos* (1936), and one of the most brilliant and epochal scholarly achievements in American historical writing, Perry Miller's *The New England Mind* (1936). After World War II, books on the Puritans that took them seriously and on their own terms rushed forth in remarkable volume. Now the literature available is rich: Edmund S. Morgan, *The Puritan Dilemma: The Story of John Winthrop* (1958) and *Roger Williams: The Church and the State* (1967); Darret Rutman, *Winthrop's Boston: Portrait of a Puritan Town, 1630–1649* (1965); Perry Miller's classic small volume *Errand into the Wilderness* (1956); Robert Middlekauff, *Puritans and Yankees: The Winthrop Dynasty of New England, 1630–1717* (1962). Philip Greven has given us a bold interpretive study, *The Protestant Temperament: Patterns of Child-Rearing, Religious Experience, and the Self in Early America* (1977).

A rich recent book on New England social and cultural history is James Axtell's *The School upon a Hill: Education and Society in Colonial New England* (1974). To consider the long-range transformation of Puritan life, see Richard Bushman's thoughtful book *From Puritan to Yankee: Char-*acter and Social Order in Connecticut* (1967). For a broad perspective on the Indian wars of the colonial period from the white person's point of view, see Alden Vaughan's *New England Frontier: Puritans and Indians, 1620–1675* (1965). Metacom's crusade is described in Douglas Leach's *Flintlock and Tomahawk: New England in King Philip's War* (1958). Charles M. Segal and David C. Stineback, eds., *Puritans, Indians, and Manifest Destiny* (1977), is an extensive collection of primary documents of the period, with a long introduction. The economic transformation of the Puritan commonwealth into a busy mercantile province is explored in Bernard Bailyn's *The New England Merchants in the Seventeenth Century* (1955).

4

The Beginnings: The Middle Colonies

TIME LINE

HISTORY IN AN INDIVIDUAL LIFE

WILLIAM PENN

The good admiral did not know what to make of his son. Off at college in the early 1660s, William Penn was forever taking up with radicals and left-wingers, mystics and Puritans—the counterculture. Admiral Penn sent William off to France and Ireland to clear his head and give him worldly tastes, but it was hopeless: young Penn was soon in an Irish jail for consorting with George Fox's new sect, the Quakers.

A brilliant writer and a well-built, good-looking, athletic man in his mid-twenties, Penn now took up his forty-year struggle for religious freedom and democratic government. In and out of jail, his pen going at a great rate wherever he was, he poured forth a stream of powerful writings. Of aristocratic standing and a close friend of royalty, everything he did caught the public eye. The Quakers were plain and simple people—unlearned, quiet, and humble. But in the world at large, which they distrusted, they had this spectacular courtier, this gifted intellectual and devout believer, fighting their battles, bringing respect and high stand-

ing to their cause, and writing eloquent explanations of their faith. God is not an external deity, wrote Penn, He is in each of us, in our hearts. "That which People had been vainly seeking Without, with much Pain and Cost," he said, "they by this [Quaker] Ministry, found Within. . . . *For they were directed to the Light of Jesus Christ Within them, as the Seed and Leaven of the Kingdom of God . . . a Faithful and True Witness, and just Monitor in every Bosom.*" Thus we have no need of churches, priests, elaborate ritual; we need only meet together and commune in silence with the inner Light.

In 1670 he preached in the open London streets and was promptly clapped in jail, his meeting being called unlawful, seditious, and riotous. But there was no specific law making his act illegal, and the scholarly and eloquent Penn, arguing his own case before a vindictive judge, exposed this fact. When the judge instructed the jury to find him guilty nonetheless, it refused, even when fined and jailed. The Court of Common Pleas then issued a historic decision: Juries must be free to decide guilt or innocence on their own; judges could no longer dictate to them.

Penn was a passionate Whig, and in the turbulent politics of the 1670s and 1680s he worked actively to secure three of the fundamental rights of the English: property ("that is, Right and Title to your own Lives, Liberties and Estates"); representative government; and trial by jury. Once again, out of a persecuted minority had come the basic ideals of liberty and constitutional rights. In 1681, after the crown had granted him Pennsylvania, this visionary man faced the challenge of his life. "As my understanding and inclination have been much directed to observe and reprove mischiefs in government," he observed, "so it is now put into my power to [create] one." The result, in Pennsylvania (and in West Jersey, also under a Penn-written constitution), was the most liberal and enlightened government of the seventeenth century.

Overview

Between New England and the South lies a region whose common name today—the Middle Atlantic States—conflicts with its geographic position, since it lies considerably north of the center of America's eastern coastline. The term arises instead from the position of these states between the two regions that through much of America's history have been its opposite poles and greatest rivals, New England and the South. The historian can tell the story of the colonies from Maryland southward by concentrating on just two or three great themes: plantation agriculture, race, and the emergence of a powerful aristocracy. In the colonies that spread outward from John Winthrop's Boston, the narrative can focus upon Puritanism, freedom from manor lords and bishops, and a communal, utopian village culture. From these two regions, furthermore, have emerged two towering cultural images, the Yankee and the Southerner. Each presents a clear and historically resonant personage drawn from its dominant English-originated population: the dour, hard-working, pious New Englander on the one side, determined to reform the world and make it pure; the gentlemanly, elegant, lordly cavalier on the other, given to the habit of command and quick to fight to protect his independence and honor.

The Middle Colonies never produced such symbolic personages, though there was Benjamin Franklin as the enterprising capitalist and ingenious scientist. The Middle Colonies were too diverse, mixed, complex, many-tongued, and many-churched. This *pluralism*, in fact, was and is their distinguishing characteristic. It makes the historian's task more difficult, for the story of the Middle Colonies follows not one or two paths but many. In this, however, it is a story that perhaps foreshadows best the American society that was to come. The Middle Colonies were the land of English Quakers, Dutch Reformed, Scottish and Scotch-Irish Presbyterians, German Lutherans and Calvinists and Pietists, Roman Catholics, Jews from many lands, New England Puritans, Africans, and Swedes. They had to learn how to get along together, which in practice meant a highly active internal politics out of which would eventually emerge the beginnings of the American two-party system. There was also the great geographic diversity of the Middle Colonies—their mixture of rich farming regions, mines, and timbered forests; their two large port cities linked to urban England; and their vast interiors, turning in upon the continent and away from the Atlantic. The region displayed, therefore, a very complex economy, in contrast with the single-crop South and New England with its simple farming villages and fisheries.

The Dutch Regime

Characteristically, the history of the Middle Colonies begins not with the English, but with a people who would become the first large (European) ethnic minority in the English Empire, the Dutch. Upon arriving in 1624 they founded New Netherland, a vast colony that encompassed both the Hudson and the Delaware valleys. They established small outposts on the Delaware (in 1638 Swedes would create New Sweden at the present site of Wilmington, on the Delaware, which the Dutch would later absorb), but their main interest was in the valley of the Hudson. On the southern tip of Manhattan Island they built New Amsterdam (later New York City), and at the juncture of the Mohawk and Hudson rivers, Fort Orange (later Albany). A vigorously mercantile people, the Dutch had little but commercial goals in mind in their new colony. Soon New Amsterdam was a multilingual community, as it has been ever since.

In 1629 the Dutch created the *patroon* system, which permitted anyone settling fifty adults on the land to become lord over a vast manor that would include 12 miles of waterfront along a navigable river, or 6 miles on both sides, and would extend inland as far as they wished. Only one great manor dates from the Dutch era: Rensselaerswyck, encompassing the three present counties around Albany. The basis was laid, however, for a unique establishment (after the English took over the colony in 1664 and vastly expanded the patroon system) of aristocratic and near-feudal landholding arrangements in New York that resembled the land system in rural England. This not only stifled the colony's growth, since relatively few immigrants wanted to settle where they would have to pay rents and feudal dues to a manor lord, it created a privileged circle of landowners. They gathered around the royal governor for protection, working to preserve their almost medieval baronies against the bitter attacks of less affluent people.

Among the historical memories in New York is "an aristocratic tradition which for better or worse has colored our state's thought and feeling beyond what one may find in other northern states. . . . The feudal spirit was apparent . . . in the whole land system of the colony. It was intended, quite obviously, to develop here a great community of landlords and tenants unlike any other colony, save, for a short time, Maryland. For the growth of the province it was anything but fortunate to grant immense domains to men of influence, compelling others to pay them quarter rents in perpetuity or pay them profits in small sales of farm improvements. But it stamped a pattern on New York which was more or less respected far down into the nineteenth century, and which became an ineradicable element in its tradition." (Dixon Ryan Fox, Yankees and Yorkers [1940])

The Dutch found New Netherland a difficult colony to govern. English Puritans moved in from Massachusetts Bay Colony, taking up land the Dutch claimed in Connecticut and settling Long Island so thickly as to make it a Puritan enclave. There were also the Indians, whom the Dutch hated and began massacring in the 1640s. In turn they were themselves horribly devastated. To reestablish order, Peter Stuyvesant came from Holland in 1647 as governor, remaining in that post until the English conquest. A strong and vigorous man, he brought 8,000 more people to New Netherland, making New Amsterdam a thriving trading community of 2,500 settlers.

The English Take Over

In 1660 Charles II and the Stuart dynasty were restored to the throne of England. An expansive, confident London government now resolved to make its scattered colonies in North America into an English Empire (see Chapter 2). An essential step was to clear the Dutch authorities out of their New Netherland colony and create a unified band of English colonies from Maine to the Carolinas. England had always claimed the Hudson and Delaware valleys on the basis of early explorations, and when the government sent an expedition to the mouth of the Hudson in August 1664 it called the action not an act of war, but a rightful acquiring of territory not yet formally occupied. The people of New Netherland had no wish to fight, and English settlers were in any event second in numbers only to the Dutch themselves. Peter Stuyvesant had no choice but to surrender without a struggle.

Charles II now gave New Netherland to his Catholic brother, James, the Duke of York. James immediately granted New Jersey as a proprietary colony to English courtiers, and then set about devising a system of government for the huge property he had retained, which he called New York Colony. Above all, New York was to produce a revenue for him: that was the whole idea. This meant establishing

taxes, to be collected by a governor he would appoint. Would there also be an elected assembly, so that the people of New York, as in England itself, would be taxed only at their own assent (or by that of their representatives)? Not at all. The Stuarts detested parliaments; Charles I, the father of Charles II and James, had been beheaded by one. Instead, James simply issued the Duke's Laws. Completely authoritarian, at the same time they confirmed all land titles and guaranteed freedom of worship to everyone. A governor chosen by the duke and an appointed council would govern New York Colony. In local government, appointed justices of the peace would administer most matters, though each village was also allowed to elect its own officials. Each community was authorized to establish a church, supported by taxation, which would be that of the majority in that village. Thus, the Puritans on Long Island and the Dutch Reformed in the Hudson Valley could worship in their own ways.

Protest Erupts

New York Colony grew slowly, for huge land monopolies stemmed the inflow of settlers, but by the 1680s its Hudson Valley and Long Island farmlands and the flourishing fur trade had attracted about 15,000 residents. Led by the Puritans of Long Island, New Yorkers for many years bitterly protested their "slavery" under an autocratic government. Every other English colony had an assembly of some sort, but not New York.

Repeatedly New Yorkers insisted that they were equal in rights to the English at home; repeatedly they were coldly informed that this was not so. For one thing, royal officials said, did not the new Navigation Acts (1660–63) control their trade by requiring all colonies to buy only from England and to send their major products only to England? What was the point of an empire, high officials in London said, if it did not exist for the purpose of enriching the mother country? At home, the king had been forced over many generations to allow Parliament to have a great share of authority over taxation and the making of laws. However, people settled in faraway colonies, all of which had been established under the sole authority of the king (not of Parliament), had no "rights" won in this way by themselves. The colonists could quote the Magna Charta to their heart's content in angry manifestos to the royal government, insisting that from the time King John signed

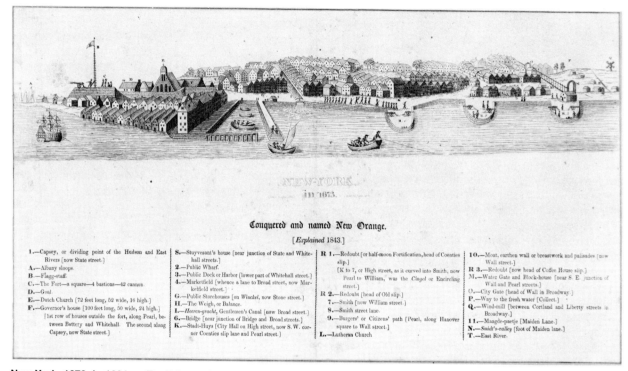

NEW-YORK.
in 1673.

Conquered and named New Orange.

[*Explained* 1843.]

1.—Capsey, or dividing point of the Hudson and East Rivers [now State street.]	**S.**—Stuyvesant's house [near junction of State and White-hall streets.]	**R 1.**—Redoubt [or half-moon Fortification, head of Coenties slip.]	**10.**—Moat, earthen wall or breastwork and palisades [now Wall street.]
A.—Albany sloops.	**2.**—Public Wharf.	[K to 7, or High street, as it curved into Smith, now Pearl to William, was the *Cingel* or Encircling street.]	**R 3.**—Redoubt [now head of Coffee House slip.]
B.—Flagg-staff.	**3.**—Public Dock or Harbor [lower part of Whitehall street.]		**M.**—Water Gate and Block-house [near S. E. junction of Wall and Pearl streets.]
C.—The Fort—a square—4 bastions—42 cannon.	**4.**—Marketfield [whence a lane to Broad street, now Mar-ketfield street.]	**R 2.**—Redoubt [head of Old slip.]	**O.**—City Gate [head of Wall in Broadway.]
D.—Goal.	**G.**—Public Storehouses [on *Winckel*, now Stone street.]	**7.**—Smith [now William street.]	**P.**—Way to the fresh water [Collect.]
E.—Dutch Church [72 feet long, 52 wide, 16 high.]	**H.**—The Weigh, or Balance.	**8.**—Smith street lane.	**Q.**—Wind-mill [between Cortland and Liberty streets in Broadway.]
F.—Governor's house [100 feet long, 50 wide, 24 high.]	**I.**—*Heeren-gracht*, Gentlemen's Canal [now Broad street.]	**9.**—Burgers' or Citizens' path [Pearl, along Hanover square to Wall street.]	**11.**—Maagde-paetje [Maiden Lane.]
[1st row of houses outside the fort, along Pearl, be-tween Battery and Whitehall. The second along Capsey, now State street.]	**6.**—Bridge [near junction of Bridge and Broad streets.]	**L.**—Lutheran Church	**N.**—*Snidt's-ralley* [foot of Maiden Lane.]
	K.—Stadt-Huys [City Hall on High street, now S. W. cor-ner Coenties slip lane and Pearl street.]		**T.**—East River.

New York, 1673. In 1664 an English naval force persuaded the Dutch, headed by Peter Stuyvesant, to surrender, and New Amsterdam was renamed New York. Here it has been briefly recaptured by the Dutch.

that document in 1215 the sovereign was bound to collect taxes only with the assent of the community. But these arguments fell upon deaf ears in London.

New Yorkers increasingly balked at paying taxes, and in 1683, when the duke's revenues from this source had dwindled more than he could abide, he finally allowed the summoning of an assembly in New York Colony. That body promptly drew up a document that would irrevocably guarantee their rights, once signed by the duke: a Charter of Libertyes and Priviledges. But events in England were moving against the New Yorkers. Whigs had been agitating powerfully to have the Catholic Duke of York declared ineligible to succeed Charles II on the throne. In response, King Charles brought Whigs under harsh royal persecution. Anyone who taught that the king's power (his "prerogative") was not absolute was in danger. Even the Whig philosopher John Locke (see Chapter 1) had to flee to Holland. Now, any proposal aimed at limiting the government's power over the colonies was certain to be condemned. "All planta-tions," stated the Lords of Trade (who administered the Navigation Acts) "were of the King's making,

and . . . he might at any time alter or dispose of them at his pleasure."

It was now, in 1684, that the independent char-ter dating from 1629 of the Massachusetts Bay Col-ony, that community of stiff-necked Puritans who often violated the Navigation Acts, was finally re-voked. Henceforth, Massachusetts was a royal colony, administered by a royal governor and an elected as-sembly. Also, New York's proposed Charter of Liber-tyes and Priviledges was denied royal assent and quashed. The colonists were *not* English people in the constitutional sense; they did not have the rights of the English at home.

New Jersey, the Scots, and Presbyterianism

Meanwhile, the proprietors of New Jersey were trying to attract settlers. They offered liberal land grants, religious liberty, and an elected assembly. Therefore, many kinds of people arrived to take up farms: Puritans from New England; Baptists and Quakers; Lutherans (Swedes) and Dutch Reformed. The local government of New Jersey blended New England's *town* system of government with large encompassing *counties* administered by commissioned magistrates.

Hundreds of Scots settled in New Jersey, bringing in their Church of Scotland form of worship, or, as it was called in America, Presbyterianism. From the beginning they made New Jersey the special seat of the Scottish population in America. This Scottish presence was symbolized by the (Presbyterian) College of New Jersey (later called Princeton University), which was founded in 1746 and had close intellectual ties to Scotland. Presbyterianism arose in 1683, when Reverend Francis Makemie of Glasgow, Scotland, arrived in Maryland. Until his death in 1708, he traveled throughout the colonies preaching, writing, suffering imprisonment for speaking in Anglican territory, popularizing the ideas of Presbyterians, and, in 1706, founding the first American presbytery.

It was Presbyterianism, with its federal structure linking its many congregations, that, first among the Christian churches, achieved an intercolonial organization. The Scots and the Scotch-Irish (those from the province of Ulster in Northern Ireland) would in later generations spread Presbyterianism widely in the American colonies. They brought with them an intense dislike of the English and of their Church of England. Centuries of history marked by bloody warfare between Scotland and England lay behind these feelings. The Presbyterians, like the Puritan Congregationalists of New England and New York Colony, were Calvinists. That is, they founded their theology on the writings of a sixteenth-century leader in the Protestant Reformation, the Frenchman John Calvin. Thus, both Congregationalists and Presbyterians stressed the need to struggle against corrupt humanity's tendency to sin, and (for the greater glory of God) the need for each person to work hard, practice self-denial, and ward off Satan.

A New Holy Community Emerges

By the turbulent 1680s, when England and its empire were being shaken by so many controversies over autocratic power and constitutional liberties, a new kind of people were making themselves heard. In 1647 an Englishman named George Fox had searched and searched, in spiritual agony, for the true road to God. There were so many contending voices! Puritans on one side, behind the powerful Oliver Cromwell, and Anglicans on the other, and a babble of other sects in between. Suddenly he heard a voice within him say, "There is one, even Christ Jesus, that can speak to thy condition." Then, Fox said, "my heart did leap for joy." Christ is *within* us: He speaks to us all directly and individually, if we will but listen to His voice, which is the Inner Light that illumines each quiet, devout soul and guides it correctly.

Authority, in short, is not to be found in some outward church, or even in the Bible (though the latter was of course central to all faith). It was to be found in the voice of the heart, which is God's voice. Neither clergy nor rituals were needed. Even taking the sacraments in church was unnecessary. One's whole life was instead to be a continuing baptism, in the sense of resisting fleshly evils, and a continuing communion, in the sense of a union with Christ.

The purpose of a religious gathering, which Quakers called a meeting, was to commune jointly, in silence, with the indwelling spirit. If a member felt called to rise and speak, he was to do so freely and without concern for his lack of clerical training. Quakers were distrustful of learning, for they felt it led to the sin of pride. True preaching came not from a learned and arrogant ministry, they believed, but from within the body of the meeting in the persons of "god-called" ministers.

In their life style the Quakers closely resembled the Puritans—though New Englanders hated them and bitterly persecuted them when they arrived in Yankee country. They lived and worshiped as a strongly communal people. They formed monthly and quarterly representative meetings and a yearly meeting, which began in London in 1668. These meetings knit together a widely scattered movement and tied American Quakers more directly to England than any other American sect. A continuing flow of advice, ideas, and preachers, as well as money, passed across the Atlantic from the London meeting.

The Quakers insisted upon living orderly, methodical lives of thrift and self-denial. Every person should have a "calling," a productive life of work in this world. Even when in jail, Quakers busily set about working at crafts. These habits helped to make them prosperous merchants, leading to the wry jest that they were people with one foot in the meeting house and the other in the counting house.

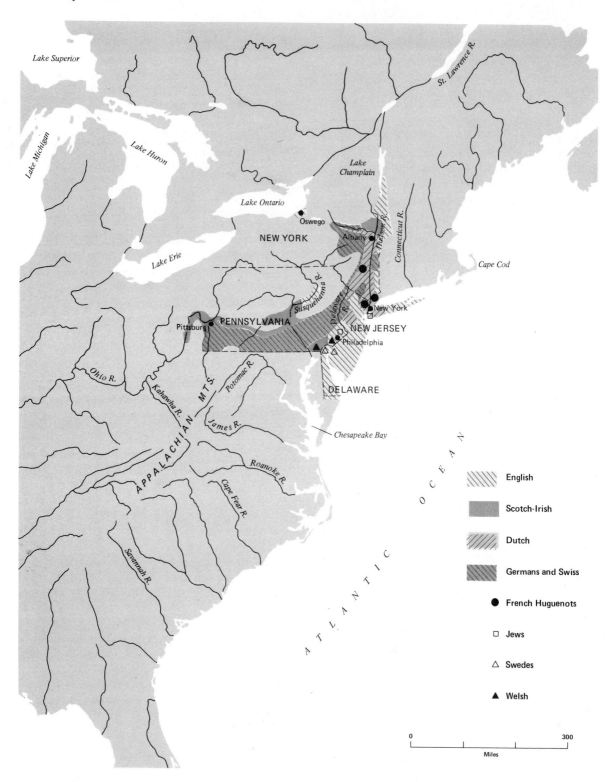

Colonial Settlement by Nationality in the Middle Colonies, 1770

Quakers: Theologically the Opposite of Puritans

The Quakers, then, were another *believing* people, like the Puritans. They too were passionately religious, they too dreamed of creating a dramatically new way of living, a utopia based in a dramatically new religious faith. Quakers, however, held theological views quite opposite to those of the Puritans. They had little real sense of sin in this life. Why? Because they thought humanity basically good, not evil.

Quakers believed in something that horrified everyone else—that we may become perfect in this life. After all, they would say, God is in each of us (not simply in the Puritan "elect"). If there is evil in the world, it lies in external institutions of power, hierarchy, and military violence, not within the individual human heart. Where Puritans thought of God as supreme *authority*, and in his image built strong institutions of government, in which the magistrate, the judge, was central, Quakers thought of God as

supreme *love*. In that spirit they sought to build societies where power and hierarchy had no place.

Thus, Quakers tried to apply the Sermon on the Mount in the most literal sense, creating a world of love and innocence in the here and now. They aided the poor and unfortunate, and were the first to condemn slavery. They believed in complete equality between men and women—women had leading roles as charismatic leaders in the Quaker movement—as well as between everyone in society. This led to the wearing of plain clothes and the using of plain language. They would not refer to anyone as "Mister" (which originally meant "master"), called the king "Charles" instead of "King Charles," and always used the familiar forms "thee" and "thou" instead of the more formal "you" in personal conversation. Because "hat honor" was insisted upon in seventeenth-century European life (inferiors always took off their headcovering in the presence of superiors), Quakers wore theirs even in the king's presence.

Quakers were mystics. They believed it possible to live the perfect life of love for all peoples, and they would not bear arms, participate in any wars,

The Quaker Meeting, **by Egbert van Heemskerk, c. 1690, illustrates the Quaker belief that silence during religious worship is essential for the revelation of one's Divine Light.**

or even pay taxes to support them. God alone was their sovereign; they would take no oaths to any worldly government (they were savagely persecuted for this, for loyalty was vital to most people in these violent times). They would not pay tithes to support a state church, for to them churches were not of God, and therefore unnecessary.

Quakers Search for a Haven

The Quakers grew in numbers, reaching perhaps 60,000 by the 1680s, but this was in the face of harsh repression. It was common for a Quaker congregation to be fined thousands of pounds for not attending the Anglican services, for Quakers by the thousands to be imprisoned or to have their livelihood denied them for not taking oaths. What they wanted, therefore, was to find a place of refuge abroad, some

place in the king's empire where they might live in peace—and, they hoped, attract converts by the grace and purity of their lives and religion. For years this searching went on, into the islands of the Caribbean and on the North American mainland.

In 1674 a group of Quakers, including the gifted William Penn, joined to buy the western half of New Jersey as their place of settlement. As an oppressed minority they were acutely conscious of the need for guaranteed civil and political rights, and the constitution that William Penn wrote for West New Jersey—the Concessions and Agreement—was strikingly liberal. It established an annually elected assembly that was fully independent of the executive. Settlers were guaranteed full due process in court (confrontation of accusers, the right to cross-examination, and the admission of evidence), and trial by jury. There was to be neither imprisonment for debt nor capital punishment, both novel provisions centu-

The octagonal meetinghouse in Burlington, New Jersey, built in 1682, showing the simple functionalism of Quaker architecture.

ries ahead of their time. Everyone in West Jersey was also guaranteed complete religious freedom, for there would be no established state church. Liberal land provisions were offered to attract settlers, and within a few years hundreds of settlers, mainly Quakers, had arrived. (All of New Jersey became a royal colony in 1702, the two halves being merged under a unified government that was provided by New York Colony until 1738.)

The Launching of Pennsylvania

A far grander "holy experiment" was set in motion in 1681. King Charles II had owed a large debt to William Penn's dead father, and to repay it he granted to William Penn—a close friend of the Duke of York—a huge proprietary colony (that is, Penn personally owned the land, and had absolute powers of government): Pennsylvania, including what is now Delaware, which had already been settled by Swedes and Dutch. Now, half a century after John Winthrop had taken his company of Puritan settlers to New England to begin their attempt at building a utopian Christian society, Penn and the Quakers set out on a similar adventure. However, though they were so like the Puritans in their ways of living (if not in their religious beliefs), in one great particular they differed—they could abide dissent. Indeed, allowing people to dissent, and to believe in and practice their faiths in their own diverse ways, was the bedrock of the Quakers' social policy. In turn, this principle would create so great a babble of tongues and faiths in their colony of Pennsylvania that it would seem at times impossibly turbulent.

Penn vigorously advertised his vast possession throughout Britain and southern Germany, to which he made journey after journey. In truth, he had much to offer. His Frame of Government, which he drew up in 1682, began with the words, "Any government is free to the people under it . . . where the laws rule and the people are a party to those laws." Both assembly and council were elective. Civil rights of the most advanced type, including religious liberty, were guaranteed to all. There were other devices, such as headrights (bounties for bringing over settlers), by which the proprietor hoped to induce rapid settlement. He offered free tools, stock, seeds, and the right to buy land in installments.

As governor of the province, Penn retained final decision-making power in his own hands, and to his intense dismay he found himself constantly embroiled in battles with the legislature. These occurred during the four years he was in London, struggling to maintain his proprietorship against enemies. There were times when he sought, in despair, to sell out his proprietorship. It seemed to bring him nothing but trouble and enormous debts. Quakers, as it turned out, did not make very peaceful or suppliant legislators.

Delaware, then called the Lower Counties, was likewise difficult to govern. Its settlers were not Quakers but Dutch and Swedes who had been there long before Penn's experiment began. They were resentful of rule from Philadelphia and constantly restless. Eventually, in 1704, they were given separate status and their own government.

Prosperous Pennsylvania

Despite its political turbulence, Pennsylvania was outstandingly prosperous from the beginning. Its rich farmlands attracted a constant stream of settlers, who produced a bountiful supply of food to be sold abroad. Philadelphia was quickly settled by experienced merchants from London and from towns elsewhere in the colonies. By the mid-eighteenth century they had made Philadelphia the third commercial city in the British Empire, after London and Bristol.

Through personal religious ties, Quaker merchants had contacts all over the North Atlantic commercial world, from Germany to the Caribbean. It was not uncommon for an intermarried network of merchants to connect Madeira, London, Barbados, Newport, and New York, all of them assisting one another. In London itself there was a vigorous community of Quaker merchants who aided their counterparts in Philadelphia. In the same letters in which they sent religious news back and forth, they took care also to report on prices, crops, and finances.

Pennsylvania's wealthy men soon invested in western lands, reselling at higher prices to incoming farmers. Many of them sought land for the same reason that the aristocracy in England did—to provide social eminence as well as income. Quaker merchants also were not long in starting to build iron foundries. Because of this, Pennsylvania has been uniquely identified with the metals trade since colonial days. Based upon this and other enterprises, an aristocracy grew up in Pennsylvania comparable to that of the planters in the Chesapeake and Carolina colonies, the patroons in the Hudson Valley, and the merchant princes of Boston.

The Paradoxes of Pennsylvania

It has been said that people sin as soon as they begin to act. Certainly the Quakers, to whom all things seemed simple while they were a persecuted sect in England, found that implementing their ideas produced unexpected results. A frugal people who emphasized plain living, they became wealthy. Believers in equality, their hard-working virtues and concern for success created an aristocracy. They expected Quaker unity, but from the outset they found themselves bitterly divided. Perhaps most mocking of all to their hopes, their vigorous championing of religious liberty brought such swarms of Lutherans, Presbyterians, Methodists, and even Catholics into Pennsylvania that in the eighteenth century they were reduced to a small minority. Within half a century of their beginnings, they were dissenters in their own colony.

The most severe problem facing Quakers was created by their pacifism. Though Quakers might refuse to support warfare out of sincere belief, had they the right to endanger the lives of the non-Quakers whom they had welcomed to tolerant Pennsylvania and who lived on the turbulent frontier? William Penn and the Quakers regarded Indians as equal to themselves, as human beings, and for many decades kept peaceful and just relations with them. This was so deeply rooted a fact in Indian-white relations that during the frontier wars of the eighteenth century, which saw bloody fighting between white frontiersmen and the Indians, Quakers, wherever they lived in Pennsylvania, were never attacked. But the other peoples who took up land on the frontier were often locked in combat with the Indians, and they hated the Quaker-dominated Philadelphia authorities for not aiding them. Because the everyday world of imperial and governmental affairs produced many dilemmas of this sort, it is understandable that all but one of the deputy governors of Pennsylvania, who ruled the colony in Penn's absence, were not Quakers, for they could do things with government authority that Quakers could not.

The Dominion of New England

In Charles II's last years, as we have seen, he moved sternly to put down his critics and to strengthen royal authority at home and abroad in the empire. Centralization was the ruling principle. After 1685, when his Catholic brother succeeded him as King James II, this broad campaign gathered strength. James decided that the answer to colonial complaints and agitations was to terminate all separate, self-governing colonies north and east of Pennsylvania (including their troublesome elective legislatures) and put them under one centralized, autocratic creation, the Dominion of New England, headquartered in Boston. Established in 1686 under Sir Edmund Andros as governor, it had a brief and extremely turbulent career.

Grievances erupted immediately. The colonists were still insisting that they were Englishmen and that their rights were equal to the English living at home. The colonists opposed taxation without representation and demanded, without success, the reestablishment of legislative assemblies. Even town meetings in New England were restricted to one meeting a year, an alarming limitation on local self-government.

The Glorious Revolution of 1688

England itself was soon in turmoil, owing to a great national fear that a Catholic on the throne would mean the destruction of all liberties. Just across the English Channel lay Catholic France, the ancient enemy, and under the powerful Louis XIV it was completely autocratic, as was the other nearby Catholic enemy, Spain. Indeed, for centuries into the future, Protestants in Anglo-America (who constituted the overwhelming majority in the British Isles and the English colonies) regarded Catholicism and autocracy as synonymous, and therefore at permanent war with England and Anglo-American civilization. When James II gathered Catholic advisers around him, dispatched Catholics to govern the colonies (who brought priests with them), and moved strongly to free Catholics from legal disabilities, the alarm of Protestants everywhere mounted. James's officials bloodily suppressed Protestant protests against his policies. When he dismissed Parliament and refused to govern with its assistance, a revolutionary situation exploded.

English Whigs now appealed to the Protestant ruler of Holland, William of Orange (whose wife Mary was James II's Protestant daughter) to invade England and, with his wife, take up the English throne. In November 1688 William landed at Tor Bay and the Glorious Revolution, as it has always been called in English history, was soon over. Whig theories of government and the constitution had won: Parliament was supreme, and in the Bill of Rights (1689) English liberties were guaranteed (see Chapter 1).

The Glorious Revolution in America

The colonists cheered mightily when they learned of these events. In Massachusetts they quickly overthrew Edmund Andros and the Dominion of New England, and in each colony they reestablished local governments that were locally controlled. However, the colonists soon learned that though they might believe that the principles of the Glorious Revolution applied to them, the new king—indeed, the English in general—did not. The Lords of Trade had rather liked James II's colonial policy: its centralization of authority and its elimination of a large group of troublesome, independent-minded separate colonies. Only in this way, they believed, would England's empire actually be administered for England's benefit in trade and defense.

Each colony, therefore, had to worry through years of troubled negotiations with London to win for itself a part of what the Glorious Revolution had won for England. Massachusetts appealed for restoration of its old charter of 1629, which would have allowed the full rebirth of the independent Bible Commonwealth, but King William would have none of that. Slowly, then, by skillful argument and maneuver, Massachusetts's agent, Increase Mather, finally secured the issuance, in 1691, of a new royal charter, thereby giving permanence to Massachusetts's system of local self-government, though it remained a royal colony.

Rhode Island and Connecticut were allowed to resume self-government under their old charters, which was all they wanted: that is, being left alone. New Jersey became again a quiet proprietary colony. Maryland had thrown off the proprietary government of the Catholic Lord Baltimore, and in the final settlement in 1691 it received the status of a royal colony with an elected assembly. But no charter guaranteed its powers. The results of the Glorious Revolution in New York were especially violent and tragic. A fiery and impetuous German, Captain Jacob Leisler, had led a rebellion in that colony in 1689 that had thrown out the Catholic royal authorities, had proclaimed William and Mary sovereigns, and had taken over all military and government power. There quickly gathered around him all those who detested the great landholders and the monopolies held by Albany and New York City merchants over wheat and fur sales and processing. With this following, Leisler assumed the governorship and established a representative assembly.

He was a German, however, not an Englishman, and when his negotiators arrived in London they were treated with disdain. The merchants' and landowners' oligarchy that had dominated New York Colony sent angry protests to London that he was stirring up tumults and radicalizing the colony, especially when he broke up the monopolies and jailed landholders who had been accused of collaborating with the former governor. Leisler was a stubborn man, and when royal officials sent to New York City in 1691 to reassume the government of the colony arrogantly refused to show him their royal commissions of authority, he held onto the city's fort. His men began firing randomly upon (and killing) people in the vicinity. The German gave up the fort and turned over control of the colony to the king's officials only after days of parlaying and the trading of insults. Promptly charged with treason, he was hanged. The entrenched oligarchy approved heartily of this peremptory execution, though in later years a political coalition gathered around the name and memory of Leisler to mount bitter political campaigns against the merchant and landholding oligarchy.

As a royal colony with an elected assembly, New York reenacted the body of essential civil and political rights that in 1683 it had claimed under the abortive Charter of Libertyes and Priviledges. But William quickly vetoed the legislation. It was acceptable for the king to establish assemblies and allow them to make laws and levy taxes, but this was entirely at the king's pleasure. There were to be no enduring statements of colonial rights in noncharter royal colonies.

Colonial Settlement in 1700

By 1700 some 250,000 settlers lived in the colonies: 92,000 in New England, 53,000 in the Middle Colonies, 88,000 in Virginia and Maryland, and 16,000 in the Carolinas. In all, this represented a doubling, perhaps even a trebling, of the colonial population in the forty years since the Restoration.

The population still lived close to the seacoast. In Pennsylvania and New Jersey, colonists lived close to the Delaware River. The westward limit of settlement in New York lay at Schenectady, as it had since the 1660s. Beyond that point was the empire of the powerful Iroquois. Deerfield, a stockaded town on the Connecticut River, marked the frontier in New England. North of the populous regions around Boston, there was only a thin scattering of settlement up the Maine coast.

The Interior

The continental interior remained Indian country. The Frenchmen of New France (centered in Quebec City and Montreal on the St. Lawrence River) had early made their way up the St. Lawrence and Ottawa rivers and across the Great Lakes, moving among the interior tribes. As early as 1623, Frenchmen had reached Lake Superior, a thousand miles west of the struggling new colony in Massachusetts Bay. Soon the French had crossed over to the Mississippi and down that great stream to the Gulf of Mexico. Through the wilderness interior, French traders and French influence stretched in an arc of forts and trading posts from Quebec to Louisiana.

The French simply wanted furs. French hunters and trappers settled among the Indians, taking brides and founding families. Their few cabins and small garden plots, scattered here and there in the wilderness, were no threat to the Indian world but rather a vital complement to it. Through the French, the Indians secured the trade goods that they came to depend on. These new articles not only made Indian life easier, but they also gave the Indians new strength against their enemies and their ancient adversaries, hunger and cold.

At the same time, French Jesuit priests, incredibly brave men whose courage appealed to the Indians, moved far into the interior to spread the word of Christ and link the Indians even closer to France. The legendary and powerful king far away in Paris became their "father." Indians who called at French forts could always count on little goodwill gifts, supplies of hunting ammunition, and provisions. The Indians (except for the Iroquois) fought against the British on the French side for a greater reason than mere military convenience: The relationship between the Indians and the French was warm and trusting, as well as mutually profitable.

The Indians' long relationship with the white men had left its mark on their culture, and though [many] stubbornly resisted being Christianized by the ever-present Jesuits, they had substituted the ironware and manufactured goods of trade for the tools and imple-ments of their earlier and cruder existence. Instead of stone axes, clay pots, fur mantles, and needles of bone, they now used European hatchets and knives, brass kettles, cloth from France, and awls and needles of steel, and in place of bows and arrows they had come to rely almost entirely on guns and powder both for hunting and to defend themselves against their enemies. Since the French had not tried to appropriate the Indians' lands or coerce them into abandoning their independence, the new and higher material culture had increased the natives' self-respect as well as their power, and in their isolation from the strong urban centers of white civilization along the Atlantic coast [in the eighteenth century] proud, young warriors . . . came to assume that their people enjoyed military equality with the white men. (Alvin M. Josephy, Jr., The Patriot Chiefs: A Chronicle of American Indian Resistance [1969])

The Iroquois

The Five Tribes of the Iroquois were different from the other Indians whom the colonists encountered. Occupying the Mohawk Valley in New York, their powerful confederacy with its 10,000 people terrified all the other interior tribes. They undertook widely ranging campaigns over vast distances, sending other Indians fleeing in terror before them and redistributing the whole interior pattern of tribal residence.

Curiously, however, when not at war they seemed exceptionally humane and sophisticated. The Iroquois based life within their confederacy on arrangements for individual freedom and government by consent of the governed that contrasted sharply with the situation in most European countries. Their sachems (principal chiefs) were known as "powerful reasoners," wise and formidable men who relied on a clear and distinct set of ideas for guidance. Moved by some inexplicable genius, they had been able to construct a powerful and enduring confederacy in the midst of an Indian world characterized by fragmentation and constant warfare among tribes. Federal councils settled common issues within the confederated tribes after long discussions, not by the use of force.

Modern studies sufficiently acute to bridge the gap between the Indian and white people's ways of thinking have uncovered what seems a likely explanation. An extraordinary Indian named Hiawatha was the moving force behind the creation of this remarkable confederation. Born in one of the Five Tribes about 1450—he was not a Minnesota Chippewa, Longfellow to the contrary—he undertook to unify

The cruelty of the Iroquois in war is demonstrated here, although, otherwise, they were a humane people.

the then constantly warring Iroquois tribes by moving back and forth from tribe to tribe, trying to teach them to live peacefully with the rest of the Five Tribes.

Ancient hatreds and suspicions, however, barred Hiawatha's way. Then another extraordinary, man, Deganawidah, inspired Hiawatha with ideals even more transcendent than that simply of unity among the Five Tribes. A wandering prophet and mystic, reputedly of virgin birth, he had had visions in which he saw humanity as a soaring spruce tree, rooted in the fertilizing soil of three sets of double principles of life: sanity of mind and health of body linked to peace between individuals and groups; ethical righteousness in actions linked to equity and justice among peoples; and physical strength and civil power linked to the power of the *orenda* (the extended family in which descent is taken from the mother), which was the basic unit in Iroquois society. These ideals, Deganawidah saw in his vision, could be extended to encompass all mankind, bringing peace and unity to everyone.

He inspired Hiawatha with his great vision and these ideals just when Hiawatha was most discouraged and unsuccessful. Joined in a common crusade, they were able to convert their most inveterate enemy, the great chief of the Onondagas, Atotarho. The government of the Iroquois confederacy was fashioned thereafter under the guidance of Hiawatha and Deganawidah. A completely civil confederacy, it did not allow warriors to be representatives to the federal councils, for they might tend to take warlike stands. Each tribe had a given number of representatives, who could be removed for wrongdoing by their own tribes. The "capital" of the Iroquois League moved about; it was located near the present town of Cazenovia, New York (south of Syracuse), when white people came into contact with the confederacy.

The Iroquois fully accepted, too, Deganawidah's inspirational three double principles and were fired with a zealous passion to extend the new order to all the Indian world. Like the Muslims of the Middle Ages, they undertook holy wars with the hope of establishing eventual peace among all peoples, founded upon the new values and beliefs. First they sought to extend their system by persuasion, but the other tribes failed to understand the revolutionary new way of life and government. It was for this reason that when the French first appeared in the seventeenth century, they found the Iroquois engaged in fanatical campaigns against all those other tribes with whom the French, coming up the St. Lawrence, had established friendship. Without realizing the significance of their actions, the French immediately sided with the tribes who were trying to fight off the Iroquois, giving these tribes temporary but startling new strength by providing them with firearms.

So the Iroquois, the most powerful peoples in the interior, took the British as their friends in order to secure firearms and support against the French. To cement this relationship, the Iroquois became the middlemen in the fur trade, delivering to Albany what would otherwise have gone to Montreal. Armies of more than a thousand men—amazingly large bodies of men in Indian warfare—wore down other tribes throughout the basin of the Great Lakes. They ruled virtually uncontested over an empire of thousands of square miles, from the Atlantic to Lake Superior, from Canada to the Tennessee River.

Throughout their empire the Iroquois tried to teach the conquered tribes the ideals of Deganawidah. They discouraged fighting among the tribes and sent parties of experienced chiefs to conciliate and arbitrate disputes. Some tribes voluntarily asked for Iro-

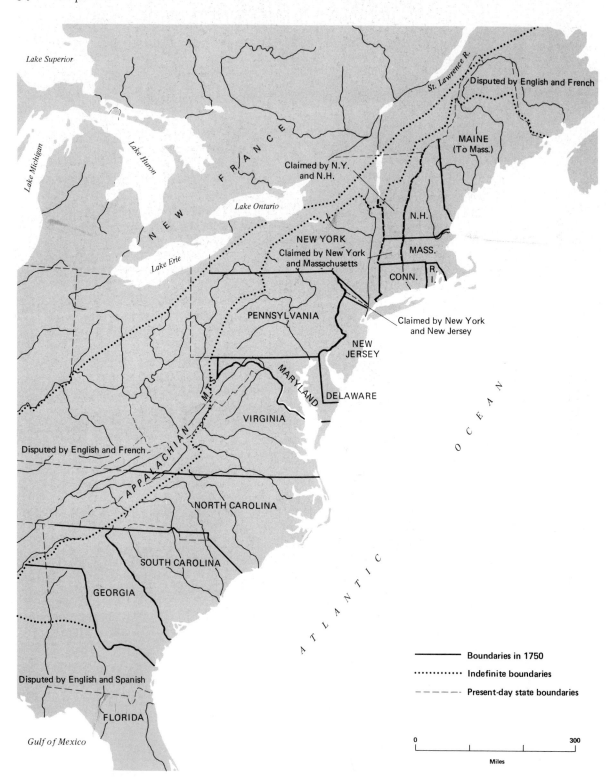

Lake Superior

Lake Michigan

Lake Huron

N E W   F R A N C E

Lake Erie

Lake Ontario

St. Lawrence R.

Disputed by English and French

MAINE
(To Mass.)

Claimed by N.Y.
and N.H.

N.H.

NEW YORK

Claimed by New York
and Massachusetts

MASS.

CONN.

R.
I.

Claimed by New York
and New Jersey

PENNSYLVANIA

NEW
JERSEY

MARYLAND

DELAWARE

VIRGINIA

Disputed by English and French

A P P A L A C H I A N   M T S.

NORTH CAROLINA

SOUTH CAROLINA

GEORGIA

A T L A N T I C   O C E A N

Disputed by English and Spanish

FLORIDA

Gulf of Mexico

—— Boundaries in 1750

········· Indefinite boundaries

– – – Present-day state boundaries

0   300

Miles

The British Colonies, 1750

quois protection, often against the white man. Fragments of tribes that had been decimated by white attacks made their way to the land of Hiawatha, seeking shelter and peace. Through two hundred years of almost constant troubles, Hiawatha's confederation retained its unity against the world, both red and white. Its defeat finally came in the American

Revolution, during which the Iroquois took the side of their ancient allies, the British. Thus ended an extraordinary military empire devoted to humanitarian ideals of brotherhood and peace, conceived and realized by an Indian people before the coming of the whites—and taught today in the traditions of the Iroquois who still live in the Mohawk Valley.

BIBLIOGRAPHY

Books that were especially valuable to me in thinking about and writing this chapter: E. Digby Baltzell's recent *Puritan Boston and Quaker Philadelphia: Two Protestant Ethics and the Spirit of Class Authority and Leadership* (1979) is a fascinating exploration of the Quaker mind. Edwin B. Bronner, *William Penn's "Holy Experiment": The Founding of Pennsylvania 1681–1701* (1962), greatly enriches, with its close focus, the broader picture provided by Frederick B. Tolles, *Meeting House and Counting House: The Quaker Merchants of Colonial Philadelphia, 1682–1763* (1963). David S. Lovejoy's *The Glorious Revolution in America* (1972) gives us our first comprehensive account of this event, and thus a fresh perspective on the American Revolution a century later. Continuingly useful is Wesley Frank Craven's *The Colonies in Transition, 1660–1713* (1968). Alvin M. Josephy, Jr.'s *The Patriot Chiefs: A Chronicle of American Indian Resistance* (1969) is a sensitive study, like all his other books on the American Indians.

There is an extraordinary upsurge of scholarly interest in the Middle Colonies. We now have newly written general histories of great value: John E. Pomfret, *Colonial New Jersey: A History* (1973); Joseph E. Illick, *Colonial Pennsylvania: A History* (1976); and Michael Kammen, *Colonial New York: A History* (1975). Part of a fine new series, *A History of the American Colonies in Thirteen Volumes*, edited by Milton M. Klein and Jacob E. Cooke, they contain extensive bibliographic essays.

Most attention in recent scholarship is paid to the eighteenth century, though there is Gary B. Nash's *Quakers and Politics: Pennsylvania, 1681–1762* (1968), and Robert C. Ritchie's *The Duke's Province: A Study of New York Society and Politics, 1664–1691* (1977). Van Cleef Bachman has closely examined New Netherland in *Peltries or Plantations: The Economic Policies of the Dutch West India Company in New Netherland, 1623–1639* (1969), as has Thomas J. Condon in *New York Beginnings: The Commercial Origins of New Netherland* (1968).

For a detailed essay on hundreds of articles, dissertations, and books on the Middle Colonies, see Douglas Greenberg, "The Middle Colonies in Recent American Historiography," *William and Mary Quarterly*, 3rd series, 36 (1979), 397–427.

5

The New People: American Life and Thought in the Eighteenth Century

TIME LINE

HISTORY IN AN INDIVIDUAL LIFE

BENJAMIN FRANKLIN

Whom do we think of first when we think of the Enlightenment in eighteenth-century America? Of course—Benjamin Franklin, the first famous American, an international figure whose face was seen everywhere in European shop windows in the 1770s. His image adorned countless medals, rings, snuffboxes, and dinner plates. Amiable, skeptical, simply dressed, his pithy, wise sayings in *Poor Richard's Almanack* (which, from Philadelphia, he had annually published from 1732 to 1757) on everyone's tongue, Franklin seemed the very symbol of the Enlightenment: reasonable, logical, balanced, practical and this-worldly.

Eighteenth-century philosophers said everything "natural" was good; that "natural religion" (not formal churches and creeds) based in our nature-given reason was our true reliance; that in science, the study of the natural world, we find the valid guide to truth and God's natural laws; that our rights are rooted in nature. The plainest and most natural people, uncorrupted by power and sophistication, were able, it was said, to see things most clearly and wisely.

And so they idolized Franklin, with his rude fur cap, his own gray hair (no wig), his plain manners, and his shrewdness: the sage from the North American wilderness, a reborn Socrates with his prudence and his questions and his searching mind. With little formal education, by the age of forty-two he had become wealthy as a printer and writer. In that year, 1748, he had settled down to the true passion of his life, science. Electricity fascinated European scientists, and suddenly out of America came word of a series of brilliantly conceived, amazingly precise experiments carried off by the backwoods philosopher Benjamin Franklin, experiments that pushed scientific knowledge far beyond where it had been. By "very small means," a great scientist observed, "he established very grand truths." Shortly he took the ancient terror of lightning from the skies by proving, in his famous experiment with the kite, that it was simply another form of electricity, which could be drawn off to the ground by metal lightning rods pointed up from rooftops. Honorary doctorates poured upon him from the most eminent universities. The careful application of reason, guided by planned experimentation, had solved a great natural danger and put it into humanity's control.

But soon he was sent off to England to represent the colonies in their long argument with the Crown and Parliament. When the Revolution broke out he went to France, where he was loved and admired, to win its support and eventually an alliance. Then he was one of the men chosen to negotiate the Peace of 1783, which brought the new United States an immense set of boundaries reaching to the Mississippi River. The year 1787 found him, a kindly man of immense prestige and more than eighty years of age, in the Constitutional Convention in Philadelphia, where his tactful good sense eased the debates. Not everyone liked him; indeed, he had harsh and bitter critics who distrusted such fame, such a talent for easy, sophisticated, skillful maneuvering. But when he died in 1790 thousands mourned him, and the generations since have been kind to his memory, for in an extraordinary century none was more extraordinary than he.

Overview

As early as 1700 two distinct economic worlds had taken form in the colonies, generally north and south of Pennsylvania's southern border. One exported two crops, tobacco and rice, to Europe, and was in the process of shaping all its ways of living and thinking around a central institution: slavery. The other consisted primarily of small farmers free of feudal obligations to anyone superior to them. These two societies were unlike anything in the British Isles and Europe generally.

Until about 1700 northern farmers raised food primarily for themselves and their families. Then they began producing wheat and livestock for the market: for the slowly growing cities along the seacoast, for the West Indies, and Europe. To ease this emerging commerce, by the 1720s a paper currency was generally in use, bringing with it visions of profit and affluence. At the same time, the quiet colonies were entering boom times. Immigrants were beginning to pour in from Germany and Ireland in the 1720s, and thousands of slaves were being purchased in the South. A high rate of survival among American-born white children, who were reared in far healthier surroundings than children in Europe—eight live children in a family, as against four in Europe, was common—accelerated the rise of population, as did a relatively low death rate. In 1700 there had been

New York City, looking across the East River toward the city, from William Burgis's A South Prospect of New York, 1719, showing the busy commerce and the Dutch architecture as well as the woods close behind on Manhattan Island.

approximately 250,000 people in the colonies. By 1775 there would be about 2,250,000 (and 5,300,000 by 1800). Transatlantic trade flourished, and settlement expanded widely from the limited coastal beachheads of the seventeenth century into the rich back country, soon reaching the Appalachian Mountains and entering their long interior valleys. With mounting affluence and trade, people, books, and ideas moved back and forth across the Atlantic in rising volume.

By the middle of the eighteenth century the simple colonial world of 1700 had quite vanished. In its place was British America—a swelling, turbulent, highly mixed, and unstable community reaching from Maine to the borders of Spanish Florida (Georgia, standing as a buffer to the Spanish, had been founded in 1732).

The Colonial City: Crucible of Change

You could walk clear around the town in half an hour, if you moved along. The smell of the countryside was near; a bee busily at work could easily call upon flowers on either side of the community. Cows, tethered behind New York City's wooden houses, gave each household its milk. Walkers needed to keep a wary eye out, for front doors were opened to throw household wastes into the streets, where wandering hogs, the town's only refuse service, fed upon them. The streets were narrow, and the crush of wagons and horses and shouting drivers could make the place ring with noise even at night. Complaining about how hard it was to sleep in such surroundings was already an urban habit. The crowded conditions were not, however, because New York City in 1700 was a vast metropolis—it held about 5,000 souls—but because most people walked to work, and it was important to live as close as possible to the docks and merchant houses. Thus, the entire town was compressed right at the southern tip of Manhattan Island, below Wall Street.

As in the other two principal colonial cities, Philadelphia and Boston, which were also little more than overgrown villages, everyone knew practically everyone else. Relationships were personal, face to face. There was little need for the written word, for most of life proceeded orally, in direct conversation. Time moved slowly. Clocks were rarely in evi-

dence and told only the hour, it not being necessary to be more precise than that. When arriving vessels rose above the horizon under their cloud of sail, they moved at a stately pace to their anchorages and were unloaded at an ambling gait.

New York City was already an astonishing potpourri of ethnic mixture. Founded on commerce alone, it reached out indifferently to all the Atlantic basin for its work force. Something more than a dozen languages were spoken in the town. And of course there were slaves. The Dutch and English merchants and officials of New York City took rather quickly to buying and using black men and women from Africa, when they became available in the mid-1600s. In fact, in 1700 about 14 percent of the town's population was black.

All of the colonies' principal towns stood, at 1700, at the opening of what would be for them a century of sweeping change. At no time before the Revolution would more than one in twenty Americans live in cities, but their influence spread deep into the hinterland. As historian Gary B. Nash writes, "the cities predicted the future. . . ." It was here that modernization, in its many dimensions, made its first appearance.

During the half-century between 1690 and 1740, Boston grew to 17,000 residents, New York to 9,500, and William Penn's "green country town" of Philadelphia quadrupled, to 9,000. Indeed, by the time of the American Revolution Philadelphia, at 30,000 people, would be the third largest community in the British Empire. Why such growth? Because the interior of the northern colonies was finally being settled, and their general population was rising. The swelling output of foodstuffs for export which came from all these new farms, as well as their increasing demands for English goods, produced a heavy trade into and out of the seacoast towns.

Great Wars and Their Impact

Something else, however, was also at work: a long series of wars between England and France that struck the colonies—especially New England—with great force. King William's War (1689–97) and Queen Anne's war (1702–13) began the cycle. Then came a long interlude of peace, broken by an explosive outbreak from the 1740s onward of another series of great international conflicts. They brought economic booms and busts, as heavy demands were made upon the colonies to provide supplies and foodstuffs. Warfare also "opened up new forms of entrepreneurial activity," Nash writes, "such as smuggling, piracy, and military contracting, provided the basis for new urban fortunes as well as new urban misery, altered the social structure, and exposed the towns to the vagaries of the market economy to a degree previously unknown."

New England in particular, being closest to the French in Canada, was called upon to supply thousands of troops. It was not unusual for a fifth of the able-bodied men of Massachusetts to be off to the wars in these conflicts. Because the fighting was bloody, this meant a heavy loss of life. Many thousands of widows and children were left behind, and for the first time a permanent class of poverty-stricken people made its appearance in colonial life. At the same time, to pay the high costs of war, Massachusetts had to begin levying heavy taxes and issuing paper currency. This led to fantastically complicated public issues to work out, for which the colonials were simply unprepared. Bitter political controversy erupted, for it was said that the taxes were unequally levied, and the new currency quickly began losing its value.

The result? For the first time, the masses became politically sensitized and mobilized. Formerly, as is generally true in traditional cultures, they had been relatively passive, dutifully allowing their betters to do the governing. However, they were now being sharply squeezed by the new economy, while at the same time they saw some among them growing rich and living lavishly. Loosely organized "interest groups" took shape; traditional lines of authority were challenged; and a politically inflammatory turbulence became characteristic of city life.

In these circumstances a "political press," formerly unheard of, made its appearance, to the outrage of the authorities. It even became custom to form political clubs and issue lists of nominees—"tickets"—of those to be supported for office. These new techniques made their earliest appearance in New York City, because within that town of ethnic mixture the cultural hostilities which give the most powerful thrust to political rivalry operated with great intensity. One of the first casualties of the new politics was the traditional habit of those below being deferential to those above. To their anger, the upper classes also found that they had to appeal to the "lesser sort" to win, for margins of victory over hated rivals were narrow.

The New Ethic of Individualism

Thus by the mid-1700s the static economics of the 1600s had given way to fluidity, growth, and the early phases of modernization. The number of new towns established in Connecticut in the thirty years after 1700 was double the number founded in the thirty years before that date. Its population had grown 60 percent in the years 1670 to 1700, but it swelled by almost 400 percent in the following three decades. Everywhere, as new towns were established and population grew, opportunities for trade increased and affluence appeared. Out of New England's port cities came a growing swarm of merchant vessels journeying on the triangular trade to England, Africa, the West Indies—and home again to the colonies, with rum and slaves. Dozens of new roads were hewn through the New England forests, and to handle the swelling activity, coastal towns enlarged harbors, wharves, and warehouses. New England towns loosened, sending out more and more families to live on their own, granting ever-larger holdings of land, and observing a brisk buying and selling of properties. Per capita income among Connecticut's whites rose perhaps 80 percent from 1720 to 1770.

Consequently, we find Americans taking on an optimistic aggressiveness that was dramatically unlike the quiet passiveness of the prior century. In fact, before the alarmed eyes of colonial clerics, a new ethic was emerging: *individualism*. Flourishing most prominently in the seacoast towns, which inlanders regarded as wicked and corrupt in the best of circumstances, the new spirit called for each person getting ahead on one's own, charging what the market would bear, and ignoring the welfare of the community at large. This was most alarming; public spiritedness had been the very core of the earlier ethic, especially in New England. Cotton Mather, the eminent New England divine, had preached in 1710:

> *Let no man seek his own, but every man another's wealth. For men to overreach others, because they find them ignorant, or screw grievously upon them, only because they are poor and low, and in great necessities; to keep up the necessaries of human life . . . at an immoderate price, merely because other people want them . . . 'TIS AN ABOMINATION!*

However, even in the countryside the new ethic of enterprising individualism was seeping in. To supplement the modest crops New England's thin soils produced, Yankee farmers turned their imaginations to many crafts and enterprises: making cider, building weirs in the rivers to catch fish, weaving cloth, working iron as blacksmiths or wood as carpenters, making shoes, raising hay to sell for cattle feed (meat was always in demand), digging stones to build walls, hiring themselves out to merchants, running malt houses and flour mills, building barrels, and carting produce. People began traveling the countryside to sell buckles, pins, and buttons, or to open small stores and establish taverns. Soon some of them were becoming prosperous merchants and innkeepers.

"Puritan" was being joined by "Yankee" in the New England psychology. People felt much freer now to pursue their own enrichment, and they did so, the historian Richard L. Bushman writes, "with an avidity dangerously close to avarice." The social energy released by this ever-more confident individualism exerted tremendous pressure against New England's traditional ways of living. In the seventeenth century Puritans had valued *order* above everything else. Now a fluid economics was breaking up that stability, a development that to the pious had inevitable consequences: chaos, pride, confusion, irreligion, and sin. Where was the austerity of life of the true Puritan or Quaker, the laboring for God's glory and not for one's own?

Ironically, the colonies were the ideal place for the new ethic of individualism to rise and flourish. On the edge of the great fertile continent of North America, with its apparently limitless resources, there was so much opportunity for anyone who was imaginative and ready to take risks. Furthermore, new enterprises could be started up without the feeling that they were getting in the way of anyone else. In the old European homelands it was customary to believe that if one person profited, it was probably at the expense of others, but this assumption weakened in America. Indeed, people could take on that distinctively modern notion—the one that lies at the heart of most economic theory—that when one person got wealthy, this was simply creating more wealth for all, to the benefit of all. The idea arose that the economy is not static, with only so much pie to cut up for everyone, but is potentially dynamic, creating ever more value to add to the total stock.

Boston and Philadelphia were expressly founded to be moral outposts of purity and community spirit in a selfish world, and in those communities the long-standing ideals of working for the common good persisted well into the eighteenth century.

Nonetheless, all the dynamics at work in the Atlantic economy were pushing in the opposite direction. Being frugal and concerned for others faded in the face of the impulse to be aggressively individualistic, and to enjoy the pleasures of self-indulgence. More and more, people made their living by selling things for whatever they could get, whether or not the price was exploitive; more and more they subsisted by speculating in buying and selling land; and by the 1740s, when the public-be-damned spirit was widely in evidence, the clergy in the cities (though not in the hinterland) said little about it.

The South and the Expansion of Slavery

The boom of the eighteenth century also swept into the Southern colonies. Southern planters joined whites in the Caribbean islands and Latin America in calling for more slaves from Africa. And by 1700 a new crop was making its appearance. About 1685 it had been discovered that the flat coastal lowlands of South Carolina were ideal for raising the ancient grain brought from the Orient to Europe in the Middle Ages: rice. Slaves taken to the region around Charleston were put to work in large gangs on extensive rice plantations.

The harsh climate in the swamps and wetlands, and the region's endemic tropical diseases, brought horrifying death rates to the slave populations. However, high profits allowed the small white population to live in safety and luxury in Charleston and, when the colony of Georgia was founded in 1732, in Savannah. Directing their plantations from a distance (i.e., they did not live in the presence of their slaves and come to know them as individual persons), they regarded the cost of replacing those who had died as simply an unavoidable cost of operation. The rice plantations sent 18 million pounds of their crop to Europe in 1730; by 1770, exports had reached the huge total of 76 million pounds, and the price had even risen 10 percent. Thus, black slaves, despite their high death rate, continued to be highly profitable. By 1750 they constituted 60 percent of the Carolina population. In 1775, South Carolina alone held 100,000 slaves.

The other great region in the South lay around the Chesapeake Bay. Here the economy was built around the tobacco plant, which was raised most efficiently on small farms. Because of overproduction, tobacco prices remained fairly low, keeping profits down. Thus, Virginia planters could not generally afford large slave gangs. They tended, in fact, to buy more black women from Africa than did rice planters, in order to acquire cheaply, through later childbearing, the slaves it was hard for them to acquire directly. This in turn allowed for a healthier and more vigorous family life among Chesapeake Bay slaves, who in any event were freer of sickness because they did not work in disease-ridden swamps and in large gangs, where contagious diseases spread rapidly. The Virginia slaves therefore flourished through natural increase in a fashion strikingly different from the situation farther south, and especially from that in the cruel Caribbean island sugar plantations. There were over 170,000 slaves in Virginia in 1775, who amounted to almost half of the colony's population.

Tobacco production, though not highly profitable, nonetheless grew to more than 100 million pounds annually by the mid-1700s, and with it came a rising population. There were 90,000 people in the Chesapeake region in 1700; seven decades later there were 685,000. Thus, Virginia and Maryland together were numerically the largest and wealthiest of all the colonial regions, almost a third of the colonial population living within their borders. (This would give the Chesapeake region a role of major prominence and power in American national politics for many years after independence.) Also, as population growth and heavy tobacco cropping depleted soil fertility, there was a significant shift to a new crop: wheat. In the 1770s Virginia was shipping out a fourth as much wheat as New York and Pennsylvania—the breadbasket colonies—together.

The Realities of Slavery

Shaping everything in Southern life, however, was the massive shift away from the use of white servants to the use of black slaves. Planters were used to working their laborers hard, for profits were low and high productivity was the only apparent salvation. But as long as the workers were white and English, there was a certain limit to how harshly they could be punished, how long they could be worked, and how simply they could be fed and housed. Now there was no limit to the work or time that could be demanded, no limit to the punishments exacted (even death and dismemberment were allowed by law).

Nothing but the barest economic necessities governed diet and shelter. Women could be made to work in the fields, and children as well. Provision need not be made for time off to study in school or worship in church. Slaves themselves even produced a crop: children.

But unlike white workers, who would toil reasonably well to ensure that they would be freed at the end of their original term of service, blacks had no incentive whatever to work hard. Slave masters therefore had to rely on the inflicting of pain far more than had earlier been the case with white workers. Beatings became harsher, more savage, more repetitive. Fugitive slaves could even be freely, legally killed for their crime. To make money, the planters had to take on a much harder, more callous way of life, for they had to be ready to maim people with whom they lived in daily terms of physical intimacy. It was not a common thing to do, but it might be called for, and an elaborate code of laws, practices, and attitudes was evolved to make it appear right and proper, indeed a duty.

In the eighteenth century, of course, this was a situation not limited to the South. From Pennsylvania northward there were scattered concentrations of black slave populations, particularly in towns and cities. New York had the highest proportion, with perhaps 15 percent of its population black; New Jersey and Pennsylvania contained 8 percent; and in New England as a whole the figure was 3 percent. In general, by the 1790s a higher proportion of the whole population was black than ever again in American history: some 20 percent.

Fears of Slave Revolt

With black people growing in numbers far more rapidly than whites, there was great fear of slave rebellions, which in fact began taking place, on a small scale, as early as 1663 in Virginia. This led to the creation of stringent, often savage slave codes in all the colonies. These laws were built on two concepts: *absolute* authority of masters over slaves, and the belief that blacks were "of barbarous, wild, savage natures [and] wholly unqualified to be governed by the laws, customs, and practices" that applied to whites. New York, with its many slaves, had a tough code of slave laws; in South Carolina, where by 1765 there were two blacks to every white person, regular slave patrols gave the countryside a military character.

Men owning thousands of acres and hundreds of slaves had few checks on their passions. Arrogance among the planters was common, especially in the low Carolina country where wealth and large plantations were prominent. When a planter had slaves valued at perhaps £30,000, he could consider himself practically on a par with a great English lord. Southern planters became known throughout the empire for their pride and lordly airs. While many were kindly and generous in their dealings with ordinary people—with whom, in the last analysis, they shared the mutually binding status of being white—others displayed only contempt for what they called the rabble. Nowhere else was the colonial aristocracy so firmly rooted. Nowhere else did they gravitate so naturally to positions of command in military and governmental affairs.

Slaves were forbidden to wander off their plantation without a "ticket" from their master or overseer. They were never to be allowed to congregate in large numbers, carry clubs or arms, or strike a white person. Masters were given immunity from legal prosecution should their slave die under "moderate" correction. . . . All white persons were authorized to apprehend any Negro unable to give a satisfactory account of himself. In areas of heavy slave concentration white men were required to serve in slave "patrols" which were supposed to protect the community especially at night and on Sundays. . . . In addition, slaves committing felonies were tried in specially constituted courts which typically consisted of a justice of the peace and two (other) slaveowners. Official punishments ranged from a specific number of stripes "well laid on" all the way to burning at the stake (often but not always after strangulation), a punishment not restricted to the southern colonies or to Negroes and not entirely abandoned for Negroes until the nineteenth century. The codes devoted much attention to the most persistent and potentially dangerous problem of slave control—running away. Probably more time, money, and energy was expended on this problem . . . than on any other aspect of administering the slave system. (Winthrop D. Jordan, White Over Black: American Attitudes Toward the Negro, 1550–1812 [1969])

Rivaling the specter of slave revolt as a source of tension in the South was the obvious and widespread mingling of the races. Miscegenation flourished in the slave system, particularly where blacks were most numerous and under the strictest, most dehumanizing controls. One of the great paradoxes in race relations is that the heaviest intermingling occurred precisely when black Americans were the least free, not after the ending of slavery. Whites in the twentieth century have often insisted that greater freedom and social equality for black Americans will lead to a corresponding rise in interracial sex relations, but historically, miscegenation appears to have declined in direct proportion to the freeing of the black man and woman from white subjection.

Nothing aroused such powerful anger in white men as the thought of black slaves forcing themselves on white women, a common and obsessive fear. Despite protests and disallowances from London, southern states often used castration, sometimes in an astonishingly routine way, as a punishment or "gentling" treatment for black men. Few things so aided the rise of English contempt for Americans—indeed, Northern contempt for Southerners—as the manner in which slaves were treated from the Chesapeake southward.

British America Becomes More Pluralistic

In 1718 the British government began worrying about labor shortages at home and discouraging emigration of English people to America. It still wanted, however, to make its empire stronger and more prosperous, so it opened the door to immigration on a major scale from new sources.

The immigrants came first from Germany. Savage wars and grinding social oppression sent thousands of German refugees to England around 1710. Soon the royal authorities were shipping them off to New York Colony. However, the Germans found the great feudal manors of the Hudson Valley not to their liking, and they headed for the freer environment and rich soils of Pennsylvania, to which in previous years William Penn had already attracted some German settlers. Into the valley of the Susquehanna, west of the "Quaker counties" around Philadelphia, began to come many thousands of Germans, who have made that part of the colony to this day the special seat of the Pennsylvania Dutch. (Germans refer to their language as *Deutsch* and their homeland as *Deutschland*.) A third of Pennsylvania's population was German by 1775, and in the colonies as a whole they numbered 250,000, or about a tenth of the population.

As they filled in the valleys of southeastern

Pennsylvania, many Germans learned that by following the Great Valley of the Appalachians southward into the western sections of Maryland, Virginia, and the Carolinas they could find rich farming land at a cheaper price than in Pennsylvania. Perhaps half of the eighteenth-century German migrants moved down the valley, occupying the Virginia back country by the 1730s. Twenty years later, Germans were down in frontier North Carolina and moving eastward to settle in the Piedmont. Many more arrived in the port city of Charleston, South Carolina, and moved into the interior of that colony, encouraged by a large free grant of land offered to all new white settlers. Indeed, in mid-century Charleston became second only to Philadelphia as a port of entry for German settlers, and the white population of South Carolina doubled in the years 1755 to 1775.

German Culture

The Germans who arrived before 1750 were primarily from the many pietistic Christian sects of their home country (i.e., evangelical, devotional, very simple in organization): Moravians, Mennonites, Amish, Dunkards. Whatever the sect, it emphasized a heartfelt, personal religion, not tied to a complex creed or theology but loving, warm, and Bible-centered. The pietists insisted on individual godliness and austerity and simplicity of life. Frowning upon higher education, they rejected "modern" society. Close, communal, inward-turning, they avoided contact with anyone outside their faith and devoted themselves to hard work and prayer. They were the Plain People. They believed in nonviolence (they maintained excellent relations with the Indians; the Moravians worked especially hard at this), democracy within the Church, and the equality of all persons. The pietists usually settled as congregations, not as separate families or individuals, and they developed a deep attachment to the land they pioneered. The Plain People, unlike most Americans, were not mobile. Even in the twentieth century, many remain where they put down roots centuries ago.

After the pietists came the Church People from Germany—that is, members of the large state churches in the homeland, the Lutheran and German Reformed. (The latter was like the Dutch Reformed, the Congregationalists of New England, and the Scottish Presbyterians in drawing heavily upon the theology of John Calvin.) By 1775 the Church People

far outnumbered the Plain People, so that it was primarily from these more numerous Lutherans and German Reformed that German culture in Pennsylvania derived.

Lutherans were by far the greatest in numbers. Indeed, the Lutheran churches, which spring not only from Germany but from Scandinavia and parts of eastern Europe, eventually became third in size in American Protestantism. In their ideas about God, life, and humanity they were much like the Anglicans. They regarded their church as part of the ancient and catholic (that is, universal) Christian Church, which had its beginnings in the time of the biblical apostles and thus was coequal with Roman Catholicism in reaching back to Christ himself. Lutherans demanded a learned ministry, for the scholarly sermon was essential in their service. They preached that people are saved by faith alone, and that this faith, even the desire for it, depends upon God's initiative in each person's life. Human beings cannot be righteous on their own; they are too far below god, too steeped in sinfulness, for that. Indeed, even after being saved through faith, people remain sinners.

Lutheranism always insisted on the duality of humanity's condition, on the fact that people are constantly being pulled toward good and toward evil, often at the same time. They maintained that both the sacraments and godly preaching were essential, and that Christ does appear in the communion service, in His human body as well as in His divine spirit. For Lutherans, the goal in all of human life must not be extremes, but the *via media*—a blending and balancing of mutually contrasting elements.

The Germans who came to America were primarily peasants, not city workers or merchants, and they cherished good, careful farming and self-sufficiency. Proud of their culture and their language, they stayed to themselves and out of the politics of the colonies they lived in. Working with their own hands was important to them, and they would not use slaves. Thus, their farms were efficiently run and lovingly tended, and Germans soon stood out from other colonial farmers in being exceptionally prosperous. This aroused jealousy; their clinging to a separate language and avoidance of English made them seem strange and secretive. In consequence, the Germans were detested. Benjamin Franklin said their women were thick and ugly, and that they knew nothing but work. They were commonly called "the dumb Dutch": plodding, unimaginative, unchanging, thick-headed. On their side, the Germans bitterly resented the prejudice of the British.

The Scotch-Irish Arrive

The Scotch-Irish from Ulster, in northern Ireland, arrived soon after the Germans. English laws at home discriminated harshly against Presbyterians, and crushed Ulster's growing industries by denying them the right to sell in England. Also, there were devastating famines that drove the Scotch-Irish to America. First they tried settling in New England in the 1720s, since the Puritans and Presbyterians were both Calvinists in theology. But the clannish, scornful Yankees looked down upon them and harassed them, so that most departed for liberal Pennsylvania. Coming in five waves of immigration from Ulster during the 1700s, the Scotch-Irish in the colonies had swelled to a population of 250,000 by the time of the Revolution.

The Scotch-Irish were an unusual people in that they had already been frontiersmen at home. In the seventeenth century they had crossed to Ireland from Scotland to take up lands vacated by the Catholic Irish, who had been massacred or driven into the hills. They transformed barbaric Ulster into a thriving province of vigorous agriculture, wool production, and linen manufacture. All the while they were between two hostile enemies—the Catholic Irish and the Anglican English—which made them cherish their own faith with a passion unknown even in Scotland itself, the home of Presbyterianism. The Scotch-Irish hated the Catholics, and fought with them constantly. Thus, a grim life in Ulster, and before that in hard-bitten Scotland, had bred into the Scotch-Irish a fighting temper and a dour outlook upon life. "All mankind," says the *Shorter Catechism* of the Westminster Confession, the historic creed of Presbyterianism, "by the Fall, lost communion with God, are under his wrath and curse, and so made liable to all the pains of this life and to hell forever."

Like the Germans, the Scotch-Irish densely settled southeastern Pennsylvania (though the two peoples avoided each other). Eventually, they moved far westward to establish Pittsburgh. But many went to the rich lands of the Great Valley, moving down into the Maryland and Virginia back country after 1730. Given the right in 1738 in Virginia to establish Presbyterian churches, they took over the local vestries and parishes, created originally for the Anglican Church, and used them for their own purposes. In the 1740s they reached the southern end of the Great Valley and moved eastward into the vast, hilly Piedmont of North Carolina and South Carolina. Together with smaller numbers of Germans, the Scotch-Irish spread out by the tens of thousands to people the western Carolinas.

The Political Impact of the New Peoples

The arrival of this tidal wave of Scotch-Irish in British America forecast an eventual earthquake in its politics, for the Scotch-Irish hated the English. They particularly hated the Church of England and Anglicans, their ancient enemy at home, and they felt much the same way about London and Parliament. Indeed, they detested anything English. Both their homelands, Scotland and Ireland, were restive under English domination. Out of them came a steady stream of radical republican ideas that made the Scotch-Irish constant critics of monarchical institutions, bishops, and landed aristocracies. They knew they were regarded with contempt by the English, who called them drunkards for their love of their ethnic beverage, whiskey, and violent savages, because they had lived with guns for generations and seemed to thrive on fighting.

Pennsylvania was a colony run by Quakers who were English in their ethnic background, and they were greatly alarmed by the arrival of the Scotch-Irish. The two groups were almost instantly at odds with each other. Centuries of bloody history between the Scots and English lay between them, as well as sharp differences in life style. Quakers were pacifists; they believed in a kindly, loving God; and they opposed drink, swearing, and rough living. The Quaker-dominated government in Philadelphia would provide no arms or support to the Scotch-Irish in their battles with Indians, and this embittered all relations between the two peoples.

In the 1770s the two great Pennsylvania minorities—the Scotch-Irish and the Germans—would join forces and take over the colony, sweeping it into the crusade for independence from Britain. By the 1770s only seven of every ten white colonials would be of English background. Indeed, south of New England, which was homogeneously English, half of the white colonial population consisted of "foreigners" eager to join in expelling London's rule.

The English Migration: Its Nature

At the same time, British people continued their long, if somewhat reduced, migration to the North American colonies. Bernard Bailyn's recent twin studies,

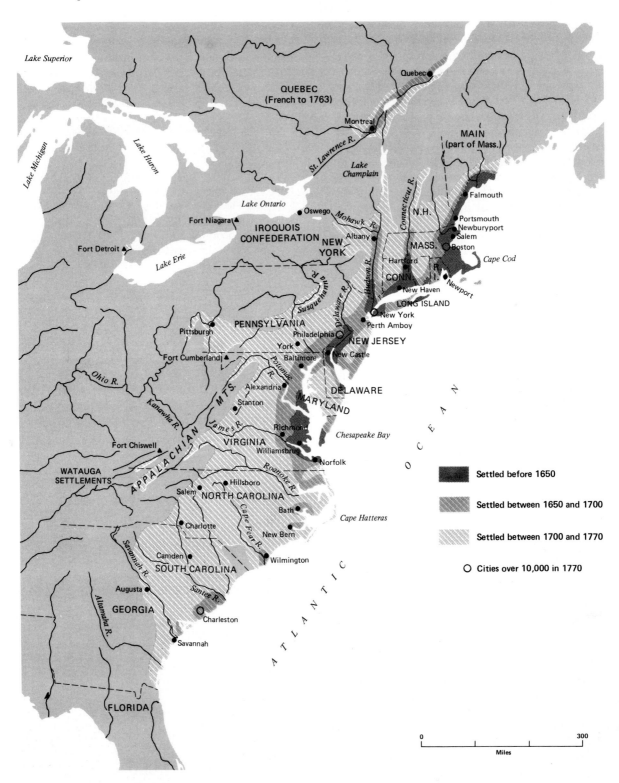

Colonial Settlement, 1650–1770

The Peopling of British North America: An Introduction (1986), and the Pulitzer-Prize winning *Voyagers to the West* (1986), tell us that at least in the 1770s—and doubtless in earlier decades—they came in two streams. One, the "metropolitan" stream, came from the south of England, centered in London and the Thames basin; the other, the "provincial" stream, came from the more remote Midlands and North Country of England, Scotland, and Ireland.

They differed sharply from each other in their nature. The metropolitan migrant was usually a young, single man, not desperately poor but middling in the working classes. He probably had his apprenticeship behind him, and had simply decided to make his future in North America. Borrowing money to make the journey, he repaid it by four years of bonded labor. Among the metropolitan migrants Bailyn found few women or children, few families. "Vigorous and at least in some minor way skilled . . . these emigrants were bound to contribute to [colonial] productivity. . . ." They went primarily to the mid-Atlantic colonies of Pennsylvania, Maryland, and Virginia, the rapidly growing places with much opportunity for young men with craft-skills and a readiness to work hard.

People from the outlying provinces, by contrast, came almost entirely in sizable families, including a remarkable number of young girls. Journeying "essentially intact," with few indentured servants among them, they moved freely as soon as they arrived in the colonial world, contributed quickly not only to economic growth but, unlike the metropolitans, also to American population growth. What did they want most of all? *Land!* It was these people who moved right to the frontier and began pushing it back as they opened new farming country. Unlike earlier migrants, they did not go to New England, for here the land was already much taken up, and large, healthy, flourishing families were sending out their sons and daughters to open the remaining country. The 1770s provincial migrants, then, were drawn particularly to the colonies of New York and North Carolina, where wide frontier farming areas were still open (and to Nova Scotia, too, in what would become Canada).

The Anglican Surge

Through the eighteenth century, friction among colonials was intensified by a campaign, mounted from London, to make Anglicanism as dominant in British North America as it was at home. As early as the 1690s the College of William and Mary had been founded in Virginia, the heartland of colonial Anglicanism, to serve as a seminary to train Anglican priests. Following harsh controversies, the Church of England became the legally established church not only in Virginia, the Old Dominion, but in Maryland in 1702 and in North and South Carolina in 1706 and 1711. Not long afterward, an autocratic royal governor in New York Colony would decree Anglicanism the established church in the four counties in and around New York City.

As population soared and the flow of trade and ideas across the Atlantic quickened, so did a strong trend toward Anglicization—the adoption of ways of living like those in England. The upper classes in America aped English styles and manners. Judges began wearing wigs and scarlet robes, and the courts and royal administration in London exerted ever more authority over colonial affairs. Because in the royally governed colonies, such as New York and Massachusetts, social and political prestige came with being Anglican, the wealthy and ambitious were increasingly attracted to the Church of England. The royal governors were of course Anglicans, which made the social circles that gathered around them gravitate naturally to that church, and to hold public office or military rank, sometimes even to sit in the assembly, required Anglican membership. However, there was more than self-advancement involved in the decision to join the Anglican Church. Thousands of ordinary colonials found the Anglican theology attractive. This was especially true in the northern colonies, where the Church, precisely because it was generally not the legally established body, worked harder and more imaginatively at missionary activity than in the South.

Samuel Johnson (not the famous author of the dictionary), who took Holy Orders in the Anglican Church in 1722, "was one of the more dramatic exemplars of the American 'discovery of England' in the eighteenth century. He immediately became one of the exponents of that 'colonialism' which looked upon all things American as primitive and unrefined, as compared with the culture of England, and he consciously set about to raise the level of the culture of his native land. This 'colonial' or 'provincial' attitude was typical of the more conservative [i.e., Anglicizing] elements in American cultural life. . . . He believed in order, discipline, and respect for the powers that be, and the Anglican church seemed to him to be an effective way of maintaining order and discipline in religion while preserving the right of the individual to work out his own salvation within the churchly institution; he even hoped and labored for the day when an Angli-

can episcopacy might become a religious bond binding the colonies to the culture of the mother country." (*Max Savelle,* Seeds of Liberty: The Genesis of the American Mind [1948])

The Anglicizing trend was but part of an increasing intermingling of Britain and its colonies as the 1700s advanced. Letters, pamphlets, newspapers, copies of speeches, scientific apparatus, and medical treatises passed swiftly back and forth across the Atlantic (the journey one way could take as little as three weeks). British radicals looked to America as the proving ground of their ideas, and they maintained an eager correspondence with American reformers. The non-Anglican Protestant churches, alarmed at the Anglican surge and concerned that they might lose their liberties, stayed in increasingly close touch with their counterparts in Britain, coordinating strategy. Meanwhile, by the 1770s every sixth British vessel was involved in the trade with America, and that trade was mushrooming year by year.

The Rise of Newspapers

No influence was as powerful in tying Britain and the colonies closer together as the emergence of a newspaper press in the eighteenth century that was modeled directly upon the newspapers of England. Frequently, the colonial papers were composed largely of reprinted British articles and items of news. The first successful newspaper was the *Newsletter*, established in Boston in 1704 by the local postmaster. Soon other such enterprises were under way, soberly reporting the political turmoils in England as well as events economic and political around the world. Benjamin Franklin was shortly on the scene with his enormously popular *Pennsylvania Gazette*, which ran until 1815.

The most lively and provocative newspaper of the day was John Peter Zenger's *Weekly Journal*, which began in 1733 in New York City. Always argumentative, continuously free with criticism of the authorities, Zenger found himself thrown into jail in 1734, charged with seditious libel for criticisms of Governor William Cosby. Until this time it was a commonly accepted doctrine that simply to criticize any branch of government was enough to put an editor in jail, on the ground that it made the people think ill of their rulers. However, Zenger's lawyer, Andrew Hamilton, successfully argued before the jury that it was not seditious libel for a person to make *truthful* allegations against the government, and

the accused was freed. This principle, however, was not widely accepted in politics and the courts for a long time.

The issue of freedom of the press was kept alive in the transatlantic community by a succession of spectacular prosecutions. Perhaps the most dramatic was the John Wilkes case in England. The accused was a member of Parliament and editor of the *North Briton*, which in the 1760s attacked the Tory government unmercifully. Charged with seditious libel, Wilkes fled to France for a time, then returned to be triumphantly reelected to Parliament by his London constituency. He was thrown in jail, fined, expelled from Parliament, and then reelected and expelled twice more. By this time the number 45 (the number of the April 23, 1764, issue of the *North Briton*, which began all the trouble) was a transatlantic sensation. Rioters in London scrawled it on walls all over the city, screamed it at the authorities, and elected Wilkes mayor of London in 1774 behind the symbol. In New York in 1770, a man named Alexander McDougall was imprisoned in a seditious libel case (in which the colonial assembly, rather than the governor, pressed the prosecution). On the forty-fifth day of that year, forty-five of his supporters gathered to dine on forty-five pounds of beef, offered forty-five toasts to the liberty of the press, and then stood outside McDougall's jail cell to send forth forty-five cheers for his cause.

The newspapers had a profound educational effect on the colonial mind. When troubles with England began, Americans already had a fund of information about political turmoil and oppression in England to draw on. Probably no other influence was so important in preparing Americans to be wary of the autocracy of the British government. Americans learned to distrust the British ministry, for their journalists had for decades been taking the side of the antigovernment radicals in England who had vainly been assaulting corruption, undemocratic government, and attacks on civil liberties.

The Colonial Family

Government was small and inactive in America. Therefore, the family was very strong, even more so than in England, where ancient governing institutions and an established aristocracy held great authority over individuals, their economic life, and their interrelations.

The form of family the colonials brought with

them from Britain was much like that familiar to modern Americans: the nuclear family, in which husband and wife and their children formed a household. (The "extended family," in which brothers and sisters and grandparents all lived together, with their children, was not in the English tradition.) Land was generally granted to the head of the household—the father. As the generations passed and the original tight village communities broke apart, families tended to live in separate, isolated homesteads. By the 1750s, intermarriage between households in thousands of small towns and villages in the northern colonies had built a strong web of relationships that helped make community life stronger than it had been. Nonetheless, nuclear families remained the basic social units in colonial life.

They were large, busy families. Half of the population consisted of children, and the population grew rapidly: by 25 percent every ten years in New England, and by 35 percent in the Middle Colonies, where heavy in-migration occurred. As long as they could, fathers divided up their lands to provide for their maturing sons and their families, but by the 1750s this was less and less feasible. This development began to fuel a westward movement into frontier regions by the younger nuclear families. Thus, the American family witnessed a growing emancipation from parental supervision as the century proceeded, a fact that may have led parents to adopt a more cherishing and loving relationship with their children during the years they were at home than was the case in Europe. At the same time, the concentration of most social and economic life within the smaller conjugal household made it easier for Americans to be mobile, to leave their original settlements and establish a new world of their own elsewhere.

The American Woman

Within the family, the need to be almost entirely self-sufficient made for a close interdependence between husbands and wives. There was no question which of the two was legally and culturally superior. In America, as in every human society of which anthropologists have record, male supremacy was the rule (which is not the same as saying it was a law of nature). This was expressed most dramatically in the possession of land by men, not by women (unless they became widowed), since land was the economic basis of almost all of life.

Women, however, were partners in the common enterprise—the home. Their labor and skills were essential if the family on its isolated farmstead would survive and prosper. Clerics often spoke in the biblical image of women as derived from Adam's rib: "Our ribs were not Ordained to be our ruler; they are not made of the Head to claim superiority, but out of the side to be content with Equality." Not equality in political power, social and economic status, or intellectual leadership—the authority structure in the community at large was incontestably male. But equality in the home, which then meant for most people just about everything, there being little else: no large and complex communities, no great corporations, no distant careers for most men to pursue. Instead, there was the farm and the home; this was where people lived their lives, from birth to death.

Women and men usually worked separately, the one in the house and the kitchen garden, the other in the fields and with the livestock, but the two activities flowed into a single economic unit. Women cared for and slaughtered the poultry; planted, looked after, and harvested the vegetables; tended and milked the dairy cattle; and made the cheese, butter, and cream. There was the salting of meats, the pickling and preserving of vegetables and fruits, and the brewing of beer and the pressing of cider. In addition, wives made wool, wove cloth, and sewed. (Well past 1850, perhaps even 1900, most of the clothes worn by Americans were sewed by women at home.) They also dipped candles, and cared for family health by preparing home remedies and soap.

Essentially, in colonial America men raised crops and manufacturing was women's work, save perhaps for shoemaking, iron forging, and leatherworking. Preparing meals was but the last stage in the manufacturing process, and this was done by means of open fireplaces; there was no running water. When planting and harvest time came, the women went out to help in the fields. Bearing children was in addition to all this, as well as rearing them, but for both these activities only a minimal amount of time was available; women had so many other things to do. Finally, women were often engaged in nondomestic economic pursuits in the small colonial towns: as shopkeepers, millers, butchers, teachers, and skilled craftspeople. In general, these activities took place either in the home or in its immediate vicinity.

Nonetheless, wives were to obey their husbands—reverently. Colonials thought of the home as a "little commonwealth" in which the man's authority provided government and law, even if he were harsh and immoral. Everyone, in fact, was thought to occupy a certain position on the social hierarchy; all of life was thought to be arranged on the Great Chain of Being, and subjection to husbands was women's role.

On the other hand, Puritans and Quakers seemed determined to treat women as persons of substance and value. Men were lectured endlessly not to be dictatorial, and colonial courts often moved in to protect women and children from brutal mistreatment. Puritan ministers urged wives not to make idols of their husbands. Marriage was made a contract that could be broken, not a permanent, divine state, as under Catholicism. God and His son Christ were to be women's proper objects of worship. And, of course, the wife's crucial role in the household, which had to be self-sufficient in a world where 90 percent of the people lived on the farm, gave "Adam's rib" a strong position. In addition, even Puritan teaching made conjugal love—love between married people— a tender and lofty part of life, but its practice was not treated as primarily the woman's concern. Couples were entreated endlessly to express their affection, to regard each other as one flesh, and thus to avoid the "civil war" that can tragically mar such little commonwealths. In short, there was a distinctly modern quality in Puritan marriage.

Getting married was a woman's declaration that

she was ready to start giving birth regularly to children, usually an average of eight during her lifetime. Childbirth was always a life-threatening process; in every thirty births, one of the mothers died. Therefore, as the time for birth approached, women commonly made preparations as well for their death. Childbirth was the "sentence," the "curse," and the "travail of women." At the same time, to pious colonials it was an act filled with divinity. The New England minister Cotton Mather said, "It is a Child of God that you now have within you. What a Consolation!" Delivery was by skilled midwives, and it was the rare mother who did not suckle her own children. Using wet nurses was condemned as "very criminal and blameworthy," for the mother held a "bottle in her breasts."

Higher Learning in Colonial America

Higher education in America originated with the founding of Harvard College in 1636. A religious people, the Puritans were determined to have a supply of learned ministers. For this reason they provided public support for the college from the beginning, since it was so important an arm of the whole governing arrangement. Its curriculum, however, was not just theological. The college was also vitally needed

This "Bodleian Plate" shows William and Mary College, second oldest in America, founded in 1693. The top left building housed an Indian school.

to train laymen for their duties of leadership as law-yers, doctors, country squires, and statesmen. Wholly a college for New Englanders (none came to this Puritan school from the Hudson Valley or the South in the seventeenth century), it formed the heart of New England's cultural life.

In Anglican Virginia, the publicly supported College of William and Mary was created in 1693. For a considerable period it was little more than a grammar school, but in time its growth to full colle-giate status made it no longer necessary for planters to send their sons to Britain for studies, a process that often returned them to the Southern colonies unfit for plantation life and impossibly arrogant to-ward inferiors.

The third of the early colleges, Yale, was estab-lished because in the eyes of strict Puritans Harvard had become a dangerously liberal and unorthodox place. As one reverend put the matter, "places of learning should not be places of riot and pride. [Stu-dents] should be sent thither to prepare them for public service, and had need to be under the oversight of wise and holy men." In 1701 an institution called the Collegiate School was established at Saybrook, Connecticut. In 1716 it was moved to New Haven and named for Elihu Yale, a wealthy New England-born merchant in London who contributed £500 to support the college. A staunchly conservative and religiously orthodox institution, Yale remained throughout the eighteenth century a stronghold of those who held to the most rigid form of Puritan Congregationalism.

The Enlightenment in America

One of the many great imports flowing into America from England after 1700 was a new way of thinking about God, nature, and humanity: the Enlightenment. Founded in the scientific revolution of the seven-teenth century, and especially in the work of two towering English thinkers, the scientist Isaac Newton (1642–1727) and the psychologist-philosopher John Locke (1632–1704), Enlightenment thought was con-sciously rational, moderate, and this-worldly. (Later, after 1750, it would grow more radical and revolu-tionary, and would derive from France and Scotland.) As such, Enlightenment thinking became for a small minority of educated Americans—many of them, like Benjamin Franklin, self-educated—the alternative and rival to classic, traditional Protestantism. Hence-forth, these two ways of thinking would intermingle

in the American mind, producing a curious and con-tradictory blend of biblical faith and rational, human-istic philosophy.

The New Learning arrived with a dramatic suddenness in 1714, when Yale received a gift of books on Newtonian science and Lockean psychology. Newton simply wiped away the old view of the uni-verse, brilliantly demonstrating how a few laws of physics could explain the motions of all heavenly bodies. This marvelous order and harmony, he be-lieved, was the clearest possible demonstration of God's reality and existence, and of His real intentions for humans as well as natural life. Educated people who read Newton no longer saw the universe as controlled by an infinite number of spirits, each with its own star, planet, or comet to supervise. The skies seemed swept clean. All was geometry, serene trajec-tories, predictability, and calm certainty. The uni-verse was not a jumbled, busy, erratic place of strange conjunctions and mysteries; it was now a lucid, regu-lar, balanced, and, above all, *reasonable* place.

The lesson was quickly drawn from this new concept. How had Newton dispelled the mysteries? By relying on reason, taking nothing for granted, rejecting dogmas, utilizing mathematics, and keeping only to what could be scientifically shown as true. Above all, he practiced *empiricism*: He stuck to facts and built from them. If such a method was so effective in science, why not in philosophy, politics, and reli-gion? Find the uniformities, the "natural laws," and the truth will be revealed.

John Locke applied this way of thinking so per-suasively in social and human affairs that he became the preeminent philosophical influence in eighteenth-century thought, especially in America. He was fasci-nated by the power of reason, though he did not think it all-powerful. A moderate man in everything, he held that some things could never be explained by humanity's reasoning powers, that there were lim-its to what we could know on our own. About God, for example, he said we could know little, other than that He is the author of the universe and a pervasive influence in human life. People therefore need the Bible, Locke said, for only in revelation from God could they learn essential divine truths that reason, unaided, could never reveal. However, he believed true Christianity consisted of only a few essentials, and therefore he not only urged, but practiced, a wide toleration of all Protestant beliefs.

But in ordinary life, Locke taught, reason is so powerful that we should rely upon it entirely, dispensing with superstition and "established" truths.

Everything should be critically examined in a spirit of calm scientific inquiry. We should gather *facts*— by the use of our senses, observing nature—and then reflect upon them diligently to find truth. Reject all dogmas, avoid all emotionally excited enthusiasms, and be skeptical of things that others take on faith alone. What is humanity? asked Locke. We are born with a mind as blank as a white sheet (a *tabula rasa*), on which experience makes entries from the moment of birth. There are no innate ideas implanted in us by God (as was widely taught in his time). Rather, everything we know comes from what *experience*—the evidence of our senses—and reason, reflecting upon that experience, tell us.

Among a small educated minority, this way of approaching the world created a preference for what was called natural religion, or deism. If natural laws govern everything, such people asked, how could we explain Christ's alleged miracles? Wasn't nature itself God's truest Bible? Look at the world at large, and what do our senses tell us? That Christianity was believed only by a fraction of the world's people. The "scientific" method in religion, therefore, called for a simple procedure: discover what things *all* people (that is, "civilized" people) believe in, wherever they are. By this means, true religion could be found. This came down to a belief in a supreme deity, God; in a code of ethics divinely established, which tells us how to live; and a belief that there is an afterlife in which people will receive rewards and punishments for their deeds in this world. Churches, Christianity, and all outward expressions of religious faith were simply local superstitions and wholly unnecessary.

The Religious Reaction

Intellectual history—the history of ideas—reveals that powerful new ideas always produce reactions. In Europe and America many preachers soon were attacking the Enlightenment and its "natural" religion. Pietists in Germany, John Wesley and what would later be called his Methodist movement in England, and many others insisted that religion is incomplete if it is just a set of intellectual beliefs. It must instead be a deep and transforming experience. "Rational" religion (such critics said) gave people the sin of pride: They exalted their rational powers and forgot their human weaknesses and sin. Full devotion to Christ must be expressed every hour of every day; He must fill and permeate one's being. *Conversion* must be the central event of one's life.

Preaching these ideas, John Wesley and George Whitefield, two Anglican priests, led a religious revival that swept England in the late 1730s. Enormous crowds in the fields listened enraptured. Storms of released feelings struck multitudes as Whitefield, an especially dynamic preacher, warned of the terrible sufferings that lay ahead for the unbelieving and held out salvation to all who truly believed in Christ. The decision, he said, was up to each person. God had given everyone sufficient grace to choose good or evil. If people listened and searched within, they would feel the increasing presence of God's grace in their hearts. Make a full surrender to the forgiving God, he said, truly allow Christ to take up residence in the heart, and an enormous sense, sudden or gradual, of having been granted salvation would come over those who were sincerely penitent.

The experience of being "saved" was a false one, John Wesley said, if it was not followed by a new way of life. "Faith working by love," his fundamental motto, must lead to cleansed lives. People must be methodical in their religious habits (thus the term Methodist) and thrifty, vigorous, and productive in daily work. A genius at organization, and, as an Anglican, a strong believer in a hierarchical church, Wesley created in Methodism a kind of Church of England for the masses. He began by establishing a Methodist society in London, then spread Methodism by interlinking groups all over England, particularly in the teeming and churchless working-class districts. Each local society was tightly organized, presided over by laymen, and open only to card-carrying members who paid small but regular dues. Meeting regularly, in midweek prayer gatherings and Sunday observances after Church (Methodism for a long time was intended as a supplement, not a rival, to the Church of England), Methodists together probed their sinful lives. They printed books cheaply and spread them widely, thus creating the first mass taste for reading.

The Great Awakening

There was great excitement when the famous Whitefield arrived in America in 1739. He was greeted by enormous crowds from one end of the colonies to the other. Everywhere he preached "vital" religion as against rational religion. So fantastic was the response that he was called the Wonder of the Age. Emulated by many American preachers, he thus helped to launch the revival frenzy that swept the colonial world in the years 1739 to 1744, the Great Awakening.

Each church reacted differently. Quakers stood aloof from such vast and turbulent gatherings, for their faith stressed contemplation. Anglicans drew back in distaste. They detested "enthusiasm" and were devoted to the view that reason is the candle of the Lord. Many colonials gravitated to Anglicanism in their dislike for the Great Awakening. On the other hand, the pietistic German sects just entering the colonies were devoted to revivalism, as were some of the Lutherans.

The Baptists flourished mightily. A small movement based in Roger Williams's Rhode Island, they numbered perhaps a dozen congregations in 1740. By 1775 there were an astonishing 500 Baptist congregations throughout the colonies. They were on their way to becoming one of the two largest Protestant denominations in America; Methodism was the other. All along they had been preaching Great Awakening doctrines. They had insisted that baptism could take place only when a person was old enough to understand the Christian message and make a conscious personal *decision* for Christ—the central doctrine preached in the Great Awakening. Most Baptists believed that anyone who was moved by the Spirit could become a minister, whether or not the person was educated. The important point was that the individual must be God-called.

Following Williams's inspiration, the Baptists were thoroughly democratic and unconcerned with ritual. They made no pretense at being a "church," but allowed each congregation to go its own way. Baptism now found frontier America a wonderfully fertile field in which to grow. Great numbers of Scotch-Irish in the southern back country left the Presbyterian fold in these years. They disagreed with the Presbyterian emphasis on learned ministers, stern predestination, and a firmly controlled federal organization, preferring to join the more open and flexible Baptists. Likewise in New England, whole groups left the Congregational church to become Baptists. In this way, Baptism joined Presbyterianism and Methodism in becoming a denomination strong in both the North and the South.

Because the Methodists thought of themselves as a society supplementary to the Church of England, their separate existence did not begin until a quarter of a century after the Great Awakening. With the arrival of Francis Asbury in 1771, sent as a missionary by John Wesley, Methodism in America began its meteoric rise. In 1784 the Methodist Episcopal church was formally organized, Asbury and another man serving as bishops. Spreading widely in the nineteenth century, Methodism, with its origins in Anglicanism and its close similarity in organization, service, and creed to that church, became the form in which the more liberal religious beliefs of the Church of England became permanently diffused in American life.

For the Calvinist churches (the Dutch and German Reformed, Congregationalists, and Presbyterians), the Great Awakening was a cruel trial. Important Calvinist ministers were leaders in supporting the new revival of faith. They had, in fact, made beginnings in this direction years before Whitefield arrived. Others, however, violently opposed the Awakening as "enthusiastic," and too much imbued with free-will ideas. It was too ready, these men said, to open the church's doors to anyone who claimed a salvation experience. Order and discipline, so crucial to Calvinism, seemed thrown out the window. The nature and necessity of having been "saved" became a great issue that split these churches wide open. What was left, many asked, of the venerable scheme of salvation—the stages of introspection, study, and training—if an instantaneous "conversion" could accomplish the same task?

Jonathan Edwards

As the revival progressed, all colonials awaited New England's reaction, for that region had been long recognized as America's foremost "plantation of religion." It was Jonathan Edwards's revival at Northampton, Massachusetts, in 1734 and 1735 that seemed to many to be the real beginning of the American revival. In New England, where there was much anxiety about rising affluence, individualism, and the breakup of old ways, the underlying tension exploded with especial violence. Enthusiasm achieved unmatched heights, reaching near delirium in its early stages.

Edwards utilized this enthusiasm and recast Calvinism to align with revivalism, thus becoming the most important Puritan theologian since John Calvin himself. The joy of the Great Awakening, he said, was good and proper. It was a delight that rushed in on people as their entire beings reacted to the love of God and to the beauties He had created in this world. But Edwards was a true Calvinist. God, in his mind, was still the blazing, awesome, all-powerful, and wholly majestic Being who willed all things and was the center of faith. Considering the perfection of God, Edwards said, people could see in contrast how prideful, lustful, and selfish they were in their self-centered, petty lives. Consider the universe that God had made, how perfect and harmonious it was; consider the beauties of the plants, of all that was of God. Astonished and overwhelmed by all this, people would be drawn to God, as in nature all things were drawn by gravitation to a common center.

Left to ourselves, he said, we are bound for hell. Such a fate was appropriate for creatures so warped and corrupted. This made God's salvation all the more ravishing to consider. Only a truly loving God could have given such delights to such unworthy creatures. The sense of salvation was a wondrous thing. Thereafter, he said—agreeing with John Wesley—the saved person would live a new life. This would be, in fact, the proof of whether or not the "salvation" was a genuine thing or just an enthusiastic delusion. But Edwards had a different sense from Wesley of what a new life meant. It meant living not only a moral life, but also a life in which people worked for the regeneration of all society, in its institutions and social arrangements as well as in its religion. Working across the boundaries of religious sects

Jonathan Edwards, brilliant young Congregational clergyman in Massachusetts, whose preaching in the 1730s helped ignite the Great Awakening.

with others similarly regenerated in other churches, the new elect would transform the world. There had thus appeared once more, in the Great Awakening, the powerful motivations that had impelled the seventeenth-century Puritans, the first radicals.

The Impact of the Great Awakening

The Great Awakening and the new modernizing culture in the colonial cities collided in a cultural and political earthquake of historic proportions. George Whitefield concentrated especially on preaching in the colonial towns, where teeming crowds gathered. In Boston in 1740, something like 15,000 people surged onto the Common to hear him.

The seacoast towns were ripe for an explosion. Their common people were being pressed cruelly by inflation, taxes, and bloody war, while a few at the top, looking out for their own profit, seemed to be opulently skimming off the cream. Now came preachers who challenged traditional sources of religious authority and called upon each person, however humble, to find religious salvation by direct contact with God's saving grace. They also poured scorn upon aristocratic fashion and the accumulating of wealth.

The Great Awakening thus spread a radically egalitarian doctrine, and this set off aristocratic alarm, especially among the Anglicizing, pro-Church of England new wealthy class. Soon one of the great revivalist preachers, Gilbert Tennant, was in Boston being called "a monster! impudent and noisy," whose "Beastly brayings" were putting dangerous new ideas into the heads of the poor. As the masses turned out ever more enthusiastically to listen to men like James Davenport attack the rich and powerful, Boston's middle and upper classes, recoiling from the Great Awakening, warned of "anarchy, levelling, and [the] dissolution [of society]." The Boston grand jury declared Davenport insane. Charles Chauncy, aristocratic minister of the [Anglican] First Church and its wealthy parishioners, cried that such radicals were making "strong attempts to destroy all property, to make all things common, wives as well as goods."

No other colonial event left a more profound impression on American life than the Great Awakening. It was the first cultural movement all the colonists experienced together. For the common people, it "involved an expansion of political consciousness and a new feeling of self-importance," the historian Gary B. Nash writes, for "people partook of spontaneous meetings [much condemned as disorderly and out of control by proper authorities], assumed a new power in ecclesiastical affairs, and were encouraged repeatedly from the pulpit to adopt an attitude of skepticism toward dogma and authority." Especially in Boston, ravaged by war and social tensions, the Awakening introduced a public temper far more ready than before to be critical of the pro-English, Anglican-leaning upper classes. Thus, in Nash's "urban crucibles," where the future was being prepared, a culture of protest, angry at aristocracy and the English, was forming. New England Puritanism, set aflame by the Great Awakening with a passion for reshaping the world, threw itself eagerly into the argument with England when the pre-Revolutionary troubles began.

The Awakening had other results as well. It led to an upsurge of social kindliness and reform, giving strength to such burgeoning movements as penal reform and care of the insane and the unfortunate. Blacks listened eagerly to the new word of equality before God. Some became noted preachers. Revivalism seemed to call out to black men and women to take part, especially in a situation where traditional church organizations were loosened. They particularly flocked to the Baptist and later to the Methodist churches, though they entered practically every other sect as well. Whitefield determinedly preached to mixed congregations of blacks and whites, noting gratefully in Philadelphia, as he left, that "near fifty Negroes came to give me thanks for what God had done to their souls."

Newly revived by the Great Awakening, the various denominations founded new colleges. Harvard was already over a hundred years old; Yale and William and Mary were almost half a century old. All three had been founded under the earlier notions of the role of state and church, when the college was assumed to be primarily a seminary to train ministers and therefore could and did claim state support. Now the second wave of colleges sprang up. Still mainly denominational, they were created in colonies where religious freedom and heterogeneity had been the case from the beginning, and at a time when state and church ties were coming under attack.

Even Anglican King's College (later Columbia University), founded in New York City by grant of King George II in 1754, took pains to assure the populace that it was not just for Anglicans. It had to solicit funds from the public, since it received none from the government. In Philadelphia the wholly secular College of Philadelphia (later the University of Pennsylvania) was established in 1755. The Presbyterians founded the College of New Jersey (later Princeton University) in 1746; Rutgers—The State University, chartered as Queen's College in 1766, was linked to the Dutch Reformed churches; Dartmouth appeared in 1769 as another Congregational college; and Brown University was created (as Rhode Island College) in 1764 by the Baptists.

So it was that by the blending of diverse streams a new culture was emerging in America. Slowly but surely, the colonials acquired a sense of their common traditions and of their common future. Already America began to be praised as a refuge for the poor and the oppressed of Europe. Religious freedom, new peoples, the rise of intercolonial links—all these were combining to create a new sense, that of being an "American."

BIBLIOGRAPHY

Books that were especially valuable to me in thinking about and writing this chapter: I've drawn much from Gary B. Nash's recent work, *The Urban Crucible: Social Change, Political Consciousness, and the Origins of the American Revolution* (1979). On the revolution in economic thinking which saw productivity as the source of wealth, see Joyce Oldham Appleby, *Economic Thought and Ideology in Seventeenth-Century England* (1978). Richard D. Brown has given us a provocative work in his *Modernization: The Transformation of American Life 1600–1865* (1976). Important to me also were James A. Henretta, *The Evolution of American Society, 1700–1815: An Interdisciplinary Analysis* (1973); Henry F. May, *The Enlightenment in America* (1976); Richard L. Bushman, *From Puritan to Yankee: Character and the Social Order in Connecticut, 1690–1765* (1967); Edmund S. Morgan, *American Slavery American Freedom: The Ordeal of Colonial Virginia* (1975); Mary

P. Ryan, *Womanhood in America: From Colonial Times to the Present* (1975); Winthrop D. Jordan, *White Over Black: American Attitudes toward the Negro 1550–1812* (1969).

In Robert Kelley, *The Cultural Pattern in American Politics: The First Century* (1979), I have explored the rising ethnic and political tensions in mid-eighteenth century British America. The eighteenth century is a complex period, and many themes in its history have been studied. Those that point to the Revolution will be dealt with in the following chapter. A valuable survey is Richard Hofstadter, *America at 1750* (1971). A major topic recently of interest to historians is the old issue of the growing *differences* between American life and British life. Read, for example, Bernard Bailyn's *The Origins of American Politics* (1968); Jack P. Greene, "An Uneasy Connection: An Analysis of the Preconditions of the American Revolution," in Stephen Kurtz and James Hutson, eds., *Essays on the American Revolution* (1973), pp. 46–53; and Richard L. Merritt, *Symbols of American Community, 1735–1775* (1966). Michael Zuckerman's *Peaceable Kingdoms: Massachusetts Towns in the Eighteenth Century* (1970) is a fine example of the newer social history telling us new things. *Quakers and Politics: Pennsylvania, 1681–1726* (1968) by Gary B. Nash provides a revealing look at this major colony and its inner changes. For the broad patterns of schooling and education, see Lawrence A. Cremin's great work, *American Education: The Colonial Experience, 1607–1783* (1960), as well as Bernard Bailyn's brilliant short essay, *Education in the Forming of American Society* (1960).

Two major works published in the 1960s link the Great Awakening (in different ways) to internal changes: Alan E. Heimert, *Religion and the American Mind from the Great Awakening to the Revolution* (1966), and Carl Bridenbaugh, *Mitre and Sceptre: Transatlantic Faiths, Ideas, Personalities, and Politics, 1689–1775* (1962).

For the urban centers, see Carl Bridenbaugh, *Cities in the Wilderness* (1955). Michael Kraus, *The Atlantic Civilization: Eighteenth-Century Origins* (1949), is valuable on the transatlantic culture. For the ethnic groups, see James G. Leyburn, *The Scotch-Irish: A Social History* (1962), and Robert Henry Billigmeier, *Americans from Germany: A Study in Cultural Diversity* (1974).

Merle Curti's *The Growth of American Thought* (1964) is an irreplaceable study of the whole sweep of American intellectual history. His recent magisterial work, *Human Nature in American Thought: A History* (1980), in its early chapters explores the colonial mind. Sidney E. Ahlstrom's award-winning massive work, *A Religious History of the American People* (1972), offers a rich, swiftly moving, readable, and scholarly panorama.

On women and the family, see a brilliant study by John Demos, *A Little Commonwealth: Family Life in Plymouth Colony* (1970); Page Smith's engaging book, *Daughters of the Promised Land: Women in American History* (1970); a solid, perceptive book by W. Elliot Brownlee and Mary M. Brownlee, *Women in the American Economy: A Documentary History, 1675 to 1929* (1976); and a valuable recent work edited by Michael Gordon, *The American Family in Social-Historical Perspective* (2d ed., 1978). A provocative, bold interpretation is Edward Shorter's *The Making of the Modern Family* (1977).

6

The New People Seize Independence

TIME LINE

HISTORY IN AN INDIVIDUAL LIFE

SAMUEL ADAMS

England, he cried, was corrupt: a den of profiteers and graft-taking politicians, whores and parasites, arrogant bishops parading pomp and finery, overblown government, and a power-hungry monarchy. Sam Adams of Boston, devout Puritan and man of politics, hated the aristocrats who administered Massachusetts for the Crown and whose taste for luxury and the opulent commerce that fed that luxury seemed certain to destroy the moral heart of New England. He flung himself into the anti-British campaign with a passionate intensity. A thin, heavy-jawed, old-looking little man in his mid-forties at the time of the Stamp Act crisis in 1765, Adams's brilliance in politics and his smoking pen quickly made him the storm center of New England resistance. America, he believed, must separate from Britain or, infected by the materialistic and moral contagions seeping across the Atlantic from London, lose its soul. Only then could a "Christian Sparta," now imperiled, be revived in America.

Adams never let the controversy die. As leader of the Massachusetts radicals, it was he who organized the Non-Importation Association, which, becoming intercolonial, forced the Stamp Act's repeal. Then he scratched out a bold Circular Letter, adopted by the Massachusetts House of Representatives in February 1768 and then by seven other colonies, which denounced the principle of taxation without representation, denied that Parliament had any such power, and called for united colonial action against London. When in 1769 British troops were placed in Boston to enforce the Townshend Duties, it was Adams who kept publishing lurid accounts of rapes, beatings, and other atrocities perpetrated by the redcoats. After the Boston Massacre early in 1770 he poured out a flood of bitter articles for local newspapers, denouncing like the biblical Jeremiah the wickedness of British officialdom and warning that concealed conspiracies in London aimed at ending all colonial liberties. In 1772, at his urging, the intercolonial Committee of Correspondence was formed "to state the rights of the Colonists . . . and . . . communicate the same . . . to the world."

Soon the fateful ships were arriving in Boston with their tea, the last commodity upon which a London-imposed tax still had to be paid. On Adams's motion, a great crowd in Faneuil Hall in December 1773 demanded that the tea "be returned to the place from which it came. . . ." When this was refused, Adams rose from his post as chairman of the gathering and uttered an agreed-upon signal: "This meeting can do nothing more to save the country." Shortly, the "Mohawks" were at the docks and throwing the tea into the harbor.

Adams had achieved his goal. This final act of impudent defiance produced an explosion of rage in London; the Coercive Acts of 1774, instantly passed by Parliament, practically ended self-government in Massachusetts; and the tumble of events leading inevitably toward revolution was in motion.

Overview

Great wars ravaged the eighteenth century. They began in 1689 when England and France began fighting each other for European supremacy, and they did not end until the defeat of Napoleon at Waterloo in 1815. These conflicts—sometimes called the Second Hundred Years War between the two countries, the first having taken place in the Middle Ages—involved colonial possessions around the world and most of the other countries of Europe as well. They were the first of the world wars.

France, then the colossus of Europe, struck repeatedly for continental supremacy, and the English, determined to maintain a balance of power to preserve their own independence, led fighting coalitions that turned back the French. Savage fighting and bitter campaigning against the French forces in Canada, where New France had existed in a long string of settlements along the St. Lawrence River since Samuel de Champlain founded Quebec in 1608, took place in each war. From time to time the English colonists even made bold but unsuccessful expeditions to conquer Canada.

By the middle of the eighteenth century, the scene was changing. By then some American colonists were topping the Appalachian rise and moving into the valley of the Ohio. The crucial fact now was that both Britain and France claimed the continental interior. French fur traders had in fact long ranged the vast Great Lakes basin and the upper Mississippi Valley, trading with the Indians, with whom they maintained cordial relations. The French government quickly realized that if the populous British colonists were allowed to pour into the interior, their claim to that region and their profitable trade would be endangered. The French acted decisively. In 1749 they sent an expedition to take military possession of the Ohio Valley and establish forts throughout the region.

The British government and its colonists had to respond. Ultimatums were delivered, and fighting broke out in 1754. Within two years the conflict had exploded into a worldwide struggle, the Seven Years War. When the Peace of Paris was signed at its close in 1763, ending what Americans call the French and Indian War, the region west of the Mississippi remained in Spanish hands, but all the rest of North America, including Canada and Florida, became British. With this vast domain and with the islands, colonies, and trading posts Britain gained around the world, that nation had achieved a maritime, commercial, and colonial supremacy such as few other powers had ever enjoyed in world history.

Loyalty and Continental Dreams

It was all so settled and serene. The British Empire was solid, secure, a grand edifice certain to last for centuries. There it was, stretching from Hudson's Bay and the Arctic Circle in the north to the wide Caribbean in the south, a vast chain of twenty-one mainland and island colonies with a population running into the millions. It supported an immense moving web of seaborne commerce that funneled wealth into its many towns and cities, and especially into Great Britain itself.

The jewels of the empire were the flourishing thirteen British colonies of settlement on the North American coast. How did their peoples feel in 1763? They were proud of being part of such a majestic empire, and intensely loyal. They had fought well and hard to help win the great victory against the French, and most of them gloried in the name "British." Especially along the seacoast, where those of specifically English descent concentrated, people aped London styles, delighted in small English social rituals like teatime, and pored over London newspapers to keep up with the latest fads. England, said admiring colonials like Benjamin Franklin, was "home," the "wise and good mother."

The colonials were grateful to Britain and its long and bloody wars against the French in North America. "The outcome [of these conflicts]," writes historian Ralph Ketcham, "meant literally life or death to the colonies, still in tender immaturity and threatened on all sides by what they rightly regarded as aggressive French or Spanish despotism." The colonials broke into a storm of hosannas when General James Wolfe captured Quebec in 1759. They regarded Wolfe's death in that same victorious battle as yet another example of Great Britain's readiness to sacrifice even great heroes to give its colonies lasting protection. The relationship between London and the colonies was by no means free of frictions, but nonetheless, Ketcham writes, from the colonials came "constant, effusive, and heartfelt expressions of love for Great Britain."

Now, the British victory spawned a great dream in the colonial mind: that with French power wiped out in North America and the British Crown incontestably sovereign over the vast interior as far as the Mississippi River, the colonials would be free to pour over the Appalachians and settle the green and fertile lands of that immense region. "All the country from the St. Lawrence to the Mississippi," exulted Benjamin Franklin, "will in another century be filled with British people."

In reality, however, these good relations and these grand hopes would soon be rudely broken. So huge had been the British war effort that London was staggering under an immense war debt. Furthermore, its expanded empire was much more costly to administer and defend. The king's ministers were worried day and night by one gigantic, obsessive problem: Where in heaven's name would they find the money to govern and defend this large new empire? How, indeed, could they make it more efficient, and less costly to rule?

A Great Public Policy Decision

The British had before them, in short, a complicated public policy question to solve, one of the most fateful in all their history. What is meant by "public policy"? The British government, faced by a complex problem, had to work out a decision as to what to do about it (a policy). Specific legislation containing the essence of that decision had to be put before Parliament and enacted. Then the government had to select a group of people to carry out—i.e., implement—the policy thus settled upon, and put them to work.

Looking back from our vantage point, we know that in the years 1765 to 1775 the British government failed at this task. Catastrophically, stunningly, irretrievably, it failed. The British drove their formerly grateful and loyal North American colonies first into a mounting rage, then into revolution. Meanwhile, during the vain effort Britain made at trying to put down that revolt, it got itself into, and lost, a disastrous world war. When it was all over, the first British Empire (there would later be another) was shrunken to discouraging bits and pieces, and the world's first new nation to appear in the modern centuries had come into being: the United States of America.

How do we explain this remarkable sequence of events? It will help to look at this great failure in policy-making with a modestly systematic approach. Of the many things that shape policy-making, in this chapter we will look at three: what each side *knew* about the other; how they *imaged* one another; and how they *defined the problem*.

Ignorance and Images

Though the British had ruled their empire for more than 150 years, the small land-owning elite that actu-

British critics of their government's policies toward the Americans satirized it savagely. Here we see King George III as an ass in an ermine cloak presiding over a solemnly foolish Privy Council, a muzzled "Jon Bull" bulldog (the British populace) kept silent on the floor. On the wall map, a jagged split divides England and America.

ally made public policy for Great Britain (the masses had little to do with it) was in fact surprisingly ignorant of the colonies. The aristocracy did not emigrate, nor save in rare instances did it travel to the colonies to observe conditions with its own eyes. The thirteen colonies were simply a kind of abstraction: Until the troubles began, little was heard of the colonies save during wartime, since they in effect governed themselves.

The elite certainly did not know or care to know the colonial mind, any more than it cared to understand the other "outsiders" to British life, the Welsh, Scots, and Irish, or the illiterate, poverty-stricken English masses. When the colonials later reacted angrily to taxes levied upon them, the London government was genuinely surprised, even though earlier warned. Then, as it stumbled on from error to error, it did so on the basis of astonishing delusions, such as that most of the colonials were actually loyal to the Crown, angry at the rebellion, and eager to welcome and assist royal troops in putting it down.

Despite their profound ignorance of the colonials, the English had distinct images in their minds as to what they believed the colonials were like. Put most simply, the English regarded the colonials as crude, inferior, distasteful people who did not seem to know their place. After all, it would be said, consider the Americans' social origins. They were either moralistic, plain-spoken and plain-dressed Puritans and Quakers—Dissenters—who in English life were distinctly unfashionable and looked down upon; or they were "self-made" men like Benjamin Franklin, not men of established family or status; or they were slaveholders, and thus rather disgraceful people who whipped their "servants" and begat children upon their helpless black women slaves; or they were rude outlanders, like the Scotch-Irish and Germans. Who could pay them any respect? In short, one of the convictions most firmly rooted in the English mind, as the historian John C. Miller has written,

> was the superiority of true-born Britons to the American colonists. . . . [They were] regarded as degenerate Englishmen or as the "scum or off-scouring of all nations"—"a hotchpotch medley of foreign, enthusiastic madmen"—a mongrel breed of Irish, Scotch, and Germans, leavened with convicts and outcasts.

There was an ancient cultural attitude at work here: the concept of honor. Warrior in its origins, a gentleman's honor made heavy demands upon him, most of all that in every circumstance he must be brave, prickly of how he was treated, and ready to fight rather than accept slights upon his reputation. Duels were a common feature of eighteenth-century aristocratic life in England. Honor required too that a gentleman never bow to anyone socially inferior. He must insist upon being paid proper respect by those below him. "Insolence" on their part (i.e., any show of independent judgment) was infuriating. This made it impossible even to think of compromise with the colonials (a name the English could give a stinging, contemptuous snap). "Is not everything English maddened in our bosoms," an Englishman exclaimed, "at the remotest thought of crouching to the creatures of our formation? Have we erected Colonies to be our masters?"

When the troubles began, therefore, the British ruling classes quickly came to define the problem in starkly simple terms. What they really faced, they believed, was not simply a financial problem and a taxing issue, but rather a *challenge to their honor and authority*. The colonists, it was said over and over again, were "children" and England was the "parent." Worse yet, the Americans were ungrateful children. Had not Britain protected them again and again, at heavy cost in treasure and lives, from their enemies the French? Was not their vast Atlantic trading fleet protected by the British navy? Their "insolent" challenge to England's authority (regarded as unlimited) could not be allowed. The colonists must in all circumstances be dutiful and *obey*.

The Troubles Begin

In this frame of mind, the British government moved ahead vigorously in the early 1760s. First, it tried to halt the westward movement of the colonials into the interior, for their migration produced burdensome Indian wars. Holding that the region west of the Appalachians belonged to the Indians, London wiped out all colonial land claims beyond those mountains and began governing the area directly from England. The fur trade with the Indians was regularized and placed under royal officials at centralized locations. However, in 1763 the brilliant Indian leader Pontiac, angered at the autocratic and insensitive way British officials exercised their authority, set off a bloody war against the colonials in a desperate attempt to oust the British and win the return of the French. When he was finally defeated, chastened British authorities established the Proclamation Line of 1763 along the crest of the Appalachians and decreed that the outraged colonists were not to go beyond it until a more effective Indian program was developed.

To tighten their regulation of imperial trade and raise within the colonies a revenue out of which the costs of their government could be borne, the British in 1764 passed the Sugar Act, the first law ever passed by Parliament specifically to raise money in the colonies. It placed new or higher duties on a wide range of imported products. Then came, in 1765, the fateful Stamp Act. It taxed all newspapers, pamphlets, licenses, commercial notes and bonds, advertisements, leases, legal papers, and other such documents.

This was clearly levying taxes without getting the consent first of those taxed, and we might expect the English to have been highly sensitive on this point. After all, control of taxation by the community at large, through Parliament—a power that body had won in generations of struggle with the king and even at the cost of civil war—was trumpeted abroad as the foundation stone of Britain's uniquely free and libertarian constitution. But when the king's ministers were warned that the colonials would protest, the warning was brushed aside with irritation.

Parliament, it was insisted, could do anything it wished to do. Was it not supreme in the British system of government? "[The] one argument [Prime Minister George Grenville] would not listen to," writes historian Robert Middlekauff, "was a challenge to Parliament's right to tax. . . ." Colonial representatives tried again and again to get him to give up the idea of a stamp tax, but he was adamant. Furthermore, the very thought that the colonials might protest made members of Parliament angry. Said Charles Townshend sardonically:

And now will these Americans, Children planted by our Care, nourished up by our Indulgence until they are grown to a Degree of Strength and Opulence, and protected by our Arms, will they grudge to contribute their mite to relieve us from the heavy weight of that burden [of debt and taxes] which we lie under?

Reaction in the Colonies

A raging controversy erupted in the colonies. The Stamp Act struck, ironically, right at the most powerful and articulate groups in the colonies: merchants, businessmen, lawyers, journalists, and clergy. They, of course, defined the situation entirely differently from the British. Taxation without consent! It was not to be borne. Liberty, freedom from oppression— *that* was the issue!

In the last chapter we saw how an explosive political climate had been building in the colonial towns. An egalitarian prickliness and outspokenness among the formerly passive common people had emerged which made them far more ready than before to react angrily and openly to British aristocratic arrogance. Stung by the Stamp Act, the colonial elite quickly organized an intercolonial resistance movement, tapping the common people's anger, which brought all business temporarily to a standstill. Mobs in New York City roared through the streets, destroying government papers and buildings. When similar events took place in Boston and Charleston, the Stamp Act was effectively nullified by violence.

The colonials were adamant that the Stamp Act was unconstitutional—i.e., it was beyond the authority possessed by Parliament—and therefore void. On May 30, 1765, Virginia's House of Burgesses had resolved that it had "the only and sole exclusive right and power to lay taxes . . . upon the inhabitants of this Colony [who were] not bound to yield obedience to any law" coming from Parliament that sought to tax them. This bold stand by the largest and most venerable of the colonies encouraged the others to follow suit. Determined to show a common front, in October 1765 the colonies sent representatives to meet in the Stamp Act Congress in New York City. There the historic Stamp Act Resolutions were adopted, which denied unequivocally any right on London's part to tax the colonies without their consent.

Resolutions of the Stamp Act Congress, October 19, 1765: That His Majesty's liege subjects in these colonies are entitled to all the inherent rights and liberties of his natural born subjects within the kingdom of Great Britain. . . . That it is inseparably essential to the freedom of a people, and the undoubted right of Englishmen, that no taxes be imposed on them but with their own consent, given personally or by their representatives. . . . That the people of these colonies are not, and from their local circumstances cannot be, represented in the House of Commons in Great Britain. . . . That the only representatives of the people of these colonies are persons chosen therein by themselves, and that no taxes ever have been, or can be constitutionally imposed on them, but by their respective legislatures. . . . That all supplies to the Crown being free gifts of the people, it is unreasonable and inconsistent with the principles and spirit of the British Constitution, for the people of Great Britain to grant to His Majesty the property of the colonists. . . . That the increase, prosperity, and happiness of these colonies depend on the full and free enjoyments of their rights and liberties, and an intercourse with Great Britain mutually affectionate and advantageous.

In March 1766 Parliament angrily accepted the inevitable and repealed the Stamp Act. But at the same time it struck back at the colonists by passing the Declaratory Act, which stated that in any event Parliament was completely sovereign over them. The colonists concentrated upon the fact of repeal and ignored the potentially inflammatory Declaration, expressing their feelings in an outburst of oratorical loyalty to the empire. The troubles seemed ended.

Colonial Images of Britain

On the colonial side the Stamp Act crisis had a detonative effect: It smashed directly into the predominant colonial images of the British. As it happened, colonials to this point had been almost as ignorant of the realities of English life as the aristocracy in Great Britain was of them. England was far away, most colonials knew it only in books and in stories, and those of English descent tended to build idealized images of the "mother country." They extravagantly admired English culture, and exulted in the inherited Whig ideas of liberty which they thought were supreme in England, with its "glorious" constitution.

Young John Adams would eventually be one of the Revolution's leaders, but before the troubles began he had "rejoiced that I was an Englishman and gloried in the name of Briton." For him, writes the historian Ralph Ketcham,

> *Shakespeare, Bacon, Milton, Bunyan, Locke, Newton, and Pope had expressed, in matchless English, the ideas and values that gave meaning and purpose to his life. Without them he would be empty and adrift, and they seemed disembodied apart from the "blessed realm" of England where they had lived and died.*

However, England in the Stamp Act crisis was now revealed to be an *arrogant* England. It was an England apparently quite indifferent to its own Whig heritage of freedom, a Tory England which in its drive to bend the colonies to its will would violate its own most cherished ideas.

Just below the surface of professed loyalty to Britain there had always been mixed feelings in the colonial mind. This should not surprise us. Whenever a people are dependent upon another nation that is wealthier, more powerful, and in a position of near-parental cultural dominance, they are inescapably ambivalent in their attitudes. Thus, attraction toward and love of Britain existed side by side with resentment and hate. Hundreds of thousands of the colonials, for that matter, had ancient reasons to dislike the English. The Scotch-Irish, the Germans, and the Dutch resented English prejudice, while non-Anglicans among the English-descended were prickly toward the Church of England. For most of the eighteenth century the Church of England had been pushing hard to infiltrate Congregational New England.

It had already been made the legally established church in the Southern colonies—that is, it was like a branch of the government—and in the four counties in and around New York City. Anglicans constantly urged London to establish a *bishop* in the colonies, who in the English system would be an awesome public figure, outranking even the colonial governors. Scotch-Irish Presbyterians bitterly opposed the campaign to make Anglicanism as powerful in the colonies as it was in England, and they fought harsh political battles with the Anglicans in New York Colony, in Pennsylvania, and in the South. In these controversies they could usually count on the support of the German Lutherans and Calvinists (the German Reformed), for they too were alarmed at the Anglican surge.

So violent were these conflicts within particular colonies that in the mid-1700s the argument over church and state, and over having an Anglican bishop, was debated more heatedly and persistently by the colonials than any other issue until the troubles with Britain began. Many non-Anglicans believed that Britain's efforts to take stronger control over the colonies sprang primarily from an Anglican plot to prepare the way for an Anglican takeover and a wiping out of religious freedom.

The Role of the British Army

The British had kept a standing army in the colonies after the end of the French and Indian War, a body of about 6,000 troops. The colonists, who had never had such a force in their midst before, could only ask themselves in alarm, whatever for? No matter how reasonable London's explanations that the soldiers were needed to govern the Indians of the interior, some conspiratorial purpose threatening American liberties was widely suspected. Then the Quartering act of 1765 ordered the colonial assemblies to provide housing for troops stationed within settled portions of the colonies. All complained of this, New York's assembly most of all, for it had the largest body of soldiers to support.

Angered at this "insolence" and embittered by the "base ingratitude" of the Americans, the government in London resolved to force the colonies to comply. In 1767 it peremptorily suspended the New York Assembly until it obeyed the Quartering Act, which in time forced that colony grudgingly to agree. What remained in the colonists' minds, however, was a rankling grievance and a brooding distrust of London.

The Townshend Duties

In June 1767, Chancellor of the Exchequer Charles Townshend got Parliament to establish tariff duties on all glass, paper, paint, and tea imported into the American colonies. The British were delighted, for this measure cleverly got around the colonials' stated objection to "internal" taxes. But the Americans were outraged, for the effect of the new imposts, however laid on, was the same: The revenue gained by the British would pay the salaries of royal governors and judges in the colonies and make them independent of colonial legislatures. Then a new royal bureaucracy, in the form of a board of customs commissioners, was sent to the colonies to collect the duties. Also, four admiralty courts were established in the chief ports to hear disputed cases, in whose proceedings juries would not be used. The total effect of these laws, if they had come into full force, would have been literally to transform the nature of the empire, placing the colonials under centralized controls such as had never existed before.

A protest movement immediately welled up. It was led by Massachusetts, under the direction of Samuel Adams. He got Boston, New York City, and Philadelphia to boycott British goods in retaliation against the new laws. Then he drafted the protesting Circular Letter, adopted by the Massachusetts legislature in February 1768. By the time angry officials in London learned of the letter and sent instructions to dissolve the sitting of the Massachusetts legislature, seven other colonies had already formally approved the document.

English Realities

By now, the fully awakened colonials were paying close attention to what was going on in London and learning a great deal about the realities of English life, which were most alarming. England was not simply a country of great writers and philosophers, and of soaring ideals of human liberty; it was also a country of aristocratic arrogance, oppressed tenant farmers, mass illiteracy and ignorance, and shocking poverty. It was also a country in which liberty seemed very much endangered—indeed, under grave assault.

What colonials now came fully alive to in British politics was an envenomed political battle going on there between Whigs and Tories. The colonials, of course, cheered the Whigs, who traditionally stood for civil rights, religious freedom, and the supremacy of the elected legislature over the monarchy. However, when George III had become king in 1760, the people he chose to run Britain's government leaned toward Tory ideas. They were royalists who insisted that the Crown could do what it wanted whether or not Parliament agreed; and who were quite ready to buy votes in the House of Commons, if necessary, to get their way—that is, to undermine the hallowed British constitution. In religion, royalists emphasized Church of England supremacy, and put religious Dissenters under great pressure to become Anglicans. Through the use of political spies and prosecutions for "sedition," they harassed those who criticized the government. Indeed, English political life seemed like a violently boiling pot. Whig newspapers screamed abuse at the authorities, who in turn were obsessed by paranoid convictions that enemies, subversives, and conspirators were everywhere.

Colonials read about all this in the newspapers that came in a steady stream from England, and were deeply disturbed. Observing what the Crown was then seeking to do on their own side of the Atlantic, they too drifted toward the belief that conspiracies were at work. Many concluded that a cunning Tory plot was in motion throughout the empire to undermine liberty, a plot which aimed first at destroying liberty in the colonies, and then erasing it in the mother country as well. When for the first time a large British bureaucracy was introduced into the colonies by the Townshend Duties to gather taxes (out of which its own salaries were to be paid), colonists told themselves that British political corruption was being introduced into colonial life to negate its freedoms. The new royal tax collectors, who received their salaries out of collections, outraged the colonists.

> *Between 1768 and 1772 they engaged in what . . . contemporary colonial opinion . . . judged was little less than "customs racketeering," as they employed legal technicalities and unscrupulous methods to plunder large amounts from colonial merchants, including such future Revolutionary leaders as John Hancock. . . . The more blatant abuses came to an end after 1770 after the commissioners and their supporters lost influence in Britain, but the damage had been done, and it was their wholesale attack on American liberty and property, not American opposition to the old navigation system or addiction to smuggling that caused the intense colonial hostility to the new board.* (Jack P. Greene, ed., The Reinterpretation of the American Revolution, 1763–1789 [1968])

Now the colonials began listening more closely to a political fringe group in England, the Radical Whigs. For years they had been calling for social equality, for government by the common people, and a reduction in royal power. They preached a "republican" ideology that demanded the end of titled aristocracy, social and economic privilege, and the established church. England should be transformed into a democratic country, austere, equalitarian, and virtuous. Over and over they attacked centralized power. Corruption (in the form of the buying of votes in Parliament by the king's ministers) seemed to have become the chief means of government, undermining freedom and the constitution. The balance between Crown, Lords, and Commons, which since the Glorious Revolution of 1688 had guaranteed British liberties, was being destroyed.

The "New People" Discover Themselves

Running like wildfire through the patriot movement in the colonies was an exciting discovery: The colonials learned that they were a *different* people from the English. The thirteen colonies, which formerly had had little to do with each other, awakened to a crucial new fact in their lives: *They shared a common enemy.* Unconsciously and automatically, this *gave them a sense of common identity*, and a *common purpose.* Few things are more powerful in creating a sense of unity than a common antagonist. A shared sense of the enemy is the most powerful single force that creates and sustains ethnic groups, religious movements, political parties, and nations. Without

an enemy, even ethnic groups slowly lose their coherence and begin dissolving.

But what would this "new people" on the coast of North America call themselves? Formerly, they had referred to themselves as "British." During the years of mounting tensions, however, this practice had become unpopular. There was, in fact, an alternative. For a hundred years colonials occasionally had referred to themselves as living in what they called "America," or "these American parts." In the 1730s and 1740s, as the thirteen colonies swelled in population and self-awareness, we see the name popping up more frequently, as in publications like *The American Magazine* (founded in 1741).

For some time, as it happened, the British in the mother country had not been able to bring themselves to call the colonials "British." So they too needed a collective name to refer to this diverse, irritating, and newly militant crowd of peoples who were giving them so much trouble. We find, therefore, that it was the British who first began referring with considerable frequency to the colonials simply as "Americans," a name that for them seemed to carry a note of disdain and inferiority. Then in the 1760s an intriguing thing happened: The colonials, eager to distinguish themselves from the British, seized upon what to the mother country was a derogatory name and began using it with mounting pride. Everywhere it appeared in the newspapers, in political oratory, in the names of new-founded learned societies (as in Benjamin Franklin's American Philosophical Society, established in Philadelphia in 1769), and even in literature, as in Philip Freneau's widely praised 1771 production, *A Poem on the Rising Glory of America.* So it was that the "Americans" got their lasting name, product of a sudden realization on both sides of the Atlantic, during a great and historic argument, that a new people whose separate existence had not formerly been recognized had come into being on the North American continent.

The Meaning of America

What, however, did "America" mean? What was it all about? Proclaiming a new identity, during a climactic argument with a "parent," was an act that called for an explanation, a purpose, a sense of meaning. The Americans grasped first at history. They called up the memory of the original founding of the colonies, insisting that they were still defenders of the religious and political liberty, and the ideal of self-government, that their ancestors had left Europe to found in the New World. They also trumpeted over and over that they were the true heirs of the ancient tradition of English liberty, won during centuries of struggle against tyrannical kings. It was the "rights of Englishmen," they said, that America had been called into being to protect and nourish.

Soon, however, it was far more than the past that they looked to. As the Americans plunged more deeply into their argument with Britain, to their mounting excitement they came to realize that they already had that "republican" way of life that the Radical British Whigs—whom most politically conscious colonials had long admired—had been vainly calling for in the British Isles. The American colonies were already remarkably democratic; their governments were small, simple, and austere; and there was no heavy superstructure within the colonies of a resident monarchy, a titled nobility, and a powerful Church of England. There were (save in New York Colony) no manor lords holding immense tracts of land, or the oppression of tenant farming. The new "America," its people could now say, had a noble task: It was to lead all humanity to a new, more just, and more humane way of life much larger than that simply encompassed in the English past.

Republicanism: What Did It Mean?

As the Americans seized enthusiastically upon the ideology of republicanism and made it their national political faith—their core idea as a new people in the world—we must take a moment to understand what it meant. Essentially, republicanism had one central belief: that the truly just society is one which gives the fullest possible liberty to individuals to live their lives as they see fit. Republicans recognized that, of course, every society needs to have a government—that is, a system of organized power—to establish laws and enforce them. But power was always at war with liberty, republicans insisted: It was greedy, aggressive, working for absolute supremacy for those who held it. There had to be, therefore, a "constitution" or an implicit and accepted agreement on the form of government that was above all parties and that could not be lightly meddled with. But even this government depended upon the existence of *virtue* among the people at large: a ruling temper and source of values that would instinctively keep governments in check and insure civility and liberty.

How could a society be virtuous if it were wealthy, luxurious and shamelessly immoral, like England, and ruled by a self-indulgent aristocracy? Corruption was monarchy's characteristic habit of government (republicans said): the buying of votes in Parliament, the handing out of privileges and high-paying but useless offices. From such practices came swollen government, destructive of liberty. A republic would do without monarchy, large government, and aristocratic rule, rooting small, limited governments in the virtuous common people.

Indeed, republicanism challenged practically all aspects of traditional English life. As its now self-conscious propagandists, American republicans had a belief that it was their mission to display for the entire world a new and revolutionary social order. An obscure colonial people, hitherto largely ignored by educated Europe, Americans found themselves surging to the front of the stage as defenders of liberty, brave strugglers for a cause of worldwide significance. They became the toast of intellectual circles in Europe, for America's way of life was seen as "philosophy teaching by example." And yet they were detested by traditionalists, by monarchists, in the Old World. Republicanism was as hated by its eighteenth-century enemies as communism has been by its twentieth-century antagonists.

Monarchists insisted that the common people were selfish, greedy, jealous of wealth, and turbulent. They needed rule by a strong and titled aristocracy independent of their control. If sovereignty were not lodged in a single person, the monarch, there would be no stability or order, and therefore no law or justice. Social hierarchy, to traditionalists, was divine in origin. Those at the top, through education, good family, and wide experience, were much more virtuous than the ignorant, passionate masses. Law and order—this was the important thing. Centralized power would ensure it. Thus, to be a republican, many believed, was to be guilty of insane designs for overturning society, true religion, and morality, and for plundering all who held property and wealth.

Republicans answered angrily that it was the *people* who were the truly virtuous part of society, for they had not been corrupted by power and wealth. Only when the people ruled would there be true social justice; only they were properly the sovereigns, collectively, in the land. Anyone holding public office should be elected by them, and subject to popular opinion (an appalling idea to monarchists). The source of debauchery and luxury, republicans claimed, lay in the ruling aristocracies, who were lazy and supported wholly by the labor of others. There should be social equality (though not "leveling"). The government, if it were to be truly just, should be rooted in the virtuous people, and all power, being dangerous, should be divided, scattered, and localized.

In their sermons the colonial clergy had traditionally used England as a wicked symbol of moral corruption and degradation, and had praised the simple austerities and pieties of life in the colonies. Now, after 1763, the religious enthusiasms built up by the Great Awakening swept full force into the patriot cause. The New Light clergy cried out that America's dreams of moral purity were endangered. Angered at the Anglican campaign for supremacy, they joined in a close political alliance with those who were alarmed at British political corruption and its threat to the colonies. Resisting British autocracy, clerics insisted, would not only secure liberty but also ward off London's depravities.

If a war were to come, these militant clerics welcomed the prospect. They gloried in historical memories of the long struggle in Britain for religious freedom, and they hungered to play again that sainted role. A conflict, they said, would purge Americans of their sins, and enable them to build in the New World the Zion of the Lord for which they had prayed since the days when the Puritan settlers had planted their "city on a hill" in New England.

The Cultural Crisis in New England and Virginia

There was a deep cultural crisis within colonial life out of which all of this flowed. New Englanders condemned impiety, luxury, and the other moral corruptions that they said threatened to come to America from England, because profound changes were in fact going on within New England's ways of life. Its traditional village-centered existence, focused in each town's Congregational chapel and in a cohesive, tightly bound sharing of moral values, was breaking down. The seaboard towns had become so much a part of the transatlantic British trading world that commercialization, and all that this meant in modernization, was flooding in. Individuals were breaking loose to live their lives according to new values, and to look out for themselves. They paid less attention to churches and ministers. The transition from Puritan to Yankee was far advanced.

Samuel Adams, the radical leader, believed that only by wrenching the colonies free from England could the righteous and cohesive community be revived; only by separation could a Christian Sparta be revitalized in America, providing to all the world a model of virtuous, godly life. New England republicans, in short, were *moralistic* republicans, people who believed that a true religious faith and a shared moral way of life should interpenetrate the state and its government. Wholeness and purity, team spirit, a kind of medieval corporateness, a family feeling of living and working together in a shared enterprise—it was these values that inspired New Englanders and drove them onward in their hopes for the future.

Virginia, too, was deeply troubled in the mid-century decades. Its wealthy and lordly planters, in their wigs, carriages, and London fashions, were carrying on their books a huge debt to British merchants. Tobacco prices were dropping, yet their way of life was growing more costly. Caught in a classic condition of colonial dependence upon the British economic system, they recoiled against this status, resenting its indignities.

There was a great fear, indeed, that the connection with Britain was corrupting Virginia's moral character. The chronic extravagance that over many generations the tobacco trade had built into life in the tidewater mansions was, by its lavish and ruinous impact, seen to be destroying Virginia's virtue and livelihood. Many insisted that the colony was on the verge of ruin, for too many Virginians had taken as their model the high-spending and self-indulgent ways of the English upper classes.

Virginians were proud and prickly individualists; that is, they were *libertarian* republicans. The yeoman farmers, small farmers, and great plantation owners of the colony prided themselves on being sturdily self-sufficient. They were armed men, they made regular use of their weapons, and this was central to their sense of independent manhood. By the 1730s a white laboring class had practically disappeared; hand labor had become associated with being black. Large and small planters were all white men, which created a strong bond between the classes, a sense of unity and equality, even though Virginia was an elitist community in which the proud aristocracy monopolized government. "Republicanism" was ardently popular, an irony in a social order founded on slavery. But the historian Edmund S. Morgan has suggested that it was perhaps the very presence of slaves that made whites passionately republican, for the example of what it was like not to have liberty was before them every day.

Virginia's political leaders did not look forward to the building of a Christian Sparta in America. Rather, they envisioned a country of free (white, male) individuals, each possessed of an unfettered opportunity to engage in the "pursuit of happiness," a goal profoundly different from the one that inspired Puritan New England. Virginians were also localist in their sentiments, and distrustful of any attempt to build strong, centralized governing systems, whether in London or—much later—in Washington, D.C. Skeptical of clerics, irreverent, free-thinking, and benefiting from a slave system abhorred by most Northerners (who were soon to end it within their own states), Virginians were devoted to a variety of republicanism quite different from that championed by the Yankees.

The Cultural Conflict in the Middle Colonies

New Yorkers disliked the Yankees, thinking them a righteous, preachy, excessively moralistic people. The Anglican mercantile and financial ruling circles in the New York City aristocracy were loyal to Britain, and fully committed to British commerce and its modernizing influences. They resisted to the end all efforts at rebellion and independence. Most swung in a body to the Tory side during the Revolution.

However, the Dutch farmers of the Hudson Valley, the Scotch-Irish Presbyterians who settled in the same region, and the Yankees who had crossed the Sound to populate Long Island had for many years opposed the Anglican aristocracy. That the Anglican Church was the legally established faith in the four counties in and around New York City permanently polarized the colony's politics.

A Calvinist coalition gathered in the mid-eighteenth century behind the Presbyterians William Livingston and George Clinton—who dominated New York politics until well into the 1790s. Fervently republican, they tried to end the state-church status of the Anglican establishment and to keep America free of the corrupting, commercializing influences of British financial and political power. As they took over New York's governing system during the Revolution, they swept away the overwhelmingly aristocratic regime of former years, in which ordinary people had had very little say in government. They brought into the legislature instead a new breed of

simple, plain men from the humbler classes. They lacked the tone and polish of the Anglicized elite, hated England, hounded Loyalists, and treated New York City's commercial aristocracy with wary dislike. In short, they were *egalitarian* republicans.

In Pennsylvania a similar conflict had long been brooding between the ruling Quaker oligarchy of Philadelphia, predominantly English in ethnic origins and loyalties, and its bitter enemies, the Scotch-Irish Presbyterians—who, with the Germans, had flocked to this fertile colony by the tens of thousands in the eighteenth century. Quakers condemned the Scotch-Irish as "Quarrelsome, Riotous, Rebellious, dissatisfied with . . . Kingly Government." The classic slurs against Scots and Scotch-Irish that the English had always used were freely bandied about: that they were robbers, crude and unclean hill people, makers and consumers of bad whiskey, bigoted and violent Calvinists who were intolerant of everyone else, mere "white savages."

Thoroughly angered, in 1766 the Presbyterians created their own party in Pennsylvania politics, with support from many of the Germans, in order to push the patriot cause against England. They also linked themselves to the anti-elite, anti-Anglican, and anti-British consciousness among Philadelphia's workingmen and artisans which, guided by historian Gary B. Nash's *The Urban Crucible* (1979), we have earlier seen growing so explosively in the port cities of the colonies. While in Boston and New York the working classes certainly flung themselves into the anti-British crusade and helped bring on the Revolution, in Philadelphia they took an even more dramatic and leading role. They became, as the Presbyterian leaders called them, the core of the emerging republican order, together with the independent yeomanry of the countryside.

When the crisis year of 1775 arrived, the Quakers called upon all Americans to be loyal to the king and washed their hands of the revolutionary cause. The Scotch-Irish and Germans then almost bodily expelled the Quaker and Anglican-dominated government of the colony. With the artisans and workingmen, they together drew up a boldly republican frame of government under which they henceforth ruled Pennsylvania. Deeply egalitarian, it called for annual elections, an all-powerful legislature, and a wide suffrage. Thus, in Pennsylvania, as elsewhere in the colonies, the Revolution had perhaps its deepest roots in a local cultural conflict, in which the English cause was identified with the losing side.

The Loyalists

In recent years we have begun to pay more attention to those people, perhaps a third of the population, who dissented from all this rebelliousness—the Loyalists. In some cases Loyalists—usually called Tories—were back-country people who supported the Crown simply because they were so angry, for their own local reasons, with the ruling patriot circles along the coast, as in the Southern colonies. Others were Loyalist because their ethnic group was favored by the Crown and persecuted by the colonial majority, as in the case of the Highland Scots in the Carolinas and in western New York. Other minorities, like the Quakers of Pennsylvania, looked to the London government for protection against those in the colonies who hated them on religious grounds. Thus, Loyalism numbered thousands of common people among its adherents.

Most important, because they gave Loyalism its most articulate leadership, were those among the aristocracy—bankers, tradesmen, lawyers, and officials, usually urban in their origins and setting—who were Loyalists because they were willing participants in the commercialization and modernization that British rule and British trade entailed. London was the center of their lives and interests. They *favored* the Anglicization of American life: the rise of the Anglican Church and its influence, of English cultural influences, of the power of English trade and the aristocratic English forms of governing. Such men found protection, identity, and assurance in being part of the British Empire, and were convinced that an independent America would soon collapse.

The Middle Colonies were shot through with Loyalism. Many in them left the empire reluctantly, for as the "wheat colonies" they were doing well within it and had few major grievances. New York City was strongly Loyalist. The seat of the British army in North America, heavily Anglican in its social leadership, English in its tone, and closely linked to London, it quarreled endlessly with the rural patriots in that colony. Philadelphia, too, with its Quaker citizenry and aristocracy and its major role in the British trading empire, was a stronghold of Toryism—or at least of a skeptical neutralism. (Those who said, in effect, a plague on both houses and supported neither side, thinking each was equally bad, made up yet another nonpatriot group.) From the beginning of the Continental Congress's sittings, therefore, the Middle Colonies took an equivocal, confused role in that body quite unlike that played by the New England and Southern colonies.

The Climax

In mid-1768 the royal governor of Massachusetts, looking out on his turbulent province, was convinced that nothing less than military force would bring the situation back into control The royal customs commissioners had even had to flee Boston when, in June of 1768, they seized John Hancock's sloop *Liberty* and were thereafter pursued by an angry mob. Boston seemed on the verge of insurrection.

Coercion: This was now the decision. The British were resolved to *make* the colonists obey by the threat of force—not realizing how little such threats do to cow strong-minded people, and how much they serve simply to inflame the situation further. In 1768 London instructed General Thomas Gage, the royal commander in chief in America, to pull back his units from the interior and place them in seaboard towns; a formidable force of five regiments was lodged in Boston. This unprecedented act called up for the colonists the memory of earlier times when kings in England had tried to crush protest by such heavy-handed use of standing armies. Now those colonists who had accused London of having hidden tyrannical purposes for its troops in the colonies were confirmed in their prophecies. Boston's mood soon turned ugly; physical clashes erupted between citizens and soldiers. In March 1770 a sentry, under attack by a mob, called for aid, a file of soldiers arrived, a confused scuffling occurred, and weapons were fired. As the sounds died away three Bostonians lay dead, two more were dying, and six had suffered wounds. The Boston Massacre had occurred.

Clearly, the British army could not be used to enforce the new laws in America, short of total war against the civil populace. Severely chastened, the ministry in London withdrew the troops and repealed all the Townshend Duties save those on tea. For a time an uneasy calm prevailed, but it was not to last long. In 1772 Britain announced that it would pay directly the salaries of governors and judges in Massachusetts, and the uproar began again. In December 1773, after months of mounting oratory, pamphleteering, and tension, British commercial vessels carrying tea arrived in Boston harbor. Following a great public meeting in Faneuil Hall under Sam

Adams, colonists dressed as Indians went to the wharf and threw the tea into the harbor.

This tore everything apart. The British had been getting angrier by the month at the colonials, and at this act of defiance they erupted. The Coercive Acts of 1774, rushed through a Parliament seething with a determination to force the colonials to submit to Britain's will, practically wiped out self-government in Massachusetts and closed Boston's port. Virginia, in response, moved to give support to Massachusetts by calling for another congress of all the colonies.

The First Continental Congress met in the fall of 1774, drew up declarations of rights and grievances, and called for nonimportation of British goods. Colonial militias in Massachusetts began drilling and practicing musketry in the countryside. In April 1775 General Gage in Boston was told to take the offensive against the Massachusetts troublemakers, now declared traitors to the Crown. He was to stop the training of militia and to gather up all arms and ammunition in colonial hands. On April 19 Gage sent a body of 800 soldiers to Concord to commandeer arms. The result: the battles of Lexington and Concord. Soon his troops were fleeing back to Boston with nearly 300 casualties, and American campfires burned

all around Boston. The American Revolution had begun.

The War

The colonies were electrified by the battles of Lexington and Concord in April of 1775. Within a few weeks the Continental Congress raised an army, issued a currency, and declared the ties between the Crown and Massachusetts dissolved. The Congress adopted the name United Colonies and prepared for unbending resistance. Almost everyone looked to George Washington of Virginia to be the commander of the colonial army. Taller than most men, quiet and thoughtful, giving in his manner the impression of strength and authority, he was one of the few colonials with extensive military experience, and the only man to come to the Continental Congress in uniform. Commander in chief of Virginia's troops in the French and Indian War, he had experienced years of hard fighting, after which he had retired to Mount Vernon to live as a gentleman farmer. Now forty-three, he was one of the older and more mature men in the Continental Congress. When to all this was added the fact that he came from proud Virginia, the largest and most populous colony, whose enthusiastic adherence to the revolutionary cause was absolutely essential, the choice of Washington as commander in chief was inevitable. On July 3, 1775, he arrived in Cambridge, Massachusetts, to take command.

On the surface it seems extraordinary that the British did not quickly win the war. They had far greater material and financial resources than the colonials, outnumbered them at least four to one, and had fifty ships of war to each American vessel. The most powerful empire in the world was pitted against thirteen unorganized colonies, and no colonial revolt since Roman times had ever been successful.

But the strategic task before the British was enormous. They were fighting a war 3,000 miles from home in a huge wilderness continent occupied by a people most of whom were in arms. The very dispersion of the American population—the fact that New York, Boston, and Philadelphia could all be taken and held for long periods, as they were, without affecting the outcome—made the military problem insoluble. Shortly, too, European enemies fell upon Britain, so that the American Revolution became part of a world war in which British resources were stretched terribly thin.

One result of the attempt to enforce the tea tax.

Most important, the London government still failed catastrophically to understand what it faced. The colonial secretary, Lord George Germain, was contemptuous of the colonials. He described them all as cowards who would run at the first sight of British redcoats. He was confident that the war would end with one decisive military compaign. He scorned all concessions, would have no dealing with rebels, and had only one prescription for ending the rebellion—unconditional surrender and a harsh settlement. King George agreed.

The British were calmly confident, too, that most Americans would rise up against the traitors as soon as a sizable British army arrived in their midst. The entire war was thought of as a massive rescue operation to free the American people from the power of a small group of desperate rebels. "I never had an idea of subduing the Americans," said one British general. "I meant to assist the good Americans to subdue the bad ones." This misconception profoundly affected British operations. Every commander searched for that fabled land of the Tories, the region of warm loyalism, where British sovereignty might be reestablished in the colonies on a solid foundation of popular support.

The Loyalists themselves, though pitifully weak, constantly encouraged the London government to believe in the myth of a Tory majority. Consequently, Lord Germain lived in a kind of dream world

in which the Revolution was always close to settlement, making him deaf to all contrary advice.

The Rebel Side of the War

The Americans rushed to war in a mood of holy self-dedication. Repeatedly it was said that God had chosen America to establish liberty for all the world, and that now the great challenge facing the American people was to show themselves worthy of that divine task. Could they do it? Europeans scoffed that republics could never survive precisely because the common people were not brave enough or disciplined enough to sacrifice their lives for the common welfare. They believed it took an honor-reared aristocracy, leading closely drilled masses of awestruck soldiers, to win wars.

Americans replied that they were uniquely courageous, uniquely ready, as a freedom-loving people, to give their all for liberty. They talked much of how the "minute-men" of local militias would spontaneously spring forth to win the war. No need of strongly disciplined regular armies, with haughty officers, for them! In their thoughts Americans dwelt upon posterity, and how it would honor them for their brave performance, their bloody sufferings, in the holy cause.

But was their national character truly up to

The Battle of Bunker Hill in April, 1775, actually fought on less easily defended Breed's Hill, was later considered a moral victory by the colonists. The outnumbered American soldiers retreated after the third assault by the British. However, the English gave up hopes of taking Dorchester Heights.

View of The ATTACK on BUNKER'S HILL, with the Burning of CHARLES TOWN, June 17, 1775.

the challenge? Were they worthy defenders of liberty? Deep doubts on this score plagued the American mind. They grew more troublesome as the war dragged on and it became clear that, left entirely to themselves, most Americans did not seem ready to fling themselves endlessly into the horrors of the fighting. After the original enthusiasm of 1775, when a "rage militaire," as historian Charles Royster terms it, swept the Americans, it was clear that the militia, which turned out only for short-term fighting, could never be relied upon to win the war. There would be long dreary stretches of exhaustion and despair when fighting-age men would have to be forced to join up; when taxes to support the fighting would be paid reluctantly, if at all; when it seemed like the whole enterprise had degenerated into corrupt self-seeking profiteering and evasion of duty. This was much of the reason, in fact, why the war stretched on and on: The revolutionaries themselves often failed to give it the personal or material support it required.

George Washington, therefore, had enormous problems to face on his side of the fighting, and it was remarkable that he eventually won. His army was so weak, undermanned, ill-equipped, underpaid, and often starving that the only strategy he could adopt was the war of attrition—wearing down the enemy's strength by making hit-and-run attacks against vulnerable points. It was impossible to think of standing up to the disciplined British army in full open-field combat, which involved massed musket volleys and bayonet fighting. American troops were simply not trained or ready for this intensively drilled fighting with compact bodies of troops, nor did Washington have the military equipment, or even the officers, sergeants, and corporals familiar with such tactics. He got Congress to authorize the forming of a regular Continental Army, which eventually he was able to train and modestly equip, but it consisted of only a few thousand troops, and it was always a precarious fighting force.

Strategically, therefore, Washington always had to be on the defensive, waiting for major moves to be made by the other side. Ultimately, he and the American leadership had to rely upon a rising opposition to the war among Britons at home to win it for them. This required making it unmistakably clear that no matter what arms, men, and funds were poured into the conflict by London, the fight could not be won. It also meant working hard at talking some of England's enemies into joining the fight on the colonial's side, which finally led to an alliance with France in 1778 and the accession of French armies and the French navy to the patriot cause.

This strategy was not easy for Washington, for in warfare he was by nature a headstrong, impetuous, combative man; he had to school himself rigorously to hold back, striking out only when the advantage in a local situation was on his side. In fact, between 1778 and 1781 Washington's army and that of the British hardly fought at all in the Northern states, but simply held on grimly to what they had and watched the other side.

The Course of the War

Within a brief period after the battle of Concord, practically all royal authority disappeared from the thirteen colonies. Rebel governments were established in each, and the Continental Congress in Philadelphia provided a rudimentary national government. What the British had now to do was to fight their way back onto the continent, reestablish royal governments in all the colonies, and defeat the colonial army. At first their only foothold was at Boston, where they were under siege.

On June 17, 1775 (a month before General Washington's arrival) the British under Major General William Howe decided to seize the Dorchester Heights, which looked down on Boston and its bay and thus commanded the entire scene. The colonials got in their way, however, putting a thousand men in entrenchments dug on Breed's Hill and, behind it, on Bunker Hill. After 1,500 scarlet-coated soldiers had been rowed across the channel between Boston and Charlestown to land on the beach just below the field of battle, and with eighty naval guns firing on the colonial position, General Howe sent his men rushing toward the entrenchments on Breed's Hill, their bayonets lowered for the assault. He and his soldiers were contemptuous of the "mere colonials," believing they would break and run at the first attack. However, as historian Robert Middlekauff describes the scene,

> *When the column of scarlet got to within fifty yards of his position, [the colonial commander] . . . ordered his troops to fire. At that range, fire into a dense column could not miss, and the front ranks of the Fusiliers disintegrated, pitched about by the heavy musket balls. They were brave men and bravely led; their officers urged them forward despite the massed fire . . . . [but they] were devoured by musket fire*

until ninety-six died on the beach where, as another sadly noted, they "lay as thick as sheep in a fold." Not even the highly disciplined Fusiliers could stand this slaughter for long, and in a minute or two they pulled back: some said they broke and ran.

Elsewhere on the field of battle British soldiers were also falling "in thick grotesque piles." General Howe, who was with them, was appalled. "The sight of his troops . . . chopped into a disordered crowd by the hot lead from the rail fence produced in Howe a 'Moment that I never felt before,' a moment of horror and . . . surely of fear that his command was about to be defeated and perhaps destroyed."

MAJOR BATTLES DURING THE REVOLUTIONARY WAR

More fighting ensued; renewed British assaults finally drove the colonials off of Breed's Hill, for they were running out of ammunition, and finally off of Bunker Hill itself, but the British gave up on their effort to take Dorchester Heights. A thrill ran through the colonies: Militia men, untrained common Americans, had repelled the flower of Britain's storied army! It was a glorious confirmation of the basic American and republican argument about the common people. By March 1776, the British had to evacuate Boston, for their position there was untenable. By sea they moved their army to New York City.

Within days of their arrival, the Continental Congress finally ended its long argument over whether to try simply to get London to negotiate grievances and then resume life as part of the British Empire, or to actually break from the Crown and declare independence. In January 1776 a young Englishman, Thomas Paine—who had arrived in Pennsylvania from the mother country two years before—had published an electrifying pamphlet, *Common Sense*, which circulated everywhere. How could a continent, he said, remain permanently subservient to an island? The Americans had a great world destiny to fulfill by declaring their independence and providing corrupt Europe an inspiring example of republicanism in practice. John Adams and Thomas Jefferson argued endlessly in similar terms within the Congress. They won their great victory when the Declaration of Independence, largely of Jefferson's authorship, was adopted on July 4, 1776.

The Towering, Nation-Defining Statement: The Declaration of Independence

No document would be more central to American life in the following centuries, save the Constitution of 1789. Here, to every succeeding generation, was the towering statement of what America was all about. Because the United States of America was the first *new* country in the world, a conscious creation, a fashioned object brought freshly into being, this self-concept, this description of who they were, was something America's people badly needed. In what became immortal and internationally celebrated words, the Declaration of Independence proclaimed to the world at large that America was a special kind of country; that is, it existed to embody certain key human ideals.

First, that *all men are created equal*, an astonishingly radical concept not only then but now. Equality! In a profoundly hierarchical world in which equality nowhere existed, nor was anywhere advanced as an ideal to be attained (in fact, most of the world's peoples, certainly its ruling elites, scorned it), what did this exciting new concept mean? Equality in what ways? By what means? The blazing center, the red meat of American republicanism, the dream of equality would be one of those ever-receding ideals that draws people persistently toward it, as in periodic tidal surges of reform they seek to bring it into full reality—only to find that their efforts are incomplete, for each generation discovers new and deeper meanings in the word.

Second, the Declaration proclaimed that by divine gift each person has "*certain unalienable rights*" that stand free and clear of all governments and may not (rightfully) be meddled with by them, since humanity's rights were not created by government. As the U.S. Supreme Court would later say, rights are "personal and present" in each individual human being. They are, so to speak, *possessed* as irrevocable property, as original human endowment simply by being alive, and thus are legally inviolable, though governments may in practice wrongfully invade them.

This, too, was then a radical idea in the world, and still largely remains so. That in 1988 a presidential candidate in the United States could be referred to by his opponent, in language clearly intended to be derogatory, as a "card-carrying" member of the chief national organization dedicated to protecting those rights, the American Civil Liberties Union, reveals how uncomfortable many even in the United States still are with the whole concept of *rights* as primary to everything else in American life. And what were the rights announced in the Declaration? They were "*Life, Liberty, and the pursuit of Happiness.*" Indeed, the Declaration says, the very reason governments exist is to protect these rights.

Lastly, the Declaration asserts that governments gain their powers only *from the consent of the governed. . . .* In an era when people everywhere were governed by monarchies and absolute autocracies, this was yet another of the Declaration's radical utterances to the world at large. Sovereignty, that is, *final* authority, residing ultimately in the people! Astonishing. Revolutionary. And thus, to Europe's titled aristocracies, deeply alarming.

The British Are Slowly Driven from Most of the North

It was in June 1776 that the British army under General William Howe arrived in force off New York City. It soon landed on Staten Island, putting 32,000 men ashore. Over on Manhattan, General Washington and the American army dug fortifications at the island's southern tip and waited through the summer months for the attack to come. Supplies were so short that Washington's untrained men could only fire two rounds in practice; nearby houses had all lead taken from them for bullets; and long lines of trenches were dug across the island. When the Declaration of Independence was proclaimed on July 4, 1776, Washington had it read to the troops, reminding them that the great cause of human liberty and human rights depended on their courage and fighting readiness.

However, by late August his troops were low in spirits, many were diseased, supplies were short, and the militia, always unreliable, was deserting "almost by regiments." First, the British sent Washington's men fleeing in the Battle of Brooklyn Heights. Then, in mid-September, General Howe landed on Manhattan island to the rear of the Americans, who frantically decamped to Harlem Heights, and in later weeks moved eventually over to New Jersey. New York City, which was a strongly Tory and loyalist town in any event, was now quite lost to the rebels, who were in full retreat. The name of General Washington became synonymous with a dreary series of defeats and withdrawals.

Meanwhile, an impossible and ultimately tragic gamble had been launched in the north. In June 1776, in a burst of soaring overconfidence, Congress had authorized General Washington, then still before Boston, to send off an expedition to drive the British army out of Canada and take that immense colonial province, if not "disagreeable" to the Canadians themselves. A brilliant young commander, Richard Montgomery, fought his way northward through the upper reaches of New York to the St. Lawrence River, and in November he took Montreal with his small force of about 300 soldiers.

Then he marched downriver to Quebec City, where he joined General Benedict Arnold and his detachment of about 700 men. They had just completed an incredibly arduous two-month journey through wintertime Maine, and now, half-frozen, hungry, and diseased, they stood before the town's formidable and heavily defended high stone walls. (Quebec City remains today the only walled city in North America). While it was still dark on the morning of December 30, 1776, with a screaming blizzard blowing, Arnold sent his force in an assault against the walls. Montgomery was quickly shot dead, and Arnold himself shortly fell with a grave wound. Soon the entire attack had failed catastrophically, with over 400 Americans captured. The northward thrust had totally failed.

Trenton Turns the Tide

However, in a brilliant strike, Washington had already rebounded from apparent weakness in December 1776 to surprise and completely defeat a British force at Trenton, New Jersey. In the first months of 1777 there was savage fighting, the issue seesawed back and forth, and Washington's image began to rise. In America and abroad he became a symbol of strength, great bravery, and occasional flights of astonishing military daring. And yet in September 1777, the British forces under General Howe won the Battle of Brandywine, near Philadelphia. Howe then proceeded to occupy that city, carrying Britain's cause to perhaps its highest point.

A month later the defeat of British General John Burgoyne at Saratoga, New York, shattered the British strategy. Burgoyne was to have split the colonies in two by striking down from Canada to New York City, while Howe was to overwhelm Washington's army in Pennsylvania. Burgoyne's defeat, and the gritty endurance of Washington's army at Valley Forge, where he wintered his troops in 1777–78, put both objectives out of reach.

This, in turn, had a powerful impact on the French, who ever since their humiliating defeat in the Seven Years War (1756–63) had been thirsting for revenge against the British. They now concluded that the American Revolution was no brief flash in the pan, and that by helping the Americans they could shatter the British Empire. In February 1778 the French openly joined the battle on the American side by signing a formal alliance with the Continental Congress. By June, Howe had disconsolately to evacuate Philadelphia; a month later the French fleet arrived off the Delaware capes, and the Americans now had on their side what they had grievously lacked before, a powerful naval force; and the harried British,

frustrated in the North, shifted their hopes to military campaigns in the South. Retaining their northern bridgehead in Tory New York City, they now headed out again in search of the legendary land of the Tories—and in truth, there was much loyalism in the Southern back-country. In 1779, one of Britain's leading generals, James Robertson, solemnly informed Parliament, then engaged in an investigation into why the war was not yet won, that two-thirds of the Americans were loyal to the king. The Declaration of Independence, he said, was just a document scribbled out and distributed by "a few artful folks." All the Loyalists needed, he said, was some help in throwing off these wretched traitors and "Congress's tyranny."

The Thrust Shifts to the Southern States

The British army, commanded in the South by Lord Cornwallis, was ordered to strike into South Carolina from Georgia and take its chief city, Charleston. In December 1779, a huge fleet of more than a hundred troop-carriers and warships left New York Harbor and sailed south to provide reinforcements. For a month it battered through violent winter winds and storms to reach Savannah. Here the troops put ashore, won the Battle of Savannah, and marched north to begin a long and bloody siege against Charleston. The British finally took that city and received the surrender of the American army encamped there in May 1780.

Cornwallis was now instructed to pacify all of South Carolina, reclaim North Carolina from the rebels, and push on into Virginia. But his was a grimy, difficult task, for violent informal battles between loyalists and rebels among the Americans were soon setting the Carolina countryside aflame, battles which the Loyalists usually lost. ". . . [T]hroughout 1780 and well into 1781," writes historian Robert Middlekauff, "nasty, brutish conflicts occurred in the interior of South Carolina . . . [many being] small-scale raids, neighbor against neighbor . . . [and others] directed against British posts, supply trains, dispatch riders. This sort of warfare, deadly little fights, shootings, and burnings, brought out the worst in people. . . ."

In August 1780, Cornwallis won a stunning victory at Camden, South Carolina, over a large

American force sent down by Congress to attack his army. Its commander, Major General Horatio Gates, fled the field ignominiously, leaving his army behind to scatter wildly through the countryside. The British, in short, had now defeated two rebel armies in the South—but Camden seemed, nonetheless, to give the British cause no relief. Rebel raids and ambushes against Cornwallis's forces continued, and the legendary loyalists of the Carolinas gave him little help, most of them having by now learned to keep their heads down.

The Tide Turns: King's Mountain

Within a month after the battle at Camden, Cornwallis's forces marched to Charlotte, North Carolina, but in October 1780, disaster struck. A fine Loyalist force had been put together under a veteran Scots commander, Major Patrick Ferguson, who had fought bravely in British wars on the European continent. At nearby King's Mountain, Ferguson's troops flung themselves at an incoming rebel force composed of frontiersmen. Ferguson lined his musket-firing men up in close-packed European fashion. They fired coordinated volleys at the rebels and followed up by the classic bayonet charges, which in Europe were usually decisive.

The frontiersmen, however, played by different rules. They nimbly gave ground before the clumsy loyalist charges, and then moved from tree to tree to pick off Ferguson's men with their long and much more accurate frontier rifles. After an hour of this carnage, Ferguson himself, who had foolishly led a charge astride a white horse, lay dead, and bloody heaps of slain loyalists were everywhere. The angry rebels, savage in their hatred of loyalists, shot and stabbed the wounded and others trying to surrender, later hanging nine of them.

King's Mountain was a stunning defeat for Cornwallis, for the countryside now clearly belonged to the rebels. Soon he had to retreat back to Camden, South Carolina, there to hunker down with his harassed army in the face of constant small-scale rebel attacks at every exposed outpost or supply train. The raids, indeed, seemed never to stop. Remarkably brave and determined rebel commanders, such as Thomas Sumter and Daniel Morgan and William Campbell of King's Mountain fame, ranged widely over the wherever they could find them.

Nathanael Greene Takes Over

Now, in October 1780, General Washington sent one of his most experienced and trusted officers, Nathanael Greene, to create once more a full-scale rebel army in the South to drive the British out. A thoughtful New Englander who had immediately taken up arms when the Revolution began, Greene had fought in the earliest battles around Boston and had led a major force in Washington's famous Trenton victory. He believed deeply in America's "glorious cause." He was convinced that troops fought well only when similarly inspired, and he often spoke to them about their crucial role in this great struggle for human rights. At the same time, as commander in the South he labored endlessly and with much success to get his men the proper food and clothing and arms that to this point they had grievously lacked. Troops ignored and starved and left to wander about in scraps of clothing, he said, could hardly be expected to do more than take to their heels at the first whiff of gun smoke.

Greene knew that head-on attacks against the disciplined British would never win. He had to fight, he said, a "fugitive war," for he had only militia to rely on and they performed best in short, intense battles around the fringes of the British army, rather than in long campaigns of frontal assault. In January 1781, a sudden battle erupted at Hannah's Cowpens (a lonely meadow) near Camden, South Carolina. Under Daniel Morgan an American force composed largely of militia but built around a core of disciplined regular army units from Maryland and Delaware held firm in the face of a strong British bayonet charge. Steady fire from the American line killed hundreds of advancing British troops; skillful tactics caught them in wild and vulnerable charges where they could be mowed down from the flank, and soon the British were a totally defeated force, hundreds being taken as prisoners.

Then the Americans disappeared into the wilderness, and a later British force, which hastened out from Camden under Lord Cornwallis, could find no one. Finally in March 1781, Nathanael Greene gathered his forces at Guilford Court House to give formal battle. A terribly bloody struggle ensued, from which the Americans finally retreated, but it left both sides grievously wounded. A reflective Cornwallis fully realized, now, that he could no longer rely on the Loyalists for help, and that whatever hap-

The British surrender at Yorktown, from a French engraving. De Grasse's fleet is shown massed at the water's edge.

pened, he was far out in enemy-dominated territory where conclusive victories would always elude him. His army, meanwhile, drained by the savage fighting and the constant guerrilla attacks, was weakening badly. Frustrated, he decided that the major scene of battle in America had to be shifted to the Chesapeake Bay. Here, British forces from New York and the Carolinas could combine to fight climactic battles against Washington's troops in Virginia.

In April 1781, Cornwallis gathered up his army and began the long march to Virginia, leaving occupation troops behind. After his departure, however, Nathanael Greene's army raged back and forth over the Carolina countryside. Soon the British remaining there were forced to retreat entirely to Charleston and Savannah to wait out the war.

British Defeat

In August 1781, Cornwallis's army was established in a major base at Yorktown, Virginia. He had chosen this bay-side location because it gave him direct access to the sea, and to water-borne reinforcements in sup-

plies and men, when they arrived from London. However, within a month of his arrival, a French, rather than a British, fleet arrived in American waters, and it quickly sealed off Yorktown from naval support. Washington and his army were at that moment engaged in a long siege of New York City, and Cornwallis felt safe. But the daring plan was conceived of moving Washington's army secretly from New York to Virginia, some 400 miles, much of it by water. Arriving in Williamsburg, the capital of Virginia, Washington's army, which contained perhaps as many French troops as American, had only a short march until it was encamped outside Cornwallis's fortifications. A force of 16,000 troops was now laying siege to a British army of possibly half that many men.

For almost a month, from late September 1781 until late October, the allied force bombarded Cornwallis with seventy cannon. On October 19 Cornwallis gave up. His men marched out, defeated, their band playing "The World Turned Upside Down."

Though it was not then realized, the military side of the American Revolution was over. Yorktown was a deathblow to British military hopes. The news

English

French

Spanish

United States

North America, 1783

but after the defeat at Yorktown there was no more fighting of any consequence in America.

English Whigs, who had long condemned the war, regarded Yorktown as the finishing blow to a conflict that to them had been disastrous from beginning to end. "I cannot put on the face of the day, and act grief," one of them said. "Whatever puts an end to the American war will save the lives of thousands—millions of money too." The national debt had almost doubled, the navy was weak and undermanned, and the army was 30,000 men short of its needs. The empire appeared to be falling apart under the blows of its many enemies. The government's majority in Commons wasted away until February 1782, when a motion was passed to give up all efforts to subjugate the Americans. Peace talks began in Paris, and in September of 1782 the British and Americans came to terms. The Peace of Paris was signed a year later, on September 3, 1783.

The United States had secured its independence. Lord Shelburne, prime minister since 1782, had decided to grant generous terms and lay the basis for a friendly relationship. Thus, the United States secured a vast domain east of the Mississippi and south of the Great Lakes and the St. Lawrence. (Excluded were East and West Florida, given back to the Spanish, and the region beyond the St. Croix River to the north of Maine, which remained in British hands.)

The British people raged angrily when they learned of the generous terms, and Shelburne's government was forced to resign, but the deed had been done. On December 4, 1783, the British evacuated their last stronghold in the former thirteen colonies, New York City and Staten Island. On that day, General Washington took leave of his officers at Fraunces' Tavern, New York. The first successful colonial rebellion since ancient times had come to an end. The first "new nation" had appeared.

of it came like a thunderclap to Lord North, the British prime minister. He staggered as though shot and "opened his arms, exclaiming wildly, as he paced up and down the apartment during a few minutes, 'Oh God! it is all over!'" He soon recovered his courage and moved resolutely on, hoping for the best,

BIBLIOGRAPHY

Books that were especially valuable to me in thinking about and writing this chapter: For the present edition I have learned a great deal from Robert Middlekauff, *The Glorious Cause: The American Revolution 1763–1789* (1982); Rhys Isaac, *The Transformation of Virginia 1740–1790* (1982); Charles Royster, *A Revolutionary People at War: The Continental Army and American Character, 1775–1783* (1979); Ralph Ketcham, *From Colony to Country: The Revolution in American Thought 1750–1820* (1974); Richard L. Merritt, *Symbols of American Community 1735–1775* (1966); Carl Bridenbaugh, *The Spirit of '76: The Growth of American Patriotism before Independence* (1975). Highly useful

is a remarkable new reprinted edition of a contemporary British publication, *The Annual Register*, edited by David H. Murdoch, under the title *Rebellion in America: A Contemporary British Viewpoint, 1765–1783* (1979). On British images of the colonials, I have also turned to John C. Miller's enduringly valuable *Origins of the American Revolution* (1943). Gary B. Nash, *The Urban Crucible: Social Change, Political Consciousness, and the Origins of the American Revolution* (1979), has been essential.

In Robert Kelley, *The Transatlantic Persuasion: The Liberal Democratic Mind in the Age of Gladstone* (1969), I have developed the concept of the central role of the "enemy" in all political culture. John A. Armstrong, *Nations before Nationalism* (1982), establishes persuasively that without an enemy, ethnic consciousness does not arise. Two brilliant books by Bernard Bailyn explore the "conspiracy theories" agitating the American mind, and the profound differences between British and American political culture: *Ideological Origins of the American Revolution* (1967), and *The Origins of American Politics* (1968). Stephen E. Patterson has given us a bold analysis of Massachusetts tensions as being rooted in the traditionalism-modernization conflict in *Political Parties in Revolutionary Massachusetts* (1973). Jackson Turner Main explores the localism-cosmopolitanism perspective in *Political Parties before the Constitution* (1973). I have also found Edmund S. Morgan's *American Slavery American Freedom* (cited for Chapters 2 and 5) valuable. On the Revolution itself, I have drawn upon Russell F. Weigley's *The American Way of War: A History of United States Military Strategy and Policy* (1977).

Robert Kelley, *The Cultural Pattern in American Politics: The First Century* (1979) explores in detail such themes as republicanism, modernization, the cultural crisis in the colonies, and ethnic and religious hostilities. John Shy gives us a fresh and exciting understanding of how the "standing army" in the colonies helped bring on the conflict in his *Toward Lexington: The Role of the British Army in the Coming of the American Revolution* (1965). Pauline Maier presents a rich description of pre-Revolutionary politics in *From Resistance to Revolution: Colonial Radicals and the Development of American Opposition to Britain, 1765–1776* (1972). Stephen Kurtz and James Hutson, eds., *Essays on the American Revolution* (1973), is a group of brilliant essays by leading historians on several aspects of the period.

Richard L. Bushman, *From Puritan to Yankee: Character and the Social Order in Connecticut, 1690–1765* (1967),

shows in one New England colony the fundamental changes underway in the eighteenth century. Carl Bridenbaugh, *Mitre and Sceptre: Transatlantic Faiths, Ideas, Personalities, and Politics: 1689–1775* (1962), illuminates the controversy over the drive to establish an Anglican episcopate. Robert Zemsky, *Merchants, Farmers, and River Gods: An Essay on Eighteenth-Century American Politics* (1971), focuses on Massachusetts, showing the central role of different social groups in its politics. Patricia U. Bonomi, *A Factious People: Politics and Society in Colonial New York* (1971), provides a fresh picture of that colony's tangled public life, as does John W. Pratt, *Religion, Politics and Diversity: The Church-State Theme in New York History* (1967). James H. Hutson's *Pennsylvania Politics 1746–1770: The Movement for Royal Government and Its Consequences* (1972) is a skillful study of Quaker-Presbyterian rivalry, and much more. An important study, quantitatively based, is Wayne L. Brockelman and Owen S. Ireland, "The Internal Revolution in Pennsylvania: An Ethnic-Religious Interpretation," *Pennsylvania History*, 41 (January 1974), 125–59; see also Owen S. Ireland, "The Ethnic-Religious Dimension of Pennsylvania Politics, 1778–1779," *William and Mary Quarterly*, 3rd series, 30 (July 1973), 324–48.

Jack P. Greene's *The Reappraisal of the American Revolution in Recent Historical Literature* (1967) is an excellent, well-written, and complete bibliographical essay. Winthrop Jordan's absorbing book *White Over Black* (1968), analyzes the effects of the Revolution on slavery, and on white America's thinking toward black America. Of great value too are Arthur Zilversmit's *The First Emancipation: The Abolition of Slavery in the North* (1967), and Benjamin Quarles's *The Negro in the American Revolution* (1961). To follow the diplomacy of the war's ending, see Richard B. Morris's *The Peacemakers* (1965).

7

Forming the Nation

TIME LINE

HISTORY IN AN INDIVIDUAL LIFE

JAMES MADISON

It was one of the most important single historical research efforts in American history. The small, scholarly, neatly dressed Virginian sat at his desk and mustered all the resources of his carefully collected library on history and public affairs to answer one question: What had gone wrong with confederacies before? There was no question that under the Articles of Confederation the United States in the 1780s had collapsed into wild confusions. The whole experiment of an American republic seemed ready to evaporate. What, then, had the great Revolution been fought for? Was the world forever fated to be ruled by monarchies?

So James Madison toiled on in 1786 and 1787, staying away from theories and sticking to humanity's actual experience as shown in history. He had been elected a delegate to the upcoming Constitutional Convention in Philadelphia, and, equipped with perhaps the clearest, calmest, and most reasonable mind of his generation, was preparing a statement of fundamental guidelines that would allow the convention to start and complete its work effectively. All history, Madison concluded, showed that "a sovereignty over sovereigns, a government over governments," could only fail. Each state of the United States was at that point entirely independent, and that was "utterly irreconcilable with the idea of a [single] sovereignty [over all]."

The independence of the states had to be limited, severely. Furthermore, any new common government, if it were to be effectively supreme, had to be rooted in the people at large, *not* in the state governments. If it had the power to pass legislation affecting only the state governments, rather than bearing directly upon individuals, it would fail.

What should such a government have authority over? It should have absolute power over all matters that affected every state, such as finance, commerce, and foreign policy. (Indeed, Madison even went so far as to insist that the central government be able to veto any law passed within a state, so as to control "disputes between different passions and interests in the State.") The strength and authority of this central government must be buttressed by a national judiciary independent of the voters and supreme, in its decisions, over the state courts. The single-house legislatures in the states had frightened all observers with their abrupt, erratic, and overbearing behavior. Madison therefore decided that stability and wise legislation made a *two*-house national legislature essential, each balancing the other and elected by different constituencies to different terms. There would be a Senate (from the ancient Latin word meaning "elder," which the Romans used for their senior legislative house), representing in effect the aristocracy, and for the whole people a House of Representatives. To ensure a just voice for the people, the new government's framers had to establish representation in these legislative bodies according to population. And, to cap it all, there must be a nationally elected executive, who would administer the laws and preside over the nation.

So, indeed, did the convention proceed, following in almost all of its features Madison's Virginia Plan. This quiet, dignified man, good-humored and always reasonable, guided his proposal to success. He had become, by general agreement, "the father of the Constitution."

Overview

For thirteen years, from 1776 to 1789, the supreme question among the American people was this: Would they be able to successfully build a new nation? In November 1777 the Continental Congress took the first step by drawing up a basic frame of government, the Articles of Confederation. Finally ratified by all the states in 1781, the Articles created a political entity called *The United States of America*. As the 1780s proceeded, however, the grave weaknesses of the Articles became ever clearer. The specific problem lay in an abstract, but very real, issue: Where was *sovereignty* (i.e., final authority) located? As it stood, each state was sovereign to itself, which meant thirteen sovereigns. If the Americans intended to build a nation, this was an impossible situation. Above the states, the only national body was the Congress; there was no national executive or judiciary. Composed simply of delegations chosen by the state legislatures, each of which had an equal vote, the Congress was hobbled by the requirement that important legislation be passed by a two-thirds majority. Its chief function was to carry on the foreign relations of the United States, but with no revenues of its own it could not build a navy or an army, and was held in contempt by all the world's powers, great and small. Domestically, the Congress could regulate the value of coin issued by itself and the states, but it was not empowered either to establish tariffs or to regulate commerce.

Politics in the Continental and Confederation Congresses

The larger outlines of national politics soon displayed themselves after the Continental Congress began sitting in 1774. The delegates from the various states all called themselves Whigs and republicans, their common enemy being the Tory and monarchist government of Great Britain, but it was clear before long that they fell naturally into four groupings, each of which had its center of gravity in one of the three geographic sections: New England, the Middle States, and the South.

The Yankees were moralistic, pious republicans whose politics were shaped by the traditional New England notion that the community must be as corporately unified as a holy family. In this perspective, government existed to look actively after the economic welfare of its citizens and to concern itself with their inner spiritual lives as well. The moral health of the whole depended upon that of each of its citizens. Thus, for the Yankees an organized political commonwealth had a touch of the sacred about it, for its purpose was to glorify God, to embody in human life His divine concerns and laws. The community was to be a righteous assembly of sober, Bible-reading, pious folk who looked to their church and its ministers for leadership and instruction.

The Revolution, for New Englanders, was a great opportunity to cleanse the American soul by pulling free from corrupt England. A Christian Sparta would be built, said Sam Adams of Massachusetts, for all the world to emulate. Indeed, so persistent was the Yankee self-consciousness, so vigorous and prideful their Calvinist puritanism, that outside their region New Englanders were constantly accused of wanting to shape the whole country in their image, to build a universal Yankee nation. There was much truth in the accusation, for the Yankees did in fact identify the nation and its fortunes with themselves, and looked upon the rest of the American population—especially the slave-keeping Southerners, with their aristocratic habits and tastes—as gravely in need of moral instruction and political regeneration.

Southern republicans, in contrast, were this-worldly people who did not care to have clerics telling them how to live. They stressed their vision of America as a place where free (white) individuals were to be at liberty to live as they saw fit and to advance themselves by their own efforts. Governments should be small and inactive, concerning themselves just with the maintenance of law and order and the security of property. When Southerners talked of human rights their habit was to speak of them as coming from nature rather than from God, and they recoiled from the righteous Yankees. They shared with them, however, a bitter anger toward the mother country and a belief that the British tie was morally corrupting. Therefore, New England and the South joined forces as "The Party of the Revolution," as the historian H. James Henderson terms them, pushing the colonies resolutely toward revolution and independence.

The people of the Middle States were much more mixed among themselves, for their region was multiethnic, contained strong urban as well as rural elements, and held a babble of diverse tongues and religions. Prominent among them were the Presbyterian, Scotch-Irish republicans of Pennsylvania and New York, who, with their German and Dutch Cal-

Pulling down a statue of George III, from a contemporary French engraving.

vinist allies, were bitingly anti-English and strongly democratic. Localist and traditional in orientation, hostile to everything smacking of Anglicization in cultural life, economics, and politics, they were the most egalitarian of the rebels.

However, a strong group of nationalist republicans also came from the Middle States. These were men of the merchant and financial circles in Philadelphia and New York City. Reluctant rebels who were understandingly tolerant of the Loyalists, they nonetheless supported the ideas of separation of church and state, an end to monarchy and its regal institutions in America, and independence rather than submission to the will and controls of London. With their deep ties to prewar British commerce, they were relatively Anglicized and cosmopolitan in outlook and values, and tenaciously committed to the dream of vigorous economic development and the idea of close and cooperative relations between business and government. They advocated a strong national government led by men whose vision was continental rather than local, men who would carry the American people toward a commercialized, urban, and modernized future. Led most notably by Robert Morris, the Philadelphia financier, the nationalist republicans had

among them such gifted young men as Alexander Hamilton of New York.

The Peace and the Western Territories

Peace, and the Treaty of Paris in 1783, brought a powerful new nationalizing force into American life: the gift of the huge western territories between the Appalachians and the Mississippi. This priceless acquisition caused enormous excitement in Virginia and Pennsylvania. Virginians such as Thomas Jefferson and James Madison, conscious that their state already had a deep bridgehead into the interior in what was to become Kentucky, believed that Virginia would seize a great future for itself by leading in the opening and development of the western territories—a future in which slavery might be left behind and a new Southern way of life founded. Pennsylvania, with the Ohio River beginning at Pittsburgh and opening an easy highway westward, was excited by similar expectations.

With Jefferson as its chief ideologue, a new

dream emerged in the American mind. The West and its apparently limitless fertile lands and resources would provide a vast new theater in which republicanism, at present in confusion and disarray, would receive a new lease on life and realize itself most completely. A westward-moving frontier of free individuals, farming their separate plots of land and seeking their own futures with little reliance upon community or government, would rescue and revivify the American nation. It would thus be saved not only from the corruptions of Great Britain—the Revolution, it was hoped, had achieved this—but from the wickedness and warping influences of eastern cities. Luxury and urban environments would be left behind as a sturdy, liberty-loving American society of frontiersmen and yeoman democrats built Jefferson's "empire for liberty" in the great interior.

Organizing the Western Lands

The Confederation Congress succeeded in solving one great problem: that of organizing the western territories. Arguments had gone on for years over these lands. Several states, notably Virginia and New York, had vast interior claims based on their colonial charters. Others had none at all, but vigorously contended that they should have equal access to the West. The confusion was especially severe in the lands north of the Ohio (the Northwest Territory), where many claims overlapped. The only solution was for each state to cede its western claims to the Confederation Congress and let that body decide on its administration.

Urged on by Jefferson, the Congress decided that states erected in the western territories would have equal standing with the older ones. Then, in the Northwest Ordinances of 1784, 1785, and 1787, it decreed that slavery would not be allowed in the Northwest Territory—that part of the western lands above the Ohio River. Also provided were successive phases of territorial government, in which Congress would have a large influence, culminating in full-fledged state self-government. (The Southwest Territory, below the Ohio, was organized by the federal Congress in 1790 as slave country.)

Congress then installed a systematic pattern of land surveying in the Northwest Territory that was designed to ward off the endless lawsuits and other difficulties that had afflicted the older states, in which land had been surveyed and sold in parcels of any size and shape. Square townships, 6 miles on a side, were to be surveyed sequentially and sold in one-square-mile sections of 640 acres or less. In a decision with great implications for the future, it was also provided that in every township in the national domain, section sixteen (the square mile in the middle of the township) would be reserved for the support of a public school.

The Loyalists

As soon as the treaty of peace was signed, the Loyalists were driven out. Clinging to their beloved king, and to their dream of an American society that would in fact move not toward democratic republicanism but toward an increasingly Anglicized model, the Loyalists had fought valiantly on the royal side. Their military units numbered perhaps 60,000 men. Even when remaining noncombatant, they were harshly persecuted. Loyalists were denied citizenship, the protection of the courts, and often the right to pursue professions, hold property, or engage in free speech. They were jailed, sent to detention camps, tarred and feathered, and summarily deported. Thousands of Tories perished before the war was over. Confiscations of their property occurred on a huge scale, some state governments openly using this device during the war to raise money for the rebel cause.

Loyalists fled by the thousands, mainly from the Middle Colonies. Refugees settled along the St. Lawrence River west of Montreal and along the north shore of Lake Ontario, then an unpeopled wilderness. Far greater numbers went to Nova Scotia, perhaps 30,000 by the end of 1783, and to Prince Edward Island. Others founded what became New Brunswick. Life was hard in these new settlements, disease endemic, and loss of life heavy. Meanwhile, the Americans did nothing to repay Loyalists for confiscated property. It is not surprising, then, that from their beginnings the English-speaking Canadian colonies were hostile to the United States, just as the French-speaking *Canadiens* of Quebec had always been toward the thirteen colonies.

To Anglo-Canadians, everything that reminded them of the land from which they had been driven was heartily detested. Republican government, democracy, equality, separation of church and state, the supremacy of popularly elected bodies in the government—these were condemned in Canada as "Americanizing" ideas. Though the Canadians eventually developed a full range of elective institutions, they did so within the British framework of a constitutional monarchy and a cabinet-dominated Parliament.

Turmoil in the States

In the 1780s a great crisis built up in the states. It sprang, fundamentally, from radical ideas on that now-perennial question: *sovereignty*. In the Revolution the Americans had wrenched sovereignty over themselves out of British hands, but where would they now put it? One part of the answer was clear and unequivocal. The Declaration of Independence had proclaimed the thirteen former colonies henceforth to be "Free and Independent States," each with full powers of self-governance. Thus, it was now said, each state was sovereign in itself.

However, where was sovereignty to be lodged *within* each state? Who had final authority? Under the British Crown, the established idea had been that in daily practice (i.e., save in circumstances of actual revolution), sovereignty had to reside in Parliament—which technically consisted of king, Lords, and Commons all together. Therefore, the various state legislatures, regarding themselves as the heirs of Parliament's authority, now thought of themselves as the sovereign authority within their own boundaries. Were they not, it was said, the elected representatives of the people?

State legislatures seized their new power with great enthusiasm. They believed that, like Parliament, they could do literally anything. And in fact, they stood practically alone. The egalitarian and democratic radicalism of the revolutionary years had produced drastically republican constitutions in each state in which the power of state governors was almost nonexistent—in Pennsylvania the office was effectively eliminated—and in some states court systems were practically done away with. The legislatures, therefore, had no serious institutional rivals to their power, no balancing mechanisms, no external checks to their actions.

They freely confiscated property without compensating owners, issued floods of paper money that quickly depreciated, and—listening to mobs of borrowers—made it impossible to recover debts. The legislatures invaded judicial authority, taking cases out of the courts and adjudicating them on their own authority. They even passed ex post facto laws, laws whose effect was retroactive to some earlier time. This made actions illegal which, when done, were not illegal at all—a grossly unjust thing to do. At the same time, they raised tariffs against the trade goods of other states, carried on diplomacy with foreign powers, and generally went in their individual, diverging directions, creating chaos in interstate relations and making a laughingstock of the United States of America.

Sovereignty in the Community at Large

The sovereignty issue, however, struck even more deeply than this. An explosive new idea had been set loose in these turbulent years of revolution and domestic turmoil. It was simply this: Sovereignty should not reside in any government at all! The more radical republicans insisted that in the Revolution the American people had seized sovereignty for themselves. It was now in *their* hands, and they were not going to relinquish it to some group of self-important legislators who, with all power in their hands, would be corrupted by it and exploit the community at large.

During the Revolution the people had got used to resorting to mob action and vigilante government to get what was needed, and now great numbers of ordinary men began rioting and terrorizing legislators and judges to get their way. Shays's Rebellion in Massachusetts (1786–87), which sought to aid debtors by forcibly closing down the court system, was the culmination of these disturbances. For the first time Massachusetts leaders, who had before been thought the most democratic, liberty-loving radicals of them all, began to talk of the need for building a strong national government to keep the masses in order.

An important new fact to remember was that within each state there was now no official body to appeal to if a freewheeling legislature, or the aroused citizenry themselves, got laws passed that were oppressive to minorities. In the former imperial times, the British government had exercised a veto power over colonial enactments or the decisions of colonial courts, but this protective superstructure was gone. Everything seemed in the hands of triumphant and unlimited majorities in the state legislatures which shifted like kaleidoscopes, upsetting all stability and distorting government. Minorities had no protections,

Western Lands Ceded by the States

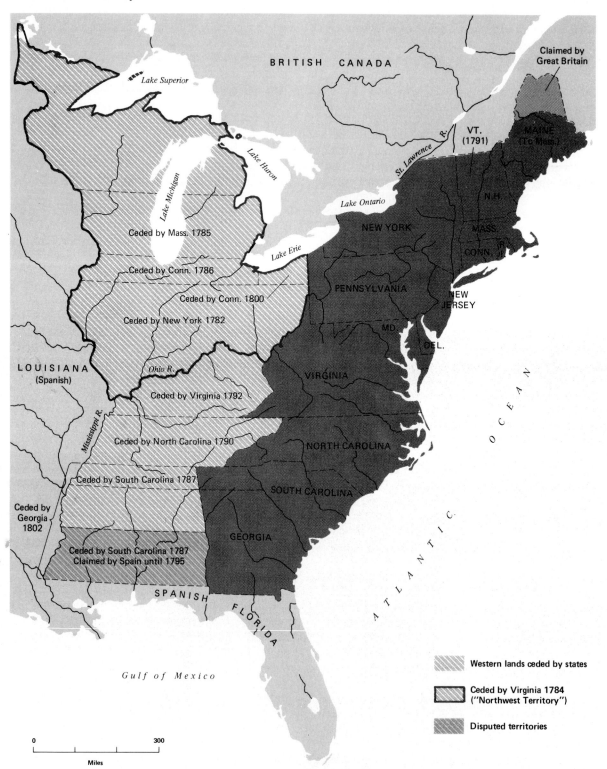

BRITISH CANADA

Claimed by
Great Britain

Lake Superior

Lake Huron

Lake Michigan

Lake Erie

Lake Ontario

St. Lawrence R.

VT.
(1791)

MAINE
(To Mass.)

N.H.

Ceded by Mass. 1785

NEW YORK

MASS.

Ceded by Conn. 1786

CONN.

R
J.

Ceded by Conn. 1800

PENNSYLVANIA

NEW
JERSEY

Ceded by New York 1782

MD.

DEL.

Ohio R.

LOUISIANA
(Spanish)

VIRGINIA

Ceded by Virginia 1792

Mississippi R.

Ceded by North Carolina 1790

NORTH CAROLINA

Ceded by South Carolina 1787

SOUTH CAROLINA

Ceded by
Georgia
1802

GEORGIA

Ceded by South Carolina 1787
Claimed by Spain until 1795

SPANISH

FLORIDA

ATLANTIC OCEAN

Gulf of Mexico

Western lands ceded by states

Ceded by Virginia 1784
("Northwest Territory")

Disputed territories

0   300

Miles

whether they were the wealthy who could not collect debts, or such persecuted religious minorities as the Baptists of New England, the Quakers of Pennsylvania, and the Anglicans of New York.

Moving Toward a New Constitution

Was this, people asked, what they had fought a war and gone through such sacrifice to achieve? It was widely said that if power had been misused by the British, liberty was now being misused by the masses. George Washington observed that in building a republican system that depended heavily upon uncontrolled legislative bodies in each state, Americans had probably had "too good an opinion of human nature. . . ." As Thomas Jefferson remarked, "An *elective despotism* was not the government we fought for." A search for order began, in time developing an irresistible momentum. The nationalist republicans of the Middle Atlantic States and the elite leadership of Virginia (as distinct from the egalitarian republicans who dominated many state legislatures in the 1780s) talked urgently of the need to construct a strong national government. The need, James Madison decided, was to build a national government that reached down through the troublesome, jealous states directly to the general body of the people at large to get its own independent source of authority—of sovereignty—but was remote enough from their direct control, and sufficiently balanced in its internal distribution of powers, to prevent either rich or poor, the many or the few, from creating tyranny.

What we see taking shape, in the latter 1780s, was a new national crusade. A decade before, in 1776, Americans moved by tremendous zeal had gathered in each state to build "republican" state governments, dedicated to egalitarian and libertarian ideals, to take the place of the old royal institutions. They had been inspired by a belief that they were creating democracy. Now a new dream emerged, held by men who called themselves Federalists. They aimed at creating a great and enduring *federal* republic that in its inner structure would prevent what they saw as the excesses and follies of localistic democracy. Thus, they would be building a United States of America that would be strong, that would survive in the world, and that would actually be able to govern that immense domain, that half of a continent, which had come to it in the Peace of 1783.

There were also powerful influences upon the popular mind that were leading in this direction. Many Americans were nationalists because they had seen in practice, during the Revolution, the impotence of the Confederation Congress, including its inability to pay the army. Others had lived in areas long devastated or occupied by British forces, and could appreciate the need for a strong national government to provide protection. Many were driven to advocate a strong national government because of the shame they felt at their country's low status and vulnerability in world affairs—everyone from the British to the Barbary pirates of North Africa held the American nation in contempt. Westerners knew a vigorous central government was needed to get the British out of the forts in the Northwest that they still occupied, and to keep the mouth of the Mississippi, which lay in Spanish territory, open to American boats. Certainly, the entire West would remain forever in Indian hands, many said, unless there was an army, properly funded and supported. People who lived in seacoast towns knew what it was like to send out ships that were mistreated by other nations because there was no American navy.

In 1786 Maryland and Virginia met to solve mutual commercial problems, making a bistate agreement on tariffs, the use of the Potomac, and a patrolling navy. Seizing upon this precedent, Virginia, led by James Madison, issued a call to all the confederated states to send delegates to a gathering in Annapolis to consider the commercial problems facing the whole nation. When only five states sent representatives, Madison and Alexander Hamilton of New York got the Annapolis convention to call upon Congress to convene a fully fledged constitutional convention in Philadelphia in May 1787. Soon the alarmed states picked up the initiative and began electing delegates; the Confederation Congress gave its belated endorsement; and in May 1787 the Constitutional Convention gathered in the State House in Philadelphia for four hot and muggy months of wrangling, debating, compromising, and distraction by events outside the hall.

The Grand Convention

It was an arresting sight. Singly and in small groups, fifty-five delegates to the Constitutional Convention arrived in Philadelphia, by water and by land, after long journeys from their homes. General George Washington himself, an awesome figure to all and one of the world's towering personages, actually left Mount Vernon to preside, bringing his sober good sense and august presence to the scene. When he arrived, the people of Philadelphia turned out to greet his carriage with shouts, salutes, and bells. Wise, venerable, internationally famous old Benjamin Franklin was also there, bringing to the deliberations one of the sanest and canniest intelligences America has ever produced. There was brilliant young Alexander Hamilton of New York, Washington's protégé, and the extraordinary young Virginian James Madison, still in his thirties, out of whose head would come the guiding concepts that would shape the new Constitution. Indeed, looking over the list of delegates in faraway Paris, where he was America's diplomatic representative, Thomas Jefferson remarked that the gathering was "really . . . an assembly of demigods."

This was the general opinion. The *New-York Journal* called the gathering in Philadelphia "the Grand Convention"; another New York City newspaper said it held the "collective wisdom of the Continent"; the *Pennsylvania Herald*, similarly impressed, found it "a wonderful display of wisdom, eloquence, and patriotism." Even Virginia delegate George Mason, himself a man revered for his insight into human affairs and one of Jefferson's demigods, broke from his usual crusty style to tell his son, after looking over his colleagues in Independence Hall, that "America has certainly, upon this occasion, drawn forth her first characters." They were, said Hector St. John de Crevecoeur, "the most enlightened men of the continent." Practically all were known widely throughout America, while many, in addition to Washington and Franklin, were even well known abroad. And they were hardly of poor, common stock. The delegates were, instead, aristocrats. They were also men who from early in life had had long careers of honorable public service.

Some were planters or large farmers; others were lawyers, merchants, state officeholders, physicians, and small farmers. Then there were the men almost impossible to classify, like Franklin and James Madison. Whatever their calling, however, they all shared one thing: a long, toughening experience in public life, fighting and directing a great revolution, running governments, and winning independence. In the words of the Declaration of Independence, they had committed their lives, their fortunes, and their sacred honor to the American cause. Three of them, in fact, had even sat in the long-ago Stamp Act Congress of 1765, while eight had signed the Declaration itself. And most of them had served in the Congress of the United States under the Articles of Confederation, learning at first hand the grave weaknesses of that document.

Early on, a pervasive *esprit de corps* developed in this gathering of old comrades in arms. Half a dozen men in the room had voted George Washington into command in 1775; others, since that fateful year, had labored in common tasks from one end of the United States to the other. "They were, indeed," writes Clinton Rossiter, "a continental elite, the nearest thing to an 'establishment' that could exist in those days of poor communications, limited horizons, and divided loyalties." Whatever else this meant, it usually created in these men an ability to think continentally and not just of their own regions. Practically all of them had gone to Philadelphia because they were nationalists, because they deplored America's alarmingly fragmented condition. Where presently there were thirteen small and bickering republics, they intended now to create one great one. Their goal, in simplest terms, was to create a strong common government for the whole of the United States of America that would establish a single nation where now, as it was widely said, there was only a "rope of sand."

The Form of the National Legislature

The first question the convention had to decide was whether to create another congress of independent states, perhaps a stronger one this time, or to establish an *independent* national government with a legislature empowered to make binding law. The former idea was embodied in the New Jersey Plan, and when it was rejected, the convention had made its most crucial decision: It had determined to free the new government entirely from the hobbling, jealous, dictatorial power of the states.

What form was the new national legislature to take? Everyone agreed that it should be composed of two houses, the lower one to represent the people at large by direct election. There was the example of the British Parliament, always a persuasive one, and the experience of the past decade, which had demonstrated how autocratic an unchecked single legislative house could become. (In most states the powers of the upper house had been largely taken away.) In what way, however, should the upper house be chosen? Alexander Hamilton insisted that its membership be appointed, for life, from the upper classes; nothing else would control the common people's passions. Others said that America was not a place in which social rank should be given permanence in the form of a special legislative body.

At this point the convention agreed upon the Connecticut Compromise, by which each state legislature would choose two senators. Thus, the proponents of the Constitution were given a persuasive argument in the later discussions over ratification of that document. When localists condemned it, the proponents could say that "the people will be represented in one house, the state legislatures in the other." Appealing to the smaller states, they could say that the Senate was their protection against the excessive power of the larger ones.

The Powers of the National Government

The role of the small states in the convention was in fact an important one. The very thing they wanted was a strong central government to balance against the large states. The result was that after the Connecticut Compromise had been adopted, the convention, under the leadership of James Madison, proceeded to establish a long list of powers for the national government: regulation of interstate and foreign commerce, foreign affairs and defense, and Indian affairs; control of the national domain; and the establishment of uniform rules of naturalization. Most important, the national legislature was empowered to levy "taxes, duties, imposts, and excises." This gave it the vitally important independent source of funds that alone would allow it to survive and be effective.

Just as important—and as revealing of the fears aroused by the turmoil in the states—were the powers forbidden to the states. They could carry on no foreign relations (some had actually sent ambassadors abroad), nor could they coin money, pass ex post facto laws, impair the obligations of contracts (that is, relieve individuals of their debts), or establish tariffs. The states, furthermore, were guaranteed "a republican form of government" by the Constitution and were promised that if domestic violence passed beyond the control of local authorities, federal assistance would be provided, if asked for by the state legislature or executive. Of crucial significance was the provision that "this Constitution, and the laws of the United States which shall be made in pursuance

thereof; and all treaties made, or which shall be made, under the authority of the United States, shall be the supreme law of the land; and the judges in every state shall be bound thereby, anything in the constitution or laws of any state to the contrary notwithstanding."

The Chief Executive

There was to be a chief executive, of course, but how was he to be chosen? Gradually the convention found itself supporting a notion that startled even some of the most devoted centralizers: the establishment of a fully independent and powerful executive office, chosen by no existing agency of government but by a special body, an electoral college, that would expire after having carried out its task. Appointed by each state "in such manner as the legislature thereof may direct," electors would be apportioned to each state in proportion to its total number of representatives and senators. This would give either the people at large the indirect power of choosing the chief magistrate, if electors were popularly elected, or the state legislatures, if they retained the power to themselves. (South Carolina was to do so far into the nineteenth century.) Either way, the president would be independent of the national legislature.

Should the president choose his chief ministers from the membership of Congress, as the British king chose his cabinet from the members of Parliament? The convention shied away from that suggestion. The delegates were too familiar with how the king had used the power to appoint legislators to lucrative offices in the executive branch to corrupt the whole system. Should the executive officers under the president be appointed by Congress, others asked, so as to keep him in check? No, came the reply, for this would reverse the problem. There was only one answer: Establish a completely independent executive with full powers to appoint his own assistants (subject to Senate confirmation of major appointments) and with real powers of government in his hands.

A Strong Judiciary

Remembering the assaults on judicial power that had been rampant in the states, the convention was determined to establish a strong and independent judiciary. An example it drew upon was the judiciary in Britain, which had been made free and powerful in the Glorious Revolution of 1688. Before then, judges had held offices at the monarch's pleasure; afterward, they held them on "good behavior"—that is, they were in office permanently unless they committed some crime. Although no written constitution provided a basis for ruling a parliamentary act null and void, British judges were nonetheless powerful. Large areas of law were simply left for them to devise in their own rulings. Also, a great body of inherited constitutional practice was relied on that gave judges authority to rule laws invalid.

The delegates in the convention were determined to ensure the judiciary's independence. This they achieved by establishing a separate judicial department in Article III of the Constitution. The Supreme Court was vested with the judicial power of the United States. Its judges (and those of such lower courts as Congress might see fit to establish) were to "hold their offices during good behavior."

The Founding Fathers and Slavery

The Revolution had fundamentally changed the status of black Americans. The ideology in the Declaration of Independence, which served as the guiding inspiration of the colonists' cause, set the notion that all men are created equal running loose and powerfully through the entire era. What of the slaves? it was quickly asked. Pennsylvania's Quakers had long condemned slavery, and even many in the South thought it an evil and fervently wished it would eventually pass away. The British authorities urged slaves to flee their masters and aid the royal cause, and tens of thousands of them did in fact run away,

The triumphal arch erected for the 1789 inauguration of George Washington.

View of the triumphal ARCH *and* COLONNADE, *erected in* BOSTON.

even if they did not go behind British lines. George Washington ordered that free blacks be allowed to enlist, and out of some 300,000 soldiers on the patriot side, perhaps 5,000 were black, most from the northern states.

A widespread movement to allow manumission (freeing) of individual slaves had a considerable effect, even in the South. From 1780, when Pennsylvania first provided for the gradual abolition of slavery within its borders, the northern states progressively eliminated the institution above the Mason and Dixon line (Pennsylvania's southern border), New Jersey completing the process by passing its enabling legislation in 1804. In 1787, after Thomas Jefferson had failed to get the Confederation Congress to outlaw slavery in all the territory west of the Appalachians (by one vote!), a great victory for antislavery was achieved when the Northwest Ordinance barred slavery from the region north of the Ohio River.

In the Constitutional Convention, a bitter argument erupted over the question. Northern delegates believed that slavery should get no recognition whatever in the new constitution. South Carolina and Georgia men, however, demanded that in computing representation in the House of Representatives slaves be counted equally with whites. Finally, to save the Union, a compromise was agreed to whereby slaves would count as three-fifths of a person—a compromise condemned by Northerners in later years, for it gave the South far more power than it would otherwise have had in the national government. However, in an equally crucial decision reached after fiery debate, Congress was empowered, after twenty years, to prohibit the slave trade.

This effectively shut off the South from the immense Atlantic trade in black slaves, which delivered to Brazil alone over a million and a half such persons from 1807 to 1860. An open slave trade would in future decades have engulfed the United States with a truly huge enslaved population in the South, would by the three-fifths clause have given the South overwhelming power in Congress, and would probably have delayed indefinitely even the solution of a civil war. Forced after 1808 to derive its slaves from the states of the upper South, the Deep South in the years of the cotton boom so drained slaves from Maryland, Kentucky, Delaware, and Missouri that these states decided to remain with the North when the Civil War began, a decision with fateful consequences for the South.

In short, although the revolutionary generation could not bring itself to assault slavery where it was strong, in the Southern states, or to deny it recognition in the Constitution, the Founding Fathers did leave it a crippled institution, clearly disapproving of it as an obviously "peculiar" arrangement. In the Declaration of Independence they had bequeathed the ideas that were eventually to help destroy it. Ambivalent and indecisive, as Thomas Jefferson's famous inability to free his own slaves while condemning the institution as a curse testifies, they nonetheless so reformed slavery's fundamental status in the new nation that eventually, by the purification of war, it was eliminated.

The Constitution's Root: Sovereignty from the People

The most exciting and novel idea developed by the Constitutional Convention was its decision on the origin of sovereignty. The document they were writing, James Madison said, could never be considered a supreme law unless it came directly from the people themselves, who were ultimately the nation's sovereign power. Legislatures were never sovereign; they were only agents appointed to carry out powers delegated by the people. Ignore the state legislatures, therefore, and base the new document on the will of the people at large. And so it was written, "We the people of the United States . . . do ordain and establish this Constitution for the United States of America."

The document should therefore be ratified not by state legislatures, but by special ratifying conventions elected by the (male, white) people (in some cases there were also property qualifications). This would put in concrete form the fundamental notion that the people were, in this great proceeding, creating their governmental system afresh. Placing sovereignty with the people also provided the perfect answer to the opponents of the Constitution, who were called Antifederalists. They protested that powers were being taken from the states, and the old Articles of Confederation wrongfully overridden. "Strange it is," observed one advocate of the Constitution, James Sullivan, that the Antifederalists "should suppose it unjustifiable for the people to alter or amend, or even entirely abolish, what they themselves have established." "Who but the people," asked Edmund Pendleton, "can delegate powers?"

The Argument over Ratification

The argument over ratification began on the day the Constitution was signed by George Washington, as president of the convention and deputy from Virginia—September 17, 1787. Localist and egalitarian republicans such as Sam Adams of Massachusetts and George Clinton of New York were alarmed. Their Antifederalist following condemned the proposed plan as antidemocratic, tyrannical, and a bald effort to reestablish the aristocratic order that had been overturned in 1776. The Federalists—predominantly nationalist republicans—did in fact believe that "the best people" had lost control of politics, and that the real problem arose from the fact that the existing structure was so fragmented and localized that it gave preeminence to parochial and narrow-minded men. Creating an immense continental arena for government, which they believed only those of education and vision could understand and administer, would inspire the elite to reenter politics and give the nation the spirited leadership it lacked.

The Antifederalists, like the Loyalists in the revolutionary period, were disorganized and bereft of a real alternative, save more of what the country already had. They seemed, also, to be in awe of the Federalists, who were college-educated, cosmopolitan, marvelously fluent, and accustomed to command, in contrast with the unlettered democrats and county politicians who opposed them. The Antifederalists, however, were able to secure a commitment to the addition of a Bill of Rights to the Constitution. By this historic achievement, the egalitarian and libertarian-republican traditions entered permanently into the Constitution. Moralistic republicanism lost out at the federal level, for the Constitution was a rigorously secular document, decreeing absolute separation of church and state. This was in fact one of the great achievements of the revolutionary era.

It was widely believed at the time that large countries had too many different interests, climates, and habits for a single legislature to be able to make laws for them equitably. In proof, Antifederalists pointed to the British empire, which had become autocratic when Parliament had sought to govern it in detail. It was inevitable that minorities would be oppressed. James Madison, however, answered this charge masterfully in *The Federalist*, a brilliant series of pamphlets that he composed with Alexander Hamilton and John Jay and published during the ratification controversy in New York. In small repub-

lics, he said, one or another of the relatively few social and economic groups could easily secure a lasting ascendancy, trampling on the rights and freedoms of others—as in the states in recent years. "What remedy can be found in a republican Government, where the majority must ultimately decide," asked Madison, "but that of giving such an extent to its sphere, that no one common interest or passion will be likely to unite a majority of the whole number in an unjust pursuit?" In a large country, interest will balance interest, section will balance section, and tyranny will be impossible to establish.

The smaller states and Pennsylvania swung behind the Constitution, but the two large states, Virginia and New York, reluctant to give up their greater power and independence, held back. Then, with the clear understanding that a Bill of Rights would be established, and with the great weight of Washington and Madison behind the new document, Virginia narrowly ratified the Constitution. This news completely disorganized the Antifederalists in New York, who until that point had things going entirely their way. Alexander Hamilton now launched his most powerful attack, openly threatening that if the state did not ratify, the city of New York might secede and ratify on its own. A bare majority confirmed the document, and the last holdouts, remote North Carolina and intensely democratic and localistic Rhode Island, had no choice but to come along. In a triumphant mood of unity, the first elections for the new federal Congress gave the friends of the Constitution a huge majority, and the experiment was fully launched.

In Retrospect

Looked at in broad perspective, the national government now established had a familiar aspect. In effect, the old federal empire as it had existed under the British before 1763 had been re-created, with important modifications. It was, in short, a remarkably Anglicized form of government, in the eyes of egalitarian republicans, and one warmly supported not only by nationalist republicans but even former Tories—the old elite. Thus, the "second revolution" was a moderate swinging back toward older, more Anglophile ways, and a partial retreat from the radical, egalitarian republicanism of the revolutionary era. London had been transferred to America, put under the control of the Americans, and given the taxing powers denied to Parliament. The distribution of

Congress voting independence, engraved by Edward Savage, after 1788.

powers between the states and the national government was almost exactly that which had existed between London and the colonies. Local affairs were left in the hands of local legislatures—roads, police, schools, most legal matters, care of the poor and insane, and the punishment of criminals. The list of powers given to the federal government—foreign affairs, control of interstate commerce, and the like— was the list of responsibilities that had been in London's hands.

However, what had been created in the new Constitution was nonetheless a strikingly republican government, which means that it diverged sharply from anything in the past or in contemporary Europe. The British Parliament, for example, claimed that it was itself "the people," in distilled, representative form. On this ground it insisted that it had unlimited authority. In America, the opposite principle was asserted: "The people" are the community at large, and they remain apart from and outside of the governments they have created. The people grant such governments only limited power to act. They hold to themselves, by specific constitutional provision, their own "rights," which by definition come from nature and are *outside governmental authority*. In the new American system, elected officials of any sort whatever—even the president, America's "king"—were to be nothing more than limited trustees for the community. They were to have no independent authority of their own. Indeed, no particular branch of the government established by the Constitution could

The assertion that Betsy Ross made the first Stars and Stripes in her upholstery shop in Philadelphia, commissioned by a committee represented by George Washington, Robert Morris and George Ross, was never authenticated.

claim to be acting with the full authority of the people, nor could all the branches together assert that power.

The Constitution was profoundly republican, too, in its inner nature. Republicanism had held that power corrupts; therefore, as James Madison said, power must be *divided* and *balanced*. "It is of great importance," Madison wrote, "not only to guard the society against the oppression of its rulers, but to guard one part of society against the injustice of the other part. Different interests necessarily exist in different classes of citizens." A thoroughly Madisonian government resulted.

There were different branches in the federal government that stood entirely independent of each other and yet had somewhat overlapping powers; there were staggered elections, to ensure that no one mood in society could take over the entire apparatus; and the Senate and House were even elected from different political bases, on the one hand from the state legislatures and on the other from the people at large. The president himself was elected in yet another way. Then there was a vertical division of powers, between the federal government and the states, which gave concrete expression to the general belief that most of government would still take place locally, where the people could watch it closely. To ensure all of this, as republicanism had insisted, there was a written constitution enacted by the people at large which stipulated the form and functions of the governing system, and explicitly protected the rights of citizens as beyond its authority.

The purpose? To enable free (white, male) Americans to live as much as possible as they wished; to build a society based upon *individualism*. To this end, governments were to be small, limited in powers, relatively inactive, simple, and inexpensive. However, in a system in which the only power holding everything together was the will of the people, whether in fact the people *were* virtuous, and wise and self-disciplined enough to govern themselves, remained the central question that would worry Americans for centuries into the future.

By comparison with contemporary Europe, republicanism—the radicalism of these centuries—was certainly in full flower in America. Placing sovereign power in the people contrasted sharply with all existing practice. The device of ratifying conventions gave the Constitution from the outset a powerful moral authority, and the new system expanded American politics, formerly confined in scattered small political arenas, to continental scale. This, in turn, elevated the whole nature and spectacle of American public life. Now people could say, in truth, that they were engaged in a grand experiment for all of humankind.

A great and numerous people had thus created, in one of the more measured and solemn constituent proceedings in modern history, a lasting frame of government, now the oldest written constitution in the world. It is not without its serious flaws. The Civil War revealed one of them: its inability to hold the nation together without resort to force. Another results from the Constitution makers' remarkable success in dividing the powers of the federal government to prevent tyranny. The nation is so large that, as Madison had predicted, majorities have been difficult to form. Even when they do appear, the Constitution has so many roadblocks built into it that it is frustratingly difficult to accomplish anything. American history has therefore gone forward in convulsive bursts. Only when massive sentiment has built up has major legislation been enacted. Such occasions have been rare. Deadlock is the normal condition of the American national government. Over long periods of the nation's history, this led impatient men to resort to corruption to make the system move in the directions they wished.

Deadlock as a characteristic condition has also led to the buildup of enormous frustration in different historical periods on the part of particular aggrieved groups—farmers, laborers, ethnic groups—and the periodic outlet of this frustration in widespread violence. When to all this is added the fundamentally conservative outlook of most Americans, created by the fact that their relative affluence has given them a devotion to property and a prickly individualism, it can be seen why the nation has often suffered long periods of turbulence. In a system of balanced power, reform energies are often blunted and ineffective. Through much of American history the greater flexibility and usable power of the business community has meant that government has stood aside while entrepreneurs have directed the actual affairs of the nation.

However, in the 1970s the nation learned again that an unbalanced constitution—in this case, toward a preponderance of power in the office of president— has its own grave dangers. From this perspective, the very qualities of cautious movement that the Constitution makers built into the document are seen to have major virtues. They can and have provided stability and continuity. The capacity of the Constitution in most of the nation's history to absorb and soften colliding forces that would otherwise, if given quick access to power, send the nation off on extreme

Ratification of the Constitution, 1787–1790

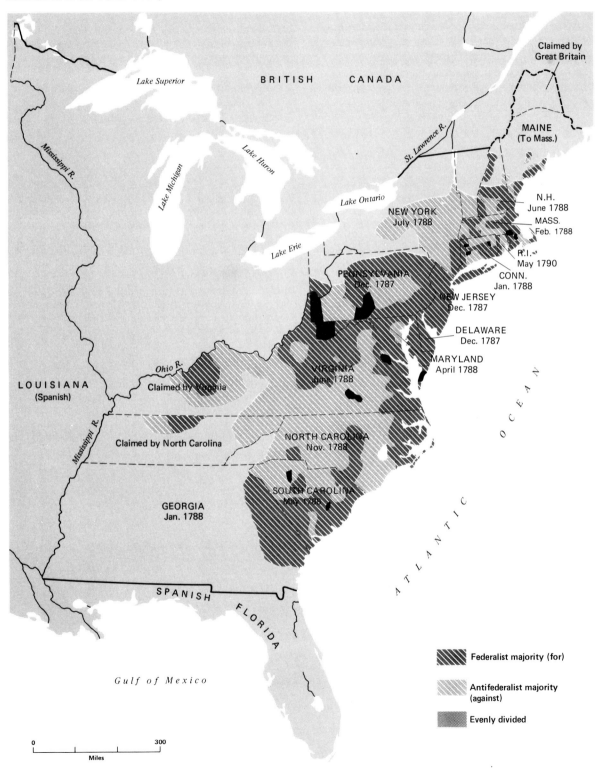

BRITISH CANADA

Lake Superior

Lake Michigan

Lake Huron

Lake Erie

Lake Ontario

Mississippi R.

St. Lawrence R.

Claimed by
Great Britain

MAINE
(To Mass.)

N.H.
June 1788

MASS.
Feb. 1788

R.I.
May 1790

CONN.
Jan. 1788

NEW YORK
July 1788

PENNSYLVANIA
Dec. 1787

NEW JERSEY
Dec. 1787

DELAWARE
Dec. 1787

MARYLAND
April 1788

VIRGINIA
June 1788

Ohio R.

Claimed by Virginia

LOUISIANA
(Spanish)

Mississippi R.

Claimed by North Carolina

NORTH CAROLINA
Nov. 1788

SOUTH CAROLINA
May 1788

GEORGIA
Jan. 1788

SPANISH FLORIDA

Gulf of Mexico

ATLANTIC OCEAN

Federalist majority (for)

Antifederalist majority
(against)

Evenly divided

0   300
Miles

courses of action, has given the system solidity and resilience. This, in turn, has had much to do with creating in the American people a fundamentally calm and rooted faith in their structure of government.

The making of the Constitution rescued the American people from paralysis and fragmentation. By creating a strong government that had popular participation built into it, the new structure released the energies of the people. It gave them disciplined

form under a clear national authority and yet protected them, usually, from the excesses of their own impulses. It was hardly a divine achievement, as some in subsequent generations would have it. The Founding Fathers were not gods descended briefly to earth to work a miracle. They were, however, seasoned, widely experienced, and remarkably talented men who created an extraordinarily successful system of government for the American people.

BIBLIOGRAPHY

Throughout I have been guided by Gordon W. Wood's important book, *The Creation of the American Republic, 1776–1787* (1969), which transformed our understanding of this epochal process. I have drawn much, too, from H. James Henderson's superb study, *Party Politics in the Continental Congress* (1974), and Alfred F. Young's massive study, *The Democratic Republicans of New York: The Origins, 1763–1797* (1967), as well as from Richard Hofstadter's reflections on the Constitution in his *The Progressive Historians: Turner, Beard, Parrington* (1968). From Clinton Rossiter's *1787: The Grand Convention* (1966) I derived the portrait of its members. In Chapter 3 in *The Cultural Pattern in American Politics: The First Century* (1979), I have offered a cultural interpretation of these events, including a discussion of the Loyalists, citing appropriate historical literature.

Students interested in plunging deeply into the core ideas of the new American republic will find Paul K. Conkin's *Self-Evident Truths* (1974) absorbing reading. In an intriguing work of major stature, *We the People: The Economic Origins of the Constitution* (1968), Forrest McDonald emphasizes the role of local events within specific states in the creation of the Constitution. Merrill Jensen, in *The New Nation* (1950) and *The Articles of Confederation* (1958), gave us powerful arguments on the theme that the governmental system replaced by the Constitution had in fact been quite democratic. Jackson Turner Main's *The Antifederalists: Critics of the Constitution, 1781–1788* (1961) highlights the ideological differences between Federalists and their opponents, maintaining that the split was one between advocates of aristocracy and advocates of democracy. E. James Ferguson's *The Power of the Purse: A History of American Public Finance 1776–1790* (1961) makes exciting reading on the public debt issue. R. R. Palmer's prizewinning study, *The Age of the Democratic Revolution* (2 vols., 1959, 1964), offers a grand panorama, setting the American Revolution in the world scene. Peter S. Onuf has given us an intriguing new perspective, linking the new constitution to the effort to organize the western lands, in *The Origins of the Federal Republic: Jurisdictional Controversies in the United States 1775–1787* (1983).

8

The New Nation: The Federalist Era

TIME LINE

HISTORY IN AN INDIVIDUAL LIFE

ALEXANDER HAMILTON

What kind of a republic should the new United States become? Nationalist republicans had an immediate answer: It should become a great nation of "power, consequence, and grandeur." Its government should work closely with entrepreneurial capitalists to develop the continent's resources, forming a powerful and profitable partnership (that is, powerful for the nation and profitable for the entrepreneurs). To realize this great dream, they looked confidently to the leadership of a sophisticated gentleman from New York City who in 1790 became the nation's first secretary of the treasury: Alexander Hamilton.

Though only thirty-five, Hamilton was already a national figure. Born in the West Indies, he had moved to New York and enthusiastically joined the fight for independence. General Washington's aide in that struggle, he was a brave officer in combat, and thereafter a leading figure in the Continental Congress, the Annapolis Convention, and (to a lesser degree) the Constitutional Convention. Known to have a brilliant mind and a keen grasp of political economy, this rather small, elegantly dressed New York lawyer of soldierly bearing struck many as vain and arrogant and others as charming, patriotic, talented, and elo-

quent. The achievements of great men were for him the chief events in history. "He did not think," writes his biographer John C. Miller, "that the people had leadership, political wisdom and initiative in themselves—leadership came from the exceptional individuals, the 'natural aristocrats' and the rich and educated."

In his hopes for the new United States, Hamilton took as his model Great Britain itself: complex, continually developing, industrial, and—above all—powerful. He detested the separate states. In the Constitutional Convention he had even proposed that they be made little more than subordinate departments of the central government. As the historian Jerald A. Combs has written, Hamilton more than anything else "believed that the United States as a nation should seek the same glory, the same heroic stature, that he himself pursued throughout his life."

The government, in short, should concern itself not with the masses but with the leaders of society. There should be an intimate link between those in power and "the rich and well born." The government should look especially to the needs of those businessmen whose concern was to develop the nation's own industrial system, rather than those who were engaged in supplying raw materials to foreign nations. Self-sufficiency based on an inward-looking mercantilistic system: That should be America's policy, just as it was the goal of the ruling authorities in Britain, whose policies Hamilton so admired. Hamilton called for protective tariffs and bounties to encourage industry; he did not get them. But he did get the most important thing of all: a great and powerful Bank of the United States, which would effectively give the nation's leading men of finance the means by which to shape the economy, directing it toward what Hamilton considered the proper goals—industry and power. Around this remarkable man gathered the Federalist party, and around his enemy, Thomas Jefferson, the Republicans. American two-party politics was born.

Overview

As George Washington took up his duties as first president of the United States in 1789, the question before everyone was: Would this latest experiment at self-government by the American people survive? Could a "republic," in fact, endure? The record thus far had not been encouraging. This feeling of national insecurity made the public life of the 1790s exceedingly bitter. Everyone seemed to believe that if their political enemies got power, they would destroy the republic, either through the errors of their ideas or because they secretly wished its destruction.

Thus, though it was commonly believed that political parties were to be shunned as inherently disloyal collections of self-seekers and subversives, the 1790s had not advanced far when two great national parties began to appear, first among the political elite and then among the mass of the voters. With Federalists ranged against Jeffersonian Republicans, this first of the national party systems formed the context within which the new nation hammered out its initial decisions. During Washington's two terms (1789–97), and John Adams's troubled single term (1797–1801), nationalist republicanism was dominant. A banking and funding arrangement was established that provided a powerful nationalizing force in the economy. Treaties were made with Britain and Spain that cleared the West of their troops and made possible the first large-scale pushing back of the Indians north of the Ohio River, opening that region to settlement. And the first new states were admitted (Vermont in 1791, Kentucky in 1792, and Tennessee in 1796).

At the same time, whether to be friendly or hostile toward Britain, the mother country, created harsh controversy. The onset of the French Revolution intensified the debate. A quasi-naval war with France broke out on the high seas, leading to the first "witch hunt" in national politics. Federalists called Jeffersonian Republicans traitors for their friendliness toward the revolutionary French regime. In the Alien and Sedition Acts, they threatened to crush freedom of speech and the press and to drive out all troublesome immigrants. In the election of 1800, a surging egalitarian and libertarian republicanism swept the Federalists out of national supremacy, placing Thomas Jefferson in the White House. Thus emerged a Southern ascendancy in the federal government that was to last, with brief interruptions, until 1860.

The Two Parties and Republicanism

When the federal government first began its operations, many believed that a conspiracy existed, among certain aristocratic circles, to reestablish a monarchy. That system, after all, was practically the universal form of government in the world. Many members of Congress, much as they revered George Washington, worried that a president would make the "bold push for the American throne" that men like Patrick Henry were predicting. Indeed, some of those men who during Washington's first term began to take on the name of *Federalist*—on the ground that only they truly believed in the idea of a strong national government—were known to be skeptical about republicanism. Keenly aware of these feelings, Thomas

The inauguration of George Washington as the first President of the United States on April 30, 1789, marked the beginning of what was at the time an uncertain experiment in republican government.

Jefferson's followers called themselves *Republicans*, implying that the Federalists were actually monarchists at heart.

This conviction created the now ludicrous but then serious argument over what titles should be used in referring to the president, the vice-president, and the other officers of the federal government. Many agreed with John Adams, who felt that ordinary citizens would obey only those whom they held in awe. He proposed using such references toward President Washington as "His Elective Majesty." Others were violently opposed. The only way out was to settle on the simple "Mr. President" for the eminent person who then held the executive office.

So briefly over, there was much about this argument that revealed deep and fundamental differences. The need for deference, for those lower in the social scale to bow and be respectful to those above, was central to the aristocratic mind, and infuriating to the democratic, egalitarian republicans. Nothing had been more central to the troubled relationship between Britain and the American colonies than the British habit of authority. Tugging at forelocks, bending the knee, and acting submissively toward superiors were for many men precisely what they had felt themselves to be fighting against in the Revolution.

What Kind of Economy?

Much more serious was the question: What kind of economy should the new nation build for itself? This was a pressing issue because people believed it was directly connected with another, even more important, one: Would the American republic, that new nation in the world, survive? Everyone agreed that a republic could not endure unless its citizens were virtuous. After all, in the new republican way of living the people themselves were to be society's ultimate authority. If they were lazy, selfish, immoral, and unwilling to sacrifice their own interest for the general welfare, the great new experiment would collapse. What did this have to do with national economic policy? Virtue, it was said, relied heavily on how the citizens of the republic made their living.

Here lay the core of the matter: Was each individual American economically independent? Or were they subject to someone else's authority and command? Were they self-supporting, or subservient and dependent? It was said that a servile people, like the serfs of czarist Russia, could not ever be strong,

upstanding republican citizens—and that no so-called republic composed of such people would ever last long.

Once again, Britain served as the chief model in the argument that now erupted. No one wanted to see America acquire the oppressed laboring class—ignorant, dull, drunken, and diseased—that Benjamin Franklin had seen in England and described, in distaste, to his fellow Americans. England was so cursed, said Thomas Jefferson and James Madison, because it had evolved into a corrupt "old age," economically speaking. Britain, they insisted, was a country enervated by luxury, dragged down by an immense national debt and the grabbing up of all the land by an oppressive landowning aristocracy. A large independent class of farmers living on their own land could not exist in Britain because there was no land left for them. The result was overpopulation: great masses of idle, landless people lying about in dissolute uselessness. To put their surplus population to work, said American critics, the English had been forced to build factories, where jammed-together crowds of working-class families, living in grim conditions, labored like dull cattle at their deadening work.

What American republicans like Thomas Jefferson wanted, as historian Drew R. McCoy has recently written, was "a society of independent, moderately prosperous, relatively self-sufficient producers who would succeed in staving off the dangers of an overly advanced, commercialized existence." Out of such people, a sturdy, austere, hard-working, and intelligently directed republic could be constructed. The ugly class divisions to be seen in Europe between the wealthy, propertied few and miserable masses of degraded poor should never appear in the United States of America.

Proposed Solutions

As we will see, these considerations prompted Jefferson and his followers to believe that America should remain as long as possible a simple farming country, each (white) family living on its own land. To ensure this, they believed that America needed a steadily expanding western frontier of open, unoccupied land where aspiring young men and women could settle and build independent households.

Other Americans, however, disagreed. They regarded a purely farming life as usually an ignorant and lazy occupation. People of this persuasion warned that America's soil was so fertile and so easily available that few had to work hard. Something was needed, therefore, to spur ordinary Americans out of their alleged natural sloth, so that they would become vigorous, industrious, self-disciplined, and productive. New Englanders in particular worried about this matter. At all costs, they said, idleness and the depraved morals that idleness brings had to be warded off. As a Massachusetts clergyman put it in 1782, everything "should be put forth to make the people industrious," for in industry is to be found "the life of all states." Indeed, sophisticated people like Alexander Hamilton of New York City said that a bit of luxury was not in itself a bad thing, if the lure of being able to buy it got the masses to working hard.

What did people of Hamilton's persuasion believe was the answer? America should be made into an industrializing country. This, in turn, would bring cities into being, thus creating profitable nearby markets for American farmers. At the same time, to tap even more potential markets for American farm goods, foreign commerce should be stimulated. The result, it was said, would be to give Americans new appetites, new and higher expectations as to the kind of

lives they could live. Farmers would be stimulated by these beckoning markets to work hard to raise more crops, and then to use their profits to raise their standard of living. A flourishing foreign trade, Hamiltonians said, would also bring America more into contact with the outside world, replacing its present crudity with a more cultivated way of life. From this perspective, commerce was seen not as a bad thing, but as a civilizing force.

Nationalist Policies

It was a historically fateful choice, therefore, when George Washington, as the nation's first president, brought Alexander Hamilton to his cabinet as secretary of the treasury. Hamilton soon sent a series of proposals to Congress which aimed at creating a centrally organized national economy. The first task, he said, was to establish sound credit for the government, and in the process to attract the support of the nation's leading financial men. No government could endure without the ability to borrow, as the last days of the Articles of Confederation had shown.

The first presidential mansion, in New York City, was occupied by George Washington until 1790.

WASHINGTON'S RESIDENCE IN NEW YORK AS PRESIDENT.

The entire national debt, and all the state debt as well (which at that time existed in the form of badly devalued bonds), should be called in and replaced at face value with federal bonds. The revenues of the new federal government would be pledged to pay the interest and capital of the new negotiable bonds. In one stroke, life would be given to the stagnant financial system. One consequence of this policy would be the enrichment of those clever individuals at the centers of influence who had bought up large quantities of national and state bonds from the poor at a fraction of their face value. But the paying in full of the entire debt would assure the world that the credit of the United States was sound.

These proposals led to a bitter struggle in Congress that went on for the first six months of 1790. Party lines that had begun vaguely to form in the controversy over presidential titles now rose stark and bold. Hamilton's plan would primarily help the North, for most Southern states—Virginia most of all—had already largely paid off their state debts and a good portion of the national debt held within their boundaries as well. Now they would be paying double, and to speculators in the North! (Four-fifths of the national debt was owed to Northerners.)

It was, in fact, becoming increasingly clear that in the new federal Congress one of the basic rivalries that would shape the conduct and outcome of practically every question was an inherent hostility between Yankees and Southerners. They really did not like each other. They regarded each other's ways of life with contempt. New Englanders were offended by the lordliness and luxurious ways of the Southern aristocrats; their casual habit of living constantly in debt; and their reliance upon an evil institution, slavery, while Thomas Jefferson and James Madison talked of democracy and equality. How could the country possibly be placed in their hands? Southerners disliked the outspoken moralism and religiosity of the New Englanders, were stung by their righteous condemnations, and worried about what would happen to their interests if the Yankees got the full control of the national government that they seemed to hunger for. Thus, when in July of 1790 Madison and Jefferson finally agreed to Hamilton's funding proposals, they did so only with the agreement that the seat of the national government be established in the South, on the Potomac River. In this way, they and their supporters in the South reasoned, it would be more likely to be friendly to Southern interests than if it continued to be in New York City or Philadelphia.

Hamilton's Banking Plan

To administer the government's finances and to supervise the currency system, Hamilton decided, in late 1790, that a national bank of the United States should be chartered. Modeled directly on the Bank of England, which for a hundred years had made the British pound the model of fiscal soundness, it would be primarily a private bank, though part of the board of directors would be selected, and part of its stock would be owned, by the government. It would be much more than an ordinary bank: It would receive all the nation's revenues, handle all the government's money, and be free to invest, in ways it saw fit, the enormous supply of tax money that would gather in its vault. It would also have the power to supervise the currency issued by state-chartered banks by being able to demand that they redeem their notes in hard cash at the national bank. With these large financial powers and the largest single pool of capital in the country, the national bank could develop the nation's economy in the most fruitful directions—as conceived by the aristocratic gentlemen who sat on its board of directors. Nothing better embodied nationalist republicanism. Briefly debated, the plan was passed by Congress in February 1791.

Then the storm broke. The argument in Congress may have been brief, but it had been intense. Southerners, led by Madison and Jefferson, were strongly opposed, as were many throughout the country who feared the giving of such great powers over the nation's economic life to a few men sitting in Philadelphia. There was fear of monopoly, of exploitation, of the invasion of local life by financial influences beyond local control. Jefferson and Madison, speaking for such fears, sought to persuade President Washington to veto the bill on the ground that it was unconstitutional.

Washington was in a quandary. Should he sign the banking bill, even though such trusted advisers, and even Attorney General Edmund Randolph, another Virginian, urged him that it was unconstitutional? Jefferson argued that the Constitution should be strictly interpreted, and that the federal government should do only what was specifically mentioned and called for in that document. Alexander Hamilton, in one of his most powerful state papers, argued instead that the Constitution should be considered as a document that prescribed the *ends* of government, not its *means*. Whenever a law was clearly related to achieving the ends of government, and was not specifically prohibited by the Constitution, then that legislation was constitutional and should be approved. The government was given all "necessary and proper" powers to achieve the "general welfare." By this argument, which convinced Washington, Hamilton successfully established the principle of *broad construction* of the Constitution.

All this, however, left a strong aftertaste. Throughout the country, people believed that the debt-funding and banking programs, taken together, constituted an insidious plot to impoverish farmers and make unscrupulous and wealthy speculators the lords and masters of the United States. They regarded them as part of a sinister campaign to reintroduce English ways into America, to sow "the seeds of every vice and calamity in our country." From this time on, Virginia became the leading center of resistance to Hamiltonian Federalism. New England formed the other end of the rivalry, persistently voting Federalist. The Middle Atlantic states, with their mixed ethnic, religious, and economic composition, played a balancing role.

Hamilton's Mercantilism

In December 1791 Hamilton made his boldest and most ambitious public policy proposals yet: In his "Report on Manufactures" he sent Congress a *plan* for America—a plan that aimed at nothing less than the revolutionizing of its life. If Hamilton had his way, government would not sit back passively and just maintain order, it would move in actively to shape the national economy, rather than letting it simply evolve in whatever way it more or less unconsciously chose to evolve. An industrializing America should be created by positive intervention.

Hamilton had two things in mind. First, he hoped an industrializing America would transform its people, whom he thought slow-moving and unambitious, into vigorous, hard-working, sturdy republicans. Equally important was his conviction that a thriving industrial economy centered on prospering cities would make the United States of America a strong nation capable of defending itself in a world

of constant wars and threats of wars. Such a nation could play a bold and powerful role in international affairs, a prospect Hamilton relished. The world, Hamilton would say, was not a placid and comfortable place, but rather one of insecurity and danger. This was why the strong nations in the world practiced *mercantilism* (their governments intervened directly in their economies to build power and wealth, treating all national production as an organic unit). They had fortress economies, regarding other countries as their economic rivals. Using every means they could find to develop their own economic resources, build their own wealth, and hamper the growth of other nations' economies, they operated on the assumption that what impoverished others enriched themselves.

Hamilton proposed *protective tariffs* (import taxes on foreign goods that would make them expensive and thereby give an advantage to local manufacturers), bounties to promote new industries, premiums for improvements in the quality of products, awards to encourage invention, especially of labor-saving machinery, and exemption from duties on essential raw materials brought from abroad. As a result money would not be sent abroad to buy goods, but would remain at home to develop American industry. Southern raw materials could then be used in Northern factories, so that commerce and wealth would link the sections of the nation instead of dividing them as at present.

The South was not charmed. These proposals appeared to be simply another plan devised by clever Northern businessmen to exploit Southern farmers. Heavily dependent on foreign trade, Southerners opposed anything that would reduce it. Forced to buy manufactured goods elsewhere, since they had no factories, they wanted to be able to buy them in the cheapest market. If tariffs made cheap foreign goods too expensive to purchase, they would have to buy costly American-made goods and in effect would be paying a direct tax to American industrialists. Northern businessmen would be made rich not by their own efforts, but by governmental favors given to support "infant industries."

Great numbers of ordinary people in the Northern states agreed with these Southern views, as did those who by their political philosophies were inclined to suspect corruption in any scheme in which the government worked directly with businessmen. The Tariff Act of May 1792, therefore, included many of Hamilton's recommendations, but it was not a genuinely protective measure. After its passage, furthermore, American businessmen continued to invest in land, shipping, and speculative schemes such as banks, turnpikes, and canal companies. They avoided the unfamiliar and doubtful field of manufacturing.

The French Revolution in American Life

In 1793, American political life was torn asunder by the impact of the French Revolution. In that world-shaking upheaval, the French monarchy was overthrown and the king and his queen beheaded; church and state were separated and the Roman Catholic Church plundered; and thousands of the wealthy and powerful were executed at the guillotine as a violent social radicalism convulsed French society. Its goal was the establishment of "liberty, equality, and fraternity."

Thomas Jefferson regarded France as America's true mother country. He deplored the violence of the revolution that broke out in France in 1789—he was there at the time as America's minister—and believed the French should not have gone further than to establish a constitutional monarchy and adequate legislative institutions. On the whole, however, he regarded the cause of the French Revolution and its goals as the cause of common people everywhere. The Federalists, on the other hand, hated and feared the French Revolution for its attacks upon established religion, its flouting of established authority, and its direct attacks upon the propertied aristocracy. They were committed to law and order as the only means by which the naturally greedy and envious attitudes of the poor—as they believed them to be—could be restrained. Unruliness of any kind, to the Federalist mind, was horrifying. Social revolution was destructive and sacrilegious.

President Washington declared that the United States would be neutral in the war between Britain and France that began shortly after the French Revolution took place. Soon, however, the Americans were angered by the British, who issued an Order in Council prohibiting American ships from carrying provisions to or from French islands in the Caribbean. They kept the order secret for a time, and in early 1794 scooped up 250 unsuspecting American vessels, most of which lost their cargoes as *contraband*, a term the British interpreted to mean far more than just munitions. They also took American sailors off their vessels and impressed them into the British navy on the ground that they were British subjects.

A storm of protest welled up in the United States. James Madison called urgently for retaliatory economic measures to force Britain to its knees. Madison and Thomas Jefferson were desperately anxious to keep open the trade American farmers had with the West Indies—a trade then highly lucrative and important. Why? Because the longer Americans could make money selling their farm produce abroad, the longer would they be content with remaining a farming country. Thus the onset of industrialization and urbanization, which people like Madison and Jefferson so much feared, and Hamiltonians called for so insistently, would be delayed, perhaps put off indefinitely. Madison now broadened the charge against the British: They were not only responsible, he said, for plundering American ships on the high seas, but they were encouraging and aiding the Indians who were then waging bloody warfare on the American frontier. One thousand of Britain's 6,000 troops in North America still occupied forts on American soil. Something drastic, Madison insisted, must be done to end this oppression.

War with Britain seemed about to break out at any moment. President Washington, hopeful of solving the matter by diplomacy, promptly dispatched Chief Justice John Jay to England in March 1794 to open negotiations with the London government on all outstanding difficulties between the two countries. The entire nation sat back to await the outcome.

The Whiskey Rebellion

Part of Hamilton's fiscal plan had been to raise funds by levying a heavy excise tax on whiskey, amounting to one quarter of the net price of each gallon. Not then a drink of gentlemen, whiskey was an Irish and Scottish ethnic liquor originally called *uisge beatha*, which in Celtic means the "water of life." Resentment quickly flared among the Scotch-Irish farmers of western Pennsylvania, for whom whiskey was both commercially and culturally important. In the fall of 1794 gatherings in that region listened to inflammatory speeches. As is usual in such meetings, the need for release in violent language resulted in extreme and rash statements. There was even talk of marching on Philadelphia, then the seat of the federal government, and taking it over by force.

Though such a thing was absurd, Washington

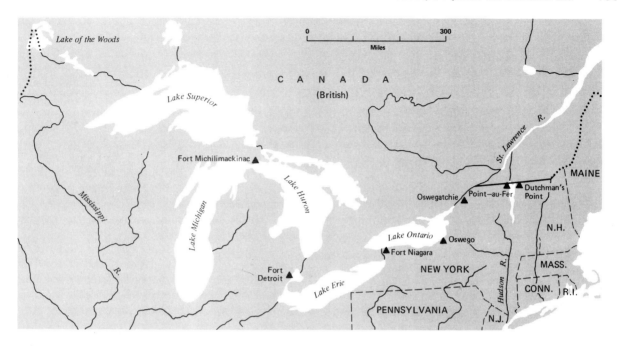

British Military Posts after 1783

and Hamilton regarded these protests as nothing less than the beginning of the French Revolution in America. They had been alarmed at the appearance of so-called democratic societies that had recently been springing up around the country to praise the French Revolution and to demand democratic reforms in the United States. A local democratic society in western Pennsylvania was linked to the turmoil, and they therefore leaped to the conclusion that a French-inspired plot was behind it all.

To demonstrate that the new federal government would absolutely not tolerate any contempt for law and order, a force of almost 13,000 militia was called up—a body of men larger than Washington had commanded at any time during the American Revolution—and marched westward, with Hamilton urging it on, to search out rebels. A few men were captured; two were tried and convicted and then pardoned as mentally incompetent. Jefferson's comment on the whole fiasco summed up the reaction of many: "An insurrection was announced and proclaimed and armed against, but could never be found." President Washington, in his subsequent report to Congress, caused a national sensation by blaming the rebellion on the democratic societies, thereby condemning by implication a great many Jeffersonian Republicans of high social and political standing who were members of such bodies.

Jay's Treaty

These events were hardly concluded when John Jay returned from Britain with a treaty. He had been required to carry on his diplomacy in London under severe handicaps. Hamilton had secretly informed the British that the United States would do nothing to enforce its demands that the British evacuate forts they still held on American soil. Furthermore, British spirits were high because they were winning their war with France. They wanted to settle the differences with America, but not if it meant giving in on their recently claimed right to disregard the extensive neutral rights for ships that the United States had adamantly claimed in its treaties with other foreign powers: that free (neutral) ships made free goods (that is, goods beyond meddling with by combatants), and that neutrals could trade freely in everything but arms with belligerents.

Jay had to give up these rights if anything else was to be gained. Nothing was even said in the treaty about impressment of American sailors. In fact, it provided that henceforth American ports could not be used as bases for privateering operations against British vessels. (*Privateers* were armed private ships authorized to capture enemy commercial vessels and wage war against enemy warships.)

However, the British tacitly accepted, finally, the fact that the new American nation was going to survive. They agreed to evacuate their forts in the Northwest, which they had been holding in expectation of imminent American collapse. At the same time, they opened the West Indies and India to limited American trade. These last provisions were to be highly profitable to the United States, setting off a booming trade. From 1795 to 1800 American exports to the British Empire trebled, and the United States became Britain's best customer.

The Republicans—who consisted generally of those who had hated Britain with the greatest intensity during the Revolution—burst into thunderous protest when they read Jay's treaty. To them it represented an insulting and unbearable toadying, once again, to British power. Turning to the general population, they mounted protest meetings all over the country. In these turbulent, impassioned days, the two opposing political parties reached their full development. Henceforth the terms Federalist and Republican were the everyday commodities of political discussion. When the treaty was ratified by the Federalist-dominated Senate, Republicans had a polit-ical club to use against their enemies, and they wielded it constantly thereafter.

The Indians and the West

The United States had secured sovereignty over the eastern half of the Mississippi Valley in 1783 in a peculiar form. The French and the British had never asserted that their control over this vast region affected Indian ownership of the land. In 1763, during Pontiac's uprising, the British had reaffirmed native rights to all territory west of the Appalachians. They tried to halt purchases of this land by the colonists and to void those already made.

In actuality, few settlers had gone west of the mountains by 1783. The region north of the Ohio was still wholly in Indian hands. When the United States assumed sovereignty, it agreed that it did not thereby gain title to the land. It had simply acquired the exclusive right to come to agreements with the Indians concerning the land, to buy it from them if they assented. Each tribe was dealt with as a resident "nation," and agreements took the form of treaties

Indian Wars in the Northwest, 1790–1794

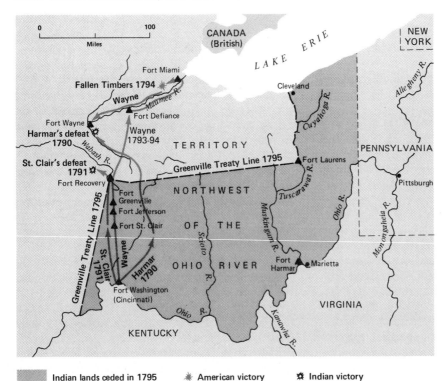

Indian lands ceded in 1795   ✳ American victory   ✪ Indian victory

confirmed by the Senate, despite the strange fact that these "nations" seemed also to be living on land over which the United States claimed sovereignty. This confusing policy was not ended until 1871.

The Indians had every legal right to fight against incursions into their lands. When in the 1770s Daniel Boone led settlers out into what became Kentucky, and when in 1782 North Carolina gave western lands to its Revolutionary veterans without so much as asking the Indians, war immediately broke out. American troops soon mounted expeditions of punishment, repeatedly forcing the Indians to evacuate the lands they had been defending. The color of legality was given to these arrangements by agreements with chiefs for the sale of lands that other members of the tribes did not recognize, on the ground that chiefs had no authority over land belonging to the entire tribe.

The Indians north of the Ohio were particularly resistant to white incursions. In the 1790s they inflicted severe losses on all settlers and troops sent into the region. After the United States had spent some $5 million of its limited funds on this seemingly endless warfare, the Indians were finally crushed by General Anthony Wayne in the Battle of Fallen Timbers in 1794. For $10,000 the Indians agreed to sell the southeast quarter of what later became Ohio, as well as the sites of Detroit, Chicago, and Vincennes, Indiana. Peace was restored, and settlers could flock in unmolested. The westward movement swept on majestically and, as the Federalists feared, the tight little eighteenth-century world that American politicians had always known was transformed. As the western frontier expanded, New England, the heartland of Federalism, would be left behind and its influence would wane. Thus, it distrusted the West and sought to limit its growth when votes were cast in Congress on the issue.

Pinckney's Treaty

For years Spain had refused to come to an agreement as to the exact boundary of the United States in the Southwest, for the Spanish claimed an enormous part of that region. They had also adamantly refused to make legal any kind of arrangement allowing Americans in the West to have free use of the mouth of the Mississippi River, which lay within the boundaries of Spanish-owned Louisiana. The Jay Treaty, however, jarred them out of this adamant mood. They conceived the notion that Britain and America were

moving so closely together that soon they would join forces against the Spanish.

In late 1795 Thomas Pinckney, the American minister to Spain, found that the atmosphere for diplomacy had changed markedly. He quickly secured the Treaty of San Lorenzo, which provided that the line of 31 degrees north latitude, the northern line of the present state of Florida, was the proper boundary line. Free navigation of the Mississippi was also allowed to American citizens. This carried with it the right of free deposit of commercial goods on docks at New Orleans for later pickup by ocean-going vessels. Spain also agreed tacitly to end its support of Indian attacks against American settlers.

The Election of John Adams

In 1796 George Washington decided not to run for a third term. His vice-president, John Adams, came forward as the chief Federalist candidate in the presidential election of that year. The Republicans looked immediately to Thomas Jefferson, who had returned from France to serve as Washington's secretary of state from 1790 to 1793, and had then retired from public life to live quietly at Monticello, his estate in Virginia. Since political parties were now well formed (though the idea of actually having them was generally disliked), the Republicans were able to fight so vigorous a campaign that Adams defeated Jefferson by only three electoral votes.

Under the existing constitutional arrangements, Jefferson, as runner-up in the electoral vote, became vice-president. From this post he worked day and night in the succeeding four years to build the Republicans into a strong national party. He knit them together so successfully by his constant letter writing and consultation as to make him the first national leader of a political party in American history.

John Adams was a strange man. One of the most penetrating political thinkers in American history, he was limited in his effectiveness as president by an almost complete inability to make himself popular. Regarding humanity as fundamentally passionate and power-hungry, he was convinced that the common people should not be allowed enough power to dominate the government, for they would use this power to attack and impoverish the wealthy. To Adams's mind, the propertied aristocracy was the ballast of the state, as well as its natural leadership. Unlike Hamilton, however, he distrusted banks and bankers. He and Jefferson heartily agreed that commercial activity was potentially destructive, a fruitful source of corrupt wealth and misplaced power. An aristocracy of ill-gotten wealth would destroy the natural aristocracy of birth, genius, and merits.

The French Hysteria

Fearful of social strife and always on the lookout for anything that threatened to equalize the ranks of society, Adams regarded the French Revolution with loathing. The French government, seeking to halt American trade with British possessions, had captured over 300 American vessels in 1795 alone, commandeering their cargoes as contraband. Determined to solve this issue by diplomacy and not by war, Adams sent negotiators to France. However, they were refused admittance to negotiations with the minister of foreign affairs unless they paid him a huge bribe and agreed to a further large contribution to France's war chest.

When these "XYZ" demands—so named for the letters Adams assigned to the French negotiators, whose names he withheld from public release—reached the American public, there was an explosion of national wrath. Even those regions strongly Republican in feeling turned violently against France and demanded war. It swiftly became a test of patriotism to support the president, who called upon Congress to authorize a limited war on the seas against French vessels, to be conducted while he continued to carry on toughly worded negotiations with the French government. Announcing a state of limited hostilities, he secured funds to build up the navy, protect American shipping and coastal areas, and manufacture arms. American diplomats in France were withdrawn, all French diplomats were expelled from the United States, and all treaties with France—including the alliance dating from revolutionary days—were abolished.

The First "Witch Hunt"

The United States was now launched on its first search for "subversives" and "traitors." Vigilante committees were organized by Federalists to keep an eye on prominent Republicans, including Vice-President Jefferson himself, on the ground that as Republicans they were necessarily conspiring with the French to subvert and destroy the American na-

tion. Adams himself fanned the flames. In the spring of 1798 he issued a stream of public letters attacking the loyalty of the Republicans, whom he invariably linked with the French enemy. Mobs roamed the streets looking for anyone brave enough to continue praising the French Republic and its revolution, and John Adams for a brief time was genuinely popular.

A preacher in Boston, Timothy Dwight, declared that the United States had been invaded by a secret organization, the Society of Illuminati, dedicated to overthrowing government everywhere. It had brought on the French Revolution and was determined to destroy all churches. These delusions, which were seized on enthusiastically, turned large numbers of clergy, especially the Congregationalists of New England, into allies of the Federalists. Jefferson had long been known to be of highly liberal views of religion, and now he and his Republican followers were damned as ungodly scoundrels who aimed at destroying all religion and morality in America.

Leading Congregational clergyman Timothy Dwight warned that America was being subverted by French-spawned conspiracies of free-thinking intellectuals who wished to destroy religion and all lawful authority.

The Alien and Sedition Laws

Convinced that they alone were truly loyal to the United States, the Federalists decided to crush all opposition. In June and July of 1798 Congress, dominated by the Federalists, enacted the Alien and Sedition Laws. *Sedition* was defined as conspiracies against the government and scandalous statements uttered against it, the Congress, or the president. Those guilty of such crimes could be fined and imprisoned. A Federalist newspaper, defining the law in popular terms, stated simply: "It is patriotism to write in favour of our government, it is sedition to write against it."

Fifteen indictments for "seditious libel" were brought; ten people were convicted and fined or imprisoned. When newspaper editors were actually thrown into jail, a shock so powerful ran through the Jeffersonians that they moved decisively to bring an end to the long eighteenth-century argument over freedom of the press. Since the trial of John Peter Zenger in the 1730s, the controversy had slowly converged on the position that "freedom of the press" meant essentially that the government had no power to exert *prior* control over newspapers by issuing licenses to print them. This left open, however, the traditional principle that editors could be prosecuted *after* the fact for what they had printed. The Zenger case had seemed to establish the principle that seditious libel could not be pressed against an editor if the things he said were true, but in practice even this basic theory was not generally accepted.

It is widely assumed now that the First Amendment to the Constitution took care of the problem once and forever. But that was definitely not the case. It simply denied Congress the power to require licensing of newspapers, while leaving state control of the newspapers exactly as it had been before—wide open to abuse. But the Sedition Act in 1798 brought an abrupt end to the tradition of prosecuting editors for seditious libel, for in defense arguments during Sedition Act prosecutions, lawyers began to argue persuasively that *words alone* should never be regarded as seditious, but only concrete steps taken to undermine and overthrow the government. This argument won out. When the Jeffersonians came to power in the election of 1800, they not only let the Sedition Act expire but they arrived on the scene clutching new books that eloquently laid out the modern argument for freedom of speech and press.

President Jefferson himself briefly retreated from this position in 1804, when he allowed the prosecution of a New York Federalist editor for his criticisms of the president, alleging seditious libel. But the case failed, ironically with Alexander Hamilton as lawyer for the defense pleading the cause of freedom of the press. Thereafter the notion that Americans could be put in jail merely for words and not for acts against the government was in peacetime no longer the ruling principle in courts of law.

As the Sedition Act showed the Federalists' hypersensitivity to "disloyalty," the Alien Act showed their hostility to immigrants. The Federalists regarded every new non-English arrival in the country as potentially a dangerous revolutionary and certainly a future Republican. Thus, the act empowered the president to restrain, arrest, or deport any alien he deemed a danger to the nation. Many Federalists wanted to prevent any further immigration at all. They revealed thereby their fundamental role as the spokesmen of the English-descended in American life, who identified the nation with themselves and thought all others essentially un-American, inferior, and subversive. The act, however, compromised by simply increasing the period of residence necessary (from five to fourteen years) before citizenship could be claimed.

The Quasi-War

Few Americans actually wanted a full-scale war with France. Congress did not declare war; it simply enacted in July 1798 a law extending naval operations to all the seas of the world, allowing the navy to capture armed (not unarmed) French vessels anywhere, and giving the president power to commission privateers. Thus began an intensely frustrating conflict that satisfied no one. The country was in a state of perpetual crisis while it went on, torn as to whether to go forward or to pull back. Federalist extremists wanted to expand the war, and made life miserable for John Adams by attacking him endlessly for not doing so. Republicans wanted to scuttle the entire enterprise.

While major naval engagements on the high seas proceeded, in which the American frigates *United States*, *Constellation*, and *Constitution* won a string of victories, roundabout diplomatic maneuvers reaching toward a peace settlement were conducted. Finally, in 1801, a convention was signed that brought the quasi-war to an end. By its terms the United States was released from its alliance with France, which eliminated France's favored position in American trade and politics, and the United States gave up its claims for indemnity for the capture of ships and cargoes.

The Decline and Fall of the Federalists

As the nation approached the presidential election of 1800, partisan debate in the newspapers reached levels of unparalleled ferocity. The Alien and Sedition Laws created widespread outrage, as editors and even a congressman—Matthew Lyon of Vermont, an immigrant Irishman—were thrown into jail for criticizing the president. Virginia and Kentucky adopted legislative resolutions in 1798 and early 1799, written by Jefferson and Madison, that called the Alien and Sedition Laws unconstitutional. The resolutions seemed to imply that the states were in fact sovereign and could nullify national legislation deemed obnoxious. Other states refused to pass similar resolutions, but the ominous note of disunion had been sounded.

The Federalists had gathered a sizable vote in the Southern states in the 1790s, since many of the Southern aristocracy admired Washington and liked to be thought of as in his camp. But Federalism was too clearly a Northern and especially a New England creed, and it could not long remain popular in the South. Besides, the most rapidly growing regions in the Southern states, as elsewhere in the nation, were predisposed toward egalitarian and libertarian republicanism. They were heavily populated by simple farmers who were becoming aggressively democratic (not, of course, with regard to black Americans). Like their counterparts in much of the northern countryside, they were fundamentally localists who wanted everyone else to leave them alone. They disliked the idea of a strong central government, with its taxes and what they supposed were its corrupt links to bankers and to urban, modernizing influences.

Thousands of Southerners were looking eagerly to the West, hoping to see it rapidly develop. Federalists, on their side, were consistently known to distrust and dislike the West—they opposed the admission of Tennessee as a state—as a land of ungovernable

democrats who would make their beloved New England an ever more isolated section of the nation. They thought of the United States instead as the westernmost segment of a transatlantic trading and cultural community that centered on Great Britain, always their admired model.

A surging Jeffersonian Republican tide began to overwhelm the Federalists everywhere in the late 1790s—even, temporarily, in New England. In that region, as oftentimes in other parts of the United States as well, Federalist areas were usually those that were static, ingrown, and conservative, whereas Republican sections were dynamic, expanding, and mobile. The Congregational Church was still the established church in Massachusetts, Connecticut, and New Hampshire, and its intimate links to the Federalists sent Baptists, Methodists, and other religious outgroups flocking to the Jeffersonian party, with its constant cry of separation of church and state. A rising working-class consciousness in the four largest commercial centers—New York, Boston, Philadelphia, and Baltimore—had pushed those cities strongly into the Republican column by 1800. Scotch-Irish Presbyterians, so strong in New York and Pennsylvania, loudly attacked Federalists as pro-English. The Germans of Pennsylvania, recognizing the hostility of the Federalists to minority groups that were not English in descent and culture, began swinging heavily toward the Republicans. Everywhere the proportion of eligible voters going to the polls mounted rapidly, and this massive politicization of the mass of American white males coincided with Republican victories.

The Federalists had held national power for a dozen years because in general the Middle Atlantic states had aligned themselves with New England. When instead they swung Republican and lined up with an increasingly unified Republican South, the shape of the next sixty years in American public life was settled. With brief intermissions, an alliance between the Middle Atlantic states and the South, in which Southerners took the leading role, was largely to govern the nation. The election of 1800—thereafter called the "Revolution of 1800"—that carried Thomas Jefferson to the White House and gave the Republicans a majority of three to two in the House of Representatives initiated a tradition in which men from the slaveholding states held the presidency for fifty years, save for the single terms of John Quincy Adams (1825–29) and Martin Van Buren (1837–41).

Mass Political Parties: The American Innovation

We must stop for a moment and take note of what had happened, by 1800, in the new American republic, because it was an event of world importance. For the first time anywhere in human affairs, *mass political parties* had appeared. The Federalists and the Jeffersonian Republicans were nationwide popular organizations entirely without precedent in any other nation. While elsewhere in the world authority was still held by tiny aristocratic circles, or, as in Britain, in somewhat larger ones, in the United States a dramatic new era had opened. In rudimentary but nonetheless effective form, the two American national parties mobilized hundreds of thousands of voters behind agreed-upon candidates for office, and they did so election after election.

Thus, the promise of the American republic was being in fact realized: Through the instrument of this new creation, the mass political party, ordinary people had become in practice, and not just in theory, the sovereign power. It was their decision, given voice through an organized party, that chose who would govern. When the Jeffersonian Republicans won in 1800, they called their victory a "revolution" because for the first time in world history a ruling party had been removed from power *by use of the ballot box alone*.

The "first party system," as political historians call the Federalist-Jeffersonian Republican rivalry which sprang into being in the 1790s, was not a highly organized operation. It was, after all, but the first stage of a long learning process in mass politics that the American people had now begun. In fact, in these years people did not realize they were building the world's first mass two-party system. "Parties" were actually condemned as harmful and disruptive. The whole idea was that everyone should band together in unity and cooperation behind the banner of *one* party so the country would not be divided. The only problem with that ancient concept was that in an open and free society it did not work. People differed, strongly and fundamentally, about the kind of America they wanted to build, and they persisted in drawing apart from one another and gathering behind opposing banners. Eventually, as we will see, the notion formed that two opposing parties, offering alternative visions to the people of what America should be as well as opposing candidates

pledged to those visions, was an essential part of the democratic system of government.

In any event, from Thomas Jefferson's time a two-party national rivalry, with brief periodic eruptions of third parties, would be the essential form within which Americans would conduct their public business. A "dialogue of the parties" has gone on continuously, a nonstop argument before the people at large in which each party has offered contrasting ideas as to what the national agenda should be, and how best to realize American values.

We cannot say, of course, that this has been an easy or a comfortable and fully satisfying situation. In the best of circumstances mass politics (like their predecessor, aristocratic politics) are messy, confusing, frustrating, and discouraging. Americans have understandably regarded the whole process with impatient distrust, and indeed in some important sense as a great failure. Nonetheless, mass party politics—the "American system," as Europeans called it in the nineteenth century—have been in reality one of America's few genuinely distinctive contributions to the world. Certainly, they are at the very center of American culture, forming its most characteristic and (to those from abroad) most striking feature, aside from America's affluence. As foreign observers noted again and again, in the nineteenth century American life became peculiarly *politicized*. From top to bottom, party politics became its passion, its all-absorbing focus of attention, rivaled only by the equally powerful lure of making money and getting ahead in life.

We will observe a regular series of "party systems," each of them lasting from twenty to forty years, or about long enough for one generation of Americans to come into active national leadership and then be succeeded by a later one. The first party system would persist until it collapsed in the 1820s. After a brief period of confusion, the "second party system" would take shape in the 1830s under President Andrew Jackson, with his followers the "Democrats" faced off against their enemies, the "Whigs." In the 1850s, a lurid and crisis-streaked decade, the second party system itself would fall to pieces, to be succeeded by another one, and the United States would stumble toward national disunion and civil war.

Before that wild and disordered time, however, the United States of America would go through a half-century of explosive internal development and vast outward expansion. To that extraordinary period, we next turn our attention.

BIBLIOGRAPHY

Books especially valuable to me in thinking about and writing this chapter: I've relied much on Drew R. McCoy's absorbing new work, *The Elusive Republic: Political Economy in Jeffersonian America* (1980); Lance Banning's *The Jeffersonian Persuasion: Evolution of a Party Ideology* (1978) is a fine analysis, thoughtful and good reading; Richard Buel, Jr., *Securing the Revolution: Ideology in American Politics, 1789–1815* (1972), offers another skillful exploration of republicanism in this era; John C. Miller's *Alexander Hamilton and the Growth of the New Nation* (1964) is keen, thorough, and beautifully written; and Rudolph M. Bell, *Party and Faction in American Politics: The House of Representatives 1789–1801* (1973), is a valuable quantitative study of bloc voting. On foreign policy, I've relied heavily on two skillful books: Jerald A. Combs's *The Jay Treaty: Political Battleground of the Founding Fathers* (1970), and Alexander De Conde's *The Quasi-War: The Politics and Diplomacy of the Undeclared War with France, 1797–1801* (1966). For an absorbing exploration of how historians have interpreted American foreign policy, see Combs's *American Diplomatic History: Two Centuries of Changing Interpretations* (1983).

John C. Miller's *The Federalist Era, 1789–1801* (1960) is a basic book on the period. Alfred F. Young's *The Democratic Republicans of New York: The Origins, 1763–1797* (1967) is an essential study, as are Harry Marlin Tinkcom, *The Republicans and Federalists in Pennsylvania 1790–1801: A Study in National Stimulus and Local Response* (1950); Lisle A. Rose, *Prologue to Democracy: The Federalists in the South, 1789–1800* (1968); and Paul Goodman, *The Democratic-Republicans of Massachusetts: Politics in a Young Republic* (1964).

Richard Hofstadter's *The Idea of a Party System: The Rise of Legitimate Opposition in the United States, 1780–1840* (1969) is the basic work on this subject. Daniel Sisson, *The American Revolution of 1800* (1974), is good reading; Gerald Stourzh, *Alexander Hamilton and the Idea of Republican Government* (1970), is an absorbing study; and Noble E. Cunningham, Jr., *The Jeffersonian Republicans: The Formation of Party Organization, 1789–1801* (1957), is a major work, basic to our understanding of the first party system. On Massachusetts' attitudes toward the South and toward federalism, see James Banner's fascinating *To the Hartford Convention: The Federalists and the Origins of Party Politics in Massachusetts, 1789–1815* (1970). Linda K. Kerber brilliantly dissects the Federalist mind in her *Federalists in Dissent: Imagery and Ideology in Jeffersonian America* (1970). Martin J. Dauer, *The Adams Federalists* (1968), is important. See also Chapter 4 in Robert Kelley, *The Cultural Pattern in American Politics: The First Century* (1979).

Stephen G. Kurtz's *The Presidency of John Adams: The Collapse of Federalism, 1795–1800* (1957) emphasizes the importance of President Adams's decision for peace during the quasi-war with France. Page Smith's *John Adams*, two vols. (1962), contains rich material from Adams's personal papers, and Zoltan Haraszti's *John Adams and the Prophets of Progress* (1952) explores his political philosophy.

James Morton Smith's *Freedom's Fetters: The Alien and Sedition Laws and American Civil Liberties* (1956); John C. Miller's *Crisis in Freedom: The Alien and Sedition Acts* (1951); and Leonard W. Levy's *Legacy of Suppression: Freedom of Speech and Press in Early American History* (1960) provide a solid understanding of these issues.

9

The Age of Jefferson: Expansion and War

TIME LINE

TECUMSEH

He was "one of those uncommon geniuses," ran the American general's report to Washington, D.C., "which spring up occasionally to produce revolutions and overturn the established order of things. If it were not for the vicinity of the United States, he would perhaps be the founder of an Empire that would rival in glory that of Mexico or Peru." The *Indiana Centinel*, looking back upon the brilliant Tecumseh in 1820, seven years after his death, remarked that "his greatness was his own, unassisted by science or the aids of education. As a statesman, a warrior and a patriot, take him all in all, we shall not look upon his like again."

Tecumseh was a Shawnee chief who was widely known for his merciful treatment of prisoners, rare in Indian warfare. He also had the rare gift of being able to think of the Indian people as a whole rather than just his own tribe. We are all one people, he insisted; we will survive if we band together in one compact group against the white man. In the Ohio River basin in the first decade of the 1800s, he built a wide following around his insistence that the land belonged to all the Indians in common, not to individual tribes, and that therefore no tribe had the right to sell any of it to the United States—as many chiefs,

benumbed by drink and corrupted by gifts, had been doing.

Tecumseh drew heavily upon a sweeping religious movement among the Ohio Valley Indians begun by his brother Tenskwatawa, called the Prophet. If the Indian peoples forsook the white man's alcohol and his culture and returned to their ancient ways of living, Tenskwatawa said, the Master of Life had promised that he would make the white man disappear. Vastly appealing to the desperate, harassed Indians of the valley, the Prophet's religion had an electrifying effect. Tecumseh himself went from village to village, trying to persuade the Indians to turn away from the drunkenness that was destroying them and return to the vigorous manhood of their past.

Angered in 1809 by the Treaty of Fort Wayne, in which bribed chiefs gave up 3 million acres of Indiana land to white settlement, Tecumseh thrust forward to become the preeminent leader of mounting Indian resistance to white encroachment. Fired by his vision of a powerful Indian confederacy, Tecumseh, a dramatically compelling orator, traveled enormous distances, visiting one Indian community after another to plead for unity in action. He pointed to the example of the United States itself, which had surmounted weakness in division by joining together in federated strength. The Indians, he insisted, must fight as a unified people.

In 1810 he had a dramatic confrontation with Governor William Henry Harrison of Indiana Territory in a great gathering of white soldiers and Indian warriors. Two strong and determined men bent upon wholly contradictory courses of action, they enraged one another and could come to no agreement. War was inevitable: It began in 1811 at Tippecanoe, and flowed on into the War of 1812. Before the conflict was over, the great Tecumseh was dead. His body was never recovered, but his spirit had caught the admiration of his time, remaining in the memories of white and red alike for generations thereafter.

Jefferson's Political Outlook

On March 4, 1801, Thomas Jefferson left his boardinghouse in Washington, D.C., and in the company of two friends walked quietly to the steps of the Capitol, where he took the oath of office as president of the United States. In the simplicity of this act, Jefferson expressed his belief that government should be as quiet, unassuming, and invisible as possible. Pursuing simplicity further, he avoided the usual forms of aristocratic dress, such as short trousers, hose, ruffs, and wigs. Instead, he moved about Washington in old clothes, a fact that angered the upper classes. His appearance, a British diplomat observed contemptuously, was "very much like that of a tall, large-boned farmer." As president, Jefferson opened what may be called the Age of Jefferson, since this extraordinary man dominated the tone and thought of the years from 1800 to the mid-1820s either directly, as president, or through his two close followers, James Madison and James Monroe. He is, of course, the founder of what is called Jeffersonianism, one of America's two core political faiths.

Jefferson had begun his political career as a man who distrusted the British, and he became one who detested them as well. Throughout his career he fought the importation into the new American nation of anything that smacked of England. He attacked Alexander Hamilton bitterly for trying to remake America in the British image—to Jefferson an image monarchical, corrupt, plutocratic, industrial, and wretchedly urban, implying a debasement of the masses and a slavish relationship among social classes.

Devoted to the philosophical skepticism and rationalism of the Enlightenment, he disliked churches and orthodox religions. Jefferson had led the struggle in Virginia after the Revolution to break the links between the state and the Anglican (Episcopal) Church. People should be free, he said, to believe whatever they wished, as long as they left others to themselves.

He believed in the wisdom of the common people, though by "the people" he meant farmers and independent craftsmen, not factory workers, who, he felt, lacked independence, were too much dominated by their employers (remember, the secret ballot was a century away). Since "the people" were uncorrupted by power, he thought ordinary individuals much better judges of what should be done than the self-seeking, aristocratic elites that ran the governments of the world. He also believed that dishonest, scheming men are always among us, contriving to get into positions of power and work with the elite to exploit the masses. In short, Jefferson believed there is no natural harmony of interests among the social classes. At all times a struggle goes on between the common people and the aristocracy, for the wealthy strive continually to take advantage of their favored position. (*Note:* The deep paradox in Jefferson's generous ideas about "the people" did not extend to blacks and slavery. Though he deplored the institution he kept slaves all his days, and he regarded them as inherently inferior.)

Jefferson's Economics

Jefferson felt that Hamilton's program would corrupt the American people by making them money-mad. It would draw them away from honest endeavor into speculative and socially destructive activities. During the difficult times of 1798, Jefferson insisted that the depression from which the nation was then suffering arose chiefly from the floods of paper money that were issued. The center of all the nation's difficulties, Jefferson and his followers were convinced, lay in Hamilton's Bank of the United States, which to them was the focus of a web of speculators and monarchists.

Likewise, Jefferson condemned protective tariffs. He agreed with the Scottish economist Adam Smith who, in his famous book *The Wealth of Nations* (1776), had attacked tariffs as corrupt and wasteful. Businessmen, Smith said, energized the economy, creating wealth and jobs, but their greed for profit continually led them into activities that worked against the public interest. Businessmen were always seeking to monopolize and to charge the public the highest possible price while paying the lowest possible wages. Furthermore, they continually asked the government for favors, the granting of which resulted in discrimination against everyone else.

The only answer, Smith believed, was to establish completely open competition. No one should get any help from the government. Open competition would prevent the emergence of monopolies, guarantee low prices, and ensure abundant production. In the world's economy, this meant no protective tariffs. Everyone should be able to buy from the cheapest supplier, whether at home or abroad. The more the world's economy was based on free and open trading, the richer everyone would be, for each nation would produce what it was best suited to produce. An international division of labor would result; economic jealousies would disappear; peace and order, as well as prosperity, would come about.

As Jefferson put it, America should "throw open the doors of commerce, and . . . knock off all its shackles, giving perfect freedom to all persons for the vent of whatever they may choose to bring into our ports, and asking the same in theirs." This would permit America to remain an agricultural country—an admirable thing, Jefferson felt, because farmers were good and moral men. Businessmen, industrialists, and financiers, on the other hand, tended to be corrupt. Jefferson was fond of saying that America's workshops should remain in Europe, for industries would only create cities crowded with ignorant, riotous mobs. He opposed any program, therefore, that would make America an urban, industrial, and bank-dominated nation.

> *A certain serenity of spirit set Jefferson and [James] Madison apart from the rest of the founding fathers. . . . They were ambitious, but they were never driven by the intense, gnawing anxieties that dominated a man like Hamilton. Hamilton relished conflict; Jefferson and Madison hated it. . . . Hamilton was dashing and arrogant; Jefferson and Madison were calm and deferential. Hamilton was a dandy; Jefferson was careless of personal appearance, and Madison wore little but black. Hamilton strutted, Madison stooped, and Jefferson shambled. . . . [For] them the purpose of government was not national glory, but the protection of individuals in the pursuit of legitimate private interests. Jefferson and Madison thought the United States should seek not wealth but simplicity, not power but liberty, not national glory but domestic tranquility, not heroism but happiness. Hamilton's search for glory subordinated domestic to foreign policy. At home he sought merely to build a power base for the ultimate source of national greatness—foreign affairs. The pursuit of national happiness undertaken by Jefferson and Madison reversed these priorities. (Jerald A. Combs, The Jay Treaty: Political Battleground of the Founding Fathers [1970])*

Jefferson's Localism

Jefferson was intimately tied to his state. He always spoke of Virginia as "my country," and his heart was firmly lodged in his hilltop Virginia estate, Monticello, where he built his remarkable mansion and lived for forty years. In this he was close to the inner heart of American life, for most Americans thought primarily of the region in which they spent

America's Renaissance man, Jefferson was a brilliant political philosopher, architect, naturalist, agriculturalist, and political leader. He dreamed of a western "empire for liberty" for America and secured the Louisiana Purchase.

their lives, and not of the whole nation. Hamilton spoke for people whose horizons were national and who had dreams of a national economy directed by themselves from a central, urban location. Jefferson spoke instead for those whose horizons were still essentially local, whose affections were firmly rooted in the village, hillside, and surrounding countryside. Distrust of Washington came naturally to a people who had long been trained in distrust of London.

Jefferson's localism derived also from his belief that the government must be as close as possible to the people, so they might more easily watch over it. Small societies, he wrote, were the most moral ones. For this reason, as much government as possible should take place in the local community. The national government should be limited almost solely to foreign affairs. As far as their internal problems were concerned, the various states should largely govern themselves, as they did before 1763.

Jefferson as President

Accordingly, Jefferson began his presidency by drastically reducing all spending. A number of foreign legations were closed, the court system was severely cut back so that it consisted essentially of just the Supreme Court, and the military system was heavily curtailed. "Peace," he said, "is our passion." At the same time, he ended all internal taxation, thus terminating excise taxes, such as those on whiskey. The government, Jefferson contended, should get all its money (aside from land sales) from import levies, for it was primarily the upper classes who bought items from abroad.

Though he would have liked to sweep away Hamilton's financial system, the charter of the Bank of the United States did not expire until 1811. But the national debt, which Hamilton praised as a means to hold the wealthy to the government—for they owned the bonds—could be eliminated. Jefferson worked out a plan for paying it off within a relatively few years.

Jefferson and the Trans-Mississippi West

Jefferson had always been the most western-minded of America's leaders. As he described it, America's task was to create an "empire for liberty," a nation huge enough in size and power to protect itself and preserve the ideal of republican self-government. In the 1780s, long before he became president, he was thinking of settlement on the Pacific Coast, of building a Panama canal, and of creating a free United States of North *and* South America. Everything depended on the Far West being held by weak Spain, rather than by strong Britain or France, until the new United States was capable of taking it over "piece by piece."

This would not be a militaristic expansion, he believed, but an inevitable outward spilling of the burgeoning American population. Common people moving westward to open new land would establish the empire for liberty. In the pursuit of his dream, two years after he became president Jefferson sent his personal secretary, Meriwether Lewis, and William Clark on their famous expedition across the continent, even though Spain ruled the region at the

time the journey was planned. In the years 1805–1807 Lieutenant Zebulon M. Pike explored the sources of the Mississippi River and then the territory that is now Colorado (where stands the peak named for him) and New Mexico.

The Louisiana Purchase

Before Lewis and Clark reached St. Louis to ascend the Missouri, Napoleon Bonaparte had decided to rebuild the French empire in the New World. He talked the Spanish into ceding back to France the great province of Louisiana, given to them by the French in 1763. In May 1801 news of the French-Spanish agreement reached Jefferson informally, and he promptly warned the French minister of grave consequences if the French actually took over Louisiana and New Orleans. Jefferson asked Robert R. Livingston, then in Paris, to try to persuade the French to sell New Orleans and West Florida to the United States so that the Mississippi and the other rivers draining into the Gulf of Mexico from American territory would be wholly in American hands. For two years Livingston fruitlessly pressed the American case while American hostility toward France mounted.

The situation became explosive when, in October 1802, the Spanish official still administering New Orleans—the French had not yet arrived to take over—suspended the American right of deposit on the docks of New Orleans, an action immediately, if erroneously, blamed on Napoleon. A huge trade was already floating down the Mississippi. One-third of the vessels clearing New Orleans were American ships. Angry outcries arose in the western settlements. Jefferson, alarmed, secured congressional authority to call on the states for 80,000 militiamen, as well as an appropriation of $2 million to aid his negotiations with France.

Events then moved swiftly. The right of deposit was restored in New Orleans, and Napoleon decided to drop the enterprise of taking over Louisiana. For reasons to this day not fully explained, he decided to sell Louisiana to the United States rather than return it to Spain. On April 11, 1803, he informed his finance minister of this intention. The bargain was struck. The United States would pay some $15 million to France and would receive New Orleans in return *and* the great province of Louisiana, which ran vaguely off to the Rockies (themselves only dimly

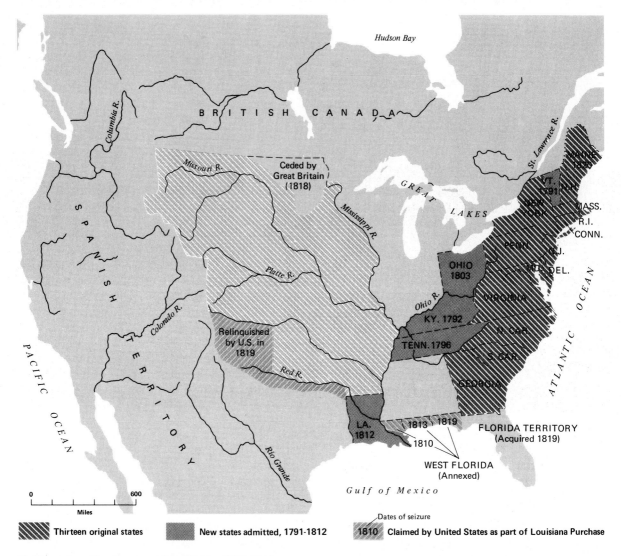

The Louisiana Purchase and New States, 1791–1812

known), encompassing the western half of the Mississippi Valley.

The Federalists might criticize, but the Louisiana Purchase was wildly popular in the country. For this if for no other reason, in the election of 1804 Jefferson received almost all the electoral votes, only 14 out of 176 going to the Federalist candidate, Charles Cotesworth Pinckney. The purchase was a dazzling stroke, a fantastic event. The area of the country was increased almost one and a half times. Over 800 million acres of land was purchased at a cost of approximately 1.8 cents an acre. The United States, having become one of the largest nations on earth, now found itself confronted with a great na-

tional treasure that each returning traveler described in ever more glowing terms. The American adventure in the Far West had begun.

The Creation of the First Trans-Mississippi State: Louisiana

The westward movement of the American frontier of settlement into the enormous trans-Mississippi West could now begin. Most of the vast Louisiana Purchase, however, was still Indian country and un-

A portrait of Meriwether Lewis painted on his return from one of the most successful and well-documented explorations in history. His account of this expedition which began in the spring of 1804 and lasted until September of 1806, remains one of the few reliable sources of information on Indian dress, customs and attitudes at the beginning of the century.

of Louisiana. Almost half a century later, Louisiana was ceded to the Spanish, at the end of the French and Indian War (1763), when the French empire on the North American continent was extinguished. (The French, as we have seen, took it back for a brief period before handing it over to the Americans in 1804.) Spanish rule did little, however, to dissipate the predominantly French culture and society that still reigned strongly in New Orleans. Indeed, the French (or "Creole") tone of life in and around New Orleans would now intensify, for among the 14,000 settlers who rushed into this rapidly developing region within five years after the Louisiana Purchase, many were French refugees from the war-ravaged West Indies.

President Jefferson moved promptly to provide an American government, organizing the southern part of the Louisiana Purchase to the 33rd parallel, the present northern boundary of the state of Louisiana, as the Territory of Orleans. (Northward, the rest of the Louisiana Purchase was organized as the Territory of Missouri, with the small fur-trading community of St. Louis, founded by the French in 1764, as its capital.) By 1810, when the census revealed that Orleans Territory held a population of 75,000, Congress authorized formation of a new state, to be called Louisiana. It was admitted to the Union as the first state west of the Mississippi in April 1812. New Englanders protested, for Louisiana was a slave state. However, slavery had been legal in the whole of the Louisiana Purchase under the Spanish and the French, so that in actual fact *all* of the west bank of the Mississippi River, clear to the border with British North America, was already open to slavery.

The Character of Louisiana

Louisiana would always be a special place in the United States. Catholic, French-speaking, cosmopolitan, Louisiana's people diverged sharply in their beliefs and in their ways of living from the overwhelmingly provincial, Protestant, and British-descended people of the rest of the South. In this connection, we must remember that the French and the English had been fighting each other, in the Old World, for centuries, and these animosities toward English-speaking people were still deep in the minds of the Louisiana French, who looked to Paris in admiration and cultural loyalty and to Washington, D.C., in distaste. They were lastingly resentful at the abrupt

safe for settlers. The southernmost part of the Louisiana Purchase, on the other hand, was a different scene altogether, for in and around the port city of New Orleans lived tens of thousands of predominantly French people, as well as others of Spanish background. Many of the French were the famous Acadian refugees, called Cajuns, who in the 1750s had been driven by the British out of Nova Scotia, in present-day eastern Canada.

New Orleans was already an old city, by North American standards, for the French had founded it in 1718 to be the base from which they would seek to develop their vast northward-stretching colony

American takeover, which took place entirely without their having any say in the matter. Fearing the intrusion and domination of English-speaking frontier Americans, they were able, in the writing of the state's constitution, to shape voting districts so that the French remained dominant in the state legislature, a position rarely achieved by a non-British people in American public life.

New Orleans, the entrepôt to the vast continental interior, would become by far the largest city in the pre–Civil War South, being borne to almost fabulous heights by the cotton trade of the Southern states and the wheat of the Middle West. Carrying the lurid reputation of French-style glamorous and festive living, it would be a rare center of elegance—and wickedness—within the predominantly Puritan, Protestant-pious, American nation. Louisiana would also be the only state in the Union where the Roman Law (technically termed the "civil law"), in its modernized form of the Napoleonic Code, would be, and remains, the basic legal system.

Historian Ray Allen Billington has captured the ambience of New Orleans, describing it as a place where

> *devout Catholics paid homage [to their faith] in imposing cathedrals which towered above iron-balconied homes . . . merchants in Parisian styles rubbed elbows with leather-clad traders, and riotous festivals enlivened existence in a way unknown to inhibited Americans. . . . By 1812 cleared fields [occupied by cotton and sugar plantations] extended along the Mississippi to the northern boundary. . . . Eight years later 153,000 people lived in the state, which was thoroughly settled except for a few northern and western areas.*

Crisis Abroad

But in the same year that Jefferson purchased Louisiana and carried his administration to a peak of national praise and affection, events began across the Atlantic that were to send him back to Monticello at the end of his second administration a shattered, grieving ex-president. Napoleon and Britain began fighting again, initiating a grim and bloody struggle that was to last, with one brief intermission, until 1815, when Napoleon was finally brought to his knees and his continental empire shattered. Napoleon made himself emperor of France in 1804, and before long he had almost all of Europe in his hands. Even Russia had come to terms; only Britain held out against him. He had now become the devil incarnate to the British people, a dictator bent on destroying the independence and liberty of every people on earth. Even Thomas Jefferson and the Francophiles in America watched Napoleon's rise to power with alarm.

By 1805 the war had settled into a long stalemate, and the British and French pursued it by indirect devices rarely used before. Both sought to starve the other into submission by cutting off supplies from the outside. Both also began eagerly capturing American vessels and commandeering their cargoes, the French largely through the use of privateers. Hundreds of American vessels were halted and taken off to prize courts.

Because the British dominated the seas, their activities were more serious. Furthermore, they had already begun halting American vessels and impressing into their navy seamen who, they claimed, were British in nationality. As it was not generally accepted that a man could renounce his loyalty to one country and become a citizen of another, pleas of American naturalization were brushed aside. By 1812 almost 10,000 American seamen had been impressed by the British.

The Search for an Alternative to War

The history of the United States from 1807 to 1812 is the story of one long search for ways to solve these problems without resorting to force. Thomas Jefferson wanted peace. This did not mean he was a pacifist. Almost as soon as he entered the White House he had sent a naval force to put down the Barbary pirates of the North African coast. He was determined to halt the paying of American tribute and to force the North African deys and pashas to respect the American flag. Several years of naval jousting had culminated in 1805 in the landing of marines in Tripoli and the securing of a formal treaty of amity and commerce.

In his mind, America's ships and goods were so vital to Britain and France that the combatants would come to terms rather than be permanently denied their use. In 1806 the Non-Importation Act (effective 1807) tried vainly to force the British to terms by denying them the right to sell British goods in the United States. This was followed by the Embargo Act of late 1807, which boldly halted trade with all the world. Months of economic chaos followed in the United States, but there were no corresponding diplomatic benefits. With the nation on the verge of disaster, Jefferson had to confess failure. Just before he left the presidency in March 1809, he signed an act repealing the embargo. Variations on the embargo, under Jefferson's successor, were similarly unsuccessful. Meanwhile, America's export trade, which had been $130 million in 1807, fell to $45 million in 1811, dropped to $25 million in 1813, and reached rock bottom at $7 million in 1814.

The British remained adamant. They could not understand the American side of the question at all. The fight against Napoleon was so overwhelmingly important for the liberty of all nations that the rights of neutrals would simply have to be a casualty of war. Furthermore, the British disastrously underestimated American anger. They simply could not believe that the United States could be driven to war.

The Republic in Peril

This was, however, the case. No nation can endlessly bear humiliation, least of all a young nation engaged in carrying out a precarious experiment in new forms of government.

Who could say that the Republic would survive? Impressment and violation of neutral rights, so arrogantly carried out year after year, seemed to demonstrate that the Republic could be toyed with by the powerful monarchies. If the new American nation could not make any forceful effort to protect its rights, it would never survive once Napoleon was gone. The great monarchies, convinced that America was spineless, would pick the country apart as soon as they had finished their struggles in Europe.

A New Generation Seizes Leadership

And then, for the first time since America had become a nation, a deep tidal change swept in to transform the country's political culture: A new generation of young leaders arrived on the scene, filled with a sense

This early view of the U.S. Capitol at Washington clearly shows its rural character; it was a city of "magnificent distances."

of great and imperative things that needed to be done and burning to achieve them. We will see this *generational revolution* occurring, periodically, throughout the rest of our story as the opening act of periods of historic change, whether they be the Civil War, the Progressive Era, or the New Deal. When these generational shifts occur, the entire mood of the country shifts. Those currently running the country had themselves once been young and zealous, but long years in office tends to make people skeptical and cautious, certainly old and gray. In their place, the new young leaders bring in fresh energy, a reborn sense of possibilities, and soaring ideals. Being young, they tend to be militant, combative, ready to take on enemies, and eager for a struggle of some kind, whether it be in the service of a compelling cause of domestic reform or in a patriotic uprising against a powerful external (or even internal) adversary.

It was this recurring tide in American politics that began to rise and announce itself in the congressional elections of 1810, which took place while an enormous anger against Great Britain was surging in the South and West. Now, what the historian Merrill D. Peterson in his absorbing work *The Great Triumvirate: Webster, Clay, and Calhoun* (1987) calls "the second generation of American statesmanship" started to arrive on the scene. This new corps of young men had had no part in the founding of the Republic, that glory had been denied to them, and now they were driven by one supreme goal: to preserve the Republic in a new time of danger, and thereby win historic rank with their towering predecessors, the sainted Founding Fathers.

The Mood of the New Generation

Seventy of these first-term congressmen sat in the Capitol in Washington. They were called "war hawks" because they seemed to be bursting for a fight with the British. Their leader was a charismatic Kentuckian, Henry Clay, a man only thirty-four years old and already prominent for his fiery patriotism and his compelling oratory. Much like another young man 150 years later, John F. Kennedy of Massachusetts, who in 1960 led a similar rising of impatient young people against older ones, Clay was contemptuous of what seemed to him the over-cautious leadership and the timid, pacifist policies of the Virginia presidents. Quickly elected Speaker of the House,

he got Congress promptly organized for war, crying out: "What are we to gain by war? What are we not to lose by peace? Commerce, character, [and] a nation's best treasure, honor!"

The Powerful Role of Honor

Honor, or having a good name, being esteemed in the eyes of the community (or the world) at large, being held in respect, having a reputation as a person of courage and of value: All over the world, for most people this desperately important concern has always been at the center of life. Any slight against a person's honor, certainly one long continued, has traditionally been a source of great anguish and pain that finally demands redress. Protecting one's standing as an honorable person has been one of the deepest of human impulses, far down in the bone and sinew of existence. People will *die* for honor—which puts it in a very special category in human history.

As far back in the past as we can see, this powerful impulse has been at work. No other force has driven people more swiftly and angrily to violence, to fighting and dueling and interfamily feuding and to war itself, than the wild, often ungovernable, imperious passion of protecting one's *honor*, or the honor of one's family, ethnic group, or nation. The history of tribalism, as in the almost constant intertribal fighting of the Native American peoples before the Europeans arrived, or those of the Scottish highland clans and of the ancient Greeks, is filled with warfare over this and often no other cause.

The surprising fact is that we have only recently begun to rediscover how powerful this sentiment has been in human history, how central a place we must give to honor if we are with any real insight to explain violence and war. When the British and the Americans began fighting in 1812, or the Germans and the Western Allies in 1914, or late-twentieth-century street gangs in Los Angeles: All of these occasions see the same force at work. Only in 1982 did the historian Bertram Wyatt-Brown, in his remarkable work *Southern Honor: Ethics & Behavior in the Old South*, first awaken us once more to the centrality of this ancient force in human culture, which he believes explains more than anything else why the South went to war against the North in 1861.

The Cry for War, and War Begins

In the Congress that convened in November 1811, the rage for redeemed honor against Britain raised a storm of angry voices in the Capitol's corridors and produced cascades of heated oratory. One of the young war hawks, John C. Calhoun of South Carolina, whom Clay had appointed to the crucial post of chair of the House's Committee on Foreign Relations, cried out that America must turn away from peaceful diplomacy. It had only brought the Republic, he said, humiliation and contempt—that is, dishonor. "We have said, we will change," Calhoun proclaimed, "[and] we will defend ourselves by force."

When President James Madison finally asked Congress on June 1, 1812, to declare war on Great Britain, many in that body responded enthusiastically. By going to war, Calhoun said, the present-day "sons of America [would] prove . . . to the World that we have not only inherited that liberty which our Fathers gave us, but also the will and power to maintain it." Fighting Britain would be in the war hawks' eyes, then, no less than a Second War for American Independence. On June 18, 1812, six days after Madison had asked for it, Congress voted a declaration of war.

But not unanimously. Congress had had to struggle through bitter debate to reach this conclusion, for the pro-British Federalists, who came primarily from New England, fervently opposed war with Britain, casting their votes unanimously against it. Then, to make matters worse, when the war actually began, disaster followed disaster. At every level the war was run badly. Madison was not a fighting president. He lacked the political skill to bring the nation along behind him, and he hesitated to pressure Congress, for he had an unswerving faith in separation of powers.

Madison had, in truth, enormous tasks. He had to raise huge amounts of money, but was faced with a Republican Congress that hated taxation. At the same time, the British navy had so reduced American overseas trade that import duties, the principal source of the government's income, had shrunk to the disappearing point. By the fall of 1814, after two years of war, the national government was practically in a state of collapse. So low was public confidence that bond issues had to be sold at half their face value. The Bank of the United States had been allowed to expire by its Republican enemies in 1811, so that when war came the government had no national machinery of finance available. It could not even transfer its funds from one state to another without great difficulty, for it had to rely on state banks. Those parts of the country with the most money, notably New England, were the ones where opposition to the war was the strongest. The Federalists in Massachusetts sought to end the war by withholding financial and other support.

By the time the war was but a few months old, American troops had been swept from Detroit, Fort Dearborn (Chicago), and Mackinac in a series of engagements notable for the stupidity and cowardice of American leadership and brilliance and courage on the British and Canadian side. The whole Northwest was thrown open to invasion and Indian attack, and many settlers fled from their homes. Battles along the Niagara frontier were directed just as poorly by the Americans, as they were elsewhere along the New York–Canadian border.

The navy was far more experienced and skillful than the army, and early in the war the small force of American vessels won some stunning victories. These came as a relief to the American people, who were shocked at the disasters on the frontier. The British navy was enormous and resilient, though, and by early 1814 it was back in control. The blockade of the American coast (New England was spared at first, since so many there opposed the war) was complete, and the American navy was reduced to a minor role. Most of its vessels eventually were tied up in blockaded ports. Clouds of American privateers sallied forth to lay waste in the British merchant marine, especially in the seas around the British Isles, but British losses were minor compared with the catastrophe that struck American trade.

Tecumseh: The Greatest Indian Leader

Meanwhile, the Shawnee chief Tecumseh had risen in the West. After his spectacular confrontations with Benjamin Harrison in 1810, he had journeyed far and wide, seeking to persuade the formerly warring Indian tribes, who had fought for centuries, to forsake their ancient animosities and unify against the white man. He had to work against strong resistance, for mutual hatreds were often too intense to override. However, by 1811 Tecumseh had won an enthusiastic following among many Indians in the northwestern tribes, especially among the younger braves.

General William Henry Harrison, governor of the new Indiana Territory (established in 1809), in November 1811 led an attack on Prophet's Town, Tenskwatawa's and Tecumseh's headquarters on Tippecanoe Creek in northern Indiana, while Tecumseh was exhorting tribes in the South. Harrison won a doubtful victory, which was trumpeted abroad as a smashing triumph for the whites.

Tecumseh renounced American sovereignty, declared himself loyal to the British, and took a large band of Indians with him to join the British at Fort Malden, just across the river in Canada from Detroit. From this location he played a major role in inflicting the defeats on the Americans in 1812 that drove them out of the Northwest, opening it all to the Indians and the British.

American Resurgence: 1813

Determined to repossess the Northwest and rid it of the Indian menace led by Tecumseh, Madison's government bent its energies to this task in 1813. By the fall of that year, Oliver Hazard Perry's naval victory on Lake Erie had enabled the Americans to take control of the lake from the British and thereby put British outposts in the Detroit region in danger. The British army decided to retreat from Detroit, despite Tecumseh's protests. Caught at the Thames River (in what is now western Ontario) by a fresh force of 3,000 American troops under Harrison, the British force was overwhelmed by a cavalry charge. In the battle Tecumseh raged and bellowed, his great voice echoing through the forest as he spurred on his warriors. Hit several times, he pressed on. But then he was killed, the Indians fled in confusion, and their fight against the Americans collapsed. For years it was rumored that Tecumseh was still alive, ready to come out and lead his people, but in fact no white person ever saw him again. The back of Indian resistance was broken; Tecumseh's dream was lost; the old Northwest was secured for American settlement; and the most extraordinary Indian leader in American history had died.

The British Offensive

In early 1814 Napoleon was defeated. The British could now turn their energies wholly to their war with the United States. Thousands of veteran British troops were sent to Canada and other North American locations. The British people looked forward with anticipation to roundly chastising the Americans for "knifing them in the back" when they were engaged in a desperate war with the great tyrant.

In June 1814 Sir George Prevost, the governor general of Canada, was instructed to invade the United States with the most formidable army ever to campaign on American soil to that time. Some 15,000 men were in his force, and only 4,000 American defenders waited for him at Plattsburg, New York, on Lake Champlain. But British hopes were soon dashed. A small American fleet was handled so skillfully that, in the battle of Plattsburg Bay, the entire naval force the British had put on the lake to support their operation was either blown out of the water or captured. The demoralized Prevost, who was already drawn up before the American lines at Plattsburg, made a few feints, but then lost the nerve to drive his stroke home. Without naval support he had few hopes of victory in any case, since the Americans could slash his supply columns and constantly come in on his rear. He withdrew to Canada, taking back to Montreal the magnificent army that had left in such high spirits, meeting there only scorn and abuse. The northern invasion had failed.

The Burning of Washington, D.C.

The Chesapeake Bay had known catastrophe in 1813. A British fleet had entered the bay and ranged far and wide, causing much disaster. In August 1814 another British naval force arrived. Troops landed on the Maryland shore and marched to Bladensburg, where they defeated an American force hastily scraped together to stop them. This left the road wide open to Washington, D.C. The Americans had earlier burned York (Toronto), the capital of Upper Canada (now the province of Ontario), and the British had a score to settle. While Madison and his govenment fled in all directions, they marched on the capital and systematically burned the government buildings. Then they turned north to Baltimore, but were thrown back with heavy losses when they at-

The White House after it had been burned by British troops in the War of 1812. It was the whitewash afterwards applied to cover up smoke discoloration that gave the building its name.

tacked that city. Fort McHenry was bombarded through the night, but to no avail. (Francis Scott Key, an observer, was inspired by this defense to write the verses to "The Star-Spangled Banner.") Frustrated and now seriously weakened, the British withdrew to embark on their fleet and resume naval activities.

The general situation in the United States was extremely grave. During these months the government's financial credit practically disappeared and the various states began arming themselves in their own defense. The central government seemed unable to mount a military effort any longer. A great victory was badly needed.

Jackson in the Southwest

The great victory came through the extraordinary person of Andrew Jackson of Tennessee, who was now beginning his meteoric rise to blazing national prominence. An unusually tall man of natural dignity and soldierly bearing, Jackson was a wealthy landowner and slaveowner in his late forties who had already been a judge, a congressman and a United States senator of strong Jeffersonian loyalties, and a major-general of the Tennessee militia. He was also a rock-hard Scotch-Irishman who hated the British (whom, as a boy, he had fought in the Revolution), and was violently sensitive on questions of personal honor. Living up to some ancient warrior code, Jackson had fought a number of duels and other shootouts, thereafter suffering a lifetime of pain from the bullets lodged in various parts of his anatomy.

The cause of American republicanism was the passion of Jackson's life. Again and again, he called it the hope of (white) humankind for justice and freedom, and condemned European monarchism as an evil, inhumane force still actively working through the British (and the Spanish in Florida) to overthrow America's noble experiment in republican self-rule. He was also convinced that the American republic faced another immense problem. It could never grow to full nationhood, he believed, it perhaps could not even survive, if huge Indian "nations" continued to be lodged within its boundaries.

The vast Southwestern Territory had been created by Congress in 1790 to include the region that would later become Tennessee, Alabama, and Mississippi. If it were ever to be occupied and settled by white Americans, in Jackson's belief something drastic would have to be done about the Indians. The

Five Civilized Tribes—the Cherokee, Creek, Choctaw, Chickasaw, and Seminole peoples—occupied not only most of the Southwestern Territory, but large parts as well of western Georgia and of Florida.

Jackson insisted that this was far too much land for the Indians actually living there. The 8,000 Creeks, for example, had an area of 40 million acres, equivalent to roughly half the size of California. They should be made, he said, to give up their wandering ways, and their pattern of living by the hunt. How? By having the land available to them greatly reduced. This, Jackson believed, would stimulate them to settle down to farming and local industries. And then into the lands taken from them, American settlers, and American republicanism, could flow.

From the time American settlement had begun in Tennessee in the late 1770s, a guerrilla warfare between whites and Indians had flared and flickered, creating bitter animosities on both sides. As a young man Jackson in the 1790s had flung himself wildly into these random frontier battles. He "vibrated," it was said, with a passion to punish the Indians, whom he thought thieving, blood-thirsty, dishonest savages who never lived up to their agreements when land was bought from them for white settlement (purchases many Indians regarded as fraudulent). He was also bitterly angry at the Spanish, who from Florida aided the Indians by sending them arms and ammunition.

To Jackson, the War of 1812 was a glorious opportunity to strike back at the British, the Spanish, and the Indians all together, and finally make the Southwest a secure and integral part of the American republic. Gathering his troops to lead them into battle, he cried out to them in a powerful address,

> Who are we? And for what are we going to fight? *Are we the titled Slaves of George the Third? The military conscripts of Napoleon the Great? Or the frozen peasants of the Russian Czar? No—we are the free born sons of America; the citizens of the only republick now existing in the world; and the only people on earth who possess rights, liberties, and property . . . which they dare call their own.*

His immediate objective lay in the Creek nation (located mainly within what is now Alabama), where warriors earlier inspired by Tecumseh's oratory, who called themselves Red Sticks, had greeted the outbreak of the War of 1812 by joining the British and attacking the whites. Jackson quickly led an invading army of Tennesseans (joined by a number of pro-American Creeks) into the Creek nation. Through

1813, his men pushed in on the hostile Creek settlements from all sides, but with little success. Then in March 1814, Jackson broke through, killing almost 600 warriors—most of the Red Sticks—in the Battle of Horseshoe Bend.

Horseshoe Bend is a victory of towering importance in American history. It sealed the eventual doom of the Five Civilized Nations by initiating the process of clearing out the Indians and making possible white settlement. It also sharply diverted the course of the War of 1812, which to this point had been a dismal failure for the Americans. After Horseshoe Bend, Jackson was able to scour the rest of the Creek nation to enforce pacification, and permanently break the military links between the anti-American Creeks and the Spanish. These steps, in turn, forced the British to drop their plan for sending a large invasion army, already on the high seas for America, through Spanish Florida to join up with the militant Creeks and seize the Old Southwest. Then Jackson called all the Creek chiefs together. In the Treaty of Fort Jackson, extorted by bribery and threats of force, he forced them—even if they had fought, as many had, on the American side—to cede to the United States more than 20 million of their 40 million acres.

The Climactic Victory: The Battle of New Orleans

The British were by now looking for another invasion route. Reluctantly, they had to settle for an attack on New Orleans, which was hidden behind great swamps and delta lakes and watercourses. In late 1814, their invasion fleet arrived off the Gulf Coast with an army of 10,000 men. After a desperate struggle, they succeeded in getting their army and its cannon through the swamps to an open stretch of ground just outside the city. Here they were met by the always-energetic Jackson (European observers were astonished at how swiftly he could move his army about, and at the boldness of his tactics), who after a lightning campaign into Spanish Florida had hurried to New Orleans. He pulled in some 5,000 men from many locations, and disposed them behind cannon and cotton bales across a narrow neck of land some 600 yards wide beside the Mississippi River. To reach the city, the British had to march up this passageway, and directly into Jackson's fortifications. Once again, Jackson issued a ringing oration to his troops:

Natives of the United States! the British are the oppressors of your infant political existence—they are the men your fathers conquered . . . remember for what and against whom you contend. For all that can render life desirable—for a country blessed with every gift of nature . . . and for liberty, dearer than all, without which country, life, property, are no longer worth possessing . . .

In a series of increasingly bold and courageous assaults, the British battered Jackson's army as the last days of 1814 and the first days of 1815 passed. Repeatedly thrown back, and outmaneuvered by Jackson's skillful generalship, the British gathered for a climactic battle. Their entire red-coated army massed in formation and marched straight across the plain for the American position. Cannon bellowed, riflemen packed four deep behind Jackson's lines poured out volleys of fire, and a terrible carnage began. In a brief time the Americans found themselves looking out upon a plain covered with thousands of red-coated men writhing in agony or piled dumbly in windrows. A third of the British army had been butchered, and the rest was fleeing in disorder. In a truce that followed so that sweating surgeons could minister to the groaning wounded, the British discovered to their shock that behind the American lines, only thirteen men had died.

The most powerful amphibious force ever to assault the American mainland had been hammered into defeat. Behind the American lines the victors watched the British mournfully file away to their ships, carrying the dead body of their commander, Sir Edward Michael Pakenham, out to his grieving wife. Jubilation spread on the American side, through the army, through New Orleans, and northward out of the city on the backs of galloping horses, the reports of the triumph electrifying the entire nation. The victory desperately needed to confirm the independence and vitality of the American Republic had been won.

Americans began to think that perhaps God had sent Jackson to save the Republic in its hour of trial. To the end of his life he was the Hero of New Orleans, the celebrity of his time. Wherever he went, especially on his 1815 journey to Washington, D.C., to receive the gratitude of his government, admiring crowds turned out to cheer him. Though he had his critics (mainly Federalists from New England who thought him a wild savage), most Americans believed that he, Andrew Jackson, had restored the security, the faith, and the self-respect of the United States of America.

The End of the War

News came thick and fast to Washington, D.C., in the first weeks of 1815. Jackson's stunning victory sent a wave of relief through the government. Then it was learned that a peace treaty had been signed in Ghent (Belgium) a few days before Jackson's victory. Almost simultaneously word arrived that a special convention called in Hartford, Connecticut, by a group of New England states, had demanded changes in the national constitution and implied secession if its demands were not met.

The British had grown weary of the American war. When the Duke of Wellington himself, the victor over Napoleon, had refused to take command on the ground that the war could not be won, the matter was settled and a peace based on a complete standoff transpired. The Treaty of Ghent provided simply for restoration of the situation as it had stood before the war, the status quo antebellum. Nothing was said about impressment or neutral rights. The Americans agreed to grant amnesty to the Indians, and even to hand back the Creeks' land (which Jackson angrily refused to do, putting an end to it). Problems concerning rights in the fisheries, the navigation of the Mississippi, armaments on the Great Lakes, and boundary disputes were referred to commissions for later settlement.

It has traditionally been said that the treaty signed in Ghent before Jackson's victory made that feat of arms superfluous. This is not true. The Republic had been in peril; now it was saved. An outburst of national pride erased the memory of stumbling defeats and shattered hopes and in a twinkling revived the prestige of the national government.

The Federalists and the Hartford Convention

The Hartford Convention effectively killed the Federalist party, for its bold resolutions, which hinted at disunion, were made to look both ridiculous and disloyal by Jackson's victory and the Treaty of Ghent. Federalists were condemned as subversives who had harmed the war effort, had connived with Britain to help its navy, and would have taken the United States down to ruin with them out of pure spite and a frustrated desire for office.

The Hartford Convention, which met in secret

sessions from December 15, 1814, to January 5, 1815, had official representatives from Massachusetts, Connecticut, and Rhode Island and unofficial delegates from Vermont and New Hampshire. Its declaration called upon the states to resist "unconstitutional" acts by Congress, such as the calling out of the state militia, and demanded seven constitutional amendments:

1. To reduce Southern power in the nation by eliminating the three-fifths rule, which counted slaves in that proportion for the purpose of apportioning the members of the House of Representatives among the various states.
2. To reduce western growth by providing for the admission of states to the Union only by a two-thirds vote of Congress.
3. To prevent future harm to New England commerce by making no embargo legal beyond sixty days.
4. To prevent the use of commercial coercion against any other nation without a two-thirds vote of Congress.
5. To require a two-thirds vote of Congress for declaration of war.
6. To make it illegal for naturalized citizens to hold federal office.
7. To allow a president to serve only one term, and to require that successive presidents could not come from the same state.

Federalists had not been inactive in the years since 1801. A new generation of young Federalists took up the Republican style in political campaigning. They formed committees, established partisan newspapers, and created nominating bodies, national conventions, campaign funds, and even secret political societies. They were able to dominate the politics of several states, and in New England, their heartland, they were still putting forward candidates as late as 1823.

The traditional core of the party, however—consisting of old-line Federalists—was so out of step with the whole movement of American life that it is hard to believe the party could have gone on for long. Many Federalists were so dismayed at the onrush of egalitarian politics that they simply withdrew from public life. They mourned the increasing loss of the society they had known, the world in which the masses silently followed and the aristocracy did the speaking and leading. They confidently expected the nation to collapse under Republican rule. What else was one to think of "democrats" who had such crude manners, who wore long pantaloons

and brutus haircuts (the hair worn moderately long and square-trimmed), rather than knee breeches and tie wigs? Jeffersonian rule seemed to be the rule of arrogant and disobedient youth. The young people of the country seemed to be engaged in a rebellion against age and authority. Noah Webster even proposed that the voting age be raised to forty-five.

From the time of the Louisiana Purchase, this kind of Federalist had begun to think and talk about breaking the nation apart. The Federalists feared the West and its growth. They feared, too, the rising numbers of Irish and other non-English immigrants. Ethnocentric to the end, they passed a resolution at the Hartford Convention that called for denying federal office to naturalized citizens.

America at War's End

So matters stood at war's end. The American nation had received a powerful boost to its sense of nationhood. The same had happened north of the border: Canadian nationality was born in the desperate and bloody fight to throw the Americans back. As is so often true, a sense of common identity came out of the struggle against a common enemy. Thereafter American emigration to Canada was discouraged by the Canadian government, vigorous efforts were made to populate Ontario with immigrants from Britain, and the emergence of a separate and lasting Canadian nation on America's northern border was assured. The War of 1812, as it is known to Americans, was also in effect the Canadian war for independence.

The long controversy with Britain, beginning in 1807 and culminating in the war, had important effects on the United States. Jefferson himself had come to realize that a wholly agrarian nation was a country without means of protection. A balance between industry and farming was vital for the nation's health. Unable to buy things from abroad during the embargo and the war, people set up a clamor that they be manufactured here. Capital formerly invested in trade and commerce flowed to New England for the building of factories. Cotton production increased sixteenfold from 1807 to 1815, and woolen production quintupled. Because goods had to be transported by land and river—the British navy having largely closed the sea lanes—overland transport systems were greatly improved and heavily used. Western cities grew rapidly because foreign goods were not available and had to be manufactured locally. Pittsburgh's rise, symbolic of this new trend, was meteoric. Ironically, Hamilton's "Report on Manufactures" did not begin to do for manufacturing what Jefferson's embargo and the war did. And yet the Jeffersonian political tradition retained all of its anxieties about the power and greed of the business and financial community. What would the Jeffersonians, in the future, do about the new economy that, willy-nilly, they had by 1815 helped to set in motion?

BIBLIOGRAPHY

Particularly helpful to me in writing this chapter was Merrill Peterson, *The Great Triumvirate: Webster, Clay, and Calhoun* (1987). On Thomas Jefferson, I have relied on my own researches, as reported in the chapter on this complicated man in Robert Kelley, *The Transatlantic Persuasion: The Liberal-Democratic Mind in the Age of Gladstone* (1969). He may be sampled in person in J. P. Boyd, ed., *The Papers of Thomas Jefferson* (many volumes). Merrill Peterson's *The Jefferson Image in the American Mind* (1960) is a perceptive study I've found valuable in many ways, and his *Thomas Jefferson and the New Nation: A Biography* (1970) is a wise and informed analysis. Dumas Malone's celebrated six-volume work *Thomas Jefferson and His Time* (1948–1983) is now complete. For a controversial look at Jefferson's personal life, see Fawn M. Brodie's *Thomas Jefferson: An Intimate History* (1974).

The nature of Louisiana political culture recounted in Richard P. McCormick, *The Second Party System: Party Formation in the Jacksonian Era* (1966), is valuable; Ray Allen Billington's book, *Westward Expansion* (1967), is essential on the westward movement of settlement. On the larger national party politics of the period, important to me were David Hackett Fischer's *The Revolution of American Conservatism: The Federalist Party in the Era of Jeffersonian Democracy* (1965), and James Banner, Jr.'s *To the Hartford Convention: The Federalists and the Origins of Party Politics in Massachusetts, 1790–1815* (1970). In Robert Kelley, *The Cultural Pattern in American Politics: The First Century* (1979), Chapter 4, readers may look into a more detailed study of Jeffersonian politics than I have been able to present here. Shaw Livermore's *The Twilight of Federalism: The Disintegration of the Federalist Party 1815–1830* (1962), is essential.

All students of the War of 1812 are in debt to Robert H. Brown's important *The Republic in Peril: 1812* (1964), from which this chapter has drawn much. On Andrew Jackson I have benefited greatly from the first volume of Robert V. Remini's superb three-volume biography, *Andrew Jackson and the Course of American Empire 1767–1821* (1977). R. David Edmunds' recently published *Tecumseh and the Quest for Indian Leadership* (1984) helped me a good deal. Bernard W. Sheehan's rich and fascinating book, *Seeds of Extinction: Jeffersonian Philanthropy and the American Indian* (1973), is essential. J. C. A. Stagg's much-praised *Mr. Madison's War: Politics, Diplomacy, and Warfare in the Early American Republic 1783–1830* (1983) takes us deep inside Madison's motivations, and the troubled course of the War of 1812.

Henry Adams viewed both Jefferson and Madison in a critical light in his brilliant *History of the United States During the Administrations of Jefferson and Madison*, nine vols. (1889–91). Marshall Smelser rejects the unfavorable appraisal of Jefferson and Madison in his *Democratic Republic, 1800–1815* (1968), but depicts Jefferson as a cautious moderate rather than a crusader. The partnership between the two giants of the Republican party is admirably explored in Adrienne Koch's *Jefferson and Madison: The Great Collaboration* (1950). Irving Brant's six-volume biography of James Madison (1961) probes the political life of this complex man in detail.

Reginald Horsman cites European upheaval and British impressment of American seamen in *The Causes of the War of 1812* (1970), a view similar to that of Bradford Perkins in *Prologue to War: England and the United States, 1805–1812* (1963). The military course of the war receives thorough treatment in Harry L. Coles's *The War of 1812* (1965), and the negotiations resulting in the Treaty of Ghent are best described in Samuel F. Bemis's Pulitzer prize book, *John Quincy Adams and the Foundation of American Foreign Policy* (1949).

10

The Nationalist Era

TIME LINE

1792	Captain Robert Gray discovers the Columbia River and establishes American claim to the Pacific Northwest
1803	Supreme Court claims power to rule laws unconstitutional in *Marbury* v. *Madison* decision
1810–22	Latin American revolutions
1811	No-Transfer Resolution
1816	The "Madisonian Platform" enacted: Second Bank of the United States founded; First protective tariff erected; James Monroe elected fifth president of the United States
1818	General Jackson invades Florida; Anglo-American Convention establishes joint occupation of the Oregon Country with boundary at the 49th parallel
1819	Transcontinental Treaty cedes Florida to the United States and establishes Louisiana Purchase boundary; *McCulloch* v. *Maryland* decision rendered by Supreme Court declares supremacy of federal government over states in exercising constitutional powers; Panic of 1819 begins; depression lasts to 1823
1820	Missouri Compromise
1822	Denmark Vesey conspiracy in Charleston, South Carolina; Latin American countries recognized
1823	Monroe Doctrine
1824	John Quincy Adams elected sixth president of the United States; *Gibbons* v. *Ogden* decision rendered
1828	Tariff of Abominations; Andrew Jackson elected seventh president of the United States

Charleston, South Carolina, in the 1830s. (No portrait of Denmark Vesey exists.)

DENMARK VESEY

He was a bold, angry man. A slave for his first thirty-three years (at which point he purchased his freedom), Denmark Vesey in his fifties was a prosperous Charleston, South Carolina, carpenter. He ranged up and down the coastal region fuming at slavery, rebuking blacks who stepped into the street to let white men pass, and reading to his friends everything he could learn of Santo Domingo, the Caribbean island where in 1791 the slaves had thrown off their white masters. He helped to found the first African Methodist church in Charleston in 1817, making it a center of black consciousness, and he would quote passages from the Bible which he said authorized slaves to kill their masters. Vesey knew well the attack on slavery made in Congress by New York's Rufus King during the Missouri Compromise debates of 1820, and he would expound on the Declaration of Independence. Like many other blacks in South Carolina, he also had a knowledge of and pride in African tribal identities, for tens of thousands of South Carolina slaves had only recently been brought across the Atlantic.

Whites in South Carolina were in a more frightening situation than other white Southerners. They were outnumbered by their slaves in the low-country regions. In the swamp plantations, blacks lived in horrible conditions, dying in great numbers of malaria and other diseases. Only the compulsion of slavery could keep them there; the land would be valueless without the institution. Their white owners lived elegantly in Charleston, avoiding the malarial outlands, but they lived in dread as well. Not only would they be bankrupt overnight if slavery ended, they were also in the midst of a vast black population that might at any moment rise in revolt. Whites seemed to be living on a rumbling volcano.

Then a house slave warned them: Denmark Vesey had organized a conspiracy! At midnight on June 16, 1822, six rebel battle units would launch a closely coordinated attack aimed at seizing the city's armories and then the city itself, and massacring the whites. What then? A mass exodus to the Caribbean? Back to Africa? It was never clear. In the critical hours while Vesey and his chief conspirators were arrested, the entire white population lived in terror. Investigation afterward revealed that the freest of the slaves, the house slaves and craftsmen, were the most prominent in the conspiracy. Revolt does not come from the most hopelessly downtrodden, but from those with some freedom to form a respect for self, some sense of the nearness of liberty.

The punishment was savage: after a closely guarded trial in which there was no jury and those accused were not allowed to confront witnesses, thirty-five blacks were executed, many of them in a public mass hanging. Over thirty more were deported from the state, and others were given public whippings. Vesey approached his death calmly, and his associate Peter Poyas urged a prisoner being tortured to "die like a man." From the gallows Poyas cried to watching blacks, "Do not open your lips; die silent, as you shall see me do!" South Carolina, indeed the whole South, never forgot Denmark Vesey. Only at the last moment had the best-organized black uprising in the Southern states been quashed.

Overview

The United States emerged from the War of 1812 with a vast sense of relief. The security of republicanism as a form of government, and the survival of the United States as a successful experiment in self-government, seemed now assured. There was a surging sense of proud *nationalism*, created by the victorious last days of the war. Now for a brief time, with a new sense of the importance and usefulness of the national government in achieving common aims, the American people for a time eagerly put their federal regime in Washington to active use.

However, by 1828, local loyalties were once more pushing aside any interest in a strong central government. Indeed, as a general rule most people paid little attention to Washington. It was so remote from the rest of the country, it had so little to do—for a number of years Congress itself was more numerous than the entire executive branch—that years went by without anything much at all being done in the scattered little capital on the Potomac. The dying away of party organizations with the decline of Federalism provided little in the way of an organizing impetus. The national government almost faded from view.

The Era of Good Feelings: 1815–19

A time of apparent well-being followed the war. The nation was prosperous; a calm and magisterial man, James Monroe of Virginia, became president in the election of 1816; the West was opening; and the future looked promising. Monroe firmly opposed the very idea of political parties, believing that everyone should work harmoniously together, and he labored to bring Federalists into friendship with Republicans. When he visited Boston in 1817 to comfort Federalists and call for national unity, his appearance was so benign and reassuring that the tour became a triumphal progress. The Boston *Columbian Sentinel* exulted that the nation could anticipate an Era of Good Feelings. This happy phrase, coming from a Federalist paper, circulated quickly about the country.

Monroe was practically unopposed when he ran for his second term in 1820, and by the mid-1820s the Federalists had just withered away. This was true even in New England, where they held on the longest as a kind of "lost cause," a last embodi-

ment of the deep Yankee conviction that New England, the seat of true religion, morality, and political wisdom, should rule the nation. Bereft of an enemy, the Jeffersonian Republicans fell apart into many warring factions, gathering behind a number of different leaders and losing all semblance of existence as a political party.

The Madisonian Platform

In 1815, however, it was the powerful postwar mood of nationalism that shaped all national policy. Uplifted by this feeling of team spirit and national union, in 1816 nearly the whole of the Congress, Republicans and Federalists alike, joined together to enact a remarkably centralizing series of measures. Practically Hamiltonian in character, it was the wartime president James Madison himself who proposed them; together, they were called the "Madisonian Platform."

At the heart of this program was what the country had learned from the War of 1812. First, Madison said, the United States clearly needed roads and canals, built by the national government; the states had to be physically knit together. It had been fiendishly difficult to get troops and supplies transported over America's enormous distances. Second, the war had taught that America needed certain industries of its own to provide the basic necessaries for fighting. During the conflict, many factories had been started up for this purpose. Now, in peacetime, cheap goods from Britain were flooding the American market, and domestic manufacturers were closing down. American labor costs were high, and British factories were more highly mechanized. New England's cotton mills, Pittsburgh's iron smelters, Vermont's wool shops, and Kentucky's hemp industries were in great difficulties.

To protect the nation's security, therefore, Madison recommended that a tax (tariffs) be put on certain imported goods when they entered the country to make them costlier to American consumers. This would offer protection to domestic producers. In effect, the consumer would be paying a subsidy to American producers by being forced to pay higher prices in order to keep them in business. This was, of course, potentially very unfair. Who could tell whether a tariff was actually necessary to prevent a local factory from closing down? Critics would say that it was instead simply an unfair privilege given to the factory owner, allowing that person to charge the public higher prices and thereby delivering to the owner unearned profits.

As the Scottish economist Adam Smith had warned in his book *The Wealth of Nations* (1776), protective tariffs could simply be corrupt arrangements for exploiting the consumer. In time, this obvious fact would push itself forward to claim tremendous national attention in the United States and make the "protective tariff" policy an enormously controversial subject in American public life. At this time, however, Congress was impressed by the argument that such a policy would make the country more secure, as well as encourage development of its industries, and it enacted in 1816 the nation's first "protective tariff." It established import tariff rates at about 25 percent, a relatively moderate level.

The Southern states would in time develop a towering hatred of tariffs, for they did not develop a factory system of their own to provide their needs, and tariffs made them pay higher prices (usually to Yankees, for New England became the nation's first industrial base) for clothing for their slaves and other manufactured articles. However, so strong was the national consensus behind the "Madisonian Platform" in the immediate postwar period that it was none other than John C. Calhoun of South Carolina who introduced the tariff bill in Congress, saying that soon the South too would have factories.

Creation of the Second Bank of the United States

The War of 1812 had highlighted another folly: not having a national banking system. With only the states chartering banks, and no central clearing house for moving money back and forth between the states, the federal government's money could not be easily transferred from state to state to pay its expenses, such as those of a war. There was also another problem: The states were handing out bank charters with a lavish hand (over 200 by 1815), and as each of them was free to print and issue their own paper currency (producing money of many different sizes, shapes, colors, and denominations), runaway inflation threatened.

It was important, Congress realized, to have some national agency that could ascertain whether these many paper currencies were as valuable, in reality, as they claimed they were. Was the $10 bill of the Merchant's Bank of Boston really worth (in gold) $10? The country needed, in short, a stable

and uniform currency. Madison recommended that a new national bank to provide some central supervision over the country's money supply be created to replace the one that, in 1811, had been allowed to die. Calhoun introduced the bill in January 1816. Soon the Second Bank of the United States was in existence, located once more on Chestnut Street in Philadelphia (then the country's "Wall Street," or commercial financial center) within a stone's throw of the headquarters of the old First Bank of the United States. (Both buildings may now be visited in Philadelphia's Independence National Historical Park.)

The Bank's Powers

Thus, for the second time, the national government had exercised its (presumed) authority to charter corporations, and once more, a bank. It was to be privately owned, though partially public because one-fifth of its board of directors would be appointed by the president of the United States, with the Senate's approval in each case. Established to create national and international confidence in the nation's economic stability, the Second Bank of the United States had strong powers. It kept the national government's tax revenues—the largest single pool of capital anywhere in the country—in its vaults. These it could then lend out, on interest, in ways that in the minds of the bank's board of directors would develop the country's economy most wisely. Thus, a powerful economic force, directed by a small elite group behind the bank's closed doors, had come into being.

The Second Bank was also authorized to issue paper money, which in this case people believed they could rely on, for the tax revenues of the federal government itself stood behind it. The bank was also charged with the huge regulatory task of keeping tabs on the paper currency issues of the hundreds of state banks. There was a powerful motive for each bank to print off floods of paper currency. It was this that they lent to borrowers, on interest, and the more loans, the more profits. By periodically showing up at a state-chartered bank to check on its operations, the Second Bank of the United States worked to ensure that the state banks had the necessary backing in gold and silver (called "specie") in their vaults (usually about one-fifth) for the currency they had issued. The goal: making certain that anyone could show up at the bank's window and get a $20 gold piece in exchange for the $20 piece of paper currency, from that bank, that one held.

The Second Bank was also given the authority to create branches all over the country to carry on its business. One crucial point: Henceforth, all federal taxes, or other payments to the national government, would have to be in gold or silver coin, or in a currency properly *backed* by specie. This would be a powerful force working in the direction of making sure that the nation's currency, whoever printed it, would be what was called "sound."

John Quincy Adams and National Expansion

James Monroe's administration achieved foreign policy triumphs that profoundly shaped the future. Though not much supported by facts, the United States had insisted since 1803 that West Florida was included within the Louisiana Purchase. On this ground, in 1810 President Madison had appropriated that region of Spanish Florida between the Mississippi River and the Pearl River (which forms part of the boundary between present-day Louisiana and Mississippi), following a local uprising of American settlers there. In 1812, it was annexed to Louisiana. Meanwhile, Spain's Latin American colonies had begun to revolt. There was a possibility that Britain or some other power might aid the Spanish by taking over such colonies as Florida and holding them for Spain.

In January 1811, therefore, Congress adopted one of the most important foreign policy statements in American history—the No-Transfer Resolution. It warned Europe that the United States could not "without serious inquietude see any part of [Spain's colonies] pass into the hands of any foreign power." If necessary, the American government would temporarily occupy territory to prevent such transfers, subject to future negotiations when the Napoleonic Wars should finally cease. Under authority of this resolution, Madison occupied the rest of West Florida, from the Pearl River east to the Perdido River, in 1813.

John Quincy Adams was United States minister to Russia when Madison took the rest of West Florida.

> *Czar Alexander spoke to him about the subject one day when they met promenading on the banks of the Neva.*
>
> *"I hear you have lately made an acquisition."*
>
> *"I suppose you mean in Florida," Adams assumed . . . "This was a part of the territory ceded by France to the United States in the Louisiana Treaty. Spain, however, has entered into a controversy with us about it, upon which negotiations were pending at the time when [Napoleon took over the Spanish government]. Since then the people of that country have been left in a sort of abandonment by Spain, and must naturally be very desirous of being annexed to the United States."*

In 1790, when the first U.S. census was taken, only 5 percent of the population was urban. By 1820, cities such as Albany were beginning a period of major growth.

The Emperor smiled and bowed. "One keeps on growing bit by bit in this world, . . ." he acknowledged.

To Alexander, Florida was like Finland.

The two men took polite leave of each other and continued their separate walks. Their two countries, the expanding Czardom of the East and the growing Republic of the West, also continued their respective national promenades east and west from opposite sides of the globe, finally to confront each other amidst the chill fogs of the Bering Sea. (Samuel Flagg Bemis, John Quincy Adams and the Foundations of American Foreign Policy *[1949])*

In 1818 the time for the promised negotiations with Spain had come. By then, Adams was secretary of state, and he was determined to use the opportunity to acquire East Florida (the present state of Florida)

John Quincy Adams, a portrait begun by Stuart and completed by Sully. He was the last Yankee to be elected president, save for Franklin Pierce in 1852 (and he was a Democrat, hardly of the classic Yankee lineage), until Calvin Coolidge in 1924.

as well. Also, the Louisiana Purchase still had an undefined western boundary that had to be settled with Spain. Adams wanted the boundary defined so as to open a corridor to the Pacific for the United States. This would strengthen United States claims to the Pacific Northwest, which were based on the discovery of the Columbia River by Captain Robert Gray, who had sailed 10 miles up the stream in 1792 and named it for his vessel. By an established international principle, this gave the United States a claim to the entire region drained by the river and its tributaries. An American fur trading post later operated near the mouth of the Columbia, as Astoria, until the British took it over during the War of 1812. Other nations—Britain, Russia, and Spain—also claimed the Oregon Country, as the whole region from California to Alaska and from the Rockies to the Pacific was called.

Florida Acquired and the Northwest Opened

Under President Monroe, General Andrew Jackson had been instructed to enter East Florida to punish Seminole Indians for their raids into American territory. He began his expedition in March 1818 and soon transformed its objective into the clear and simple one of seizing East Florida. In a few weeks Jackson took the fort of St. Marks, ran up the Stars and Stripes, executed two British subjects whom he charged with inciting Indian attacks, seized Pensacola, put an American governor in charge of the province, and declared that the revenue laws of the United States were in force.

These events sent the Spanish into a rage, created war rumblings in London, set off celebrations in the West, and drew harsh criticisms in Congress and the cabinet. Adams, however, took an approving stance. Though he detested Jackson personally, he saw that the general's actions had given American diplomacy the necessary lever. He then issued a grave warning: The United States would vacate East Florida this time, but if Spain did not place large enough forces in Florida to subdue the Indians, so that the American government had to launch similar operations again, "another unconditional restoration [of East Florida to Spanish hands] must not be expected."

Adams's statement, which ran to twenty-nine eloquent and colorful pages, dramatically expressed the bold new American nationalist mood. It delighted

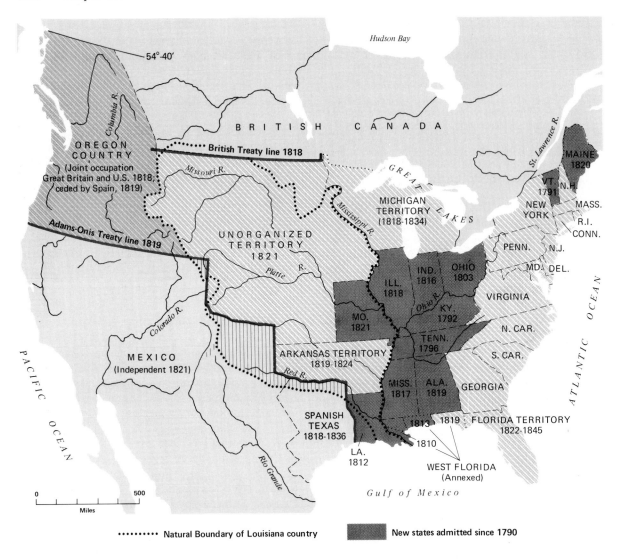

Hudson Bay

54°–40'

B R I T I S H   C A N A D A

OREGON COUNTRY
(Joint occupation Great Britain and U.S. 1818; ceded by Spain, 1819)

········· British Treaty line 1818

Columbia R.

Missouri R.

Mississippi R.

G R E A T   L A K E S

St. Lawrence R.

MAINE 1820

VT. 1791 N.H.

NEW YORK   MASS.
R.I.
CONN.

MICHIGAN TERRITORY (1818-1834)

Adams-Onis Treaty line 1819

UNORGANIZED TERRITORY 1821

Platte R.

Colorado R.

PENN.   N.J.

MD. DEL.

IND. 1816   OHIO 1803

ILL. 1818

Ohio R.

VIRGINIA

MO. 1821

KY. 1792

TENN. 1796

N. CAR.

MEXICO (Independent 1821)

ARKANSAS TERRITORY 1819-1824

Red R.

S. CAR.

MISS. 1817   ALA. 1819

GEORGIA

SPANISH TEXAS 1818-1836

1813   1819   FLORIDA TERRITORY 1822-1845

1810

Rio Grande

LA. 1812

WEST FLORIDA (Annexed)

PACIFIC OCEAN

ATLANTIC OCEAN

Gulf of Mexico

0 ———— 500
Miles

········· Natural Boundary of Louisiana country   ▉ New states admitted since 1790

The United States, 1822

the country and quieted doubts over the legality of Jackson's foray. Thereafter, Adams began a bargaining session extending over many months, concerned with all outstanding issues, not simply Florida. In this effort he had one purpose—to open an American corridor to the Pacific Northwest. He proposed that the western boundary of the Louisiana Purchase be established on a line running northward along the front range of the Rockies to the forty-second parallel (the line of the present northern boundary of California) and *from that point directly westward to the Pacific.* When the Transcontinental Treaty was signed in Washington in February 1819, the way to Oregon was wide open. Spain ceded to the United States

whatever rights it possessed north of California, which immensely strengthened American claims.

Always active, Adams by this time had also concluded an agreement with the British—the Anglo-American Convention of 1818. This established the boundary between the United States and British North America at the 49th parallel, from the Great Lakes to the Rockies; opened rich fisheries to American seamen off the Labrador and Newfoundland coasts; and proclaimed that the whole of the Oregon Country would be open to citizens of both countries without prejudice to the claims of either party. At ten-year intervals, the question of how to divide the territory would be reopened for further examination.

John Marshall, third and one of the most influential Chief Justices of the Supreme Court, owed his long tenure (1801–1835) in part to his personal qualities of charm, logic, and intellectual persuasiveness.

(In 1824, Russia relinquished all claims south of 54°40′, the southern tip of the Alaska panhandle.)

The Supreme Court Emerges as the Great Arbiter

While Adams was expanding the nation's boundaries, Chief Justice of the United States John Marshall was making the federal government constitutionally ascendant over the states. He did this through the power of "judicial review," which allows the U.S. Supreme Court to:

1. Issue rulings as to *what the law is* (i.e., interpret a law), which are binding on all other institutions of government;

2. Say whether or not something a government has done is *constitutional* (i.e., legal);

3. Ordain how the *powers* of government created by the Constitution are *divided between the federal and state governments*.

The Supreme Court, in short, is America's constitutional watchdog, which means essentially the guardian of the nation's liberties.

"No other country," writes the distinguished constitutional authority Archibald Cox in his book *The Court and the Constitution* (1987), "has given its courts such extraordinary power." Surprisingly, there is no explicit language in the Constitution that gives the Supreme Court the power to review the constitutionality of federal laws. Nonetheless, there the Court stands, a tremendously active and powerful body that does not legislate but simply issues rulings, and these rulings shape the most fundamental national policies.

The courts, in fact, are a great departure from the norm in a democratic republic. These powerful officials, the federal judges, are not elected; they are appointed by the president, with the Senate's approval; unlike most state judges they hold their offices for life, or during what is called "good behavior." (This is a legal term that means as long as they do not become felons; that is, someone who has committed a crime.) Indeed, because the courts were so glaringly undemocratic in nature, Thomas Jefferson bitterly distrusted them and wanted sharply to limit their powers. Over the generations, many people have shared this distrust.

Where do the courts' powers come from? To begin with, their powers come down to them from far back before recorded history. Even the most primitive societies have judges to settle disputes. Most directly, the American courts inherit their fundamental powers from the English kings, who were the first national "judges" in that country, centuries ago. This is where we get the name "court," for such institutions are the present-day descendants of the king's court, where the monarch made his rulings. Thus, their authority to issue orders (i.e., "writs" and "injunctions"), and make rulings as between parties in a dispute, is the ancient king's authority.

Hence, when a judge issues a decision, he or she is in fact making law; not "statute law," which is what legislatures make, but law nonetheless. Also, when someone refuses to obey an order from a court, that person is said to be "in contempt of court" (in contempt of the king). Such individuals can therefore be fined and thrown into jail almost without limit.

The Colonial Origins of Judicial Review

Before the American Revolution, the colonies had become used to the idea that there was a supreme court in the governing system, in this case the Privy Council in London (a committee of the House of Lords), which had the power to "disallow" laws that particular colonies had enacted on the ground that they violated a superior law—that is, that of Britain. The Privy Council also heard appeals from colonial court decisions and issued rulings in particular cases.

Then, during the arguments leading up to the Revolution, the colonials had argued passionately that there was an unwritten "constitution" in the British Empire. It consisted, essentially, of the traditional ways in which the kingdom of Great Britain and its empire were governed. This unwritten constitution had been formed, Americans insisted, over many centuries, beginning with the Magna Carta (Great Charter) of 1215, in which the king agreed not to tax the nobility without their prior assent. Thus, the colonials insisted, when the London government taxed them without representation, it was violating this ancient "constitution," making the royal government's actions invalid. The authorities in London, of course, never accepted this concept. To this day, there are no "constitutional" limitations on what the British Parliament can do, when it passes law. Parliament is supreme.

In due course, the Americans went on to develop the radical new idea of constitutions as *supreme laws made by the people at large*, not by legislatures, which are superior to anything enacted by a mere Congress or a state legislature. That is, the Americans put the government *under the law*. This was a dramatically "republican" means of protecting the people and their rights against dictatorial government. Many nations in the world have since copied the concept and practice. Rarely, however, have such constitutions had the unquestioned moral and legal authority that the United States Constitution possesses among the American people.

The Constitutional Origins of Judicial Review

In the Constitution, there is a historic statement of towering importance in American life. In Article VI we read: "This Constitution and the laws of the United States . . . shall be the *supreme law of the land* and *the judges in every State shall be bound thereby* . . . [emphasis added]." Also, in the Judiciary Act of 1789—one of our most important laws and one that is still in effect—Congress put Article VI into operation by formally giving to the United States Supreme Court the power of reviewing state court decisions to see if they violated the national constitution. This meant that the Supreme Court could invalidate a state law if it was at issue in a state court decision.

This created something that Americans often forget: Although the state legislatures are not under Congress, and the state governors are not under the president, the state courts are under the U.S. Supreme Court! In this crucial dimension of the American system of government, there is not a federal arrangement of divided sovereignty, but one pyramidal system of courts that runs from the lowest municipal courts right up to the Supreme Court in Washington, D.C. And for most of the Supreme Court's first century, it was primarily the constitutionality of state-enacted laws that it ruled on.

The Case of Marbury v. Madison

However, what about *federal* laws, that is, those passed by Congress? Here, the Constitution is silent as to who is to decide upon constitutionality. In the country's very first years, the Supreme Court was a quiet body that heard few cases in any event. Then in 1801 everything changed, for in that year President John Adams chose as Chief Justice of the United States (Note: not "of the supreme court") a distinguished public figure who had been on General Washington's staff during the Revolution—John Marshall of Virginia. He would be Chief Justice for thirty-four years, until 1835! And he would be a confident one, determined vigorously to use the powers of the Court. Marshall, after all, was a Federalist, and this meant that he believed that government, in all its branches, should be strong and active.

His chance to stake out a powerful role for the Supreme Court came early, in the year 1803, when Thomas Jefferson was president. In 1801, just before John Adams's term as president had expired, Adams had appointed one William Marbury, a Federalist, to be a federal judge—and then forgot to give him the actual appointment papers. When Jefferson entered the White House, he refused to turn them over. Marbury finally brought suit against the then-secretary of state (James Madison), asking the Supreme Court to issue an order (a "writ") requiring Madison to release the official appointment papers.

Instead, the Court declared that the federal law empowering it to issue such orders to the executive branch violated the separation of powers, and was therefore unconstitutional. Thus, the canny Marshall had used a trivial issue to stake out a principle of great importance, knowing that Jefferson would never challenge him. Henceforth, it was established doctrine that the Court had the power to review the constitutionality not only of state laws but also of laws enacted by Congress. In actual fact, not until the 1850s would the Court ever seek to put this power again into effect.

There is an important point to make here: Because the courts have no police forces or armies of their own, they must ultimately rely on the federal or state executive branch voluntarily to enforce their decisions, and on the relevant legislatures voluntarily to abide by their rulings, and the people voluntarily to obey. In short, the court system in the United States must depend on its *moral authority*, which is something judges work hard to protect. They do so by always making sure that their decisions stick as close as possible to prior decisions, so that no big disturbing changes are introduced that would get people angered and disobedient. This is called following *precedent*, which is summed up in the legal maxim of *stare decisis*, Latin for "the decision [i.e., the principle of a relevant prior decision] stands."

Marshall and the States

In 1819, in the case of *McCulloch* v. *Maryland*, Marshall used the Supreme Court's great legal powers to deal with a severe challenge to the national government from the states. Maryland had tried to eliminate the Second Bank of the United States within its borders by taxing the bank's local branch out of existence. Marshall's response was to lay down some of the most powerful nationalizing principles in the history of American constitutional law. Maryland argued that the establishment of a national bank was unconstitutional, since nowhere did the Constitution explicitly authorize Congress to create one. Marshall replied: "Let the end be legitimate, let it be within the scope of the Constitution, and all means which are appropriate, which are plainly adapted to that end, which are not prohibited, but [are] consist[ent]

with the letter and spirit of the Constitution, are constitutional." In the exercise of such powers, he went on, the federal government is supreme over the states, and may not be interfered with by them. Maryland's tax was itself unconstitutional, for the "power to tax," as he said in another utterance that became famous, "involves the power to destroy." If the states could tax federal agencies, then the statement in the Constitution that it and the laws made under it "shall be the supreme law of the land, is an empty and unmeaning declamation."

In a further assertion of national supremacy, in 1827 Marshall threw out an attempt by Maryland to establish its own tariff (*Brown* v. *Maryland*), saying that the constitution granted Congress exclusive control over foreign and interstate commerce. Then, in 1831, Marshall ruled that a state could not relieve distress within its boundaries by issuing any kind of currency. The purpose of the constitutional prohibition, he said in this case, *Craig* v. *Missouri*, was to prevent the states from driving out good money with bad.

The Steamboat and American Unity

By the end of the War of 1812, a world-shaking new invention had appeared: the steamboat. Its implications for America were beyond calculating. To this point Americans had settled primarily next to or near the sea, for water transportation from point to point was infinitely easier than slow, laborious, and costly land-transport using horses or oxen traveling over dirt roads that in wintertime became quagmires of mud. Navigating into the interior was also difficult, for it meant going against the current. Now, however, the steamboat could make the nation's rivers open highways, easily traveled. In fact, the entire interior of the country, at least to the Mississippi, was open now to rapid development. The steamboat, in short, could potentially open up and tie together America's enormous continental domain, in which to this point its people had been, in effect, drowning.

Robert Fulton had put the first practical steamboat, the *Clermont*, into the water in 1807, with the backing of a skillful, imaginative entrepreneur, Robert Livingston. Earlier, when the idea had seemed ridiculous, Livingston had gotten the New York legislature to grant him a monopoly of all steam transportation on the Hudson River. Soon he had secured also a state-granted monopoly from Louisiana for all steamboat traffic entering the Port of New Orleans. This was a staggering thought. One man potentially could control steamboat transportation practically throughout the whole interior of the country! Another thought was just as daunting: Soon, perhaps, there would be many competing state-chartered steamboat monopolies.

The Mighty Case: Gibbons v. Ogden (1824)

Shortly, people began violating these monopolies by putting their own steamboats into the rivers. Thus, there came into the courts what Lawrence M. Friedman in his book *A History of American Law* (2d edition, 1985) calls "the mighty case of *Gibbons* v. *Ogden*." When one Thomas Gibbons began sending steam-powered ferry boats across the Hudson River (entirely within the boundaries of New York state), Ogden, who shared Livingston's monopoly, got an injunction against Gibbons from the New York courts. Promptly, Gibbons took the case on appeal to the U.S. Supreme Court.

Consider the enormous issue posed in this case: Could different states grant monopolies over steamboat transportation to different entrepreneurs, so that everything would have to be trans-shipped from boat to boat at state lines? Was there to be no check on how high the fees could go, no competition? In short, was America to be divided into as many separate economic areas as there are states, each engaging in commercial warfare against all the others? Or would it be one immense, open, free-trade theater with no internal barriers to trade?

The Founding Fathers had foreseen this problem. To ward off this kind of economic fragmentation (they had seen it already under the Articles of Confederation), into the Constitution they had written a provision that gave the federal government a tremendously important power: Under Article I, Section 8, in what would become the famous *Commerce Clause*, the Constitution declares that Congress shall have authority "To regulate Commerce with foreign Nations, and among the several States. . . ." (For most of American history, practically all federal legislation on economic issues has relied on this clause for its fundamental authority.) When *Gibbons* v. *Ogden* got to the Supreme Court, Chief Justice Marshall therefore had in the Constitution a specific

clause he could apply to it. He knew, of course, just how crucial were the principles involved. As a Federalist, Marshall was a deep-dyed nationalist, and he knew that national unity depended fundamentally on economic unity.

The attorneys for Ogden argued that Livingston's monopoly affected transportation only *within* one state, which meant the federal government had to stay out of the dispute. But Marshall would have none of this. In a ruling of immense importance for all later American history, he decreed that "Commerce among the States cannot stop at the external boundary line of each State but may be introduced into the interior." Vastly expanding federal authority, he held that the Constitution meant for Congress to have supreme authority over the navigable rivers (wherever they were in fact navigable). The states, as sovereign entities, owned the rivers within their boundaries, of course, and they too could regulate their use, but only reasonably, not by means of monopolies. As soon as they began to interfere with the free movement of interstate commerce (which included commerce coming from abroad, as through the Port of New Orleans), then what they were doing was unconstitutional. And certainly steamboat monopolies hindered the free use of the rivers. Thus, the Court ruled them illegal.

The effects of *Gibbons* v. *Ogden* were immediate and profound. Within a year, forty-three steamboats were sailing out of the City of New York, instead of six as formerly. And the entire economy of New York State was, accordingly, vastly energized—as was any part of America to which steamboats could penetrate, or their economic influence could be felt. John Marshall had created one national economy, where for a time it looked like there would be many separate ones.

The Slavery Question Explodes into National Politics

Meanwhile, in the new frontier of settlement beyond the Mississippi that Jefferson had opened up in the Louisiana Purchase of 1804, settlers had been rushing in by the thousands to take up land. In 1818 the Territory of Arkansas was carved out of the Louisiana Purchase, and in the same year those people who lived in the Territory of Missouri, in and around St. Louis and spreading westward in a broad band along the Missouri River, petitioned Congress for statehood. In early 1819 a bill to create the State of Missouri was duly reported to the floor of the House of Representatives.

Suddenly something happened that had never happened before: The question was raised in Congress whether new states could have slavery, about which the federal government had said nothing to this point. (It was the old congress of the Confederation that had decreed the Northwest Territory, above the Ohio River, to be free of slavery.) A relatively unknown congressman of vaguely Federalist leanings, James Tallmadge, Jr., of upstate New York, proposed the stipulation that admission for Missouri would be subject to the requirement that further importation of slaves into Missouri cease and that slave children born after statehood be freed following their twenty-fifth birthday.

Southerners reacted in astonished anger. "You have kindled a fire," one of them shouted in Congress, "which seas of blood can only extinguish!" Thomas Jefferson, observing national events from his retirement at Monticello, recoiled as if hit by an electric shock. It was like "a fire bell in the night," he said, and thousands of Southerners agreed with him. To have Congress even consider the slave question was infuriating to them, for they insisted that the Constitution gave no power whatever over the institution of slavery to the federal government, slavery being a creation wholly of local law that predated the founding of the nation. A kind of implied compact of silence on the topic had to this point screened slavery questions out of congressional discussions. Furthermore, as we have earlier seen, slavery in the area called the Louisiana Purchase had been entirely legal under the French and Spanish, and it continued to be legal under American sovereignty. White settlers in Arkansas and Missouri had been freely taking slaves there to establish plantations; the deep and legally legitimate roots of the institution beyond the Mississippi seemed beyond any doubt.

The national policy here had been similar to that exercised over slavery everywhere else: *nonintervention*; silence; no action. Where slavery did *not* exist in the United States, as in the free states and in the Northwest Territory, it had been terminated or excluded only by conscious, explicit enactment. James Tallmadge now proposed that this be done once more, only on this occasion through the unprecedented instrument of the federal government, and in a huge new state whose white people did not want to abandon slavery.

The Black American in the Northern States

Several things must be considered in assessing the Missouri controversy. The Northern states had ended slavery within their boundaries. Many resented the fact that slave states could count their bondsmen as three-fifths of a citizen when having apportionment in Congress computed, and this kind of irritation seems to have provided much of the motivation behind the Tallmadge amendment.

In the Middle West the line between slave and nonslave states was blurred. Illinois had just been admitted to the Union in 1818 with a constitution that was practically a slave-state document. It allowed indentured service and a kind of limited slavery. A punitive Black Code regulated the lives of free blacks, and the immigration of any more into the state was prohibited by a law that, though rarely enforced, posed a constant threat to those who later entered Illinois. Practically every other new state carved out of the Northwest Territory emulated Illinois. They either barred blacks completely, or let them come into the state only after presenting documentary proof of their freedom and posting a bond, which could be as high as $1,000, guaranteeing their good behavior. In Illinois, a violator could be advertised and sold at public auction.

In the Northern states generally, free blacks were denied the right to vote. Blacks were also prevented in a number of states from giving testimony in cases where a white man was involved. This meant that a black could with impunity be assaulted, robbed, or killed by a white man, unless another white would testify against the assailant. Ohio did not revoke its law on this subject until 1849. Blacks were also generally excluded from juries and were not allowed to be judges. This meant that they were always tried by all-white juries, judges, and laws. It is hardly a coincidence that they occupied jail cells in numbers disproportionate to their population. They were commonly arrested for minor legal offenses such as vagrancy. Competent legal counsel was normally unavailable, and it was not unusual for blacks to receive longer sentences for the same crime than white criminals. Accusations usually meant convictions. Public opinion convicted them before a trial was even held.

While statutes and customs circumscribed the Negro's political and judicial rights [in the Northern states], extralegal codes—enforced by public opinion—relegated him to a position of social inferiority and divided northern society into "Brahmins and Pariahs." In virtually every phase of existence, Negroes found themselves systematically separated from whites. They were either excluded from railway cars, omnibuses, stagecoaches, or assigned to special "Jim Crow" sections; they sat, when permitted, in secluded and remote corners of theaters and lecture halls; they could not enter most hotels, restaurants, and resorts, except as servants; they prayed in "Negro pews" in the white churches, and if partaking of the sacrament of the Lord's Supper, they waited until the whites had been served the bread and wine. Moreover, they were often educated in segregated schools, punished in segregated prisons, nursed in segregated hospitals, and buried in segregated cemeteries. . . . To most northerners, segregation constituted not a departure from democratic principles, as certain foreign critics alleged, but simply the working out of natural laws, the inevitable consequence of the racial inferiority of the Negro. . . . Integration, it was believed, would result in a disastrous mixing of the races. . . .

Newspapers and public places prominently displayed cartoons and posters depicting [the black's] alleged physical deformities and poking fun at his manners and customs. The minstrel shows, a popular form of entertainment in the ante bellum North, helped to fix a public impression of the clownish, childish, carefree, and irresponsible Negro. . . . As late as 1860, a group of New York Negroes, in an appeal for equal suffrage, complained bitterly that every facet of northern opinion had been turned against them. "What American artist has not caricatured us?" they asked. "What wit has not laughed at us in our wretchedness? has not ridiculed and condemned us? Few, few, very few." (Leon F. Litwack, North of Slavery: The Negro in the Free States, 1790–1860 [1961])

However, for all their agreement on the inferiority of the black American, white Northerners and Southerners now began to draw apart on the question of *whether slavery should be allowed in the territories.* Many Northerners were outraged at the possibility of such slave expansion, for to them this would mean massive invasion of the territories by black men. Wanting the new territories to be "white men's country," they detested this possibility. If pressed, they might say that slavery was an evil, but most of all they wanted it to stay where it was.

What was startling for Northerners to observe was that in the years after the Revolution, and especially after the great cotton boom that began after 1800, Southerners were no longer apologetic and defensive about the institution of slavery; they were assertive and aggressive. The Bible itself had been turned to for arguments "proving" that slavery was

divine in origin. Thus, when the Missouri issue erupted before Congress, it was explosive and violent precisely because Southerners were now confident of themselves on the issue, they had a booming economy behind them, and they were far more determined to have their way than in the past.

The Missouri Compromise

The House of Representatives accepted Tallmadge's amendment and sent a bill for a free Missouri to the Senate. A major crisis quickly erupted. As the question came up for debate in the Senate, an ugly atmosphere filled the chamber. Northern speakers had now reached the point of attacking slavery itself. There were pointed references to the words in the Declaration of Independence that all men were created equal. Particularly disturbing to Southerners was the accusation that slavery was a moral wrong. Above all, however, Southerners were alarmed that Congress would even engage in a discussion of slavery. Charles Pinckney of South Carolina, who had been a delegate to the Constitutional Convention of 1787, rose to say that the Constitution gave Congress no authority whatever over the slavery issue. Missouri itself was far less important, he said, than "keeping the hands of Congress from touching the question of slavery."

Nathaniel Macon of North Carolina described plantations as warm, loving institutions where there were only "glad faces and the hearty shaking of hands" when owners returned to their slaves from visits away. Relations between masters and slaves were far more easy and genial than between rich Northerners and their hired lackeys, he said. William Smith of South Carolina went even further. Slavery, he said, was ordained by God. "Christ himself gave a sanction to slavery," Smith said. "He admonished them to be obedient to their masters; and there is not a word in the whole of his life which forbids it. . . ."

The pro-slavery people, however, were up against an adamant anti-slavery-extension bloc of Northerners. The best that Southerners could get was to offer a compromise in which each side got something (a *quid pro quo*). Senator Jesse B. Thomas of Illinois, a native-born Virginian, proposed an amendment stating that: If Missouri were admitted with no anti-slavery restriction, in what remained of the Louisiana Purchase slavery would be "forever prohibited"; that is, above the line of 36° 30′ north

A power in Congress for more than forty years, Henry Clay helped frame the Missouri Compromise and the Compromise of 1850.

latitude, the southern boundary of Missouri. (The large area remaining in the Purchase would henceforth be denominated "unorganized territory"—that is, it would simply be left to the Indians, with no organized American government, even territorial, over it.) Maine, as it happened, was also seeking admission as a state, having formerly been a separated part of Massachusetts. The simultaneous admission of both Missouri and Maine would maintain the even balance between slave and non-slave senators in the Senate. With Henry Clay providing skillful congressional leadership, the Missouri Compromise of 1820 was enacted in this form: The Thomas amendment was adopted, and a slave Missouri and a free Maine were admitted to the Union.

The Compromise's Significance

To reach this point, we must note, Southern representatives in Congress had made enormous concessions to anti-slavery-extension opinion. First, in effect they had agreed that, save for the northward-thrusting state of Missouri, the line dividing the nation into free and slave states established by the old Northwest Ordinance of 1787 would be extended right on through the Louisiana Purchase to the nation's then-

existing western boundary. Second, by implication, Southerners were accepting a point of very great importance: the thesis that Congress did indeed have the power to legislate on slavery in the nation's territories. And third, they had agreed to a grossly uneven division of the vast Louisiana Purchase, the nation's largest remaining expanse of federal territory. The sum result: An enormous area *formerly open to slavery*, under law, was now to be free territory, like the Old Northwest. The Compromise, ultimately, was an immense anti-slavery-extension victory.

In all of this, there was a deep flaw that later years would uncover: Pro-slave people would never in fact let this new policy be put into effect. When it came to actually *implementing* it—that is, allowing what remained of the Purchase to be, in reality, formed into free organized territories and subsequently free states—Southerners would find themselves unable finally to accept that arrangement. Indeed, pro-slave Missourians would eventually move in decisively to nullify it by violence. This would not occur, however, until thirty more years had passed.

The Denmark Vesey Conspiracy

In 1822, two years after the Missouri Compromise, a free black in Charleston, South Carolina, named Denmark Vesey was alleged to have formed a conspiracy among household slaves. Unless the bonds of slavery were clamped down hard, black men seemed surprisingly (to Southern whites) like their white masters in striking out for freedom. Vesey and his followers, it was also said, had been directly stimulated by the debates over Missouri. "[W]hoever remembers the inflammatory speeches on the Missouri bill," one South Carolinian put it, "must be aware, that no subject, in which the question of slavery may be directly or incidentally introduced, can be canvassed, without the most malevolent and serious excitement."

Before this time it was not unusual for South Carolinians to describe slavery as a bad thing, though a necessary evil. Now the word went out. The institution was not to be questioned. *Not a word* that put slavery in even the smallest light of reproach could be allowed. Black churches were closed down, since plots were apparently brewed there. Masters were prohibited from freeing their slaves—freedmen were regarded as highly incendiary influences—and no free black was to be allowed into the state. Every black

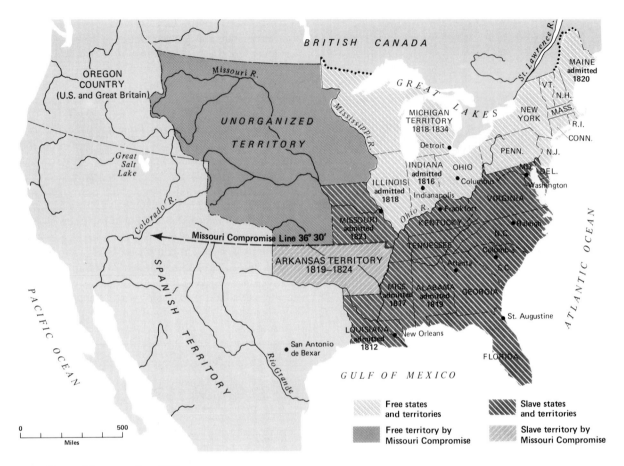

The Missouri Compromise, 1820

seaman arriving at Charleston was jailed until his boat left. When foreign nations protested and federal courts ruled the action unconstitutional, the South Carolina Senate defiantly asserted that "the duty of the state to guard against insubordination or insurrection . . . is paramount to all *laws*, all *treaties*, all *constitutions*."

The United States and Latin America

The United States had been watching with great interest the revolts against Spanish rule that had erupted in Spain's Latin American colonies in 1810. Many were flattered because Latin Americans were apparently imitating the American Revolution and fashioning governments modeled after that in the United States. Dead in the Old World, republicanism seemed to have taken fresh life in the New. Others were interested because of the great trade opportunities opened by the removal of Spanish mercantilist restrictions. By the 1820s, the United States was buying and selling millions of dollars worth of goods in Brazil alone.

All of this led to a historic debate on a crucial question: What should be America's relation to the outside world? Should the American people, inspired by their cause, follow a course of what would later be called "missionary diplomacy"? That is, should their national government work actively to spread democracy, to change the world in what it believed to be a progressive, pro-republican direction? Or should the country stick, instead, to providing simply a *model* for all the world to emulate; should it teach by example only? By following this course America would avoid international activism, with all of its uncertainties and complications.

Henry Clay of Kentucky had strong views on this question. He was an activist, and like many Americans he was alarmed at what was happening in the world at large. After 1815 and the defeat of Napoleon, Europe had fallen swiftly back under the rule of feudal monarchies; the republican dream seemed to have dwindled down to just the United States itself. Now, therefore, Clay urged that America, the exemplar of democracy in the world, had a great mission: to intervene actively in international affairs to push forward the cause of free institutions.

Looking at the Latin American wars for independence, Clay urged passionately that the United States encourage them. As he said in a major speech in 1818, "We behold the glorious spectacle of eighteen millions of people, struggling to burst their chains and to be free." They were battling, he said, not only for independence but also for liberty and self-government on the model of the United States of America, and were thus continuing the American Revolution. The United States should give them what is called "diplomatic recognition," a specific legal step which meant that, henceforth, the formal relations America had with all other nations would be opened to the Latin Americans as well. By this step, the United States would be declaring to all the world that the rebelling Latin American countries *were* independent nations (the European nations, loyal to monarchical Spain, were holding back), and that the rule of Spain over them was dead.

On whether the United States should follow an activist foreign policy, John Quincy Adams took a different view from Henry Clay. He insisted that America could not try to influence the internal affairs of other nations without getting involved in complex and unpredictable difficulties that might lead to war. The United States, he said in a Fourth of July oration in 1821, would be a "well-wisher to the freedom and independence of all," but would avoid grandiose efforts to liberate all those who lived under monarchies. The United States might become "the dictatress of the world [but] would no longer be the ruler of her own spirit" if it sought to manage the affairs of other nations. The nation should "go not abroad in search of monsters to destroy."

Even to Adams, however, it was another thing to stand aside passively while European powers intervened in the Western Hemisphere. Continental monarchs had been badly frightened by Napoleon, and they regarded rebellion anywhere with loathing. Rumors were rampant that these monarchs intended to adopt Spain's cause in the New World and return the former colonies to Spanish rule. To help prevent this, in March 1822 the United States became the first nation outside Latin America to recognize formally the five most successful rebelling countries: Argentina, Colombia, Chile, Peru, and Mexico. The Spanish government, the United States said, could never reassert its sovereignty over these nations. Diplomatic representatives would be exchanged, commercial treaties would be negotiated, and trade between the United States and Latin America would be fully opened.

The Monroe Doctrine

The British, meanwhile, had taken a major role in Latin American affairs. They were pleased with the rebellions, for British traders quickly dominated the new Latin American market. The British had far more goods and much more advantageous prices to offer than anyone else. Like the United States, Britain wished to see the Latin American countries remain independent and open to world trade. George Canning, the British foreign secretary, undertook vigorous diplomatic action in Europe to ward off action against the rebels. London now proposed to Washington that the two governments issue a joint statement guaranteeing the independence of the new Latin American countries.

President Monroe was disposed to agree with this proposal, as were most of his cabinet members. But John Quincy Adams had other ideas. He was determined to make the United States a vigorous, independent nation that took its *own* course in world affairs. Furthermore, he detested Great Britain. The British, he firmly believed, were the great rivals of the United States. He recoiled at the thought of the United States being a "cockboat in the wake of the British man-of-war." Adams converted Monroe to his view by appealing to his sense of nationalism. The president, indeed, decided to go further. Instead of just making a diplomatic reply to the British, as Adams had in mind, he wrote a bold statement that he was to make public to all the world by sending it in a formal message to Congress on the second of December 1823.

The American continents, Monroe asserted, were no longer "to be considered as subjects for future colonization by any European power." The two hemispheres were so separate from one another in their ways of life and government that each must refrain from interfering in the affairs of the other. The United States, in fact, would regard "any attempt on [Europe's] part to extend their system to any portions of this hemisphere, as dangerous to our peace and safety." In plain language, America would fight to keep them out. In this statement, the United States was setting itself up as the guarantor of Latin American independence.

The Monroe Doctrine was not backed up by force, however, for the United States did not equip itself with a sizable army and navy to enforce its policies; such a step would have been enormously costly. Indeed, it was the British navy that actually protected both Latin America and the United States from any possible assault from the European continent. Canning's forceful diplomacy, which he was conducting in Europe at the same time Monroe was drawing up and publishing his message, had much more to do with ensuring Latin American independence than Monroe's bravado and rhetoric. But the assertion had been made, soberly and unequivocally, at a time when Monroe could not yet know of Canning's maneuvers. It was bold; it could be applied thereafter or not, as circumstances might dictate; and such utterances have a way of influencing world affairs even though no overt act is committed.

European statesmen called it "blustering," "monstrous," and "arrogant." Latin American countries were delighted. They reproduced the statement and passed it from hand to hand, and their revolutionary leader Simon Bolivar publicly praised it. Their ardor cooled, however, when they found that it was little more than words. When they applied for alliances, they were rebuffed. When they asked for material aid, they learned that America intended taking no action unless an invasion came from Europe. America's Latin American relations, thus launched, were so filled with contradictory statements that resentment on the part of Latin America could be the only result.

The Election of 1824

The first party system, founded in the Age of Jefferson, was coming to an end. The decline of the Federalists into a local party based in New England and then their disappearance left the Republicans with no one to oppose. The "enemy" plays a powerful role in politics, both in providing an opposite pole against which to define party positions and in posing a clear and present danger that, having to be fought, induces unity. Without that enemy, the Republican party Thomas Jefferson had built broke up in the 1820s into factions and dissolved. At the same time, national

voting in presidential elections fell off precipitously, for the organizing power of a national party and the presence of a specific political enemy were absent. To many people this was good; political parties were thought to be divisive, disloyal, and a cause of disorder. For others, however, it soon became clear that a great continental republic could not survive without parties to focus and organize across state lines the political desires of the people.

The immediate question in 1824 was real and pressing: Who would succeed Monroe as chief executive? There were four candidates: John Quincy Adams of Massachusetts, William Crawford of Virginia, Henry Clay of Kentucky, and—clearly the most popular—Andrew Jackson, the Hero of New Orleans. All the other candidates carried the grimy look of men who had rolled and tumbled in the petty politics of Washington. Jackson alone appeared fresh, a grand and inscrutable figure cast to fit a large mold. No one seemed to know what he stood for. That did not matter; indeed, it probably helped him. In the uncertain political situation of the time, he was described as the man who could bring order out of chaos. He seemed honest, virile, and majestic in a crudely natural way.

In the balloting of 1824, Jackson received by far the largest popular vote. He was without question the favorite in the country. But no one had a clear majority in the electoral college. There were 99 votes for Jackson, 84 for John Quincy Adams, 41 for Crawford, and 37 for Clay. It was now up to the House of Representatives to make the decision, each state casting an equal ballot and thus nullifying the weight of popular votes. By constitutional provision, the House had to choose from among the three top candidates.

A storm of bargaining began. Of all the understandings made, that between Adams and Clay was crucial. What they actually said to one another is not known. It is doubtful that so scrupulous a man as Adams would have made an open bargain, promising the secretaryship of state to Clay in return for electoral votes. Adams seems, rather, simply to have indicated that the future would find the government much more favorable to old Federalists and to men of Clay's orientation if he (Adams) were president. The result was a victory for Adams, for Clay supporters in the House swung their votes to him. When Adams later gave the post of secretary of state to Clay, an outcry of "corrupt bargain" went up that dogged both men ever after.

John Quincy Adams as President

So began John Quincy Adams's four sterile years in the White House. Unhappily for Adams, the times were not congenial to a nationalist in the White House. They were certainly not friendly, moreover, to a Yankee nationalist who carried an air of superiority, felt himself surrounded by enemies, and resorted frequently to scorn and sarcasm in reply to criticism.

His first message called boldly for far-ranging programs of national development led by the government in Washington. He asked for huge expenditures for internal improvements and called for the founding of a national university and other such agencies. He also instructed his hearers that "liberty is power," that to have the most liberty the country must have a strong national government. He poured scorn upon the idea of limited government. He also brushed aside the notion that the nation's leaders should follow popular belief. While other nations were advancing, he said, "were we to slumber in indolence or fold up our arms and proclaim to the world that we are palsied by the will of our constituents?"

Rage and ridicule greeted Adams's message. It was tactless and politically suicidal. It was widely remembered that his own father had signed the Alien and Sedition acts. Now here was the son again singing the praises of strong, European-style, irresponsible government. Even Henry Clay could not follow him. Thomas Jefferson burst out in anger from Monticello that federalism had been reborn in John Quincy Adams. Liberty was not power, he said, but rather the restraint of power.

The Tariff of Abominations and the Election of 1828

In 1828 Congress took up the tariff again. In a highly confused proceeding, it passed a measure that was the product of so many complicated bargains and under-the-table deals that around it inevitably hung an aura of corruption and greed. Initially designed to aid those who produced raw materials rather than those who worked them into finished goods, the final tariff dispensed favors to producers and manufacturers in the Northern states. The South was enraged. Cotton was at a ruinously low price in the Liverpool Exchange in England, and now what Southerners called the Tariff of Abominations hiked costs consid-

erably. Woolen cloth, extensively used in slaves' clothing, had its tariff raised markedly, and its price correspondingly increased. Iron, sail cloth, and hemp for making rope were also favored, all of which hurt shipbuilders, who complained vigorously.

It was the South Carolinians, however, who acted on their anger. South Carolina congressmen gathered in the home of Senator Robert Y. Hayne after the tariff's passage. They were convinced that their place in the Union was growing ever more perilous because the Northern states were combining to exploit Southern plantation owners. In the hope that Andrew Jackson would modify the tariff, it was agreed that nothing would be done until after the election of 1828, but the mood remained militant. It was at this moment that John C. Calhoun, now an *ex*-nationalist, retired to his home in the uplands of South Carolina to begin writing a statement that

The Election of 1828

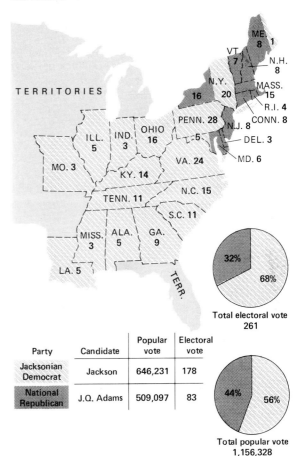

Party	Candidate	Popular vote	Electoral vote
Jacksonian Democrat	Jackson	646,231	178
National Republican	J.Q. Adams	509,097	83

was later adopted as the South Carolina Exposition and Protest. The whirlwind that Jackson was to reap in the Nullification Crisis was already brewing. (This controversy will be discussed in Chapter 15 as part of the history of the slavery controversy from 1820 to 1850.)

As to the coming presidential election of 1828, there was no longer any doubt regarding the candidates. The confusion of 1824 had disappeared. The nation was once more dividing into a two-party political configuration; that is, toward a *second* party system. There was simply the president, Adams, and his great opponent, Jackson, who had been moving toward this confrontation ever since the "corrupt bargain" of 1824. Adams, whose backers called themselves National Republicans, had little chance, though he secured a larger vote than might have been expected. He took all of New England as well as New Jersey, Delaware, and Maryland. The rest went to Andrew Jackson, who swept into the White House with the support of 650,000 votes, over 508,000 for Adams. It was a replay of the election of 1800: The South and the Middle Atlantic states of New York and Pennsylvania, with the aid, this time, of most of the new states of the West, joined to defeat New England. There was no doubt about it: In a way that only Jefferson and Washington could claim before him, Jackson was the popular choice for president of the United States.

BIBLIOGRAPHY

Books that were especially valuable to me in thinking about and writing this chapter: several recent works, Merrill D. Peterson's *The Great Triumvirate: Webster, Clay, and Calhoun* (1987), Archibald Cox's *The Court and the Constitution* (1987), and Lawrence Friedman's new edition of his *A History of American Law* (1985). I am also in debt to George Dangerfield's two beautifully written volumes *The Era of Good Feelings* (1963) and *The Awakening of American Nationalism, 1815–1828* (1965), and Samuel Flagg Bemis's authoritative *John Quincy Adams and the Foundations of American Foreign Policy* (1949). Marcus Cunliffe's *The Nation Takes Shape, 1789–1837* (1959) is a perceptive introduction to the nationalist period that highlights its links to the past and focuses on the peculiar tensions that dominated the period. James Sterling Young's *The Washington Community, 1800–1828* (1966) is a brilliant description of what the national capital was actually like as a political community.

Frederick Jackson Turner first elaborated the problem of sectionalism in his *The Significance of Sections in American History* (1932), and Charles S. Sydnor's *The Development of Southern Sectionalism, 1819–1848* (1948) illustrates this beautifully for the South. The disruptive clash over Missouri is capably discussed in Glover Moore's *The Missouri Controversy, 1819–1821* (1953).

Harry Ammon's *James Monroe: The Quest for National Identity* (1971) is a fine work. Ernest R. May's *The Making of the Monroe Doctrine* (1975) is a major new work. Arthur P. Whitaker's *The United States and the Independence of Latin America, 1800–1830* (1941) expertly probes the Monroe Doctrine and its implications. For those who read Spanish, a provocative analysis of the United States' and Britain's actions from the Latin American viewpoint is found in Jorge Abelardo Ramos's *Historia a la Nación Latino-Americana* (1968).

The election of 1824 is thoroughly inspected in Shaw Livermore, Jr.'s *The Twilight of Federalism: The Disintegration of the Federalist Party* (1962). Banking is the focus of an excellent, far-reaching study by Bray Hammond, *Banks and Politics in America from the Revolution to the Civil War* (1957). Glyndon Van Deusen's *Life of Henry Clay* (1937) offers an intriguing view of one of the consummate politicans of the era, and Robert V. Remini's *The Election of Andrew Jackson* (1963) illuminates the 1828 election.

11

The Great Transformation, 1815–1850: Physical and Human Dimensions

TIME LINE

1791–1802	Toussaint L'Ouverture leads slave rebellion in Santo Domingo and Haiti
1800	General Gabriel leads slave rebellion in Richmond, Virginia
1803	Ohio admitted to the Union
1811	National Road authorized
1815–40	Cotton boom under way in Deep South; wheat boom in Old Northwest; new states admitted to the Union—Indiana (1816), Mississippi (1817), Illinois (1818), Alabama (1819), Maine (1820), Missouri (1821), Arkansas (1836), and Michigan (1837)
1816	American Colonization Society founded
1817–25	New York State builds the Erie Canal
1820s	First labor unions formed
1830s	Railroad era begins
1834	Pennsylvania's Main Line Canal opened
1835	Cherokees take the Trail of Tears from the Southeast to the Western plains
1837	Depression begins
1840–60	Regularly scheduled ocean transport inaugurated; cloth mills built in New England; heavy immigration from Ireland and Germany; new states admitted to the Union—Florida and Texas (1845), Iowa (1846), Wisconsin (1848), California (1850), Minnesota (1858), and Oregon (1859)

ELI WHITNEY

It was the year 1801, and the president and vice-president of the United States, John Adams and Thomas Jefferson, sat dumbfounded as they watched a sight they could hardly believe. The tall, dignified Yankee before them, Eli Whitney, already famous for his invention of the cotton gin almost a decade previous, calmly took ten muskets apart, distributed the pieces into separate heaps, then sat back and offered to pick up the scattered bolts and stocks and barrels at random and reassemble the muskets. Then he did so.

Interchangeable parts! And made by machinery, so that they could be fabricated swiftly and with unvarying accuracy. Not original with Whitney (the process was actually conceived in Europe), it was nonetheless in America that this labor-saving procedure was earliest and most extensively put to use, since labor in America was scarcer and more costly. Its potential was dramatic. The entire production of the federal arsenal at Springfield, Massachusetts, amounted to 245 muskets in two years time, since each part was made painstakingly by hand to fit each particular weapon.

Whitney spent two laborious years building the machine tools—grinders and borers and lathes—necessary to make the parts accurately. Now he could start the project people had scoffed at: manufacturing not 245 but 10,000 muskets in two years' time. Actually, Whitney's methods were perhaps not even as advanced as those in use at other armories, and he took eight years, not two, to meet his contract. But the principle had been dramatically established.

He was, of course, an old hand at working revolutions. In 1792 the United States had exported about 140,000 pounds of cotton. All of it was long-staple cotton raised in the only place it could be grown, along the Southern coasts. Short-staple cotton could be grown all over the South, but the tedious labor of pulling out its many seeds had made that crop unprofitable. Whitney's cotton gin, invented in 1793 after the Yankee, visiting in Savannah, Georgia, had heard Southerners lamenting this problem, had produced a bewildering explosion of productivity and a new era in American economic history. By 1800 the United States was raising 35 *million* pounds of cotton and exporting half of it. The cotton boom, with all its historic results, was under way.

The industrial use of interchangeable parts and mass production by machines took much longer to ignite. It was a far more complex phenomenon anyway. A machine-tool industry needed to be in place before the necessary stamps and borers and other devices would be generally available. In 1815 Eli and Seth Thomas put the system to work making clocks. By the 1840s it was in use making sewing machines, farm machinery, watch parts, and Colt revolvers. American industry always had to pay a higher price for labor than its European counterpart, since it was scarcer in America, and in time industrialists put mass production to use far more extensively in the United States than in any other country. But the great inventor saw little of this. He died at the age of sixty, in 1825, a classic Yankee entrepreneur whose fertile inventiveness had helped to make the world different for his having lived in it.

Overview

America was still a quiet, preindustrial country at the end of the War of 1812. But then it exploded, seemingly in all directions, becoming an open, moving, growing, rapidly changing new country. By the 1850s, all was different. From the bursting 1820s onward, agricultural productivity began rising swiftly, a factory economy started to emerge, standards of living improved steadily (for whites) as productivity and per capita income swelled, the vast interior was invaded by hundreds of thousands of westward-moving settlers taking up cotton, corn, and wheat lands, new towns were founded by the hundreds, and old ones grew into great cities. Enterprising persons saw undreamed-of wealth before them.

States arose on all sides in the wilderness, a new one entering the Union about every two and a half years. Immigrants crowded into America to work in the new factories in the Northeast and to take up farmlands in the Old Northwest. The adoption of new ways and new things based on the fluid, rather than static, economics of this era became the order of the day. Perhaps most striking of all, by the mid-1850s the United States of America had expanded into a vast nation extending from coast to coast.

Explosive Growth in Territory

When the United States of America had begun its national existence in 1789, in European terms it was already a very large country, with 860,000 square miles. Four countries the size of France, Europe's largest nation, could fit into it and leave something left over. Then had come a fantastic event: the Louisiana Purchase of 1803. In one stroke of the pen, the United States became a truly immense republic of 1.6 million square miles, its western parts so far away and little known that it would take many years to get their precise boundary line searched out and agreed upon. Now the American nation was larger than *all of Europe*, excluding Russia. Indeed, it rivaled in size Russia itself, a fact that caught wide attention. America and Russia: Would they ultimately be, it was often asked, the leading nations of the future?

And still the expansive surge went on. As we have seen, while Europe was convulsed in the Napoleonic Wars, the American government had simply taken over West Florida, and in 1819, following protracted negotiations with Spain, East Florida had joined the American domain. A quarter of a century later came the largest outward burst of them all. In the 1840s, diplomatic agreements with Great Britain dividing up the Oregon Country and war with Mexico would bring in 1.2 million more square miles. When in 1853 the Gadsden Purchase of 29,000 square miles (in present-day southern Arizona and New Mexico) was made, the outlines of what are now the 48 contiguous states would be complete. The United States of America had become a country of continental proportions, 3,000 miles from east to west, with long seacoasts facing the Atlantic, the Gulf of Mexico, and the Pacific Ocean—and a land area (as of 1860) of 2.97 million square miles.

Explosive Growth in Population

During the years from 1815 to the 1850s, the American people also increased enormously in numbers. Since far back in the 1700s, in fact, Americans had been multiplying at a tremendous rate, considerably surpassing the population surge going on in Europe at the same time. From 1700 to 1800 the number of people in England had swelled from 6 million to 9 million, but the number of Americans had grown from 250,000 to over 5 million—and this figure was rising at a rate of *more than 30 percent every ten years*. The median age in 1800 was sixteen; about every third American was a small child less than ten years old. The United States of America was a land of adults awash in a sea of children.

This rapid growth would continue until about 1860. In 1820 there were almost 10 million Americans; in 1830 this figure had risen to almost 13 million; by 1850 the total would be over 23 million; and at the moment of Southern secession, in 1861, the United States would number 31.5 million people, of whom perhaps 4 million were black and mainly enslaved. Thus, as the demographic historian Walter Nugent observes, in the years from 1815 to 1850 the American people were still in that era of rapid population growth which he terms the frontier-rural period. With about 50 live births per thousand Americans each year (there are about 17 now, in the 1980s), Americans doubled in numbers every twenty-two years.

Where did they increase most rapidly? In the new-settled country just behind the westward-moving frontier. Here, young people were plowing new farms and forming new families, and the birth rate probably achieved *65 per thousand*—a rate higher than that in any nation in the world in the 1970s and 1980s. After 1840 the American rate slowed to about 40 per thousand in 1860. Nonetheless, because of so many births annually, until well after the Civil War most Americans were young people. By the 1860s, the median age had risen only to about twenty (in the 1980s, it is about thirty).

How do we explain this explosive growth? In part it happened because of heavy immigration after 1840, but primarily because people in the United States married at an early age, and Americans were healthier than Europeans (due to more abundant food and a more scattered population, so that disease did not spread so easily). Perhaps a fourth of all American babies died at birth or soon after, because of childhood sicknesses, but even so this was a significantly lower figure than in the European countries. Furthermore, because of earlier marriages and better health, American women were simply in the childbearing business earlier and longer. They began menstruating at age fifteen (menarche occurs at a younger age in the 1980s since diet and health have continued to improve), and in practically all cases they were soon married and having children about as rapidly as nature allowed, or generally every eighteen months to two years. This continued until menopause in the mid-forties, by which time the average American family had about five living children.

The Preindustrial Economy

Americans needed these big families, for in 1815 the United States of America was still overwhelmingly an agricultural country. Because hand labor and primitive tools were the rule, many hands were needed to work each farm. More than eight out of every ten families lived on the land, as against less than four in England.

There was also, however, a lot of manufacturing. It simply took place in the home, thus creating another demand for hard-working hands. Household manufactures had played an important role, in fact, in the emergence of American republicanism. Although Americans proudly proclaimed that they were farmers, and in the revolutionary years had insisted that republicanism flourished in its truest form among them precisely because the farming life made people virtuous and independent-minded, they had quickly seen that they needed manufactures in order to make their new republic independent of England. During

the Revolution itself, technology, in the form of what was called "useful knowledge," was highly praised. Domestic manufacturing was strongly encouraged, and this resulted in an unprecedented outpouring of textiles and other goods made in the household, or in small workshops.

After the Revolution, when British goods began pouring into the country again, a strong motive for creating a new constitution and an effective federal government was the desire to use that instrument to foster domestic industries (that is, within America, as well as within the home) and keep out British articles. The new nation, it was said, needed a balanced economy that was independent of the United Kingdom.

People still thought, however, of decentralized, household manufactures, not of factories and great cities. Thus, household manufactures and the making of goods by individual craftsmen in small, scattered rural communities would, it was believed, enhance American republicanism, not threaten it. Small-scale manufacturing flourished in preindustrial America. In the older Northeastern areas, as in parts of Pennsylvania, perhaps a third of the people made their living not just as farmers, but mainly through practicing a trade or working as craftsmen: Blacksmiths, shoemakers, weavers, cabinetmakers, and many more skilled workers were in evidence. Thousands of men, women, and children worked as butchers, tallow chandlers, soap boilers, and leather curriers, processing the products produced by the farms—wheat, pork, hides, and cheese—so that they might be exported. In the Philadelphia area there were six textile factories whose product reached 65,000 yards of cloth in 1809, but individual families working at home in and around the city produced 230,000 yards! In other words, in the preindustrial economy people generally worked at home, or in small operations nearby; there was much independence of life, since a farm was often part of the family scene; and craftsmen directed their own hours and conditions of work, subject only to the market.

The Building of Turnpikes

The War of 1812 showed how bad were the nation's roads. It had been a major undertaking just to get troops to the Canadian border. A national clamor arose for a swift expansion of improved roads. The first step taken to improve transportation was the building of turnpikes, a movement that began in the

This view of Broadway, New York City, captures the teeming activity of a highly commercial scene of the 1830s.

coastal states some time before the War of 1812. Of all the projects of this nature, the greatest was the building of the National Road. Much harassed by political wrangles—the whole question of federal support for internal improvements was a burning issue in these decades—the road nevertheless moved steadily westward. Its objective was to open the interior. Begun in 1811 at Cumberland, Maryland (a fairly central location in the East), by 1818 it had been completed to Wheeling, West Virginia; by 1833 it had reached Columbus, Ohio; and by mid-century this immense undertaking, Roman in its grand proportions, had arrived at Vandalia, Illinois.

The Canal Era

New Yorkers conceived and forged ahead with an ambitious plan. In 1817, even though most of the people of New York lived in the lower Hudson Valley, the state legislature passed a bill calling for the excavation of a canal 363 miles long, running from Albany through the almost unpeopled valley of the Mohawk River to Buffalo on Lake Erie. Opening

up the one easy route through the mountains to the interior, it would make New York State the highway of national expansion, populate the Mohawk Valley with prosperous cities, and fashion New York City into the preeminent seaport of America. Since the longest canal then constructed in the United States ran less than 30 miles, this public act required unusual fortitude and vision. The federal government refused all aid; the whole financial burden would fall on the one million people of New York State who raised the money by borrowing in London. Pushed forward with feats of innovation genuinely legendary, the Erie Canal opened in the fall of 1825 to an outburst of oratory and celebration.

The canal began a new era in national history. Settlers crowded westward through this new pathway to settle territory around the Great Lakes. Within ten years of its completion, traffic was so heavy that enlargement of the entire canal had to begin. This large volume of traffic produced excellent revenues for decades afterward. In fact, traffic on the Erie continued to rise long after the railroad age had begun, reaching its peak in 1880. It was clear now that vast developments in the American interior awaited only an adequate and economical system of transportation. Scheme after scheme was launched to connect other locations on the East Coast—Philadelphia, Baltimore, the Potomac—with the trans-Appalachian West.

The Railroad Era

The first railroading began in England in 1829, but its most dramatic development came in the United States. All of Europe had less than 2,000 miles of trackage by 1840, whereas America already possessed 3,000 miles. The need was urgent, and a continental expanse free of boundary and tariff restrictions lay open for development. Land was cheap, making railroad construction easier than in Europe, and the American economy was more innovative and less hampered by monopolies and long-established customs. The result was a railroad explosion. In 1840 the United States had as much railroad trackage as it had canals, and by 1860 the railroads in the country totaled more than 30,000 miles, divided about equally among the Northern, Southern, and Western states. The canals, even though widespread in the 1840s, were below 9,000 miles in total extent.

Because of what economists call the multiplier effect, such great improvements in transportation had a dramatic impact on the productivity of the Northern states. Farmers, manufacturers, and mine owners got higher prices, those buying goods received more for their money, the value of land rose, middlemen and bankers in good locations became wealthy, and tax money flowing to the government swelled in volume. In short, the whole society gained tremendously, not just the men who invested in each project, although laboring men seemed to benefit little.

There was not enough private capital in the country to provide the transportation net that was wanted. State governments and local communities responded by making lavish grants to railroad projects, devising attractive charters to make construction profitable, and sometimes building the railroads themselves. Congress soon joined in. Until 1850, aid was prevented by the fact that Eastern and Southern legislators tended to be envious of Western growth at the expense of older areas. Thereafter, the South gave its support to Western demands, hoping thereby to gain allies in its growing controversy with Northern states over slavery. A North–South railroad running from Chicago to Mobile, Alabama (the Illinois

Central), was given 4 million acres of federal land in Illinois, Mississippi, and Alabama.

The Transatlantic Economy

Steam had its impact in many ways, not just on the railroads. It transformed transportation on the rivers and on the lakes. On the high seas, however, steam came slowly, since there were difficult technical problems to solve. Meanwhile, the number of sailing vessels crossing the Atlantic increased rapidly. Until the 1850s, ocean transport remained primarily a matter of broad-bottomed merchantmen pushing through the seas under a cloud of sail. From the late 1840s to the Civil War was the time of the stately clipper ships. Phenomenally fast, strikingly beautiful, they coursed the world's sea-lanes at speeds never before achieved for such distances on land or on sea.

They gave way in the 1850s to the steam vessel, which by that time had been sufficiently improved to master the difficulties of long voyages over rough seas. Partly through inadequate technology and partly because they simply could not believe that steam and iron could replace their beautiful wooden vessels, American shipbuilders continued to concentrate on sailing ships. In part for this reason, dominance in ocean transport passed primarily into British hands after the Civil War.

Meanwhile, an Anglo-American economy far more vigorous than before took shape. From 1815 to 1860 there were not two separate national economies, one British and the other American, but a unified Atlantic economy in which both countries played complementary parts. Hundreds of thousands of English, Scots, Welsh, and Irish journeyed across the Atlantic to become part of American life. At the same time, British capital, enterprise, and technology poured into the American economy.

To a great extent, the economic dividing line was not the Atlantic but the crests of the Appalachians. A transatlantic partnership had developed between New York and Liverpool, Boston and London, New England and Old England, these relationships jointly providing the vigor, confidence, and capital to open the American frontier. Eastern Americans and Britons joined in developing the continental interior, opening its resources, populating its cities, and breaking its soil. The United States was Britain's principal customer. Americans bought most of their cloth, hardware, iron, and other manufactured goods

An early illustration of railroad travel showing a passenger carriage and "cow-catcher" on a locomotive.

from the British Isles. In turn, America's largest customer was the United Kingdom, to which the United States sent half its exports. Between 1820 and 1860 about half of this trade consisted of cotton bales going to northern England to be spun into cloth.

Cotton was king of the whole transatlantic economy. It crossed the Atlantic in such enormous volumes that almost by itself it paid for American purchases from Europe. Without such mountainous supplies of the raw material, the cotton textile industry of northern England would never have been built and the factory system would not have advanced with the vigor that characterized its transformation of the Anglo-American world. Liverpool flourished on the American trade, receiving yearly from across the Atlantic hundreds of vessels laden with cotton and wheat from the Middle West, and in return

sending to New York metal goods, pottery, finished cloth, and Irish immigrants. Nourished by this massive transatlantic trade, New York swelled in population, soon leaving Philadelphia and Boston far behind. At a million people, New York in 1860 was twice the size of Philadelphia.

Factory Production Surges

The great transportation innovations opened up large markets to everyone. Consequently, from the 1820s onward factory manufacturing surged, especially in New England, where water power, an enterprising and industrious Yankee culture, and an available labor supply of women and children existed together. It

Canals and Roads, 1820–1850

was soon apparent that larger operations could be much more productive than small ones in terms of the investment and the number of people employed. They could afford larger equipment, the use of more power, and the most up-to-date technical innovations. Larger machines meant labor-saving, and this meant cheaper products. The process was not, however, instantaneous: Small-scale factories dominated the economy until the 1840s, when large-scale operations began booming.

During that decade people began leaving their farms in great numbers to flock to the cities and go to work in large factories. They did this principally because, even though hours of labor were long and pay scales hardly luxurious, city workers made more than farmers (about one-third more in real income), and life in urban centers was more interesting and attractive, certainly during the early phases of industrialization. But there was a heavy cost to all of this: loss of independence and, for many independent craftsmen, of the satisfactions of their trade.

The factory system, once begun, could only result in the destruction of local crafts in small towns. Thus, a large and important group in American life, one having a great sense of personal worth and autonomy, was slowly eliminated. On the other hand, greater productivity meant that the wealth of the entire society was rising, and this contributed to a steady increase in the standard of living. There was no escape from the essential dilemma: Economic modernization brought with it both blessings and curses.

Many Americans, however, no longer agonized over what high productivity might do to national life. After the War of 1812 the Republic itself was no longer in danger. Indeed, it now seemed confirmed by battle and burstingly confident of its continued existence. Thus, the concern for maintaining simplicity of life in order to keep the Republic virtuous gave way to an intoxication with the possibilities that a booming industrial economy had for fulfillment of dreams and a more abundant life for every individual. The new productivity, it was believed, could also make people more optimistic, compassionate, and concerned for others.

Technological progress was now seen (not by everyone, by any means) as a great enhancement to the Republic. America was coming to mean prosperity and relative affluence for the common person. "Progress" was beginning to be seen as the country's most important product. In a constant outpouring of sermons, speeches, pamphlets, and books, textile mills were described as sublime instruments of a better

life, and locomotives as fabulous creations. They were the images of the new America. The leading political orator of the pre–Civil War generation, the Harvard classics professor and editor of the *North American Review* Edward Everett, spent a lifetime crying the marvels and beauties of industrialism. Republicanism and technology, he insisted, combined to put America, with its unusual freedom of economic life, in a position of promise offered by no other nation in the world.

Textile manufacturing led the way. Here, with the most dramatic effects, all procedures involved in making cloth were collected in one plant under a single management, and the making of standardized grades of inexpensive cloth was thus set in motion to tap a mass market. The marketing of the plant's entire output through one marketing agency was the next step. Mechanical power, mass production, concentration on a low-cost market, and strong financial backing made this system a profitable operation. By the mid 1840s, the rivers of southern New England (where power was available to turn looms) were dotted with cloth mills. In a brief time the system spread to the production of woolen as well as cotton cloth, the manufacturing of carpets, and such operations as flour milling, lumber milling, glassmaking, distilling, tanning, and even the making of iron.

The Appearance of Organized Labor

The expansion of the market provided factory owners with great opportunities, but also with great problems. They now faced many competitors and had to produce their goods as cheaply as possible. Every possible device was used to keep wages down, and wages were paid only every three or six months. Higher production was demanded, reduced hourly rates were given, longer hours of work were insisted on, and always workers lived under the threat of being fired.

In the 1820s, the expanding market created such a strong demand for labor that skilled craftsmen were able to form unions. They began to struggle with organized capital for higher wages and fewer hours. Thirteen to sixteen hours a day was a common work schedule. But strikes for better wages and hours almost always failed. The employers had too much power, and public opinion was on their side. Employers were "gentlemen," and it was thought monstrous for those below to make demands on those above.

When carpenters in Boston struck in 1825 for a ten-hour day, the "gentlemen engaged in building" crushed the strike, issuing a statement that the "spirit of discontent and insubordination" among workers was a disruptive idea introduced from Europe. A shorter workday, they said, would simply mean "a wide door for idleness and vice." In case after case, workers were fined and jailed for the "crime" of combining to raise their wages. Labor won a major victory, however, in the important case of *Commonwealth* v. *Hunt* (1842), in which a Massachusetts judge ruled for the first time that workers could lawfully organize unions and go on strike.

In the 1830s, skilled craftsmen in many trades were able to build vigorous unions, since the economy was booming and the demand for labor continued strong. At the same time, organized workmen entered politics, forming the Workingman's party in New York City. All this, however, ended when the depression of 1837 wiped out the labor movement's economic base. Thousands were thrown out of work. Those still employed were ready to labor for any wage and under any conditions. Their unions disappeared, and their political movements withered away, buried under an avalanche of public abuse.

Mass Immigration

Of all the folk wanderings in world history, the one that sent 5 million Europeans to America in the years from 1815 to 1860 is certainly one of the most remarkable. It was like a great flood that mounted higher and higher, exciting public amazement on both sides of the Atlantic. Americans were enthusiastic at the influx of free labor but alarmed that the incoming horde spoke different tongues and brought in Catholicism, making that faith for the first time a major feature of the American religious scene.

In the 1820s, immigration brought only some 150,000 people into the United States. Then the swift rise began. In the 1830s, the figure rose to almost 600,000. In the 1840s, the influx grew to an astonishing 1.7 million, a figure eclipsed in the 1850s by 2.3 million immigrants. Altogether, they composed a group of people greater in numbers than the entire population of the United States in 1790. A great many, perhaps 250,000, came from Canada, which sent French-Canadians into New York State and New England, and Ontario farmers into the American Middle West. Most of them, however, came from northern and western Europe. Half arrived from the British Isles (2 million of these from Ireland); 1.5 million came from Germany; Switzerland, Holland, and the Scandinavian countries provided most of the remainder.

Why did they come in such incredible numbers? Periodic depressions, dreams of improvement, hopes of establishing a religious utopia, famine, local repressions, failing revolutions—an almost infinite variety of influences moved men to ask, "How do I get to the sea?" Many people simply called it the American fever. Whole populations in Europe that had hardly even heard of America suddenly learned of it through the appearance of a huge body of books and writings that circulated all over Europe.

It should be noted, too, that immigration to America was only one aspect of a continentwide European milling about. From 1818 to 1828, a quarter of a million Germans moved into southern Russia while only 10,000 of their countrymen were going to the United States. As late as the middle of the nineteenth century, almost as many Irish were in Britain as in the United States. Furthermore, the *whole* of the New World received Europeans. The proportion of foreign-born population to native-born in the United States has never been so large as in Argentina, where in 1914 three of ten had been born abroad. There were periods in the history of some Canadian provinces in which the immigrant population outnumbered the native-born two to one.

Of all the migrations, that from Ireland was the most dramatic. That unhappy country had grown seriously overpopulated by the early nineteenth century, and thousands were forced to emigrate for economic reasons. Then came the grim potato blight of the 1840s, leading to an appalling loss of life through starvation. Whole regions became open-air charnel houses. Isolated, without food or hope of food, many Irish peasants simply sat in their one-room cottages and waited for death. Others made their way to the seaports. A million and a half people left the small country of Ireland in the decade after 1847. A comparable tragedy in the United States today would see 35 million people fleeing the country and an equal number left behind dead and dying of starvation. Perhaps only the Jews and Russians in the twentieth century have been struck as severe a blow as the Irish in the 1840s. Even today, the Irish number about half what they did a century ago. For many decades after the actual famine, hundreds of thousands of Irishmen continued to board boats and head west, for their country seemed filled only with despair and terrible memories.

By 1860, the 32 million people living in the United States included over 4 million foreign-born. Most settled in the North; only about one-eighth went to the South. Wherever they went, most immigrants headed for cities. In New York, in Chicago, and in San Francisco, half of the population was foreign-born; in St. Louis the proportion was three-fifths. The poverty-stricken Irish remained primarily in the northeastern cities, for they could not afford land, though large numbers scattered in urban centers throughout the country. The Germans spread out more uniformly in both countryside and town. Almost none settled in New England; over half went to the upper Middle West. Those from Great Britain dispersed even more widely, blending into the general population so thoroughly as largely to escape notice. Scandinavians concentrated heavily in the upper Mississippi region, and the Dutch stopped either in New York State or went on to Michigan, Wisconsin, and Iowa.

Immigration's Significance

For immigrants, entering American life was economically difficult and emotionally wearing. They came to a country where everything looked strikingly different from what they were used to at home, and where their clothes, their language, their ways of life, and often their religion subjected them to scorn. At least for the first generation, the immigrant lived as a marginal person, caught between two cultures but not a full member of either. There was no one to help them, and few were ready to understand or sympathize.

The great task in every country engaged in industrialization is to find hands free from other work that may be put to use in factories and in the huge construction projects that economic development requires. American industrialization in such cities as Boston had been forced to advance slowly until immigrants arrived. Now workers came crowding off the boats, eager to labor at anything, ready to take low wages, often unable to speak English, and disliked by existing craft unions. The 5 million immigrants gave a massive upward lift to the entire economy, probably approaching the transportation revolution in importance.

While others benefited, the immigrant generally got little. Many were forced to crowd into old warehouses or ancient mansions for living space or had to build one-room shanties. Tens of thousands of New York City's immigrants lived in basements. Immigrants were subjected to constant incursions of mass disease, which swept across them like killing winds. Tuberculosis, smallpox, typhus, cholera, and other such illnesses struck them far more cruelly than they did the general population. The world of the urban immigrant was a world of survivors who lived in dread of the next season of illness.

Alienated, exploited, shunned by the majority, immigrants developed a strong sense of ethnic identity. When they were deeply religious, their church became everything to them that Congress, president, and flag were to native-born Americans. Drawn by fellow feeling, they congregated in certain parts of the cities. Two-thirds of New York City's 100,000 Germans lived in three wards, where German was practically all that was heard, and German churches, eating places, theaters, libraries, and schools maintained German culture.

Non-British immigrant groups quickly lined up on the side of the Jeffersonian party. The early established pattern, in which the Democrats spoke for the non-British immigrants and the Federalists (and their descendants, the Whigs and the Republicans) spoke against them, has persisted as one of the most distinctive patterns in American politics.

The Frontier Moves Westward

As momentous as was the immigrant flood, the vast westward sweep of the frontier of settlement that got in motion after the War of 1812 and kept surging decade after decade was even more arresting. A wedge of settlement had earlier, by 1815, been thrust out beyond the Appalachians, into the region that became Tennessee, Kentucky, and southern Ohio. These three states together had actually reached a population in 1810 of some 900,000. But vast territories to the north and south of this wedge remained largely unsettled. In the next generation a flood of settlers surged into them that dwarfed all earlier movements. By 1850, the American frontier of settlement had swept halfway across the continent. Indeed, the frontier by 1850 included vast Texas, and had leapfrogged beyond to California and Oregon.

What fueled this tidal movement across North America? First, Americans were fortunate in that the interior of their continent was not a vast desert, as in Australia; it was not a jungle, as in Brazil; or an Arctic terrain, as in much of interior Canada. It was instead one of the world's great food-growing regions, a wonderfully fertile land blessed by a relatively temperate climate. There was at first a barrier to settlement in the Indian peoples already living there, but they were tiny in numbers by comparison with the westward-surging whites, and as had been true since American settlement began on the eastern coast, the barrier was soon removed.

We must also remember the basic demographic facts of American life. A dramatically high birth rate meant that in the older American sections there was never enough land for a father to give a farm to all his sons, so that each could begin the independent life that America promised and that Americans so highly valued. By 1800 the Eastern seaboard was crowded (given the way land was then used), so younger people began looking beyond the mountains, and trekking there to begin the same process over again.

We see, therefore, that high fertility, as Walter Nugent has remarked, was like an engine driving Americans westward. The westward movement, it could accurately be said, was born in America's bedrooms. It was a movement that, so driven, would go on decade after decade. Not until the 1920s would the ready supply of new land in the West for young men and women to go to and found independent families finally dwindle away. By this time too, Americans would be having far fewer children.

Clearing Out the Indians

Pressure for land in the plains around the Great Lakes and the Gulf of Mexico was intense as soon as the War of 1812 was over, and the government moved vigorously to clear out the Indians. Since 1803, Thomas Jefferson had been urging that the western half of the Mississippi Valley become Indian country and that Indians from the East be removed to that location. As early as 1811, 2,000 Creeks had migrated to the Arkansas country.

Many argued—Jefferson had advanced such reasons—that it would be in the Indians' best interest to send them far away from the whites, so that their own way of life could regain its strength and moral health. Certainly it is true that those Indians who were clasped most closely and compassionately to the breast of the whites, such as the coastal tribes around the California missions, have almost wholly disappeared, whereas those living apart have survived. But the process was so fraudulently carried out, and tribes so heartlessly shuttled back and forth,

that voices of protest arose. Some New Englanders, Ralph Waldo Emerson among them, began eventually to speak for the Indian, though opponents could point to the fact that New Englanders had long since driven out their own Indians. The protests were futile. Local whites in each region would brook no interference with their determination to kill the Indians or drive them out.

Some Indians north of the Ohio fought back. In 1832 the Sacs and the Foxes on the Illinois frontier rose in rebellion. In this, the Black Hawk War, an armed force containing two future presidents, Abraham Lincoln and Zachary Taylor, caught the Indians on the banks of the Mississippi and practically exterminated them. This ended resistance in the Middle West.

Indian Removal in the South

In the Old Southwest, as the region that became Alabama, Mississippi, and Tennessee was called, the issue had long since been settled by Andrew Jackson. As the federal military commander there after the War of 1812, he had simply pushed ahead on his own to apply the Jeffersonian policy of Indian removal he himself had also long called for. Nobody tried to stop him; no one dared. In fact, the national government in Washington was probably pleased. Despite bitter opposition from people like Henry Clay of Kentucky, who despised Jackson and was sympathetic to the Indians, in the years 1815–20 he forced treaty after treaty on the Indians of the Old Southwest. They required the Indians to give up such incredibly large tracts of territory that altogether they amounted to three-fourths of Florida and Alabama; one-third of Tennessee; one-fifth of Georgia and Mississippi; and even a tenth of such remote states as North Carolina and Kentucky. In effect, Andrew Jackson *created* the Deep South, the Cotton Kingdom, having earlier, by his military campaigns, ensured that it would remain part of the United States of America.

It was in the treaties dictated by Andrew Jackson that the idea of Indian removal beyond the Mississippi to what is now Arkansas and Oklahoma first became explicit policy. Removal, Jackson said, was the alternative to extinction. Indians simply could not live among whites. They became corrupted by whiskey and money and disease. By sending them far away, they would preserve their identity and culture. Such a step, he said, was "the only means we have in preserving them as nations, and of protecting them." Jackson may be accused of hypocrisy, for

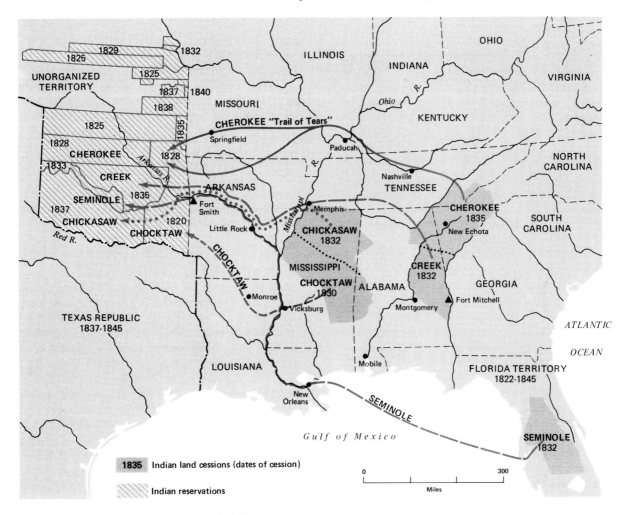

Indian Land Cessions and Migrations, 1820–1840

certainly his objective was to deliver the Southwest to white settlement, but he appears nonetheless to have been sincere in his belief, which many others shared.

Indeed, the Indians themselves seemed to admire Andrew Jackson. At his plantation in Tennessee, the Hermitage, he was year after year visited by dozens of Indian chiefs, even those who had fought him, for something in his strong-willed, courageous character appealed to them. For his part, he never appeared to harbor racist beliefs about the Indians (that is, that they were biologically inferior). In fact, an 1817 treaty he made with the Cherokees contained the first official American statement opening the possibility of United States citizenship to the Indians, if they wished to remain where they were and become farmers, build houses, and educate their children.

Jackson even approved of marriages between Indians and whites. In short, it was not the Indians as such that bothered Jackson, but their status as *tribes*, as organized and sovereign *nations*, within the larger American nation. As a passionate republican who believed that a growing, flourishing United States of America was a boon to all humankind, he was determined to sweep away the Indian nations and send them beyond the Mississippi.

The Indian nations had been, in their internal lives, outside the laws of the United States. There were no American courts within them; the Indian people governed themselves according to their own customs. This was now, Jackson insisted, to end. All Indians who remained behind, living on their ancestral lands, had to be subject to the laws of the United States. Furthermore, when organized states of the Union were created around them, then they would also be subject to state laws—that is, to their courts and their sheriffs. The cumulative result of his policies, said Jackson to Congress in 1830, would be a great advance in civilization. "What good man," he asked, "would prefer a country covered with forests and ranged by a few thousand savages to our extensive Republic, studded with cities, towns, and prosperous farms, embellished with all the improvements which art can devise or industry execute, occupied by more than 12,000,000 happy people, and filled with all the blessing of liberty, civilization, and religion?"

The Cherokees, an extraordinary people, tried to adjust by developing so flourishing a state of "civilized" agriculture and local industries that they would be allowed to remain as a separate Indian nation. They wrote a constitution and sought to secure recognition for their "state within a state" in Georgia. The Supreme Court supported their claim to be a separate nation in *Worcester* v. *Georgia* (1832), but Georgia brusquely pushed it aside. With Jackson's support, Georgians began vigilante violence to expel the Indians. A corrupted Indian faction was prevailed on to sign a treaty of removal in 1835, and the Cherokee tribe was forced to take the Trail of Tears to what is now Oklahoma. More than a fourth of the 14,000 who made the 1,200 mile trek died.

The Chickasaw and Chocktaw Indians of Alabama and Mississippi had agreed to migrate to the Indian country, but the Seminoles of Florida refused to follow the terms of a removal treaty signed in 1832, and war broke out in 1835. For seven years a few hundred warriors in the swamps and Everglades were hunted remorselessly. Over $50 million were spent in this seemingly endless guerrilla war, which resulted in the removal of most of the tribe to Oklahoma (then called the Indian Territory), although several hundred Seminoles remained in Florida. This experience in the Southern states—conducted, as in the North, in an atmosphere of illegal violence, greed, and wholesale corruption—resulted in great Indian tragedy: Half the Creek nation, one of the southern tribes moved out, did not survive the migration and their harsh early years in the West.

The Settlement of the Lake Plains

As Indians left the Old Northwest, settlers from the upland South rapidly crossed the Ohio to take up the vacated land. By the thousands they swarmed across the river, appropriating land in southern Illinois and Indiana to raise corn, and giving that region the predominantly Southern characteristic in its population and way of life that is noticeable to the present day. Half a million acres a year were sold by the government while this movement was under way. After 1830, the southern migration waned and a heavy tide began running in directly from the east, along the National Road and the Erie Canal. In this movement, population was drawn from New England, the Middle Atlantic states, and Europe. This wave of settlement occupied the northern portion of the Lake Plains. Hundreds of boats landed passengers at the end of the Erie Canal, in Buffalo, where they took small lake boats to locations further west.

Many going west were not the hardy pioneer farmers of legend, but calculating urbanites from Eastern towns who went directly to new communities on the frontier. As early as 1763, in fact, the first major city of the interior was founded when French businessmen planned the city of St. Louis. The town of Pittsburgh had been laid out a year after the French and Indian War ended in 1763, though it grew slowly until the War of 1812 stimulated its factories. A permanent settlement appeared at the site of Louisville in 1778; by 1800 Lexington was the "Philadelphia of Kentucky" and the West's largest city; and by that time Cincinnati was already more than a decade old. Such communities surprised later comers by the speed with which they acquired a mature and civilized air. Newspapers, schools, libraries, theaters, churches, local governments, and police were flourishing in areas that not long before had been wilderness.

Because land was so readily available, towns were founded all over the landscape with optimistic abandon, most of them never to be heard of again. Easterners looked over Western maps and often bought locations sight unseen. The result was that every major metropolis in the interior had already been founded by 1800, save only Chicago, Milwaukee, and Indianapolis. They grew with startling speed after that date. The state of Ohio grew four times in population from 1810 to 1830, but the city of Cincinnati grew twelvefold in that period.

Western Growth

As settlement of the Lake Plains flourished, cheap and abundant grains began to be sent east. By 1850 3 million barrels a year came down through Erie

Canal locks in canal boats. By 1860 the city of Chicago alone was sending eastward 20 million bushels of grain annually. Thousands of New England farmers were driven into bankruptcy by the competition, and they went to work in the new factories, or joined the westward movement to swell Western food production even more. In a similar development, Western sheep raising made such activity so unprofitable in New England that wool production dropped 50 percent in the northeastern states from 1840 to 1850. This began the long decline of rural New England.

In contrast, the states around the Great Lakes grew so rapidly as to astonish the nation. Detroit, a sleepy little village in 1831, when it received its first boat load of settlers, had become a booming community of 10,000 ten years later. Illinois grew swiftly as boats found their way around Michigan and discharged passengers at Chicago. Incorporated in 1833, that city had soared to a population of more than 100,000 by 1860. At the end of the 1830s, settlers were moving into Wisconsin. Some 30,000 people lived in the region in 1840, and 305,000 in 1850, a growth of 1,000 percent. A large influx from Europe played its part in the settlement of all the states around the Lakes. In a total population of 4.5 million people living in the Old Northwest in 1850, some 640,000 were foreign-born. Altogether, the world of the Lake Plains was highly varied and cosmopolitan. By mid-century it sent a formidable delegation to Congress, for all the states bordering the Lakes had entered the Union: Ohio (1803), Indiana (1816), Illinois (1818), Michigan (1837), and Wisconsin (1848). Iowa had also made its appearance (1846), and Minnesota was not far behind (1858).

The Rush into the Old Southwest

At the same time, a similarly large but not nearly as ethnically mixed population was moving into the Old Southwest. As we have seen, during the War of 1812 the United States had taken West Florida, and in 1819 it secured East Florida. This opened up Mobile and other towns along the Gulf Coast, thus ensuring planters of direct access to the sea for their downriver shipments of farm products.

The invention of the cotton gin and the development of a voracious market for raw cotton in northern England combined to produce a veritable gold rush. The price for raw cotton was so high that gigantic profits could be made practically overnight. Long wagon trains of settlers, sometimes moving as whole

families complete with slaves and plantation equipment, took the winding roads leading westward from settlements in the older South, where generations of tobacco culture had drained the soil. Almost half the whites born in South Carolina and still alive in 1850 lived outside their home state in the new settlements around the Gulf. The same was true of one-third of the North Carolinians and one-fourth of the Georgians.

In Alabama, government land sales that totaled 600,000 acres in 1816 were at 2.5 million in 1819. Prices for good land soared, and it was bought and sold in a speculative fever. Meanwhile, more and more settlers came over the western mountains. A planter in North Carolina observed in 1817, "*The Alabama Fever* rages here with great violence and has carried off vast numbers of our citizens. I am apprehensive, if it continues to spread as it has done, it will almost depopulate the country." By the end of 1819, 200,000 people had moved into the Gulf Plains. They were so busily producing cotton that half of the nation's crop came from their lands. At the same time, sugar production exploded in Louisiana. Both Mississippi and Alabama became eligible for statehood quickly, and achieved it in 1817 and 1819, respectively.

Although it seemed impossible, the westward migration of the 1830s surpassed that of the previous decade. Men found that they could recoup the cost of an expensive plantation in a year and live the life of a wealthy planter thereafter. "It would seem as if North and South Carolina were pouring forth their population by swarms," observed a Tennessee newspaperman. By 1850, so massive was this movement, almost 4 million people were living in the lower South (including 1.8 million slaves).

Thus the Cotton Kingdom came into being. With Louisiana having become a state in 1812, the Deep South formed a connected tier of states from the Atlantic coast to the Mississippi. (Arkansas was to join in 1836, Florida and Texas in 1845.) The worn-out soils of the older South were never so profitable for cotton raising; it was uniquely the Deep South that formed its special theater. The people inhabiting that region included few immigrants, and even fewer from the Northeastern states. Overwhelmingly, they were from the British and German stocks that had settled the Southern states in the eighteenth century, and from Africa. For them the North was an increasingly strange and remote world, incomprehensible—and contemptible. The people of the Deep South were heavily rural in their living patterns. Only one city in that region, New Orleans, was among the ten largest cities in the nation in 1860. Indeed, only one other Southern city, Baltimore, was in that list.

The huge boom in cotton production after 1800 meant that Southerners could now say that slavery was highly profitable, not a drain upon the nation's economy, as had been said earlier when overcropped tobacco plantations in Virginia found themselves with too many slaves and with soils depleted of their fertility. Slavery, in short, was healthy and dynamic once again, a distinct shock to many in the North. Eager for slaves, Deep South planters went to the older states along the Atlantic coast to buy their surplus blacks. An interstate trade in slaves, largely unknown before, appeared and flourished. Virginia planters found their slaves newly valuable.

Slave breeding, that most noxious of American institutions, came into being. The huge trade sent thousands of slaves from the older Southern states into the Deep South. Washington, D.C., became an important slave mart, to the disgust of Northern legislators and foreign diplomats alike. Southern whites, meanwhile, were uncomfortable about the growing number of free blacks in their midst. (Manumissions continued, perhaps increased, up to the Civil War.) Manumission was one thing; what to do with free blacks was another. No one wanted them around—in the North or in the South.

The South was deeply afraid of a slave revolt. In earlier pages, we have followed the abortive attempt at slave rebellion led by Denmark Vesey in the 1820s. Thereafter, although many slaveowners tried to exercise authority with paternalistic concern for their slaves, the tendency was to make the institution much more rigorous, unbending, and, to the slave, hateful.

In South Carolina, slave gatherings for education or for religious worship were prohibited after sunset or before sunrise. New patrol systems were established, and a lapsed system of requiring an overseer for every ten or more slaves was revived. Manumission was possible only if a magistrate and five other whites approved. Free blacks were barred from admission to the state. Similar laws were enacted elsewhere. At the same time, free blacks were surrounded by a thicket of discriminatory laws, some of them specifically aimed at ensuring that they had

The violence of Nat Turner's insurrection of 1831 and the even greater violence of retaliation shook the country.

little contact with slaves. In Georgia, they were practically returned to slavery. Meanwhile, talk began of finding someplace in the world to which the blacks could be sent, preferably Africa. In 1816 the American Colonization Society was formed for this purpose. *Something*, it was said, must be done about slavery and the blacks before it was too late.

BIBLIOGRAPHY

Students should be aware how much easily accessible basic information about the United States is available in an official federal publication, the bicentennial edition (2 volumes) of *Historical Statistics of the United States: Colonial Times to 1970*, published by the Census Bureau in 1975. As before, on demographic history Walter Nugent's superb *Structures of American Social History* (1981) has been essential to me. I have also relied much upon John F. Kasson's important work, which links the new economic order and national values, *Civilizing the Machine: Technology and Republican Values in America, 1776–1900* (1977), and upon a number of other books: a fine examination of the preindustrial order and its breakdown in James A. Henretta, *The Evolution of American Society, 1700–1815* (1973); on all issues of economic history, W. Elliot Brownlee's *Dynamics of Ascent: A History of the American Economy* (2d ed., 1979), which is indispensable; Robert Cruden's *Many and One: A Social History of the United States* (1980); Remini's biography of Andrew Jackson, cited in the previous chapter; and a brilliant analysis of the impact of the American Revolution on attitudes toward slaves and black people, Duncan J. MacLeod, *Slavery, Race, and the American Revolution* (1974).

Other available works on the chapter's general themes: Possibly the most intriguing of the books that offer a fresh look at the overall impact of economic change is Richard D. Brown's *Modernization: The Transformation of American Life 1600–1865* (1976). America's growing commitment to industrialism is carefully discussed in Stuart Bruchey, *The Roots of American Economic Growth, 1607–1861* (1965). The laboring class's optimism regarding capitalism and its consequent lack of political radicalism is highlighted in John R. Commons et al., *History of Labor in the United States*, Vols. 1–4 (1918–35). A differing and stimulating viewpoint is presented in Edward Pessen's *Most Uncommon Jacksonians: The Radical Leaders of the Early Labor Movement* (1967). A readily available and quite serviceable account of labor is found in Joseph G. Rayback, *A History of American Labor* (1966). See also Henry Pelling's comparative analysis, *American Labor* (1960).

The seminal work on transportation changes during the first half of the nineteenth century is George Rogers Taylor's extraordinary *The Transportation Revolution* (1951). More specific accounts include P. D. Jordan, *The National Road* (1948), and Walter Havighurst, *Voices on the River: The Story of the Mississippi Water Ways* (1964). A pleasurable leap through time is provided by Mark Twain's authentic and adventuresome *Life on the Mississippi* (1883). Insight into the significance of canals in one state is offered by Nathan Miller's *The Enterprise of a Free People* (1962) and Ronald E. Shaw's *Erie Water West: A History of the Erie Canal, 1792–1854* (1966). Carter Goodrich explores the active involvement of government in spurring internal improvements and economic growth in *Government Promotion of Canals and Railroads, 1800–1890* (1960).

The advent of mass immigration is sensitively discussed in Oscar Handlin's impressionistic story *The Uprooted* (1951). Maldwyn A. Jones's readable survey *American Immigration* (1960) should also be consulted. More recent and also valuable are Philip Taylor's *The Distant Magnet: European Emigration to the U.S.A.* (1971) and L. Dinnerstein, R. L. Nichols, and D. M. Reiners, *Natives and Strangers: Ethnic Groups in the Building of America* (1979).

The history of Native Americans, the Indians of North America, is in a condition of great activity. See works cited in the previous chapter's bibliography. A revised edition of William T. Hagan's older work *The Indian in American History* (1972) provides an excellent guide to the overall bibliography. A fine book on white images of Native Americans is Roy H. Pearce, *The Savages of America: A Study of the Indian and the Idea of Civilization* (1965). A controversial, widely influential study of white–Indian relations in the time period of this chapter is Francis P. Prucha, *American Indian Policy in the Formative Years: The Indian Trade and Intercourse Acts, 1790–1834* (1962). Robert F. Berkhofer, Jr.'s writings are powerful and essential to read; see his *The White Man's Indian: Images of the American Indian from Columbus to the Present* (1978).

The continual fear of slave revolts that plagued white Southerners is covered in Herbert Aptheker's *American Negro Slave Revolts* (1943). The whole question of slavery is brilliantly explored in Winthrop Jordan's *White Over Black: American Attitudes Toward the Negro, 1550–1812* (1968), and in David Brion Davis's authoritative works, *The Problem of Slavery in Western Culture* (1966) and *The Problem of Slavery in the Age of Revolution 1770–1823* (1975).

12

The Age of Jackson: A Republican Culture

TIME LINE

HISTORY IN AN INDIVIDUAL LIFE

LUCRETIA MOTT

To modern ears, the name Lucretia sounds ancient, rigid, and stern. But Lucretia Mott was quick, wry, tough, a free thinker and a radical. Respectable people sometimes left the room when she entered. A Hicksite (reforming) Quaker, she was impatient with Orthodox Quakers, who concentrated upon belief in traditional dogmas as the test for true Christianity. Mott insisted that it was what people did with their lives, how Christlike they became in helping others, that marked the true Christian.

Quakers had a special practice: They allowed their women to give sermons. Mott, always lively and bold and fluent, became a great Quaker preacher in the 1820s, traveling widely. A scoffer at authority wherever lodged, she taught that truth is to be found within us, in our hearts and consciences and minds, not in venerable books and traditions. In 1820 she helped organize a society for the relief of the poor in Philadelphia, insisting that women should be social activists.

But it was the slave issue that absorbed her. In 1833 she rose in the "women's gallery" at the organizing meeting of the American Anti-Slavery Society, electrified the gathering with her ringing eloquence, and became one of the signers of its Declaration of Sentiments and Purposes. Soon she had a Female Anti-Slavery Society organized, which people thought a brazen thing for women to do. Calling for the immediate emancipation of the slaves, the most radical position on the question, Mott was a stormy figure in the movement. Southern whites called her "the modern Borgia, the planner of wars and murders," and doubtless most Northern whites agreed. When in 1840, at forty-seven years of age, she was elected a delegate to the American Anti-Slavery Society convention, it promptly split over the issue of letting women be members. That year she also attended the World Anti-Slavery Convention in London, once more as an elected delegate, and was again denied the floor.

Walking together from the meeting to their rooms, Mott and a young American woman named Elizabeth Cady Stanton resolved to hold a woman's rights convention in the United States. In July 1848 the much-condemned meeting convened in Seneca Falls, New York, with Mott, "the Benjamin Franklin of the woman's movement," its guiding spirit. From this convention came the famous paraphrase of the Declaration of Independence, its Declaration of Sentiments, which asserted that "all men and women are created equal. . . ." Women should have equal status in marriage, property rights, wages, and the custody of children; the right to make contracts, to sue and be sued, and to testify in courts of justice; and the power both to vote and to hold office. (Mott, a seasoned agitator, thought this last premature and likely to stir derision.) A torrent of national ridicule poured in. Woman, it was said, "the angel of the family altar," had been shamed. This first national eruption of the woman's movement did not survive long, for the slavery question and the Civil War soon took everyone's—including Mott's—attention. But the cause now had its heroic figures, in Mott and Stanton, its historic declaration, and its clearly stated goals. Mott lived until 1880, a salty reformer to the end, and died nationally revered.

Overview

We have seen that from 1815 through the 1840s—the years that may be termed Jacksonian America, after its dominating figure—the United States of America went through a time of wrenching change. Population soared; the nation's territorial expanse exploded to become continent-wide; and the country became fully enmeshed in a swiftly growing transatlantic, Anglo-American economy. It is hardly surprising that Americans began thinking, therefore, in new ways. We learn from historian Patricia Cline Cohen that people were fascinated by *numbers*, by the kinds of quantitative information about the nation at large (the "state"), such as population and trade, that were now beginning to be called "statistics." Such things caught everyone's attention, Cohen writes, because they "signaled America's rising power and glory; numbers commanded respect because they measured and weighed the very aspects of American life of which the people of the republic were most proud . . . material growth, progress, improvement, and abundance."

Little children in schools (boys, not girls) were now taught arithmetic, so they could get along well in this new commercial way of life. At the same time, European visitors noted that Americans were preoccupied with "punctuality, measurement, and calculation. . . ." It was in the Age of Jackson that "cheap, mass-produced wooden clocks became standard household fixtures even in remote areas. . . ." Ordinary Americans, unlike ordinary Europeans, wanted to know what *time* it was, so they could organize their days, start becoming more efficient in their use of each hour, and keep on schedule.

At the same time, as rising prosperity pushed standards of living higher and higher, people wondered: What is happening to the Republic? Where are we headed? What *was* the American character? Was it entering on a new day of glowing progress, or being corrupted by wealth?

A New "American" National Culture

By the 1820s, when this mood of probing self-analysis took hold, it was clear to everyone that, for better or worse, a new way of life was emerging in the United States. Half a century before, in the Declaration of Independence, Americans had proclaimed a dream: that not only life and liberty, but the *pursuit of happiness*, was what a republican way of life was all about. The troubled years between the nation's founding and the end of the War of 1812 had chilled these soaring hopes, but thereafter the "American dream" (which continuing heavy immigration even now in the 1980s reveals has not yet disappeared) was reborn full and strong. At the same time, an increasingly nationwide way of living was emerging, as people moved about and a cultural blending ensued. Distinctive regional differences in ways of living would persist, most of all between the slave South and the rest of the country. Nonetheless, in this first generation to follow that of the Founding Fathers—James Monroe was the last president to have been an adult in the revolutionary era—an "American character," a shared national culture, seemed to come into being.

We must remember that while this basic national culture was being created, white Americans were ethnically homogeneous in a way they were

The enthusiasm of Jackson supporters who on Inauguration Day, 1829, pursued the new president into the executive mansion, forcing him to flee, is illustrated in this lithograph entitled "All Creation Going to the White House."

never to be again. The first census of 1790 had revealed that more than half were of English descent, most of the rest being from Scotland, Germany, and Holland. That is, most were British Protestants, and almost all of them came from what was called "Anglo-Saxon" northern Europe. (The term *Anglo-Saxon* refers to the ancient Germanic tribes of northern Europe who in the 400s expanded across the North Sea to found England and Lowland Scotland.)

Until the latter 1840s there was little immigration to change this pattern, so that the American way of life now being put into enduring form, to which later immigrants would have to assimilate or react against, had a certain monolithic character. One of America's great teachers, Princeton's Charles Hodge, exulted in 1829 that the United States of America was one nation having "one language, one literature, essentially one religion [Protestant Christianity], and one common soul."

Americans as Visitors Saw Them

America, as a democratic republic, fascinated Europeans, who lived under monarchies and were governed by hereditary aristocracies. Visitors came from many countries to study the United States and write books on it, the most famous of them being the Frenchman Alexis de Tocqueville. His two-volume masterpiece, *Democracy in America* (1835), remains to this day the classic study of Jacksonian (and therefore enduringly American) culture.

Whether the visitors toured the country in the 1820s or in the 1850s, we find them saying surprisingly consistent things. They all pointed to how *politicized* daily living was in America. Ordinary Europeans were usually passive and inactive in public affairs, for they assumed government and politics were the preserve of the aristocracy. Not so in America, where government was clearly everybody's business. Whenever an American sat down, he seemed immediately to get into an animated conversation on politics with whoever was around him. The two national parties, the Whigs and the Democrats, had thousands of busy party workers, running organizations which extended from the national capital down into every precinct and ward. Elections seemed to be going on all the time; parades and bands marched through the streets; and attentive crowds turned out to listen to hours of political oratory. Politics in America, in short, formed the country's nonstop folk theater in which

practically all (white males) took a part, worked together, rehearsed, gathered funds, handed out roles, and headed off en masse to the balloting—only to start working right away on the next such event.

Furthermore, Americans were outspokenly, irritatingly proud of their country. Given half a chance, they would boast expansively about anything and everything connected with the United States of America, their "grand and glorious" republic. In these paeans of self-praise, what did they most eagerly talk about? Their *political institutions*. Here was the particular sense of national identity that Americans shared. While those in older nations might point to ancient buildings or a richly developed art and literature, in America people pointed instead to their most prized national creation and asset: the freedom each white citizen possessed, and their democratically elected governments, from each particular small town to Washington, D.C.; to the vote free to all white males (a reform completed in the 1820s), and political careers open to everyone, even those of humble rearing; to guaranteed rights for all (white) citizens; to a simple, open, and independent court system built around trial by jury; to free speech and uncontrolled newspapers; to free and equal churches, none of them with any privileges over the others (this would be given great emphasis); and to the separation, diffusing, and balancing of governmental powers, so that no tyrants, no Napoleons, could seize power.

In truth, the contrasts Americans were fond of making between their own way of life and that in monarchical Europe were based in reality. By comparison with Europe, government in the United States was so small and carefully limited in powers as to be almost nonexistent. The United States was in reality the kind of laissez-faire country that Adam Smith had called for. Americans were left largely alone to do whatever they pleased, a fact that astonished Aleksandr Lakier, one of the first Russians ever to visit the United States and the first to write a full-scale book about it. As he journeyed through the country in 1857, with the contrast of his own czarist-ruled, autocratic, officialdom-dominated country always in mind, he asked himself: "Who keeps order? How does all this move about . . . without a word [from authority]?"

Americans, he noted, were perpetually busy, perpetually fashioning some new plan for investment. They were racing ahead to open and profit from a continent whose resources appeared to be literally without limit. Lakier described the New England Yankee as a man of "feverish activity . . . who never

An illustration of the Jacksonian passion with politics.

knows rest and always wants work and business. . . ." This capacity for *work*, for keeping at a task until it was completed, and the confident American assumption that all obstacles could be surmounted, astonished Lakier. Clearly thinking of Russia and its millions of serfs, where a work ethic had never developed, Lakier remarked to himself how transforming it was to put people in charge of their own lives and let them profit directly from their labors.

Individualism

By the Age of Jackson, individualism had become almost a national religion. Americans, we must note, had no monopoly on the trait. Walter E. Houghton's absorbing book, *The Victorian Frame of Mind, 1830–1870* (1957), tells us that in England and Scotland, in these very years, the British were also developing an individualistic, go-ahead, stress-filled, and rapidly changing way of life. However, individualism in America seemed a thing apart. There were almost no restraints on what anyone wanted to do, whether

in custom, law, or morals. We know that there was great inequality, actually, in levels of income in Jacksonian America, but nonetheless people of initiative and enterprise, whatever their actual situation, entertained bold dreams about what they could do. Looking at a New York City crowd, Aleksandr Lakier mused that for each person there was

> no limit to his enterprise when the goal is financial security if not self-enrichment. Not everyone, by far, achieves this desirable state, and here as everywhere there are many poor people. But nowhere [else] do they strive so for the realization of this ideal and nowhere do they achieve it more frequently.

Americans, therefore, were hopeful and optimistic (and apparently remain so, by comparison with other peoples, if we may believe surveys of world opinion in the 1980s). Orators, ministers, and pamphleteers in Jacksonian America insisted that the United States was destined to become a great country, the most progressive and advanced nation the world had ever seen. Thus, Americans said to themselves, they must be teachers to the world. They must demonstrate by the example of their efforts how a just, free, and prosperous way of living could be created.

British radicals and reformers, for their part, looked at the life of ordinary white Americans and found the United States the very blueprint that Great Britain should follow. Free votes, free schools, free churches, free (readily available) land, and free speech: These, the hallmarks of the American republic, were praised abroad by its friends as the formula of freedom. As Britain's famous reformer, Jeremy Bentham, put it with simple emphasis, the Americans had it better.

The Center of It All: Equality

What was it that most caught the eye of the visitors? *Equality* (save, of course, for black Americans). As Aleksandr Lakier wrote:

> [All] are as one . . . no differences divide society into fossilized strata . . . all consider themselves equal in social rights and consequently no one expects to be deferred to in accordance with his honors, service, or wealth. In his own circle each person will have his place but in society all are equal; everyone has the right, neither more nor less than that of his fellows, to be respected. . . . each person is equal to every other in his right to discuss and interpret. There are no people inferior to others, there are only the rich and the poor, and the latter serve the former until they themselves become rich.

Tell an American, Lakier later remarked, "about class divisions in other lands, and he becomes ecstatic about the equal state of each and all, without distinctions of wealth, origin, or connections, in his own country . . . [separating out] only the colored (with whom whites want to have nothing in common, not even the air they breathe), and ladies (who are considered higher beings . . .)."

Americans were notably egalitarian even in behavior. They did not like the elaborate manners of Europeans, which seemed aimed at showing who was superior and who inferior. They insisted on being treated equally, in a style considerably more informal and open than Europeans were used to. There were always middle-class Americans who felt uneasy in the presence of sophisticated Europeans and aped their class-conscious ways, but the "American" style in manners was widely in evidence. Englishmen, accustomed to maintaining a social reserve, found Americans overly forward, pushy, and rude. On their side, Americans believed they were only maintaining

the upright and assertive air of what was then referred to as a "sturdy republican," who counted no one to be above him.

The Entrepreneurial Spirit

In this aggressively democratic and egalitarian new society the *entrepreneurial* spirit, the spirit of enterprise and risk-taking, flourished. America, it was said, was booming; therefore, be a boomer! Restlessly, confidently, swarms of people arrived yearly in the Deep South to settle, break the soil, plant a few crops, and then sell out to newcomers and move on. Even in the Lake Plains, few farmers planned to stay where they first settled. The objective was to turn a virgin field into a farm, grow wheat, dig a well, put up a house and outbuildings, and offer the property for sale. Land values constantly rose, for more buyers were always crowding in. People simply threw themselves into the lap of the future, expecting to be caught safely with the added bounty of a sizable profit. *Speculation*: it was a fever. Any new spot that appeared to be well situated for a city received a rush of buyers. Everyone, it seemed, bought and sold town lots. By the mid-1830s, enough building lots had been sold in New York City, it was said, to care for a population of 2 million; in New Orleans, for a million.

Banks boomed and collapsed, railroad projects made millions or went bust, town lots were snapped up by the first purchaser or sat dusty and unsold while the "city" glimmered and disappeared. Steamboats were launched and blew up, went aground, or sailed grandly up and down rivers, leaving their great plumes in the sky and making their owners princely fortunes. For many Americans, the risks were invigorating. Boom and collapse: It all seemed in the nature of things for the hardy individualist, the far-sighted entrepreneur, the man who was willing to do anything to get on the wave and ride it.

> The American is really like that [remarked Aleksandr Lakier]: full of courage, he strides forth boldly, and he will reach his goal without fail. He knows this well and that is why there are no limits to his enterprise; and he loves his dream as if it were actuality, because he is convinced of its realization.

In this future-oriented environment, the "self-made man" (i.e., his wealth and standing came not by inheritance, but from his own efforts) was much praised. He was the model for everyone, whereas in Britain self-made men tended to be looked down on as crude social climbers. European observers noted in distaste that Americans seemed to talk continually of money as proof of one's standing in life, rather than of family and role in public service.

And yet being a self-made man meant having qualities much admired: working hard for the pleasure of accomplishment, competing enthusiastically, investing prudently. Such Americans, in short, were building lives of industrious enterprise that long ago, in eighteenth-century New England, first appeared in the busy, profit-making Yankee. In truth, wherever New Englanders migrated and settled in the Middle Western states, that region quickly became a brisk and go-ahead place.

Alexis de Tocqueville observed a new kind of man as he traveled about Jacksonian America. Individualism of the American variety, Tocqueville mused, was a new thing in history. Traditional societies might know of *egotism*, but not *individualism*. That attitude was a "mature and calm feeling" that led each man to separate himself from others, form his own world of family and friends, and leave the larger society to fend for itself. It dissolved the organic compactness people had always known. Where life was stable, as in the old country, men knew who their forefathers were and felt that they already knew their descendants, for each generation lived the same life, in the same location, as those who went before. But the American democracy made "every man forget his ancestors . . . hide his descendants, and separate his contemporaries from him. . . . [The] woof of time is every instant broken, and the track of generations effaced. Those who went before are soon forgotten; of those who will come after no one has any idea: the interest of man is confined to those in close propinquity to himself."

Such a society made for a lonely existence, in which people felt they owed nothing to, and could expect nothing from, anyone else. Insofar as their destiny was to be shaped, they alone could shape it. Each man was thrown "back forever upon himself alone. . . . The system threaten[ed] in the end to confine him entirely within the solitude of his own heart."

The Sense of American Mission

The America of Andrew Jackson, in short, was a nation and a society of young people bursting across their continental domain and swept by a romantic feeling that their country had a transcendent national

destiny. America's first great historian, George Bancroft, rejoiced that his nation would "allure the world to freedom by the beauty of its example." How could America help but exert, asked Charles Hodge, "a greater influence on the human family than any other nation that has ever existed?" God himself, people said, had America under his special care. Had he not saved the country in the spectacular victory at New Orleans? Had he not given it there a miraculous second chance to fulfill its great task? Clearly, Americans said, God had a great work in the world for them to perform.

Side by side with this boastfulness and confident counting on the future there was another mood as well, one not so often revealed to foreign visitors. America's bursting national prosperity and affluence filled a good many people with gloomy foreboding. In 1842 Reverend Caleb Stetson warned:

> [T]he basis of our *civilization* is wealth. The love of money is almost the universal passion. The inordinate pursuit of it for the gratification of avarice, vanity, pride, and ambition, has deeply corrupted the principles of the country, and nearly destroyed all generous public feeling.

Prosperity, such critics said, had in some way turned a republic of devout and freedom-loving idealists into an unprincipled mob of greedy, self-regarding dollar chasers. Others worried about the very newness, and therefore precariousness, of republican government. Americans knew that they had a heavy responsibility to prove before multitudes of European skeptics that a democratic republic could govern itself wisely and effectively. The young Massachusetts politician Daniel Webster, using terminology widely current in the Jacksonian years, said in the mid-1820s that "this lovely land, these benign institutions, the dear purchase of our fathers," constituted a "sacred trust" for all generations of the future.

All prior republics, Americans well knew, had failed miserably. The republican idea was built on the assumption that the people at large had certain qualities which no one could be sure they possessed: solid common sense; a capacity for self-denial; and a concern for the public welfare. It was often said

*Asher Durand's **Kindred Spirits**, a painting from the Hudson River school, showing Thomas Cole and William Cullen Bryant delighting in nature. Classically romantic, the painting is rich in detail and has an air of wonder at the mystery of nature.*

Andrew Jackson, president from 1828 to 1835, polarized American politics and inaugurated the second party system.

that earlier republics had lapsed into corruption, demagoguery, and ultimate failure precisely because, in reality, the masses lack these qualities. (We will see these gnawing doubts about democracy, and about the wisdom of the people at large, surface again and again in future generations. They have never, in fact, gone away.)

The new spectacle of *mass* political parties was itself a cause for alarm. They were, of course, quite unprecedented, existing nowhere else but in America. Turbulent, raw, loud, and aggressive, the mass political party made many turn away in distaste. By the 1840s Americans generally had come to accept the argument that political parties were necessary in a democratic government, but nonetheless the word "politician," as Lakier noted, was commonly a term of reproach, as it certainly was in Europe. The political parties themselves seemed quite uninterested in the general welfare. Instead, they voiced the demands only of those who voted their ticket. Divisiveness, selfishness, pride: All of these seemed encouraged, not damped down, by democratic politics.

What was the answer? It was given many times, in every imaginable setting. To realize their republican dream, Americans said, they must develop nobility of *character*, loftiness of *virtue*, and earnestness of *religion*. "Such an outlook," the historian Paul

C. Nagel writes, "became the center of national meaning." Daily events were scrutinized anxiously to see if the necessary qualities of virtue were emerging in the people at large. Using the biblical imagery they were most accustomed to, Americans grieved that "mammon" (greed, wealth and luxury) and "passion" (emotional excess and instability) were tearing down the Republic.

One foreign observer visiting America in 1836 remarked that "the population of the United States is beyond that of other countries an anxious one." Americans were a "careworn people," for they were struggling with the frustratingly difficult task of resolving one of humankind's ancient paradoxes: How can life be orderly, if it is also free? The more liberty, so it seemed, the more disorder and immorality, as each person argued and scrambled for what he or she wanted. Human frailty appeared stubbornly to resist the heavy demands that republicanism placed upon it.

The Great Hope: Revived Protestant Christianity

To make themselves virtuous, Americans turned with fervent hope to God. Lyman Beecher, a prominent Congregational divine, warned in 1829:

> Our republic is becoming too prosperous, too powerful, too extended, too numerous, to be governed by any power without the blessed influence of the Gospel.

In reality, the Founding Fathers had not been particularly Christian, in a churchgoing sense (save in New England). Historians of religion estimate that in the twenty-five years following independence, less than 10 percent of the American people were formally church members. From this perspective, it could hardly be said that the United States at its founding was a Christian nation. However, around 1801 Americans had begun to hear of tumultuous revivals of Christian faith out in the frontier regions of Tennessee and Kentucky. The War of 1812 intervened, but by the 1820s the Second Great Awakening, as it is called, had swelled into the first nationwide cultural movement. It was a great crusade to convert Americans to Christianity, and it went on well into the 1840s.

Its ultimate objective was to build a distinctive American culture that would endure and inspire the world, and specifically to do this by transforming the United States into a fervently Christian (Protestant) community. If confusion and disorder were the distinguishing ills of the new mass democratic way of living, then Christianity, it was hoped, would bring stability and true morality and national health to anxious America.

The dream of a revived Protestant Christianity swelled into a grandiose conception that the United States of America would become God's righteous empire in the world. Was it not, Protestants asked, the largest Protestant nation in the world? Even today, seven of ten American citizens identify themselves as Protestants. Fired by this inspiration, Evangelical Protestants, especially Methodists and Baptists, began in the 1820s a decades-long campaign to purify America, to shape all its manners, laws, and values in the mold of a Protestant kingdom. The campaign swept into politics and government, as we will see. In fact, a formal doctrine evolved in the American courts that the United States was essentially, that is to say *legally*, a Christian country. On this ground, laws in the thirteen original states which denied the vote or officeholding to Jews were ruled constitutional. (The last of these restrictions would not finally disappear until after the Civil War.)

In the Age of Jackson the geography books children read in the public schools and the spellers and readers they used pictured the United States of America as a Protestant island in an overwhelmingly Roman Catholic and infidel (non-Christian) world. The history of Americans was written to tell a story of Puritan Christians, the elect of God, journeying to the New World to found God's special enclave of the true faith, where it had since been winnowed and sifted into a high state of perfection.

And it stood embattled, cried evangelicals. No refrain was more constantly sounded from their pulpits than the warning that Protestantism in America was being assaulted by the pope and Roman Catholicism. Before the large Irish and German immigration of the 1840s there was only a tiny Catholic community in the United States, but nonetheless determined efforts were made to prove that it was a threat. So, too, it was said of the few atheists and free thinkers America still had left after the mood of the eighteenth-century Enlightenment had faded.

Yankees: The Crusade's Leaders

It was Yankee Americans—New Englanders in their home states and in the Midwestern regions to which they migrated—who were the most confident and outspoken in their triumphant Protestantism. And New England was their model, for all America to emulate. There, they said, was the place in America where the strongest Protestant faith could be found, and the purest morals and public life.

What of the South? The South, Yankees scoffed, was not really religious. It consisted, they would insist, of "NOTHINGARIANS." What else could one say, Yankees asked, of people who were not only slaveowners but who also performed the crime of turning the Bible into a source of supposed proofs for the rightness of their system?

Nonslave America, then, was the Promised Land, the evangelists said, and Northern Americans were now the Israelites called on to show the true faith to the world. After 1815, Americans came to believe that Protestantism had a global mission, and for the first time evangelicals began to go abroad as missionaries, journeying first to Burma. At the same time, those in the Eastern states looked on the uncivilized American West as another huge mission field, where Christ must be brought to the unsaved masses. The supreme task, said one of the most respected Congregational clergymen, Horace Bushnell, was "to fill this great field with Christian churches and a Christian people." To evangelicals, an integral part of the Christian message was to teach people to become sober, hard-working, self-denying, and enterprising, in the traditional Yankee mold.

The righteous empire had its ranks of heroes, widely praised. Clergymen, fundraisers, missionaries going abroad to dangerous foreign lands, those who gave their lives to directing benevolent societies, leading revivals, packing their goods on a horse's back and becoming circuit riders, and journeying through all weathers to church after church in the raw wilderness of the frontiers: These were celebrated figures who were much admired, their lives being offered as models to devout young people. The religious life had a powerful appeal to this generation of Americans, as shown in the remarkable fact that while the overall population grew 88 percent from 1832 to 1854, the numbers of clergy swelled 175 percent.

At the same time, an intricate network of interdenominational societies, often directed by laymen and with women playing an important role, sprang into being to direct and support the evangelical crusade. Jacksonian Americans, Tocqueville said in wonderment, were amazingly ready to form voluntary societies and to work hard in them to do all sorts of things—help the poor, clean the streets, free the slaves, build libraries, provide firefighting companies. And among these, church-connected societies were prominent. They held revival meetings, published magazines and newspapers, and formed an extraordinary interstate complex of evangelical Protestant activities.

Evangelicals also founded many colleges to offer Christian-oriented higher education to the young, among them Miami in Ohio, DePauw, Oberlin, Knox, Denison, Wabash, Colgate, and Williams. Meanwhile, the Sunday school was founded as an institution where small children were taught to read as well as to understand the Gospel.

The Mormons

Of all the many new religious movements that flourished in this period, none was as striking as the Church of Jesus Christ of the Latter Day Saints—the Mormon Church. In the spring of 1820 a young man named Joseph Smith, bewildered by the conflicting claims of the many sects that competed for his support went into the woods to pray for divine guidance. "I had scarcely done so, when immediately I was seized upon by some power which entirely overcame me. . . . [Then I saw] a pillar of light exactly over my head. . . . When the light rested upon me, I saw two personages, whose brightness and glory defy all description, standing above me in the air. One of them spake unto me, calling me by name, and said, pointing to the other—'This is my beloved Son, hear him!' " These spiritual beings then told Smith that the time had come for a new revelation from God to lead people once more on the true path. A fresh beginning was to be made in Christian history, and he, Joseph Smith, was to be its prophet.

This new revelation, which Smith issued to the world in 1830 as the *Book of Mormon*, was indeed startlingly new. The scene of Adam and Eve and the Garden of Eden, Smith would later say, had taken place in North America (in Missouri), not in some place far away. Until the Flood, when Noah and his people and animals were carried to dry land in the Near East, North America had been at the center of the human experience. From the Tower of Babylon tribes had returned to these shores, and in North America they had had a long history, which the *Book of Mormon* recounted.

They had been visited in the New World by Jesus Christ after his death and crucifixion in Jerusalem, and he had taught them the true faith. Warfare between the North American tribes subsequently broke out, and the darker of them (the Indians) had exterminated those of lighter skin. But before their disappearance, a scribe named Mormon had buried

their history and sacred beliefs in a hill in western New York, near Palmyra. It was this book, Smith said, that divine inspiration led him to uncover, translate, and publish as the basis of the regenerated Christian faith. Thus, as those Christians in the United States who called themselves Protestants were also saying, in these years of the Second Great Awakening, Smith held out the exciting message that God had chosen America to be the place where he would once more labor in his cause, and offer eternal life to the world's peoples.

For this was what Mormons believed was happening: a return to earth, after centuries of silence from the heavens, of true Christianity, to replace the corrupted version that then existed. Theirs was the Church of Jesus Christ of the *Latter* Day Saints, as they termed themselves, responding to a new outpouring of divine guidance primarily through Joseph Smith, an excitingly vital and visionary man who until his death would report a continued receipt of revelations, but also through his successor presidents of the church.

The Mormons Trek Westward

From these events came a religious movement unparalleled in growth and vitality in American history. Forming a closely organized communal society under the direction of Joseph Smith, the Mormons began preaching their faith to the world and drawing converts from all over America and Europe. Intensely moralistic, strongly resembling in their faith and practices the patriarchal Hebrews of the Old Testament, they formed a "special people" whose ideas varied so markedly from those of the Christian sects around them that they suffered unremitting persecution. The *Book of Mormon* had hardly made its appearance when the Mormons moved to Kirtland, Ohio, the first stop in their forced wanderings. Preaching that the end of the world was at hand, they insisted that members of the Mormon Church would inherit the earth, a doctrine nonbelievers found offensive.

In the late 1830s the Mormons trekked to Missouri, where again they encountered hostility, this time violent. Mob action culminated in the indiscriminate murder of Mormons, including women and children. The governor of the state decreed in 1838 that "the Mormons must be treated as enemies and must be exterminated or driven from the state, if necessary, for the public good." Some 15,000 Mormons then fled to Illinois, where they founded a city-state, Nauvoo, on the banks of the Mississippi. The community

The first Mormon refugees evacuate Nauvoo, Illinois, beginning their long trek westward to Salt Lake City, Utah, after mobs had murdered Joseph Smith.

flourished to the point where it held a strategic voting position in the state's politics. This created hostility that swelled gigantically when reports of a new revelation came out of Nauvoo: that polygamy was divine. In the explosion that followed in June 1844, Joseph Smith was captured, placed in jail, and then murdered by nonbelievers.

Then, in its time of extreme distress, the Mormon movement was saved and vastly invigorated by the gifted leadership of Brigham Young, whose actions in these critical times are regarded as miraculous by members of the faith. Young gave the Mormons order and stability once again and prepared them for the occupation of a new Zion to be founded in the Far West, preferably in some location outside the United States. He set out with a party to search beyond the Mississippi for such a place, "not knowing," he later said, "at that time, whither we were going, but firmly believing that the Lord had in reserve for us a good place in the mountains, and that He would lead us directly to it."

The Mormons in the Salt Lake Basin

Brigham Young found it in the remote basin of the Great Salt Lake, then Mexican territory. He then led the Mormons in their incredible march. By the end of 1846, 15,000 Mormons, 3,000 wagons, and 30,000 head of cattle had crossed Iowa to the banks of the Missouri River. From there, they left in small

parties for the long journey across plains and mountains. By 1860 the Mormons had been so successful that the Territory of Utah (American domain after the Mexican War) held 40,000 people, who had opened up almost 80,000 acres of farmland by extraordinary feats of engineering and irrigation.

"Will we remain here?" Mormons asked Brigham Young. "I answer, yes," he replied, "as long as we please to do the will of God, our Father in Heaven. If we are pleased to turn away from the holy commandments of the Lord Jesus Christ, as ancient Israel did, every man turning to his own way, we shall be scattered and peeled, driven before our enemies and persecuted, until we learn to remember the Lord our God and are willing to walk in his ways."

What was Mormonism's most essential belief? That of all the human institutions God has created, the family is the most sacred. Within its arms we find eternal life, if the marriage of husband and wife at its inception has been duly solemnized in appropriate Mormon ritual. Marriages, thus "sealed," last beyond death into heaven itself, where God, whom Mormons regard as our physical as well as spiritual father, awaits. Smith taught that through the Mormon Church, individual persons could even aspire to godhood themselves; that is, to becoming creators of worlds and peoples. Traditional Christianity in most of its forms was pessimistic, but the Mormon faith was sublimely optimistic about humanity's future. The Mormon Church was also, in dramatic contrast to an aggressively individualistic and competitive America, warmly, lovingly, devotedly communal and familylike.

The subsequent history of the Mormon Church forms the most striking chapter in the history of American religion. The Church of Jesus Christ of the Latter Day Saints, now a worldwide movement, counts, in the 1980s, over 4 million Americans in its family. It remains strongly communal, growing in vitality and numbers. It comprises the most formidable and lasting religious and social legacy (of a nonpolitical nature) to modern America from the Age of Jackson.

The Rise of Unitarianism

When we follow the Second Great Awakening, we are following what was happening, spiritually and intellectually, to most of the American people in the Age of Jackson. However, for a much smaller group, the well-educated and established people of New England, things were different. Their spiritual life was stirred too, but not at all in the same ways. They were appealed to, instead, by a calm and thoughtful new faith: Unitarianism.

It was closely linked to the science and rationalism of the eighteenth-century Enlightenment, as well as to the growing humanitarianism of the nineteenth century. Brought to the United States in the 1790s by the famous scientist Joseph Priestley, who had been driven out of England for his religious beliefs, Unitarianism soon drew Thomas Jefferson into its ranks. Its name came from Unitarianism's central belief: that the concept of the Trinity—God in three persons: the Father, Son, and Holy Spirit—does not stand to reason. God, to Unitarians, is a single person; Christ, while divinely inspired, was merely a human being charged by God to teach humanity the message of love.

Beyond that, God has left human beings entirely on their own. His spirit does not move about here on earth, as evangelicals believed, entering people's souls and doing mighty things in the world. For Unitarians, religion was not passionate and God-centered; it was calm, thoughtful, and humanity-centered. They did not go to great revivals, but spent long afternoons in book-lined studies, reading widely in humane literature (not just in the Bible), and reflecting on the human condition.

Unitarians agreed in one important particular with the Evangelicals: They rejected the older Calvinist notion that humanity is so depraved and fallen that we have no free will and can make no choices on our own. William Ellery Channing, a quiet New England clergyman who by the mid-1820s had emerged as the spiritual leader of the Unitarians, taught that it degraded both God and humankind to teach classic Calvinism. God is not, he said, an angry and willful deity who sends men and women to suffer endlessly in hell for small transgressions. Our every instinct is not, as the Puritans had taught, corrupt. God is love, not anger and law.

Human beings, Channing said, are fundamentally good and reasonable—if they are given a chance to be. Educate them, clear away all superstition, and they will steadily rise in understanding, maturity, and goodness. Our highest human duty, Channing believed, was to do everything we could to clear away the barriers that prevent people from fully realizing their human nature, from growing in freedom and responsibility into the dignity of human personhood God intended us to experience.

People who later became leading literary figures—Ralph Waldo Emerson, Henry Wadsworth Longfellow, Oliver Wendell Holmes, and others— came under Channing's influence. From him they learned that their task in life was to care lovingly for their fellow creatures. Among such New Englanders, Unitarianism inspired reform movements that attacked slavery, worked for the spread of free public schools to the common people, labored for reform of prisons and insane asylums, and crusaded against war.

Romanticism

However, many young people in the New England middle classes found Unitarianism too pale, too limited, too calm and reasonable. They were caught up instead by a much wider cultural mood, European in its origins: *romanticism*. Rising in Europe in the late eighteenth century, it swept out into the whole of the Atlantic community. In the arts, in literature, indeed in all human feeling and action, romanticism took hold of Europe in the years around 1800 and suffused transatlantic culture for half a century. Romanticism said life is lived validly only when we are passionate, active, and vitally engaged with all of experience and all of our being, not just with intellect and dry reason.

Romantic painters turned away from the calm and balanced rationalism of eighteenth-century art to paint nature not as serenely simple, but in all its profusion and complexity. Romanticism was fascinated by biology, not by mathematics; by life in its infinitely irregular forms, not by numbers and universals. The English naturalist Charles Darwin, a true Romantic, spent years studying the particular way earthworms lived in the soil, painstakingly described a fly's wing or an ant's "courageous" response to the approach of a spider, and painted word pictures of a natural world filled with spirit and feelings. Romantic writers described the grotesque next to the sublime; their works were so crowded with the richness of life that it was difficult to see form in them. William Wordsworth's poems on the beauties of the English Lake District, for example, abounded with visual images.

Romantics praised genius and energy. Europeans found these qualities in Napoleon, Americans in Andrew Jackson. Whatever one did, it should be on a large scale—a huge painting, a massive book, a new geological calendar for the history of the world. In the religious life, one must grapple with nothing less than the vast majesty and power of the whole universe, or with God himself, and experience the soaring ecstasy of the revival experience.

Ralph Waldo Emerson: Philosopher of American Individualism

A generation of educated young people in the Northern states, seized by romanticism, turned for guidance to Ralph Waldo Emerson, America's poet-priest from the mid-1830s to the Civil War. Emerson spoke, for that matter, specifically to college youth. At one campus after another, Emerson would arrive for short visits to give his apparently captivating talks to eager crowds of students. Many in those crowds, later in life and in major positions of leadership, would say that Emerson's words had turned their lives around.

Colleges, in his time, were empty places of little learning and juvenile carousing, much of it vicious and demeaning. Emerson would say: Study, study hard. Get system and order into your life; do not waste it in sloth and dissipation. Dedicate yourself to a great cause, mobilize your spirit and your genius—each person, he would say, has a particular genius—and prepare for a life of heroism, of great achievement, of rising out of the petty and the merely sensual and commonplace. For decades Emerson wrote his wise, pithy essays in the small historic town of Concord, Massachusetts, and sent them out to a wide national readership, or he journeyed great distances to lecture in town after town.

Everywhere he preached to his age the great message of personal salvation he believed himself to have hit upon: individual self-reliance. The physical and philosophical terrors of life, Emerson would say, may be met solidly only if we do not depend on external sources of truth. We must turn within. We must develop a serene, sturdy, and vigorously active self-reliance, finding our guiding values within ourselves. A healthy society depends ultimately, he would say, not on its institutions, but upon the strength, instinctive insights, and leadership of heroic and self-reliant individuals.

What made this almost anarchic philosophy valid, in Emerson's mind? God, the Oversoul, he said, dwells in each person, and we may rely upon his guidance. The spirit that we sense within us is a fragment of the transcendent, of the divine; it is the ultimate reality. The world surrounding us is an illusion, a kind of shadow show whose material

delights can corrupt us into sensuality. As a true Romantic, Emerson said we are guided most validly not by reason, but by our instincts. A reasoning and informed mind are essential to valid thought, but as much as possible each person should be spontaneous and "natural," rather than abstractly logical and scientific.

The Transcendentalists

The most spectacular of Emerson's followers, younger people who called themselves Transcendentalists, idolized their master and took his home in Concord, Massachusetts, as their spiritual center. They formed communes such as Brook Farm and Fruitlands dedicated to demonstrating that competitive individualism could be cast aside. In a truly loving community all could share equally, labor equally, make decisions without anyone being in "authority," and usher in the good society of brotherhood and sisterhood.

In these communities a purely natural existence was sought. The corruptions of modern society and its oppressive institutions would be replaced by a completely open and unforced way of life. Owning everything in common, the members would eliminate the exploitations of private property. Devoted to each person being free to express him- or herself, since restraints of any kind on the individual were harmful, they had difficulty agreeing upon common enterprises. Forms of clothing were devised that were "natural"; only vegetables were eaten; wheat was thrown on the ground without undertaking the "unnatural" act of plowing it; and anything from a cow was regarded as unclean. Logical planning, orderly foresight, and calculated, practical action were disliked. It was ironically suitable that the Fruitlands commune practically ended one autumn when the men went off to a reform meeting instead of harvesting the wheat.

New Literary Imaginations

Powerful literature emerged from transcendentalism, some inspired by it, some inspired against it. "I was simmering, simmering, simmering; Emerson brought me to a boil," wrote Walt Whitman. And Emersonian are Whitman's famous lines,

I celebrate myself, and sing myself
And what I assume you shall assume
For every atom belonging to me as good belongs
to you

An ardent Democrat, Whitman was truly romantic in the sweep of his vision, the vast range of subjects in his poetry, and his determination to do nothing less than to sing the song American. He loved busy cities, swarming immigrants, the vitality and expansiveness of America. He loved also the quiet and calm of meadows and remote beaches. In *Leaves of Grass*, the book of poems he brought out in many editions through his long life, which lasted into the 1890s, he said: "The United States themselves are essentially the greatest poem." Depicting hope and debasement, shining beauty and rottenness, and the manysidedness of life, his poems were given form not by their meter, which is shambling, but by their powerful human content.

Far different was Henry David Thoreau, Emerson's intimate young friend. Totally rebellious against all constraints, he saw an America befouled by materialism and power. Enraptured by the beauties of nature, he was happiest contemplating nature in the "wise passiveness" urged by Wordsworth and the Oriental mystics. A celibate, he withdrew entirely from society in the mid-1840s to live two years by himself at Walden Pond, near Concord, Massachusetts, ruminating the ills of the nation and the glories of nature.

Thoreau regarded the factories of New England with disgust. To him, machines were infernal gadgets that rendered life too complicated for wholesome existence. The pursuit of wealth had made men monsters. Government, too, had become evil. The war against Mexico embodied, for him, a lust of power gone mad. In *Civil Disobedience*, which he wrote at Walden Pond, he presented the most powerful attack in American literature on the inherent malevolence of the state. Individuals, he said, must refuse to follow immoral orders. They must follow the "higher law" of their own natures. The principle of majority rule was fallacious, for "right" was not quantitative—in his famous words, "Any man more right than his neighbors constitutes a majority of one already." The state robs us of our human nature. We must defy it at all times and reduce its operations to the tiniest sphere possible.

Nathaniel Hawthorne was also close to Emerson. However, he soon proclaimed his disenchantment with transcendentalism. Emerson's philosophy, he said, was too bland, too Platonic, too smooth. It made little place for the existence of evil. A realistic view of humankind, he believed, would see it as bloody, passionate, and selfish, not spiritual and touched with divinity. The cause of the world's ills

lay not in circumstances—aristocracy, oppressive churches, weaponry, drink, tobacco, propertyholding, and undemocratic constitutions—but in our corrupted hearts. He could not share the perfectionist faith that led so many Transcendentalists to work in reform movements. Clear all the corrupting circumstances away, he said, and suffering will remain.

Hawthorne had little faith, too, in the individualism of those alienated young people who followed Emerson. Such people, he said, separated themselves from the rest of the world on the ground that they were morally more right or intellectually more capable than the common people. But all they really did was express arrogance and come to a bad end. They were monomaniacs who paid little attention to their own weaknesses and passions and who, in their moral anarchy, destroyed one another. In Hawthorne's novel *The Scarlet Letter*, the central figure was such a person, whose alienation and apparent saintliness sprang from his having committed a monstrous sin that he sought to hide. In this situation, his morality came apart. Much preferable to withdrawal, Hawthorne felt, was to find those things that bound suffering humanity together. There is love as well as evil in our hearts, and we must be given ways of sharing that love. Insanity awaited those who were denied affection and lived sterile, inward-turning, solitary lives.

The Age of Reform

Historians of the United States and of Great Britain have traditionally labeled the years from 1820s through the 1840s the Age of Reform. The famous Reform Bill of 1832 in Britain, angrily fought over and debated, finally gave the vote to about 200,000 men in the middle class. (Britain was still far from being a democratic country; in a nation of 12 million, only 650,000 men voted, after the reform of 1832. During the 1820s, universal male white suffrage—that is, no "property tests" for the right to vote—became the norm in the United States.)

In both countries humanitarian reforms in the prisons, the asylums, the schools, and the factories set off extended controversies. Two spectacular political battles—the Bank War in the United States and the repeal of the Corn Laws in Britain—gave expression to powerful demands that the "interests" and their monopolies be broken. All of this took place within a remarkably interactive Anglo-American community. People and ideas passed back and forth across the Atlantic with striking ease, and reformers of many persuasions drew inspiration from one another. Here we will look at the Jacksonian age of reform in several of its key aspects: in the schools, in what the country began doing with criminals and the insane, and in the realm of women and the family.

Common School Education

A campaign for common school education surged widely in the Northern states, the South remaining a land of widespread illiteracy until after the Civil War. Where the issue was debated, it was tremendously exciting and controversial. To be educated: that was the mark of the established classes. To be illiterate and ignorant: that was the curse of the poverty-stricken, the mark of being lower class and without much chance in life. Common people desperately wanted schooling, especially for their children. This, it was insisted, was the most powerful single way that republican government could help its citizens realize their talents, and make the American experiment in republicanism succeed.

As the Jacksonian age opened, few schools in America were worthy of the name. Most were costly private institutions or schools open only to members of particular faiths. New England retained a traditional commitment to the idea that each community should maintain a public school, but in fact its system was in deplorable condition. School terms were short, usually two or three months out of the year, and the teachers were undertrained and underpaid. Many were retired sailors or disgruntled clergymen.

The function of the elementary school was assumed to be a religious and moral one. The Bible took the principal place in the curriculum. Boys, and sometimes girls, were rigorously trained in the catechism. Subjects were taught not for their particular utility, though reading had practical value, but because they were regarded as valuable for disciplining the mind. Different kinds of education were given to different classes of people. The poor learned how to be obedient, industrious, and thrifty. The wealthy learned the larger ideas by which elites ran the country.

Ferment in Education

But there was now great interest in changing all this. The country was in a ferment of educational theorizing. How best could a genuinely republican system of education, which would create an educated and self-reliant citizenry, be built? At first there was talk of having a national system of education, directed and supported by the federal government, but states rights and localism soon brought this to an end. Many powerful social influences, indeed, wanted to frustrate the whole project of public education.

Most of the wealthy regarded education not simply as their monopoly by right, but as something positively dangerous for the lower classes. Conservatives said that education would give the lower classes appetites they could not satisfy and thereby make them unhappy, dissatisfied with their places in life, and inclined to riots and disorders. The poor should receive little more than literacy training. And whatever was done should be very cheap.

There was criticism from some church quarters as well. Public education, many ministers said, was a thing of the devil. The whole concept was linked with that impious man Thomas Jefferson, and therefore associated with free thinking and un-Christian influences. Since the Bible was not to be taught in public schools, this made the proposal clearly a radical idea brought in from revolutionary France. It was a conspiracy designed to subvert America, to make it a godless, immoral republic. The attacks emanated primarily from such state-church interests as the Congregationalists in New England, who had traditionally exercised strong influence over the schools.

After 1830 the clamor for reform grew insistent. A good education should be provided not only for children, but also for working-class adults. Liberals had a complete and trusting faith that educational reform would solve *all* the nation's problems. Providing education on an equal basis to everyone, old and young, rich and poor, would remove all social, economic, and political inequities. The monopoly of education enjoyed by the upper classes would disappear, just as their monopoly of voting had been wiped away and their monopolies in economic affairs were being attacked.

Horace Mann

Horace Mann was the leading figure in this cause. Reared in Massachusetts, as a boy he had undergone the savagery of the typical common school. A lawyer and a socially conscious Unitarian, he entered the legislature, helped pass major educational reforms, and resigned both his legislature post and his lucrative legal career to become the first state superintendent of education in Massachusetts in 1837. His action surprised many, for his financial sacrifice was great. But Mann had always been moved by a powerful urge to do something for the benefit of the great republican experiment Americans were engaged in, and thus (he believed) for all the world. As he said many years later to his students at Antioch College, "Be ashamed to die until you have won some victory for humanity."

Mann's office gave him moral leadership but little direct power. Through many devices—a series of powerfully written annual reports, his *Common School Journal*, and in meetings, orations, and special training programs—he spread his message. He was a missionary, an evangelist, just as were the ministers of the Second Great Awakening. Perfection lay ahead for all, he seemed to believe, if people would only follow the road of true and enlightened education. He widened curricula, brought in trained teachers, lengthened the school year, sought to create a happier atmosphere in the classroom, and led teaching in the direction of reason and science.

Mann resembled his forebears in believing that the school should be an agent of moral instruction. In his mind, the common school was the means for erasing greed and wickedness; more than this, for blending diversity with moral unity. A coherent republic would be created in the hearts of all Americans though they might speak different tongues, work in different careers, occupy different class positions. Moral instruction, he believed, would flow automatically from the rational study of history, literature, and the arts. There was no need to pound morality into children by use of a catechism and the rod. Properly directed, the schools of America would be the means of creating an ethically disciplined and unified republic.

Of course, such a school should be secular. A Unitarian, Mann abhorred control by churches. It should also be publicly supported so as to be available to all. So successful was he that he got the state legislature to expend millions on schools, establish normal schools to prepare teachers, and greatly increase salaries to attract better-qualified men and women to the profession. Public elementary schools became standard in Massachusetts. He even brought life to the high school system. Established by law in 1827 in that state, the system had been largely moribund until Mann established some fifty new high schools, providing free public education at the secondary level at many locations in Massachusetts.

Inevitably, Mann attracted bitter opposition from social conservatives and orthodox churches. But by the time he had come to the end of his career in Massachusetts in the mid-1840s, he had done as much as any one man to revolutionize public education in America. The influence of Mann's ideas spread through the Northern states, so that by 1860 the campaign for free common schools had largely been won in the North. In this victory, the United States was far in advance of Great Britain, where sectarian and aristocratic hostilities prevented such progress for many decades.

Care for the Socially Deviant: The Institution

In Jacksonian America a dramatic new concept emerged in what to do with criminals, the insane, orphans, and the poverty-stricken who could not support themselves. Lawbreakers were no longer simply to be whipped, fined, put in stocks, or hanged; the mentally disturbed and the orphan and the indigent were not to be left to the casual mercies of the home and neighbors. In Jacksonian America, when the country was turning confidently in individualistic directions, Americans paradoxically conceived the idea of large central institutions as places in which to put the socially deviant: almshouses, penitentiaries, insane and orphan asylums.

The first thing done, after the Revolution, was to sweep the savage punishments inherited from British law out of American codes. What else, it was asked, should more properly happen in a democratic republic where the people, and not aristocrats, made the laws? Where humane treatment was to be the rule? In former times, the idea of long-term incarceration as punishment was not thought of, for there was literally no place to put criminals for this purpose. They were either expelled from the community, humiliated by being put for a time in the stocks (a wooden frame with holes in it for hands and feet), fined, or whipped. The death penalty was decreed for many crimes we would consider quite ordinary, and the common treatment for someone guilty for the third time of breaking the law was to hang him or her. By 1820, however, the American states had largely ended death sentences for all save a small group of heinous crimes such as rape and murder.

Now, as the spirit of reform gathered force in Britain and America, the eternally puzzling question of crime and punishment was being actively debated.

The ideology of the American republic insisted that the common people are essentially wise and good. Certainly, it was said, they would be so in a republic, where they would be freed from the distortions of aristocratic government. Therefore, something external to the criminal, not something essentially bad inside, must be causing him or her to become a lawbreaker.

Studies made in the 1820s of the actual life histories of criminals in the state of New York—an early example of what would later be called social science—pinpointed, people believed, the cause for their deviance: the collapse of family and community controls in a rapidly changing society. The badly reared child who was allowed simply to wander about and get into bad company was the one who later ended up in trouble. Society, these studies showed, was filled with temptations—particularly those found in saloons, brothels, and dissolute theaters. The social environment was the problem. Therefore, the answer, it was believed, was to build large central institutions and put the criminals inside their walls instead of whipping or hanging them. There, in a controlled environment, they would be remade into good and hardworking people by being taught orderly habits of labor and self-control.

In New York and Pennsylvania, the new ideas were given tangible form. With great public attention and pride, "penitentiaries" were constructed. Two goals would be achieved: reform of the criminal, and simultaneously protecting and stabilizing society at large while the process was going on. The penitentiary, "free of corruptions and dedicated to the proper training of the inmate," historian David Rothman writes, "would inculcate the discipline that negligent parents, evil companions, taverns, houses of prostitution, theaters, and gambling halls had destroyed." By the 1830s, penitentiaries were proliferating all over the Northern states, and the new American idea had become world-famous. Sing-Sing and the Elmira Reformatory in New York, and the Eastern State Penitentiary in Pennsylvania, received a steady stream of visitors from abroad. It was, in fact, to visit American prisons that Alexis de Tocqueville had journeyed to America in the mid-1830s.

The same ways of thinking and planning were directed also to that other perennial issue, what to do with the mentally disturbed? Insanity, like crime, was said to be produced by a harmful social environment. Confidently, reformers said it could be cured, and in a fashion similar to the penitentiary. Rescue the insane from their local communities, where they were tied to a tree or consigned to dark back rooms, and bring them into a publicly supported institution. Here, in a tranquil, pleasant, rural setting, free of the stresses of everyday life, disordered people would find their way to sanity once more.

As Americans in later generations were to learn, institutions founded for good reasons could become nightmares of repression and indifference. However, in Jacksonian America, the penitentiary and the asylum seemed shining symbols of the new and humane way of life that a republican country could establish.

The Revolution among Women and in the Family

The reform impulse running through American life in the Jacksonian years reached into the lives of women and into the family, accelerating long-range trends and in some cases inducing the passage of new laws. Profound changes had been coming to American women since the colonial days of "Adam's rib," when husbands and wives lived in isolated farm households and shared in the support and direction of the large colonial family. The new currents moved, paradoxically, in two directions: toward a growing sense of self-worth and personal independence for women, and toward an increasing concentration of women in the role of mother and householder.

Nothing so caught the eyes of European visitors as the behavior and standing of American women. As soon as Aleksandr Lakier got off the boat in Boston, he found himself "busy reflecting on the independence of women walking alone, without escorts, and looking as boldly at the men as the men looked at them." Falling into conversation with an American man about this remarkable sight, Lakier observed that "My European eyes were not admiring their hats or ankles . . . but rather what to a visitor from Europe is simply the fantastic freedom of the woman, her independent gait, and on the other hand the politeness and courtesy with which she is treated by men."

It was clear, too, that women and men lived separate lives, especially within the cities and among the city's middle classes. This pattern had been long emerging, beginning around the middle of the 1700s, when in the growing seacoast cities, in middle- and upper-class homes, a sharp separation between men's and women's spheres evolved. While men went out to the merchant houses, shops, and banks, women stayed at home and, with the family's affluence rising, hired household help. Among such families there emerged European ways of living, including the idea that respectable ladies were to be adornments to their husband's household, not hard-working participants in everyday economic life.

After the Revolution, with increasing urbanization and industrialization (still, of course, affecting a minority of the population), the "separation of the spheres" began to take place in more and more American families. Women came increasingly to be thought of as remaining in the home, that being their world exclusively, while the men built railroads, founded industries, and directed the nation's affairs.

Coincident with this development, between the Revolution and about 1830, the "modern family" began to take form, especially in the towns and cities, though its appearance in countryside homes can also be detected. Young men and women began choosing their own marriage partners; parents had less influence, save perhaps in the form of a veto (not wholly disappeared in the twentieth century). Couples chose each other for love and founded their marriages in mutual respect, women enjoying a growing personal influence and freedom within the family. The patriarchalism of the earlier generations, when husbands dominated both at home and outside it, was replaced with an arrangement much more democratic, in which the home was exclusively under the sway of the wife and mother.

Women's primary tasks were to raise and care for the children and keep the household going. They were considered morally superior to their husbands, though legally and socially inferior to them. As to the family itself, its focus shifted from a common economic enterprise, such as a farm or a household (or nearby) industry, to the rearing of children.

Finally, women were having fewer offspring. America had been a land of children: In 1790, half of the population was below the age of fifteen, so high was the birth rate (for every 1,000 children there were only 780 adults). After 1800, however, the birth rate among white Americans began dropping. Where in 1800 there were 1,844 children under ten years of age for every 1,000 white women of childbearing age, in 1860 this figure was 1,308, a decline of 30 percent. The immigrants who began pouring into the country in the 1840s quickly made up the gap, so that the American population thereafter grew at the same rapid rate as in 1800, but the internal demographic trends were well established.

The Gradual Revolution

It is important to understand that this description of the emerging "modern family" is that of an ideal, a direction, an orientation, not of a condition like turning on a light, in which illumination floods in and remains constant thereafter. The American family moved steadily in this direction generation after generation. To say that women began having fewer children is not to say that they suddenly began having only one or two offspring, but that the average family of eight children began slowly to drift downward in numbers. It would continue to do so for at least a century.

The increasing autonomy and freedom of women within the family, and that institution's focus on children, were gradual processes. For an American woman of 1990 to look at the life of an American woman in 1830 would be to see someone still fenced in by great limitations, still responsible for heavy labor in traditional activities at home—washing, canning, preparing food, sewing by hand, and experiencing frequent pregnancies.

The doctrine of the two spheres was associated with a romantic idealization of women that could be stifling. In clothing, this was literally true. Modesty was extreme: respectable women had to be covered from the chin to the ground. Showing an ankle to the public gaze was a shocking thing. In their relations with men, women were still depicted in contemporary literature as clinging vines, whereas men were the sturdy oaks. Or women were said to be like the moon, revolving around the (male) earth and receiving light and inspiration from it. Morally superior to animal-like man, they were to be queenly beauties gliding along in their separate paths: delicate, tasteful, refined, sensitive, loving, gentle, pure, devout.

In the Jacksonian years of reform, public schools in many Northern states began teaching both girls and boys at the elementary level, and by the 1850s girls commonly attended the new public high schools. Aleksandr Lakier, in that decade, stood in a Boston schoolroom and watched in wonderment as both sexes studied together, the course of study for the girls being "no less or easier than that for the boys. . . . I think the basic education that girls receive in school," he went on, "explains more than anything else the respect that American men, without exception, accord to women. . . . The girls freely answered the purely governmental questions as if they had been trained for political office. . . . According to our way of thinking this would be unnecessary for women, whose sphere is limited to domestic matters. But in America women are looked upon differently."

Republican Motherhood

Ever since revolutionary times, Americans had believed that women had a crucial task before them: being *republican* mothers. What went on in the home had actually not been paid much attention before the Revolution. In colonial times, historian Mary Beth Norton writes, "women had been viewed as wholly domestic beings whose influence in the world was confined to their immediate families." All this began to change when Americans started building their country. If civic virtue was the indispensable basis for a republic, where else would it begin but in the home? The republican mother was to fill her home with patriotism, and to rear her children with great care so that they became—especially the boys—devout Christians, honorable and active citizens, and sturdy competitors in a society based on free competition.

Mothers for the first time were being told, in other words, that what they were doing had high public significance; that they were important not only in shaping their daughters' characters, but in their impact on their sons as well—and therefore, on adult men. Pouring her life into her family (i.e., moving purposefully into a concentration on the separate sphere of the home), the republican mother was to send her husband and children out into a difficult world as strong individualists. "At times," writes Norton, "it even seemed as though republican theorists believed that the fate of the republic rested squarely, perhaps solely, upon the shoulders of its womenfolk."

In Jacksonian America, therefore, it was asked, how could women as mothers teach their boys about public affairs and to care for the public welfare, if they were not themselves knowledgeable? We see once again how republicanism shaped even daily American life and its intimate institutions. To make the Republic flourish, girls as well as boys were allowed into the new public schools. And the extended impact upon women themselves, in those parts of the country where they shared in schooling with the boys, was of great importance. Probably no other single influence was so powerful, over the long haul, in liberating women from older limitations than the

determination of educational reformers that the public education system being built in the Age of Jackson would be for both boys and girls.

Jacksonian reforms affected women in their marital status as well. In law, women had had the status of something like a grown-up child when they married. In theory, the husband was to be completely and absolutely the master; in reality, the relationship was becoming something else. A man could legally control his wife's property and any earnings she might receive, and his signature was necessary for her to enter into a valid contract. However, in the 1820s and 1830s legal restrictions on women began to change, as did so much in family relations. Although the courts generally held that there had to be a sovereign in the family—the husband—he had none of the rights to beat and otherwise abuse his wife that legend describes. Many states began giving wives greater rights over their property and allowed them to run businesses, make contracts, claim their wages, sue in court in their own name, and have joint control over their children.

Personal Autonomy

These legal changes reflected something much deeper that was going on in American culture. "In America," Lakier said to his Russian readers in one of his more arresting observations, "a woman is as independent as a man; she enters life boldly, moves through it alone if fate does not send her a husband, works as much as possible, and writes and teaches." Obviously, though he wrote these words after having traveled widely in both North and South, he could not have been talking about all American women everywhere. Nonetheless, there was a reality to what he saw. Lakier was not the only European visitor to comment on it, and it was a reality that was spreading. American women were awakening to a new sense of self, of personal importance and autonomy. American individualism, that assertive way of living so widely remarked on, was surfacing as an impulse among women as well as among men.

The result was a revolution in society's basic institution, the family. It was commonly remarked by European travelers in the United States that American women were freer in their marriages than their counterparts in Britain and on the European continent, no matter what class they belonged to. It was also regularly said that they were more valued, respected, cherished, and given more rights and standing.

In light of these considerations, the falling birth rate becomes more understandable. Clearly it occurred in significant part because women were searching for more personal independence within the family, and of course it could not have occurred at all unless women had wanted it to. (Two of the three commonest birth control methods of the time were either directly or largely under women's control: coitus interruptus required the man's cooperation, but abortion and simple abstinence did not.) Having babies was that part of a woman's life that affected her more than anything else, for it kept her tied down and dominated by the wishes and needs of others.

Thus, the decline in the birth rate that began with the opening of the nineteenth century may be thought of as a gauge showing the slow advance, through the century and beyond 1900, of women's autonomy within the family. The radical idea that women should have a right to control the number of children they bore was circulating before the nineteenth century was half gone. It was a sensation when Victoria Woodhull, radical feminist and advocate of free love, went about the country in the 1850s lecturing on the subject, but its practice had been a private reality for years.

As the fundamental basis for marriage (as against the traditional motives of economics, social standing, procreation, and family alliances) love itself was the ultimate individualizing influence, for it put to one side all other considerations in choosing a life partner. Also, it immediately gave to women more standing in the marriage. Among Quakers and Puritans, where loving marriages had long been stressed, women had always tended to be more independent and important in the family as well as outside it. The extraordinarily loving marriage of John and Abigail Adams, as intimate during Adams's presidency as in its earlier years, has regularly attracted attention, and certainly the life of Lucretia Mott was a dramatic demonstration of Quaker attitudes.

Of course, this ideal of a marriage of loving companions that was now appearing would still be widening and growing in American life a century later, in the 1920s, as we shall see; it was hardly the universal standard before the Civil War, nor one fully realized. The central role of love in manwoman relationships, however, was clearly emergent. Romantic novels built around the theme of love in marriage began flourishing in Jackson's time; women began to win divorces on the simple ground of husband's adultery (that is, the loss of his affection to someone else); and they scorned other women who married for money and standing. Courtship now became a prominent and lengthy element in the forming of a marriage, for it was necessary to have time to find out whether two people were genuinely in love and compatible.

The Cult of True Womanhood

What has been called the Cult of True Womanhood, which extravagantly idealized women as morally elevated persons, emerged full-blown in the Jacksonian years. We see that it presents contradictory aspects. It has been condemned as a male tactic to get women to accept their house-bound role, to keep them inferior and dependent. On the other hand, the Cult of True Womanhood also seemed to parallel in time a much heightened valuing of American women as persons.

Fredericka Bremer, a Swedish feminist who visited America in the 1840s, spoke admiringly of the unusually high standing given women in America. She especially esteemed their role as "the center and lawgiver in the home"—that is, their responsibility for the ethical and spiritual civilizing of children and husbands. Alexis de Tocqueville in the 1830s remarked that in his native France men who raped women were given only light punishment, whereas in America rape brought a sentence of death.

There is evidence that most women preferred having their separate sphere in which they were dominant. They tended to avoid joining communal, utopian societies in which segregation by sex was not practiced and men and women did largely the same things. The growing importance attached to the rearing of children seemed to make this now exclusively female task far more valued and respected than before. As mothers became the parent most directly and "naturally" connected with their children's rearing, and as the future of America came more and more to be linked to the healthy training of its children, the task of motherhood was elevated in public esteem.

As the century proceeded, the concentration of women's work in the home accelerated. By the 1840s employers in the new factories had shifted to the hiring of men rather than women. (Figures for the cotton textile industry in 1816 showed 66,000 women at work, 24,000 boys, and only 10,000 adult men.) In the first place, women were felt to belong at home. Second, industrial tasks began requiring more skill, and men were usually better educated.

Possibly connected with this reduction in heavy work outside the home, by the 1840s women's life expectancy was longer than that of men, the reverse of the former pattern. (Having fewer childbirths, with their risks to life, also helped women live longer.) By 1910, the concentration of women in the home was so general that although more than half of Americans lived in cities, only one of twenty married white women worked outside the house.

The Century of the Child and the Age of Youth

It has been fashionable among scholars to write that until the nineteenth century children were regarded simply as little adults and punished severely for not living up to adult standards; and that beyond harsh discipline, little attention was paid to them. Recent study indicates, however, that at least for the past several centuries people in Britain and America have loved their children pretty much as they do now, and that they have understood that childhood is a distinct and separate time of life, with its own particular needs.

Beginning in the early nineteenth century there was a great deal more systematic study of and writing about childhood and parenting, as there was about so much else in life. This may have made people more self-conscious about the whole experience, if not any more fundamentally concerned about their own children. Indeed, a new literature written especially for children flourished in Jacksonian America. Appearing at the same time were books providing mothers with detailed instructions on how to rear their offspring, how to love them and instruct them properly. "There is scarcely any subject concerning which I feel more anxiety than the proper education of my children," an early nineteenth-century mother wrote. "It is a difficult and delicate subject. . . ."

The greater systematic pains being taken with rearing children went hand in hand with the rise of the concept of the republican mother, whose nurturing of her sons and daughters could affect the health of the nation at large. It also paralleled the freeing of women to concentrate on this task. By the early years of the nineteenth century, the mother was openly identified as the person with primary responsibility for raising the child, and a strong emotional bond characterized the relationship between mothers and children. Furthermore, in America's increasingly complex economy, children needed careful rearing and a good education if they were to do well in life. For this reason too, parents began to take greater pains with each child. More money was spent on schooling, and children were kept in the classroom longer.

One result of these converging influences, which together led to smaller families, was a shifting of the national population's center of gravity upward, to the years of youth and young adulthood. In the 1830s, the number of children below sixteen and the number of people in their twenties and early thirties were equal. By the 1870s, there would be 1.25 adults for every child. In short, while before 1800 America had been a land of adults interspersed among crowds of small children, by the midcentury decades there had appeared in American life a huge group that had not existed in such proportions before: people in their late teens, twenties, and early thirties.

Their very numbers, and their characteristic high spirits, thrust young people upon the American consciousness. The country's mood shifted in the Jacksonian years toward an idealization, a tremendous vogue, of youth. In 1835 a social observer could write: "Nothing but what is elastic and youthful, is in fashion. Our legislators, our professional men, must all be young to be popular. A man of fifty is considered almost superannuated with us." The earlier reverence for age faded markedly, as well as all the things associated with the older generation: its clothes, ways, beliefs. (By 1860 the median age for white males was almost twenty.) "Young America" was in full momentum: expansive, impatient, eager for change, individualistic, romantic.

BIBLIOGRAPHY

For American ways in the Age of Jackson, and how they thought and worried about themselves, I have relied on a number of books: as always on Alexis de Tocqueville's *Democracy in America* (1835–36, and many subsequent editions), as well as on: Arnold Schrier and Joyce Story, trans. and ed., *A Russian Looks at America: The Journey* of *Aleksandr Borisovich Lakier in 1857* (1979); relevant sections in John Higham, *From Boundlessness to Consolidation: The Transformation of American Culture, 1848–1860* (1969); Richard L. Rapson, *Britons View America: Travel Commentary 1860–1935* (1971), for long-term characteristics; and especially on two superb books, Paul C. Nagel's

This Sacred Trust: American Nationality 1798–1898 (1971), and Fred Somkin's *Unquiet Eagle: Memory and Desire in the Idea of American Freedom, 1815–1860* (1967). In Robert Kelley, *The Transatlantic Persuasion: The Liberal-Democratic Mind in the Age of Gladstone* (1969), first chapter, I have sought to describe the broad transatlantic Anglo-American culture and economy. Marvin Meyers' *The Jacksonian Persuasion: Politics and Belief* (1957) offers a keen analysis of the mood of the time. Morton Borden, *Jews, Turks, and Infidels* (1984), tells us of the nineteenth-century struggle by American Jews to throw off the civil disabilities that made them legally second-class citizens.

I have explored the Second Great Awakening in: Martin E. Marty, *Righteous Empire: The Protestant Experience in America* (1970); Paul E. Johnson, *A Shopkeeper's Millennium: Society and Revivals in Rochester, New York, 1815–1837* (1978); Whitney R. Cross, *The Burned-Over District: The Social and Intellectual History of Enthusiastic Religion in Western New York, 1800–1850* (1950); Daniel Walker Howe's *The Unitarian Conscience: Harvard Moral Philosophy 1805–1861* (1970); and Sidney E. Ahlstrom, *A Religious History of the American People* (1972). Concerning the Mormons, I have drawn upon two absorbing works: Ray B. West's *Kingdom of the Saints: The Story of Brigham Young and the Mormons* (1957), and Klaus J. Hansen's recent much-praised study, *Mormonism and the American Experience* (1981). Jacques Barzun's brilliant and enduring *Classic, Romantic, and Modern* (1961) is essential on romanticism's overarching mood, and Merle Curti, *Human Nature in American Thought: A History* (1980) is essential on all these themes.

Among other sources I used Paul K. Conkin's important essay on Emerson in his *Puritans & Pragmatists: Eight Eminent American Thinkers* (1968). Burton J. Bledstein, *The Culture of Professionalism: The Middle Class and the Development of Higher Education in America* (1976), is also important on Emerson and the "youth culture." The Transcendentalists speak for themselves in two excellent collections edited by Perry Miller, *The Transcendentalists*

(1959), and *Margaret Fuller: American Romantic* (1963). Many works are available on Emerson, Thoreau, Hawthorne, and their literary era.

A brilliant examination of one of the era's central reform efforts is David J. Rothman, *The Discovery of the Asylum: Social Order and Disorder in the New Republic* (1971). A recent study of the impact of common school education is Daniel Calhoun's *The Intelligence of a People* (1973). Carl Degler's *At Odds: Women and the Family from the Revolution to the Present* (1980), which was important to me, has elicited excellent scholarly approval since its appearance. On the concept of republican motherhood, see Mary Beth Norton's recent studies: *Liberty's Daughters: The Revolutionary Experience of American Women, 1750–1800* (1980), and her essay in *The American Historical Review*, "The Evolution of White Women's Experience in Early America," 89 (June 1984), 593–619. A new and intriguing work, Linda A. Pollock's *Forgotten Children: Parent-Child Relations from 1500 to 1900* (1983) gave me a fresh look at this major topic, and I have continued to rely on Mary P. Ryan's *Womanhood in America: From Colonial Times to the Present* (1975), and W. Elliot Brownlee and Mary M. Brownlee's *Women in the American Economy: A Documentary History, 1675 to 1929* (1976), as well as Eleanor Flexner, *Century of Struggle: The Women's Rights Movement in the United States* (rev. ed., 1975). Page Smith's *Daughters of the Promised Land: Women in American History* (1970) is useful in evoking the mood.

Richard D. Brown's pioneering study, *Modernization: The Transformation of American Life 1600–1865* (1976), is provocative. David Hackett Fischer has written a path-breaking and intriguing book that studies the shift in the attitude of the era's various generations, *Growing Old in America* (expanded ed., 1978). Relevant chapters in Robert Cruden's *Many and One: A Social History of the United States* (1980) are valuable. Ronald G. Walters, *American Reformers 1815–1860* (1978), is the strong new general work on this topic.

13

The Age of Jackson Center Stage: The National Debate

TIME LINE

1829	Inauguration of Andrew Jackson as president
1830	Veto of Maysville Road bill
1832	Higher tariff enacted; Anti-Masonic party active
1832–33	Nullification Crisis
1832–36	Jackson's war on the Second Bank of the United States
1833	Compromise Tariff lowers tariff in stages over a ten-year span
1834	Whig party formed
1836	Jackson issues Specie Circular; Martin Van Buren elected eighth president of the United States
1837	Van Buren proposes Independent Treasury System
1837–41	Depression
1840	William Henry Harrison elected ninth president of the United States; *Caroline* affair
1841	John Tyler becomes tenth president upon death of Harrison; Robert Peel becomes prime minister in Great Britain
1842	Protective tariff reestablished; Webster-Ashburton Treaty settles Maine boundary
1844	James Polk elected eleventh president of the United States
1846	Walker Tariff establishes low United States tariff; British eliminate protective tariffs by repeal of Corn Laws; independent Treasury enacted

HENRY CLAY

Henry Clay of Kentucky: Young men like Abraham Lincoln of Illinois loved him, idolized him. For twenty years, he was regularly talked of for the presidency. The Whig party seemed to be built around Clay, and the dream many shared of a more civilized, more gentlemanly, more respectable America seemed to depend upon his success. The word "charismatic," more than a century later used of John Kennedy, would have been applied to Henry Clay in his time had it been thought of then. What was his secret? Why was he so fascinating?

Clay was a classic symbol of the Other South: the Whig South that rejected the barbarism, the violence, and the poisonous hatred of Yankees that characterized the Democratic South. He thought the Yankee ideal admirable: the vision of an America led by a well-educated elite modeled along the lines of the English gentleman. Sending his son to Harvard (as did Lincoln in later years), he returned from a visit to Yankee-land "full of admiration and esteem for them. . . ." He agreed with Alexander Hamilton's basic conception, and that of New England Federalists,

that America should strike out to build its own industries, foster the growth of cities, become economically independent. This, Clay said, would make the United States a land for industrious, hard-working young men anxious to get ahead.

It was Clay who first spoke of the "self-made man." The slothful indolence of the typical Southern plantation was not for him, though in operating his hemp-growing Kentucky plantation he had become the largest slaveowner in the state. Rather, he believed a busy, enterprising, vigorous society should be nourished and encouraged by the central government. At the same time, by developing its own resources and building a balance between farming and industry, America would become a strong and tightly knit union, a great family of mutually supportive states. Clay was, in short, a strong *nationalist*, as against the localism and state-centered loyalties of the Democrats.

Though Clay, like Jefferson, owned many slaves throughout his career, he deplored the institution and argued for its extinction, though he knew not how to do it and did not like abolitionists. In 1832, he called unsuccessfully upon Congress to begin annual appropriations of $10 million to buy the slaves' freedom. Hostile to the influence of military men like Andrew Jackson in public life, in the mid-1840s he condemned the annexation of Texas and attacked the Mexican War as being founded upon a mad rage for expansion, as well as upon obvious lies by the president, James K. Polk. As a loved and respected elder statesman, in his mid-seventies he played again his role as the Great Compromiser—a title he had won in the Missouri Compromise debates of 1820–21—by helping to bring about the Compromise of 1850 and thereby (for a time) settle the status of slavery in the territories won in the Mexican War. But two years later Henry Clay was dead. Before long, so was his party.

Overview

In March 1829 a mob of enthusiastic supporters followed Andrew Jackson to the White House after his inaugural address, creating such bedlam that the new president fled the exccutive mansion to escape the crush. The event symbolized for Jackson's enemies and friends alike the beginning of an era. Either the rabble had taken over, or the day of the common man had arrived.

Andrew Jackson's presidency was a mythic event. He was "the Hero," with popular-vote majorities behind him not to be matched until the twentieth century. During his eight years as president (1829–37) he towered over American political life. For eight more years until his death in 1845, he continued to influence public affairs powerfully. It was his protégé, the young James K. Polk of Tennessee, who with his support became president in 1845, completed the Jacksonian economic revolution, and in a rebirth of Jackson's impetuous military expansionism, swept America to the Pacific Coast.

Thousands of ordinary people, awakened to a new sense of their dignity and power, found in the Scotch-Irishman Andrew Jackson the supreme expression of the egalitarian republican values that had elevated them. Distrusting the learned and the aristocratic, they trusted instead a sturdy military man who lived by his natural, untutored, and, so it was said, unselfish instincts. He was the "nursling of the wilds," a man of "fiery heart." They admired both his style and his character, and he captured their loyalties as have few other presidents.

Jackson polarized American politics and inaugurated the second party system. His followers, who called themselves Democrats, won most of the presidential elections in the Age of Jackson over the Whigs, who coalesced as Jackson's opposition. Until 1840 national politics concentrated primarily on domestic economic problems. From then until 1848, foreign problems and expansionism were dominant. Through both periods there ran the ever-growing problem of slavery. Expansion and slavery will be discussed separately in subsequent chapters. For the present we shall concentrate on the Jacksonian response to the problems created by the beginning of modern economic conditions. That is, we will focus on the national debate over the ever-pressing question: In the matter of America, what is to be done?

Jackson and the Economy

In the early 1820s, Henry Clay had crusaded nationally for what he called his "American System." It would consist of protective tariffs, to make foreign goods expensive and allow new American industries to rise and flourish; a centralized banking system; and a vigorous program of internal improvements (roads, ports, and canals) to ease transport. When Andrew Jackson began his presidency in 1829, something very like Clay's system was in existence as national policy.

How did Jackson feel about it? In 1830 he appeared to indicate his leanings when he vetoed the Maysville Road bill. Although the proposed road would have been a segment of the National Road, Jackson said the bill was unconstitutional because the part built would have been wholly within the one state of Kentucky. He insisted also that the government should return to the Jeffersonian model by spending as little as possible. This action was revealing, for it showed the way Jackson was principally to use his power as president and national leader— by saying no.

Speaking in Cincinnati, Ohio, in 1830 Henry Clay, angered at Andrew Jackson, praised the American System and its effects:

> To the laboring classes it is invaluable since it increases and multiplies the demands for their industry and gives them an option of employments. It adds power and strength to our Union by new ties of interest, blending and connecting together all its parts, and creating an interest with each in the prosperity of the whole. It secures to our own country, whose skill and enterprise, properly fostered and sustained, cannot be surpassed, those vast profits which are made in other countries by the operation of converting the raw material into manufactured articles.

> It naturalizes and creates within the bosom of our country all the arts, and, mixing the farmer, manufacturer, mechanic, artist, and those engaged in other vocations together, admits of those mutual exchanges so conducive to the prosperity of all and everyone, free from the perils of the sea and war—all this it effects while it nourishes and leaves a fair scope to foreign trade. . . . (Calvin Colton, ed., The Works of Henry Clay . . . [1904])

The Bank War

The banking system touched a sensitive Jacksonian nerve. The president was from the West, where the Second Bank of the United States had been condemned as a "monster" since a massive wave of foreclosures it had launched in the panic of 1819. One of the few things that Jackson had actually read about in books was the South Sea Bubble, an inflationary boom and collapse that had shattered the British financial system in the early eighteenth century. He had also personally struggled for many years under crushing burdens of debts to banks. From these influences he derived an abhorrence of speculation and bankers. He also knew that the Second Bank of the United States was a nest of his political enemies. Nicholas Biddle, president of the bank, and his financier friends were confirmed Clay men who detested Jackson. Always obsessed with his "honor" and sensitive to all personal slights, Jackson bridled at their criticism.

The facts of the struggle may be briefly summarized. From his first message to Congress, Jackson expressed doubts that the Second Bank of the United States was either constitutional or necessary. When he kept the matter alive, friends of the bank took alarm. In 1832 matters quickly climaxed. Henry Clay, nominated for the presidency by a convention of National Republicans, denounced Jackson's views on the bank. A daring stratagem was then adopted: The bank's charter would be presented to Congress for renewal that year, though it ran to 1836. If Jackson vetoed the recharter bill, his action would be a major issue in the coming presidential campaign. If he did not, the bank's survival would be assured.

Jackson: Bank Veto

Jackson was enraged. "The bank," he told Martin Van Buren, "is trying to kill me, *but I will kill it!*" When the recharter bill came to him he issued a ringing veto that electrified the nation. It was a violent attack on the moneyed, and a passionate appeal to the lowly. No president had ever done such a thing before. The veto message, Biddle wrote to Henry Clay, "has all the fury of a chained panther. It is really a manifesto of anarchy." A Boston newspaper fumed, "For the first time, perhaps, in the history of civilized communities, the Chief Magistrate of a great nation . . . is found appealing to the worst passion of the uninformed part of the people, and endeavoring to stir up the poor against the rich."

In his bank veto message of 1832, Jackson condemned explicitly the "rich and powerful, [who] too often bend the acts of government to their selfish purposes." Distinctions are inevitable in human life, he said, for some people are more talented than others. But "when the laws undertake to add to those natural and just advantages artificial distinctions . . . to make the rich richer and the potent more powerful, the humble members of society—the farmers, mechanics, and laborers—who have neither the time nor the means of securing like favors to themselves, have a right to complain of the injustice to their government." The bank, he went on, had been an unconstitutional institution since its founding. It was destructive in its operations, and it represented far too great a concentration of power in private hands. Everyone would be at the mercy of the small group who directed the bank, for they were "irresponsible to the people."

Jackson attacked over and over again the "monopoly" control the bank had over the nation's finances, and the way this power had "operated as a gratuity of many millions to the stockholders." And who were the stockholders? They were foreigners (i.e., British), together with men drawn from the very richest class of Americans. How could they conceivably "have any claim to the special favor of the government"? With a rechartered bank, and its monopoly powers, they could continue subverting the rights of the states and endangering the liberties of each American. It was far better to close down the institution and reinforce the local agencies of national life.

The country was actually weakened, Jackson said, when its central institutions were strengthened. "Its true strength consists in leaving individuals and states as much as possible to themselves. . . . Many of our rich men have not been content with equal protection and equal benefits but have besought us to make them richer by act of Congress." Thereafter, Jackson warned, it was his intention to "take a stand against all new grants of monopolies and exclusive privileges, against any prostitution of our government to the advancement of the few at the expense of the many."

In the election of 1832, Clay was buried in an electoral landslide. Close to 688,000 votes went to Jackson, about 530,000 to Clay. The electoral college total stood at 219 for Jackson and 49 for Clay. (Eighteen electoral votes went to minor candidates.) As one editor who grieved at the defeat of Clay put the matter: "It is the duty of every good Christian to pray to our Maker to have pity on us."

Jackson then instructed the secretary of the treasury to ignore the Second Bank's charter and withdraw all federal funds from the vaults of the Second Bank. When that official refused on the ground that such action was illegal, Jackson discharged him and placed in the office a man who would do his bidding. Clay men howled tyranny, but the funds nonetheless were withdrawn and placed in a group of state-chartered banks around the country, which were promptly called pet banks. The Second Bank continued for a time after 1836, under a different name and a Pennsylvania charter. But Biddle's leadership of the institution had grown erratic, financial conditions were shaky, and it closed its doors forever early in 1841. The United States would never have such an institution again.

Veto and Financial Reality

Without doubt, the veto faithfully expressed the way many people viewed the Second Bank of the United States, but the reality of the banking system, recent studies have revealed, was something quite different from the way Jackson described it or understood it. Its "monopoly" consisted simply of being the sole bank that received the government's funds and transferred them about the country. The banking system as a whole was open to all comers. States chartered them by the hundreds. The national bank dominated certain parts of the financial system, but it had no monopolistic control.

Jackson condemned the bank for draining currency out of the Western states. In fact, it did not do so. He talked as if debts owed to the bank were paid to its stockholders, which was not the case. The Second Bank was depicted as an evil centralizing agency that expanded and contracted the volume of currency at will, thereby inflating or deflating prices

President Jackson slays the hydra-headed bank monster, assisted by Van Buren and the comic character Major Jack Downing.

in order to give profits to those on the inside. In reality, the bank almost never acted as a regulator of the money supply despite the standard assumption by historians since then that it did so. This is the classic function of what is termed a central bank, but only in limited ways did the Second Bank carry out central bank operations. Primarily, it spent its efforts trying to insure that money printed by state banks was adequately backed by specie or other reliable securities, such as government bonds.

Jackson, then, slew a monster that hardly existed. It is important to note, however, that he also did not kill a "central bank" as it is generally conceived. Modern historians have usually maintained that Jackson's destruction of the Second Bank removed an essential regulatory mechanism, prompting a riotous expansion of the currency supply. This was not so. In fact, when the Second Bank actually did

caused distinct political party.

try to control the volume of money, it bungled things. Furthermore, its existence was not essential to maintain the honesty of the currency issued by state banks. Whether or not the bank was in existence, state banks kept a check on one another's issues by promptly presenting each other's bank notes for redemption.

In Jackson's mind, nevertheless, and in the minds of the thousands who supported him, the bank was a real monster, just as in the minds of Jackson's enemies it was a vital part of a healthy economy. Its destruction, therefore, was as real an issue in politics as if the beliefs about it were true. Political passions gathered around the cause as filings gather around a magnet. In direct response to Jackson's policies, several political factions coalesced in 1834 to form the Whig party, which appeared first in New York City and then spread rapidly throughout the nation.

Who Were the Whigs? *Anti Jackson*

What was this strange business, the ancient name of a British political party appearing among the Americans? It was not an accident. The men who chose the name Whig for their new political party, which was soon strong in every state in the Union, said they were doing what Britain's Whigs had been doing since the 1600s: trying to fight the tyranny of an autocratic monarch, in this case "King Andrew." Jackson, they said, was dangerously inflating the true powers of the American presidency. He rode roughshod over his cabinet; threatened South Carolina (as we will see) with military force; insisted that the president could disregard laws he thought unconstitutional, such as the Bank's 1816 charter; and refused to carry out a Supreme Court ruling that sought to protect the Indians in Georgia. Jackson issued more vetoes of congressional enactments than all his predecessors put together, advancing, as he did so, a novel claim: That the president's veto power could be used not simply to strike down enactments which were legally or constitutionally faulty, but those which he, in his own independent judgment, thought bad policy.

Jackson said he did these things as the voice of the people at large against the organized interests of privilege and wealth. Whigs recoiled from this concept of the presidency. They were uncomfortable anyway with manhood suffrage and egalitarian democracy. Whigs were certainly republicans, but they

The Election of 1832

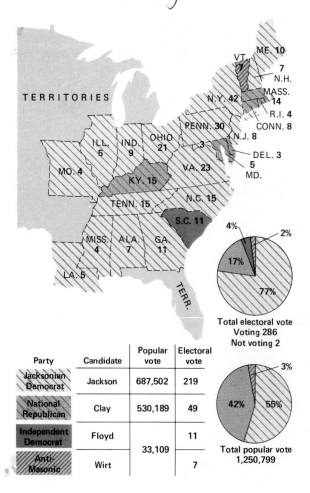

Party	Candidate	Popular vote	Electoral vote
Jacksonian Democrat	Jackson	687,502	219
National Republican	Clay	530,189	49
Independent Democrat	Floyd		11
Anti-Masonic	Wirt	33,109	7

Total electoral vote
Voting 286
Not voting 2

Total popular vote
1,250,799

were also elitists who believed the people should elect their representatives from among the educated and the well-established. Thereafter, the electorate should stand back prudently ("prudent" was a word Whigs often used) and let those representatives, in their superior wisdom, jointly manage the country.

The president, on his part, should be a quiet, careful chairman of the board who dutifully carried out what Congress enacted. To the Whig mind, Jackson was a man of passion, certainly not a gentleman or a man of learning and sober thought. And thoughtful gentlemen, Whigs believed, working together as a team, should run the United States of America, rather like paternalistic fathers were supposed to govern their families or a board of directors runs a business corporation.

The Whigs as an Ethnocultural Community

Whigs thought of themselves, to put it most simply, as the very heart of the country, as its most virtuous and enlightened and truly republican element. In a nation overwhelmingly English in its language, law, religion, and basic institutions, they were the most self-consciously English of all. Their heartland lay in New England, which was the region physically closest to England, and Whigs took every chance they could to return to the mother country and renew their contacts with a way of life they admired so much, except for its monarchical institutions. Whigs characteristically described themselves as America's "sober, industrious, thriving people." We might term them America's "core culture"—that is, the kind of people whose way of living presented itself as the model for everyone else, and would eventually become nationally dominant. Historian Ronald Formisano refers to the Whigs as the Center, and their political opponents as representing the Periphery.

In the North, most Whigs were devout churchgoers, and usually of pious Congregationalist or evangelical Presbyterian stock. Proudly Yankee, they carried with them an outspoken New England consciousness and identity wherever they migrated: into western New York state, and the upper Middle West—northern Ohio, Michigan, northern Indiana and Illinois, Iowa, and southern Wisconsin. In their transplanted settings, Yankees formed New England Societies to serve in each community as their club, their collective voice, and often their political arm.

In the slave states, Whigs were men of the "other South," as historian Carl Degler terms it. That is, they were those generally urban Southerners (a minority in the overwhelmingly rural South) who admired Yankee ways of hard work, punctuality, and thrift, and who wanted to see the South become more Northern—that is, more concerned with schooling and industry and towns. Merchants, bankers, professional men, and many of the large plantation owners—these were the people who led the Whigs in the Southern states. Like the Northern Whigs, they looked to aristocratic England in admiration, and took the traditional ways and ideas of English country gentlemen as their model.

Joining them in the Southern Whig party were many thousands who lived in upland Appalachian areas, where there were few slaves and where slaveholders were disliked. In the South, too, there were non-British ethnic groups who shared these views and voted Whig: the French of Louisiana and the Germans. In fact, Southern Whigs made up together so large and important a part of the Southern population that they actually won a slight majority of popular votes cast in Southern elections in the years from 1836 to 1848.

Whigs both North and South admired "respectability." Their ideal way of living was that of the solid, churchgoing man of property. Personal morality in matters of dress, recreation, and sexual relations was important to them. They regarded the rough-and-tumble egalitarianism of the frontier and the urban working-class districts with disdain, and were particularly alarmed at the disorder and violence which everywhere seemed to rumble and flare in Jacksonian America. They recoiled from the murderous Protestant-Catholic battles in cities like New York and Philadelphia; the chronic violence of slavery, with its whipping and branding; the strong-arm taking of Indian lands; and lynching (mobs taking the law in their own hands to hang people accused of capital crimes). In Congress, legislators attacked legislators; in the Northern states abolitionists were mobbed and murdered; and in the South men seemed always to be knifing each other, carrying on blood fuels, or dueling.

In every state, Whigs publicly deplored America's violent temper, and "saw themselves as the party of all who love law and order and peace and prosperity," as Daniel Walker Howe, the Whig's most perceptive historian, has recently written. They joined Henry Clay in blaming the violence on Andrew Jackson's political following, the Democrats. Was he not, they would ask, the prince of all who used guns and strong-arm methods to get their way? Was he not the supreme expression of a kind of aggressive masculinity that Whigs deplored? Of a fanatical readiness to kill and maim to avenge slights to one's "honor"?

The Whigs' Moralism and Nativism

Moralistic and strongly Protestant, the Whigs, as Formisano has observed in his skillful study, *The Birth of Mass Political Parties: Michigan, 1827–1861* (1971), "constituted the evangelicals' best hope to Christianize America through politics." Sunday dancing, grog shops, suggestive dress, gambling, debauchery, bigamy, brothel keeping, seduction, lewdness—all of these, Whigs believed, must be sternly controlled by righteous men in positions of power if the American republic were to endure and God was not to be mocked. Whig newspapers said it clearly: The righteous had no choice but to save the world from evil, and those committing evil from themselves.

A tidal wave of drinking and alcoholism seemed to engulf America after the War of 1812, and Whigs actively labored in a nationwide temperance crusade that sprang to life in the 1820s and struggled along through American politics for generations thereafter. Also, too many Americans, zealous Christian believers said, were violating the Sabbath. To work against this evil, Whigs lent strong support to demands calling for laws to be passed halting all movements on Sunday, all recreation, everything but going to church and thinking of God. Whigs were also offended by what they saw as sexual impurity, and they crusaded for strict controls. In 1843, for example, when a Democratic-controlled legislature in Michigan amended and loosened laws that punished adultery and fornication, Whigs rent the air with cries of outrage.

As the aggressively British and Protestant party, the Whigs attracted the support of those native Americans who recoiled at the influx of non-British or non-Protestant immigrants. Particularly distasteful to them was the life style of the Irish Catholics and Germans, for they were both heavy drinkers, the first of whiskey and the latter of beer. They also thought Sunday a fine day for picnics and folk dancing. Whigs welcomed immigrants from the island of Great Britain, of course (the English, Scots, and Welsh), for in the face of a growing Irish Catholic influx they looked on all Protestants from the British Isles as political friends and allies.

In Britain, Irish Catholics were widely regarded by the Protestants as an inferior, almost savage, people. In both the United States and Britain, those prejudiced against Irish Catholics described them in the same terms used by others of an equally prejudiced outlook to describe the black American. The Catholic Irish were said to be apelike (cartoons uniformly depicted them in this form); childish and emotionally unstable; ignorant, indolent, primitive, politically naive, greedy; musical, amusing, likable at a distance;

Attempted assassination of Jackson in 1835 by Richard Lawrence, both of whose guns misfired. There is nothing peculiarly modern about the impulse to murder presidents.

impulsive and never able to calculate ahead; and excessively lustful. "Respectable" people did not understand how Democrats could work with them.

The Irish were not alone in being disliked, though no other immigrant group was described in such terms. There were also the Germans and other continental immigrants who entered the country in great numbers after 1820. A Whig newspaper angrily attacked the Democrats in 1840 for winning an election by using the votes of an "avalanche of Germans, Irish, Swiss, Prussians, French, Russians, and Poles." There was one exception to this list—the free blacks of the Northern states. The Whigs offered them the only sympathy they got, and where they could vote they went down the line for the Whig ticket.

For all their elitist temper, the Whigs were not simply a party of the middle and upper classes. Jackson may have said that his party was that of the "farmers, mechanics, and laborers," but thousands of such people voted Whig. This is why in most elections the Whigs split the popular vote fairly evenly with Democrats. Workers in industries that were hurt by British competition voted the Whig ticket, as did those who feared that immigrants might take their jobs. Many detested Catholics or any non-British alien. It is true that Whigs drew a strong vote in the higher-income levels, but this was primarily because Protestantism and Anglo-Saxon origin were more characteristic of upper- than of lower-income groups.

Also, Whig values appealed strongly to people in all walks of life. Getting ahead, following upright ways of life, putting leadership in the hands of the wealthy and the eminent—these attitudes were by no means unpopular. Henry Clay was widely admired by humble people because they thought Whig ideals admirable and Whig dreams for America appealing. Abraham Lincoln, as one of his Democratic relatives regretfully recalled, "allways Loved Hen Clay's speaches," and yet he was clearly not from the upper class. Lincoln was, nevertheless, a devoted Whig.

The Whigs' National Vision

Whigs were culturally traditional people who often called themselves "conservatives." However, in their economic values they were modernizing reformers. Like Alexander Hamilton before them, they wanted to thrust America in new directions. Rather than see Americans spreading willy-nilly westward and taking up farms, Whigs wanted to see them cluster together in thriving, industrious cities where their labor was needed in factories.

Whigs saw progress in the rise of manufacturing and new technology. They exuded unyielding and sometimes ecstatic cheer when they looked at swiftly rising factories. In an earlier chapter we have seen the great New England orator, Edward Everett, enthusiastically praising industrial development, and are not surprised to note that he was a Whig. Did industrialization create class divisions, as its critics asserted? Not at all, Whigs said, for everyone was a laborer, and everyone a capitalist. If workers and employers were angry at each other, it was only because "outside agitators" had come in and filled workers' heads with nonsense about exploitation. Society's natural condition, Whigs said, was harmony between the classes in a familylike relationship. Labor and capital were but complements of one another, not natural enemies.

The Whigs' Long-range Impact

In egalitarian Jacksonian America, Whigs were not as successful politically as the Democrats. They simply did not enjoy the new mass party politics in the way Democrats seemed to. Nonetheless, as Howe rightly points out, the Whigs probably had the most powerful long-range influence upon American life. As investors, bankers, employers, and industrialists, they set America moving toward what it has since become: an urban and industrial country tied compactly together by complex transcontinental transportation networks and an intricate financial web. Whigs were the people who pushed the United States toward a national way of life that became predominantly entrepreneurial in mood, risk-taking in strategy, and fascinated by economic development.

This was not a process, however, that Whigs believed could get going simply on its own steam. Letting all people merely do what they wanted to do—i.e., following a policy of *laissez-faire*—would mean drift and inefficiency. Though Whigs too regarded European governments with distaste, thinking them far too powerful and oppressive, they believed that Americans had gone too far in the other direction. They needed, Whigs believed, to get over their love affair with pure and unfettered individualism. They needed to think of the whole nation as a family that required paternalistic leadership. If there were to be real progress, a *plan* needed to be imposed from above, in the same way that God has imposed his plan of salvation upon humanity. Then the United States of America, Whigs believed, would achieve an "organic unity of society," a phrase they liked to use.

Ever since the 1820s, Henry Clay had offered the national plan that Jackson now supported, in his call for an American System. The United States, Clay said, could never build factories as long as British goods, made with cheap labor, flooded into its ports to undersell anything made in America, where the cost of labor, because of its relative scarcity, was always higher. To become truly independent from Great Britain, the United States must erect protective tariffs to keep out foreign goods and allow factories to spring up within its own borders to produce the things people wanted. This, in turn, would have many admirable results. It would open a wide array of opportunities and occupations to gifted young Americans, so they would no longer be limited just to farming—and Whigs were passionately interested in releasing this spirit of enterprise, in seeing common people rise from poverty to wealth and property. Industrialization would also mean jobs for workers, and it would mean cities and trade.

The Whigs and Modernization

Above all, Whigs said, a protective policy would make a self-sufficient national community out of America, and therefore one no longer dependent on other nations and "colonial." Southern cotton could be sent northward as raw material to fuel New England's textile mills; the Northern states could send finished goods back to meet Southern needs; and the Middle West could grow the food that all needed. To make all this possible, Clay and the Whigs called year after year for ambitious programs of tax-supported "internal improvements" (roads, ports, canals, and eventually railroads) to open up the country and make interstate trade flow more rapidly and more widely.

The building of a modern society required, however, citizens whose habits and skills were *modern*. How to make them so? By building public schools and getting the children into them. This would make Americans literate, ambitious, and disciplined. Whigs led the crusade for public schools, and organized and managed them. Horace Mann himself, the nation's leading educational reformer, was a Whig who urged the building of centralized school systems directed from the state capitals.

Whigs, in short, were classic Yankees (or those who shared Yankee values) in that they wanted government at all levels to intervene actively in cultural and economic life. We have earlier used the term *nationalist* republicans to refer to such people in Alexander Hamilton's time. From this perspective, government, God's earthly magistrate, exists to be used, to promote the general welfare in many ways. At the level of the local community it should supervise private morals and behavior; at the state level it should build schools, erect prisons and insane asylums, and borrow money to build canals; and from the national eminence of Washington, D.C., it should turn the whole nation into a self-sufficient industrial society by enacting protective tariffs and a national bank, and supporting internal transportation projects.

The Democrats' National Vision

Andrew Jackson's political following called themselves the "Democratic Party," adopting the name officially in 1840. How did they see America? To the Democrats, the booming economy was a source of alarm, not of optimism. In them we see the paradox of a nation obsessed by the race for wealth but torn by doubts that the game was worth the candle. Communities expanded and collapsed, personal fortunes gyrated wildly, and everything stable seemed on the verge of being swept away. America, the Democrats maintained, had once been an innocent, happy, and virtuous nation. Now it was a corrupted society caught up in an orgy of speculation. Jackson's followers wanted to restore the honest and agrarian Old Republic—an idealized fiction that nonetheless was real to them and motivated them to battle their political opponents.

The situation, Democrats said, was a simple one—the honest yeomen and mechanics of America had been *robbed*. Nothing else explained their suffering. The Democrats maintained that a massive, sinister conspiracy among the wealthy had taken over the nation, working primarily through the national bank. Many of these conspirators performed "artificial" functions in the economy, producing nothing. They traded stocks and bonds, manipulated paper currency, and speculated in land. Confusing everyone with the complexities of mysterious financial operations, entrepreneurs made the economy a chancy, restless, and insubstantial system. They were clever men who lived by their wits, and they exploited ordinary men who lived by the sweat of their brows. Democrats regarded business corporations as particularly dangerous. Organized capital was too powerful, they said, too exploitive of society.

The capitalists, said Samuel J. Tilden, a young friend of Martin Van Buren's, "had banded together all over the world and organized the *modern dynasty of associated wealth*, which maintains an unquestioned ascendancy over most of the civilized portions of our race, and which is now striving to extend its dominion over us."

But although openly critical of many businessmen, the Democrats were hardly an antibusiness party. Many businessmen and bankers were Democrats. Small businessmen were often Jacksonians, for they resented the privileges that central bankers and stockbrokers and tariff-protected industrialists seemed to have. Men of modest enterprises—corner grocers, cobblers, traveling salesmen—who had little economic power and had always to be nice to people of "quality," expressed their resentments in election parades crying the virtues of Andy Jackson and the wickedness of Henry Clay and his rich supporters. Party politics gave them a chance to strike back at their enemies, even if only by winning an election and angering the Whigs. Political life, in this sense, was a great public drama in which everyone, if he wished, could act out his feelings.

Other businessmen were Jacksonians for more calculating reasons. They might be bankers engaged in loans to overseas traders, who were hurt by the way protective tariffs cut down on British imports. They might be shipowners, cotton producers, export merchants, or any one of the many businessmen whose vital interests were linked to an open international market, to getting American raw materials abroad and buying what they needed from the cheapest source, whether national or foreign. What mattered in casting a ballot was not class membership, but the specific location of a man's business in the national economy.

Adam Smith and the Democrats

For their economic theory, Jacksonians—like Thomas Jefferson before them—looked to the writings of the Scotsman Adam Smith. His *Wealth of Nations*, now half a century old, was their ultimate authority. Smith's purpose had been to show how to create wealth and distribute it most equitably. No government, he said, could know enough to direct an economy centrally. Ignorance of actual local conditions would lead to distortion of the economy and harm

its capacity to be truly productive. Tariffs and other methods adopted ostensibly to stimulate the economy actually hindered the creation of wealth, even though they might help individuals reap excessive profits.

Furthermore, to get such favors businessmen would use graft and corruption, thus harming the government as well as the economy. All links between government and business were inherently corrupt. There should be economic *laissez-faire*; i.e., the government should let each person make his own way without assistance. Smith warned specifically of the harmful effects of specially chartered corporations. Such monopolistic creatures, he said, cramp the economy while making a few men rich. The road to social justice and an equitable income for everyone, poor as well as wealthy, was to fight monopoly wherever it appeared and to open everything to competition. The power of the marketplace would discipline businessmen by stimulating them to produce abundantly when prices were high and forcing them to throttle back when prices dropped. It would weed out shoddy merchandise and prevent anyone's acquiring the power to exploit the community.

The ultimate objective in Smithian economic policy, then, was the same as in Jeffersonian political policy—to localize everything. Let the market regulate in the light of local conditions, not the distant and misinformed government. Then the economy would grow genuinely dynamic and productive, wealth would mount, and if no one were given special privileges all would profit. An egalitarian and libertarian republic would be the result. That is, all would have an equal chance to get ahead, for no one would receive special advantages; and a small and inactive government would leave people alone to handle their property and make their profits as they saw fit.

Jacksonians and the Money Supply

A key element in Jacksonian thought was the belief in "sound money." A currency system so constituted, they believed, would be a powerful agency for social justice. The objective was to create a supply of money that would fluctuate slowly in volume, thereby ensuring relatively stable prices. Workmen, farmers, ordinary people who did not have inside ways of profiting from currency gyrations, and consumers in general—all wanted a low and stable price level. The Whigs, who wanted abundant supplies of money to boost the economy, seemed to favor inflationary measures. They were concerned with helping producers, who received their income from selling. In the Whig view, banks should be able to print paper money if they had reliable business securities in their vaults as well as gold or silver. In that way, the currency supply would expand as business expanded, for the more loans a bank issued (receiving a mortgage or a note of indebtedness in return), the more money it could print.

Jacksonians condemned monetary expansion. The inflation it seemed to bring with it, they pointed out, was a cruel burden on the poor. Workmen, lacking powerful unions, had little power to raise their income when prices rose. Men like William Leggett and Samuel J. Tilden, whose economic writings influenced Jackson and Van Buren, urged that only gold should be used to back currency, thus making it sound money. Radicals on the issue, such as Senator Thomas Hart Benton of Missouri, called for "hard money" alone—that is, currency composed wholly of gold and silver. But most Jacksonians supported the sound-money system.

Such an arrangement, Jacksonians believed, would nip inflationary spirals in the bud. As prices rose in the United States, foreign creditors, who did an enormous business with Americans, would demand payment in actual gold instead of in depreciated currency. Bankers, having sent their gold abroad, would have to reduce the amount of paper money they issued, which would bring prices back down before they fluctuated very far from a "natural" level. If deflation took place, the opposite would occur. Gold would flow into the country because it would be more valuable here than abroad (that is, it would buy more goods). Banks would issue more currency, and the price level would rebound.

This theory, derived from the British economist David Ricardo, is called the price-specie flow mechanism, and it dominated the thinking of economists for a century. Another general term for this system is the *gold standard*. Essentially an internationalist financial policy, it aimed at achieving stable prices and stable economies and disciplining businessmen.

The essence of the system, Democrats said, was for it to operate automatically and "naturally." Artificial efforts to control the volume of currency through the device of a national bank would only set things awry. Insist on a gold-backed currency and let the international gold standard operate freely, and businessmen and farmers could carry on their operations confidently. Laborers and consumers would be spared the agonies of inflation.

In New York, among other states, Democrats

secured reforms for a sound-money system by requiring banks to maintain adequate supplies of gold to back their currency (reserve requirements). They also established joint funds that could prevent the collapse of individual banks. This made New York's banking system unusually strong and stable and prompted the nation to shift its financial reliance to New York City and away from Philadelphia. To clean out the "shinplasters" (depreciated paper currency) from most transactions, by 1836 more than a dozen states had prohibited their banks from printing banknotes of less than five dollars.

The Democrats and Egalitarian Government

Jacksonians, as firm egalitarians, welcomed manhood suffrage and praised the virtues of the common man. Government posts, they believed, should be open to everyone, not reserved to aristocrats. "Rotation in office" was their party cry. They also displayed a preference for strong executive leadership. Jackson was the Old Hero, and they admired his bold actions. Then and afterward, the Democratic party tended to rely on strong executives who dominated their cabinets and sought actively to lead Congress and the public in their direction.

Seeking to base their support in the population at large, Democratic presidents have characteristically tried to break free of control by congressional committees. When the Whigs (and their descendants, the Republicans) were in the White House, congressional committees directed the nation's affairs. When the Democrats took over, with a Grover Cleveland, a Woodrow Wilson, or a Franklin Roosevelt, power seemed to travel the length of Pennsylvania Avenue and lodge in the executive mansion.

The Democrats as an Ethnocultural Community

If the Whigs were the party of the core culture, of the Center, the Democrats were the party of the outgroups, the minorities, the nonconforming—of what Ronald Formisano has termed the Periphery. They, of course, insisted that it was their party, the Democrats, who were the true republicans in America, pointing to their descent from Thomas Jefferson as proof. America, they held, was genuinely a republic only if every (white) person were treated equally, no matter what their religion or way of living. America's philosophy must not be the old way of forcing cultural homogeneity on everyone, but the new idea of leaving people alone to live as they wished, the new concept of cultural *laissez-faire*. If the Whigs were modernizers in economic terms, Democrats were preaching cultural modernity, for certainly being allowed, in mid-twentieth-century language, to "do your own thing" was not the traditional way.

Liberty, freedom from governmental intrusion into private morals—this was what, to Democrats, being an American rightfully meant. If this resulted in people being free to drink, or go to the theater, or even to have multiple wives, as among the Mormons, or own slaves, as among Southerners, this was what liberty required. Democrats battled against Whig crusades for alcoholic temperance, for a holy Sabbath, for controlling dress and sexual relations and saloons. With Jefferson they rejected the idea of a "Christian party in politics," and disliked seeing Protestant clerics "meddling" in politics. Church and state must be *separate* in every way. Democratic political headquarters in places like New York City were well-known centers of agnosticism; Democrats held that Jews should be allowed to vote and hold office; and in the very heartland of Whiggery, Massachusetts, they even argued that atheists should have equal civil rights with everyone else.

The Democrats' demand for freedom from Yankee efforts at making everyone else live according to their pattern and values extended to public education. This put them into a strange position, since Thomas Jefferson had held that an educated citizenry was the ultimate hope for republicanism, and he had labored for years in the cause of public education. However, the Democrats were the party that, as we will see, attracted to their ranks the Irish Catholics and the German Lutherans, and both of these peoples wanted to be free to have their own parochial schools so that they could raise their children in their particular faith. Also, Democrats almost by instinct recoiled from anything that Whigs actively supported—what the "enemy" does, in politics, is in some ways the most powerful of all forces in shaping what people do in public life. So when Whigs called for public schools, Democrats were distrustful. The result was that Jacksonian Democrats were not very active workers for public schools, often condemning the idea as another Yankee plot; that is, as an effort to get control of the children and stuff Puritan ideas into their heads.

Democrats certainly retained, however, another

of Jefferson's ideas: a warm and welcoming attitude toward immigrants. Inheriting Jefferson's distaste for England, they attracted the Irish Catholics en masse, making the Democrats the "Catholic party" from the beginning of American history to the present. Even in South Carolina the cause of Irish freedom against the British was hailed by Democrats. In the Northern states, which were so dominated by the British-descended, anyone who felt like an outsider gravitated to the Democrats: the Germans, New York Dutchmen, French-Canadians, the tiny Jewish community. (In the Southern states, paradoxically, the general culture and way of life was so overwhelmingly Jacksonian Democrat that it was the Whigs who served as the party of the minorities: urbanites, those hostile to slavery, and the French of Louisiana.)

Democrats and Black America

Of course, Democratic openness to the minorities in the Northern states did not include free blacks. Both in the South and in the North, Democratic politicians distinguished themselves sharply from Whigs by their outspoken distaste for black Americans, calling the Whigs (and their Republican inheritors) the party of "niggerology" because many among them were so uncomfortable about slavery and worked to give free black Americans a better status in Northern life.

Democrats disliked blacks and abolitionists for many reasons. Many Jacksonians opposed abolitionism on the ground that it distracted attention from social issues within the Northern states. Jacksonian workers' organizations distrusted abolitionists, for they seemed to be indifferent to the "wage slavery" that existed in Northern factories. Although opposed to slavery as an abstract proposition, workers concentrated instead on their own objectives.

Martin Van Buren and the Dutch farmers from whom he sprang were moved by additional considerations. They had owned slaves, did not like having them taken away, and opposed social and political equality for black men. The Catholic Irish of New York City competed with black Americans for unskilled jobs and so grew to hate them. The Irish feared a flooding of labor markets in the North by released slaves. Last, abolitionism was eagerly supported by evangelical Whigs, and Democrats were always suspicious of clericalism in politics. The hostility of Democrats to moralistic reforms tended to make them insensitive to the plight of the slave.

The Second Party System

By the mid-1830s, as we now see, a new two-party confrontation had appeared: Whigs against Democrats. Historians refer to this as the Second Party System. By using this terminology, they aim at alerting us to the fact that American politics are usually fairly stable over long periods of time. The great voting blocs tend to be lined up on one side or the other, and there they stay. In the Age of Jackson, Yankees predominantly, though not unanimously, voted one way (Whig); Irish Catholics predominantly, and in this case almost unanimously, voted another (Democratic). When these stable voting patterns are in place, what is called a "party system" exists. The two parties will battle energetically to pull people away from the other side, and fluctuations do occur in particular elections, but overall the broad pattern endures and is predictable.

Generally, these party systems have lasted for about a generation or two, or from twenty to forty years. What brings them to an end? In the first place, while older voters keep voting the same way, the younger ones who regularly enter the voting community get restive. They had not themselves participated in the dramatic events that created the original loyalties. The Bank War in Andrew Jackson's presidency, for example, became more and more a remote event for them. Therefore, unless there is something that keeps them faithful to the party of their parents, party loyalty slowly falls off; voting blocs no longer vote quite so predominantly on one side or the other.

Then a powerful new crisis takes place. This shakes everyone up, challenges old loyalties, and brings what are called "critical elections." In these crisis years, political parties are reshaped. Conventions become turbulent, marked by great ideological polarization, and the two parties find themselves far apart on the issues. Typically, this is the time when "third parties" appear, demanding things the two major parties are trying to avoid. The emotional content of political life escalates, with voters and politicians both growing more dogmatic. Voters throng to the ballot booths in unusually huge numbers, and whole groups shift from one side to the other.

After this flash point, a new order of things, a new "party system," appears. What typically happens is that the victorious party, shaken up and reorganized from top to bottom, and with a new mandate of national support, enters office to launch major changes in national policy. Thereafter, the new party system becomes stable again, and another long period of relative stasis begins. We will see this pattern working itself out periodically in American history, but here we will return to follow what happened after the Second Party System was fully on the scene; that is, during the years of Jackson's successors.

Van Buren to the White House and the Independent Treasury

In 1836 Martin Van Buren, Jackson's Dutch vice-president from the state of New York, was nominated to succeed him as president. Against several Whig candidates—they could not agree on a single one—Van Buren won the election and immediately faced a fresh economic crisis—the Panic of 1837. Farmers

The Election of 1836

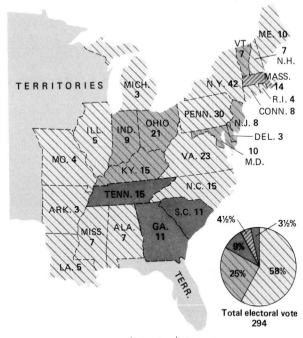

Total electoral vote
294

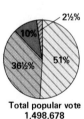

Total popular vote
1,498,678

Party	Candidate	Popular vote	Electoral vote
Democratic	Van Buren	762,678	170
Whig	W.H. Harrison	549,000	73
Whig	White	146,000	26
Whig	Webster	41,000	14
Independent	Mangum	None	11

were not hurt badly, for they could continue raising their own food, but urban workers suffered cruelly. Banks collapsed, factories slowed, men were thrown out of work by the thousands, and mobs stormed New York City flour warehouses. In May 1837, the banks suspended specie payments, so that no one could redeem paper currency in hard coin.

Van Buren blamed the bankers, saying they had speculated wildly with the funds that depositors had put in their banks, thus producing an inflationary spiral that led to an inevitable crash. His response: Get the federal government's own money, which since Jackson it had deposited with many "pet" state banks, out of the bankers' hands, and therefore cut back drastically on their ability to speculate. In September 1837, Van Buren asked Congress to create an Independent Treasury System, which would allow the federal government to take its money out of the state banks and keep it in its own depositories around the country, to be carefully husbanded.

This would achieve the ultimate reform that radical young Democratic reformers had been calling for over many years: complete separation of bank and state, which they said was as important as separating church and state. Thus, a powerful blow would be struck against privilege, they argued, and a major step would be taken toward stabilizing the economy.

Radical Democrats were therefore delighted with Van Buren's proposal. Frank Blair of Missouri called it "the boldest and highest stand ever taken by a Chief Magistrate in defense of the rights of the people . . . a second declaration of independence." A Bostonian Democrat compared Van Buren to Jackson: "Like his predecessor he now stands at the head of radical democracy." Whigs cursed the scheme. "The message is a heartless, cold-blooded attack on our most valuable and most cherished classes of citizens," wrote one Whig paper. "He had identified himself wholly with the loco-focos [radical Democrats in New York City]," mourned another, "come forth a champion of the most destructive species of ultraism—and aimed at the vital interests of the country a blow, which if it do not recoil upon the aggressor, must be productive to the country of lasting mischief, perhaps of irretrievable anarchy." The Whigs' major complaint was that such an Independent Treasury System would take capital out of circulation at a time when it was needed for economic development.

Like Andrew Jackson's veto of the rechartering of the Bank of the United States in 1832, Van Buren's plan for an Independent Treasury System became a symbolic issue that was bitterly fought over in national politics for *years* into the future. Back and forth it would go, first enacted by the Democrats, then repealed by the Whigs. Finally, under Democratic president James K. Polk, in August 1846 the Independent Treasury Act was enacted permanently, never to be repealed. Thereafter, the Treasury served as a special sort of bank. It cared for the federal government's funds, keeping them in its own vaults, and issued a kind of paper currency, called Treasury Notes, as well as gold and silver coins, to pay the government's expenses. It also exercised considerable influence on the economy. If inflation threatened, it could let gold and silver pile up in the Treasury, thus withdrawing specie from private banks and contracting the supply of paper money in the country. By such devices, the Mexican war was conducted without an inflationary spiral. In times of stringency the Treasury could release specie in the hope of accelerating recovery. Government and banking had been formally separated by the Independent Treasury System, but the federal government and the nation's currency arrangements continued to be inextricably interwoven.

The Election of 1840

In 1840, Van Buren was nominated for a second term by the Democrats, although many of them were not enthusiastic about him. The Whigs chose William Henry Harrison of Tippecanoe fame. They mounted an enormous national campaign, unprecedented in the multitude of devices used to whip up enthusiasm—parades, bands, banners, free cider, torchlight processions, and endless oratory. Indeed, the election of 1840 signaled the demise, after half a century of national life under the Constitution, of the old belief that political parties were evil, disloyal creatures to be shunned and condemned. Being a "party man" was for many Americans (by no means all) a glorified ethic in public life. Political activity was America's national theater, a mass drama in which hundreds of thousands participated, year after year. Intricate structures of committees and party conventions bound the whole system together, from the top to the lowest precinct. Absolute loyalty to the cause was demanded. There were practically no "independents," and to vote against the party nominee (secret voting had not yet appeared) was much condemned.

Democrats were much stronger than the Whigs

in their party commitment, probably because they consisted so heavily of the minority outgroups who had to stick closely together in order to win. Political parties were their means of rebelling against the power of the socially dominant. "Army style" politics resulted, party oratory being studded with words like recruitment, drill, discipline, campaign operations, attacks, conquest, foes, rank and file, and *obedience*. There were no national sports for the masses to follow, and no common folk activities, save evangelism, to give ordinary people the excitement of participating in great national events and causes. Therefore, hundreds of thousands went to hear the open-air speeches of national leaders, and the speech-making went on for hours.

Harrison swept the election, but within a month after taking office, he died of illness. Virginian John Tyler, a former Democrat, became the first vice-president to assume the presidency upon the president's death. Soon he and the two powerful Whig senators Henry Clay and Daniel Webster were locked in angry, jealous wrangles for party supremacy, and the first Whig presidency was bogged down in impasse.

Transatlantic Conflict and Reunion

Attention shifted now to foreign affairs. Britain and the United States seemed to be close to war again. A rebellion against British rule in Canada in 1837 had failed, but American sympathies and private aid had enraged the British. Also, Britain's campaign against the slave trade led to hostile encounters between American vessels and British boarding parties, which put Southerners in an angry mood. Massive defaulting on state debts in the West had caused British investors to lose about $150 million. In Maine, a vaguely defined and much disputed boundary had created the Aroostook War of 1839, in which Maine took forcible possession of the Aroostook Valley and drove out Canadian lumbermen.

The most critical problem arose from the destruction in American waters by Canadian authorities of a small American steamer, the *Caroline*, which had been supplying Canadian rebels during the 1837 uprising. In 1840 a former Canadian official indiscreetly boasted in an American saloon of having played a role in the burning of the *Caroline*. He was promptly clapped in jail and indicted for murder, for an American had lost his life in the affair. At this point the British public, goaded to exasperation by the succession of difficulties with America, began rumbling about war.

Fortunately, a major transition occurred in British politics. In 1841 Robert Peel, an extraordinarily gifted and politically powerful man, became prime minister. For the next five years he led one of the great reforming governments in British history. In large part his government was inspired by the same outlook on economic affairs, national and international, that had inspired the Jeffersonians and Jacksonians in the United States. Peel and his spectacular protégé, young William Gladstone, conceived it their task to reshape the British economy along the lines called for by Adam Smith. Tariffs and monopolies should be eliminated, thus freeing the national economy to be dynamic and opening the nation to free trade with the world. This, it was believed, would cheapen food prices and all other necessaries for the poor; it would go far to end special privilege in economic matters; and by ending commercial rivalries it would start the world on the road to international peace.

At the same time, the British and American economies were growing more in need of each other than ever before. The vast expansion of farming in the American Midwest created large supplies of grain and farm products that needed overseas markets. Denied entry into British markets by the Corn Laws (Britain's high protective tariff against foreign grains), American farm prices sagged. The growing American population, meanwhile, wanted the cheap and abundant manufactured goods produced by British factories. These pressures forecast major policy changes on both sides of the Atlantic.

Such developments, however, were still in the future. For the moment the diplomatic problems remained. British Tories, long contemptuous, indeed fearful, of American democracy and republicanism, trumpeted demands for harsh settlements. But Robert Peel did not believe in aggressive foreign policies, and he earnestly wanted to establish a better relationship with America. In 1842 he sent Lord Ashburton, a banker with friendly ties in America, to begin negotiations in the United States. Fortunately the Canadian jailed as a result of the *Caroline* affair had been released on the strength of a newly discovered alibi. It was clear to the two governments, however, that the time had come to clear up all controversy.

The resulting Webster-Ashburton Treaty of 1842 achieved several things. It assigned a compromise line in Maine that finally settled that ancient

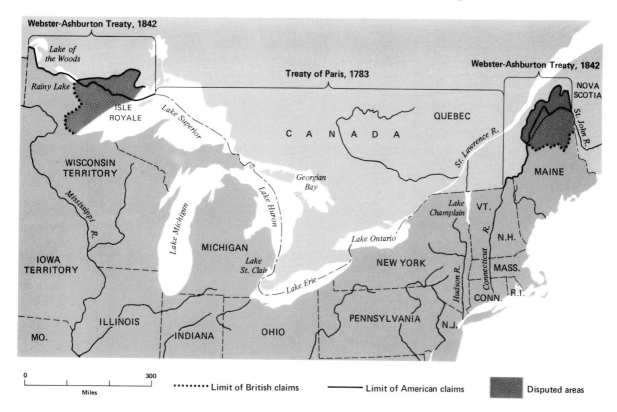

Webster-Ashburton Treaty, 1842

Treaty of Paris, 1783

Webster-Ashburton Treaty, 1842

Lake of
the Woods

Rainy Lake

ISLE
ROYALE

Lake Superior

C A N A D A

QUEBEC

NOVA
SCOTIA

St. John R.

St. Lawrence R.

MAINE

WISCONSIN
TERRITORY

*Georgian
Bay*

Mississippi R.

Lake Huron

Lake Michigan

Lake
Champlain

VT.

N.H.

IOWA
TERRITORY

MICHIGAN

Lake
St. Clair

Lake Ontario

NEW YORK

Hudson R.

Connecticut R.

MASS.

CONN.

R.I.

Lake Erie

ILLINOIS

MO.

INDIANA

OHIO

PENNSYLVANIA

N.J.

0   300
Miles

•••••••• Limit of British claims   ——— Limit of American claims   ▓ Disputed areas

The Webster-Ashburton Treaty, 1842

dispute, and it established Minnesota's boundary with Canada. (In such a way, as it later turned out, that the immense iron deposits of the Mesabi Range came to the United States. Canadians have long pointed to this treaty as an example of the way Britain sacrificed its interests in the cause of good Anglo-American relations.) In addition, the treaty also gave free navigation of all bordering waters to both America and Canada. Finally, both sides promised to maintain warships off the West African coast to curb the illegal-slave trade.

James K. Polk: A Jacksonian Democrat as President

A great new issue was now surging into national politics: *territorial expansion.* In 1836 a huge part of the Republic of Mexico, comprising what is now the State of Texas, a region settled primarily by people from the United States, revolted and established the Republic of Texas. (This subject will be explored in the next chapter.) By the early 1840s thousands

of Americans, especially in the Southern states, were calling for the United States to annex Texas.

Martin Van Buren opposed this step, which made his renomination for the presidency, in 1844, problematical. When the Democratic national convention met, he had a majority at the outset, but not the necessary two-thirds. (Southern demands had got this requirement in the party's rules in 1832, for it would give the South a powerful veto over who the party nominated. The rule would not be removed until Franklin Roosevelt's time, in the 1930s.) The nomination finally went to Andrew Jackson's own choice, an astonishingly young man (forty-nine) who was pro-expansion, James K. Polk of Tennessee, former governor of that state and from 1835 to 1839 Speaker of the House of Representatives.

Henry Clay, meanwhile, was buoyed by an enormous national swell of Whig support as he headed for the election as his party's nominee. He too opposed the annexation of Texas, as did Whigs generally, for he was convinced that it would mean war with Mexico. Hoping to eliminate the Texas issue altogether from the campaign, he and Van Buren had simultaneously published letters opposing annexation. Now, however, with Polk the Democratic nominee, expansionism faced antiexpansionism in direct confrontation. In an intense electoral campaign that overshadowed even that of 1840, Clay was just barely defeated.

Of 2.7 million votes cast, Polk received only 38,000 more than Clay. Indeed, had Polk lost New York State, he would have lost the election. Only the entry there of a tiny movement, the abolitionist Liberty party, saved the day for Polk. Some 15,000 votes were cast for its nominee which, it was generally conceded, would otherwise have gone to Clay. Those votes were fateful; Polk won New York State by only 5,000 votes.

Polk was a strong and determined man who knew what he wanted to do, and he had a precociously modern sense of how a president should go about achieving his objectives. Devoted to Andrew Jackson, he inherited the Hero's ideas about a strong executive. Polk felt that as president he should lead his government vigorously. He thought of himself as the one public official elected by the whole nation, an attitude that strengthened his belief that he possessed unique moral authority. No other nineteenth-century president practiced this kind of leadership as systematically and effectively. He was the first chief executive to take office with an actual program in mind, and it would be difficult to find any other occupant of the White House so successful in accomplishing what he set out to do. Watching the Congress carefully to get his program through, he kept track of each man's voting record and constantly whipped laggards into line with a determined use of patronage and every other device he could muster.

Strengthening the Transatlantic Community

Polk was determined to reshape the nation's economic policies, and he succeeded so well that most of what he did survived for decades. He reestablished the Independent Treasury System. He moved vigorously to open the nation to foreign, primarily British, trade, thereby veering away from the economic nationalism that Clay had so painstakingly erected since the 1820s. Thus, his major objective was to lower the tariff. In his dramatic first message to Congress in 1845, he characterized the Whig tariff of 1842 as "so framed that much the greatest burden which it imposes is thrown on labor and the poorer classes, who are least able to bear it, while it protects capital and exempts the rich from paying their just proportion of the taxation required to support the government."

The year 1846 saw a remarkable feat of transatlantic cooperation that brought victory to Polk's low-tariff crusade. The goal was a dramatically simple one: America would lower its tariffs against British manufactured goods, in return for which Britain would throw open its markets to American wheat. When Polk's secretary of the treasury, Robert J. Walker, sent Congress a report explaining why and how the tariff should be lowered and holding out the prospect of reciprocal action on the British side, it was eagerly picked up by the free-trade advocates in Britain and circulated widely among members of Parliament. Robert Peel's campaign to repeal the Corn Laws (Britain's protective tariff on wheat) achieved, then, a dramatic victory, in significant measure because of the implied transatlantic commitment to open American markets to British goods in return.

News of the event was hurried onto the mail steamers. James Gordon Bennet of the New York *Herald* had a courier waiting at Halifax, Nova Scotia, to catch the earliest word, and by galloping horses and the earliest telegraph lines—the first had been opened only the year before, between Baltimore and Washington—the news was rushed to the Capitol. On June 15, 1846, an extra of the *Union* proclaiming the repeal of the Corn Laws hit the streets in Washington, and Polk's triumphant supporters in Congress soon won passage of the Walker Tariff.

By no means a free trade document, since it did not eliminate tariffs, the Walker Tariff aimed at a "tariff for revenue only." That is, the rate was established at just that point where the most revenue was produced, not the most protection. That was always at a low enough level to encourage extensive imports and therefore an abundant revenue. Such an arrangement necessarily provides moderate protection. The result, however, was to lower drastically American barriers against British and other foreign goods. The Walker Tariff of 1846 returned the United States to the economic relationship with the outside world it had had in the days of Jefferson, while Peel's repeal of the Corn Laws gave American farmers for the first time free and unhampered access to the British market, with its millions of city-dwelling consumers. Transatlantic trade now swelled enormously.

The Smithian Revolution Reaches Its Peak

With this transatlantic achievement the Democrats and their British counterparts, who would shortly found the "Liberal Party" in British politics, had carried through most of Adam Smith's program. Smith had called for an end to the mercantilist state, in which the government intervened in the economy to aid business by means of tariffs, bounties, and chartered monopolies. (The advent of general incorporation laws in most states after 1848, to be discussed in Chapter 16, ended the era of specially chartered corporations.) Mercantilism's principal effect, Smith had said, was to enrich the privileged and to exploit everyone else. It resulted in a limited and restricted economy bound by illogical and regressive regulations.

Wiping out special privileges and rigorously separating the government from the economy, Democrats and British Liberals said, would unleash the economy. These moves would set off dynamic forces that would provide everyone with a steadily rising affluence. In such a free economy, the principal devices for controlling businessmen so that their appetites would aid the general welfare were a competitive market and a sound-money system.

There are many paradoxes in this system. On one hand it would unleash the economy, and yet on the other it would try to curb speculative and inflationary pressures. Its principal weapon against inflation and speculation was sound money; its principal device for freeing the economy was to widen

Daguerrotype from the late 1840s showing President James Polk, his wife, and a group of friends. The first young president (he was 49), Polk was perhaps also the first to come to office with a positive agenda of achievements to realize, and he secured them with remarkable success.

the market through elimination of tariffs and monopolies. As it turned out, Smithian economics were better at freeing the economy (creating economic liberty) than at controlling the businessmen and their speculative instincts. The success of Smithian economics, in fact, was in creating a dynamic economy, as subsequent decades demonstrated. The failure was in so releasing the businessman from all control that he grew into a giant figure who dominated society, thus gravely threatening the egalitarian ideals that inspired the Democrats in these economic reforms.

There is no reason to doubt the sincerity of the men who appealed to Adam Smith's ideas, saying they were working for the "common man," just as there is no reason to regard those ideas as free from contradictions. Every idea system has both creative and destructive tendencies, which often work concurrently. Each reformist ideology presents features, when it becomes an orthodoxy, that later reformers find repellent. Democrats believed that Adam Smith's ideas provided an answer to poverty, aristocratic and capitalist exploitation, and war. If they did not get lasting peace, they certainly seemed to get prosperity. In one of the most extraordinary demonstrations of how events can apparently confirm ideas, the completion of the Smithian revolution was followed by a period of remarkable prosperity. Probably stimulated by the sudden influx of gold and silver bullion

from the California and Nevada mines after 1849, both the United States and Great Britain experienced an economic expansion in all directions from the 1850s into the 1870s.

After the miseries of the worldwide depression of the 1840s—the Hungry Forties of famine and unemployment and sullen outbreaks of political and social violence—the prosperity of the 1850s produced the euphoria of the Anglo-American mid-Victorian years. For a generation, until the collapse of the mid-1870s, everything in economic life seemed to confirm what Adam Smith had predicted: The dynamic *laissez-faire* economy would elevate everyone. People could take comfort, year after year, in the way the average person's standard of living was bounding upward. For a time the shocking inequities that were developing, especially among the laboring poor, could be ignored. In the 1850s the United States (and Great Britain) experienced its most explosive economic boom. After the Civil War it continued with undiminished zest.

Against this background, in the twenty years from the mid-1840s to the mid-1860s the United States rushed westward to the Pacific, fell into fatal disputes about slavery, and underwent one of the bloodiest civil wars in history. It is to the exploration of these great problems that the next chapters will be devoted.

BIBLIOGRAPHY

There is a very rich historical literature on the Age of Jackson, the first great era of continental mass politics, and I can here only indicate some of the works relied on to develop the account and interpretation presented here. For a beginning, Glyndon G. Van Deusen's *The Jacksonian Era: 1828–1848* (1959) in the New American Nation Series remains sound and essential. Students will enjoy reading Arthur Schlesinger, Jr.'s exciting book, his Pulitzer Prize-winning *Age of Jackson* (1945), also enduringly valuable. On bank and financial issues, I found Peter Temin, *The Jacksonian Economy* (1969), an eye-opener, and John M. McFaul's *The Politics of Jacksonian Finance* (1972) immensely revealing.

Daniel Walker Howe's brilliant book, *The Political Culture of the American Whigs* (1979), has given me major new insights, and two superb books by Ronald P. Formisano give us the ability to see Whigs and Democrats at work within two states: *The Birth of Mass Political Parties: Michigan 1827–1861* (1971), and *The Transformation of Political Culture: Massachusetts Parties, 1790s–1840s* (1983). Two older works continue to be central to my understandings: Marvin Meyers' *The Jacksonian Persuasion: Politics and Belief* (1960), and Lee Benson's ground-breaking exploration of the ethnocultural origins of politics, *The Concept of Jacksonian Democracy: New York as a Test Case* (1964). Robert Remini's multivolume biography of Andrew Jackson tells us fresh new things about this central figure, whose public meanings have been so well explored in John William Ward's *Andrew Jackson: Symbol for an Age* (1953). In two related studies I have explored the Age of Jackson extensively: in *The Cultural Pattern in American Politics: The First Century* (1979), and *The Transatlantic Persuasion: The Liberal-Democratic Mind in the Age of Gladstone* (1969).

The Age of Jackson has stimulated sharply diverging views, especially on the question of how egalitarian it was. A leading scholar who takes strong (anti) views on this subject, Edward Pessen, presents a rich account in his *Jacksonian America: Society, Personality, and Politics* (rev. ed., 1978). Alcohol consumption and alcoholism in the Jacksonian years may be explored in a remarkable book, W. J. Rorabaugh's *The Alcoholic Republic: An American Tradition* (1979). On attitudes toward the Irish, see L. Perry Curtis, Jr., *Apes and Angels: The Irishman in Victorian Caricature* (1971). William G. Shade, *Banks or No Banks: The Money Question in the Western States, 1832–1865*

(1973), explores, through sophisticated quantitative analysis and a sensitivity to cultural styles, what this issue meant at the grass roots to different kinds of people. James Roger Sharp, *The Jacksonians versus the Banks: Politics in the States after the Panic of 1837* (1970), also sees the conflict as a protest against economic modernization. Joel H. Silbey, *The Shrine of Party: Congressional Voting Behavior 1841–*

1852 (1967), demonstrates the great power of the two parties, by the 1840s, in holding voters' and politicians' loyalty. On the party systems, see Walter Dean Burnham, *Critical Elections and the Mainsprings of American Politics* (1970), and Chapter 2 in Paul Kleppner, *Who Voted? The Dynamics of Electoral Turnout, 1870–1980* (1982).

14

Surge to the Pacific

TIME LINE

HISTORY IN AN INDIVIDUAL LIFE

FATHER JUNIPERO SERRA

In 1749 a learned scholar in his mid-thirties teaching in an ancient university on the Spanish island of Majorca in the Mediterranean made a startling decision: He cast a brilliant career behind him and left for Mexico. Father Junípero Serra's passion was to live among the heathen as a missionary, and bring them to Christ.

At Mexico City he found a great urban center of 80,000 people, far richer in its cultural life than the distant English colonies, and already two centuries from its founding. From there he journeyed 200 miles into the frontier to found a mission. In the awesome wilderness of the Sierra Gorda, he spent years on end without returning to civilization. Instead, he taught the Indians the crafts and agricultural skills of Spain, and each day rang his bell to call them to mass for their regular encounter with the Christian's Holy Savior. Working as a common laborer himself in the hot sun, he built churches whose Mediterranean architecture linked the Mexican frontier with ancient Rome.

Under his hand, the Indians learned to be masons, carpenters, blacksmiths, painters, and decorators.

At the same time, this God-obsessed man prayed long hours daily, often until four in the morning. "We don't know," said the sentinels, "when Father Junípero sleeps." An ascetic Franciscan, he was caught fast by St. Francis's ideals: self-sacrificing love for others, austerity of life, an uncompromising love of God, and hard daily labor in ordinary tasks. Serra ate sparingly of fruit, vegetables, and fish, avoided meat, and read the Holy Scriptures aloud at meals. When in grief at his own imperfections, he would stand in the choir loft in the evening hours and flog and lacerate his body with rough canvas in memory of the sufferings of Jesus Christ. An arresting preacher, in one seven-year period Serra walked more than 5,000 miles to speak from pulpits in widely scattered churches.

Then, in his mid-fifties this unvanquishable man made a second great decision. In the year 1769, as leader of a small party of Franciscan missionaries, he joined an expedition of Spanish soldiers, sailors, and settlers heading northward to colonize the coast of a legendary, almost unknown country: far-off California. By eighteenth-century standards already an old man, slight and almost frail in body, before his death fifteen years later he would found nine missions and Spanish-Indian communities along the California coast from San Diego northward to Monterey, thereby opening for God and Crown a new province of Catholic Christendom and the Spanish Empire. Serra brought Spanish culture to the Indians, and his faith and love. He brought also tragedy, for the populous native peoples of California had had no contact with European diseases. Within half a century of Serra's arrival, epidemic death was sweeping the coastal tribes to extinction. Even those Europeans who clasped the Indians with love to their breasts, who hated weaponry and war, killed them.

The Spanish Borderlands

The western half of the Mississippi Valley—the Louisiana Purchase—contained hardly a single American in the 1820s save for small populations in Missouri and Louisiana. Beyond it, from the front range of the Rocky Mountains to the Pacific Ocean, and south of the 42nd parallel (the present northern border of California), was an enormous area that had been part of the Spanish Empire for centuries. When the Republic of Mexico won its independence in 1821, the immense imperial provinces that occupied this area—Alta California, Nuevo México, and Texas—were made a part of that republic. However, though they made up half of the Mexican nation in territorial extent, they contained even as late as the 1840s (the decade of the war between Mexico and the United States) only 1 percent of its population (about 80,000 people of Mexican citizenship).

The Mexican settlements in these provinces, therefore, were few and tiny in the 1820s. Spain had long ago settled New Mexico (primarily the upper valley of the Rio Grande), beginning in 1598, out of a fear that Sir Francis Drake's recent exploits in the Pacific Ocean meant the approach of the English to their northern frontiers. That did not occur, however, and the small villages of Taos, Santa Fe, and Albuquerque, a thousand miles from Mexico City, were largely ignored by the central authorities thereafter. Texas was briefly occupied by missionaries in the seventeenth century, and through most of the next century was left to the Indians. In 1800 it held only three small settlements: San Antonio, Goliad, and Nacogdoches, containing perhaps 2,000 *Tejanos* all told.

By 1820 the province of California had been occupied by the Spanish for half a century. Twenty-one missions, founded after 1769 by the Franciscans under Father Junípero Serra and his successors, dotted the coastal valleys from San Diego to the upper San Francisco Bay area. Four *presidios* (forts) were located at San Diego, Santa Barbara, Monterey, and San Francisco. The capital of the province was at Monterey. Two *pueblos* (civilian towns), Los Angeles and San José, completed the roster of settlements. Aside from the Indians—who were unusually numerous, perhaps 130,000 when the Spanish arrived—there were about 3,000 *Californios* in 1820, who were descended from a few hundred soldiers, settlers, and their families sent to the province from Mexico in the 1770s. Extensive deserts and hostile Indians made it almost impossible to reach California from Mexico by land. The sea voyage could take months because of contrary prevailing winds. In effect, California was a remote island far away from the Spanish Empire, left to its own resources.

Mexican Rule over California

The three northern provinces of California, New Mexico, and Texas were an enormous distance from Mexico City and the ancient heartland of what became in 1821 the Republic of Mexico. It was almost 2,000 miles in a direct line from Monterey, in California, to Mexico City (or about the distance to Chicago, Illinois), and much farther than that by sea and overland travel. The crucial question for Mexico, as it began its independence, was: Would it be able to integrate these far-distant provinces, separated from the mass of the Mexican people by great expanses of desert, into the national life of Mexico itself, make them in fact and not simply in law a part of the Mexican republic? Would Mexico be able, in the long run, to hold onto them? The new Republic of Mexico meant little to the people of California. As residents of a separate province of the Spanish Empire, they had never revolted against Spain, nor had they thought of themselves as part of a "Mexico." They called themselves simply *Californios*. When Mexico sent officials to govern the province, trouble soon erupted. The first Mexican governor arrived in 1824; four years later the *Californios* rose in their first revolt. In the following fifteen years there were nine more rebellions against Mexican governors.

Meanwhile, to stimulate population growth in the northern provinces, the Mexican government had launched far-reaching programs of economic development. A colonization act passed in 1824 allowed anyone who was a Mexican citizen to acquire, practically free, grants of land of up to 48,000 acres provided he put the property to use. In California a clamor arose that the well-developed mission lands, held in trust for the Indians, be made available for *rancho* grants. In 1833 the Mexican Congress complied. Amid graft and corruption hundreds of *ranchos* were quickly granted on the former mission lands, most of them in southern California and along the coast to San Francisco Bay. Thus was founded California's history of large, private landholdings as opposed to small farms.

The Indians got nothing. Before secularization they had been practically imprisoned in the mission villages. Now they were freed from all controls. They held some of the mission lands briefly, but these were soon taken from them. Whole tribes had disappeared because of the ravages of European diseases. The 30,000 surviving Indians scattered widely, many becoming *vaqueros* (cowboys) on the great *ranchos*, thus forming the first pool of unorganized and easily exploited rural laborers in California. Since that time, a succession of such groups has undergirded the state's agricultural economy—ex-miners, Chinese, Hawaiians, Hindus, Japanese, and, around 1900, a renewed influx of Mexicans.

The Revitalization of New Mexico

Over the centuries, a different way of life from that in California had evolved in New Mexico. The Indians there were powerful and aggressive, unlike those in California, and their frequent attacks had created among the *Nuevo Mexicanos* a preference for living in towns for protection. Homes were built like fortresses, windows were barred, walls were thick, and patios were large and enclosed to guard stock in time of danger. Living along the upper Rio Grande and its tributaries in order to obtain irrigation, the New Mexicans left their villages each day to tend cultivated fields of corn, beans, wheat, and chili. The Roman Catholic Church in this region was very old and deeply rooted. Large sheep herds flourished, and were periodically driven southward to Chihuahua, 600 miles from El Paso.

The distinctive character of life, however, was one of great isolation and simplicity. Contacts with the heart of Mexico were few, and trade articles from that region hard to secure. In 1803, the Louisiana Purchase suddenly brought the American border quite near—indeed, a relatively few miles northeast from Santa Fe through Raton Pass. By the early 1820s some enterprising American traders had found their way to Santa Fe, across the plains from St. Louis, to begin commerce.

Meanwhile, the Republic of Mexico awakened sleepy New Mexico by terminating the traditional Spanish policy of closed frontiers. New Mexicans could now welcome trade with the Americans, over what was soon called the Santa Fe Trail. For twenty years, until troubles between Mexico and the United States in the 1840s closed off this commerce, the Santa Fe trade flourished. New Mexico's geographical and commercial separation from Mexico itself had opened this large province to American economic and cultural expansion. Learning of New Mexico's remoteness from and indifference to Mexican rule, Americans became convinced that sooner or later the province would fall into their hands.

Mexican Development of Texas

The province of Texas (actually part of the larger state of Coahuila-Texas, ruled from Saltillo) was practically empty in 1820. If the new Republic of Mexico hoped to retain it, it could not remain so. Accordingly, it was thrown open to settlement, the government hoping to attract immigrants from Europe and the older parts of Mexico. However, few Mexicans came because Texas had no mineral wealth, and large landholdings in Mexican ownership relied, as elsewhere in the Mexican world, upon *peonage* (the labor of landless workers bound to compulsory servitude). This semi-feudal system could not grow rapidly.

Land, therefore, was granted to *empresarios*, who brought in settlers from the American states. The first of these grants went to Stephen F. Austin, whose father had been a naturalized Spanish subject in the former province of Louisiana. By the end of the 1820s his grant in the valleys of the Colorado and Brazos rivers held the farms of many hundreds of American settlers, each of whom had sworn loyalty to the Republic of Mexico. In a population of about 30,000 in Texas, 25,000 were Americans; only some 5,000 were Mexicans.

Austin had screened his settlers carefully. They had agreed to convert to Catholicism or at least not to practice their Protestant faiths. The purpose was to settle a community of industrious and sober men who would work hard as farmers and be good Mexican citizens. It was the success of Austin's efforts that led the state of Coahuila-Texas in 1825 to open its borders to any American of "sound personal habits and morals" who would swear loyalty and dispense with Protestantism. Thousands of families were attracted to Texas by the abundance of land offered at low cost, the huge wandering herds of wild cattle, and the opportunity to raise cotton. A "Texas fever" swept the lower Mississippi Valley in the late 1820s, and the influx boomed.

The new arrivals, however, were impatient with Mexican culture and ways, prickly, and independence-minded. In time, Mexican authorities grew concerned that few from Europe or Old Mexico were entering Texas. It was becoming a province in large parts of which only English was spoken. The prohibition against Protestantism began to cause grumblings. Equally serious was the issue of slavery. Mexico decreed an end to the system in 1829. Loud protests came from Texas, where cotton plantations were the mainstay of the economy, and a special dispensation exempted Texas from the decree. Nevertheless, Texans continued to worry about the problem.

The Expanding Sioux

Far to the north, fur traders had for generations been observing and trading with the outspreading Sioux tribes of the northern Missouri River country and the Great Plains, in what would later become the Dakotas, Nebraska and Kansas, and eastern Colorado and Wyoming. This tremendous region was not a static scene of tribes occupying certain areas since the beginning of time, but one of great internal flux since far back in the eighteenth century. Here, in fact, the "invasion" was not by white people, though French, Spanish, and British fur traders had long been among the Indians. Rather, it was by the nomadic and warlike Sioux tribes.

They had been moving westward since the early 1700s from the Missouri River into the Great Plains, conquering sedentary, agricultural village tribes like the Arikaras (and in effect turning them into serfs) and driving out the Omahas, Cheyennes, and Iowas to take over their fur-trapping lands and buffalo grounds.

The warfare among the Plains Indians, in other words, was not simply an eternal sniping back and forth at "hereditary enemies" with no significant change in territorial areas resulting, as has been the traditional view, but a great battle for valuable resources in which the Sioux took over immense territories formerly occupied by other Native American peoples, including such traditional holy lands as the Black Hills. By this process they became the dominant trappers and traders of the prairies, getting guns, horses, and European trade goods in return for fur, buffalo hides, and pemmican (preserved meat). They were aided by periodic incursions of smallpox and other European diseases brought in by European and United States fur traders, because the village Indians, in their more closely packed settlements, were more vulnerable to contagion than the wide-ranging, nomadic Sioux.

Meanwhile, Sioux buffalo hunting so decimated the herds that the Sioux had to keep moving west-

ward, northward, and southward, spreading ever outward, to find more populous herds. In the process they killed off and drove out such other Native American peoples as the Pawnee along the western Platte River and its tributaries, and the Mandan from their villages far up the Missouri in what are now the Dakotas. The Omaha and Ponca tribes eventually fled in panic from the merciless Sioux. While the other tribes declined steeply in population, the Sioux kept increasing in numbers, reaching perhaps 25,000 in the 1850s. The great smallpox epidemic of 1837 probably cut the Indian population of the Plains in half, but the roaming Sioux largely escaped the devastation.

In the 1840s citizens of the United States began migrating westward through the Platte Valley, on the Oregon Trail, to settle Oregon and Utah and move in among the *Californios*. This drove away buffalo from a wide corridor through the plains, and established another avenue for epidemic diseases (a cholera epidemic on the plains followed in 1849–50). Since the Crows and Pawnees were in the track of this migration they took its brunt, which further helped the Sioux widen and consolidate their empire. In 1843, in a dramatic coup, they destroyed a major Pawnee village, killed scores of its people, and reduced the tribe to desperate appeals to the Americans for help. Thirty years later, just before the Battle of the Little Big Horn with United States troops under General George A. Custer, the Sioux administered the crushing blow to the Pawnee, killing 100 of them in a major attack and forcing the Pawnee to undertake a long migration south to settle in the Indian Territory (what is now Oklahoma). By this time too the Sioux had driven the Crows into the Rocky Mountains, taking over their plains territory.

The Lure of the Oregon Country

The Americans had acquired co-ownership of the vast Oregon Country—as the enormous region running from California's northern border to Alaska was called—with the British in 1818, but the Hudson's Bay Company and its trappers dominated most of the region. Then in 1831 a group of Indians accompanied a group of American fur traders to St. Louis in order to observe the white man's way of life. They were said to be in search of the white man's Bible. This story swept through the churches of the country, and in a brief time the first missionaries were on their way to the Oregon Country.

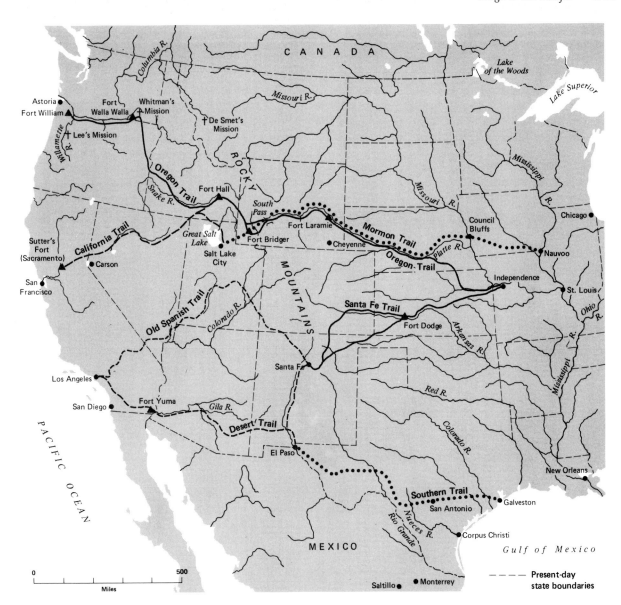

Trails to the West

Few Indians were converted, but high hopes and ardent support attached to this sacred adventure. The missionaries established the first lasting American settlements along the lower Willamette River. Farmers in the Missouri region, having heard so much of the rich soils of Oregon, began taking their families across the Plains to the valley of the Willamette. By 1840, more than 100 farms and 500 settlers had made for a significant community, considerably larger in numbers than the British community at Fort Vancouver on the Columbia.

More than 100 settlers made the trek in 1842, and in 1843 a veritable army of pioneers departed from the Missouri frontier to head out through the valley of the Platte to the Rockies and on to Oregon. A thousand migrants, taking almost 2,000 cattle and oxen with them, made the six-month journey of 2,000 miles so successfully—not a life was lost—that thousands more followed them in 1844 and 1845.

As always, the influx of settlers brought the question of sovereignty to the fore. In 1843 the settlers established a temporary government to last until

Skilled Swiss artist Karl Bodmer offers detailed illustrations of Indian artifacts and social customs.

"such time as the United States of America extend their jurisdiction over us." The time for a joint occupation of the Oregon Country had come to an end.

The Lure of California

Because it was foreign territory, California did not attract American settlers as soon as Oregon, nor in such numbers. Some Americans, however, lived among the *Californios* in the 1830s. They were resident agents sent out by New England merchant houses. Their task was to conclude purchase agreements for hides and tallow for the Boston ships, which now regularly visited the California coast. Thomas O. Larkin in Monterey and other such men assumed leading positions in the life of the province, often marrying into *Californio* families. Their ability, in fact, to accommodate to *Californio* culture shows that cultural conflict between Mexicans and Americans need not have occurred. Their education and knowledge of the distant civilized world assured them influential roles in every public question.

By the 1840s farmers on the Missouri frontier were learning of the fabulous land grants that Mexico issued in California. People also heard tall tales of California itself: never-ending sunshine and a province so blessed by nature that disease was said to be almost nonexistent. Everyone knew, furthermore, of the constant rebellions against Mexican rule that

went on in California. It seemed a land ripe for the plucking. All it needed, people confidently asserted, was an influx of American settlers and its ownership would automatically transfer from the reputedly weak and palsied Mexican hand to that of the vigorous Americans.

In truth, governmental authority had almost vanished in California. In one period of little more than a year, four different men held the governor's chair. From 1836 to 1840, as we shall see, the province actually declared its independence, because of General Santa Anna's ending of federalism in Mexico in 1834. In 1844 a new governor arrived from Mexico with a body of 300 troops. Within weeks he was sent packing, and all Mexican control vanished. For the next two years of California's existence as a nominal part of the Republic of Mexico, the province was under the governance of two *Californios*, one a military official with authority over the north and the other a civilian with authority over the south.

Americans Dream of Annexation

In 1841 the first party of American immigrants struggled over the Sierra Nevada into California after an exhausting trek from Missouri. They established themselves in the Sacramento Valley, where they would be far from the *Californios*, who lived along the coast. Other small parties followed in the next few years, so that by the middle 1840s a few hundred Americans were living in the valleys north and east of San Francisco Bay. Before long they too, like the American settlers in Oregon, began working up plans to get the United States to take over.

In the fall of 1845, Thomas Larkin, the canny New Englander who served as American consul in Monterey and had been conducting business in California since arriving in 1832, sent an important message to President Polk. As an intimate member of California's ruling circles, he reported that the *Californios* who governed the province appeared to be extremely friendly toward the United States. Larkin quoted them as telling him "that they will fight all troops Mexico may send here to the last drop of their blood, and . . . they wish to govern themselves, the country, but prefer to see the United States troops, to those from Mexico, to govern the country."

Larkin's news was well founded. So eminent and widely respected a figure in California as Colonel Mariano G. Vallejo frankly considered American annexation not only inevitable but also preferable to any other possible solution of California's chronic anarchy. Polk, delighted at the prospect of peaceful acquisition, immediately made Thomas Larkin a confidential agent of the State Department and charged him to do everything in his power to swing *Californio* public opinion in this direction.

Frémont and Rebellion

By the time these words arrived in California in April 1846, events had already made them obsolete. A young U.S. army captain, John C. Frémont, had suddenly appeared in California a few months earlier. Sent west by the American government to search out trails and potential railroad routes, his ostensibly scientific party was accompanied by a suspiciously large contingent of armed men. Soon he had started a brief military skirmish near Monterey with the California authorities that put the whole province in an uproar, and had fallen in with the restive American farmers in the Sacramento Valley. They were in turmoil over rumors spread by settlers close to Frémont that an enraged Colonel José Castro, the military commandant, intended to kill all the Americans he could find and drive the remainder from California. In June 1846 a militant group of Americans living north of San Francisco Bay took matters into their own hands. At Frémont's urging, while gathered in the small mission town of Sonoma, they ran up the

Bear Flag, and proclaimed the existence of a new nation, the "California Republic."

Frémont now openly took charge of the Bear Flag cause. He marched on Monterey, sending Castro's force fleeing southward. On the ninth of July, 1846, he arrived in Monterey and learned that a much larger conflict was under way. Seven American naval vessels lay anchored in Monterey harbor, and the American flag floated over the former capital of Mexican California. The United States and the Republic of Mexico had been at war for two months.

Trouble in Texas

The war with Mexico had complicated origins. First of all, in 1836 the Americans in Texas had successfully risen in rebellion and established an independent republic. Nine years later this republic was annexed to the United States, an event that led to the outbreak of hostilities.

Fundamentally, the Texas revolution arose from an irresolvable conflict of cultures. Many Americans in Texas regarded Mexican ways of life as inferior and debased. Within the province of Texas itself, those of Mexican descent had become a minority group held in contempt. Mexican ways of governing, furthermore, seemed tyrannical and arbitrary. Many Mexicans in other provinces agreed. Texas was not, in fact, the only Mexican province to rise in revolt. The Republic of Mexico was racked by rebellions year after year.

The Texans had weighty grievances. The capitol of Coahuila-Texas, Saltillo, was 700 miles away from the American settlements, and the people of Texas had little representation in its legislature—a situation justified by Coahuila's much larger population. The Americans asked time and again for Texas to be separated from Coahuila and allowed to have its own local government, but the Mexican authorities, understandably, feared that this would lead to secession. As early as 1829 an investigating commission from Mexico City had warned that the pattern of American settlement and later rebellion would eventually lead to Texas's annexation to the United States.

The centralized form of Mexican government resulted in important decisions being made far away from the local regions. Land titles, immigration regulations, custom duties, control of the military—these and other vital matters were frequently changed by apparently arbitrary decisions from above. Local government was nonelective. Mexican law gave large powers in each community to an appointed *alcalde* (magistrate). Trials were held in Saltillo, on the basis of written documents put together by the local *alcalde*. The accused had no right to be present; there were no juries; there was no confrontation of accusers, or any other civil rights to which Americans were accustomed.

Texans were further angered in 1832, when the state of Coahuila-Texas placed a ten-year limit on the continuance of slavery. Few Texans viewed this prospect with anything but fear and anger. To them, the restriction was not a question of human rights, but of another tyrannical Mexican assault on the security of property. In 1833 Stephen Austin carried to Mexico City a proposed constitution for a separate state of Texas, but he was first elaborately ignored and then thrown into jail.

Then occurred the event that tore everything apart and set the disintegration of the Republic of Mexico in motion. In 1834 General Antonio López de Santa Anna, originally chosen president of the Republic of Mexico as a reform candidate, abruptly proclaimed himself dictator, wiped out the federal system of government that had been established in 1824, and established a completely centralized regime. At this news, the always restive northern provinces of California and New Mexico—which had never felt a strong loyalty to the Republic of Mexico, within whose borders they had been placed without their request—revolted against the central government and in effect became independent. Indeed, the region of the Yucatan Peninsula, far within what is now Mexico, did the same, submitting to central control only after a long fight that lasted until 1843.

Revolution in Texas

The situation in Texas, with its overwhelmingly large American population, was even more explosive. In November 1834 the Texans declared a conditional independence, demanding, like California and New Mexico, that the 1824 federal constitution be reestablished. In late 1835, with an enraged Stephen Austin back in Texas, General Santa Anna brought an army of 4,000 men there to quell the rebellion. A last desperate attempt was made by Austin's followers to secure a compromise. Even in this extremity, a majority resisted the fateful step of throwing off their oaths of allegiance to the Republic of Mexico. Santa Anna would not agree, however, to local self-govern-

ment, and on March 2, 1836, the Texans issued a declaration of independence. Bloody fighting remained before that declaration was confirmed.

The defenders of the Alamo Mission in San Antonio, which included Mexican Texans as well as American, were overwhelmed and wiped out by the Mexican army a few days after the declaration was issued. Two weeks later a force of 350 Texans was captured and all were killed in cold blood at Goliad. Aware that Santa Anna intended no mercy, the Texans gave supreme authority to Sam Houston, the commander of their army. While he retreated eastward to gather and train his troops, settlers in droves began fleeing after him, heading for American sanctuary.

On April 21, 1836, Texas won its independence. Houston surprised Santa Anna and his army of 1,500 men near the San Jacinto River. Some 800 Texans overwhelmed them, killing more than 600 Mexican soldiers in retaliation for the earlier massacres. Santa Anna was captured and forced to sign peace treaties. The southern and western boundary

Sam Houston, first president of the Republic of Texas. A bluff and courageous patriot, he was given to showy and unusual clothes and unusual views, speaking passionately for the rights of Indians and against Southern secession.

of the Republic of Texas was fixed at a point far beyond its location under Mexican rule—at the Rio Grande, which flows into the Gulf of Mexico at a point 150 miles to the west and south of the Nueces River, the former boundary. (Upstream, this translated into an enormous accession of territory, since the Nueces is relatively short and the Rio Grande, rising in the Colorado Rockies, is almost 2,000 miles long.) The treaties were repudiated by the Mexican Congress, the only body legally empowered to ratify them, but Texan independence had unquestionably been established.

Annexation Protested

Texas immediately appealed for annexation to the United States, but President Jackson declined. Northern Whigs—who were traditionally opposed, like the Federalists before them, to western expansion—called the Texas revolution a plot to increase the size of the slaveholding South. Eight Northern legislatures announced their opposition to annexation, and thousands of individual protests poured into Congress. There was the substantial possibility as well that annexation would lead to war with Mexico, a prospect most Americans deplored. The United States government extended official recognition of Texan independence in March 1837, but for the time being that was as far as it was willing to go.

William Ellery Channing, the Unitarian leader and pioneering pacifist, protested in 1837 against Texan annexation in a letter to Henry Clay:

> Having unfolded the argument against the annexation of Texas from the criminality of the revolt, I proceed to a second very solemn consideration, namely, that by this act our country will enter on a career of encroachment, war, and crime, and will merit and incur the punishment and woe of aggravated wrongdoing. The seizure of Texas will not stand alone. It will darken our future history. . . . It is strange that nations should be so much more rash than individuals . . . of all the precipitate and criminal deeds, those perpetrated by nations are the most fruitful of misery. . . . It is full time that we should lay on ourselves serious, resolute restraint. Possessed of a domain, vast enough for the growth of ages, it is time for us to stop in the career of acquisition and conquest. Already endangered by our greatness, we cannot advance without imminent peril to our institutions, union, prosperity, virtue, and peace. . . . We give ourselves an impulse, which will and must precipitate us into new invasions of our neighbors' soil. Is it by pressing forward

> in this course that we are to learn self-restraint? Is cupidity to be appeased by gratification? Is it by unrighteous grasping that an impatient people will be instructed how to hem themselves within the rigid bounds of justice? . . . Our Eagle will whet not gorge its appetite on its first victim; and will snuff a more tempting quarry, more alluring blood in every new region which opens southward. To annex Texas is to declare perpetual war with Mexico.

Such wars, Channing went on, will corrupt the nation. Texas will be populated by "adventurers" looking for more booty: "the proscribed, the disgraced, the outcasts of society." The nation's future will be placed in their reckless hands, and they will be uncontrollable, the most states'-rights-conscious of all American citizens. America should be helping Mexico, not hurting her. That nation has "looked to us with a generous trust. She opened her ports and territories to our farmers, mechanics, and merchants." American influence might have been helpful and peaceful.

> And what is now the case? A deadly hatred burns in Mexico toward this country. No stronger national sentiment now binds her scattered provinces together than dread and detestation of republican America. She is ready to attach herself to Europe for defense from the United States. All the moral power which we might have gained over Mexico, we have thrown away; and suspicion, dread, and abhorrence have supplanted respect and trust.

> It is sometimes said that "the mixed, degraded race of Mexico must melt before the Anglo-Saxon." Away with this vile sophistry! There is no necessity for crime. There is no fate to justify rapacious nations any more than to justify gamblers and robbers in plunder. (The Works of William Ellery Channing [1848])

The Texas Republic

For nine years Texas was an independent nation. France and Britain accorded recognition in 1839 and 1840, and the Netherlands and Belgium followed shortly. Immigrants poured in, raising its population from 30,000 in 1836 to an astonishing 142,000 in 1846. Meanwhile, with British encouragement the Republic of Texas flourished as a cotton producer for English textile mills. As the United States remained steadily indifferent, at least officially, to annexation, the people of Texas began to lose their interest in that possibility and to take pride in their role as an independent country—even if it was one whose very existence the former ruler, Mexico, still refused to recognize, maintaining a state of war.

With steady immigration from the United States, Texas became ever more American in language and culture. A German colony of some 6,000 to 10,000 people arrived in the 1840s to settle in eastern Texas (and provide, eventually, a solid source of votes for the Whigs, after annexation, and the Republicans after that). Dutch immigrants arrived steadily, and so did settlers from France. By 1850, so many slaves had been brought in that the proportion of slave population to white was greater even than in Kentucky or Tennessee. Thousands of substantial slave-holders, in fact, migrated from the Deep South across the Sabine River into Texas after the Panic of 1837 to rebuild their fortunes.

Texan leaders began dreaming of huge westward expansions, creating a great nation in the Southwest that would extend to the Pacific and stand as a rival to the United States. The English government was pleased, and for a time seriously considered whether or not to stand as protector of Texan independence to halt the continuing growth of the American nation. A Texan expedition was sent to New Mexico in hopes of securing that Mexican province and attaching it to Texas, but it ended in humiliating defeat.

Independence was in fact a difficult and precarious course to pursue. The nation's finances were chaotic, for the costs of self-government ran far beyond the country's revenue. Its paper money rapidly lost value. In 1842 a Mexican army sacked San Antonio. Thereafter, such raids occurred with alarming frequency, and a new flight of refugees began. Efforts at retaliation against Mexico led to a bloody defeat, an entire Texan army being marched off to a Mexican prison in 1842. Intermittent warfare continued in 1843. In 1844 President John Tyler of the United States grew alarmed that Texas would become a British protectorate, and he reopened negotiations with Texas on a treaty of annexation. It was laid before the Senate in April 1844, only to be defeated.

Manifest Destiny

But circumstances were different in the United States now from those in 1837, when the annexation issue had first been seriously presented. Prosperity returned in 1842 after years of depression; settlers were streaming to the Oregon Country and clamoring for American rule to be extended to that vast region; California

seemed besieged by never-ending rebellions and ready to cast itself adrift from Mexico; Texans had for years presented periodic requests for annexation; Canadians had (briefly) revolted in 1837, for a time holding out prospects that they might be ready to join the United States; and practically every year another state in the Mississippi Valley was added to the roll call of the Union. Population was pouring into the country from abroad, huge migrations were under way within the nation itself, and industry was beginning to expand.

In these circumstances, a new national mood emerged. Why not open the way, many people said, for non-American states to enter the United States and enjoy what were felt to be the blessings of republicanism? All who were so inclined should be given the opportunity to join the Union, said Democrats, who, as Jeffersonians and Jacksonians, were traditionally expansionist. It was America's Manifest Destiny to expand.

It is important to note, however, that traditional descriptions of Manifest Destiny have not always been accurate. It was not necessarily an aggressive philosophy calling for military expansion in all directions. In most quarters, especially in the Democratic newspapers of the northeastern states (where it was eagerly advanced), Manifest Destiny was an idealistic, nonviolent, and noncoercive philosophy. It called for opening the Union to all, but expressly condemned the use of force.

Whig newspapers and politicians uniformly rejected Manifest Destiny. Since the Republic's beginnings they had been hostile to the West and had resisted expansion. Western growth would isolate New England even more and bring in more Democrats. The Atlantic seaboard and industrialization took their attention. They preferred to see the Oregon Country become a self-governing republic, living in friendship with the United States through its devotion to similar principles, but not a part of the nation. But Democratic newspapers in the Northern states cried out the new message unceasingly, especially those of the new immigrant Irish Catholics, who saw expansionism as a way of pushing back British power in North America.

Many intellectuals were devoted to peaceful Manifest Destiny, Emerson and Walt Whitman among them. The Middle West, when it talked of Manifest Destiny, was more belligerent and aggressive, more ready to take action to achieve the goal. The South, though eager for the annexation of Texas—indeed, desperate for it—was the least concerned with Manifest Destiny. Southerners cared little for Oregon or Canada, and they were hostile to the idea of taking in Mexico or any other region with a numerous dark-skinned people.

There was a pervasive and romantically agrarian cast to Manifest Destiny. The whole idea was linked to a hunger for land and an equally passionate belief that the greatest benefit any society could bestow on humankind was to bring land into cultivation. Everywhere Americans said that no nation had a moral claim to territory left empty and undeveloped. Why do Americans want the Oregon Country? asked John Quincy Adams. "To make the wilderness blossom as the rose, to establish laws, to increase, multiply, and subdue the earth, which we are commanded to do by the first behest of God Almighty." Also undergirding Manifest Destiny was the belief that the United States was obligated to train backward peoples in self-government. Was not Mexico illiterate, badly governed, torn by rebellions? it was commonly asked. What better task for the American nation could there be than to accept the peaceful adhesion of Mexico so that it could be tutored by those who knew how to create security, prosperity, and enlightened government?

The Background of Manifest Destiny

More than just the prospect of gaining new territories released the spirit of Manifest Destiny. The transportation revolution so swiftly uniting the country had made it possible to dream new dreams. People everywhere talked of a railroad across the entire continent and of what that would mean. Congressmen could then travel from Oregon to Washington, D.C., in less time than it used to take them to get to the capital from Ohio! The telegraph, another new phenomenon, seemed almost magically to shrink time and distance.

Hoping to open trade to the Orient with its fabled riches, the American government since Jackson's administration had made periodic attempts to buy the bay of San Francisco from Mexico. Daniel Webster, who opposed the annexation of Texas, nevertheless favored acquiring San Francisco, insisting that it was worth twenty times all of Texas. In 1844, treaties were negotiated with China that opened several of its parts to American traders. This made even more pressing the desire for ports on the Pacific coast.

Manifest Destiny also drew much of its vigor from the reforming spirit that filled the air in the middle 1840s. Young people in the Northern states were taking up reform movements of all kinds, among them public education, prison reform, communal societies, the labor union movement, and the struggle for women's rights. The Boston *Times*, using a term that quickly became a national slogan, praised the spirit of "Young America." Congress was filled with young representatives and senators. At forty-nine, James K. Polk was by far the youngest president yet, and this was widely noted. The *United States Journal* trumpeted that the new spirit of youthfulness "was felt in boyhood in the triumphant election of James K. Polk; and in manhood it will be still more strongly felt in the future administration of public affairs in this country." The youthfulness of many Manifest Destiny adherents suffused the entire movement with a sense of moral purity, of honesty of motive beyond doubt.

Even the communicatons network added to the excitement. A revolution in news-gathering methods joined with a revolutionary expansion in readership to create the first mass market for journalism. The spread of literacy along with the invention of the high-speed printing press in the 1840s created an astonishing outpouring of cheap newspapers. These were fed news by the telegraph and carried swiftly into the countryside by the railroad. The penny press came into being, riding to huge circulations on the back of sensationalism in news coverage—scandal, lurid political intrigue, and Manifest Destiny. It is extraordinary how closely this development, which preceded the Mexican War, paralleled a similar revolution in sensationalist journalism that preceded the Spanish-American War half a century later, expressing a similar upsurge of national sentiment for expansionism.

James K. Polk Takes the Lead

These national influences, however, did not bring on the Mexican War or dictate the course of events following the war's outbreak. To be sure, they created among the large parts of the population an openness to expansion. But in what form and by what means? The presidential campaign of 1844 was fought on these questions, and Polk was elected with a bare plurality of popular votes over Henry Clay on the basis of an expansionist party platform stating that "the re-occupation of Oregon and the re-annexation of Texas at the earliest practicable period are great American measures." The cry "fifty-four forty or fight!" (referring to the demand for *all* of the Oregon Country) resounded through the country. Nonetheless, at best Polk's election was an uncertain mandate. But he did not hesitate. The nation was to learn that the president of the United States has enormous and almost unchecked powers in foreign policy. If any single person may be considered responsible for the war with Mexico and the acquisition of New Mexico and California, it was James K. Polk.

Polk's election emboldened President Tyler to push ahead with the annexation of Texas. Since he could not obtain a two-thirds majority in the Senate for ratification of the treaty, with Polk's help he secured the passage of a joint resolution in both houses offering annexation to Texas. Hours before he left the White House Tyler dispatched a messenger carrying news of the offer of annexation to the Republic of Texas. When Tyler's offer went out to Texas, Mexico angrily broke off diplomatic relations with the United States. What now? With his first act, Polk intimated what he planned to do. He sent word to the Texans that if they agreed to join the Union, he would support Texas's claim to the Rio Grande boundary. In May 1845 came a dramatic event: Upon Britain's urgings, Mexico agreed to recognize Texan independence if it did not thereafter join the United States. However, after some debate a Texan national convention called for the purpose in July 1845 decided unanimously for annexation as a state in the American Union.

Polk's Diplomatic Offensive

And so, Texas was now part of the United States of America, its state government being formally installed at Austin in February 1846. But where was its western boundary? At the Nueces, or at the Rio Grande? No mention of the question had been made in the resolution of annexation precisely because of its questionable nature. The land between the Nueces and the Rio Grande was settled neither by Texans nor by Mexicans. Texas maintained an outpost just beyond the Nueces at Corpus Christi, and Mexico did the same on the northern bank of the Rio Grande.

When Polk's offer to Texas to support the Rio Grande boundary became known, therefore, a storm of criticism erupted from Whigs and Northern Democrats alike. Polk's critics were even angrier when they discovered that he had dispatched a sizable army under General Zachary Taylor to take up positions at Corpus Christi. He had also assembled one of the strongest naval forces in American history in that part of the Gulf, under the command of an eager expansionist, Commodore Robert F. Stockton.

Polk was unmoved by the criticism. He sent word to the United States naval commander in the Pacific to "at once possess yourself of the port of San Francisco, and blockade or occupy such other ports as your force may permit," if the commander learned that war had broken out between the United States and Mexico. It was this instruction that led to the occupation Frémont discovered in process when he arrived in Monterey with his Bear Flag army.

Polk took advantage of another longstanding controversy with the Mexicans—the matter of American claims against Mexico. In the periodic revolutions within Mexico since 1821, American businessmen had been subjected to sudden and arbitrary seizures of their property. By an international adjudication to which Mexico had agreed, the claims for reparation against Mexico were set at about two million dollars. Actually, by 1845 they were considerably higher than that. Mexico, however, was unable to pay either its American bills or those owed to other nations. Polk hoped to cause such friction over the issue of American claims that the Mexicans would come to the bargaining table. Lacking money, they would cede California and New Mexico as part of an overall settlement in which the United States would pay many millions to Mexico to compensate for the difference in value between the damage claims and the value of the territories themselves. Pursuing this policy, Polk instructed General Taylor to take no hostile steps whatever at Corpus Christi. The American army was to be there merely as a pressure, not as an invading force.

Through the long summer of 1845 Polk labored to get Mexico to reestablish diplomatic relations. Characteristically, however, he kept insisting that the negotiations take place on American terms. Mexico was to accept as a closed issue the annexation of Texas to the United States, together with its Rio Grande boundary. The negotiations were to concern themselves only with appropriate reparations and mutual settlement of claims. The Mexicans could not accept such conditions. No Mexican regime could remain in office if it did, so strong was Mexican public opinion against the United States. Indeed, one government was overturned simply for having opened discussions with an informal intermediary. There was a longstanding fear in Mexico of American expansionist attitudes toward Mexican territory. Manifest Destiny, to the people of Mexico, meant something entirely different from what it meant to American idealists.

Acquiring the Oregon Country

At the same time, Polk was carrying on prolonged negotiations with Britain over the division of the Oregon Country. For years the British had offered to split the Oregon Country along the line of the Columbia River while the United States had offered to divide it along the line of the 49th parallel. This meant that only one area was in dispute: the western half of the present state of Washington, which includes the magnificent "ocean in the forest," Puget Sound. Polk was determined to get that harbor. Puget Sound would provide a priceless base of operations for commerce throughout the North Pacific area.

In December 1845 Polk asked Congress for authority to give Britain the year's notice, called for in the treaty of 1818, necessary for bringing an end to the joint occupation. He went on to insist that the United States had a valid claim to the whole of the Oregon Country, clear up to 54°40′ north latitude, the southern boundary of Russian Alaska. If settlement was not reached within the year 1846, he said with ominous firmness, then questions of national honor would become paramount—that is, war might result.

By April 1846, when Congress authorized Polk to terminate joint occupation, the United States and Great Britain seemed on the brink of war. But economic considerations saved the day. British prime minister Robert Peel finally realized that American markets were more important than Puget Sound. His great project of repealing the protectionist Corn Laws and throwing the nation open to free trade would have much greater chances of success if good feelings were reestablished with America and a mutual lowering of tariffs could be achieved.

The British public was also beginning to doubt that the interests of the Hudson's Bay Company in an extremely remote part of the world were worth another war with America. The British government, buoyed by this feeling, sent a compromise treaty to the United States government, offering to divide the Oregon Country at the 49th parallel, save for the part of Vancouver Island that jutted south of that line. To match the British concession, Polk was asked

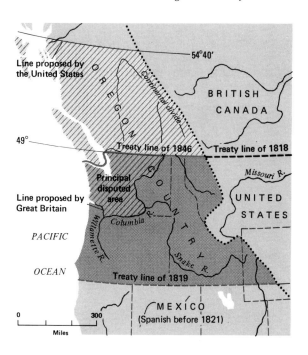

The Oregon Controversy, 1818–1846

to agree to perpetual free navigation of the Columbia River by the Hudson's Bay Company. Within a few days Polk accepted the offer, and on June 15, 1846, the Senate ratified it. The Oregon question finally was closed, and a vast new region became U.S. territory.

The War with Mexico

War had broken out with Mexico by this time. Polk's policy of trying to bully and bribe the Mexicans had not worked. The Mexican government would not be so treated. Polk's emissary to Mexico City, John Slidell, left the capital in a huff when the Mexican government refused to deal with him. "Depend upon it," he wrote Polk, "we can never get along well with them, until we have given them a good drubbing." Polk immediately sent General Taylor to the northern banks of the Rio Grande in March 1846 in hopes of provoking a Mexican attack. None came, and Polk vacillated, for at this time a war with Britain was still a possibility. In a rising chorus Northern Democrats joined Whigs in demanding that negotiations be restored on a basis that would not offend Mexico. "Why should we not compromise our difficulties with Mexico as well as with Great Britain?"

For the Mexicans, the war was a disaster from beginning to end.

asked a Chicago newspaper. It was extremely doubt-ful that Congress would agree to declare war.

General Taylor threw up a fortification so close to the Rio Grande that his artillery commanded the square in the Mexican town of Matamoros on the other side of the river. The Mexican commander understandably warned Taylor off, threatening to launch an attack. When this news came to Polk, he decided to wait. When nothing had occurred by May 9, 1846, Polk decided to risk two wars—the British settlement was not yet made—and ask Con-gress to declare war. Before he finished writing his war message, however, news came that the Mexicans had encountered a detachment of Taylor's troops on the northern side of the Rio Grande, killing or wound-ing sixteen and capturing the rest. Polk's newspaper, the *Union*, rushed an edition onto the streets of Wash-ington with the ringing words, "*American blood has been shed on American soil!*"

Polk reshaped his message to ask Congress not for a declaration of war but simply for a recognition that a state of war initiated by Mexico already existed. Both the Senate and the House were thrown into an uproar. All debate was choked out in the House by a rule requiring passage of the necessary appropria-tion bill within the same day that Polk's request arrived. Expansionists were ready to shout approval, but Whigs and many Northern Democrats reacted in dismay. All concentrated on the key point: Was Polk correct in saying that American blood had been

spilled on *American* soil? Few had considered the Rio Grande the boundary of Texas when Congress passed the resolution of annexation. Some insisted that the land beyond the Nueces was Mexican soil, others that the matter was at least debatable. They argued that Polk had been the aggressor by placing the American army in the disputed section.

Protests in the House were in vain. The Speaker of the House would not recognize Whigs to address the body. In the Senate John Calhoun asked how a mere local skirmish could amount to a full-scale war. How could the president justify such a grave under-taking as full warfare when so little had really oc-curred? But a big majority in both houses approved Polk's request, even though many voted with grave misgivings. The Whigs felt absolutely handcuffed, for they remembered keenly that the Federalist party had destroyed itself by opposing the War of 1812. The charge of selling out to the enemy and not rallying around the flag was one they could not bear. There were also indications that the country, especially the South and the West, feverishly supported the war. Manifest Destiny itself, a doctrine so widely trum-peted by Northern Democrats, had now come back to haunt them. Who could draw back now?

It takes rare courage to oppose a president in such a grave situation, especially when large parts of the nation are eager for war. A majority of the Congress seems clearly to have deplored the outbreak of the Mexican War; its outspoken critics maintained that everything Polk had done in bringing it on was unconstitutional; yet in moments of crisis they felt the need to give the president support. Even Thomas Corwin, the Whig from Ohio who within the year was to utter the classic condemnation of the war—if he were a Mexican, he said, he would ask America, "Have you not room in your country to bury your own dead men? If you come into mine, we will greet you with bloody hands and welcome you with hospitable graves"—said "aye" to war when the issue was voted on May 12, 1846.

Who Was Responsible?

So began the conflict that, until the war in Vietnam, has most disturbed the American conscience, for in the angry criticisms of the war issued by Whigs and by anti-slavery forces at the time, and in the eyes of multitudes of critics since then, the Mexican War has been seen as an unprovoked attack on a much weaker country. There is no question that American insistence on the Rio Grande as the boundary of Texas was the immediate cause of war. In fact, however, it was not simply whether the Rio Grande or the Nueces River was the proper boundary, for the Mexicans never gave up on their claim that they owned *all* of Texas, clear to the Sabine River (the state's present eastern boundary). Mexicans were and are a proud people, and any government that accepted the annexation of Texas in any form whatever would have been angrily thrown out of office by another of Mexico's too-frequent revolutions. In short, annexation *by itself* meant war.

Europe did not then see the conflict as one between a bully and a weak neighbor, nor did the Mexicans themselves see it that way. The previous military effort of the United States in the War of 1812 had hardly been brilliant, save at the Battle of New Orleans, which had been a defensive struggle. In this war the Republic of Mexico expected to be strengthened by aid from England and France, for neither country wanted to see the American nation expand. Furthermore, Mexico had an army four times larger than America's, and it was well equipped and well trained by experienced European officers, deeply seasoned by years of almost continuous fighting within Mexico itself, and confident of victory. The Mexican army had other great advantages. It was fighting against a badly divided American people. Mexico expected to invade the United States, set off slave and Indian rebellions, then march on Wash-

ington to dictate a peace agreement. Thus, as historian William Hanchett has recently written in a published essay, Mexico "did not at all see itself as a dove being attacked by a hawk. . . . [It] aroused public opinion [at home], therefore, with aggressively anti-American propaganda and assurances of easy victory."

In recent years, too, American historians have been looking at the controversy afresh, and some of them have pulled back significantly from the "bad war" thesis. In a flood of new scholarship—more historical studies of the Mexican War have appeared since 1960 than in any comparable earlier period—revisionists note that avoiding a war with Mexico would have required not annexing Texas at all, but allowing it to become a British protectorate; giving up all interest in California and New Mexico, which in fact, at the time, appeared to mean letting those rebellious Mexican states come under European domination. William Hanchett observed:

> The United States, in short, would have had to decline to participate in the political organization of a vast contiguous region and to accept a second-class status among the nations of the world. It is difficult to imagine that even the opponents of "Mr. Polk's war," had they been in power, would have been willing to make such a sacrifice of the national interest. . . . Assessing "blame" for the Mexican war is thus a fruitless enterprise. . . .

In a revisionist work, two other historians, Seymour V. Connor and Odie B. Faulk, observe in their *North America Divided: The Mexican War 1846–1848* (1971), that "for every bit of American guilt there is matching Mexican guilt."

Conduct of the War: First Phase

The fighting began in April 1846; it ended a year and a half later when an American force fought its way to Mexico City and hoisted the American flag. Five months after that, in February 1848, the Treaty of Guadalupe Hidalgo was signed. James K. Polk got what he wanted: the Rio Grande as Texas's boundary, California, and all the territory in between.

The war was fought with small armies. Zachary Taylor's force, which invaded northern Mexico, contained about 6,000 men. Stephen W. Kearny's "Army of the West," with which he took New Mexico, numbered about 1,500. The American forces who conquered California did not reach 1,000, the largest

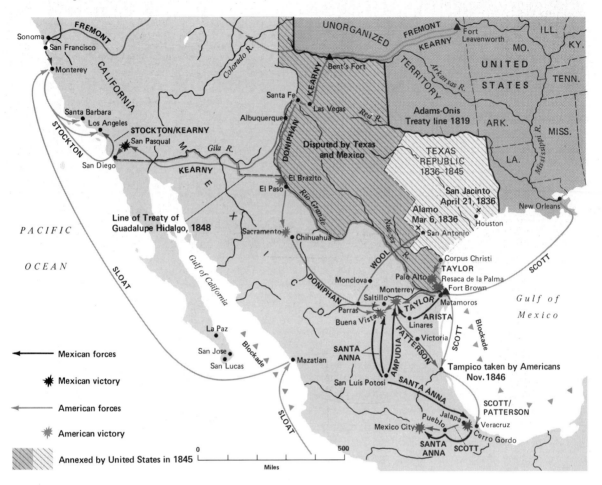

The Mexican War, 1846–1848

single attacking body being about 500 men. Winfield Scott took Veracruz by amphibious assault with 10,000 men. He made his plunge hundreds of miles into the Mexican interior with an army numbering at the outset about 14,000 men. It had dwindled to half that size by the time Mexico City was won.

For the Mexicans, however, the war was a disaster from beginning to end. The country had grave economic weaknesses that ill prepared it to fight a costly war, and it was far more internally divided between hostile, feuding factions than were the Americans. American firearms were more accurate than those of the Mexicans, and American soldiers, more accustomed to using rifles, were murderously effective in their fire. The European-trained Mexican army was accustomed to thinking of battles as being fought at a distance, and its soldiers were repeatedly overwhelmed in close combat with handgun and bayonet. The volunteers who made up the American

forces fought with a striking disregard for personal danger and, after the encouragement of early victories, with that confident boldness that so often is the key to success in infantry combat.

The Mexican War was a training ground for many of the young men who later became generals in the Civil War. The list is remarkable: Robert E. Lee, Ulysses Grant, Stonewall Jackson, James Longstreet, P. G. T. Beauregard, Joseph E. Johnston, Albert S. Johnston, William Tecumseh Sherman, George McClellan, and Joe Hooker provide the most notable names. This was also the first war in which graduates of America's new military academy at West Point assumed a role. Scott and Taylor were able to surround themselves with trained, competent, and disciplined young officers, in sharp contrast with the situation in all former American conflicts.

Polk's initial strategy was to take the territory he wanted, invade and hold what is now northeastern

Mexico, and then wait out the Mexican government, forcing it to the negotiating table by dogged tenacity. He immediately dispatched Colonel Stephen W. Karny on a long march to New Mexico in June 1846 with orders to proceed to California for the conquest of that province as well. In July the naval force in the Pacific, under Commodore John D. Sloat, followed its earlier instructions by seizing Monterey, being joined there by John Frémont and his Bear Flaggers. Together they sent a force to southern California, where most of the *Californios* lived, and occupied it without incident—though after harsh mistreatment by arrogant American occupying forces the *Californios* in southern California rose, in September 1846, to retake control of their region.

Kearny's campaign against New Mexico was relatively uneventful. Santa Fe and the other towns were occupied bloodlessly in August 1846. The acting governor and leading *Nuevo Mexicanos* greeted Kearny warmly and promised loyalty to the United States. So too did the chiefs of the Indian pueblos, saying that the Americans were rescuing them from Spanish injustice and oppression. (Some months later, a rebellion took place in Taos during which the American governor and several other officials were assassinated. Within a few days, order was restored.)

Having taken New Mexico, Kearny then marched off to California. Here, with an army of a few hundred men he quickly put down the *Californio* uprising in southern California, after the single brief battle of San Pascual (December 6, 1846). The Treaty of Cahuenga was signed on January 13, 1847, giving amnesty to all. As Kearny wrote afterwards to Washington, the *Californios* had rebelled because they had been "most cruelly and shamefully abused by our people. Had they not resisted, they would have been unworthy [of] the name of men." California, finally, was taken by the United States.

At the same time, General Zachary Taylor was throwing back the Mexicans in two sharp victories in Texas (the battles of Palo Alto and Resaca de la Palma) and then launching the American invasion of Mexico. Heading toward Saltillo, the capital of Coahuila, he arrived before the nearby city of Monterey in September 1846. After several days of American assaults that broke through defense after defense, Monterey was taken. Some 500 Americans were dead, and the stolid but courageous Zachary Taylor—a Whig—was being boomed as a presidential candidate by his delighted party colleagues back home. (This pleased the general, but it thereafter poisoned all his relations with President Polk.) Other military

and naval operations in and along the coast of northern Mexico led to practically the whole region being taken by the end of 1846.

Conduct of the War: Second Phase

Mexico, however, refused to give in. Polk realized that to get a treaty of peace he would have to invade central Mexico. Who was to be the commander of this expedition? Spurning Taylor for political reasons, Polk was forced to turn to another hopeful Whig presidential candidate in the army, Winfield Scott, the only general superior in rank to Taylor. Enormously vain, overbearing, and yet a gifted commander, Scott carried off his task brilliantly. He put the heavily fortified coastal city of Veracruz under siege in March 1847, and had it in his hands by the end of that month. A few days later he began his daring strike into the interior. It was a march of over 300 miles, during which he was cut off from his base of supplies. By careful preparation, skillful strategy, a deft use of the terrain, and hard fighting, Scott's army battered its way through all outlying fortifications to the outskirts of Mexico City, leaving thousands of its men dead and wounded along the way.

Complete demoralization ensued on the Mexican side. The populace was panic-stricken, and Santa Anna decided to withdraw, leaving the vast city open for American occupation. This took place on September 14, 1847, six months after the invasion had begun at Veracruz. On February 2, 1848, the Treaty of Guadalupe Hidalgo was signed, ceding California and New Mexico to the United States and confirming the Texan boundary at the Rio Grande. In exchange, the United States agreed to pay $15 million to the Republic of Mexico and assume all claims by American citizens to the amount of $3.5 million. The treaty arrangements also guaranteed that the Mexican citizens living in the ceded territory—about 80,000 of them—would receive civil and political rights fully equal to those of American citizens, and would have their land titles protected.

How Did Americans and Europeans Feel About the War?

This outcome to the Mexican War was utterly astonishing to the nations of Europe, whose ruling circles had for years scorned the "ridiculous" American republic as weak, lacking in courage, certainly unable successfully to fight a powerful military society like Mexico. Why not? Because a republic, which consciously strips power from elites and delivers it into the hands of the common people, would simply forever lack the vigor and the discipline and the determination to fight wars. Were not the common people ignorant, lazy, unable to discipline themselves? Did not the common herd everywhere, Europeans believed, need the guiding, strong hand of high-principled, brave, far-seeing aristocrats?

Indeed, Americans themselves had been highly uncertain on these points. Their country was so new, so untried, so fragile; "its people [were] acutely sensitive to the fact," writes Robert W. Johannsen in *To the Halls of the Montezumas: The Mexican War in the American Imagination* (1985), "that in the eyes of the world they were still an unproven experiment in popular government," one that Europeans regularly scoffed at. "Viewing themselves as an island of republicanism surrounded by the tempestuous sea of monarchical oppression . . . [to] them the Mexican War was [therefore] a giant stride in their quest

for national identity, testing American democracy as it had never been tested before." And Americans, people said, had passed the sternest test of all, war itself, with flying colors! Their country had finally earned the reputation it had always claimed, as the "model republic" in the world.

So the Mexican War, as the amazing victories burst on the world's consciousness and rolled on, one after the other, became a wildly popular undertaking in the United States. It was the country's first foreign war, fought on alien soil; it was the first to be covered extensively by reporters in the field, who published floods of exciting copy in the new mass-circulation penny press; and its progress obsessed the country. The whole vast affair, spread over thousands of miles of exotic country and amongst (to Americans) an exotic people, was seen as a fantastic romantic adventure. Far more men volunteered for service than could even be put to use. The war was quickly on stage in florid dramas, sheet music put patriotic songs into parlors and saloons, and novels hastily written around Mexican War themes poured from the presses to be snapped up by an eager national audience. The

During the Mexican War (1846–1848), a U.S. naval force seized Monterrey, which fell with little resistance.

American volunteer soldiers were of course always shown as good, kind, and courageous men far superior in character to the "dark, skulking, 'inferior' Mexican ranchero. . . ." The American invasion was even depicted as a great rescue operation aimed at liberating the Mexicans from the presumed tyranny of the Roman Catholic Church, as well as from the despotism of General Santa Anna.

The sequence of smashing victories by American armies poured a vastly welcomed flood of new self-confidence into the American spirit. Some said the cause lay in America's superior Anglo-Saxon race, but others said it sprang instead from the superiority of the country's republican system of government, which fostered individual self-respect, the spirit of enterprise, and a readiness to innovate. Ordinary Mexicans, it was said, held back from the fighting because they were under despots, and not much interested in dying for them, whereas the Americans, as citizens of a democracy, were fighting for *their* country, were fighting out of a soaring sense of patriotism. Indeed, most of the American people thought of the Mexican War as a great gesture for republicanism and human progress.

Nonetheless, there was an undercurrent of bitter criticism, emanating primarily from Whig New England. Not only were Polk's explanations regarded as highly questionable but his constant reliance on strained arguments and under-the-table manipulations made him much distrusted. He seemed to prefer devious means, thinking himself shrewd while others thought him simply dishonest. In exhaustive detail congressional critics examined Polk's thesis concerning the Texan boundary, demonstrating that at no time had the Rio Grande been the boundary of Texas while under Mexican rule. An agreement extorted from the captured Santa Anna and repudiated by the Mexican legislature, the only body legally charged with ratifying treaties, had no standing in law or principle. The president, said a Whig congressman from Tennessee, had perverted the truth in order to make the people "believe a lie."

Eventually, many of the American people of the Whig persuasion formed a picture of their president as a man who had been uncandid to the nation, devious in language, and deceitful in methods. One of the chief political issues of the time became nothing less than the character of the chief executive. Polk was distrusted, hated, and reviled. Alexander H. Stephens, a Whig who was later vice-president of the Confederacy, put these feelings succinctly: "Why,

if a man were ambitious of acquiring a reputation for duplicity and equivocation, he could not select a better example in all history than to follow in the footsteps of our President."

The New People: The Spanish-Speaking

Ten thousand lives, $100 million, a great deal moral capital and the undying anger, even hatred, of the Mexican people toward America, as alive today, for this cause, as it has ever been: This was what it cost the United States of America to win the enormous Mexican cession. It left a legacy beyond calculating. There is the permanent memory in the Mexican mind that half of the territory that the Republic of Mexico began with, upon its independence from Spain in 1821, was taken by the United States in 1846. Nonetheless, in whatever way the war with Mexico may presently be understood, few Americans could bring themselves to say now that the territory should all be given back. After several centuries under the Spanish flag, and 25 years under Mexico, it has for 140 years simply been an indissoluble part of the American nation, home to many millions of its citizens, a vast and deeply loved region cherished for its great beauty and immense resources. The conflict that won this treasure, however, has not taken its place in the nation's memory as a glorious event, but rather has been almost banished from that memory, in contrast with how it is viewed south of the border.

Among the most profound consequences of the war was the reaching out to take in, and make a part of the United States citizenry, a people sharply distinct from the rest of the American population: the Spanish-speaking *Californios*, *Tejanos*, and *Nuevo Mexicanos*. The Louisiana Purchase had had a similar effect when another foreign people, the French of Louisiana, were without their asking made a part of America—another Catholic people speaking a separate language. In subsequent years, they would make of the state of Louisiana their own enclave, preserving their ways of life and voting little in national elections while ensuring that they dominated the government of the state itself.

The number of Spanish-speaking people in the Mexican cession was very small, and they were soon inundated in California (in Texas the inundation had long since occurred) by scores of thousands of gold seekers, who rapidly made California an overwhelmingly American state in population. Not until after 1900 would a huge migration from Mexico set in, reestablishing the Spanish-speaking as a major people, in numbers, in the Southwest and California.

But the fact that people from Mexico had arrived in this region before the Americans was of great importance. From Texas to California they had dotted the terrain with Spanish names for watercourses, mountain ranges, and urban settlements. They had opened immense cattle ranges, settled towns, developed mining skills that they taught to the gold rushers in California, and introduced fundamental legal concepts (such as that of community property between [owned jointly by] husbands and wives) that were quickly adopted by American authorities.

Mexican Culture

Unlike the French of Louisiana, the Spanish-speaking peoples of the Southwest and California had their ancient homeland in North America, not in a distant continent. As we have seen in Chapter 1, Mexico, centuries old as a city-building, highly organized, civilized culture, arose from one of North America's own peoples, the Nahúas. Out of them there evolved the immense Aztec Empire centered in Mexico City that the Spaniards conquered in the early 1500s. Into it was brought Spanish culture, by an invading people who always remained a small minority, though absolutely dominant for three centuries, and a rich Mexican culture resulted. Partly Spanish, partly Indian, partly *mestizo* (the name given to those born of Spanish-Indian unions—few Spanish women came to Mexico), it focused upon the Catholic Church in a way that in early American history only the pious Puritans of New England and the Quakers of Pennsylvania perhaps could match.

Indeed, there was a brooding passion about Spanish Catholicism, arising from its centuries-old struggle to drive the Muslims out of Spain, that Protestantism seemed not to contain. Church and state were interwoven in a sacred, mutually supportive relationship massively unified against theological error and massively combined in a great crusade for Christ. Authority was absolutely centralized, in government and in worship. Indeed, within the *hacienda* itself (the large landed estate or ranch which was the typical Mexican agricultural unit), all power over

everyone resident on the property was in the hands of the landowner.

And for the Spanish-speaking *Californio, Nuevo Mexicano,* and *Tejano,* as for the Irish Catholic entering America in huge numbers in this very decade of the 1840s, the Catholic priest was everything: holy father; the only learned man among an uneducated people; the center of the community, and yet beyond it. He was chosen not by his parishioners, in the Protestant fashion, nor did he preach primarily from the Bible, which was regarded by Protestants as the sole source of the divine word. Rather, he was sent to them by a faraway bishop, himself spokesman for an even more awesome and remote figure, the Pope in Rome, whose authority was believed to come from Christ himself. The local priest was part of the great Teaching Authority of the Church, in Catholic belief created by Christ to be a separate, divine body mediating between fallen humanity and God. Thus, in itself, the Church was the source of the divine word; it was the agency that would read and interpret the Bible to the laity.

The Catholic altar was a place where in Catholic belief miracles daily occurred, during the Mass. The priest, properly ordained and given these powers, presided over the mystical transformation of bread and wine into the body and blood of the Savior. Taking regularly the sacrament of Communion (the Eucharist) was in Catholic belief far more powerful in saving the soul than the spoken word, which was given out in Protestant churches in long sermons. The sacraments were believed to be pure, sufficient in themselves, never changing in their divine power. And so too (its adherents held) was the Church: centuries old, embattled, faced by the great Protestant heresy, but in divine truth if not in daily fact the one true universal church. Meanwhile, the parishioners, properly confessed of their sins to the priest, who stood careful watch over their moral lives, were enabled regularly to feed upon the Savior. By this saving grace, as ancient doctrine taught, they were assisted in keeping their souls in precarious union with him.

For the Spanish-speaking of the Mexican Cession, the Treaty of Guadalupe Hidalgo was the beginning of the end. Their land titles were supposedly guaranteed under its terms, but in practice thousands lost their property because American courts refused to accept as valid the vaguely drawn title documents the earlier Mexican and Spanish authorities had issued. The California rancheros went through a shattering tragedy, being summoned to courts hundreds of miles from their homes—in San Francisco—where Anglo-American common-law principles, with their requirements of precision in land descriptions, and the heavy fees of American lawyers, brought about loss of their lands by either legal judgment or bankruptcy. In addition, the chaotic economic conditions that erupted with the American conquest plunged rancheros into overwhelming complications. Proud families of ancient lineage were soon poverty-stricken.

There were "few Californians [who] regretted having become Yankees," writes the historian Leonard Pitt in his *Decline of the Californios: A Social History of the Spanish-Speaking Californians, 1846–1890* (1970), but they could only reflect bitterly that they were "a ruling class militarily conquered, bereft of national sovereignty and a constitutional framework, and alienated from their land, homes, civil rights, and honor. They had retained little else besides their religion and a thin residue of honorary political influence." The Spanish-speaking were driven from the gold mines by Americans, treated with contempt for their language and culture, and given only the lowest and most ill-paid jobs. In the vast region that had once been theirs, they eventually found themselves a propertyless and practically voiceless minority.

The War's Legacy

Americans were immensely enthused about their country at the end of the Mexican War. "Our destiny," boasted the *New York Herald* in March 1848, "has been more clearly developed within the past two years than at any time before or since the Declaration of Independence." It was now a nation that swept from the Atlantic to the Pacific, it was far larger than all of Europe (without Russia), and its great and unexpected military victory had given republicanism wholly new respect in the world. The honor gained by the fighting had catapulted America, it was said, into an honored place in the "history of civilization and the human race." Many believed

that the Mexican War was the final declaration that their country had moved from youth to full maturity.

And then the most amazing thing happened: Within weeks after the Mexican War was formally ended, news began flooding in from California that its mountains were yielding buckets full of gold! As Robert Johanssen has written:

> It was easy for an astonished populace to identify a larger national purpose in the event. The object of three centuries of desperate searching had been revealed, not to men lured by visions of instant wealth nor to adventurers motivated by a vulgar greed but to the "hardy emigrant," to the citizen of a republic! What had been denied the "indolent Spaniard" had been granted the energetic [Americans]. . . . The ink on the peace treaty was scarcely dry before California disclosed its riches to its new owners. It was almost as if God had kept the gold hidden until the land came into the possession of the American republic.

Everything seemed to be going for their "beloved country." Americans, said President Polk, were clearly the "most favored people on the face of the earth." The year 1848 was certainly, he observed, the "miracle year" in a remarkable century. "Our country," insisted the *American Review*, "has entered on a new epoch in its history. From this year we take a new start in national development; one that must, more than ever before, draw the world's history into the stream of ours."

Behind the soaring spirits, however, lay a brooding question that would eventually turn the future into a nightmare, not into a glorious utopia. What were the Americans going to do about slavery in the vast territories it had taken from Mexico? As early as August 1846 a Pennsylvania Democrat of Free Soil convictions, David Wilmot, had offered a proviso to a military appropriations bill stipulating that any territory acquired by the United States as a result of the war was to be free of slavery. Violent emotions in both South and North were thereby released. Once opened, the issue of slavery could never again be closed. It remains now to examine slavery and its impact on national life from 1830 to the Compromise of 1850.

BIBLIOGRAPHY

Books that were especially valuable to me in thinking about and writing this chapter: Robert W. Johannsen's fascinating, richly detailed, and well-written *To the Halls of the Montezumas: The Mexican War in the American Imagination* (1985); an insightful essay by William Hanchett,

"Americans and Their First Foreign War," *Reviews in American History*, 14 (March 1986), 76–82. He tells us of the remarkable surge in recent scholarship on the Mexican War, especially by the revisionists, and he points to Norman E. Tutorow's extraordinary *The Mexican-Ameri-*

can War: An Annotated Bibliography (1981), which lists and discusses 4,537 titles. Matt S. Meier and Feliciano Rivera, *The Chicanos: A History of Mexican Americans* (1972), helped me greatly in understanding events in California as well as in all of the northern Mexican states; Seymour V. Connor and Odie B. Faulk, *North America Divided: The Mexican War 1846–1848* (1971), offer a spirited revisionist work that rejects the "bad war" thesis; Leonard Pitt's *The Decline of the Californios: A Social History of the Spanish-Speaking Californians, 1846–1890* (1970) was most useful. Frederick Merk's absorbing *Manifest Destiny and Mission in American History: A Reinterpretation* (1966) changed in dramatic ways our traditional understanding of this period's expansionist ideas. I also relied on the superb biography *James K. Polk: Continentalist, 1843–1846* (1966) by Charles Grier Sellers, Jr.; and Ray Allen Billington's many writings on the West and the frontier, especially *The Far Western Frontier, 1830–1860* (1956). Concerning the Sioux, I learned much from an article by Richard White, "The Winning of the West: The Expansion of the Western Sioux in the Eighteenth and Nineteenth Centuries," *The Journal of American History*, 65 (September 1978), 319–43.

Whether depicted through a dime novel or a television series, the saga of the Far West has charmed generations of Americans. Billington's admirable *Westward Expansion* (1967) as well as his comprehensive study mentioned above illustrate the high quality of scholarship among historians who have tried to portray the realities of the adventure of westward migration, a progress that often involves debunking popular legends. Thomas D. Clark's *Frontier America* (1959) is also a valuable survey, full of accurate and intriguing detail. Firsthand accounts of pioneer life are extensively used in John A. Hawgood's *America's Western Frontier* (1967). LeRoy R. Hafen and Carl C. Rister concentrate on the trans-Mississippi West in their excellent *Western America* (1950).

Before Americans surged to the Pacific, Spaniards made lasting imprints on the vast expanse of the American Southwest. Herbert I. Priestley credits the Spanish as the van-

guard of European civilization in *The Coming of the White Man* (1930), and George P. Hammond's *Don Juán de Oñate and the Founding of New Mexico* (1926) is an illuminating study of Spanish colonization and Indian policy. John Caughey's *California* (1953) and Walton Bean's *California: An Interpretive History* (1968) are fine general accounts of the alluring land named for a mystical island. Willa Cather's sensitive novels, especially *Death Comes for the Archbishop* (1927), maximize the human drama of the Spanish experience.

The most absorbing recent book on the meaning and influence of Manifest Destiny is Frederick Merk's book cited above. Albert K. Weinberg's *Manifest Destiny* (1935) remains excellent, in part because of its revealing quotations. The crucial year of expansion is highlighted in Bernard De Voto's *The Year of Decision, 1846* (1943). Diplomacy and foreign policy make up a central part of the story of westward expansion. Norman A. Graebner's *Empire on the Pacific* (1955) is an important interpretation that points to the vital role of the desire for western seaports. Frederick Merk's *The Monroe Doctrine and American Expansion, 1843–1849* (1966) probes the psychology of American expansionism under Tyler and Polk. A more detailed examinaton of Tyler's principles is found in Robert J. Morgan's *A Whig Embattled* (1954). For a good view of Mexico's concerns about U.S. expansionism, see Gene M. Brack, *Mexico Views Manifest Destiny, 1821–1846* (1975). See also John H. Schroeder, *Mr. Polk's War: American Opposition and Dissent, 1846–1848* (1973), and Chaplain W. Morrison, *Democratic Politics and Sectionalism: The Wilmot Proviso Controversy* (1967).

Two excellent one-volume presentations of the Mexican War are available: A. H. Bill, *Rehearsal for Conflict: The War with Mexico, 1846–1848* (1947), which uses as its central theme the preparation this war gave to many men who were leaders in the Civil War, and Otis A. Singletary's *The Mexican War* (1960), which emphasizes the petty military and political ambitions that led the United States into a war of aggression against Mexico.

15

Abolitionism: The Building Storm

TIME LINE

HISTORY IN AN INDIVIDUAL LIFE

FREDERICK DOUGLASS

It was 1838, abolitionism was rumbling in Congress, and in Baltimore an uneasy young black man, Frederick Douglass, boarded a northbound train. A skilled shipyard worker and a slave, he had borrowed a "pass" given to free black seamen who came ashore in Southern ports. When the conductor accepted it as Douglass's, his twenty-one years of slavery were over.

Soon he was a close associate of William Lloyd Garrison, the famous abolitionist. A gifted writer and orator who had taught himself literacy, and a striking black man whose imposing, upright figure and courageous character caught national attention, Douglass was shortly traveling widely on regular tours in the Northern states to speak for the cause. He published a best-selling memoir, *Narrative of the Life of Frederick Douglass* (1845), and endured violent physical assaults. In England in the mid 1840s, Douglass built a large following for abolitionism in America. Then, from Rochester, New York, he began publishing one of the first black weeklies in the nation, *The North*

Star. For the next fifteen years, he sent out from this pulpit a trumpet voice across the United States in the cause of black freedom and justice. He also provided in his journal an outlet for black essayists, columnists, and poets, aiming in this way to challenge the charge of black inferiority.

As the leading black American, Douglass guided the black abolitionist movement in its many conventions and declarations. At the same time, he battled against Jim Crow segregationist laws in the North, urged young blacks to acquire skills, and also threw his support behind the emerging women's movement. Douglass had long since rejected Garrison's condemnation of political action to win abolition, and he worked hard to make the Liberty party a strong influence in national politics. Then in 1858 an old friend, John Brown, visited in his home; twenty months later, Brown's assault on the Harper's Ferry arsenal was made, and the rush of the United States toward secession and war took on gathering speed.

Thirty years of life remained to Frederick Douglass after the Civil War began, and he never ceased laboring for the black cause. He insisted to Abraham Lincoln that black men should be allowed to fight in the Northern armies, and that they must be given equal status with whites as soldiers. In the Reconstruction years, he demanded the vote for black men as their main weapon in the struggle for equality and integration. On the use of jailed black men as convict laborers, the crop-lien system (which virtually made peons of Southern black farmers), the lynch law, and other civil rights issues, Douglass's voice rang out from the 1870s to the 1890s. At his death in 1895, five state legislatures mourned him, and the Washington *Post*, summing up the national view of the greatest of the Civil War generation of black men, said that he died "in an epoch which he did more than any other to create."

The Rage of South Carolina

The state of South Carolina seethed with anger in 1830. The immediate cause was the Tariff of Abominations, enacted in 1828, but the real irritant lay deeper. On every side that state felt besieged by the North. Abolitionist literature was finding its way southward in increasing volume, and the slaves seemed aroused by what they could learn of it. Because of the state's huge slave population—three blacks to every white around Charleston, as high as eight to one in the lowland districts along the coast—its white population was haunted by fears of slave revolt. South Carolina was practically a garrison state, having organized a huge militia to deal with feared black rebellion.

Worse yet, cotton prices had steadily declined in the 1820s. Squeezed between declining incomes and rising costs, which they attributed to the protectionist Tariff of 1828, South Carolina's aristocracy was in an ugly mood. In the best of times, they were unique in the Southern states for their prickliness. They could flash in an instant from gentle courtliness to savage violence, shooting down even close friends if a slight to "honor" were detected. Public men often bore the scars of dueling wounds or carried the enviable reputation of many successful encounters.

The fate of George McDuffie demonstrated the cruelty of losing. His dueling wounds never healed. Festering, slowly destroying his nerves, they made him almost a paralytic wreck. Once genial and likable, he became a brooding, permanently angry man who screamed and raved on the floor of Congress whenever South Carolina's grievances were at issue. Led by such men, it is no wonder that South Carolina was frequently swept by towering rages and in such moments given to challenging the entire nation.

South Carolinians had hoped that Andrew Jackson, elected in 1828, might lower the tariff. When he did not, they opened their campaign for its repeal. They attacked not simply the tariff's actual duties (which made the cloth they had to buy in large quantities for their slaves much more expensive), but the whole idea of "general welfare" legislation. The federal government, they insisted, should not exact tariffs to achieve a social purpose, such as aiding industrial growth, but simply to raise a revenue. Social improvement of any sort was not the proper subject of government. It was their solemn duty, South Carolinians insisted, to find some way to halt the steady encroachment of national power on the states.

Enraged by the Tariff of 1828, George McDuffie gave one of his typical speeches in Congress in 1831:

> South Carolina is oppressed [a thump]. A tyrant majority sucks her life blood from her [a dreadful thump]. Yes, sir [a pause], yes, sir, a tyrant [a thump] majority unappeased [arms aloft], unappeasable [horrid scream], has persecuted and persecutes us [a stamp on the floor]. We appeal to them [low and quick], but we appeal in vain [loud and quick]. We turn to our brethren of the north [low, with a shaking of the head], and pray for them to protect us [a thump], but we t-u-r-n in v-a-i-n [prolonged, and a thump]. They heap coals of fire on our heads [with immense rapidity]—they give us burden on burden; they tax us more and more [very rapid, slam-bang, slam—a hideous noise]. We turn to our brethren of the south [slow with a solemn, thoughtful air]. We work with them; we fight with them; we vote with them; we petition with them [common voice and manner]; but the tyrant majority has no ears, no eyes, no form [quick], deaf [long pause], sightless [pause], inexorable [slow, slow]. Despairing [a thump], we resort to the rights [a pause] which God [a pause] and nature have given us [thump, thump, thump]." (Quoted in William W. Freehling, Prelude to Civil War: The Nullification Controversy in South Carolina, 1816–1836 [1968])

John C. Calhoun, Jackson's vice-president, prepared South Carolina's argument, retiring to his home in 1828 for the purpose. Adopted, printed, and widely circulated by the state legislature as the South Carolina Exposition and Protest, it became South Carolina's official explanation of its position. The American system of government, the exposition insisted, had to be changed. No law of major importance should become effective until supported by a "concurrent majority"—that is, until each minority had agreed to it. Since each state, Calhoun believed, represented a single minority interest, his plan meant giving each the power to nullify federal laws. This, he insisted, was the *only* way the Union could survive.

Such a system was justified, Calhoun wrote, because each state was absolutely sovereign within its borders. The Union was no more than a compact among fully sovereign states that they could break at will. The power of nullification, however, was so weighty a one to exercise that it should be implemented only by specially elected state conventions. This would ensure that the issue concerned would receive the solemn consideration due a major crisis.

For three years, from 1828 to 1831, events outside South Carolina heightened its sense of alarm. In 1829 Mexico terminated slavery, which set off a controversy in the province of Texas. The same year saw a debate in Congress over the slave trade in the District of Columbia, resulting in condemnatory resolutions. In January 1831 a determined young man, William Lloyd Garrison, began publishing *The Liberator* in Boston, filling it with radical demands for the immediate abolition of slavery.

Then, in Virginia, the South's fears were realized. In the summer of 1831, a slave named Nat Turner led a rebellion in which all the white men, women, and children in a district near Richmond—a total of fifty-seven—were slaughtered. This was the bloodiest slave rebellion ever to break out in the Southern states. Although it did not spread to South Carolina, the whites there were wild with fear. They imprisoned many blacks, gathered together white women and children for protection, intensified patrols, and formed a cavalry unit to protect the city of Charleston. Governor John Floyd of Virginia described Turner's rebellion as caused by a "spirit of insubordination" spread around the South by Yankee traders, evangelical missionaries, and abolitionist fanatics.

The Nullification Crisis

Moderates in South Carolina had been able to hold back the nullification flood until this time, but now the extremists took the lead. The atmosphere intensified in 1832, when Congress enacted a new, more protective tariff. Since large parts of South Carolina were suffering a severe depression, desperation now seized its people.

Moderates and nullificationists concentrated on electing a new state legislature in 1832. When the ballots came in, they revealed a sweeping nullification triumph. The new legislature, quickly convened for a special session, called a special election for a nullification convention. By November 1832 that body had met and formally adopted an Ordinance of Nullification. It declared the tariffs of 1828 and 1832 unconstitutional, and null and void in South Carolina. The convention called on Congress to lower the tariff to a 12 percent level by the following February. If its demands were not met by then, nullification would be put into effect. If Congress authorized the use of force instead of compromising, such action would be "inconsistent with the longer continuance of South Carolina in the Union."

Every other Southern legislature condemned nullification as "unsound in theory and dangerous in practice." Andrew Jackson, for his part, was determined to uphold national authority. At the same time, however, he urged Congress to lower the tariff. Jackson then formally rejected the constitutional theory advanced by Calhoun. In his Nullification Proclamation of December 10, 1832, he declared that the federal government was supreme in the Constitution. Allowing each state a veto was nonsensical, he said, for if a government could not enforce its own laws it was nothing less than a standing contradiction, a philosophical absurdity. The power of nullification was "*incompatible with the existence of the Union, contradicted expressly by the letter of the Constitution, unauthorized by its spirit, inconsistent with every principle on which it was founded, and destructive of the great object for which it was formed.*"

Furthermore, he warned, men should know that bringing about disunion by armed force was treason. In the face of such a threat, the "First Magistrate can not, if he would, avoid the performance of his duty." Jackson then stepped nimbly to avoid using force. He moved the collection of customs to federal forts in the bay, where collectors could work unmolested. He also secured a "force bill" from Congress in early 1833, which reaffirmed his legal authority to call up state militias and national forces and granted him greater powers to use the courts to enforce collection of duties.

The situation was rapidly deteriorating for the nullificationists. Short of a direct attack on the federal forts, no alternative save defeat presented itself. Virginia then offered to mediate, and South Carolina eagerly grasped the opportunity. Led by Henry Clay, Congress did its part by enacting the Compromise Tariff, which drastically dropped the tariff in stages to a 20 percent level by 1842, but most of the reductions were to be made in the last few years of the ten-year span. At the same time, an overwhelming majority enacted the force bill. South Carolina then rescinded its nullification ordinance.

The tariff was lowered, but nullification as a principle had been destroyed. Both President Jackson and Congress had so strongly reaffirmed the supremacy of national law that the power to nullify was never again seriously advanced. Only one means of challenging majority rule was left: secession, with its probable result of civil war. This knowledge—coupled with a fortunate upward swing in cotton prices after the crisis—moderated the South's tactics during most of the next thirty years.

"Old School" Abolitionism

The Nullification Crisis changed the character of the antislavery movement, which had had strong Southern roots and for many years had employed moderate and gradualist tactics. The American Convention for Promoting the Abolition of Slavery, founded in the 1790s, had 130 local societies in the South in 1827, as against 24 in the North. Relying on conciliatory efforts to persuade Southern whites of the need for abolition, it looked to the far future as the time when slavery would come to an end and counseled blacks to be patient.

A favorite project was the American Colonization Society, which sought to solve the race problem by sending blacks back to Africa. Founded in 1816, it was based on the belief that black people could find equality only among their own race. Widely supported by such men as Henry Clay and James Monroe, it was given congressional appropriations and encouraged by many resolutions passed in state legislatures. In 1820 the first group of eighty-eight black colonists left for the West African coast. In 1822, the society founded Liberia, maintaining control over the colony until it declared its full independence in 1847.

A large segment of the American people, however, bitterly opposed the plan: those who were both free and black. In 1830 they numbered 320,000. (By 1850 there were roughly 435,000 free blacks in the United States, as against some 3,200,000 slaves.) They rejected the implication that they were not fit to live in equality with whites, and they had no interest whatever in Africa. When James Forten, a wealthy black sailmaker, posed the question of support for colonization to a crowded black audience in a Philadelphia church in 1817, the long, loud "No!" that went up unanimously from the gathering "seemed as if it would bring down the walls of the building." In its quarter-century of supervision over Liberia, the American Colonization Society succeeded in persuading fewer than 3,000 blacks to leave the United States and become Americo-Liberians.

"New School" Abolitionism

A "new school" type of abolitionism, which rejected moderatism and colonization alike, arose in response to the Nullification Crisis. Harsh, uncompromising, radical, the new movement was symbolized by William Lloyd Garrison. A twenty-six-year-old newspaperman with a prematurely bald head, steel-rimmed spectacles, and a sharp New Englander's nose, Garrison was made a national figure by the South's violent criticism of him during the Nullification Crisis. His boast in the first issue of his newspaper, *The Liberator*, "I will not equivocate—I will not excuse—I will not retreat a single inch—AND I WILL BE HEARD," was already famous. Ironically, *The Liberator* had only a tiny circulation. Few would ever have heard of it had not Southerners so violently and unendingly denounced it.

Most Northerners detested Garrison. He was frequently mobbed. His warmest friends and supporters were the free blacks, who gave him an undying affection that he returned with equal fervor. Blacks were the chief buyers and supporters of his newspaper; they accompanied him home at night through dark streets to protect him; he spoke in black churches time and again when other reformers would have nothing to do personally with blacks; he traveled with them constantly; and he argued unendingly not only for abolition but for black equality in Northern society as well—a notion repugnant to many of his white colleagues.

In 1831 Garrison helped to form the New England Anti-Slavery Society, and in 1833 he went to Philadelphia to participate in forming a national organization, the American Anti-Slavery Society. That body adopted a Declaration of Sentiments, which struck the key Garrisonian note: *immediatism*—free the slaves *now*. But how were the slaves to be freed? This was the dilemma the antislavery movement never solved. Garrison, in fact, held the national government in complete contempt. Because it allowed slavery to exist, it was a compact with sin. He even favored breaking up the Union on the ground that this would so weaken the South that it would no longer be able to keep blacks enslaved. How was slavery to be ended? By exhortation; by creating a new consciousness, a new way of thinking, among white Southerners. Through the pulpit and the printed word, the society resolved "to bring the whole nation to speedy repentance. Our trust for victory is solely in GOD."

The Declaration of Sentiments of the American Anti-Slavery Society stated, in part:

> *That every American citizen, who retains a human being in involuntary bondage, as his property is (according to Scripture) a* MAN-STEALER.
>
> *That the slaves ought instantly to be set free. . . .*
>
> *That . . . their right to be free could never have been alienated. . . .*
>
> *That all those laws which are now in force, admitting the right of slavery, are therefore before God utterly null and void; being an audacious usurpation of the Divine prerogative, a daring infringement on the law of nature, a base overthrow of the very foundations of the social compact, a complete extinction of all the relations, endearments and obligations of mankind, and a presumptuous transgression of all the holy commandments—and that therefore they ought to be instantly abrogated.*
>
> *That all persons of color who possess the qualifications which are demanded of others, ought to be admitted forthwith to the enjoyment of the same privileges, and the exercise of the same prerogatives, as others; and that the paths of preferment, of wealth, and of intelligence, should be opened as widely to them as to persons of a white complexion.*
>
> *We maintain that no compensation should be given to the planters emancipating their slaves—*
>
> *Because it would be a surrender of the great fundamental principle, that man cannot hold property in man;*
>
> *Because* SLAVERY IS A CRIME, AND THEREFORE IT IS NOT AN ARTICLE TO BE SOLD. . . .

> *Because if compensation is to be given at all, it should be given to the outraged and guiltless slaves, and not to those who have plundered and abused them. (Quoted in* The Abolitionist, *the publication of the American Anti-Slavery Society, 1 [December 1833])*

New-school abolitionism sprang directly out of Yankee America and the Second Great Awakening. Congregationalists, Presbyterians, Methodists, and Baptists led the attack. Its most intensive center of activity was in western New York, which was being settled thickly by westward-migrating New Englanders. (In the 1840s, six out of ten New Yorkers were Yankees.) Slavery was thought of as nothing more than individual sin grown gigantic through the fact that many individuals engaged in it. All that was needed was for slaveowners to recognize their involvement in sin and renounce it—just as they might renounce drink, or sexual intercourse with prostitutes, or swearing.

Seventy traveling preachers were trained by the society and sent throughout Ohio, New York, and New England to spread the message. They described the slaveholder as a man-thief, child seller, and woman whipper. As the exhorters went about the country dealing out this verbal mayhem, they were proudly called "he-goat men . . . butting everything in their line of march . . . made up of vinegar, aqua fortis, and oil of vitriol, with brimstone, saltpetre and charcoal, to explode and scatter the corrosive matter."

Violent words led to violent reactions. Wherever abolitionists went, they were bitterly hated and

Mild-mannered, youthful William Lloyd Garrison, founder and editor of the *Liberator*, published in Boston, was absolutely unyielding in his opposition to slavery.

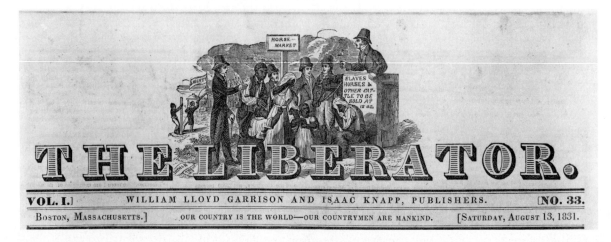

THE LIBERATOR.

VOL. I.]   WILLIAM LLOYD GARRISON AND ISAAC KNAPP, PUBLISHERS.   [NO. 33.

BOSTON, MASSACHUSETTS.]   OUR COUNTRY IS THE WORLD—OUR COUNTRYMEN ARE MANKIND.   [SATURDAY, AUGUST 13, 1831.

personally assaulted. Attacks on abolitionist newspaper offices were unrelenting, culminating in the murder of Elijah P. Lovejoy in 1837 by a mob in Alton, Illinois, when he sought to prevent the fourth destruction of his press. Abolitionists were accused of bringing on racial intermarriage and the debasement of white people.

Furthermore, people feared that the abolitionists were breaking up the Union. Ministers were discharged from their pastorates, and professors were expelled from colleges. Businessmen organized boycotts, bankers called in debts, judges lost their seats, and meeting places were regularly denied to abolitionist gatherings or burned down. The decade of the 1830s was called the "martyr age" by abolitionists, and with good reason. They said this with grim relish, however, for in those same years local antislavery societies sprang into being by the hundreds. By 1838 there were more than 1,300 societies with perhaps 250,000 members, who were overwhelmingly Yankee in ethnic background.

The Petition Campaign

As the years passed, however, no significant results came from the abolitionist movement. The antislavery societies in the South quickly disappeared after the appearance of new school abolitionism in the North. All attempts to gain a specific objective clearly within federal authority, such as ending slavery in the District of Columbia or stopping interstate slave trade, failed miserably. The South, however, never realized how weak abolitionism actually was. The violent words abolitionists put into the air seemed all by themselves extremely threatening to the South. Perhaps they were.

The examples of Nat Turner and Denmark Vesey were proof to the Southern white that certain kinds of words could not be heard in the South without causing terrible events. In July 1835, Charleston citizens broke into the local post office, took out packages of literature that had recently arrived, and burned them in the street. A clamor for censorship of the mails arose in the South, and Andrew Jackson, thoroughly angered with the abolitionists, agreed. The administration gave local postmasters enough authority to keep abolitionist literature out of the mails from then on.

Congress, meanwhile, was besieged by floods of petitions from Northern groups calling for an end to slavery. In May 1836 Southern congressmen, primarily Democrats, prevented the words of the abolitionists from even being uttered in Congress. They secured passage of a "gag rule" by the House that prevented all such petitions from being read to the body or discussed. This was a serious mistake. Northerners in general, who had little interest in black people, were aroused, for their own liberties now seemed in danger. Furthermore, the power of the South in the national government was now highlighted as if in a flare of white light. Some Northerners began to talk about a "Southern conspiracy," a "slavocracy" that was taking over the Democratic party and dominating the federal government.

In doing so they revived Northern opposition to the expansion of the Southern system. John Quincy Adams, now a representative from Massachusetts, angrily began a long campaign against the gag rule. Year after year he carried on the struggle, devising all sorts of parliamentary devices for getting his petitions into open debate. He was constantly censured and threatened with expulsion. The gallant campaign of Old Man Eloquence against all odds caught the admiration of the nation and encouraged thousands to give their support to abolitionism. In 1844 Adams finally won his long battle, securing the abolition of the gag rule.

Anglo-American Abolitionism

During the petition controversy, abolitionism reached its international high point. The same churches in Great Britain as in America led the attack on slavery, and these churches maintained close ties across the Atlantic. The British abolitionists had won the first great antislavery victory in 1807, when they secured the end of the slave trade in the empire, an event that helped to bring on the American prohibition of the trade in 1808. In 1833 British antislavery workers won the ultimate victory: the abolition of slavery itself in the empire (with compensation to slaveholders). Of course, the task was much simpler in Britain than in America, since no part of Britain itself was actually using slavery and therefore deeply committed to its continuance. It was a matter of overriding the power of the West Indian plantation owners, who had influence but not actual voting representation in Parliament.

Abolitionists such as William Lloyd Garrison looked to Britain for advice, money, and approval. That the British lionized him during a trip he made to the United Kingdom in 1833 was enough to elevate him to leadership of abolitionism in the United States. The American Anti-Slavery Society itself was fashioned on the British model. Frederick Douglass, the ex-slave who did so much to advance the abolitionist cause by his own labors and example, observed that "the abolition movement in America was largely derived from England."

In June 1840 the point of highest transatlantic excitement was reached when more than 500 Anglo-American abolitionist delegates to the World Anti-Slavery Convention gathered in Freemasons' Hall, London. For a week they debated, drafted resolutions, and exhorted one another, the chief object of the entire proceeding being to mobilize opinion in both countries against American slavery.

Schism and Dismay

Abolitionism in America, however, was already falling into disharmony and disarray. Garrison had decided that abolitionism should join forces with other reform movements, notably that for improving women's rights. Women, too, as we observed earlier, were an oppressed class and were denied the right to speak in public. When gifted women such as Harriet Beecher Stowe and the Grimké sisters entered the antislavery movement, they were forced to remain silent at meetings and were sometimes required to sit in the balcony, as at the World Convention in London.

Garrison thought this monstrous. Bringing a steamboat full of women's rights advocates to the annual convention of the American Anti-Slavery Society in New York in 1840, he succeeded in committing the organization to, among other causes, the "woman question." The result, however, was to split the abolition movement, for many angrily disagreed with this tactic. Abolitionism, they believed, should concentrate on its one great issue and not disperse its concerns and energies on other unpopular reforms. This would only increase the number of their opponents. Many specifically condemned the admission of women into the society. Why, such critics asked, could they not form their own organization? These dissidents immediately withdrew from the parent body to form a rival, the American and Foreign Anti-Slavery Society, to which most British abolitionists turned their support.

This was not the only issue that divided abolitionists. The new school type of extremist oratory had long disturbed many antislavery workers. They

drew back from Garrison, considering him an un-Christian, uncharitable man. Merely to own slaves, said such men as the Reverend Leonard Bacon, a New England Congregationalist, was not a sin in itself, for slaveowners had been born into their situation. Garrison retaliated by condemning Northern churches in the same terms he used for the United States government. As a result, most Congregational churches in New England closed their doors to abolitionists in the middle 1830s.

The key fact was that Garrison, condemning the government as wholly corrupt and anti-Christian, would have nothing to do with using politics to free slaves. He and his followers would not vote or hold office. Those who favored a political approach now looked upon the abolitionist movement with amused contempt. "If the Anti-Slavery organizations cannot find better business in [the] future than they have been engaged by, for a year or two back," observed the antislavery lawyer Ellis Gray Loring—whose financial support had saved *The Liberator*—"they will assuredly die." And they practically did. They staggered on through the 1840s and 1850s, having little influence on public life. The future lay with such men as Frederick Douglass and the white abolitionist Joshua Giddings of Ohio, who by the mid-1840s were taking the lead in turning the antislavery movement toward political action.

Black Abolitionism

Black Americans in the Northern states were enormously stimulated by new school abolitionism. It offered them for the first time a major role to play in American public life, pulled them out of their traditional political apathy, and, as the historian Benjamin Quarles has written, gave them "a heightened sense of self-respect." From the start they took leading roles in the creation of the American Anti-Slavery Society, held important posts in other key organizations, and established many societies of their own.

The schism between white antislavery advocates had one fruitful result: It brought a flood of new black workers into the movement, for as the whites fell into disarray, greater opportunities were opened to blacks. The schism had another effect as well: It led blacks to regard their white colleagues with more critical eyes. They began remarking that although some abolitionists followed Garrison in working for complete black equality, others in the antislavery movement did not want blacks in their organizations. The latter, said Samuel Ringgold Ward, were reformers who "best love the colored man at a distance." When in the same organization with blacks, white abolitionists generally assumed the superior offices and patronizingly directed the efforts of blacks.

As always, blacks found a great source of strength in their churches. Since there were few blacks in other professions—those being largely closed to them—black leaders were predominantly ministers. Driven out of the white churches by prejudice, Afro-Americans had been forming their own sects for a long time, usually along Baptist or Methodist lines. These congregations were important, for they were the only organized social institutions wholly in black hands. The black lecturer John Mercer Langston said the black church gave the black man the "opportunity to be himself, to think his own thoughts, express his own convictions, make his own utterances, test his own powers, and thus, in the exercise of the faculties of his own soul, trust and achieve."

Black Americans undertook vigorous programs of self-improvement as one important means by which they could strengthen the abolitionist cause. Such programs, as they often observed, would disprove the charge of racial inferiority. Self-improvement took many forms, from temperance campaigns to mutual-aid organizations, libraries, and literary societies. Great efforts were concentrated on establishing schools. In 1827 only ten black schools existed in the Northern states. Thereafter the efforts of black and white abolitionists changed this situation markedly.

The rise of a black press was just as notable as that of black schools. At least seventeen newspapers were published before the Civil War by Afro-Americans, their constant concern being the demand for emancipation. Bearing such titles as *Freedom's Journal* and *The Rights of All*, they boosted antislavery books, printed antislavery literary efforts, and worked to bolster racial pride. "I thank our Father," wrote Junius C. Morel, "that it has pleased him in his wisdom to order our color just as he has." One topic frequently argued was the question of which name black Americans should adopt. The editor of *The Colored American* argued for his own terminology, saying, "We are written about, preached to, and prayed for, as Negroes, Africans, and blacks, all of which have been stereotyped, as terms of reproach, and on that account, if no other, are unacceptable."

The most dramatic and effective single effort of black self-help was in aiding runaway slaves through what was called the Underground Railroad. Northern blacks often went into Southern states, at great risk to themselves, to bring slaves out. Harriet Tubman was the most famous of these "conductors," making fifteen forays into slave territory after her own escape in 1849 and bringing back more than 300 fugitives. Others were middlemen, working on Northern railroads and smuggling slaves on their way. There were also scores of black families who provided

An 1850 lithograph of Henry "Box" Brown, who escaped from slavery in Richmond, Virginia, by mailing himself north in a box 3 feet long, 2½ feet deep, and 2 feet wide.

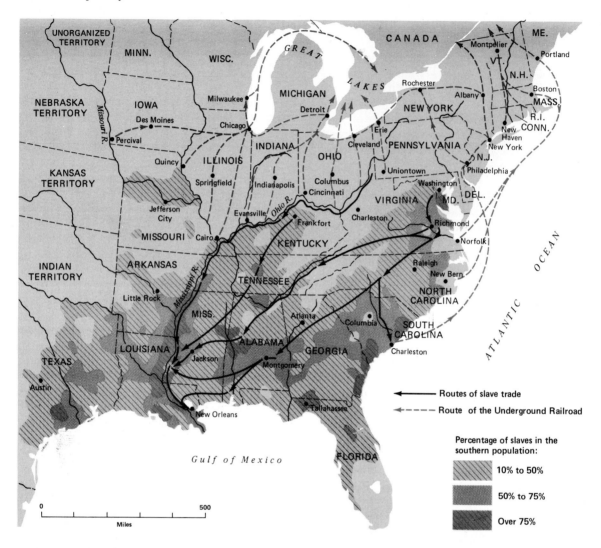

Slavery and the Underground Railroad, 1840–1860

hiding places in their homes. White workers in the Underground Railroad often did not see the men whose flight they were assisting, for they hid in black homes. "I have no confidence whatever in white people," one of them said. "They are only trying to get us back into slavery."

Blacks struggled hard to use the ballot in their own behalf, but were frustrated. In 1860 equal suffrage was available to the black man only in New England, excluding Connecticut. Elsewhere he was either barred from the polls or faced with a heavy property qualification. Often these barriers were raised for blacks while being lowered for white men. In Pennsylvania the vote was actually taken away from blacks in 1838, at a time when a more "demo-

cratic" constitution was being adopted. This was a terrible blow to black morale. The white people of Pennsylvania were enraged with abolitionists and determined to make the black man suffer.

Abolitionism Moves into Politics

Meanwhile, those abolitionists who were entering politics in the 1840s to gain their end were struggling through the question of what tactic to adopt. Many decided on creating a separate party. In Warsaw, New York, they formed the National Liberty party in 1839, with the active support of Frederick Douglass. They chose James G. Birney, a wealthy former slave owner from Kentucky, as their presidential candidate in 1840. Running on a platform that called simply for an end to slavery, he secured the disappointing total of about 7,000 scattered votes in the election of 1840.

This discouraging result led the party to broaden its appeal. It approached the election of 1844 with high hopes, strengthened by a platform that appealed to many reform interests and also condemned the annexation of Texas. Defeat, however, was again their portion. The vote that Birney garnered rose to more than 60,000, but it was clear that this kind of victory would never put an abolitionist in the White House. A third party founded on abolitionism was clearly doomed.

Other abolitionists turned to the Whig party.

Harriet Tubman, a fugitive from a Maryland plantation, returned many times to the South to free hundreds of slaves by leading them on dangerous routes to freedom in the North.

Joshua Giddings of Ohio was a leading advocate of this tactic. Elected as a Whig to the House of Representatives, he had won a dramatic battle there in 1842 after the House had censured him for his antislavery statements. He promptly resigned, returned to his Ohio district, and was triumphantly reelected. After that, the Whig party in Congress had to make room for him. Giddings then turned to abolitionists in the Northern states and appealed to them to join the Whigs, even if it meant supporting Henry Clay, a slaveowner, for the presidency. The Whigs, Giddings insisted, were actually working for the end on which all antislavery advocates agreed—removing all federal laws that aided and supported slavery. This included those that legalized the slave trade in the District of Columbia and authorized the hunting down of fugitive slaves in the North. Every vote for the Liberty party, he warned, was actually a vote for the Democrats, since it would reduce the Whig total.

Events bore him out, as we have seen. In the election of 1844 the 15,000 votes that went to the Liberty party in New York State, which would otherwise have gone Whig, gave that state, and the presidency, to James K. Polk. This in turn brought about the annexation of Texas, the Mexican War, and the Mexican Cession. "There has never been a vote of any fragment of a party," said the New York *Express*, "so extensively disastrous in its consequences or so pernicious to the ostensible objects of its authors."

The Wilmot Proviso and the Election of 1848

The war with Mexico swept up all those loose ends and discarded them. An entirely new national situation was created by the Mexican Cession of 1848. Was slavery to be allowed in the new territories? The proviso offered by David R. Wilmot of Pennsylvania in the summer of 1846—to exclude slavery from any territory won from Mexico—opened the controversy. The proviso was passed again and again by the House, but rejected by the Senate. The issue, kept thereby in the public eye, dominated the election of 1848.

The Democrats selected Lewis Cass of Michigan after a sharp internal struggle. A firm expansionist, Cass had fought gallantly as a general officer in the War of 1812, had strongly favored the annexation of Texas, had demanded that the United States take *all* of Oregon, and had eagerly pushed the war with Mexico. An opponent of the Wilmot Proviso, he was the first major figure in national politics to broach the idea of "squatter sovereignty." "Leave to the [local] people who will be affected by this question [of slavery], to adjust it upon their own responsibility," he said, "and in their own manner."

Cass's nomination outraged many Northern Democrats. Looking to Martin Van Buren as their leader, they were strongly opposed to the expansion of slavery. With Van Buren they had come to believe—ever since the party went for Polk in 1844 and not for Van Buren—that the Democratic party had come under the control of a Southern conspiracy. The most outspoken among these northerners were the Barnburners of New York State, so called because they were said to be so eager to root Southern control out of the party that they were willing to burn down the barn to expel the rats. The Barnburners, in turn, called Northern Democrats who *favored* Southern policies Hunkers; that is, they so "hunkered" for the patronage jobs that Polk and his Southern supporters could bestow that they supported the expansion of slavery. After Cass's nomination, many Barnburners began talking about running a separate ticket.

The Whigs were also bitterly divided on the slavery issue. For many years such powerful Whigs as the New England textile mill owners had assured Southerners that they had no intention of disturbing slavery. They personally deplored it, but they regarded the system as wholly a domestic institution under the sole control of the various states and beyond interference with by the North. Ever since they had begun the highly profitable business of milling cotton cloth during the War of 1812, they had worked hard to keep a good relationship with the men who supplied them their raw material, the Southern plantation owners. Northern mill owners detested abolitionists and on some occasions joined in mob attacks upon them.

The extension of slavery, however, was another matter. Although he would not disturb slavery where it then existed, said Rufus Choate to a meeting of Boston Whigs, "I still controvert the power, I deny the morality, I tremble for the consequences, of annexing an acre of new territory, for the mere purpose of diffusing this great evil . . . over a wider surface of American earth!" Young Whigs like Charles Francis Adams (John Quincy's son) and Charles Sumner were particularly aroused. In the mid-1840s, they began warning the mill owners who ran their party that New England Whigs should be more concerned with their conscience and less concerned with their cotton.

Whig leaders were determined, however, to find some way to reassure the South while putting a man in the White House who would keep slavery out of the territories. Passing over all Whig leaders whose earlier antislavery or antiexpansionist utterances had outraged the South, they chose the popular Mexican War hero Zachary Taylor. A Southerner and a slaveowner, he had lived for a long time in the Northern states and was more devoted to the nation's survival than he was to slavery, though his stand on slavery expansion was at that time unclear. The young Whigs were furious. Henry H. Wilson of Massachusetts rose on the convention floor to call Taylor's nomination "another and a signal triumph of the Slave Power" and, vowing to do all he could to defeat him, strode out of the hall in a scene of uproar and confusion.

The stage was now set for the almost spontaneous appearance, in a burst of righteous enthusiasm, of the Free-Soil party. Conscience Whigs, Barnburner Democrats, and former supporters of the Liberty party gathered in Buffalo, New York, in August 1848 to create the party and nominate a presidential candidate. Van Buren had issued a public statement just two months before, condemning slavery expansion and insisting that Congress had the constitutional power to prevent its extension into the new territories. Delighted, the Free-Soilers nominated him on a platform that called for "Free soil, free speech, free labor, and free men!" Seized by the triumphant sense of impending victory that inspired the Free-Soilers, John Greenleaf Whittier burst into poetic song:

> *O prisoners in your house of pain,*
> *Dumb, toiling millions, bound and sold,*
> *Look! Stretched o'er Southern vale and plain*
> *The Lord's delivering hand behold.*

Actually, few Free-Soilers were abolitionists. In fact, it has been fashionable among historians to say that they were really racists who wanted free soil only to keep the new territories solely for white men. But the historian Richard Sewell, in *Ballots for Freedom* (1976), has revealed that most Free-Soilers held a more complicated outlook toward black people. They were, like whites generally, prejudiced against them and concerned primarily with battling against the might of the Slave Power in America and the menace of slavery to free institutions, not with helping the black person as such.

On the other hand, however, most Free-Soilers were surprisingly able to rise above the rampant racism of their time. They criticized the usual stereotypes about black inferiority, preached the equality of all humanity, and led not only in defending, but in trying to extend, black civil rights in the Northern states—even though they stayed away from the idea of black equality in *social* relations. This, in reality, was to be the fundamental position of the later Republican party of Abraham Lincoln. As to the ending of slavery, Free-Soilers believed that preventing the extension of slavery into the new territories would lead inevitably to emancipation, since a cooped-in Southern economy, constantly wearing out its soils, would (they thought) have to give up plantation agriculture.

Free-Soilism was also founded in a repugnance toward the "Southern system." It seemed to create only illiteracy and poverty for nonslaveowning whites. The North, on the other hand, was praised by Free-Soilers as being founded on free labor and the opportunity for ordinary people to rise and better themselves. If the "slavocracy" were allowed to take over the territories, they would be lost to the kind of sturdy farmer, mechanic, and small businessman who formed the core of Northern life.

In the election of 1848 the Free-Soilers lost. But Martin Van Buren's large vote—almost 300,000 ballots—took New York State from Lewis Cass and put Zachary Taylor in the White House. Once again, as in 1844, a third party had the deciding influence on the nation's presidential choice. Slavery was bulking ever larger in national politics.

The Slavery Issues Converge

Within two years, the boiling pot of slavery controversy was threatening to erupt and bring on disunion. No decision had yet been made in Washington, on how to provide local government to the vast Mexican Cession, which was still under military rule, following completion of the war. Most crucial, of course, was the issue: Was slavery to be allowed in this new part of the United States of America?

Events on the Pacific Coast forced the crisis. The discovery of gold in California in 1848 and the ensuing helter-skelter rush to the Sierra Nevada in 1849 sent California's non-Indian population soaring from 10,000 to 100,000 people. Clearly, they could not go on indefinitely under military rule. Zachary Taylor, installed in the White House in March 1849, quickly revealed his position on slavery. He sent a

special emissary to California urging the people there to bypass the territorial stage, draw up a state constitution on a slave or free basis as it suited them—the predominantly antislavery sentiment of Californians was well known—and ask for admission to the Union. He proposed the same course of action to the people of New Mexico.

Southerners exploded in wrathful condemnation of Taylor, calling him a Southern man with Northern principles. They could do little, however, for Congress was not to meet until December 1849. Californians, for their part, had already held a constitutional convention in Monterey in September and in October 1849, ratified a free-state constitution by a vote of the people, and had a state government in operation in December. Soon their elected representatives were distributing copies of their state constitution in Washington and with the president's support clamoring for admission to the Union as a free state.

Meanwhile, Northern governors and legislatures were loudly reasserting the doctrine of the Wilmot Proviso. A petition from New York opposing slavery expansion provoked a tremendous uproar when presented in Congress, with Southerners all but declaring war on the state of New York. Similar messages soon came in from Michigan, Pennsylvania, Massachusetts, and Illinois. Southern congressmen responded by forming a solid block of opposition to the admission of any free state until all their outstanding grievances against the North were satisfactorily resolved.

The Fugitive Slave in Federal Law

The issue that most enraged Southerners was the welcome and protection that Northerners provided for runaway slaves. Estimates of property loss suffered by Southerners ran into the hundreds of thousands of dollars. From 1810 to 1850, perhaps 100,000 slaves successfully ran away, 40,000 of them through Ohio alone.

In actuality, the federal and state governments could not legally ignore this matter. Long before, in 1787, when the Constitution was written, at the urging of Southerners the following passage was put in Article IV, Section 2:

> *No person held to service or labour in one State, under the laws thereof, escaping into another, shall, in consequence of any law or regulation therein, be discharged from such service or labour, but shall be*

delivered up on claim of the party to whom such service or labour may be due.

To implement this provision, Congress enacted the Fugitive Slave Act of 1793. It said that slaveowners or their agents could cross a state line (that is, go into a free state) and seize someone they said was a fugitive slave, take that person before a federal or a local judge, and upon presenting proof of ownership (which could simply be an oral statement, or an affidavit certified by a Southern judge), be given a certificate entitling them to take the captive away to the slaveowner's place of residence.

Thus in this sensitive question a most peculiar public policy existed, given the federal nature of the United States. What it actually meant was that slavery was *not* just a local institution. Rather, here was something—being a "slave"—that stuck to someone (the legal term used was "attached") even if he or she got out to a state where the status of slaves did not even exist, was not even recognized in local laws. How could one be a slave when the laws of his or her state made slavery illegal? Thus, state sovereignty was violated to serve the interests of slaveholders in another state. State officials (judges) were required by federal law to participate in the slave-catching process, so that in effect they were made part of the law-enforcement machinery of an entirely different state other than their own. There were even financial penalties mandated for interfering in what was happening.

Furthermore, the person alleged to be a slave had none of the protections of due process of law: No trial by jury, none of the usual rigorous judicial tests of "evidence," no protection against self-incrimination (thus they could be tortured or otherwise coerced into incriminating themselves), not even any arrangement for testifying in their own behalf. The owner need only present to a compliant judge, perhaps one bigoted against black people, some sort of "proof" of ownership, and without further ado the black person was hustled off. It was, in short, an invitation to legal kidnapping, with the authority of the federal Constitution behind it.

Of course, the 1793 law relied entirely on the cooperation of local officials in the North, and many refused to give it. Also, Northern legislatures often obstructed the law by passing "personal liberty" laws that made it illegal for officers of the given state to participate in "slave catching." The result was a swelling chorus of bitter complaint from the South.

A Crucial Supreme Court Decision

Of course, sooner or later the U.S. Supreme Court would have to make a ruling in these matters. That ruling came in 1842, in the crucial case of *Prigg* v. *Pennsylvania*. (We have seen that this means that from this point on, the principles laid down would be the law of the land, just as much as if they had been enacted by Congress.) The Court ruled, first, that slavery was entirely a product of local law, and could claim as a matter of right no jurisdiction in another state. Thus, the courts and the police of the free-state governments were not required to enforce the Fugitive Slave Act of 1793. So far, so good, from the standpoint of antislavery people.

However, the Court went on to state that, nonetheless, the Fugitive Slave Act of 1793 was quite constitutional, even though it violated the rights of the alleged slave. And the provision in the Constitution could not be ignored; indeed, it was so explicit that it was self-executing, that is, it needed no law passed by Congress to carry it out. It gave the slaveowner a "positive, unqualified right" personally to recapture an escaped slave anywhere in the United States, without interference, as long as the slaveowner did not breach the peace. In short, slaveowners *carried the law of their own state with them* (this is termed "extraterritoriality"). So the free states were legally bound to accept that an accused person was a slave unless that person could prove his or her freedom. In other words, the burden of proof lay upon the accused, not on the accuser.

By implication, *Prigg* v. *Pennsylvania* dismissed the kidnapping problem as irrelevant, as well as the rights of black people in the free states. And the laws of slavery were now, in effect, made national in scope.

The Compromise of 1850

In the late 1840s Congress was a boiling cauldron of angry debate. Southern and Northern representatives argued over whether slavery should be allowed in the new territories won from Mexico, and they bitterly debated the question of fugitive slaves. There was also the knotty issue of Texas's claim that its western boundary followed the Rio Grande clear up into the Colorado Rockies, which would give it about half of the present state of New Mexico. And there was another long-festering controversy: An active slave market existed right in Washington, D.C., itself. For decades Northerners and foreign visitors had watched with disgust as "coffles" of chain-bound slaves were marched by the Capitol building itself. Year after year, Northerners had pleaded for wiping out this stain upon the national capital.

With Mississippi and South Carolina (where the proportion of blacks in the population was highest) leading the way, in Congress the South pushed resolutely toward a crisis by threatening secession if the Mexican Cession were not opened to slavery. They warned their fellow Southerners that otherwise there might be as many as a dozen free states carved out of that vast territory, thrusting the South into a permanent minority in the Senate, their fort and bastion against the North.

Bills poured into Congress proposing dozens of different solutions. Almost daily, personal combat threatened to erupt on the floor of Congress. Now the aged Henry Clay, the Great Compromiser, moved once again to center stage. Gathering up all the various slavery issues, he proposed a combined legislative package that he hoped would attract enough support to resolve the conflict.

First, the North should abandon its demand for the Wilmot Proviso. Nature itself, he insisted, would keep slavery out of the dry country of the Mexican Cession. Why needlessly outrage the South? In return, Southerners should accept the dictates of geography and climate and not demand a formal endorsement of their right to take slaves to the new territories. Allow the people of the regions concerned to settle the matter on their own, Clay urged. If Californians wished to have a free state, so be it; and the same for New Mexico. The South should also relent on the question of the slave trade in the District of Columbia, allowing Congress to terminate it. In return, however, it would receive a guarantee that slavery itself would not be ended in the District unless approved by the white people there and in Maryland. Congress, furthermore, would go on record declaring its inability to interfere with the interstate slave trade.

As to Texas, its western boundary should be drawn to exclude New Mexican territory. In return, the federal government would assume the huge public debt of Texas, most of which then consisted of almost worthless bonds. Last, the North, Clay said, should agree to the enactment of a new and much more stringent fugitive slave law.

Abolitionist Henry Ward Beecher, a minister, advocated disobedience of the Fugitive Slave Act.

Many months of argument and maneuver remained, however, before a final agreement could be made. Then death and old age began to play their role. Calhoun died, followed by Zachary Taylor in July. Taylor's successor in the White House, Millard Fillmore of New York, was a much more pliable man than Taylor, who had resisted supporting the compromise. Clay, worn out, gave up the battle and went to Newport, Rhode Island, to revive, turning over the leadership of the struggle to a young man from Illinois, the Democratic senator Stephen A. Douglas.

Short, large-headed, equipped with a huge voice and absolute self-confidence, Douglas saw that the compromise package, once broken into separate bills, might be able to secure passage. For although the majorities supporting the various bills were differently composed, taken together they were sufficient for victory. In the Compromise of 1850, the concept of *popular sovereignty*—letting the people of each region make up their own minds about slavery—became the settled principle for the Mexican Cession. In a series of climactic Congressional votes in September 1850, California was admitted as a free state; New Mexico was allowed to organize itself as a free terri-

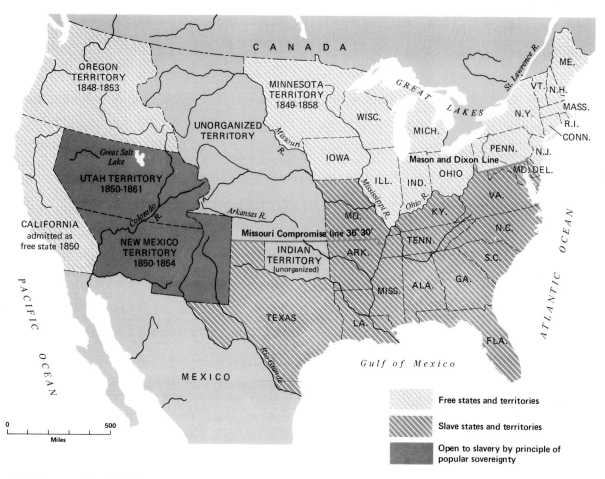

The Compromise of 1850

tory, as were the Mormons of the Salt Lake region, who formed the Territory of Utah. The Texas boundary was finally settled on its present alignment, and in return some $10 million worth of depreciated Texas bonds were paid off at full value.

The slave trade was abolished in the District of Columbia (it simply moved a short distance down the Potomac to Alexandria, Virginia), and a stringent new Fugitive Slave Law was enacted. The new system delivered the retrieving of slaves wholly into the hands of federal officials (i.e., it essentially put *Prigg* v. *Pennsylvania* into statute form), who could punish citizens with fines, imprisonment, and civil damages if they did not cooperate in enforcing the law. Special commissioners were established to hear claims concerning ownership of a slave, with no provision made for either jury trials or judicial hearings. Blacks had to prove their freedom, rather than the burden of proof being placed on the white claimant.

Moreover, the law was made ex post facto; that is, it applied to all fugitives who had been living in the North unmolested for years.

What was the practical effect of the Compromise of 1850? Hundreds of blacks in the North were arrested in the 1850s, only a tiny number of whom successfully defended their claim to freedom. Thousands fled to Canada or abroad, many of them leading figures in the black community. The Man-Stealing Law, as abolitionists called it, thus served as a powerful stimulus to anti-Southern feeling in the North, for the whole proceeding was sickening to witness. Several states, unable to bear the spectacle, enacted new personal liberty laws that provided legal counsel, guaranteed hearings and jury trials, forbade confinements in state jails, and prevented state officials from giving aid to white claimants. This led to bitter Southern charges that the Northerners had betrayed a solemn promise. The Fugitive Slave Law, in brief, caused enormous mischief, gave antislavery feelings and abolitionism a tremendous boost in the North, but was totally ineffective in halting the continued fleeing of slaves from the South.

If the South's victory in obtaining a new fugitive law turned into a costly defeat, its apparent defeat in the West turned into something not so bad. When California was admitted as a free state, it proceeded to elect senators who were usually of Southern loyalty. New Mexico was not admitted as a state for sixty years, so popular sovereignty there was no threat to the balance of power in the Senate. Utah, similarly, was kept out of the Union until 1895 because of its Mormon faith. Practically the only people who benefited directly from the compromise were the citizens of California and those who held Texas bonds. Nothing was permanently settled. Both North and South came out of the long debate convinced they had been mistreated and bearing a heavy grudge.

More immediately, however, the nation greeted the passage of the Compromise with jubilation. The great divisive issue had apparently been laid finally to rest. In Washington the event was celebrated with bonfires, parades, singing in the streets, and cannon salutes. The main buildings were illuminated that night, and crowds surged through the street crying, "The Union is saved!" Even the bland President Millard Fillmore came in for praise, for he had worked hard with Northern Whigs to get a majority in favor of the fugitive slave bill.

"I can now sleep of nights," wrote Daniel Webster to a friend. "We have now gone through the most important crisis that has occurred since the foundation of this government, and whatever party may prevail, hereafter, the Union stands firm. Disunion, and the love of mischief, are put under, at least for the present, and I hope for a long time."

BIBLIOGRAPHY

Books that were especially valuable to me in thinking about and writing this chapter: Don E. Fehrenbacher's *Slavery, Law, and Politics: The Dred Scott Case in Historical Perspective* (1981), and Harold M. Hyman and William M. Wiecek's *Equal Justice Under Law: Constitutional Development 1835–1875* (1982); William W. Freehling's beautifully written *Prelude to Civil War: The Nullification Controversy in South Carolina, 1816–1836* (1968), which evokes, almost with the power of a novel, the mind and emotions of that crucial state; Benjamin Quarles's revealing *Black Abolitionists* (1969), which shows how much of the movement was staffed, led, and inspired by black Americans themselves; Allan Nevin's rich and detailed human panorama—history written in the grand style—in his *Ordeal of the Union: Fruits of Manifest Destiny, 1847–1852* (1947); and Richard Sewell, *Ballots for Freedom* (1976).

Chaplain W. Morrison, *Democratic Politics and Sectionalism: The Wilmot Proviso Controversy* (1967), is valuable reading. Three books reveal excitingly that the subject of abolitionism is still rich ground for historians: James Brewer Stewart, *Holy Warriors: The Abolitionists and American Slavery* (1976); Ronald G. Walters, *The Antislavery Appeal: American Abolitionism after 1830* (1978); and Peter Walker, *Moral Choices: Memory, Desire, and Imagination in Nineteenth-Century American Abolition* (1978). Gerald Sorin's systematic collection of sociological data leads him to a different conclusion in a stimulating work, *New York Abolitionists: A Case Study of Political Radicalism* (1971).

The all-important issue of black Americans' involvement in the antislavery struggle receives some attention in John Hope Franklin's *From Slavery to Freedom* (1956). Leon Litwack effectively hammers out the story of black organization in the North and probes with unsettling conclusions the racial attitudes of white abolitionists in *North of Slavery: The Negro in the Free States, 1790–1860* (1961). For the controversy embedded in the colonization movement, see P. S. Staudenraus, *The African Colonization Movement* (1961). The anger and salvation of a runaway slave are vividly depicted in Philip S. Foner, *Frederick Douglass* (1964), and Larry Gara's *The Liberty Line: The Legend of the Underground Railroad* (1961) delineates the predominant role played by blacks in leading escapes from the South. On the great former slave, see particularly Nathan Irvin Huggins's important work, *Slave and Citizen: The Life of Frederick Douglass* (1980).

The antagonisms evoked by the Compromise of 1850 are richly depicted in human perspective by Allan Nevins in the first volume of his *Ordeal of the Union* (1947).

The essential issues are interpretively chronicled in Holman Hamilton, *Prologue to Conflict: The Crisis and the Compromise of 1850* (1964). Insight into the dramatis personae on the compromise stage is provided by Merrill D. Peterson, *The Great Triumvirate: Webster, Clay, and Calhoun* (1987); Richard N. Current, *Daniel Webster and the Rise of National Conservatism* (1955); Charles M. Wiltse, *John C. Calhoun*, three vols. (1944–51).

16

The Shifting Balance: The North and the South at Midcentury

TIME LINE

HISTORY IN AN INDIVIDUAL LIFE

CYRUS McCORMICK

They were constantly spinning out small inventions, the McCormicks of Virginia's Shenandoah Valley. Scotch-Irish and sternly Presbyterian in mood, they believed in hard work, trained intelligence, and putting the mind industriously at work to solve practical farming problems. Robert and his son Cyrus responded to the booming Jacksonian years by turning out a threshing machine, a blacksmith's bellows, a grist-mill improvement, a hemp-breaking machine, and a plow that worked well on hillsides.

But it was the reaper, which Cyrus invented in 1831, that caught wide attention and then exploded into one of the great technological innovations of the nineteenth century. The reaper, out of the richest grain-growing valley in the South, did for wheat farming, and thus for the immense fertile plains of the Middle West and then all the granaries of the world, what the cotton gin had done for that crop, for the South, and for the cotton lands of Egypt and India. Until a hot July afternoon in 1831 when Cyrus's reaper, horse-drawn, cut steadily through a stand of John Steele's wheat, American farmers, like farmers for

thousands of years into the past, had relied simply upon their strong right arm and the sickle. By 1848, when Cyrus McCormick had moved to set up his plant in Chicago on the edge of the immense spreading wheatlands of the upper Mississippi valley, the great wheat boom in America was ready to begin.

While Chicago grew and spread rapidly back from the lakefront, McCormick's life was totally transformed. Now he was no longer a quiet farmer who fiddled with inventions, but a great entrepreneur with thousands of employees, a worldwide market clamoring for McCormick reapers, and millions of dollars pouring in upon him that had to be managed. He enjoyed moving among the nation's leaders, being a power in the Democratic party, and finding friendships in Europe among the aristocracy. Committees of Congress, learned societies, presidents of the United States, and kings of foreign nations hailed him as the great inventor of the machine that had broken the lock on wheat raising (the fact that no more could be raised than could be reaped by hand) and released a flood of cheap food upon the world.

He was in fact the classic entrepreneur, for he was always attracted by speculative opportunities, by action, by moving swiftly. McCormick enjoyed battling with competitors, he kept pushing ahead long after he had gathered enough wealth to fill almost anyone's dreams, and whenever he won one victory he used it to win another just on the horizon. Business was life to Cyrus McCormick; he was unhappy only when he was not able to be up and doing. Thousands of miles passed beneath him in his travels, but he apparently never traveled for pleasure alone. In the 1850s Cyrus McCormick received businessmen in his hotel bedroom in Chicago, bargaining while he shaved; a dozen years later he was a Chevalier of the French Legion of Honor and living in an elaborate mansion on Fifth Avenue in New York, surrounded by a large staff and receiving a steady stream of the great and powerful. The Shenandoah Valley was far behind. Until McCormick died in 1884, at the age of 75, he was one of the nation's towering figures. With his inventive mind, he had changed the world.

The Great Migration

In the 1830s, almost 600,000 Europeans came to the United States. In the 1840s, almost three times that number (1,700,000) immigrated. Irish Catholics flooded into America, driven out of their homeland by the terrible potato famines of the 1840s, when hundreds of thousands starved to death. In the 1850s, some 2,500,000 immigrants arrived, practically engulfing the Northeastern ports. This gigantic and unprecedented movement of peoples created amazement on both sides of the Atlantic.

Proportionately, it was the largest influx of immigrants in American history. A thousand vessels carrying migrants moved back and forth across the ocean. European authorities worried that the exodus was composed mostly of young people in the prime of life. Of the quarter-million immigrants who arrived in American ports in 1856, four out of five were between the ages of ten and forty. By 1860, one out of eight Americans was foreign-born (4.1 million out of a total of 31.5 million).

Most immigrants, Irish and Jews especially, settled in Northern cities. The Jewish people did so because they had been city dwellers for centuries, the Irish because they were terribly poor, unskilled, and in need of work. A gregarious and religious people, they clustered in city tenements close to Catholic churches. Being generally illiterate and untrained, they went into unskilled work and came into harsh competition with free blacks, for whom they developed a bitter distaste.

Immigrants from Great Britain dispersed widely, melting into the population except in locations where their specific skills produced an unusual concentration of settlement. Germans made up the greatest part of those migrating from continental Europe. Avoiding New England, they settled in the mid-Atlantic states or in heavy concentrations in the upper Middle West (St. Louis, with its large German population, is an exception). Immigration from Scandinavia, especially Norway, was just beginning. Shipping routes from their part of the world led most Scandinavians to enter North America through the St. Lawrence. From there they moved on to settle in Wisconsin and nearby regions, where they found a heavily forested country much like their homeland.

Anti-immigrant Prejudice: The American Party

Old-stock Americans disliked such strange people. The Catholic Irish were especially repellent, partly because they were lawless and disruptive. In Ireland they had become accustomed to think of the law as the weapon of their enemy, the English landowners, and they brought this attitude to America. To the Irish, flouting the law was a manly activity. Some 55 percent of those arrested for crimes in New York City in 1860 were Irish.

Irish Catholics were especially hated by those of New England and British descent (the English, Scotch-Irish, and Welsh), for whom they had always been a contemptible, hardly human people. Yankees, whether in New England or out in western New York, northern Pennsylvania, and the northern Middle West—areas to which Yankees by the tens of thousands had migrated—were the most aggressively Protestant of all Americans, and the most alarmed at seeing Protestant America receive for the first time a large Catholic population. Therefore, Yankees were the most anti-Irish. Indeed, to their horror, Yankees were being inundated by the Irish in their great homeland city of Boston.

Americans of British descent recoiled from Irish illiteracy and ignorance (ironically, induced by generations of repressive British laws in Ireland), their tendency to violence and heavy drinking, and their passionate hatred of the English. Before long, American cartoonists, like those in Britain, were depicting the Irish Catholics as practically apelike. They were especially condemned for their corrupt politics—that is, their tendency to vote in one great bloc for the Democrats, traditionally the party of the outgroups (the Scotch-Irish in the North now decamped from the Democratic party to join its anti-Irish Catholic enemies), and to pass around political favors to one another. In Ireland they had had to look out for themselves, and in America, where they finally had access to political power in local elections, they intended to do no less. The Irish Catholics were like a large family held in contempt by all the neighbors and distinguished by a religous faith that created general distaste. Mutual assistance and sticking together were to them merely the means of survival.

Local anti-Catholic parties began arising in the late 1840s. By 1854 they were powerful enough to form a national organization, the "American Party." It adopted the trappings of a secret order. When

Native-born Protestant Americans hated immigrant Catholics, as shown in this lithograph of a riot in Philadelphia in 1844 between Catholics and non-Catholics. This sentiment led eventually to the founding of the American party in the 1850s.

pressed for details about the American party, its members would say they "knew nothing"; shortly, they were called the Know-Nothings. In voting strength the party grew very rapidly, in both the North and the South, drawing in many thousands of Whigs, traditionally the most anti-alien people in politics. New Englanders, of course, joined the American party in great numbers.

The Woman Question

One group which in the 1850s *tried* to enter politics were the feminists. For some women, the doctrine of the two spheres was impossibly constrictive. They hated especially the reigning idea that women should not be public figures, or speak in public save in occupations taken to be in their special sphere, such as church work. The "woman question," as it was called, thus came into national consciousness for the first time: the demand for equality of participation in public life.

Like the women's liberation movement of the late 1960s, it sprang into prominence as part of the general climate of reform agitation. In particular,

the women's rights movement was a spinoff of the abolition crusade. A tremendous furor broke out among abolitionists when an equal role was denied to women, as when Lucretia Mott was refused the right to sit on the main floor or to speak at the London convention. After all, the huge efforts being made to free black men from slavery led militant women to ask why they too should not be freed from their own form of "slavery."

Modesty required middle-class women to shun all contacts with the world at large. They were regarded as soiled if they took up occupations in which they worked alongside men or appeared before the public. A woman speaking in public was a shocking spectacle, especially if she spoke to a male audience. When a woman stood before a gathering of male temperance workers in 1853, they yelled at her for an hour and a half to keep her from being heard. The *New York Herald*, angered at her obstinacy, raged at such "rampant women . . . unsexed in mind, all of them publicly propounding the doctrine that they should be allowed to step out of their appropriate sphere to the neglect of those duties which both human and divine law have assigned them."

However, there was a small group of women

in the 1840s and 1850s who were determined to win wider rights. Led by Lucretia Mott, Elizabeth Cady Stanton, and Susan B. Anthony, they gathered at the first woman's rights convention in history at Seneca Falls, New York, in 1848. Their Declaration of Sentiments insisted that "all men and women are created equal," and deplored the "repeated injuries and usurpations on the part of man toward woman, having in direct object the establishment of an absolute tyranny over her." There followed a list of men's crimes: denying women the vote, an education, the guardianship of their children, the right to speak in pulpits and in public affairs, an equal code of morals with men, and even "her confidence in her own powers [in order] to make her willing to lead a dependent and abject life."

In the 1850s feminists began holding annual woman's rights conventions, though they were often terrorized by physical attacks. When they tried to speak in public meetings they were howled down; books were even thrown at a woman having the courage to rise in a gathering of teachers. "We cannot," said a group of Massachusetts ministers, "but regret the mistaken conduct of those who encourage females to bear an obtrusive and ostentatious part in measures of reform, and countenance any of that sex who so far forget themselves as to itinerate in the character of public lecturers and teachers." In particular, the feminist demand that women be given the vote received massive public condemnation. "It seemed," wrote Elizabeth Cady Stanton, "as if every man who could wield a pen prepared a homily on 'woman's sphere.' So pronounced was the popular voice against us that most of the ladies who had attended the convention [of 1848] withdrew their names and influence and joined our persecutors. Our friends gave us the cold shoulder and felt themselves disgraced by the whole proceeding."

So, after a few years of prominence this first surge of feminism died away, sapped by failure, apathy, and a new sensation—the Civil War. The war had a major practical impact on the position of women, for it provided work outside the home for many of them. Women became munitions workers and clerks, and transformed nursing and teaching into female professions. Many middle-class women refused at war's end to slide back into their old seclusion. Instead, they founded the women's club movement, in which they engaged in various areas of civic reform—schools, libraries, playgrounds, and charity.

The Industrial Revolution of the 1850s

The arrival of millions of immigrants profoundly affected the Northern states. Aside from their major role in the development of Western farming, the presence of hordes of immigrants eager to work provided the essential supply of available labor that allowed the North to build major additions to its transportation network and to swiftly expand its industry. The result was so explosive an expansion in the Northern economy that it transformed the whole nation.

From 1850 to 1860, the capital invested in manufacturing almost doubled, rising from $533 million to over $1 billion. The money came from many sources, such as domestic savings and investments from abroad, but most of all from a dazzling stroke of luck—the discovery of gold in California. More than $500 million in gold came out of the Sierra Nevada in the 1850s, pouring into the nation's economic bloodstream a sum that alone was equivalent to the total invested in new industry during the decade.

How was this great sum put to use? Most dramatically in a swift extension of the nation's railroads. "The railroad fever," observed a Philadelphia paper in the mid 1850s, "appears rather to increase than abate. . . . The vast results of opening the iron lines of communication, as illustrated in the unexampled growth of Chicago and other cities in the Lake region, seems to have excited a spirit among some of the rising towns that will not rest until the Great West is fairly gridironed with railroads like Massachusetts."

This expansion, in turn, produced a heavy demand for iron. A mile of track required 80 to 100 tons of rail, in addition to spikes, switches, bridges, and trestles. Iron rails wore out quickly (the longer-wearing steel rails came after the Civil War), and a heavy demand for replacement accentuated the need. American iron foundries at first grew slowly in number, for British iron was still quite cheap, due to more efficient processes and the lack of a protective tariff. By 1860, however, the iron industry had grown tremendously, especially around Pittsburgh, whence iron could be floated westward down the Ohio River. Iron in any form—rails, bar, boiler plate, wire rods, nail plate, sheet iron—was eagerly purchased. At the same time, locomotive factories flourished. The Baldwin Company in Philadelphia produced more than 1,500 locomotives before the end of the Civil War.

One dominating characteristic of the American economy set it off from British and European economies and shaped its development—the shortage of labor. Even in the eighteenth century American enterprisers had had to look more intensively for labor-saving machinery than their counterparts in Europe. The French invented the principle of interchangeable machine-made parts, but the Americans were the ones who brought it to commercial profitability. Because cheap seamstresses were not readily available, the sewing machine, which seemed hardly worth perfecting in Europe, became highly developed in the United States. By 1850 the habit of thinking in terms of machinery was ingrained, a fact that was to send American productivity per individual worker soaring far above that in Europe.

These influences were strikingly expressed in Western farming regions, where labor was always short and costly and land seemed limitless. Responding to insatiable demands, Northern industry concentrated heavily on the invention and production of farm machinery. New inventions were swiftly put to use. One enterpriser, who did nothing more than make a small improvement in a device for cutting straw, realized a $40,000 profit from one tour in the Western states. Cyrus McCormick, who invented the reaper, moved to Chicago in 1847 to build his machines and soon was selling them by the thousands. In response, acreage tilled in the open prairies spurted enormously, producing an ever-mounting demand for equipment. This led to the building of small factories in towns located all over the Middle West. Nowhere else were so many different kinds of farm tools made so well and so cheaply. Plows, corn-planters, wheat drills, revolving rakes, cultivators, and threshing machines—all excited enthusiasm and wonder when taken across the Atlantic for display in the first of the modern world fairs, the Crystal Palace Exhibition in London in 1851.

One American visitor to the Crystal Palace Exhibition wrote of the products from the United States on display: "Our handled axes, hay-rakes, grain cradles, scythes and snathes, three-tined hayforks, solid steel hoes, road-

One of the great inventions in the history of agriculture, Cyrus McCormick's reaper, here shown in an advertisement of 1851, opened the western plains to heavy grain production.

scrapers, post-hole augurs, fan-mills, smut-mills, sausage cutters, sausage stuffers, tinman's tools, permutation locks, wheel cultivators, carpenters' tools, currycombs, cornbrooms, portmanteaus and trunks, ice-cream freezers, axletrees, paint-mills, and many other things of universal use here, but in the shape and conveniences which we have given them utterly unknown in Europe, established for our industry a character independent of and unlike that of any other nation."

The sewing machine also "had its hour of triumph in London," but Cyrus McCormick's reaper won the greatest acclaim. Although it was derided at first by the London Times as "a cross between a flying-machine, a wheelbarrow, and an Astley chariot," all were astonished when in competition with other machines it marched smoothly through a heavy stand of rain-soaked wheat while the others failed. The "rough, brown, home-spun Yankee in charge jumped on the box, starting the team at a smart walk," reported the New York Weekly Tribune, "setting the blades of the machine in lively operation, and commenced raking off the grain in sheaf-piles ready for binding, cutting a breadth of nine or ten feet cleanly and carefully, as fast as a span of horses could comfortably step. There was a moment, and but a moment, of suspense; human prejudice could hold out no longer; and burst after burst of involuntary cheers from the whole crowd proclaimed the success of the Yankee 'treadmill.'" (Allan Nevins, Ordeal of the Union: A House Dividing, 1852–1857 [1947])

Meatpacking and grain milling expanded vigorously, centralized operations that had formerly taken place in small establishments in each village. Hog slaughtering became a mass-production arrangement in Cincinnati and Chicago. Richard M. Hoe designed and built printing presses that were famous for their speed—8,000 newspapers an hour. This press made possible the appearance of cheap newspapers for a mass audience.

So it went, industry after industry. Charles Goodyear patented his process for vulcanizing rubber in 1844; the Otis elevator was invented in 1851; artificial ice makers and refrigerators were already available; and in Massachusetts the invention of appropriate machinery and the division of labor had reached the point where more than twenty workers were involved in the production of a single shoe. This led to a huge increase in production. In 1843 the city of Milford, Massachusetts, produced 150,000 pairs of shoes; within ten years, one firm alone was producing almost that many. Three hundred machines were utilized to produce one complete Springfield musket, and the arsenal turned one out every eighty minutes.

The Wheat and Cotton Kingdoms Expand

America was still an overwhelmingly agricultural country, and in these pre–Civil War decades the great story in its economic life continued to be the immense expansion in farm output that had been set off in the 1820s when cotton producers in the South flooded into the Gulf Plains and wheat and corn farmers invaded the Lake Plains in force. In 1840 more than three out of four Americans at work were farmers; in 1860 the figure would still be two out of three. The westward movement was so enormous that the coastal states along the Atlantic, which in the 1790s had held almost all Americans, by 1860 had only half of them. And since the forests were thinner in the Gulf and Lake Plains and the land was more fertile and easily farmed, Western farms and plantations were more productive, per farmer, than those left behind in the older regions. Furthermore, farm laborers got the best wages in the new farms of the West, and such workers settled in that region in great numbers to provide manpower.

Migration took place primarily by families, relatively young ones that had been started in the East. Since in the older regions most farming land was taken up, these families had trekked westward to find open land and found a new farm. Because of liberal federal land policies, it cost only about $200 to buy a farm of 160 acres from the government. Indeed, this subsidy to new farmers—the handing over to them of public lands at low cost after all the steps of land survey and the provision of local government had been completed—was probably the most important single stimulus to the national economy to come from the national government in the pre–Civil War years. The Preemption Act of 1841 even allowed a farmer to go out into unsurveyed lands, "squat" on them, and have first rights to buy his farm (up to 160 acres) when the lands went on sale. (In 1862 the Homestead Act allowed people to get their land free, provided they had improved it with dwellings and other investments and had lived on it for five years.)

The Southern states had little public land, so these laws had less impact there in encouraging settlement. In the South, it was the continuing high profits to be made in raising cotton that provided the stimulus. As far back as 1801, the new cotton gin had had so dramatic an effect in increasing production that America had provided almost one-tenth of the entire world supply of cotton. With this abundant cheap source of raw material, English textile mills multiplied into a great industrial system, and the demand for cotton was soon voracious. By the 1820s the United States of America was the largest cotton producer in the world—and also the largest slaveholder in the Western Hemisphere. In the year 1850, two-thirds of the world's production came from America. Some 700 million pounds of cotton a year left American ports for Britain in the 1850s, pushing the value of America's foreign commerce from $317 million to $687 million annually in that decade.

Wheat was not far behind. Its production increased an astonishing 72 percent in the 1850s, all of this increase coming from the Mississippi valley. In an important sense American wheat was as essential to Britain as American cotton, a fact of vital importance during the Civil War. In 1851, one million bushels of wheat were exported; in 1854, eight million; by 1857, over fourteen million. A considerable dropoff then occurred, followed by a huge outpouring of over thirty-one million bushels in 1861.

The Rise of the Corporation

Northern capitalists had fresh supplies of labor, new capital from California, and opening markets in the interior. What they still needed, however, was a means of organization to exploit these opportunities. In 1848 such a means was provided. Jacksonian Democrats in New York—who were now also called Barnburners—had long clamored for an end to the system whereby charters of incorporation were granted only by special legislative acts. Quoting Adam Smith, they condemned the system as one that produced graft, special privilege, inequality, and a slowly growing economy. The power to incorporate was so potentially profitable that eager enterprisers used every means at their disposal to get such charters, thus corrupting popular government. To free the economy for dynamic growth, reduce corruption, and open opportunities for everyone on an equal basis, the power of incorporation should be thrown open to everyone.

In 1846, under the leadership of Martin Van Buren's young associate Samuel J. Tilden, such a provision was put into a new constitution then being written for the state of New York. This, in turn, led to the enactment of the General Incorporation Law of 1848, which allowed all businessmen to incorporate if they met certain minimum financial requirements. Within a few years such laws were enacted

in all the other Northern states. During the 1850s as many corporations were established as in all the previous years of America's history.

The larger impact of this development on American society was not simply to accelerate the economy's growth, but to make business corporations extremely powerful while every other group and agency remained relatively weak. The national government was small and largely without power; state governments were nerveless; and county and municipal governments had supervision only over small areas and had little authority. Farmers, laborers, professional men, retail businessmen—none were organized. There was not even one powerfully organized church, as in Roman Catholic countries. Now, in this scattered nation where no agency had more than local and limited powers, there appeared a new social institution of great influence, the business corporation.

By the end of the Civil War such organizations could pool the capital of thousands of individuals and place it under the direction of a few men whose decisions affected whole states and regions. The power of a great corporation like the New York Central Railroad dwarfed that of the scores of city councils and county boards of supervisors and even the state legislatures who "governed" the areas along its route. Large banks, corporations that mined and produced iron, big factories, and trunk-line railroads reaching from the Atlantic Ocean to the Great Lakes and beyond—these were systems of organized power in a sea of disorganization. Their social power, expressed in economics, politics, and social life, was enormous. They battled with one another, but regarded public agencies with mild contempt. They crushed workers who tried to organize, charged farmers such rates as they wished, and wiped out small businesses by underselling and other techniques whenever it appeared useful to their interests.

The result was the rapid emergence of a group of gifted enterprisers who grasped opportunities now rapidly opening before them. Despite the often destructive use they made of their power, they were widely admired. They had, after all, no real competitors for social prestige. There was in America no titled nobility with its independent sources of wealth, no proud and elitist governing class such as existed in European nations. The great businessman in the United States was all these things rolled into one person, and as the years went by he became the dominant American type. Because government was so limited in its powers and offered few opportunities for exciting careers, many of the most gifted young men in the country were drawn off into the new world of large business enterprise. A new social class was emerging in the 1850s that ruled the United States in the decades after the Civil War with the confident style that comes with power and mass adulation.

Railroads Unify the North

Meanwhile, a swift expansion in railroad lines strengthened links between northeastern states and the Old Northwest, the region north of the Ohio and east of the Mississippi. This profoundly changed former relationships between the nation's sections. For many years the South had maintained special economic ties with the Old Northwest. Southern planters, who devoted their energies almost exclusively to raising cotton, tobacco, or rice, bought huge supplies of wheat and hogs from farmers in the Old Northwest. The Mississippi River enhanced this relationship, directing the flow of trade to the cities of the South. At the same time, the South had worked hard to maintain a political alliance, too, with the Old Northwest, both sections joining to secure the passage of low tariffs and other programs of mutual interest. The South even supported federal internal improvement projects in the Old Northwest in the midcentury years in the hope that this would keep the alliance alive.

By 1850 railroads were weakening this bond by shrinking its economic base. Eastern financiers saw potentially fruitful opportunities in linking Western food to Eastern manufactures. When the depression begun by the panic of 1837 eased off in the early 1840s, they invested heavily in several trunk railroads that were building their lines vigorously westward. Both the Baltimore and Ohio and the Pennsylvania railroads reached the Ohio River in 1853, and the New York Central, created by a merger of several roads in that state, had completed rail connections between New York City and the Great Lakes by 1852.

The next step was to build a network of rails across the Old Northwest to divert the shipment of its products eastward, away from the southward-flowing rivers. Each of the trunk lines built rapidly westward, first through Ohio and then to Chicago. The next stage was the pushing of rail lines westward from Chicago to reach the Mississippi, and the extension of others down to the Ohio or to St. Louis to catch the trade along the Missouri River. The most daring project was the building of the Illinois Central, which sought to do nothing less than connect Chicago with the Gulf of Mexico, thus paralleling and taking trade from the Father of Waters itself, the Mississippi. By 1856 a connected line ran from Mobile on the Gulf to Chicago.

How did the South fare in railroad building? Within its resources it worked hard to match the North's spurt, but it fell far short. The capital was simply not available. Such lines as were built, furthermore, did not connect the South with the Old Northwest, but simply improved internal transportation. Lines were built westward from Georgia and South Carolina that tied Nashville and Memphis to the seaboard and linked with Vicksburg in Mississippi, where the South's principal East–West rail line crossed the great river to run into Arkansas and Texas. Consequently, the South became more inward-turning than ever, and was severely hurt by the swift reduction in river transport on the Mississippi that occurred when northern railroads pulled trade off to the East.

After the trunk lines were built out into the Old Northwest, feeder lines were constructed in all directions, hemstitching the region into an integrated rail network whose eastern terminals lay along the eastern seaboard. Farmers learned that swift, all-year transport was available to them, opening new lucrative markets. Where in the past they had sold most of their produce either to the South or through New Orleans to the West Indies or South America, hereafter they turned to more profitable markets in the Northeast and in Britain and the European continent. Important advantages lay in this direction. The wheat that spoiled in the damp air of the lower Mississippi kept perfectly in the brisk climate of the Atlantic seaboard. Loans to finance trade were more abundant in the many banks of New York and New England than they had been in St. Louis or New Orleans. More and more, the Old Northwest and the Northeast were welded economically into one interactive and mutually supportive section.

Slavery as a Mature Institution

While these transformations occurred in the North, the South remained a relatively static society. In these years—the period when American slavery reached its most fully developed stage—what was the institution like? Slaves were owned and used everywhere, in cities and in the countryside, in iron foundries, in skilled crafts, as household servants, and as wagon drivers. Nine out of ten slaves, however, were used as farm laborers. Of these, only half worked on *plantations* (operations with twenty or more slaves). Something more than half of the slaves in the South were used in the relatively new states of the Deep South, where conditions were at their rawest and harshest stage. Although the Upper South produced cotton, the Deep South was preeminently the Cotton Kingdom, where plantations were huge and slaves were used in large gangs.

Whether the plantation grew cotton, tobacco, or rice, the pattern of life was roughly similar. On small plantations, owners worked directly with slaves; on large ones, white overseers were hired. Where gangs were large, specially favored and cooperative blacks were given the task of being "head driver" over small groups of slaves. Rung out of their cabins by the plantation bell, slaves were led to the fields at first light. They labored until dusk, returning to their quarters not long after dinner, there to remain for the night. Cabins were commonly patrolled to ensure that slaves did not venture out after curfew, and were periodically turned inside out to make certain arms or stolen goods were not in the slaves' possession.

Slaves might be allowed the use of a few articles of personal property, but they could not own anything or trade their possessions without the owner's permission. The law stated that no slave was to leave his plantation without a pass signed by his master. Any black off the plantation without a pass could be halted and arrested by any white. A slave found more than a few miles from the plantation was legally regarded as a runaway and subject to punishment.

Most slaves were kept totally uneducated. Any violation of law, or of the owner's plantation regulations, could be, and frequently was, punished by flogging. Accused slaves were tried by "Negro courts," informal tribunals that meted out swift "justice" without safeguards for the person being tried. There were practically no limits on the punishment that owners could levy. Serious injury and death were generally avoided (the persistently rebellious slave was usually sold), but floggings were excruciatingly painful and could result in death. In such cases white men were usually safe from prosecution. Their slaves, after all, whites said, were nothing more than property.

The Realities of Slavery

Slavery was an unmitigated horror for the slaves, said abolitionists, and masters were unrelievedly brutal. Why else would 100,000 slaves flee for freedom to the North? Slavery was a civilizing, gentling school in which savages were made into productive human beings, said slaveholders. Indeed, they insisted slaves in the American South were far better off than peasants in much of Europe, or industrial laborers in England and the North, for they were cared for with concern by an enlightened master class that could not simply discard people when they became ill or old. Plantations were kindly places where black slaves were happy, compliant, and affectionate toward their masters—the classic merry Sambo.

For generations after the Civil War, American historians presented the latter view of slavery. It was deeply reinforced in the white mind in the twentieth century by the consistent presentation of Sambos in motion pictures. Since the 1950s, however, when the Second Reconstruction of black American life had its beginnings, historians have vigorously explored slavery afresh, discovering quite new things. It is clear now that though the slave system may have generated its share of Sambos—since the slave was totally under the authority of, and dependent upon, white masters and was given little opportunity to develop any sense of personal independence—a rebellious spirit flared and flickered on many plantations.

So important a witness as the ex-slave Frederick Douglass testified that most slaves stood "in awe" of whites, but that many were militant, "insolent," "surly," stole constantly from their masters and resorted to arson as a means of protest. Runaways were a constant problem, and slaves sometimes attacked their owners. When emancipation came, blacks universally welcomed it.

More recently, historians have been urging us to realize that to understand slavery we must start with the fact that it was a *human* institution. That is, it was filled with variety, contradictions, complexities, emotions, self-interest, moral concerns, and above all, human spirit, on both sides of the racial line. Also, the millions of black people in slavery had ways of thinking and acting that to a certain extent were under their control. Slavery was a system shaped by both slaves and masters. It was not simply what was described in the laws.

To begin with the most fundamental fact: Slaves were not *things*. Whatever the law said, they were in reality human beings. This was the basic contradiction in the system. A plow could not be evasive at work tasks, or burn down the barn, or escape—nor would it bleed when whipped, or develop for self-protection an elaborate, courteous politeness when dealing with the master. An intricate complex of informal customs and "rights" sprang up because the slave was a person.

The master had to have the cooperation of the slaves to make his plantation survive. This meant recognizing their humanity and treating them as well as possible. In other words, it meant creating the concept of *paternalism*. According to this view of slavery, the relationship between master and slave was really a fatherly one. The former was to provide kindly concern as well as discipline and guidance; the latter, in return for this caring direction, would provide labor and obedience. In other words, it was a reciprocal relationship.

Slaves recognized this. The master had certain obligations to them. This meant that they had a personal reality. In the American South, certain conditions enhanced the development of obligations to-

ward the slave. The legal ending of the slave trade in 1808 meant that slaveholders had to care for and nurture their existing stock of people. Also, unlike Caribbean slaveholders (and those in coastal South Carolina and Georgia), most American masters lived on the land with their slaves in an intimate, daily relationship that did in fact have a familylike quality. A master presided over white family and black slaves as if they were an extended family and he the father of it all (in the case of many slaves who were partially black and partially white, this was literally true). The result was a greater individual concern for each slave, so that the American slave force, alone in the Western Hemisphere, flourished by natural increase. The 400,000 slaves imported into the South from Africa were 4 million people by the time of the Civil War.

Changes in the Slave System

From the 1830s onward, following the Denmark Vesey conspiracy and the Nat Turner rebellion, the Southern states turned sharply away from an earlier

Cotton Production, 1840–1860

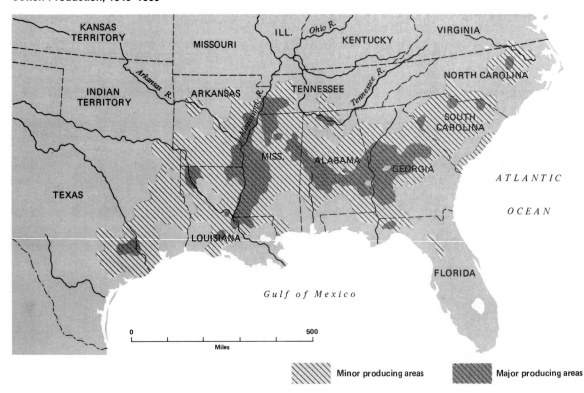

Minor producing areas   Major producing areas

trend toward manumissions and the weakening of slavery in its legal definition. Manumissions were made almost impossible, and free blacks were either driven out or placed under strict controls. But Southern whites moved at the same time to make slavery more humanized and livable for the slaves, hoping by this means to head off insurrections. Better food, better housing, better working conditions, the allowance of slave marriages, some schooling, the right to attend church services, and protection against gross cruelties: these were the things Southern reformers worked for, sometimes with success.

Material conditions certainly improved, and occasionally masters were given long jail terms when convicted of killing a slave. Oftentimes, slaveholders intervened to halt mistreatment on a neighbor's plantation when appealed to by the slaves suffering his excessive flogging. In particular regions a great many "customary rights" grew up that had no reflection in law, such as having a private garden plot to enrich the slave family's diet (upon which slaves lavished endless labor). Slaves insisted adamantly upon these rights, once granted, which further strengthened their sense that they were not simply things, but people. As early as 1836, the high court of Kentucky held that "although the law of this state considers slaves as property, yet it recognizes their personal existence, and, to a qualified extent, their natural rights."

Thus, writes the historian Eugene D. Genovese in *Roll, Jordan, Roll: The World the Slaves Made* (1974), the concept of paternalism "afforded a fragile bridge across the intolerable contradictions inherent in a society based on racism, slavery, and class exploitation that had to depend on the willing reproduction and productivity of its victims." They all lived and worked together, whites and blacks; masters and slaves formed a community, however strange it was; and there had to be some minimal arrangements for meeting self-interest and ensuring self-respect.

The Masters' Attitudes

Masters did not feel guilty for owning slaves. Rather, their racist philosophy defined black people as so inferior that they could not survive without the protection and guidance of the whites. Certainly they could not survive freedom (it was said): that condition would destroy them, through starvation and disease. Thus, slaveholders constantly said to themselves that being a slave master was both a burden and a duty;

they thought of themselves as Christians performing a laborious responsibility. From this standpoint, relying upon absolute terror and violence to get obedience was not morally possible. It was important to most slaveholders that the slave do his or her tasks out of love for the master—which meant the master loving the slave in return. This too slaves recognized, and used in every way possible to humanize their situation.

"Gratitude," "loyalty," "family": these were words that white slaveholders used frequently. They were offended almost more by the "ingratitude" of an escaped slave than by the loss of investment the fleeing represented. A rebellious slave was not merely said to be hard to handle; he was "treasonous," or "disloyal." When emancipation finally came and slaves deserted their masters en masse, after years of apparent mutual affection and dutiful labor, slaveowners were rudely shocked—and bitter beyond measure at their "ungrateful" former slaves.

The paternalist ideal had deep effects upon the psychology of Southern whites. People idealized the virtues implicit in paternalism—being firm, kind, strong, and proudly dominant—and sought to build them into their own behavior. Indeed, the great planters took paternalistic views toward the poorer whites. An ethic of self-sacrificing public service to the whole community was a prominent value among the elite. Having unquestioned power over others, being lord within one's own domain, being the very source of law itself in daily practice—all of this deepened that libertarian individualism that had so long been central to white Southern life. Men were prickly concerning slights to honor, and they were determined never to accept challenges to their personal authority over themselves, their property, and their households. Courage in the face of constant danger: This was at the heart of their character.

Ready to use violence to get their will, Southern whites could also be gracious and courteous, for this was in the paternalist code. Blacks themselves adopted this courtliness in personal address, and shared the emphasis upon bravery and fortitude in a difficult life. There was a generous openness and hospitality in the paternalist creed, an intense family-centeredness—together with arrogance, toughness, and pride. A vein of quickly tapped anger, a violent hatred of being "crossed," and a readiness to use weapons to settle personal disputes, together with an ability to be cruel when pressed: Critics and admirers joined in saying these qualities were prominent in the character of Southern whites.

The Slaves and Work

One thing is certain: The slaves were a highly trouble-some labor force to manage. Plantation owners were commonly driven to distraction by the problem of maintaining discipline and getting the slaves to work steadily and effectively. Slaves took every opportunity to slow down at their labor. "Hands won't work unless I am in sight," ran a typical entry in plantation diaries. Slaves put rocks in their cotton sacks to give them a spurious weight—a practice harshly punished when uncovered. Or, when pushed beyond the work level they had chosen for themselves, they turned uncooperative, whining, and disobedient.

Owners naturally formed the notion that their slaves were inherently lazy and shiftless, or that they were shrewd, cunning, and superhumanly ingenious saboteurs. "The fear of punishment," said one slave-holder, "is the principle to which we must appeal, to keep them in awe and order." Whips were regularly used. They seemed to symbolize the South and the heart of Southern civilization, just as did the breaking up of families by selling off their members, an appalling reality in slave life.

> A former slave woman recalled that "babies was snatched from dere mother's breas' an' sold to specula-tors. Chilluns was separated from sisters an' brothers an' never saw each other ag'in. Course dey cry; you think dey not cry when dey was sold lak cattle? . . . It's bad to belong to folks dat own you soul an' body; dat can tie you up to a tree, wid yo' face to de tree an' yo' arms fastened tight aroun' it; who take a long curlin' whip an' cut de blood ever' lick. Folks a mile away could hear dem awful whippings. Dey was a turrible part of livin'." (Leon Litwack, Been in the Storm So Long [1979])

Work: The endless problem, to whites, of mak-ing the slaves do it. And yet the masters themselves lived leisurely lives at every available moment—and the slaves knew it. Poor whites in the countryside were commonly described as lazy and shiftless. Few in the South worked systematically. In fact, it is only in modernized societies that time, the clock, even the calendar or the year, have much meaning. Slaves resembled traditional peasant peoples the world over, for whom work along the disciplined pattern of a modern factory, with its morning whistle, established lunch hour, and continuous day of unbroken labor, was simply foreign, alien, against nature.

Village people in traditional society, whatever their skin pigmentation, interweave work and play.

There are many saint's days, celebrations of weddings, wakes at funerals, times for dancing and carousing. Northern Yankee factory owners tore their hair at the impossibility of getting their immigrant laborers from European villages to work like New Englanders did. English factory owners complained in the same way about their Irish hands in the same years. They were forever wandering off to go fishing, or sitting down together to laugh and eat at odd times in the factory.

In a Southern world still preindustrial, where whites themselves worked little unless forced to it—labor being something attached to a black skin, and leisure being thought of as the reward of high social status—Southern slaves worked primarily in bursts of great effort, following the planting seasons. Their masters little respected steadiness, regularity, and sus-tained effort in their own lives, and the slaves were no different. But in situations where they were work-ing for themselves—doing extra work on Sunday for pay (a surprisingly routine practice) or cutting lumber during off-hours—they would work as hard as a Northern farmer.

Was the Slave System Profitable?

Why did Southern whites cling to so difficult and (outside the South) morally condemned a system of economy as slave plantation agriculture? There was nothing inherent in black people that prevented their being put to work in factories (as in fact some were) and evolving a system for buying their freedom. Eco-nomic historians have in recent years proposed at least one explanation: The slave-plantation system was more profitable to the white masters than any other use of their labor force and capital. Obviously, this is not a total answer, for slavery was also a system of keeping absolute control of a black popula-tion whose freedom, most whites believed, would bring massive disorders and violence.

In the 1850s, slavery was a flourishing system. The market price of a slave was twice what it cost to rear him or her. This meant that owning and using slaves in cotton farming was highly profitable, or people would not have been willing to pay so much for them. In fact, the profit from the slave's labor ran about 10 percent per year, more than could be made in Southern railroad investments or in New England textile firms. Even older slaves returned a profit, though less than those between the ages of ten and thirty-five, the best years. Ensuring productivity provided a strong motive to masters to keep their slaves healthy, fit, and in good spirits.

The historians Robert W. Fogel and Stanley L. Engerman, in their book *Time on the Cross: The Economics of American Negro Slavery* (1974), have even held that slaves were allowed a high degree of family stability, adequate medical care, light discipline, allowances of food, clothing, and housing that compared well with laborers elsewhere, and even a remarkable amount of upward mobility. This has been much disputed, however, as not an accurate picture, though in such bare statistics as birth and death rates black slaves were close to the national average.

Even the most exploited Northern workers did not have roughly half of the income that they earned taken away from them by their employers, as studies now estimate to have been the case with black slaves—to speak of nothing else in the slave condition that made their way of living grotesquely unequal to that of free laborers. Working in gangs made money for the planter, for it was more economical, but as soon as emancipation came, black Southerners refused to labor in that way any longer, preferring the psychic rewards of being a sharecropper or a tenant farmer, however precarious this made their lives economically.

Proslavery Arguments

In the years around 1830 the problem of slavery had produced many heartfelt expressions of guilt among Southern slave owners. After that, however, as the South began reacting defensively to Northern abolitionists' attacks, these expressions were little heard. They were replaced by assertions that slavery was a positive good, ordained by God from all time. When abolitionists quoted the Bible to attack the institution, Southerners did the same to defend it. Blacks, they said, were clearly the cursed descendants of Ham, whose offspring and their progeny, as described in the Old Testament, were rendered dark-skinned and destined to be "servants of servants" till eternity.

Many Southern ministers preached that God had given the South a special providential mission to play in human history. What was it? "I answer," said the Reverend Dr. B. M. Palmer, "that it is to conserve and perpetuate the institution of slavery as now existing. . . . My own conviction is, that we should at once lift ourselves, intelligently, to the highest moral ground, and proclaim to all the world that we hold this trust from God, and in its occupancy we are

prepared to stand or fall as God may appoint. . . . "This duty is bound upon us again as the constituted guardians of the slaves themselves. Our lot is not more implicated in theirs, than is their lot in ours; in our mutual relations we survive or perish together. The worst foes of the black race are those who have intermeddled on their behalf. We know better than others that every attribute of their character fits them for dependence and servitude. By nature, the most affectionate and loyal of all races beneath the sun, they are also the most helpless; and no calamity can befall them greater than the loss of what protection they enjoy under this patriarchal system." (B. M. Palmer, "Slavery a Divine Trust: Duty of the South to Preserve and Perpetuate It," Fast Day Sermons: The Pulpit on the State of the Country [1861])

Other writers, such as the most talented and widely read defender of slavery, George Fitzhugh, justified the institution by attacking the North's way of life and lauding Southern paternalism. The ideas of liberty and equality that the North professed, he said, were new in the world and were already failures wherever tried. It was ridiculous to condemn slavery, for every civilized society was based on some system of social exploitation. Blacks were only brutes anyway, though they had the form of human beings. Slavery was beneficial for them.

In the North, Fitzhugh said, ordinary whites who worked for wages were worse off than Southern slaves. Used only in the best years of their lives and then cast aside, paid wages that barely kept them alive, and ignored when sick, they were in even worse "slavery" than the black. The notion of equality was but a device for leading misguided men to accept meaningless political arrangements while being subjected to economic exploitation under the name of freedom.

The Myth and Reality of Southern Life

Ironically, many in the North looked to the afflicted South with something like warm approval. The myth that every planter was inherently a gentle aristocrat enfolded all Southern culture. Eagerly searching for literary sources that would tell them how noble aristocrats had lived in the dim British past, planters found them in the novels of Sir Walter Scott, which the South bought literally by the boxcar load. Genealogy became an obsession, and coats of arms were ardently sought.

By appealing to human qualities of dignity and selflessness the South brought in influences that in fact softened and gentled its way of life and helped keep alive the tradition of large-spirited paternalism. "The result was a kindly courtesy," W. J. Cash has written, "a level-eyed pride, an easy quietness, a barely perceptible flourishing of bearing which, for all its obvious angularity and fundamental plainness, was one of the finest things the Old South produced."

Southerners clung to the aristocratic myth with such intensity partly because the moral dilemmas of slavery were so real and pervasive and needed to be in some way disproved. There was the brutalizing effect of having constantly to discipline slaves. The whip was always in the background, together with chains, shackles, bloodhounds, mutilations, and branding iron—and the rank fact of sadistic cruelty released and unpunished. There were also slavery's sexual aspects. It has been estimated that only one in five slaves lacked some degree of white inheritance. An 1858 figure put the number of mulattoes at around 800,000. Whatever the statistics, it was abundantly clear that miscegenation was common.

Everyone, most of all the white women who were the "ladies" of the plantation, knew what went on between many white masters and black slave women. If for women everywhere in Victorian Anglo-

American life the subject of sex was taboo, for the white women in the South it was a nightmare. It was not to be discussed or written about, nor were proper ladies supposed to enjoy it. Yet practically before her eyes the plantation lady saw voluptuous sexuality displayed. Black women were everywhere regarded as sexuality embodied, in contrast with the image of chastity and purity the white woman was supposed to emulate. On the auction block, black females were commonly stripped so that prospective buyers could view them more clearly. For commercial reasons, slave girls were often taught an easy compliance. Many white boys learned to take advantage of the slave girls who were among their playmates on the plantation, and they often kept them as sexual companions throughout life.

As the diarist Mary Chesnut, a plantation lady herself, put it, "Under slavery we live surrounded by prostitutes, yet an abandoned [white] woman is sent out of any decent house. . . . Like the patriarchs of old, our men live all in one house with their wives and their concubines; and the mulattoes one sees in every family partly resemble the white children." She wryly observed that "any lady is ready to tell you who is the father of all the mulatto children in everybody's household but her own."

Miscegenation was everywhere condemned,

A view of New Orleans at the time of the visit of the Frenchman Alexis de Tocqueville. An aristocrat himself, he was, although critical of slavery, sensitive to southern charm.

and yet it flourished. Northern abolitionists did not ease the tension this obvious contradiction built into Southern life when they dwelt, as they did constantly, on the image of every Southern planter wallowing in lechery. It was for this reason—to answer the Yankee and show the goodness of Southern life—that the myth of the Southern gentleman was continually trumpeted abroad. Another such myth was that of the Southern Belle, the idealized mate to the Cavalier. Both North and South placed "the woman" on an impossibly elevated pedestal, but the virtue of the Southern family, it was asserted, was far superior to that of Northern families, as demonstrated by the spotless, mystically pure, gleaming Southern belle.

She became the symbol of Southern nationality. Armies marching off to the Civil War cheered her and proclaimed on their banners that it was for the Southern woman that they fought. Angel of mercy, she was depicted as ministering to the blacks in their illnesses, surrounding her noble husband with beauty and domestic bliss, gracing every public occasion with her smiling and uplifting presence, and teaching her children the eternal values of true manhood and gentle womanhood. Toasts at dinners, sermons in church, speeches in crowded public squares—hardly any of them did not begin and end with shouted paeans of praise in her honor. "Woman!!! the center and circumstance, diameter and periphery, sine, tangent, and secant of all our affections!" So ran a toast that was cheered again and again at Georgia's centennial celebration in the 1830s.

Yet many Southerners felt a sense of impending catastrophe. Living in a slave society, they watched the triumphant rise of equalitarianism in the North with much alarm. It was clear to them that the South could not continue for long holding on to the democratic values of the nation and at the same time whipping slaves. Such men despairingly observed the South's growing isolation. Young Southerners used to go to England for their education, acquiring a cultured cosmopolitanism; they did this no longer. There used to be much interaction with the Northern states; this too was dying away. Major churches—the Baptists and the Methodists—had split off in anger from their Northern counterparts. Virginians, especially, felt how changed things were. "And thus we, who once swayed the councils of the Union," said one of them in 1852, "find our power gone, and our influence on the wane." History, it seemed, was passing them by.

Southern Honor

A brilliant book by historian Bertram Wyatt-Brown, *Southern Honor: Ethics and Behavior in the Old South* (1982), has recently warned us that we will not understand the South before (or after) the Civil War if we believe that Southerners lived primarily by a gentle aristocratic code of careful thought and reasoned discourse. Many did, of course. The Thomas Jeffersons and James Madisons glowingly embodied that ethic, and Whigs North and South venerated the memory of Madison, that classic man of thought. As the expansive, booming prewar South took shape, however, it was Andrew Jackson who increasingly spoke for the majority, the South of the Democratic party: of Yankee-hating, violence and dueling, and an aggressively proud and touchy masculinity. This South, which would eventually sweep the Southern states into secession and war, lived by a warrior code of *honor*.

In living this way, we should not think that Southerners were at all unusual. In fact, in the world at large they were right in the mainstream. As far back as human memory goes, to ancient tribal times, most of the world's peoples have lived and breathed the code of honor, and perhaps most of them still do. It was only in a few places where life was veering off into the odd ways of modernity, as in parts of industrializing Europe and in the Northeastern American states, that a new widely shared life style that recoiled from violence and emphasized living by a code of "civility" and "respectability" was emerging. Even here, we will see people still talking of "honor" and responding to its powerful urges far into the twentieth century.

Furthermore, we should not think of a way of life like the South's code of honor as something that people take on consciously. They are born into it. They breathe it in the very air, for everyone around them thinks that way. The code of honor was for Southerners part of the "of course" universe, the things that seem so obvious, so (apparently) instinctive and "natural," that they are not even a matter for serious discussion. To be ready at any moment to use violence, even to die, to protect one's standing as a man of honor? Of course. Is there really any other way to live that would not be shameful?

This is the key, in the code of honor: shame—which means being regarded with contempt by others.

The community's judgment—this is the crucial thing. To be proud of oneself required respect from others; it required having a spotless reputation for courage and what was called "being a man." The newer Yankee way offered a sharply contrasting ethic. Yankees believed people should listen to their own God-instructed consciences and feel *guilt* (not shame, a different thing) if they were not true to their inner voices, to the gyroscope inside.

The warrior code prized having *power* over others and *prestige* in the community. It was important to be the kind of man whom other people labored for, and served. Thus, not working with the hands was itself a mark of honor. In such a society, slavery was valued not simply as a money-making system but as a powerful source of honor. Being an honorable man also meant bearing suffering, pain, and even death stoically, above all if one were fighting for the honor of one's own family. Northerners certainly venerated the family, but the passionate commitment to family, to the kinfolk, that Southerners displayed (and still display) was extraordinary.

Wyatt-Brown, drawing on the recent researches of Grady McWhiney and Forrest McDonald, makes an interesting suggestion: That the warrior code of honor may have been so strong in the South because of the kind of people who settled it. The original settlements in the Tidewater Lowlands were English, many Germans arrived in the eighteenth century, but the people who set the tone for Southern life from the time of Andrew Jackson onward were the hundreds of thousands of Scots and Scotch-Irish who had swarmed into the Southern colonies in the 1700s. They had come from the more tribal and mountainous "back country" of the British Isles, the so-called Celtic fringe, where for centuries they had been warlike herdsmen remote from the great centers of civilization. Their history of almost continual fighting among themselves and against the English, in the name of the warrior code, filled the novels of Sir Walter Scott with irresistible glamour and heroism. Published in a voluminous stream from the 1820s onward, Scott's novels—*Ivanhoe, Rob Roy, The Lady of the Lake*, and many others—were read avidly in the South. Clannishness, the blood feud, the glories of personal combat, an addiction to violence, and a passionate protection of honor: Scots and Scotch-Irish culture seemed to concern itself with little else. So too in the South, the warrior code of honor reigned supreme.

The Militant South

The language Southerners used of themselves in the pre–Civil War years, then, was entirely fitting. Talking of the South and its future, the *Southern Quarterly Review* insisted that as a "warrior race," Southerners will "found an empire, illustrious in arms, as renowned in arts. . . . [Their] empire will be peace; but the sword will share the supremacy of the spade, the camp contribute no less to the national glory than the forum and the senate."

Being militant and eager for combat was, after all, an ingrained Southern trait by the 1850s. All observers, within and outside the South, agreed with remarkable unanimity that Southerners loved to fight. It was a reputation proudly worn. Most Southerners lived in the countryside, where guns were used from early childhood; most cultivated the qualities of a master race, dominating slaves whether or not they owned any; and they praised, above all, the man who could ride fast, shoot straight, and down his adversary.

Southerners claimed unique military talents and wrote many histories of the American Revolution to explain how much the patriot victory owed to Southern military genius and valor. They claimed responsibility for the War of 1812, scornfully condemning the New Englanders who had opposed it. The Mexican War was their special pride, for Southerners had made up by far the largest body of soldiers in the American forces and had provided much of the leadership. It was to them a "magnificent dream of sport, glory, and opulence."

Everyday life kept Southerners in fighting trim. Duels were a constant feature of life among the elite, and wrestling and gouging of eyes were similarly common among the poor. In Alabama, a newspaper observed that "this stabbing and dirking [knifing] business has become so common and fashionable, that it has lost all the horror and detestation among . . . our population." A visitor in Mississippi found that his host's sons, aged eleven and thirteen, were regularly engaged in studying boxing, fencing, and shooting with rifle and handgun. At school young Southerners carried sticks and knives, and used them. Even lawyers found it necessary to carry a pair of pistols in their briefcases. Editors, frequent targets of violence, went suitably armed.

The South, with its scattered plantations and

lack of towns, had never paid much attention to providing public schools—with the result that ignorance and illiteracy remained in the South for generations after it had been largely eliminated in the North. It did, however, turn early to establishing military schools. Not only were the soldier's virtues much praised, but the idea of implanting discipline in a predominantly unruly young population seemed one solution for the turbulence of Southern life.

Several privately supported military schools existed in Southern states by 1839, and in that year the first to be founded with public support appeared—the Virginia Military Institute. South Carolinians were so impressed that in 1842 they established two public military schools, of which The Citadel in Charleston became the more famous. State universities established military programs and public funds were given to private schools so that they could begin training soldiers. Military institutes like that in Virginia were established in Kentucky, Alabama, and other states. In the 1850s the creation of such schools accelerated, and by the end of the decade military education had been introduced into more than twenty schools and colleges. By this time most of the textbooks written in the United States on infantry tactics, the use of artillery, gunpowder, or military engineering had been written by Southerners, who took much pride in the fact.

Ready to Fight

By the 1850s talk of war with the North was common in the South. It was confident talk. The South had been preparing for such a conflict for many years. Not only were military schools turning out the necessary officers, and rough-and-tumble living among the poor turning out the necessary soldiers, but also vigorous efforts were under way to build iron foundries, arms factories, and local armories. Thousands of rifles and other weapons were gathered from every possible source by the Southern state governments. Wherever the attack came from, the slaves or the North, Southerners intended to be fully ready.

At the same time, mob action began to take the place of court action against anyone suspected of criticizing Southern institutions. A professor driven from the University of North Carolina for his free-soil beliefs observed, "If the . . . spirit of terror, mobs, arrests and violence continue, it will not be long before civil war will rage at the South." The South's situation produced an intolerance of dissent that verged on dictatorship. It was only the rarely courageous public man, and then only the most eminent and impregnable, who could any longer express doubts about slavery without being mobbed, tarred and feathered, and even hanged.

The ban on dissent spread to every other aspect of Southern life, to all its treasured myths and saving rationalizations. Even proposing different courses of action—for Southerners argued intensely over the proper tactics to adopt in national politics—could be fatal. Five editors of the Vicksburg *Journal* were shot down in the course of thirteen years. Though not yet at war, the South had become a war society. No longer did the leaders who modeled themselves on the quiet rationality of a James Madison catch the Southern eye. They had been replaced by those who adopted the rhetoric of "fire eaters" like Robert Barnwell Rhett and William Lowndes Yancey, who bellowed about Yankees and poured out hatred.

This was the South that looked out on the shattering and ever more threatening national events of the 1850s. Locked into a static way of life, driven to compensate for its maddening frustrations by adopting more and more irrational and potentially explosive attitudes, the South moved steadily toward detonation.

BIBLIOGRAPHY

Throughout this book, W. Elliot Brownlee's *Dynamics of Ascent: A History of the American Economy* (2d ed., 1979), has been essential to me. On immigration and ethnic conflict, there is now a large literature. See Robert Henry Billigmeier, *Americans from Germany: A Study in Cultural Diversity* (1974); Ray Allen Billington, *The Protestant Crusade 1800–1860: A Study of the Origins of American Nativism* (1964); L. Perry Curtis, Jr., *Apes and Angels: The Irishman in Victorian Caricature* (1971); Leonard Dinner-stein and David M. Reimers, *Ethnic Americans: A History of Immigration and Assimilation* (1975); John B. Duff, *The Irish in the United States* (1971); and Michael Feldberg, *The Philadelphia Riots of 1844: A Study of Ethnic Conflict* (1975). Terry Coleman's *Going to America* (1973) gives us a graphic, closeup view of the immigration experience. The South and slavery are the subjects of a huge and absorbing historical literature. Eugene D. Genovese's brilliant *Roll, Jordan, Roll* (1974) is now the fundamental work on slavery, especially on the attitudes between master and slave. Leon Litwack's *Been in the Storm So Long* (1979) gives a slave's-eye viewpoint with sensitivity. The entire question of profitability has been much discussed, since Robert W. Fogel and Stanley L. Engerman's much-debated study, *Time on the Cross* (1974). A major work still of importance is Kenneth Stampp, *The Peculiar Institution: Slavery in the Ante-Bellum South* (1956), which made us aware that there was much turbulence and slave rebelliousness on plantations, while Stanley Elkins explored the potentiality for making "Sambos" out of slaves in Southern plantation slavery in his *Slavery: A Problem in American Institutional and Intellectual Life* (2d ed., 1968). Two books that sensitively explore the Southern mind are W. J. Cash's *The Mind of the South* (1941), an enduring masterpiece, and William R. Taylor's absorbing *Cavalier and Yankee: The Old South and American National Character* (1961).

Bertram Wyatt-Brown's remarkable work, *Southern Honor: Ethics & Behavior in the Old South* (1982), and John Hope Franklin's *The Militant South, 1800–1861* (1964), have been exceptionally helpful to me. Herbert G. Gutman's *The Black Family in Slavery and Freedom, 1750–1925* (1976) is a path-breaking study, as is also John W. Blassingame's *The Slave Community: Plantation Life in the Antebellum South* (rev. and enl. ed., 1979). A view of daily life is presented in Leslie Howard Owens, *This Species of Property: Slave Life and Culture in the Old South* (1976). Carl N. Degler has given us an important comparative book in *Neither Black nor White: Slavery and Race Relations in Brazil and the United States* (1971), and relevant chapters in Vincent Harding's *There Is a River: The Black Struggle for Freedom in America* (1981) offer superb writing and excellent description.

John McCardell, in *The Idea of a Southern Nation: Southern Nationalists and Southern Nationalism, 1830–1860* (1979),

has in an award-winning book reopened this major topic. Older and still valuable are: Clement Eaton, *The Growth of Southern Civilization* (1961); Avery O. Craven, *The Growth of Southern Nationalism, 1848–1861* (1953); and C. S. Sydnor, *The Development of Southern Sectionalism* (1948).

Industrial growth in the 1850s can be traced in several of the general economic histories cited in Chapter 10. Especially worthwhile is Douglass C. North's *The Economic Growth of the United States, 1790–1860* (1961), which emphasizes regional specialization and the tremendous demand for American cotton in Europe as main causes for economic growth. Relevant chapters in Allan Nevins's *Ordeal of the Union*, Vols. 1 and 2 (1947), discuss economic trends without neglecting the human drama of the era, and are highly recommended.

In *The Farmer's Age: Agriculture, 1815–1860* (1960), Paul W. Gates sees the Civil War as the beginning of the end of the "farmer's age." In *History of Agriculture in the Southern United States to 1860*, Vols. 1 and 2 (1933), Lewis C. Gray examined the impact of agricultural change on Southern society. Gray's accomplishment duplicated Percy W. Bidwell and John I. Falconer's study of the northern states, *History of Agriculture in the Northern United States, 1620–1860* (1925). See also William T. Hutchinson, *Cyrus Hall McCormick: Seed Times, 1809–1856* (1930).

The significance of railroads in the pre–Civil War era is strikingly contrasted in two provocative studies with differing conclusions: Albert Fishlow, *American Railroads and the Transformation of the Ante-Bellum Economy* (1965), and R. W. Fogel, *Railroads and American Economic Growth* (1964). Thomas C. Cochran explores the social attitudes of railroad builders and financiers in *Railroad Leaders, 1845–1890* (1953).

17

Disruption Begins: Bleeding Kansas

TIME LINE

1852   Franklin Pierce elected fourteenth president of the United States

1853   Gadsden Purchase

1854   Kansas-Nebraska Act; Republican party formed; first antislavery settlers arrive in Kansas

1855   Proslavery territorial legislature elected in Kansas; rival Free-Soil legislature formed; slave constitution ratified in Kansas

1856   Free-Soil Kansas government formed; attack on Senator Charles Sumner in Senate; sack of Lawrence, Kansas, by proslavery forces; John Brown attacks Pottawatomie Creek settlement; violence breaks out throughout Kansas; Governor John Geary restores peace; James Buchanan elected fifteenth president of the United States

1857   Proslavery Lecompton constitution adopted in Kansas; *Dred Scott* decision announced by Supreme Court

1858   Kansas voters reject Lecompton constitution

HISTORY IN AN INDIVIDUAL LIFE

HARRIET BEECHER STOWE

The publisher was astonished. He knew that Harriet Beecher Stowe had for years been one of America's most popular women writers, but no one had even faintly imagined what was now happening to her latest book, *Uncle Tom's Cabin*; *or Life Among the Lowly* (two vols., Boston, 1852). The publisher was being inundated with a flood of orders for it. Five thousand copies had been printed; 3,000 were gone the first day, the rest in two more. Some 50,000 copies were sold in two months; a year after its appearance, 305,000 copies of *Uncle Tom* had gone out to the world, thundering presses were working day and night to keep up with the demand, and sales were as heavy as ever. Eventually, *Uncle Tom* sold in the millions.

It was an earthquake. The South erupted in anger, pouring hatred and scorn upon Stowe not only as a liar and a fraud but for being unwomanly: She had become a public figure! Most of her preacher brothers were abolitionists; the dearest of them to her, the famous New York Congregationalist minister Henry Ward Beecher, had urged her on. After the hated Fugitive Slave Act was passed in 1850, she had vowed to strike back in the only way by which women could then reach large audiences: by the pen. "I feel as if I could be willing to sink with it," she had written her husband, "were all this sin and misery to sink in the sea. I wish some Martin Luther would arise to set this community right." For thousands of fascinated and horrified readers in the North, she had then done the nearest thing: She electrified them, making slavery a reality, and an abomination that could no longer be abided.

Stowe had hit upon the very means by which people's feelings would be most directly touched. In an age that idealized the family, that elevated women and children and loving fathers to near divinity, she created a family and then graphically, painfully tore it apart before her readers' eyes. "My vocation is simply that of a painter," she wrote to her editor as she was composing the book, "and my object will be to hold up in the most lifelike and graphic manner possible Slavery, its reverses, changes, and the negro character. . . . There is no arguing with [word] *pictures*, and everybody is impressed by them, whether they mean to be or not." No one had ever made black people the subject of a novel before, or had taken them seriously; now, for hundreds of thousands, the fate of black Americans in slavery could never again be thought of in abstract terms.

In England, Stowe was lavishly honored by royalty in later years. Abraham Lincoln himself said, when she called upon him in the White House, that he was honored to meet the woman who had started the Civil War. She never again, in her many later novels and stories, met anything like the response she won with *Uncle Tom*, but one blockbusting novel in a career—perhaps the most powerful and influential book ever written by an American—is surely enough to establish for her a lasting achievement.

Overview

The 1850s began optimistically. The slavery issue appeared to be settled by the Compromise of 1850, and the gold rush to California, with the ensuing boom in the national economy, held out hopes of an abundant future. In 1854, however, the slavery problem was suddenly reopened. The Kansas-Nebraska Act of that year and the turmoil that followed in Kansas inflamed and divided the nation as the war in Vietnam did more than a century later. By the time the Kansas issue had subsided in 1858, the presidencies of Franklin Pierce and James Buchanan were shattered, the Democratic party was ready to break apart, the Whigs had disintegrated, and a new party, the Republicans, had appeared. "Bleeding Kansas" worked a revolution in the politics of the nation and set the United States on its course to civil war.

Franklin Pierce Becomes President

The presidential election of 1852 was a national referendum on the Compromise of 1850, of which the most controversial feature was the Fugitive Slave Act. The Democrats ran Franklin Pierce, a New Hampshire politician who supported the Fugitive Slave Act, popular sovereignty in the Mexican Cession, the principle of strong states' rights, and the continuing existence of slavery. He was swept into the White House with a huge Democratic majority in Congress.

When inaugurated, Pierce announced that in his foreign policy he would not be held back "by any timid forebodings of evil from expansion." As Caleb Cushing, the attorney general, said in a New Jersey speech, "We are now the men of modern Rome"; Rome had "conquered [and] went on annexing." Some men talked eagerly of getting more land from Mexico. James Gadsden, the American minister to Mexico, arranged a treaty with that nation in 1853 by which, for $15 million, lower California and a large area in northwestern Mexico would become American territory. Northern congressmen feared a proslavery plot and scaled down the area purchased to what is now the southern portion of Arizona and New Mexico, which reputedly contained a good railroad route to California, and lowered the purchase price to $10 million. This, the Gadsden Purchase, added 45,535 square miles to the

nation and ended the continental expansion of the United States, save for the later purchase of Alaska.

The Kansas Issue Erupts

With California growing rapidly and settlers moving into Oregon and Washington, a railroad was needed to link these areas to the rest of the nation. Four routes were surveyed in 1853: from the St. Paul–Minneapolis region to Seattle; from Chicago or St. Louis to San Francisco; from Memphis to San Francisco; and from New Orleans to San Diego. The question now was, Which route should be taken?

Those Democrats who called themselves "Young America" now looked to Senator Stephen A. Douglas of Illinois as their leader. A short man of powerful physique and leonine head, the Little Giant was "young in years, bold in temper, and pugnacious in spirit." He was fascinated by the prospect of opening the West to settlement and felt uniquely chosen to lead this grand endeavor, having successfully shepherded the Compromise of 1850 through Congress. In January 1854 Douglas moved to secure two objectives: Get Southern support for a *central* railroad route across the continent, and open the region beyond the Missouri to settlement. As chairman of the Senate Committee on Territories, he proposed a bill that would establish a territorial government for the whole of the Indian country north of what is now Oklahoma and *make it possible for slavery to move into the region* on the basis of popular sovereignty. In particular, the bill would create two territories, Kansas and Nebraska, one implicitly for slavery and the other for free soil; deny Congress any role in deciding whether the territories were to be free or slave; and explicitly *repeal the Missouri Compromise*, so that slaveholders could take their property to Kansas from the very beginning, rather than at such time as a territorial legislature would decide for or against slavery.

The Northern states exploded in rage. In what appeared to Northerners to be a massive swindle, that venerable compact, the Missouri Compromise (which still governed slavery policy in the vast area that remained unorganized in the former Louisiana Purchase) was to be torn up. Thousands of Northerners concluded angrily that the nation was being handed over to a conspiracy of Southern slave owners and their Northern sympathizers. Debate over the bill raged in Congress for four months. But predominantly pro-Southern Democrats, with their command

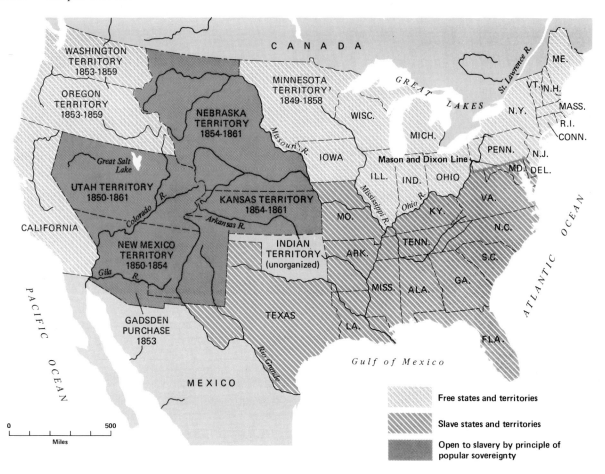

The Kansas-Nebraska Act, 1854

Map legend:
- Free states and territories
- Slave states and territories
- Open to slavery by principle of popular sovereignty

of most seats in Congress from the South, were too strong to hold back. Despite all protests, the Senate enacted the Kansas-Nebraska bill on March 3, 1854, after an all-night debate, by a vote of thirty-seven to fourteen. Two and a half months later, the House of Representatives did the same, by the bare margin of three votes.

Kansas: Proslavery Forces Become Aggressive

The people of western Missouri were determined to make the newly created Territory of Kansas a slave state. Otherwise they would be hemmed in on three sides by free states. Slaves would constantly run away, especially in western Missouri, where freedom would be just across the Missouri River. Proslavery men were especially outraged at the activities

of the New England Emigrant Aid Company. With great public fanfare it gathered funds to send organized groups of free-soil settlers to Kansas. Its work was exaggerated to gigantic proportions in the Southern mind. Everyone on the proslavery side—including President Pierce—referred constantly to the company as the embodiment of Yankee meddling, arrogance, and moral hypocrisy.

The fact was, however, that free-soil settlers continued to pour into the Territory of Kansas mainly from the states of the Northwest and the border South. They were not aggressive antislavery activists but ordinary farmers who wanted land, did not own slaves, and had no desire to see black men brought in or a slaveowning plantation aristocracy created. Meanwhile, few slaveowners came to the territory. Why go into an area where the future of slavery was in doubt, while Arkansas and Texas were eagerly welcoming slaveholding immigrants? The base for the hopes of proslavery men—the rapid arrival in Kansas of a sizable slaveholding population—never materialized.

These considerations had a critically important effect on the tactics adopted by proslavery men. However valid popular sovereignty might be in theory, *they could not bring themselves to allow it to operate in practice.* The issue, in their minds, was simply too crucial. They gave up on the democratic system and turned to fraud, intimidation, and violence on a mass scale to get what they wanted. When the first territorial election in Kansas approached in the fall of 1854—the choosing of a territorial delegate to Congress—U.S. Senator David Atchison harangued up and down the Missouri frontier, urging Missourians to cross over into Kansas and cast ballots. In the words of a later congressional investigation, a "systematic invasion" then occurred. More than half the 2,800 ballots cast in the election were fraudulent, and the proslavery delegate was elected.

With these events the Kansas problem took on a new character. A large-scale organized attack had been initiated against the nation's basic principle: majority rule. One major segment of the American population had decided to *impose* its will on another large group of Americans and seize the government of an entire territory. Furthermore, this was being done by Southerners, and ever since the gag-rule controversy of the 1830s there had been one long series—to Northern eyes—of arrogant actions by the "slave power." It appeared that the white South was going to destroy the most fundamental thing of all—the rule of law. How could any issue be more crucial? The argument over slavery had broken out into an arena without boundaries; anything might happen, and the first casualty would be the government itself. This was why the nation became obsessed with the Kansas issue. It was a crisis in which fundamental principles, of which slavery was only one, were at stake.

In March 1855 a territorial legislature was elected. By threats, wholesale stuffing of ballot boxes, and the expelling of impartial judges, every proslavery candidate save one was elected to the legislature.

Illinois senator Stephen A. Douglas, the leader of those Northern Democrats who believed slavery should be left alone, advocated popular sovereignty (local option) on the issue in the western territories, and boomed western development.

Some 4,969 illegal votes were cast in the election as against 1,210 that were valid. Meeting in Shawnee, Kansas, in August 1855, the proslavery legislature adopted the statutes of Missouri, declared slavery legal, and provided that anyone criticizing the legality of slavery would be imprisoned. Restricting the holding of office to proslavery men, it unseated the free-state members.

In response, free-soil settlers created a territorial government of their own. They condemned the slave legislature as the tool of the "demagogues of Missouri" and declared its laws null and void. Through the autumn of 1855, an interim free-state govenment sat in Topeka, drew up a new constitution, and submitted it to the voters in December. It was adopted by a vote of 1,731 to 46. In January 1856, free-soilers elected a "state" governor and legislature. They also chose a free-state territorial delegate to Congress. The free-soilers did not simply exclude slavery in their constitution and laws; they tried to exclude all blacks from Kansas, slave or free. From the beginning they took pains to declare to the nation that they were *not* abolitionists, despite the accusations of Southerners, President Pierce, and their other critics. When the Topeka authorities sent the free-state constitution out to the voters, they also put up for consideration a proposal to prevent free blacks, as well as slaves, from entering Kansas. It was adopted 1,287 to 453.

The Attack on Charles Sumner

The atmosphere in Congress was now electric, for a steady succession of spectacular events had put everyone's nerves on edge. Indeed, throughout the North a mounting obsession with slavery and its evils seemed to be seizing the popular mind. When Harriet Beecher Stowe published her *Uncle Tom's Cabin* in 1852, she and her publishers were astonished at the public reaction. The book was a strong force in making it legitimate to speak publicly of the cruelties of slavery.

In May 1856, Charles Sumner, a senator from Massachusetts, gave a two-day address on the floor of the Senate. Attacking the South and its institutions in violent and insulting language, he also personally vilified, among others, a kindly and much respected senator from South Carolina, Andrew P. Butler. That gentleman, Sumner said, "has chosen a mistress to whom he has made his vows, and who, though ugly to others, is chaste in his sight—I mean the harlot, Slavery." According to Sumner, errors of judgment were the least of Butler's defects, for he was guilty of lying whenever he opened his mouth.

Preston S. Brooks, Senator Butler's nephew and a member of the House of Representatives, determined to avenge these insults to his kinsman's honor in the only way known to the South Carolina aristocracy—by violence. On the twenty-second of May he approached Sumner at his desk on the Senate floor, where the senator sat writing letters. Brooks called Sumner's name, stated briefly that his speech was "a libel on South Carolina, and Mr. Butler, who is a friend of mine," and suddenly began raining heavy, smashing blows on Sumner's head with a thick cane. Southern senators and congressmen stood around approvingly, taking no steps to halt the beating. The bleeding Sumner staggered from the chamber and was unable to return to his seat for more than three years.

The South cheered Brooks's "chivalry." The "elegant and effectual caning" pleased the Richmond *Whig*. "The only regret we feel is that Mr. Brooks did not employ a horsewhip or cowhide upon his slanderous back instead of a cane." But the North was outraged. Protest meetings were held everywhere. "You can have little idea," wrote a conservative Bostonian, "of the depth and intensity of the feeling which has been excited in New England. The concurrence of the Kansas horrors has wrought up the masses to a state of fearful desperation." Northerners in growing numbers became convinced that the whole system of government in the United States was being overwhelmed by brute force, whether in Kansas or in Washington. William Cullen Bryant, editor of the New York *Evening Post*, expressed Northern apprehensions tellingly:

> Violence reigns in the streets of Washington . . . violence has now found its way into the Senate chamber. Violence lies in wait on all the navigable rivers and all the railways of Missouri, to obstruct those who pass from the free States into Kansas. Violence overhangs the frontiers of that Territory like a stormcloud charged with hail and lightning. Violence has carried election after election in that Territory. . . . In short, violence is the order of the day; the North is to be pushed to the wall by it, and this plot will succeed if the people of the free States are as apathetic as the slaveholders are insolent.

War Begins in Kansas

The day before Sumner was attacked, the proslavery sheriff of Kansas led an armed force of over 750 men to Lawrence. Led by a banner displaying "Southern Rights" and "South Carolina," their objective was to arrest officials of the free-state government whom the proslavery chief justice of the territory, Samuel D. LeCompte, had declared guilty of treason. The free-state governor, Charles Robinson, was thrown in jail, and the proslavery militia destroyed the town. This was the "sack of Lawrence," which became a national *cause célèbre*.

John Brown now entered the scene. A nervous, highly strung Ohioan in his mid-fifties, Brown had been reared by his devout abolitionist father to believe that he was chosen by God "to break the jaws of the wicked." In 1855 Brown followed five of his sons to Kansas, taking a wagon full of guns, ammunition, and artillery sabres. The attack on Lawrence sent him over the edge. With four sons and two other men, he set out to accomplish some act that by its ferocity would, he hoped, punish proslavery men, frighten them, and make them rue their ways.

His favorite maxim was that "without the shedding of blood there is no remission of sins." On the night of May 24, 1856, Brown and his band attacked a proslavery settlement on Pottawatomie Creek. Five innocent men were dragged from their homes and shot or hacked to death. In one incident a man and his two sons were murdered while his wife pleaded for their lives.

A cry of horror went up, North and South. "WAR! WAR!" trumpeted the Westport, Missouri, *Border Times*. And so it was to be. Proslavery men quickly launched attacks against isolated farmsteads. Missourians bearing guns patrolled all roads to Kansas, stopped river boats, seized weapons, and subjected travelers to frightening interrogations. Homes were burned and looted, free-soilers were ordered to leave—large numbers actually did flee—and from every direction came reports of bloodshed. People in Northern states gathered funds for free-soilers in Kansas for the purchase of arms. In Chicago, Boston, Syracuse, and many other cities, crowds gathered to listen to speeches and pass condemnatory resolutions.

Brown's massacre sent a wave of anger and righteous indignation through the South, leading to

Preston Brooks, attacking Charles Sumner in the Senate after Sumner spoke against proslavery forces in Kansas, became the burning example for Northerners of the Southern tendency to use violence and crush freedom of speech in the cause of slavery.

Brought to a show of arms by the crisis in Kansas in 1856, a gun crew protects Topeka, the seat of free-state government.

a flood of monetary aid being hurried to proslavery Kansas from groups formerly uncertain about the validity of the cause. Senator Atchison exulted that "in a few months, in my opinion, there will not be an abolitionist left in Kansas; they will be swept with a clean broom. Then the war will be carried elsewhere, if war we are to have." As skirmish followed skirmish—in Palmyra, Franklin, Osawatomie, and elsewhere—newspapers all over the nation gave attention to little else.

In the fall of 1856, John Geary, a veteran of difficult governmental tasks in California, was sent to be governor. In short order he pacified Kansas by dissolving the existing militia, which consisted mainly of proslavery Missourians, and forming a new organization composed of actual Kansans. Then he intercepted an invading Missouri army of several thousand men, negotiated with Senator Atchison and the force's other leaders, and convinced them that he would bring a halt to free-soiler assaults on proslavery settlers. Meanwhile, federal troops captured a large band of free-soilers who had just completed an attack and threw them in jail. Agitators on both sides were sought out and imprisoned. Calm finally came to Kansas, but not until some two hundred lives had been lost and millions of dollars in property destroyed.

The Rise of the Republican Party

Now a new era of critical elections began. By the election of 1856, the Jacksonian system of political parties—the "second-party system"—was shattered. The tide of immigrants from Ireland and Germany had already drained strength from the Whig party, for thousands of citizens both North and South left it to join the nativist American party, which was growing with explosive speed. Hatred of Catholics and of foreigners seemed to be unhinging the structure of American politics. Then came the Kansas crisis, which thrust the slavery issue and the North-South conflict into everyone's consciousness. Both the Whigs and the Know-Nothings tried to straddle the issue, hoping by ignoring it to hold onto their Northern and Southern followers, but this only destroyed them. The crisis could no longer be pushed aside.

Almost as if by spontaneous combustion, a new political party burst into being in the Northern states in 1854. Everywhere it was said by those opposed to the apparently rising South, and to its helpmeet, the Democratic party, that American republicanism was in danger as it had not been since the Revolution itself. On the one side were the Catholics from Ireland and Germany, who threatened Protestant America—

and to hundreds of thousands of Americans, only a Protestant country, one based on the idea of religious individualism, could be a republican country. Rising from the other direction was the threat of the Slave Power—the South. The Southerners, so it seemed in Kansas, had clearly turned away from the essential values in republicanism: democracy, free votes, majority rule. They appeared determined to force their supremacy on the North. The Whigs, compromisers to the end, were simply not *angry* enough at this sight for many thousands of Northerners.

The name "Republican" for the new party seemed to spring up naturally. The Democrats, it was said, had fallen into the hands of slavery, and had lost all ties with republicanism. Indeed, Republicans said that it was now their party that was the true inheritor of the legacy of Thomas Jefferson; that it was they who believed genuinely in liberty, and in the Democrats' old cry of equality. Thousands of Northern Democrats, furious with Southerners after the Kansas-Nebraska Act and the Kansas crisis, decamped for the Republican party as the only true party of Jeffersonian republicanism. So did the former Free-Soilers, the Liberty party men, and thousands of ex-Whigs who had for a time joined the anti-Catholic American Party.

Wherever Yankees were strong in numbers, the Republican party was powerful: in New England, and in a great band of territory running westward in the upper North, where New Englanders had settled. In fact, the Republican party was far more a Yankee party than the Whigs had been, for it had no Southern wing to balance the New Englanders. Inspired by the same vision of a universal Yankee nation that in revolutionary days had possessed Sam Adams, the Republicans pulled in the traditionally Whig ethnocultural groups. Evangelicals, moral reformers who wanted the government to outlaw drinking and "evil recreations," zealous Protestants (including Northern Baptists and Methodists) who hated Catholics, and Scotch-Irishmen, who traditionally looked on the Catholic Irish with contempt—all joined the new party. The Republicans inherited the atmosphere of respectability and good family that had always been a Whig characteristic, and drew in those attracted by such qualities. Then there were the economic motivations that since Hamilton's day had united people in opposition to the Democrats. The Republican party quickly became the vehicle of those business interests that wanted to see the federal government take an active role in the economy.

Republican Ambivalence toward Blacks

How to explain the swift rise of the Republican party? The traditional view, recounted in political histories for decades, was that the Republicans appeared because Northerners loved freedom and abhorred slavery and needed a new party to express this moral fervor. But in recent years a new note has been sounded—that the Republicans were not troubled by slavery as much as they were troubled by blacks. They wanted the territories to be for whites only. The free-soil forces in Kansas consistently voted to deny free blacks entry into Kansas. In short, Republicans too were racists.

Though true, this statement must be qualified. The most accurate description of the Republican attitude toward black people was that they were undecided, ambivalent, pulled forward and backward. Republican leaders genuinely detested slavery. William H. Seward of New York, perhaps the Republican party's most articulate spokesman, called for giving the vote to black Americans and urged that fundamental civil rights be granted to them. Democratic orators constantly played on Northerners' fears of blacks, but few Republicans did so. Even so, Seward publicly stated that blacks were a "foreign and feeble" element in American society that could never be assimilated, and Salmon P. Chase, another Republican of high standing, observed that the white and black races must inevitably separate. An expressed doubt ran through Republican speeches that blacks could ever be capable of achieving full equality, no matter what opportunities were opened to them. Public law should not *keep* black people down, but social inferiority was probably their natural condition, most (by no means all) Republicans believed.

What, then, was really behind the Republican party's meteoric ascent? Its members were genuinely opposed to the institution of slavery, though extremely few were abolitionists. They certainly wanted, as much as the next white man, to keep the territories white. But most of all, the Republican party grew with such startling speed because *millions of Americans in the North regarded the Kansas-Nebraska Act as the opening bell in a last-ditch struggle to save the American republic.* They believed that would happen only if the *Northern* way of life could be protected and then gain national supremacy.

The North and South were both convinced that in order to survive, their societies had to expand territorially. Who would get the West? It was crucial to both (or so they believed—and what people believe to be so is the important thing). *The North looked at the South and drew back at what it saw, and what it feared would happen to the whole country if the South won the struggle for supremacy.* Seward traveled extensively in the South in the 1830s, 1840s, and 1850s, and found "an exhausted soil, old and decaying towns, wretchedly neglected roads, and, in every respect, an absence of enterprise and improvement. . . . Such has been the effect of slavery." The existence of slavery had made the idea of manual labor repugnant to whites, so white Southerners, poor or wealthy, seemed to avoid work as being beneath them. Furthermore, all the good land had been taken up by the plantations, which left poor whites only the hardscrabble, infertile soil. Because there were practically no towns where they could find better-paid work, the ordinary poor white seemed to live a shiftless life of lolling on his veranda, drinking bust-head liquor, raising a few spindly crops, and coon hunting in the nearby woods.

Republicans and the Dignity of Labor

Meanwhile, Republicans said, slavery turned blacks into brutes who were "incompetent to cast a shuttle, to grease or oil a wheel and keep it in motion." Lacking any incentive to labor hard in the fields, they were indifferent farm workers and never acquired any real skills. And in a world without the schools that were such objects of pride in the North, few slaves could hope for a good education. Free labor, hard work, the drive to save money and be frugal, an interest in self-improvement, getting ahead, and economic progress—all these essentially modernizing values, which were crucial to Republicans and were to them the attributes of a republican people, seemed fatally lacking in the socially and economically stagnant and backward South.

The dignity of labor was a constant theme of Republican speakers. If free men could labor freely, then America would continue to be the one country in the world in which common men, by working hard and showing a spirit of enterprise, could improve their condition in life and eventually become employers of labor themselves. Republicans rhapsodized an expanding, competitive America. They admired small, independent businessmen who risked their modest capital in enterprising schemes and made the whole system whirl and spin, scattering jobs and good homes and hopes for the future to everyone.

This, then, was what fueled the explosive growth of the Republican party in the mid-1850s, and the emergence of the Third Party System, which would endure until the mid-1890s. Millions of Northerners, wedded to the belief that their system meant hope, progress, and an ever-improving way of life for all and that the Southern system meant stagnation, the debasement of labor, and the destruction of all incentive, felt the moment of national decision had arrived. An expanding South had to be stopped, its conspiratorial hold on the federal government had to be broken, or the "last best hope of earth" would be lost.

The Republicans in the Election of 1856

The Republicans held their first national convention in Philadelphia in June 1856. The gathering had almost the atmosphere of a revival meeting. The chairman of the platform committee was the venerable free-soil ex-Democrat from Pennyslvania David R. Wilmot. To the accompaniment of roar after roar, he shouted out the principles of the new party. Congress, the platform insisted, had no power to make slavery legal in a territory, nor did the territorial legislatures, for this would deprive individuals of their liberty without due process. Congress must positively prohibit slavery in the territories. Kansas must be admitted under the free-state Topeka constitution. The party also urged that the federal government assist in the building of a railroad to the Pacific Coast by a central route, and insisted that Congress had full authority to make appropriations for the improvement of rivers and harbors—Pierce having recently vetoed a bill on the ground that Congress had no such authority.

For months the colorful young explorer John Charles Frémont had been mentioned as a presidential prospect, even the Democrats making overtures in his direction. The Republicans now hoped to launch their "young, bold, and determined party [with] a young, bold, and determined candidate." Amid scenes of wild celebration, with a band playing, hats and handkerchiefs tossing, a pandemonium of yelling from the crowd, and the unfurling of a huge banner reading "John C. Frémont for President," the Republicans unanimously chose the popular young explorer. Shortly afterward the North American party—the

Northern wing of the Know-Nothings—endorsed him as well. This opened the way for the anti-immigrant, anti-Catholic groups to merge with the Republicans. Trailing sadly in the rear, a tiny remnant of the dying Whig party gathered in Baltimore in September and endorsed Millard Fillmore, who earlier had also been chosen by the Southern wing of the Know-Nothing party.

The Election of 1856

The Democrats, convening in Cincinnati, searched for a prominent party figure to be their presidential nominee who was in no way involved in the controversy, and found him in James Buchanan of Pennsylvania.

On election day 1856 there was a massive outpouring of voters. Out of a national population of about 30 million, more than 4 million cast ballots, or some 900,000 more than in 1852. Buchanan received 45 percent of the vote, Frémont 33 percent, and Fillmore 22 percent. The Democrats had won, but Buchanan was a minority president.

Significant shifts had taken place. New York, long a Democratic stronghold, went Republican, and Pennsylvania almost did. New England was in the Republican camp, and the Democrats suffered heavy losses even in their former bastion, the Northwest. The latter development meant that the long alliance between South and Northwest was permanently shattered. The whole of the region north of the Ohio was clearly within reach of the Republicans if in the next election they chose the right candidate.

A sharp split between North and South was the just-emerging Third Party System's most dramatic and ominous feature. The Solid South was born in this balloting. Every state in which slavery was legal went Democratic save Maryland, which went for Fillmore. North of the 41st parallel, which runs just north of New York City and just south of Cleveland and Chicago, the Democrats carried hardly a county. Above that line, in the upper North, was the Republican stronghold. A massive polarization between North and South was under way.

Renewed Crisis in Kansas

The peace in Kansas achieved in the fall of 1856 by Governor Geary did not last long. Land sales boomed, antislavery immigrants continued to arrive, and the populace grew increasingly restive under pro-

slavery rule. Early in 1857 the proslavery legislature in Lecompton made rules concerning the election of a constitutional convention. Fearful of the influx of antislavery settlers that would arrive with spring, the convention ordered that only those who were residents by the middle of March could vote in June for delegates to the convention. In addition, proslavery officials were to supervise the balloting. Then, in a startling move, the legislature decreed that the constitution to be written would not be submitted to the people of Kansas for popular ratification, but would be submitted directly to the president.

Governor Geary vetoed this bill but was overridden. Soon he was in danger of his life. Defied, insulted, even spat upon, he was in the midst of a community where bowie knives and revolvers were carried and assassination talk was common. He appealed to the federal commander at Fort Leavenworth for protection but was refused. On March 4, 1857, on the eve of James Buchanan's inauguration as president, Geary resigned and went east to tell the nation what the "felon legislature" in Lecompton was doing.

James Buchanan Becomes President

On March 4, 1857, James Buchanan of Pennsylvania gave his inaugural address as president of the United States. An indecisive and legalistic man, he had been born while George Washington was in the White House, had won his first election in 1813, served in the War of 1812, and later had a long public career: as congressman, senator, secretary of state under Polk, and as American minister to Russia and Great Britain. A Pennsylvania Scotch-Irishman and thus a hereditary Democrat, he simply could not understand the anger against slavery extension. Endlessly, he worried that an enraged South would secede if its demands were not met.

In his inaugural statement, Buchanan made a major assertion: The question of how much authority Congress had over slavery in the territories, he said, was essentially one for the courts to resolve. At that very moment, he went on, a case was before the Supreme Court (as everyone knew, it was the by-now famous Dred Scott case) that would settle the whole problem conclusively. "To their decision, in common with all good citizens," Buchanan intoned, "I shall cheerfully submit, whatever this may be." In fact, he already knew what the decision was going to be. Historian Don E. Fehrenbacher, in his recent magisterial study of the Dred Scott case, has established conclusively that the president was misleading the country and was trying to load the dice. Behind the scenes, and quite against accepted constitutional practice, Buchanan had been allowed to see the decision: indeed, he had had an influence on how it turned out.

The Supreme Court Boldly Intervenes

Two days later, Chief Justice Roger B. Taney of Maryland, an almost ghostly old man who had held his post since Andrew Jackson appointed him to it in 1836, read from the bench the decision of the U.S. Supreme Court in the case of *Dred Scott* v. *Sanford*, and the country was launched on a new wave of tension. A brief consideration, here, of this case will give us a revealing look at how the Constitution, the courts, and the federal system work.

Dred Scott was an elderly Missouri slave who had been in the courts since 1848 seeking to win his freedom. His argument went thus: During the years from 1834 to 1838 his master had taken Scott with him to live in free Illinois, and later in the Territory of Wisconsin (in that part of it rendered free by the Missouri Compromise of 1820), and therefore he was a free man. His case had been seized on by antislavery people as a crucial one to test great slavery issues, and for the same reason it had been resolutely fought against, on the other side, by slavery sympathizers. Everyone knew that the justices intended to issue a sweeping decision that would cover not simply Scott's status but also Congress's authority over slavery.

This was a bold and risky thing for the Supreme Court to seek to do. Never before had it ever tried to push itself forward into the political arena and "settle" a large public policy question that had been debated for years around the country and in Congress. Indeed, not since *Marbury* v. *Madison* in 1803 had the Court used the power it had asserted and exercised in that case—namely, the power to declare unconstitutional an enactment of the federal Congress. The Court had been pretty busy over the years doing that to state legislation, and we have seen that the Marshall Court had intervened strongly to build up the powers of the national government as against the states. However, as regards essentially national issues it had not followed the philosophy of what is now called "judicial activism." In fact, Justice

Taney himself had specifically held, in an 1838 decision, that the Court's powers did not extend to settling what he called "political questions." These must be handled by the popularly elected legislatures. (This is called the concept of "judicial restraint.") Above all, it was widely said and believed, the Court should "stay out of politics."

However, many like James Buchanan had come finally to despair of Congress—in other words, the democratic process—ever being able to resolve the question of slavery in the territories. So they looked to the Supreme Court, that distinctly nondemocratic institution, calling on it to rumble up its ancient medieval powers and unlimber them like an artillery cannonade to sweep the field clean. As it happened, the Supreme Court at that time was composed mainly of Southerners. Justice Taney himself secretly harbored passionate proslavery views. Now he and his colleagues gave in to the temptation to set aside judicial restraint and to intervene in an important and wrenching "political question."

The Existing Doctrine as to Slaves in a Free State

Over many decades there had been a tacit agreement between the North and the South on what happened to slaves accompanying their masters into a free state. If they were just passing through ("sojourning") with their masters—their presence there being entirely temporary—then Northern courts regarded the laws of their original state of residence as still applying to the master and slave. Therefore, the black person's status of being a slave had remained "attached" to him or her. In proceeding in this way, the Northern courts would be obeying Article IV, Section 1 of the Constitution, which states: "Full Faith and Credit shall be given in each State to the public Acts, records, and judicial Proceedings of every other State." (This is called the principle of "interstate comity.") The sojourning slaves were slaves under the laws of, say, Virginia, and the free state would give "full faith and credit" to that law.

If, however, the master actually took up enduring residence in a free state (was "domiciled" there), became a citizen of that state, and accepted the jurisdiction of its laws, then both Northern and Southern courts agreed that any slaves accompanying the slaveowner would be henceforth "forever free." After all, the laws in the free state did not recognize slavery as a legal condition for *any* of its residents. Furthermore, people thus freed were permanently freed, remaining so even if for some reason they returned to a slave state, for their freedom had been achieved under the laws of a Northern state, and under the principle of interstate comity that status would be given "full faith and credit" in the South.

The Breakdown of Interstate Comity

Beginning in the 1840s, however, Northern courts, especially in Massachusetts, had broken the implied North-South agreement. Courts began ruling that no matter how short or temporary the slave's stay, he or she was free from the moment the master brought the slave into the state (perhaps off a Boston ship for a few hours). In such situations, the courts would cite as precedent a famous decision made in England long before, by a great jurist named Lord Mansfield. In *Somerset* v. *Stewart* (1772), which involved a slave who was briefly in England, Mansfield had held with great sternness that slavery was "so odious" to the laws of England itself, where of course it had been illegal for centuries, that just by setting foot in that country, the slave had become free. The distinctions of "sojourning" and "domicile" did not apply.

In the 1840s, Dred Scott had been taken by his master back to the slave state of Missouri, and from 1848 to 1854 he sued in the state courts there for his freedom. However, in these years the whole atmosphere between North and South, after the eruption of the Wilmot Proviso controversy in 1845, had grown increasingly embittered. At the same time Southern judges were angry at their Northern counterparts for having broken the tacit North-South arrangement on slaves in free states. Therefore, the state court in Missouri turned away from the "domicile" and "comity" doctrines too. In 1854 it ruled that Scott had "reverted" to the total jurisdiction of Missouri's laws when he had returned to that state, and was a slave. As a slave he could not be a "citizen," and therefore he had no "standing" (as it is called) in court to bring suit against anyone, let alone his master.

The Core Question: Who Is a Citizen?

The core question in the Dred Scott case was in fact that crucially important issue: Who is a "citizen"? and what does it mean to be one? If Scott were a citizen, then he would be protected under an explicit and powerful statement in the Constitution (Article IV, Section 2): "The Citizens of each State shall be entitled to all Privileges and Immunities of Citizens in the several states." That is, he would have the claim of citizens for full civil rights *wherever* they were, no matter in what state: trial by jury, testifying in one's own behalf, and the like.

Antislavery people were keenly interested in Scott's case, and when the Missouri courts ruled him still a slave they provided funds for an appeal to the federal courts. Scott's legal owner was by this time a resident of New York State. Therefore, Scott could insist that, as a free man and a citizen of the state of Missouri (which he still maintained that he was), he could call on the federal courts to take action under what is called the "diverse-citizenship" clause of the Constitution (Article III, Section 2), which states that the federal courts have jurisdiction in all "Controversies . . . between Citizens of different States. . . ." His specific complaint? That he was being illegally imprisoned (kept in slavery) by a citizen of another state.

So now the question, to this point unsettled in American law, of *who is a citizen* had to be formally decided. In February 1856, a prominent Missouri lawyer of firm free-soil views, Montgomery Blair (his Pennsylvania Avenue home in Washington, D.C., is now the famous Blair House, where distinguished guests of the president reside), filed his brief (i.e., argument) in Scott's cause before the U.S. Supreme Court. In the background were the lurid, nation-rocking controversies in Kansas over slavery, and the swift rise of the new Republican party. Loud debates were once more echoing in Congress over the constitutional powers that body possessed over slavery in the territories. Politics, and the Dred Scott case, had finally come together in history.

The Supreme Court Case of Dred Scott v. Sanford

In the ensuing months of 1856, large audiences gathered in the Supreme Court chambers to listen to the arguments before the bench, which went on for hours. A key point: There was as yet no statement anywhere in the Constitution creating a status of "citizen of the United States." Americans were regarded primarily as citizens of their states. Their United States citizenship flowed from that fact, but it did not stand by itself. Blair could argue that a certain proportion of free black people were recognized as citizens in particular states (as in Massachusetts), and therefore under the privileges-and-immunities clause free blacks, *wherever* they lived, could claim the rights of a citizen, which included the protection of the courts. Henry Geyer, attorney for Dred Scott's owner, John F. Sanford, argued that for someone to be in fact truly a citizen, that person must have the *full* rights that all citizens, black or white, possessed. Free blacks in the Northern states, he pointed out, were denied many of the usual appurtenances of citizenship, such as being able to vote, or bear arms, or testify in court.

Another crucial point: Blair insisted that Scott was free not only because he had lived in Illinois but also because he had lived in Wisconsin Territory, which was free territory under the Missouri Compromise. Geyer now erupted with the same argument that Southerners for many years had loudly proclaimed: that the Missouri Compromise itself was unconstitutional, since Congress, they said, had no power over slavery whatever. After all, they pointed out, in the Kansas-Nebraska Act of 1854 that body itself had repealed the Compromise Line.

On March 6, 1857, thirteen months after the case had begun, Chief Justice Roger B. Taney announced the Court's rulings and read his own decision (several other concurring decisions were filed too, by judges in the majority, which was seven out of nine). First, Taney ruled that Scott had no "standing" to carry on a lawsuit in the courts (in effect, he dismissed the case) on the ground that *no black person, free or slave, could ever be a citizen of the United States.* That status was reserved, under the Constitution, to white people. Therefore, Scott had no right to bring a suit in the federal courts under the diverse-citizenship clause or under any clause whatever. Then, rather confusingly, Taney went on to lay down other decrees, essentially ignoring the fact that he had just thrown the whole case out of court. Congress he said, *had no authority over slavery*, and therefore the Missouri Compromise Line it had enacted in 1820 had been unconstitutional from the beginning. In other words, slavery was in the territories already, since it had been there under the French and the Spanish. This meant that Wisconsin Territory had *not* been free of slavery after all, so that Scott's residence there could not have made him free. (It was here that Taney and the Court's majority tried to settle the political controversy concerning the powers that Congress had over slavery in the territories.) But, it might be said, Scott had lived for a while in

the free state of Illinois. Surely that had made him free? No, said Taney, for in any event, Scott's legal status when he returned to Missouri "reverted" to slavery, for then he was once more under the authority of that state's laws (so much for the old principle of interstate comity). Taney had barred the door with several locks, so that if one did not do the job, the others would.

Republicans cried out in outrage that everything in Taney's decision after the ruling that Scott had no "standing" was simply Taney's personal *obiter dictum* (something said in passing that is essentially irrelevant to the main point, and not authoritative). However, Don E. Fehrenbacher concludes that this criticism does not hold up. In each of his rulings, Taney "did present the opinion of the Court," and "there can be no doubt that Taney's opinion was accepted as the opinion of the Court by its critics as well as by its defenders. In all branches of government and in popular thought, the 'Dred Scott decision' came to mean the opinion of the Chief Justice."

And its message was clear and unequivocal: The Supreme Court had now declared that not even territorial governments could exclude slavery, since they were creatures of Congress and that body could not give them powers it did not itself possess. Thus, *slavery existed in the territories already.* Only a *state* government could exclude it, in its constitution.

Reaction

The South was delighted at the Dred Scott decision, whereas the North resounded with cries of dismay. "Poor betrayed, imbruted America," mourned Emerson. What happened now to abolitionism or to the hope for black equality, if the Constitution did not apply to black men in *any* condition? "This infamous decision of the Slaveholding wing of the Supreme Court," insisted Frederick Douglass, "cannot stand." But what was to be done, with the Democrats in control of Congress, the presidency, and the Supreme Court—and the South firmly in the ascendancy in that party? Almost immediately William Seward of New York, a leading Republican, declared that there had been collusion between Buchanan and Taney. Before his inauguration Buchanan had been told what the decision would be, Seward claimed (apparently rightfully), and this rendered hypocritical his assertion in his inaugural address that he would abide by that decision, "whatever this may be."

As it happened, the Dred Scott decision affected

LIBERTY, THE FAIR MAID OF KANSAS _ IN THE HANDS OF THE "BORDER RUFFIANS".

James Buchanan robs a corpse, drunken Franklin Pierce and Lewis Cass ogle the fair maid Liberty, and a bearded Stephen Douglas scalps a victim in this cartoon satirizing the democratic leaders' failure in Kansas.

nothing but the long-run standing and powers of the U.S. Supreme Court. It had utterly no effect on slavery in the territories: for the South, the ruling in *Dred Scott* v. *Sanford* was an entirely empty victory. Within four years the federal government was at war, putting down what it described as an illegal insurrection in the South, and during that conflict it quite ignored the Supreme Court's ruling that Congress had no powers over slavery. In the Reconstruction period that followed, as we will see, one of the first things done by the Republicans, in the Fourteenth Amendment, was to create a constitutional status of "citizen of the United States" as primary over state citizenship (applying to everyone born or naturalized in the United States, save Indians not taxed, and thus to the former slaves). Thereafter, the federal government could constitutionally try to protect the rights of citizens wherever they lived. Meanwhile, the Supreme Court, carrying the burden of the Dred Scott decision on its back, fell catastrophically in pubic opinion outside the South, thus losing much of the moral authority on which almost alone it must rely for its decisions to be obeyed. It would

be many years before the Supreme Court would take up once more the philosophy of "judicial activism."

Controversy over Kansas's Constitution

Since Kansas needed a governor, John Geary having resigned, President Buchanan appointed Robert J. Walker to that office. Formerly Polk's secretary of the treasury and the moving spirit behind that administration's strong swing toward free trade, Walker was widely admired as a man of force, integrity, and intelligence. He went to Kansas declaring that the territory was unsuited by climate and geography for slavery and insisting that any constitution written there would have to be ratified by the people. He was supported by Buchanan's firm promise that the president would "stand or fall" on the issue of ratification.

The free-soilers generally boycotted the election of delegates to the constitutional convention in Kansas, and a proslavery body was elected. Elections for a new session of the territory's legislature were held, but once more massive corruption brought about the election of a proslavery majority. Governor Walker moved vigorously, however, to examine the returns. He found, in one typical instance, that in a precinct in which there were only six houses, a return was sent in with 1,628 proslavery votes. It was then discovered that the names inscribed on that precinct's official role had been copied verbatim from an old Cincinnati directory! Similar frauds elsewhere led the angered Walker to throw out many ballots and certify the election of free-state candidates. Consequently, the antislavery elements in Kansas were able to win an election for the first time. Having seized control of the legally constituted legislature, the free-staters let their illegal government in Topeka dissolve.

The proslavery faction, however, was by no means defeated. Still in control of the coming constitutional convention, it resolved to write a proslavery constitution for Kansas. When the constitutional convention gathered in Lecompton, Kansas, in October 1857, it put together a document that declared the right of property in slaves inviolable, forbade the legislature to enact emancipation without the consent of individual slaveowners, and prohibited the amendment of the constitution for a period of seven years. The convention then decided to give the voters an opportunity to vote on the constitution, but in a special and limited way: They could vote to approve the constitution "with slavery" or "without slavery." That is, one version of the document would explicitly legalize slavery; the other would just not mention it at all. Nothing would be done by either vote to change the condition of the slaves already in Kansas or in the future, since at best the constitution would merely be silent about slavery. In a balloting held on December 21, 1857—again largely boycotted by free-staters—the constitution received 6,226 favorable votes "with slavery" and 569 favorable votes "without slavery."

The legislature, however, had resolved to take a hand. It decided in December to submit the Lecompton constitution to a fair vote in January. By this time President Buchanan had come completely under the domination of Southerners in his cabinet and party. Jefferson Davis, now a senator from Mississippi, led other Southern representatives in informing Buchanan that he would lead a revolt if the governor of Kansas, Robert Walker, were not dismissed for having allowed the calling of a new referendum there. Buchanan dismissed Walker, but not before the refer-

endum had taken place. On the fourth of January, 1858, the people of Kansas voted as follows: for the constitution with slavery, 138; for the constitution without slavery, 24; and against the constitution in either form, 10,266. There was no question now as to the voice of popular sovereignty in Kansas.

Both the North and the South now had a popular referendum in Kansas to point to. Both dismissed the opposing verdict as fraudulently obtained. The legislatures of Alabama and Georgia declared that they intended to bring about secession if the Lecompton constitution were rejected by the president. Buchanan capitulated. He announced that he would urge Congress to approve the proslavery constitution. If Kansas wanted to abolish slavery after it became a state, he went on, it would then be at liberty to do so (an assertion that blinked at the provision in the Lecompton constitution that it could not be amended for seven years). The Supreme Court, Buchanan observed, had settled the slavery question. "It has been solemnly adjudged by the highest judicial tribunal," he said, "that slavery exists in Kansas by virtue of the constitution of the United States. Kansas is therefore at this moment as much a slave state as Georgia or South Carolina."

Crisis and Compromise

The North was now in turmoil. Practically every Northern newspaper, Republican and Democrat, condemned Buchanan's course. Mass meetings in all the larger cities shouted applause for anti-Lecompton speeches. Letters began pouring into Washington urging rejection of the Kansas constitution. Northern legislatures passed resolutions urging this course and instructed their senators to vote against admission. A state election in New Hampshire sent the Democrats to smashing defeat.

In Washington, Douglas openly broke with the president and began leading a Northern Democratic revolt against the Lecompton constitution. "We must stand on the popular sovereignty principle," he observed, "and wherever the logical consequences may carry us, and defend it against *all assaults* from whatever quarter." Douglas knew that his party was heading for a breakup. He was convinced that Southern Democrats had made Buchanan their errand boy and that they not only hated democracy, but also were determined to destroy the Union.

In Congress, the House resolved that the Kansas constitution would have to be submitted to a fair referendum. On August 2, 1858, Kansas rejected the Lecompton constitution by 11,300 ballots to 1,788. The controversy was finally resolved. Remaining in its territorial status and now with its free-soil legislature completely in control, Kansas waited for two and a half years and then entered the Union with a free-state constitution—after the Civil War had begun. But it entered with a constitution that gave the vote only to every *white* male. As far as the

black American was concerned, the issue had never been in doubt. The Kansas crisis, which shattered the Democratic party in the Northern states and delivered that region to the Republicans, had little to do with abolitionism or, least of all, with racial equality (though many Southerners thought it did). It was fundamentally an argument among white men, over white issues, for white objectives.

BIBLIOGRAPHY

I have been greatly aided by Don E. Fehrenbacher's landmark study, *Slavery, Law, & Politics: The Dred Scott Case in Historical Perspective* (1981), a powerful, step-by-step analysis. As in all these chapters dealing with the years from 1848 to 1865, Allan Nevins's authoritative volumes have been essential to me. On the events described in this chapter, see his *Ordeal of the Union: The House Dividing* (1947). I relied heavily also on James A. Rawley's absorbing study *Race and Politics: Bleeding Kansas and the Coming of the Civil War* (1969).

In Robert Kelley, *The Cultural Pattern in American Politics: The First Century* (1979), the interpretation in this chapter of the rise and nature of the Republican party is developed at length. The following works, on this and related themes, have been most valuable to me: Eric Foner's *Free Soil, Free Labor, Free Men: The Ideology of the Republican Party before the Civil War* (1970); Ronald P. Formisano, *The Birth of Mass Political Parties: Michigan 1827–1861* (1971); Michael F. Holt, *Forging a Majority: The Formation of the Republican Party in Pittsburgh, 1848–1860* (1969); Frederick C. Luebke (ed.), *Ethnic Voters and the Election of Lincoln* (1971); Robert W. Johannsen, *Stephen A. Douglas* (1973); Mark L. Berger, *The Revolution in the New York Party Systems: 1840–1860* (1973); Walter Dean Burnham, *Critical Elections and the Mainsprings of American Politics* (1970); William G. Shade, *Banks or No Banks: The Money Question in the Western States, 1832–1865* (1973); David Brion Davis, *The Slave Power Conspiracy*

and the Paranoid Style (1969); George M. Fredrickson, *The Inner Civil War: Northern Intellectuals and the Crisis of the Union* (1965); David Herbert Donald, *Charles Sumner and the Coming of the Civil War* (1967); David M. Potter, *The Impending Crisis 1848–1861*, completed and edited by Don E. Fehrenbacher (1976); Michael Feldberg, *The Philadelphia Riots of 1844: A Study of Ethnic Conflict* (1975); John F. Coleman, *The Disruption of the Pennsylvania Democracy 1848–1860* (1975); Carl N. Degler, *The Other South: Southern Dissenters in the Nineteenth Century* (1974). The breakup of the Whig and Democratic parties is well described in Roy F. Nichols's *The Disruption of American Democracy* (1948).

Recent books have also given us fresh new insights: John McCardell, *The Idea of a Southern Nation: Southern Nationalists and Southern Nationalism, 1830–1860* (1979); Daniel Walker Howe, *The Political Culture of the American Whigs* (1979); Bertram Wyatt-Brown, *Southern Honor: Ethics & Behavior in the Old South* (1982). More general studies of antiblack feelings among whites in the western states are E. H. Berwanger, *The Frontier against Slavery: Western Anti-Negro Prejudice and the Slavery Extension Controversy* (1967), and V. J. Voegeli, *Free But Not Equal: The Midwest and the Negro during the Civil War* (1967). The towering figure to emerge from Bleeding Kansas, enigmatic John Brown, is treated unsympathetically in James C. Malin's *John Brown and the Legend of Fifty-Six* (1970).

18

The Nation Splits Apart

TIME LINE

HISTORY IN AN INDIVIDUAL LIFE

JEFFERSON DAVIS

The newly elected president of the Confederate States of America stepped into an elegant carriage drawn by six iron-gray prancing horses. Thousands of cheering Confederates greeted him as, to the tune of "Dixie," he swept up the lofty hill in Montgomery, Alabama, upon which sat the capitol building. Jefferson Davis was taking command.

Tall, slim, straight, and dignified, Davis was the image of a Southern gentleman. Trained at West Point, his heart was in the military life. During his youth on a Mississippi plantation, he had been an imaginative dreamer excited by the idea of the South as a nation. When he and his brother built plantations near each other in the state, they spent long nights discussing the cause of the South faced by an increasingly hostile Yankee North. Davis himself was an unusually gentle and patriarchal slaveholder, and he bitterly resented the abolitionists' unending attacks upon men like himself as cruel despots siring mulatto children in their helpless female slaves. In 1845 he was elected to

Congress, but shortly he was gaining national adulation as a brave young regiment commander in the Mexican War.

Sent thereafter to the Senate, he was unbending on the slavery issue: No power existed either in Congress or in the people of a territory, he insisted, to exclude slavery from any part of the nation's newly acquired possessions. Davis bitterly opposed the admission of California as a free state in 1850, and as Franklin Pierce's secretary of war (1853–57) he pushed for more southward expansion to create more slave states. The fruit of his effort was the Gadsden Purchase of 1853, which added a large part of northern Mexico to the American Southwest.

Jefferson Davis helped to plan the Kansas-Nebraska Act in 1854, which repealed the Missouri Compromise line. Then, from 1857 on, he was a senator again and heatedly arguing for the South. A brilliant figure in the nation's eye, his honesty and his great intensity of purpose gave him high standing and great influence. He seized upon the Dred Scott decision of 1857, which held slavery legal everywhere in the territories, and angrily fought off Stephen A. Douglas's rival cry of popular sovereignty—that only a vote by territorial residents could install the system. When president-elect Abraham Lincoln declared his opposition to any more slave states and therefore to further Southern expansion, Davis rose in the Senate on January 21, 1861, and in a great oration announced the secession of Mississippi and his own decision to follow his state.

He expected war, he wanted to lead the Southern armies, and now, on February 18, 1861, he became president of the Confederacy and its commander in chief. His dream of Southern nationhood was launched. Four years and hundreds of thousands of lives later, he and his Southern countrymen would see that dream finally and utterly extinguished.

The Emergence of Abraham Lincoln

In the summer of 1858 Stephen A. Douglas boarded a train in Washington and traveled home to Illinois to begin a series of debates with the Republican who was challenging him for his seat in the Senate. By the time the debates had ended, his opponent, Abraham Lincoln, was no longer known only to the people of one state, but had become a national figure.

Over the last century, Lincoln's character has come to seem unreal and remote. It is difficult to pierce the historical crust to get at the real man within. This is a shame, for he was an appealing human being. In appearance, he was "the *ungodliest* man you every saw!" Homely and usually carelessly dressed, he stood six feet four inches at a time when most men were about five feet seven. His arms and hands were long and pendulous, and he habitually shambled about or collapsed gracelessly into chairs, all knees and elbows. His character mystified even close friends. He was either brooding silently and alone, his dark eyes shadowed with grief, or entertaining acquaintances with crude, hip-slapping jokes.

Of the two moods, melancholy was the more characteristic. "I looked up at him," said an intimate friend of their first encounter, "and I thought then, as I think now, that I never saw so gloomy and melancholy a face in my life." Lincoln had a difficult life, he saw much suffering and death among those close to him, and he rarely found much happiness. Inordinately sensitive to the pain of others, he was a tender and compassionate man. It is revealing that in addition to the Bible, his favorite and much-read books were by Shakespeare and Robert Burns, two men who found life an interesting experience but hardly one that was light and gay.

At the same time, this complex and openhearted man was driven by ambition to be a leader. He chose law for his profession, thus ensuring that the pressure of personal encounter would be a continuing part of his work. In his teenage years he practiced public speaking, and he had hardly reached voting age before he ran for the state legislature. He loved politics. The life of caucuses, debates, drawing up campaign documents, planning strategy, working in committees, guiding legislation, buttonholing and persuading and speaking—all of it was meat and drink to him. Wherever he saw a group of men he was drawn to it and soon became the center of its attention. Elected as a Whig to the legislature of Illinois in 1834 at the age of twenty-five, he was quickly chosen by his party colleagues as their head. He had rare talents for the work. He inspired trust and was transparently honest. His personal style was always a bit ludicrous, and yet his genuineness and his deftness made him an arresting figure.

Lincoln's Politics

What was his political outlook? The best way to understand Lincoln is to see him as a man of the South who revolted against the values of that society. Born in Kentucky, he was part of that predominantly Southern world in southern Indiana and Illinois created by the northward movement of settlers across the Ohio River after 1815, in which his family had participated. Although the two states were free of slavery under the Northwest Ordinance, there was much proslavery agitation against the antislavery provisions of that document. Laws were adopted that made blacks practically slaves again, and abolitionists lived in terror of their lives.

The Lower North—a band of territory roughly below the 41st parallel that includes the great port cities of New York and Philadelphia, which had strong economic ties to the South and tens of thousands of Irish laborers who hated black Americans; the bulk of Pennsylvania and New Jersey; and southern Ohio, Indiana, and Illinois—was not hospitable to New Englanders or their stern anti-Southernism. The Whigs here had long followed Henry Clay of Kentucky and his devoted Unionism, as well as his belief that the issue of slavery should be kept out of national politics or it would tear the country apart. They joined the Republicans reluctantly, bringing in a moderate and gradualist attitude toward slavery.

In Lincoln's Illinois, Jacksonian Democracy of the aggressive, expansionist, pro-Southern type was powerful and triumphant throughout most of the state, successfully holding down the Yankees who dominated its northern regions. Lincoln's own family was vigorously Democratic. But Lincoln became a Whig. His choice of party is highly revealing. Lincoln, to begin with, admired Henry Clay to the point of discipleship. In his first political speech, given in 1832, he said, "My politics are short and sweet. . . . I am in favour of the internal improvement system and a high protective tariff." He was devoted to the notion that America was a place where, more than anywhere else, poor persons could get ahead, earn a comfortable life, and thereby become independent people, sturdy republicans beholden to and dominated by no one. He much admired the essentially Yankee ideology of free soil, free labor, and free people. Lincoln sent his son to Harvard, in the Yankee heartland, and as a lawyer he worked with the great railroads and corporations of Illinois. A developing, vigorous, modernizing economy was what he desired for America.

There was much more to Lincoln's Whiggery, however. He rejected the cultural values of Jacksonian democracy as well as its economic politics. In the midst of a hard-drinking frontier society, he avoided alcohol and advocated temperance. In a community littered with spittoons and cigar butts, he did not smoke or chew. Surrounded by a way of life centered on guns and violence, he refused even to shoot animals after trying the experience once at the age of eight. While universal manhood suffrage was being trumpeted, he said he favored the vote only for those men who paid taxes or served in the militia. He favored the vote for women, an astonishingly radical position in an aggressively male-oriented and male-dominated world. He chose for his wife a spirited young woman of the elite, and they had the first Episcopalian wedding ceremony in Springfield, Illinois. Lincoln gravitated to Whiggery, one must conclude, in good part because it represented a life style he admired. Whigs regarded themselves as moral, *civilized* people in a rough, crude country.

Lincoln's Views on Slavery

Lincoln's views on slavery must be understood against this background. He was that rare Southerner who was repelled by the institution. In long trips down the Ohio and the Mississippi he saw slaves chained together and young black women stripped naked, coarsely examined, and laughed about. Always inordinately sensitive around women, this sight, and those of slaves in general, grieved him deeply. "[It] was a continual torment to me," he wrote his close friend Joshua Speed, who was strongly proslavery. "I see something like it every time I touch the Ohio or any other slave border." In the Illinois legislature in 1837 he was outraged at an excessively proslavery resolution adopted by that body, and he took the unusual step of presenting a formal protest against it. He could find but one other legislator to sign the protest with him. As a congressman from 1847 to 1849, he prepared a bill for the gradual and compensated extinction of slavery in the District of Columbia.

He voted perhaps forty times for the Wilmot Proviso (which would have excluded slavery from the territories acquired from Mexico) while in the House.

This is not to say that he was an abolitionist or that he believed in social and political equality for black people. He was too much of a white American for that. "There is a natural disgust in the minds of nearly all white people," he said, "at the idea of an indiscriminate amalgamation of the white and black men." He disliked abolitionists and refused to support forcible, illegal antislavery proceedings in Kansas. He recoiled from the notion of taking direct action against slavery in the states where it then existed, and he supported firmly, if reluctantly, the Fugitive Slave Law. He felt that slavery was built into the constitutional system and that it was imperative to the continuance of the Union to maintain the institution where it then existed.

What he wanted was to put slavery back where he believed the fathers of the nation had put it: legally protected, but kept where it was, marked out clearly as an evil institution to be detested by all people, and thus placed "in the course of ultimate extinction." If contained within the Southern states, there it would eventually die, perhaps in a hundred years—and Lincoln was willing to have it take that long. What he opposed was the growing tendency, as he saw it, to be indifferent to the moral evil of slavery and to allow its expansion into new areas if the people there approved. The situation had become so bad, he said, that anyone who condemned slavery was ridiculed, that "if one man chooses to enslave another, no third man shall have the right to object." Little by little the nation had given up on its "central idea"—its belief in equality.

Lincoln thus reveals the main paradox in American thought. He genuinely believed in the principle of equality, but he could not extend that principle in *all* its implications to black people. His political thought began and ended with the Declaration of Independence, a document he regarded as practically sacred and constantly used as his point of reference. He described Thomas Jefferson as "the most distinguished politician of our history. The principles of Jefferson," he said, "are the definitions and axioms of free society." The Declaration of Independence was what justified the United States, made the whole national enterprise worthwhile, and gave it an enduring standard toward which it should ceaselessly strive.

"I am not a Know-Nothing, that is certain," he wrote. "How could I be? How can anyone who

Photograph of Abraham Lincoln taken in 1858, when he was little known nationally.

abhors the oppression of negroes be in favour of de-grading classes of white people? Our progress in de-generacy," he went on, "appears to me pretty rapid. As a nation we began by declaring that 'all men are created equal.' We now practically read it, 'all men are created equal, except negroes.' When the Know-Nothings get control it will read, 'all men are created equal, except negroes, and foreigners and Catholics.' " When that happened, he said, he would prefer to emigrate to some country like Russia "where they make no pretense of loving liberty . . . where despotism can be taken pure, and without the base alloy of hypocrisy."

The dilemma cannot be resolved. Lincoln was an equalitarian who could not envision blacks in completely equal relationships with whites. The equality he did see for them was an equal right, as he put it, to eat the bread they had earned by the sweat of their brow, to enjoy freely the fruits of their own toil. How to achieve this? How to make slavery disappear? He simply did not know, other than by cooping it up and condemning it. It is testimony to the state of the Southern mind that these two beliefs made Lincoln a radical in Southern eyes. And, within the terms of Southern life, so he was. For a public man to have said these things in Alabama or even in Virginia would have made him a hated revolutionary. For a Southern-born man to say them in a state that was in good part an extension of the South (Illinois), and in the midst of a populace, most of whom thought black people had no claim to *any* form of equality, was perhaps no less revolutionary and was certainly just as condemned.

The Lincoln-Douglas Debates

Abraham Lincoln was a relatively quiet party worker after serving his one congressional term. He had forthrightly condemned the Mexican War and was not in public favor. But the Kansas-Nebraska Act in 1854 stung him into action. Thereafter he was extremely energetic, helping to lead the antislavery and anti-expansionist movement in Illinois and to form the Republican party. By 1858, in his state he was the most prominent figure in his party. That year Lincoln entered the senatorial contest in Illinois. He began his campaign by staking out an advanced party position on slavery. The time had come, he said, for Republicans to declare that, far from being ready to accept slavery as a permanent part of national life, they felt that even in the South it must be only temporary. Slavery would have to be extinguished, or it would grow until it became nationwide. In phrases that reverberated around the nation he said, quoting the Bible: " 'A house divided against itself cannot stand.' I believe this government cannot endure, permanently half *slave* and half *free*."

The Lincoln-Douglas debates began in Ottawa, Illinois, in August 1858 and lasted two months. Douglas called Lincoln a radical. He explicitly asserted that black people were inherently inferior to whites; Lincoln simply stated that this belief might be true. Douglas, moreover, frequently talked of blacks with revulsion in his voice, whereas Lincoln spoke in detached and sympathetic tones and simply approved the social conventions of the time—save that of slavery. He took pains to assert not simply what blacks should be denied, but what they had a right to claim—namely, "all the rights enumerated in the Declaration of Independence," which meant life, liberty, and the pursuit of happiness. In his time, millions of people regarded this claim as deeply subversive.

At the second debate, in Freeport, Lincoln asked Douglas if the people of a territory could *lawfully* exclude slavery, now that the Dred Scott decision had ruled slavery in existence in all territories and President Buchanan had insisted that only a state legislature could exclude the institution. Douglas said that, nonetheless, a territorial government could exclude slavery by failing to enact the necessary police laws, and he was immediately subjected to condemnation by his enemies in the South and in Washington. Now Southerners began to demand something new: that Congress *positively* protect slavery in the territories by direct legislation—by enacting a federal slave code—instead of simply standing passively by and relying on the Dred Scott decision.

Stephen Douglas won the senatorial election in Illinois that followed the debates. But he did so only because the electoral districts of the state were so adjusted that more weight was given to Democratic than to Republican votes, so that the legislature, which elected senators, was Democratic. Lincoln got a heavy vote in the northern districts of the state (strongly Yankee) and actually secured a popular majority. His demonstrated power in the voting booth caused politicians all over the North to prick up their ears. Illinois had the third largest population in the Union; its electoral vote was crucial; the state could go either way; and a strong vote-getter in the next presidential contest would be a great aid to the Republican cause.

The Evangelical Upsurge in the North

In 1858, an eruption of religious revivalism that amazed the entire nation took place in Northern cities. Interdenominational prayer meetings were held in banks, business houses, and railroad stations. During the noon hour, clerks in Wall Street financial houses crowded into nearby churches for common worship. The Metropolitan Theater in Chicago held thousands of worshipers daily, as did great public halls in Philadelphia. School buildings were even put to use for such gatherings in Cleveland.

The constant theme stressed in these gatherings was not simply the saving of one's soul, but the need to reform society. Many causes were given new strength—schools, temperance, the suppression of

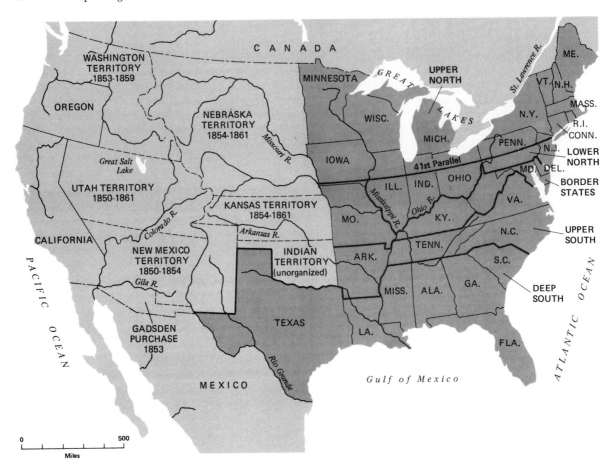

Political Regions, the 1850s

vice, the attack on corrupt politics—but the most important was the campaign against slavery as it was expressed by the Republican party. The time had come, ministers insisted, to cease being silent on the question. When in October 1858 the prominent New York Republican William Seward made a speech insisting that slavery was to be judged by a "higher law" than that of the Constitution, the churches rang with praise. God was immediately involved in these events, preachers insisted. The nation must cleanse itself of the sin of slavery.

Abraham Lincoln's biblical prose, his invoking of holy texts—"A house divided against itself cannot stand"—and his moral outrage against slavery appealed to the reawakened religious consciousness of the age. His uncertainty, too, as to how slavery was to be eliminated was shared by Northern ministers. They usually shrank from what they called "fanatical abolitionism," and they would not sanction direct action. But that the task of wiping out slavery was

a divinely appointed one they had no doubt. When the challenge of war came, Northern churches greeted it in the somber zealousness of Old Testament prophets. Many had for years been preaching that a new day of holiness was dawning in America—the nation of the earth, they insisted, that God had chosen to carry out His purposes.

John Brown's Raid on Harpers Ferry

John Brown then reappeared to strike the violent blow that crystallized emotions North and South. In July 1859 he appeared near Harpers Ferry, Virginia, a village located in what is now West Virginia where the Shenandoah joins the Potomac. The Baltimore and Ohio Railroad passed through the community, heading westward to the Ohio Valley, and a small factory and warehouse there constituted a federal armory that manufactured rifles at the rate of 10,000 a year. Brown's plan was to take Harpers Ferry, send out agents to rally nearby slaves, and, after enough of them had joined him to form a military force (he expected 500 to respond to his call), head southward carrying war and terror into the heart of the plantation world. He was convinced that the slave system would fall apart at the first blow. He did not even reconnoiter the territory to locate routes of travel. A man of faith, he believed the Lord would provide.

On a cool Sunday evening, October 16, 1859, Brown and about twenty followers walked quietly into the village and, after brief difficulties with night watchmen, took command of the armory and arsenal. Brown then sent out a party to capture two nearby plantation owners—one of them a wealthy descendant of George Washington, Colonel Lewis W. Washington—and bring in their slaves, who were ten in number. The slaves were put to maintaining guard over their imprisoned owners. Telegraph wires were cut, and the railroad blocked. In the morning a railroad supervisor, a free black citizen of Harpers Ferry, went out looking for one of the night watchmen and was shot dead. Soon a white townsman was killed and workers filing into the armory were taken prisoner.

All this time, John Brown waited confidently for the slaves of the surrounding countryside to come swarming in. Soon large numbers of armed men were streaming into the town, but they were white, not black. By noon on Monday the local militia, townsmen, and farmers were firing heavily on the arsenal. Meanwhile the alarm spread through Maryland, the District of Columbia, and Virginia. Thousands of Virginia and Maryland militia were quickly mustered and carried swiftly over the rails and by galloping horses to Harpers Ferry to join the assault. Federal troops shortly arrived, followed by Brevet-Colonel Robert E. Lee of the Second Cavalry.

When darkness fell, Brown counted his losses. Only three fighting men were left in addition to Brown himself. But he remained resolute. Listening to one of his sons groaning in his last agony, he counseled him to be courageous and die like a man. When morning came, Brown's surrender was asked. He refused save on his own terms: a provision for the escape of his men. A body of marines burst through the door, bayoneted right and left, knocked Brown senseless, and the fighting was over.

Having utterly failed in direct action, Brown

achieved the victory of a courageous martyr in the courtroom and on the scaffold. The nation watched his trial with fascination. Indicted on three charges by the state of Virginia—conspiracy with blacks to produce an insurrection, murder, and treason against the Commonwealth of Virginia—he insisted that he should be treated with the consideration customarily given a prisoner of war. His trial in nearby Charles Town, now in West Virginia, began a few days after his capture. Lying on a cot in the courtroom, "wrapped in a blanket, his eyes often closed, from time to time he started up, grim as a cornered wolf, to snap out a sharp question or deliver a curt, dry speech." The jury held him guilty on all counts and sentenced him to death by hanging. On the morning of December 2, Brown was taken to a nearby field, escorted by six companies of Virginia infantry and a troop of horses. One of the observers was the actor John Wilkes Booth; another was the secessionist fire-eater Edmund Ruffin. When Brown dropped through the trapdoor of the scaffold, the rope knotted around his neck, Colonel J. T. L. Preston cried out, "So

Photograph of John Brown, revealing the grim passion of his cause to punish the South for slavery and spark an uprising among the slaves.

John Brown is arraigned before the court at Charleston following his attack on Harpers Ferry in October, 1859. Northerners and Southerners alike reacted irrationally to this spectacular event.

perish all such enemies of Virginia! All such enemies of the Union! All foes of the human race!"

The New York journalist John Bigelow remarked that it was easier to put John Brown on a scaffold than to get him down again. Antislavery workers in the North had gained a martyr, and Southerners had their fears confirmed. Southern fire-eaters had long predicted that wild Northern abolitionists would one day start a slave insurrection. It did not matter that Brown's pitifully unsuccessful exploit—unsuccessful in its immediate objective—had demonstrated, if anything, how impossible it was to start an insurrection. The fact of the attempt was enough.

The Southern Frame of Mind

Indeed, an earthquake of historic and fateful proportions was massively reshaping the Southern mind in the crisis-filled 1850s. Southerners watched what was going on in the North with mounting alarm. Never before had the national scene changed so swiftly in directions so threatening to Southern life. In former years, antislavery Northerners had not been able to find much support for their crusade. The Whig party had been strong in both the North and the South, and it had consistently and until the Kansas-Nebraska Act successfully urged compromise and the damping down of all arguments over slavery that threatened the survival of the Union. The Liberty and Free Soil parties had, if anything, confirmed the inability of antislavery Northerners to muster more than a small following. They had certainly been quite unable to take over Washington, D.C. Yankeeism, the great enemy of the South, had seemed isolated and ineffective.

Therefore, both Northern and Southern extremists had been frustrated. For long stretches of years, as we have seen, Southerners had been as absorbed by great questions of national economic development as were Northerners, and they had worked together cooperatively across sectional lines on these issues. The Whig party, with its organic nationalism—its deep devotion to the *whole* of America—and its cultural core in Yankee, Anglicized ways of living and thinking, was powerful in the South for more than twenty years.

The reason for this was simple: Southerners were profoundly patriotic. They had led in America's founding, had been the dominant influence in its national government for most of its history since 1789, had provided most of its presidents, and were proud of being "Americans." When South Carolina and Mississippi, the two most militant centers of anti-Yankeeism in the South, had called for secession during the slavery-extension crisis of 1850–51, it was primarily the Unionist loyalties of the great majority of Southerners that kept the nation together.

We will see that even in the election of 1860, when Abraham Lincoln and the Republicans could get not a single popular vote in the South, a majority of Southern voters would still cast their ballots for anti-secession candidates. We will also see, in our exploration of the course of the Civil War, that one of the most powerful reasons why the Southern Confederacy finally fell was that it actually did not have a very deep claim on the general Southern mind. When the war was over, the complete disinterest of Southerners in continuing the war by means of guerrilla fighting—indeed, as historian David Potter has written, the mass readiness of the Southern people to return immediately to the status of citizen of the United States of America—can only be understood against this background. It was the Southerners' instinctive loyalty to the United States, which had been so much their creation, a feeling never obliterated during the Civil War ("Unionism" would be powerful in many parts of the Confederacy), that gave the conflict "its peculiarly tragic tone," Potter observes, "its pathos as a 'brothers' war.' "

In the mounting national turmoil that followed the Kansas-Nebraska Act, however, the South's basic sense that slavery was safe within the American Union, the foundation stone of Southern peace of mind, began rapidly to erode. Southerners were fully aware that the Republican party was far more Yankee than Northern Whiggery had been, that it was the vehicle for a New England supremacy, in the Union, that Yankees had sought for many decades. They were also keenly conscious of the booming industrial growth of the North, its rapidly spreading railroad net. They watched, too, the incoming flood of immigrants who avoided the South but flocked to the Northern states and swelled its population. In the days of Thomas Jefferson, the slave states had been equal in population to the North, and they had held 40 percent of the nation's white people. By the 1850s, however, the number of white people in the North was half again as large as the population of the South. If Southerners had been worried about Yankees as far back as the turn of the century, in the late 1850s they were faced with a colossus of the North that

had enormous strength if it were concentrated and turned in one direction—as now it seemed to be.

Obsession with the Yankee

Southerners now became obsessed with *The Yankee*. It was for this reason that Southerners in the 1850s turned almost en masse to the Democratic party, and Whiggery rapidly declined south of the Mason-Dixon Line, for the Democrats were anti-Yankee and the Whigs were deeply New England, at their core. Both Northern and Southern Democrats had long aimed their bitterest attacks at the archetypal Yankee. In the 1850s it mattered little where the Democratic newspaper was published, whether in Texas or Illinois, in Alabama or New York; everywhere streams of angry anti-Yankee invective were poured out by Democratic editors in an uninterrupted flow.

"The people of the New England States," observed a Texas editor in 1856, "have been as remarkable in their history, for the violence of their fanaticism and proclivity to superstition and intolerance on all subjects connected with religion as they have been for their intelligence, energy, and enterprise on all other subjects." As they observed the Yankees in politics, Democrats singled out for particular condemnation, as they had for generations, the Yankee "practice of dragging politics into the pulpit." New England ministers, they said, were the moving force in the crusade to reshape the nation at large in the Yankee image. "The Puritans of today," wrote a Tennessee editor, "like the Puritans of 1700, conceive themselves to be better and holier than others, and entitled—by divine right as it were—to govern and control the actions and dictate the opinions [of their fellow men]." New England was "always putting itself forward as the accuser & maligner of its brethren, the marplot & busybody of the confederacy, always crying over its grievances & always arraigning the other states for pretended usurpations. . . . They are unhappy unless they can persecute, either some unprotected class of their own people, or their colleagues in the confederacy." Intolerance, an arrogant belief that they had a monopoly upon truth, and "a fanatical zeal for unscriptural reforms" characterized Yankees in the present scene, as in the past when they "burnt old women for witches, banished the Quakers, tore down Catholic convents. . . ."

The ancient activist philosophy of government

that the Whigs had preached, and which the new Republican party had inherited, now became a crucial national issue. The Republicans' combined warfare against Catholicism, drink, and slavery, Democrats argued, demonstrated that the strong government ideal would be turned in cultural directions as well. What New Englanders intended to do, if they got power in Washington, seemed to be abundantly demonstrated by their record at the state level, where for years they had agitated for Sabbath laws, sought to use the public schools to Protestantize Catholic children, had exerted stern controls over sexual behavior not only outside of but within marriage, and labored to end the use of alcohol. One thing seemed certain, Southerners believed: Given the Republicans' basically Yankee, Puritan way of thinking, *sooner or later*, if they got power in Washington, *there would be an assault on slavery*, which to Southerners meant *an immediate and convulsive slave insurrection*, chaos, bloodshed, murder and rapine in the night.

If Yankees believed in a Slave Power conspiracy at work in Washington, Southerners had their own conspiratorial delusions. Abolitionists, they were convinced, secretly controlled the Republican party, whatever people like Abraham Lincoln said. Southern whites fantasized that lavishly financed organizations existed to lure slaves northward and direct Northern resistance to the Fugitive Slave Law. They believed that nests of abolitionists were placed in Kansas to prey upon Missouri, Arkansas, and Texas; regarded Northerners traveling through the South as abolitionist agents "tampering" with the slaves; circulated stories of poisonings and burnings on the plantations, allegedly plotted by Northern, even English, elements; and conceived of Yankees as "shifty, cowardly hypocrites [who] concealed their aggressive designs behind a mask of pious benevolence."

Southern Honor

Equally powerful among thousands of Southerners, as we have earlier seen, was the call of honor. Over two centuries of Southern life, honor and slavery had become so intertwined that many simply could not conceive one could exist without the other. Out of honor came an imperious insistence upon absolute authority over others, in this case over black people. As historian Bertram Wyatt-Brown has written: "White man's honor and the black man's slavery became in the public mind of the South practically indistinguishable."

The code of honor also demanded that honorable people were not to be meddled with. The predominant mood was "Don't cross me," and "Stay out of my affairs" (my domain of authority). It was monstrous, from this perspective, that Yankees should try to meddle with slavery, or tell white people in the South what to do. Out of this proud prickliness could come the quick flares of violent anger so widely noted as a trait among Southern white men, for bravery, a readiness to die in defense of honor, was the highest virtue. Thousands of Southerners, both male and female, saw the problem they faced in the election year of 1860, and in the war that followed, as a simple test of courage. Would they stand up to the Yankee?

Besides, what would happen to one's family if the dreaded Yankees had their way and ended slavery? The shame of degradation, of losing authority and having to live on a par with black people, was an intolerable prospect. We have seen that fighting to protect the honor of one's family, of one's kinfolk, was a duty in the South. In the year 1860, to thousands of white Southerners the ultimate disgrace seemed poised to engulf their families. It was the "threat of honor lost," Wyatt-Brown remarks, "no less than slavery, that led [Southern whites] . . . to secession and war."

Southern Nationalism

Thousands of Southerners who had resisted the idea of secession were now ready to listen to what Senator William L. Yancey of Alabama and his followers had been saying for years: that the time had come to form an independent Southern nation. Secessionists were people who agreed with Abraham Lincoln when he said the United States of America could not go on forever, half slave and half free. Outright advocates of Southern nationalism were impatient with those Southern politicians who would seek more compromises with the North in order to preserve the Union.

As a mood, Southern nationalism had been obvious in Southern literature since the mid-1850s. A cascade of argumentative novels poured from Southern presses in angry response to *Uncle Tom's Cabin*. They described Southern plantation life as good and gentle, and contrasted it harshly with what Southern novelists depicted as the savage capitalism of the North. Northern and Southern periodicals began raging at each other, condemning the way of life in each other's sections. Meanwhile, the leading Southern literary voices had swung strongly to Southern nationalism. Southern newspapers, pamphleteers, and public leaders were declaring "that our interest is radically different from that of the Northern people; . . . that in every aspect in which Union can be viewed, it is a permanent evil to the South."

The Election of 1860

This, then, was the frame of mind Southerners were in when the Democrats, in late April 1860, gathered in their national convention in Charleston, South Carolina, to adopt a party platform and choose a presidential and a vice-presidential candidate. Almost immediately they broke apart. The Southern delegates insisted that the platform call on the federal government to enact a slave code, and led by Senator Yancey and his followers, they walked out of the convention when they were turned down. Two months later the party met in Baltimore to try again, but without success. Southern Democrats then held their own nominating convention and chose the man who was currently vice-president, John C. Breckinridge of Kentucky. The original Democratic convention, now greatly reduced by the secession of its Southern members, chose Stephen A. Douglas.

In early May another convention gathered in Baltimore, that of the Constitutional Union party. Composed primarily of remnants of the Whig and Know-Nothing parties, it tried to soft-pedal the slavery issue by refusing even to adopt a platform, and it nominated a Border State man, John Bell of Tennessee. Much more exciting was the Republican convention in Chicago that same month, for with the Democrats split the Republicans sniffed victory. William Seward of New York was at first the leading candidate for the nomination, but it was decided that he was too strong on the slavery issue. Besides, Abraham Lincoln had already shown great strength against Douglas in the electoral booth; he came from Illinois, and the Republicans could win only if they could sweep the northwestern states; and his ideas had built up a growing national ground swell in his favor. In late February he had appeared in New York City and given a widely praised speech at Cooper Union (a great lecture hall), urging that the North hold fast against the expansion of slavery while leaving the institution alone where it already existed. By the third ballot state after state had turned to Lincoln, and as a wildly cheering convention saw the totals

mounting rapidly, the sweep became practically unanimous.

Particularly arresting to Northerners was a question posed by Lincoln in his Cooper Union speech: What could Republicans really do to convince the South that they intended nothing harmful: no abolition, no invasions, no insurrections? Not by yielding on the territorial question, he said, for the outcome there was a foregone conclusion. "This, and this only: cease to call slavery wrong, and join them in calling it right. And this must be done thoroughly, done in acts as well as in words. Silence will not be tolerated; we must place ourselves avowedly with them. Senator Douglas's new sedition law must be enacted and enforced, suppressing all declarations that slavery is wrong, whether made in politics, in presses, in pulpits, or in private. We must arrest and return their fugitive slaves with greedy pleasure. We must pull down our free-state constitutions. The whole atmosphere must be disinfected from all taint of opposition to slavery before they will cease to believe that all their troubles proceed from us.

I am quite aware they do not state their case precisely in this way. Most of them would probably say to us, "Let us alone; do nothing to us, and say what you please about slavery." But we do let them alone—have never disturbed them—so that, after all, it is what we say which dissatisfies them. They will continue to accuse us of doing until we cease saying. [Though they did not ask the overthrow of the free-state constitutions, these documents were eloquent declarations that slavery is wrong], and when all these other sayings shall have been silenced, the overthrow of these constitutions will be demanded and nothing left to resist the demand. . . . Nor can we justifiably withhold this on any ground save our conviction that slavery is wrong. . . .

Their thinking it right and our thinking it wrong is the precise fact upon which depends the whole controversy. Thinking it right, as they do, they are not to blame for desiring its full recognition as being right; but thinking it wrong, as we do, can we yield to them? Can we cast our votes with their views and against our own? In view of our moral, social, and political responsibilities, can we do this? (John G. Nicolay and John Hay, ed., Complete Works of Abraham Lincoln *[1905])*

On November 6, 1860, the votes were cast, and Abraham Lincoln secured a majority of the electoral college. His 180 votes were followed by 72 for Breckinridge, 39 for Bell, and a pitiful 12 for Douglas. In the balloting, a national shift of earthquake proportions had taken place. Since 1800 enough Middle Atlantic and Middle West states in the region of the Lower North had given their support to candidates supported by the South to keep that section generally dominant in the federal government. Now, however, a monolithic North appeared, giving the Republican party command of the presidency and Congress. The result, within months of Lincoln's election, was the fragmentation of the Union, and civil war.

Out of a total national vote of about 4.7 million, less than a majority—1.8 million—went to Abraham Lincoln. Ironically, Douglas was next in line with approximately 1.4 million. Lincoln did not receive a single popular vote in ten Southern states, and in the border states he was at the bottom of the heap. However, Lincoln won not because his three opponents divided the votes and let him, a "minority" president, sweep the prize. Rather, he won because his vote was most strategically situated. Even had all his opponents combined, he would still have carried all the states that he won, save California and Oregon, and therefore would still have become president.

Formation of the Confederate States of America

Huge numbers of Southerners were now convinced that abolitionism was coming—and that eventuality they regarded as an unthinkable horror. It was not simply that their slaves were profitable to them, and abolition would mean economic disaster; only a fraction of white Southerners, after all, actually owned slaves. Rather, the white South—especially in places like South Carolina where blacks were often overwhelmingly in the majority—was terrified by the prospect of the blood bath that it believed would instantly follow general emancipation. Books on this theme were widely read, and the subject was endlessly discussed. Slavery, whites believed, was their great protector, a massive barrier standing between themselves and the barbaric tribe, as they thought of blacks, in their midst. They insisted publicly that black people were naturally docile and warm-hearted persons who loved their masters, but Southern whites secretly feared the hatred for all whites that they believed must be rooted in the black consciousness.

Slavery was therefore the only conceivable relationship that most Southern whites could understand as a basis for their society. This was why, in part, they were so enormously angry at the North, for how could fellow white people, they would ask, so endanger other white people in the South? Especially after John Brown's raid, as historian Stephen Channing writes, "a knife [had been] plunged deep into the psyche of Southern whites, and life would never be quite the same again." South Carolinian whites were reported actually to have become deranged because of fears of a slave uprising and abolitionist invasion. Alleged agents of John Brown were arrested all over Dixie. Mysterious fires in the distance were linked to his mythical army; vigilance committees were formed, and men suspected of being incendiaries were arrested. Patrols were formed, slaves were freely arrested and punished on the public roads, visitors were often violently seized and interrogated; white men talking to black persons were jailed, mail was taken and opened; people were tarred and feathered, and a person's Northern birth was sometimes enough to lead to expulsion from the community. Populations of entire towns were summoned together for questioning to see if they completely backed the Southern cause. "[In] the end fear of the Negro," observes Channing, "—physical dread, and fear of the consequences of emancipation—would control the course of [South Carolina]."

As soon as Abraham Lincoln won the election in November 1860, South Carolina immediately called a state convention to consider secession. We must remember that until the 1930s, a newly elected president would not be actually inaugurated until March, five months later, and Southern radicals wanted to move quickly before Lincoln was actually in office. In December 1860, South Carolina's convention declared the state no longer in the Union.

Georgia, anxiously debating this step, watched three other states secede—Alabama, Mississippi, and Florida. On January 19, 1861, Georgia followed, thus making the emergence of a Southern Confederacy a foregone conclusion. Louisiana seceded in late January, and Texas on the first of February, 1861. Three days later, with great excitement, delegates from the first seven states to secede gathered at Montgomery, Alabama, to draw up a constitution. They made little change in what they created from what they had left. Much of the constitution written in Montgomery used even the same language as the one written in Philadelphia in 1787. One of the distinguishing characteristics of the Confederacy, for that matter, was that it was not created or directed by the fire-eaters who had done so much to bring on secession. Jefferson Davis became the new president, and Alexander Stephens, who had even opposed secession, his vice-president.

The new constitution described each state as "sovereign" and gave state legislatures the power to impeach federal officers whose activities were wholly within a particular state. But the new constitution was still stated to be the "supreme law of the land," binding on state officers and judges and overriding provisions contrary to it in state constitutions or laws. This was to be no paradise of states' rights, no loosely aggregated confederacy of self-governing republics. There were even the same restrictions on the powers of the states as are indicated in the United States Constitution: no foreign relations, coining of money, passing of bills of attainder, and the like. The Confederate constitution did not even provide that the right of secession was inherent in the sovereignty of each state.

What Could Buchanan Do?

James Buchanan was now in a difficult situation. He had practically no army; most of the military posts in the Southern states, save Fort Pickens at Pensacola, Florida, and Fort Sumter at Charleston, South Carolina, were soon in Confederate hands; and the president was a timid, legalistic man. In truth, he had a difficult problem, and he did follow a definite policy. Fundamentally, he was persuaded that he must give peaceful measures every possible trial. And in an act for which he is usually given little credit, he refused to evacuate Fort Sumter. At the same time, he ordered the federal commander there to defend himself to the last extremity, but do nothing to bring on hostilities. The result was a steady narrowing of the options open to either side. Questions of honor were beginning to push to the fore, and all eyes began to focus on Fort Sumter as the touchstone of the entire controversy.

For a time there were hurried, anxious, and—in the last analysis—despairing efforts to work out a compromise. All the meetings that were held (of which a peace convention, called by Virginia in early February, was the most ambitious) failed because the issues were irreconcilable. Southern delegates to these gatherings were unappeasable, even when it was proposed to add an amendment to the federal Constitution making it illegal to meddle with the domestic institutions of any state (the amendment was actually passed by Congress and voted on favorably by three states in the North). Meanwhile, the Republican leaders Lincoln and Seward would accept no arrangement that did not include the Wilmot Proviso, a wholly unacceptable requirement to Southerners. "Entertain no proposition for a compromise

CHARLESTON

MERCURY

EXTRA:

Passed unanimously at 1.15 o'clock, P. M. December 20th, 1860.

AN ORDINANCE

To dissolve the Union between the State of South Carolina and other States united with her under the compact entitled " The Constitution of the United States of America."

We, the People of the State of South Carolina, in Convention assembled, do declare and ordain, and it is hereby declared and ordained,

That the Ordinance adopted by us in Convention, on the twenty-third day of May, in the year of our Lord one thousand seven hundred and eighty-eight, whereby the Constitution of the United States of America was ratified, and also, all Acts and parts of Acts of the General Assembly of this State, ratifying amendments of the said Constitution, are hereby repealed; and that the union now subsisting between South Carolina and other States, under the name of " The United States of America," is hereby dissolved.

THE

UNION

IS

DISSOLVED!

A special edition of the Charleston Mercury hailed South Carolina's secession.

in regard to the *extension* of slavery," Lincoln wrote an Illinois member of the House committee concerned with these matters. "The instant you do, they have us under again; all our labor is lost, and sooner or later must be done over. . . . Have none of it. The tug has to come, and better now than later."

The Accession of Lincoln

So the situation remained when Abraham Lincoln came to the presidency on March 4, 1861. He took over in the face of widespread skepticism about his

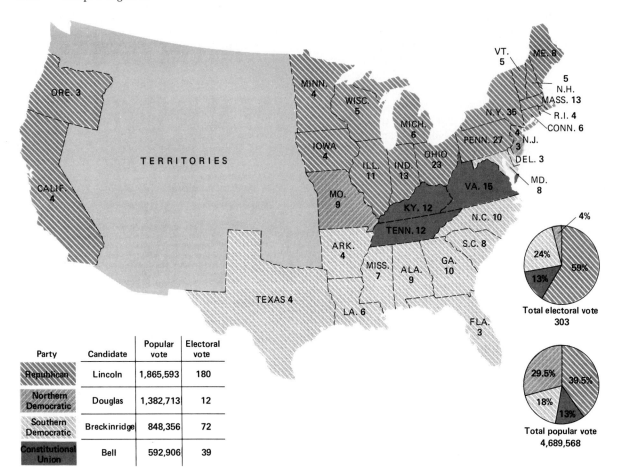

Party	Candidate	Popular vote	Electoral vote
Republican	Lincoln	1,865,593	180
Northern Democratic	Douglas	1,382,713	12
Southern Democratic	Breckinridge	848,356	72
Constitutional Union	Bell	592,906	39

The Election of 1860

character and his capacities. He was so homely that critics almost immediately began calling him a "baboon" and a "gorilla." Except for two years in Congress, he had not been part of the Washington scene. The Democrats had held the presidency for most of the previous generation; the Republican party was a new and untried organization; and no one could ever look as crude or unqualified as the little-known lawyer from the prairies of Illinois. He was thought to be a good politician, even a deft hand with the pen, but definitely a second-rate man when the nation needed the highest talents available.

Lincoln, however, was a man of great personal strength, as his presidency revealed. He never had the tough skin that might have given him peace of mind. He was not able to shake the compassion that made his tasks as war president little more than ashes and blood for him. That Lincoln was never swept up by the war spirit while all around him succumbed to it is the highest testimony to his uniqueness and

honor in history. But he had iron in him all the same. The strength of the North in the Civil War was really Lincoln's strength, for he never gave in. He was convinced that saving the Union, and thus demonstrating to the world that a democratic republic *did* have enough strength and inner resolve to keep from flying to pieces, was above all what he must do. Republicanism, enshrined in America since the Revolution but mocked in Europe, was facing its ultimate challenge, and Lincoln was the ultimate republican. Time and again the North was weary; time and again the shocking casualty lists, the terrible loss of life, and the hordes of maimed men shook its resolve and might have ended the war and the Union. Lincoln, however, held to his cause while explaining the bloody conflict to both North and South in words that were gentle, conciliatory, understanding, and yet firm and unyielding on his main goal—restoring the American Union.

Lincoln took a brief time to hear advice from

his cabinet and from his military commanders. General Winfield Scott said that it was impractical to reprovision or reinforce Fort Sumter. Most of the cabinet agreed. For a time Lincoln was in doubt, but then he decided it was unavoidable: Sumter had to be retained. The least he must do was to reprovision it and inform South Carolina beforehand so it could not claim that he was underhanded.

On the fourth of April, 1861, he sent vessels to Sumter and had a clerk in the state department, Robert S. Chew, personally inform the governor of South Carolina, Francis W. Pickens: "I am directed by the President of the United States to notify you to expect an attempt will be made to supply Fort Sumter with provisions only; and that, if such attempt be not resisted, no effort to throw in men, arms, or ammunition, will be made, without further notice, or in case of an attack upon the Fort." If a first shot was to be fired, it would have to be by the other side.

President Jefferson Davis and his cabinet anxiously assembled. It was clear that if the Confederate government did not move to prevent the reprovisioning of Sumter, the angry people of South Carolina would do so on their own. On orders from the Confederate government, General P. G. T. Beauregard sent a message to Major Robert J. Anderson, commander of Fort Sumter, demanding that he surrender before the supplies arrived. This being the eleventh of April, Major Anderson replied that if he had not received new provisions before the fifteenth his garrison would be starved out and he would have to evacuate the fort. News had already reached Beauregard that the reprovisioning ships had arrived off Charleston Harbor, however, and at 4:30 A.M. April 12, 1861, the Confederate shore batteries began firing on Fort Sumter. After forty hours of bombardment, Major Anderson, his ammunition almost gone and his fort in ruins, surrendered to Beauregard and was permitted, with his garrison, to depart.

Lincoln Calls for Troops

Lincoln moved swiftly. Relying entirely on his powers as commander in chief—Congress was not in session and would not meet for three months—on the fifteenth of April he published a proclamation calling on the states to provide 75,000 militia to put down "combinations . . . too powerful to be suppressed by the ordinary course of judicial proceedings." Four days later Lincoln declared the Confederate coastline

blockaded, an action the Supreme Court later took as the legal beginning of warfare.

Virginia and the rest of the Upper South now had a critical decision to make. Would they provide troops to put down their Southern brethren? Should they even allow federal troops to march across their territory to carry out the campaign? For Virginia, the idea was intolerable. On the seventeenth of April, two days after the call for troops, its convention chose secession by a vote of eighty-eight to fifty-five. Arkansas followed on May 6, Tennessee on the seventh of that month, and North Carolina on the twentieth. Four slaveholding states in the border region remained in the Union: Delaware, Maryland, Kentucky, and Missouri—though the issue was only narrowly decided in the latter two, and Maryland contained a significant pro-Southern minority. The border states were joined by the western counties of Virginia, following the establishment there of a Union-leaning "State" government in the summer of 1861. These counties were admitted to the Union as the State of West Virginia on June 20, 1863.

The four seceding states quickly joined the Confederacy, whose capital was moved to Richmond, Virginia. Neither the Richmond nor the Washington governments anticipated a long war. The militia Lincoln called for were to serve only three months, and the Confederates talked confidently of capturing Washington in short order and dictating the terms of peace. Enormous outbursts of public enthusiasm took place on both sides. Anger at the other side had been building up for so *many* years. Now it simply exploded, as in the beginning days of the American Revolution, eighty-six years earlier, in a *rage militaire*.

The Battle of Bull Run

By July 1861 the federal government had a force of about 30,000 men under General Irvin McDowell gathered at Centreville, a hamlet about twenty miles southwest of Washington where the railroad running down into Virginia from that city joined one coming in from the west. Opposing them was a Confederate force of about 24,000 men under General Beauregard. Tremendous pressure had built up on President Lincoln to begin the march on Richmond, and he instructed General McDowell to move forward.

On the twenty-first of July, 1861, the federal attack began. At first it went well, and the news rushed out from the fighting at Bull Run (the name of a small stream just beyond the Centreville heights,

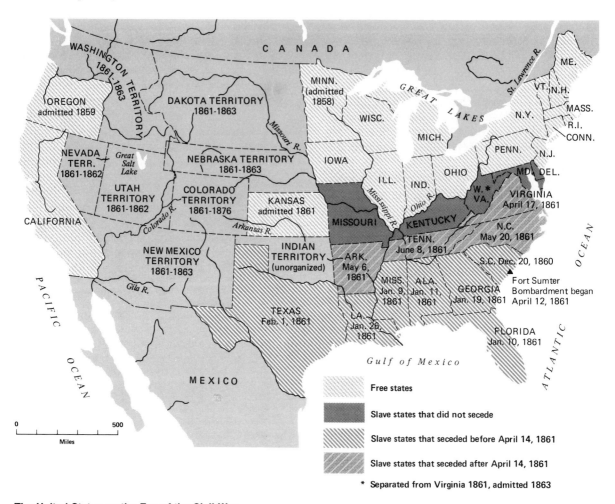

The United States on the Eve of the Civil War

where the battle took place) that the Confederates were fleeing in all directions. But the rocklike determination to hold his ground displayed by one of the Confederate commanders, T. J. Jackson—thereafter called Stonewall Jackson—provided a rallying point for the Confederate army, and the arrival of reinforcements provided fresh troops for assault.

The fighting was desperate. Thousands of soldiers charged and countercharged; artillery batteries flung shot from both sides; indescribable confusion soon reigned over much of the clamorous, dusty battleground; the heat was intense; masses of men rushed this way and that, or jammed up in long lines waiting to cross a small stone bridge. Charging Confederate soldiers screaming the "Rebel yell" had the federals

retreating by afternoon. Soon a mob of federal troops (and Congressmen and journalists, who had been watching from Centreville heights) was streaming off to Washington, desperate for sanctuary. The Confederates had won.

The South was delirious with joy. "What else," asked the Richmond *Whig*, "could one expect from a clash between the gamecock and the dunghill?" Their cause never seemed more secure. The North, on its side, was startled out of its complacency. It knew now that it was in for a long, serious war. The cheering stopped, but the recruiting doubled. No longer did men sign up for a three-month lark; they put down their names to fight until the end of the war. The Civil War had begun in earnest.

BIBLIOGRAPHY

The entire Civil War era fascinates historians, and a rich literature on it keeps pouring from the publishers. Please refer to the bibliography for the previous chapter for many works upon which I relied in Chapter 18, such as those by Nevins, McCardell, and Wyatt-Brown. See also a fascinating study by Stephen A. Channing, *Crisis of Fear: Secession in South Carolina* (1970).

Penetrating the historical crust surrounding Abraham Lincoln is a rewarding endeavor. Many works could be cited; for the present, reference may be made simply to a recent much-praised work by Stephen Oates, *With Malice toward None: The Life of Abraham Lincoln* (1977). Others written by Lord Charnwood, Allan Nevins, David Donald, Carl Sandburg, Benjamin P. Thomas, Richard N. Current, R. H. Luthin, James C. Randall, Don Fehrenbacher, Donald W. Riddle, John J. Duff, and Benjamin Quarles testify to Lincoln's unending interest, and richness of character.

Carl N. Degler, *The Other South: Southern Dissenters in the Nineteenth Century* (1974), together with David M. Potter, *The Impending Crisis*, explore brilliantly the loyalism to the Union that existed in the South, as well as secessionism. C. Vann Woodward's *American Counterpart: Slavery and Racism in the North-South Dialogue* (1971) consists of judicious and informed reflections by a distinguished historian with sensitive insights into human character.

19

The Civil War

TIME LINE

1862 General Ulysses S. Grant takes western Tennessee; James Peninsula invaded and lost by General George B. McClellan; Second battle of Bull Run; Battle of Antietam; Emancipation Proclamation issued (to take effect Jan. 1, 1863); Battle of Fredericksburg; Morrill Land Grant Act passed to aid state universities; Morrill Tariff; new national currency and national banks established; Homestead Act

1863 General Robert E. Lee's victory at Chancellorsville; Battle of Gettysburg; Grant takes Vicksburg; Grant takes Chattanooga; draft riots in New York City

1864 Grant begins "hammering campaign": battles of the Wilderness, of Spotsylvania Court House, of Cold Harbor; Grant's siege at Petersburg begins; General Sherman takes Atlanta; Sherman's "March to the Sea"

1865 Sherman takes South and North Carolina; Lee surrenders at Appomattox Court House; Thirteenth Amendment abolishes slavery; Abraham Lincoln assassinated

HISTORY IN AN INDIVIDUAL LIFE

ULYSSES GRANT

Ulysses Grant, like Jefferson Davis, was West Point-trained and a brave young officer in the Mexican War. He fought in it month after month, right up to the climactic battles outside Mexico City. Davis married the commanding general Zachary Taylor's daughter, and Grant modeled himself in habits and dress after that plain, unpretentious, rock-solid general who after the war became president. But while Davis went on to brilliant postwar successes, the quiet, inarticulate Ulysses Grant drifted off to unimportant military appointments, finally resigning his commission in poverty and disgrace (for hard drinking) at a remote encampment on the far northern California coast. He had never, in fact, liked the military life.

Grant loved horses, however; they were his passion. Possibly no other army officer has ever ridden them as well as he. So, out of a job in 1854, Grant tried farming in Missouri, and then a string of other minor occupations. Unobtrusive and colorless as ever, he was modest, he never swore, and he was almost a complete failure. Of Yankee stock, he had been well educated, his wife Julia Dent was a strong and durable woman, but somehow things had not turned out well. Then the nation's history caught him up again, this time seizing upon his hitherto unsuspected military genius and swirling him to the top. As soon as Fort Sumter was bombarded, Grant was in arms again. Shortly, as a brigadier general, he was characteristically plunging at the enemy in Kentucky. Then in January 1862 he won a dramatic victory far up the Tennessee River, where he captured crucial river forts in bold, headlong attacks. The North, weary of fumbling generals, thrilled at his blunt message to the Confederate commander: "No terms except an unconditional and immediate surrender can be accepted. I propose to move immediately upon your works."

There was a scrubby, rumpled, common look about Grant. When after more powerful, hammering victories, Lincoln brought him to Washington as commander of all the Northern armies, people hardly knew what to make of him. But Lincoln liked Grant and supported him against all criticism: "I can't spare this man—he fights." Though a friendly man, in the crowds that now surrounded Grant everywhere he seemed always, somehow, alone. But troops trusted him and followed his orders unquestioningly. In a war fought by traditionalists, Grant was an essentially modern general. He knew how to use railroads to marshal all needed resources from far away for one concentrated task; he could think "globally," of the entire war, and coordinate operations with dogged skill. And he knew that victory would come only by smashing the armies and the resources of the other side; that single battles would not win a war, but only hammering campaigns that bore in relentlessly.

At the base of Capitol Hill, in Washington, stands the most dramatically powerful statuary grouping in America, the Grant Memorial. Mounted federal soldiers gallop madly, and forever, toward the enemy. At the center of this wild energy is a quiet figure, Ulysses Grant, seated high on his standing horse, his eyes, shadowed under an old wide-brimmed campaign hat, gazing somberly down the Mall to the Virginia shore beyond, as if seeing, still, the horrors of the civil war he fought so unflinchingly to its grim finish. An observer said that Grant always looked as if he was determined to butt his head through a brick wall and on the verge of doing it. This was essentially what he did, destroying the Confederacy and reunifying the United States of America.

PART ONE:
AMERICANS FIGHTING AMERICANS

Overview

The Civil War is the one huge American conflict that has been fought on the nation's soil. It has absorbed Americans as has no other war. Whole libraries exist on the subject. The Revolution does not compare to it in bloodshed and widespread devastation. The wounded alone on the Northern side exceeded in number the total revolutionary army (275,000 to 231,000). The number of dead reached 620,000 (360,000 Northerners out of an army of about 1.5 million, 260,000 Southerners in an army of about 1 million). In proportion to the American population—about 30 million in 1860—this was a heavier loss than the shocking carnage the British suffered in World War I. In World War II, when the American population was 135 million and its military forces fought for four years all over the world, the total dead, about 300,000, was less than half that in the Civil War.

Almost every Northern and Southern community old enough to have experienced the war bears its monument to the dead, usually a pensive young man in stone leaning on his rifle and looking eternally in the direction of the enemy. In the South, the war left behind a region sharply unlike the rest of the United States, in that it alone has known defeat—and it keeps the memory of that defeat alive. As the Catholics in Ireland hold fast to the bitter memory of the Battle of the Boyne (1690), when the hated English ended for more than two centuries all hopes for independence, and as the French-Canadians never forget the fall of Quebec (1763), when the British conquered them, so the South cannot forget Gettysburg, Robert E. Lee, and the Appomattox Court House.

Lincoln, like Grant, still broods in Washington in his memorial on the Mall, and Lee's mansion still sits across the Potomac looking out from its high hill upon the Washington its master could not conquer. These conjunctions impress themselves upon each generation that visits the nation's capital, or sits in its Congress making laws, or wanders through the battlegrounds that dot the countryside from Gettysburg southward.

What Caused the Civil War?

In his Second Inaugural Address, Abraham Lincoln explained why Southerners and Northerners had plunged into this bloody struggle: It was *slavery* that caused the conflict. "All knew that this interest was somehow the cause of the war." Jefferson Davis wrote a long book insisting that it rose instead from a constitutional argument over the right of states to secede. In the twentieth century many historians, led by Charles Beard, have argued that the war was rooted in economic conflicts. The war, Beard wrote, was a second American Revolution, in which the North threw off the national supremacy of the South in order to get the things it wanted to industrialize the country: tariffs, bounties, railroads, a national banking system, and land grants. In the 1930s historian James G. Randall said the conflict was the folly of a "blundering generation" that had foolishly let slavery cloud its vision and had lost its senses.

Historians in the past twenty years have come full circle: They agree with Lincoln that one way or another, an explanation of the war must come back to the issue of slavery. At least, a determination to protect the institution of slavery is the best explanation for Southern secession. Why, however, did the North fight to *prevent* that secession? It is now clear to historians that Northern whites were not eager to end slavery, save for a minority among them, for they hated both blacks and abolitionists. The war eventually became a war to end slavery, but it did not begin that way.

Fears for Republicanism

For many years, fear over the survival of the nation had been mounting in the Northern states. Nothing was more sacred to Americans than the ideology of republicanism. Scoffed at in Europe, to Americans it was the very basis for their country. They still saw themselves engaged in a demonstration of world importance that ordinary people could govern themselves without a monarchy and hereditary nobility to do it for them, that within the people lay the greatest wisdom in government, the truest public virtue, and the highest capacity for creating a just society of liberty and equality. Monarchists insisted that republics always failed, for the people at large are too ignorant, selfish, and undisciplined ever to make the tough and punishing decisions that are needed to keep a country sound and in one piece.

Then came the appalling events in Kansas, where it appeared that Southerners, easily throwing off the restraints of republicanism, intended to get their way by any means, including violence, or else destroy the United States. Northerners were enormously angered by what to them was Southern arrogance, the characteristic "these nabobs have acquired in their custom of giving commands to their miserable serfs." It was infuriating to stand by and watch the Southerners in Kansas apparently getting their way once more. "It is the slave driver's lash," observed a Northern church newspaper in 1854, "differing a little in shape, but wielded for the same end, the enforcement of their will, and by essentially the same means—brute force instead of reason and justice."

Secession was seen by the North in 1860 as the ultimate challenge to law and order and to the republican idea. There was a genuine alarm behind all of this. The historian Philip S. Paludan tells us it was widely believed the United States was on the verge of falling apart into small clusters of states that would thereafter begin competing with each other ruinously (had that not happened already under the Articles of Confederation in the 1780s?) and fighting the brutal little wars that for centuries had flared and rumbled all over Europe. The question was real and inescapable: If the South were allowed to go, what would happen thereafter? The noble edifice of the United States of America, handed down for the good of all humankind to the generation alive in 1860, would dissolve, and the republican ideal would be lost. "*A surrender to Secession*," said a Cincinnati newspaper, "*is the suicide of government.*" "Without a Union that is free," a Chicago newspaper warned, "without a Constitution that can be enforced . . . our Republic ceases to be a government, our freedom will be quickly supplanted by anarchy and despotism."

And there was such a great *anger* against Southerners. It had been building for decades. Whether or not Northerners were concerned with slavery, there were thousands of them who were determined to put the "damned rebels" in their place. They were eager to sign up when Abraham Lincoln called for

troops, and anxious to join his cause. For his part, Lincoln was convinced that preserving the Union, the American republic, was a task of almost divine importance. "On the one side of the Union," as he declared to Congress in July 1861, "it is a struggle for maintaining in the world that form and substance of government, whose leading object is to elevate the condition of men—to lift artificial weights from all shoulders—to clear the paths of laudable pursuit for all—to afford all an unfettered start, a fair chance, in the race of life." In his Second Inaugural Address, in 1865, he put it simply: "Both parties deprecated war, but one of them would make war rather than let the nation survive, and the other would accept war rather than let it perish. And the war came."

The Two Combatants

Looked at as they stood at the start of the war, the North and the South were certainly mismatched in warmaking potential. There were 21 million Northerners in 23 states, with 1.3 million industrial workers producing more than 90 percent of the prewar nation's factory output. There were only 9 million Southerners, of whom 3.5 million were black, and the South had but 110,000 industrial workers. Thus, the North was able to produce enormously more essential war goods than could the South: seventeen times more cotton and woollen goods; twenty-four times as many railroad locomotives; thirty times more boots and shoes; and thirty-two times as many firearms.

Yet it was not as simple as this. President Jefferson Davis appealed to the prewar Southern Whigs to lead the Confederacy's economy, for they were skilled at management, and they plunged in vigorously at their task. Soon the Confederacy was building an industrial capacity that kept its armies quite adequately supplied with arms and munitions, as well as such essentials as clothing and shoes, though there was always severe difficulty in getting such things to the troops when and where they needed them. Indeed, historian Emory Thomas writes that

> the Davis administration outdid its Northern counterpart in organizing for total war. Economically, the nation founded by planters to preserve commercial, plantation agrarianism became, within the limits of its ability, urbanized and industrialized.

The Tredegar ironworks in Richmond and the Confederate Powder Works in Augusta, Georgia, were built into astonishingly huge operations, putting thousands of workers into production. By the end of the second year of war, eight government-owned armories were turning out 1,000 cannonballs and 170,000 rifle cartridges each day.

Also, the "strongest" side does not always win wars, as two other American wars—the Revolution and the Vietnam war—amply demonstrate. And in 1861 neither Southerners nor European observers believed the North could win. Southerners believed the "dollar-grubbing" Yankees were too mean-spirited and cowardly to fight for any great cause, especially if there was no money in it. They were convinced, too, that cotton was king. By withholding it from the world market they expected to force England and France to recognize the Confederacy to prevent massive unemployment, to provide arms, and to force the North to make peace.

European observers believed the Confederacy was simply too large to defeat. It was, after all, many times larger than most European nations. Two wars in America, the Revolution and the War of 1812, had shown how impossible it was to defeat a widely scattered population. In addition, the South had an easier strategic task than the North. It needed only to defend itself to win, whereas the North had to conquer the other side, a fact that went far to equalize the conflict. The South also had an apparent advantage in military leadership. Most of the officers of the United States Army had been Southerners, who now staffed the Confederate forces. (The same did not apply to the navy, a fact of considerable significance.)

From the beginning, the South had gifted generals. Robert E. Lee and Stonewall Jackson were easily superior to their Northern counterparts until the advent of Ulysses S. Grant and William T. Sherman. Southern troops were more used to living in the field than were urban Northerners; guns were an intimate part of Southerners' way of life; and since most campaigns took place in their own countryside, they had the aid of a friendly population. In the war's first two years much of the Confederate people were strongly devoted to their cause, as shown by the fact that 1 million men joined the Confederate army out of a total white population of about 5.5 million (as against 1.5 million men in the Northern army, out of 21 million). This was a fight for Southern independence, a bold and exciting concept to a suffi-ciently large number of Southerners to make the war one that would be hard fought.

Overall Strategy

The Confederacy's strategy was bold and simple: It halted all shipment of cotton abroad so as, by this economic pressure, to push Britain to intervene on the South's side (a catastrophic error in policy; it failed utterly); launched a vigorous (but unsuccessful) diplomatic campaign to secure from European powers diplomatic recognition as an independent nation; and simply waited for the Federals to come into Dixie so they could be attacked and defeated. Lincoln had to devise a comprehensive strategy of both containment and attack. He sent Charles Francis Adams, John Quincy's son, to London to warn the British that war was possible if they did not steer a strictly neutral course, and to remind them that their need for Northern wheat and markets was as important as their need for Southern cotton.

Lincoln declared a naval blockade as soon as war began. Gideon Welles, a strange-looking old gentleman buried in a spiky ruff of whiskers, was a vigorous secretary of the navy. He expanded the navy from 42 ships at the beginning to 82 by July 4, 1861, 264 by the end of that year, and a peak of 671 in December 1864. This huge force was never able to close entirely the coastline of the Confederacy, but at the end of 1862 Welles could report, with only a minimum of exaggeration, that "in no previous war had the ports of an enemy's country been so effectually closed by a naval force." Without such an effective blockade, a Northern victory would have been impossible.

Another element in Lincoln's containment policy was to retain the loyalty of those Border States that had not joined the Confederacy—Delaware, Maryland, Kentucky, and Missouri. This required placing large bodies of troops in those states—especially Missouri, where savage fighting between Rebel sympathizers and Rebel haters went on throughout the war. Lincoln had also to follow policies toward slavery that would not offend these states prematurely.

To conquer the South required invading Confederate territory. Lincoln's strategy for this was threefold: regain Tennessee, thus acquiring a base of power in the heart of the Confederacy from which armies could be sent in several directions; cut the

Confederacy in two by taking the Mississippi River, including the Confederacy's great port of New Orleans; and wage unrelenting war in the eastern theater between the two capitals, Richmond and Washington, D.C., which sat only a hundred miles apart.

What about Tactics?

So much for strategy; what were their tactics, how did they expect to win individual battles? The French military expert Baron Antoine Henri Jomini had studied Napoleon's campaigns and had laid down what he believed were the eternal principles of how to win battles in his 1837 book, *Summary of War*, which Civil War commanders studiously read. First, Jomini said, fighting *offensively* was the key to victory. Do not rely on a passive defense; that will inevitably produce defeat. Rather, *attack* and *attack*! If forced to be on the defensive, go on the attack as soon as possible.

Second, when on the attack, Jomini urged working for a *turning movement*; that is, getting around one or the other end of the enemy's line of defense, allowing an attack from the always-weaker flank or rear. A "tactical" turning movement would be confined to the actual field of battle; in a "strategic" turning movement, the attacker would try to strike far into the enemy's rear and cut his line of communications, from which came supplies and reinforcements, or down which he could retreat. Either way, if "turned," the enemy would have to give up his laboriously constructed defensive position and hastily retreat. This was especially true in Civil War battles, where the armies were huge (by comparison with earlier wars), and men, supplies, and ammunition were used up at a tremendous rate, so that lines of communication to bring in reinforcements and fresh supplies of ammunition were vital.

Over and over, through the war's four long years, both sides tried for turning movements, and they achieved them repeatedly. Thus, most battles were usually fairly short, the army that had been "turned" retreating as rapidly as possible.

Early Campaigns

For more than two years Lincoln searched for a commander who could win the war. It was a desperate, fruitless quest. First he turned to an apparently brilliant young man, George B. McClellan, who had won victories in West Virginia, had immense self-confidence—and a correspondingly low opinion of Lincoln—and was widely praised as a young Napoleon. Marvelously skillful at building the army into a well-trained and well-equipped fighting force, he was paradoxically clumsy and timid when it came to leading his troops in actual combat. In April 1862 Lincoln finally succeeded in prodding McClellan to action, and the general took his army of 100,000 men down Chesapeake Bay to the James Peninsula, from where he began an assault striking inland toward Richmond. Soon General Robert E. Lee, relentlessly on the attack, overwhelmed McClellan, who fell back with heavy losses, withdrew, and returned to Washington in disgrace.

Lincoln then tried John Pope, who was defeated by Lee in the second battle of Bull Run. Following this, the Confederate general decided to invade the North in hopes that Border State Americans in Maryland would rise in rebellion against the Northern government. With McClellan once again in command, Lee was halted in September 1862 at Antietam Creek in Maryland, where the bloodiest single day of fighting in the Civil War occurred. The battle was tragically inconclusive. More than 20,000 men from both sides lay dead and wounded; the Border States did not rise in rebellion; Lee had to retreat to the South; but still the war was as far from being won as ever.

The Nature of the War

The losses in these battles were appalling, the butchery beyond belief. In July 1862, a Union army was well dug in on Malvern Hill, southeast of Richmond, Virginia. On came the Confederates, charging en masse into the Union guns. "[R]egiment after regiment, and brigade after brigade rushed at our batteries," a Union commander later wrote, "but the artillery . . . mowed them down with shrapnel, grape, and canister; while our infantry, withholding their fire until the enemy were within short range, scattered the remnants of their columns." As the sound of cannon and guns rose to a deafening roar, the slaughter went on and on. A Confederate general whose division lost 2,000 of its 6,500 men in these "grandly heroic" assaults, as he termed them, wrote afterward: "It was not war—it was murder."

Historians Grady McWhiney and Perry D. Ja-

Major Battles of the Civil War, 1861–1865

mieson remark in their powerful book, *Attack and Die: Civil War Military Tactics and the Southern Heritage* (1982), that this sort of murder "became almost commonplace during the Civil War." A Union soldier in 1864 wrote home: "The Rebs made 3 charges on us but we stood up to the rack with our 7 Shooters [repeating rifles] & repulsed them each time & we piled the Rebs in heaps in front of us. . . ." At another battle a Southerner mourned, "O, my God! what did we see! It was a grand holocaust of death. Death had held high carnival. . . . The dead were piled the one on the other all over the ground. I never was so horrified and appalled in my life."

In the war's first twenty-seven months of fighting, the South lost the ghastly total of *175,000 men*. "The South simply bled itself to death," McWhiney and Jamieson observe, "in the first three years of the war. . . ." The Union army also endured a terrible slaughter in the Civil War, but it was relatively much less. "If the North . . . had suffered [proportionately as many losses as the South]," observes Charles P. Roland, "she would have lost more than 1,000,000 men instead of 360,000 . . . [and] in World War II [the United States] would have lost well over 6,000,000 men instead of somewhat more than 300,000."

Why did this happen? In the first place, a crucially important technical advance in armaments was completed just before the Civil War began. Soldiers could put aside the traditional smooth-bore musket, which fired a short-range, wildly inaccurate bullet, and begin shooting at each other with rifles (guns whose barrels had spiral grooves, imparting a spiral motion to the bullet which made it far more accurate over great distances). In one leap, the *defensive* had acquired a tremendous advantage over the *offensive*.

Formerly, charging bodies of men could get within a few hundred yards of musket-firing defensive lines before coming into danger, and even then the erratic musket ball could easily miss. Battles were generally won by resolute troops who overran defensive positions and bayoneted the defenders. It was by such tactics that the American army had won the Mexican War, and this lesson, learned in that conflict by many young officers who later would be commanders in the Civil War, was applied when North and South fell to fighting each other. The new rifle, however, made such tactics obsolete, for now soldiers could be shot down at more than 600 yards. The availability of more accurate cannon, plentifully made in modern factories, mowed down even

more attackers. A soldier firing a rifle from a hole in the ground could easily fight off three times his number, and with a cannon at his back several times more than that. Tens of thousands in both armies now died in useless, senseless charges, falling like wheat before a mower long before they were even close to the enemy lines.

The Generals' Reaction

The lesson was obvious: Massed charges must henceforth be avoided. Most generals, North and South, refused to accept this truth. They stuck grimly to Jomini's rules of war. Charge! Charge! was almost universally the cry through most of the war. Lamentably, it is a rule of warfare that commanders will ignore the tactical implications of new technical advances (for example, the tank and the machine gun in World War I, the linkage of tanks and tactical aircraft by radio in World War II) and send millions to their deaths needlessly because they are determined to hold to tactics that had won in the past.

However, there was more to it than this. Cultural values lay deep at the heart of this behavior. The irony is that during the Civil War the generals were warmly supported and applauded, especially in the South, for their "gallantry" in pressing such attacks. A Confederate newspaper in 1862 urged the troops to "charge impetuously. No Federal regiment can withstand a bold and fearless bayonet charge. . . . The greatest minds in the South are coming to the conclusion, that our liberties are to be won by the bayonet." And then a revealing sentence: "Those regiments that most distinguish themselves in bayonet charges will march on the true road to honor. . . ."

Honor: this was what sent men in such appalling numbers running headlong to their deaths. And the dominance of the code of honor was much stronger in the Confederacy than in the North. To take a defensive position and simply hold it was regarded as shameful. Whenever he could, General Robert E. Lee sent his men charging out of defensive positions to assault the enemy. General Thomas (Stonewall) Jackson routinely sent his troops running directly into Union guns, using them up at a breathtaking rate. Ulysses S. Grant did the same until late in the war, for in the Mexican War his hero, General Zachary Taylor, had won one glorious victory after another by the charge.

If Grant eventually gave up on the tactic, the South was still attacking until the war's very end, though there was a year of trench fighting around Petersburg, Virginia. "We want Stonewall Jackson [type] fighting . . . that . . . hurls masses against . . . the enemy's army," said a Confederate officer. "The policy of intrenching . . . will ruin our cause if adopted here." In both armies generals were often in the thick of battle, but so many Confederate generals gave personal leadership that more than half were killed or wounded in the fighting—many being wounded two, three, and four times. Most of those who died fell while leading charges. It is not surprising that such men could ignore the losses in the units they led, and mutilate not only themselves but their armies.

Celts and Englishmen

Why were Southerners so ready to die? All observers agree that, as McWhiney and Jamieson put it, "The simple fact is that Southerners were aggressive." Even in peacetime, they were "quick to anger and to fight."

> The southern habit of regarding a fighter—soldier or dueler—as a hero horrified many Northerners. "Cruel horrid custom thus to butcher & destroy men for the false code of honor," pronounced a Yankee preacher. Unlike Southerners, Northerners "were not so military in their habits," observed a contemporary, "because, though equally brave . . . , they were more industrious, more frugal, and less mercurial in their temperament. . . . The social and moral virtues, the sciences and arts, were cherished and respected; and there were many roads to office and to eminence . . . not less honourable . . . than the bloody path of warlike achievement."[1] [p. 171]

In an intriguingly bold suggestion, McWhiney and Jamieson go further to say that Southerners attacked with such boldness because they were Celts. "In the South, especially in the Carolinas and the backcountry, Celts [Scots, Scotch-Irish, and Welsh] constituted an overwhelming majority," their predominance being so strong that the non-Celts around them seemed to take on their traits. On the other hand, "Yankee culture," they remark, "was in large part transplanted English culture, [for] . . . the majority in the North were of English origins," or culturally Anglicized. In this sense, "the American Civil War was basically a continuation of the centuries-old conflict between Celts and Englishmen. . . ." (It is hardly coincidental that the Confederate flag, the Stars and Bars, was an adaptation of the traditional Scottish flag.)

For centuries, Celtic tribal warriors had been legendary for their headlong, heedless charges. From the Civil War's beginnings, therefore, they fought in this ancient way: They attacked. A people who glorified war in Celtic fashion, Southerners, like their Celtic forebears, seemed to love combat, and "usually fought with reckless bravery." In 1188 it was said of the Welsh, "In peace they dream of war and prepare themselves for battle." In 1861 a visitor in the wartime South found "revolutionary furor in full sway, . . . an excited mob, . . . flushed faces, wild eyes, screaming mouths . . . Young men are dying to fight." A Yankee agreed: *"A Confederate soldier would storm hell with a pen-knife."* In the time of the Romans and afterward, the "war cry" of the Scots tribes was remarked on, and during the Civil War the "Rebel yell" pierced the air at every fight. Hearing it, a Union soldier said, "made the hair stand up on his head." It was, said another, "that 'terrible scream and barbarous howling' . . . loud enough to be heard a mile off."

Lincoln Gives the War a Larger Purpose

For many months during the year 1862, Lincoln had been trying to do something about slavery. In February 1862 he had gotten a congressional resolution passed that called on the Border States to work out programs for the "gradual abolishment of slavery," and that would give each state "pecuniary aid to be used by such state in its discretion, to compensate for the inconveniences, public, and private, produced by such change of system." Thereafter he had talked, argued, and pleaded endlessly and unsuccessfully with the Border State governors to accept compensated emancipation.

When McClellan was defeated on the James Peninsula, an angered Congress yelled for an end to "kid-glove warfare" and whooped through a Confiscation Act in July 1862. It called on the president to seize the property of all rebels who fell into certain categories, *including their slaves*, and to put that property to use in prosecuting the war. The slaves thus seized were to be "forever free." Charles Sumner pleaded with Lincoln to go further and use his powers as commander in chief of the armed forces simply to declare that all slaves in rebel territory were henceforth free, whether or not seized. Lincoln replied that he could perhaps make such a decree covering eastern Virginia, but taking in the whole South was

Confederate volunteers at the start of the war, bold young men excited by the romance and soaring spirit of their cause: Southern independence and a chance to smite the hated Yankee.

"too big a lick now. I would do it if I were not afraid that half the officers would fling down their arms and three more States would rise."

Lincoln knew that the North was at a point of crisis in the summer of 1862. McClellan's failure at the James Peninsula demonstrated that the Confederacy was far stronger than supposed. Northern opinion needed a new inspiration to give the war drive and purpose. Emancipation, Lincoln began saying to his close associates, had become an essential war measure. "I am fixed in the conviction that something must be done." Throughout the summer, while General Pope was meeting disaster at Bull Run, Lincoln was working silently at a little desk in the White House telegraph room, drafting and redrafting a proclamation.

In August he informed his cabinet members that he intended to decree a *general* emancipation behind Confederate lines, thus giving a scope to the measure that none of them had anticipated. (He could not extend his decree to cover the Border States, for they were not "the enemy" and he lacked there the sweeping powers of commander in chief in enemy territory.) So total a step had always been rejected because of the fear that it would set off a widespread slave insurrection, endangering white women and children as well as those who still remained on plantations. Seward, the secretary of state, advised Lincoln to wait until a favorable moment in the war to announce emancipation, else it would seem a step taken only out of desperation. Lincoln accepted this advice. As an immediate measure he approved the forming of military support units out of the freed slaves already within Union lines.

After the doubtful Northern victory in September 1862, in the battle of Antietam, when Lee had been forced to retreat back to the Confederacy, Lincoln informed his cabinet, "I think the time has come now. I wish it were a better time." But it was now or never. On the twenty-third of September the newspapers headlined the news: *The president had declared all slaves behind Confederate lines free,* effective 100 days later, on January 1, 1863. As T. J. Barnett, New York Democrat, paraphrased Lincoln's words, if the South did not surrender in that period, "from the expiration of the 'days of grace' the character of the war will be changed. It will be one of subjugation and extermination. . . . The South is to be destroyed and replaced by new propositions and ideas."

The Emancipation Proclamation: "Now, therefore, I Abraham Lincoln, President of the United States, by virtue of the power in me vested as commander in chief of the Army and Navy of the United States, in time of actual armed rebellion against the authority and government of the United States, and as a fit and necessary war measure for suppressing said rebellion, do, on this 1st day of January, in the year of our Lord 1863, and in accordance with my purpose so to do, publicly proclaimed for the full period of 100 days . . . order and . . . declare that all persons held as slaves within said designated states and parts of states [now in rebellion] are, and henceforward shall be, free; and that the executive government of the United States . . . will recognize and maintain the freedom of said persons.

"And I hereby enjoin upon the people so declared to be free to abstain from all violence, unless in necessary self-defense; and I recommend to them that, in all cases when allowed, they labor faithfully for reasonable wages.

"And I further declare and make known that such persons of suitable condition will be received into the armed service of the United States to garrison forts, positions, stations, and other places, and to man vessels of all sorts in said service.

"And upon this act, sincerely believed to be an act of justice, warranted by the Constitution upon military necessity, I invoke the considerate judgment of mankind and the gracious favor of Almighty God."

Black Americans in the Civil War

Black Americans in the Northern army! As James McPherson has remarked in *The Struggle for Equality: Abolitionists and the Negro in the Civil War and Reconstruction* (1964), "the enlistment of Negro troops in the Union Army . . . was one of the most revolutionary features of the Civil War." Since 1792 black Americans had been barred from the state militias and the federal army. However, like interned Japanese-Americans during World War II, Afro-Americans wanted to demonstrate their patriotism, manhood, and courage in battling for their nation, thus winning a moral right to equal citizenship and rights thereafter. But when they offered themselves for enlistment in 1861 they were turned away. "We don't want to fight side and side with the nigger," a New York corporal said. "We think we are a too superior race for that." It was a white man's war, Union soldiers said; it was about holding the country together, and had nothing to do with blacks.

Abolitionists, who were leading the drive to secure equality for blacks, cascaded demands on Washington that the federal government accept black troops. In 1862, when the war was going badly and calls for more enlistees were not being met enthusiastically, Lincoln overrode objections and authorized black enlistments—though the black soldiers sworn in were to be used only in segregated units, a policy to be followed by the American military until after World War II.

By war's end, so enthusiastically did black Americans respond to this opportunity that some 134,000 had enlisted from slave states, and 53,000 from free states. They fought in almost every battle, and 68,000 lost their lives in the war. Black soldiers fought with great intensity and energy. They were "fighting for their homes and families," said one of their white commanders. They would risk their lives, he said, in ways white troops never would. Some black units suffered the highest mortality rates of any in the army. Overall, some 40 percent of them died or were wounded, a proportion much higher than that in white units. They were extensively used in building fortifications and frequently served as spies and scouts behind Confederate lines, where they could pass as slaves. Few were allowed to be officers, however, and they were paid a lower wage than white soldiers. (One Massachusetts black regiment served for a year without pay in protest.) The Confederates were enraged by the North's use of such troops, and they executed many after capture to serve as a warning to other blacks. Eventually, however, even the Confederacy enlisted them, though few were used for fighting.

To look ahead for a moment, we may note that four of the Border States eventually achieved emancipation. The new state of West Virginia was required by Congress to include in its constitution a clause providing for gradual emancipation when it sought admission to the Union in 1863. Tennessee abolished slavery by constitutional amendment in February 1865, the state having been almost entirely in federal hands since 1862. Maryland repealed its slave code and outlawed slavery in a new constitution written in 1864. A state convention in Missouri abolished slavery in January 1865. Only Kentucky and Delaware still held stubbornly to the institution.

In Congress a proposal for an amendment to the national Constitution abolishing slavery had come forward early in the war but had been set aside because of doubts over its legality. Never before had the Constitution been amended to bring about a social reform in the nation. However, when in 1864 the presidential election revealed that the nation followed Lincoln firmly in his determination to end slavery, the amendment was brought up again and passed in late January 1865. It was then sent to the states for ratification, achieved in December 1865, after which it became the Thirteenth Amendment.

The War Becomes Revolution

One thing was clear: The Civil War had now become a revolution for both North and South. Northern victory would mean a sweeping transformation of Southern life. The institution of slavery was now doomed. The war for the Union was now a war for freedom, if not a war for equality. Those Republicans who had been urging emancipation for a long time were ecstatic. Poets, politicians, and journalists joined in praise. Emerson declared that Lincoln's proclamation had transformed the terrible sufferings of the war, which thus far had seemed to be in vain, into necessary sacrifices in a great cause. Abroad,

the Emancipation Proclamation had a miraculous effect, especially in Britain. Many British aristocrats had backed the Confederacy from the beginning out of distaste for the "money-grubbing" democracy of the North. A grudging sympathy for the underdog had also emerged in the general British population as Lee fought so brilliantly, and his troops with such surpassing courage, against huge odds. But now a great wave of enthusiasm for the North swept over the British people. "It is indisputably the great fact of the war," said the *Morning Star*, "the turning point in the history of the American commonwealth—an act only second in courage and probable results to the Declaration of Independence. . . . Is this not a gigantic stride in the paths of Christian and civilized progress?" When the name of Lincoln was uttered before crowds, they rose and cheered tumultuously.

However, many Democrats in the North, those who all along had sympathized with the South or had hated abolitionists, condemned the proclamation. Black men would now flood Northern labor markets, they warned, and Union soldiers would quit fighting. Indiana and Illinois already had laws against the entrance of immigrant blacks, and Ohio politicians began calling for the same.

The war was now revolutionizing far more than just the South. The enormous national effort of raising, equipping, supplying, and transporting an armed force of more than a million men was teaching the North lessons in organization (the word had hardly been known before the war) and concentrated effort that it never forgot. Disciplined activity replaced confusion. A recognizably modern economic system was beginning to appear.

Although losing battle after battle, the North was actually growing stronger as the war went on. There was plenty of food, money, and jobs for everyone. Soldiers filled streets and railroad stations everywhere, and war orders crowded the mailbags of almost every business house. In every field—iron making, shipbuilding, arms manufacturing, machine-tools production, farm-machinery manufacturing, locomotive construction, printing, food canning, and scores more—the war drove small firms together to form large ones, induced the invention of machinery to replace men gone off to service, put a premium on devising efficient management, and led to the training of new and imaginative administrators. The number of corporations rose, and many of them began to carry on nationwide activities and even large-scale trade with Europe.

Blueprint for Modern America

In Congress, meanwhile, the departure of Southern legislators and the preeminence of Republicans brought about the passage in 1862 of a group of laws "so far-reaching in their effects," remarked Senator John Sherman of Ohio, "that generations will be affected well or ill by them." It was the final victory for Alexander Hamilton and Henry Clay. The republic of their dreams began now to be built.

Justin Morrill of Vermont began a revolution in American higher education by pushing through the Morrill Land Grant Act, which offered each state enormous grants of lands for the establishment of at least one college "where the leading object shall be (without excluding other scientific and classical studies, and including military tactics) to teach such branches of learning as are related to agriculture and the mechanic arts." Out of this came the land-grant universities, open to all without regard to religious affiliation. Their purpose was to train the professional classes needed for the burgeoning new national economy.

The Pacific Railroad Act began the huge undertaking that linked the Far West to the rest of the nation, vastly expanding by its land-grant and bonding provisions the principle of federal aid to private enterprise. Corporate interests were to come back to Congress again and again in succeeding decades for direct and indirect federal subsidies. In the last days of the Buchanan administration a new tariff, named for Justin Morrill, had been enacted that moderately raised duties. When the war began, the Morrill Tariff was transformed into a highly protective measure. As the historian Edward Stanwood put it, manufacturers "had only to declare what rate of duty they deemed essential, and that rate was accorded to them." By war's end some duties were at the 100 percent level, the general average being about 47 percent.

In its desperate need for money the government got authority from Congress in February 1862 to print $150 million worth of "United States Notes," soon called greenbacks. By war's end a total of $432 million had been issued in this form. Then the Republican majority created a system of "national banks": privately owned institutions that would be under the supervision of the Treasury Department and a new official called the comptroller of the currency. These banks were to buy United States bonds, after which they could issue National Banknotes in the amount of 90 percent or less of the value of the bonds they had purchased. In 1865 a federal tax on paper currency issued by state-chartered banks eliminated all forms of currency save National Banknotes, and ever since, the same kind of currency has been used from one end of the country to the other.

Last, the Republicans passed the Homestead Act. Giving "every poor man a home" appealed to thousands of Northerners, and in May 1862 the program was inaugurated. If a settler lived on a quarter-section of unoccupied public land for five years, developed it, and paid nominal fees, he would receive title of ownership. By the middle of 1864, even while the Civil War was raging, 1.26 million acres were already occupied under the act.

Behind the Southern Lines

Meanwhile, the South was in grave condition. Although winning battles, it was growing steadily worse off. Lacking gold, refusing to sell its cotton abroad, the Confederacy was also terribly weakened by an ingrained hostility to taxation so strong that it raised no more than 1 percent of income from Confederate citizens, while the North, conversely, raised the stiff proportion of 23 percent. Thus, lacking "hard" currency in its vaults, the Confederacy simply turned to the printing press and turned out floods of paper currency to serve as a medium of exchange.

Confederate paper currency fell steadily in gold value, reaching about five cents on the dollar in 1864. To make things worse, slaves often ran away, and plantations disintegrated. Everything was impossibly complicated by what in time amounted to a breakdown in the South's transportation system. Emory Thomas writes that people went hungry "in the midst of full [corn] cribs, barns, and smokehouses. A bountiful harvest counted for little if local railroad tracks were destroyed by foes or cannibalized by friends, if the road to town were a quagmire, or if wagons and mules were impressed to serve the army." There was plenty of food, but folks in the towns suffered constantly from its shortage.

In fact, everything was in short supply, and prices skyrocketed. As early as July 1862 a European diplomat in Richmond observed that there were "no . . . vegetables except potatoes and cabbages and one cabbage, one single cabbage, costs $1.25." In 1864, boots cost $200 a pair, a coat $350, a pair of pants $100, a barrel of flour $2,756, and even chickens fetched $30 a pair. A laborer's petition to the government in 1863 said wages were "totally inadequate to afford us the merest necessities of life—plain food, shelter, fuel, and clothing. We are literally reduced to destitution."

The Question of Southern Nationalism

In these circumstances, grave weaknesses in Confederate morale began to display themselves. As Richard E. Beringer and his colleagues have written in their recent book, *Why the South Lost the Civil War* (1986), Southern nationalism was actually not very strong or deep, beyond the passionate minority of true believers in the Southern cause who in a time of enormous emotional excitement had swept the Southern states out of the Union.

> *We believe that the Confederacy functioned as a nation only in a technical, organizational sense, and not in a mystical or spiritual sense. . . . Only slavery gave the South its own identity, despite the efforts of some southern writers before the Civil War to pretend otherwise. . . . Many Confederates became Confederates not because they shared a sense of unique nationhood but because they had a mutual fear of a society without slavery and white supremacy. . . . Many Confederates harbored conflicting notions of why they fought. . . . Confederate nationalists surely existed, but Confederate nationalism was more a dream than anything else.*

The Whigs had opposed secession, and Whiggism remained strong, especially in North Carolina, the cities, in the hill country of Appalachia, and among the Germans of Texas. Conscription acts were passed by the Confederate Congress, but numerous exceptions, especially those for slaveholders and overseers, caused anger in those regions settled by farmers without slaves. One man in the Alabama hill country said the war was just a slaveholders' plot and "all they want is to git you pupt up and go to fight for there infurnal negroes and after you do there fighting you may kiss there hine parts for o they care." Many conscripts deserted to form guerrilla bands that roamed large areas of the up-country South. Secret peace societies even sprang into being, as early as 1861, in such places as Arkansas, where disaffection was widespread. East Tennessee was practically in a state of rebellion.

However, one influence seemed more than anything else to firm up white Southerners' nerves, as the war grew more wearing: their deep religious faith. It was incomprehensible to Southerners that God was not on their side. For many years before the war Southern Protestantism had en masse reassured the South that slavery was a divine institution; that in fact it brought a formerly pagan people, the Africans who were now their slaves, to Christianity. Southern whites believed implicitly the classic, ancient faith that God controls events; that whatever happens is God's will; that victory was a sign of God's favor. And during the early part of the war, it seemed clearly that God was with them. Southern congregations, Beringer and his colleagues write, "threw themselves into the war effort with a fervor that seemed to know no bounds in an effort not only to win the war but also to prove to themselves that God really *was* on their side."

PART TWO: THE LONG DEMISE OF THE CONFEDERACY

The War Turns Around: Gettysburg, Vicksburg, and Chattanooga

In the middle of 1863 the war turned against the South. The Confederacy was in an absolutely desperate condition through shortage of supplies. The war had to be won, and soon, or defeat was inevitable. In late June Robert E. Lee invaded the North again, hoping to win a complete victory over the Army of the Potomac, capture Washington, and secure a peace while the momentum of victory still favored the South. With 75,000 men he passed through Maryland and entered Pennsylvania, sending out foraging columns far and wide and frightening cities as far away as New York and Pittsburgh.

President Lincoln now had another commander in George Gordon Meade. Finally, in this steady, competent soldier, he had a man on whom he could rely. On the first of July, 1863, Meade's forces caught up with Lee's army, and the battle of Gettysburg began. Everything depended on Lee winning this battle; a draw would not be enough. For once he was not in a defensive position awaiting an assault and then counterpunching, as was his preference. He had to initiate the attack. Meade collected his army of some 80,000 men on a strong position, shaped like a fishhook, running south from the little town of Gettysburg. Lee's somewhat smaller force had to extend itself around the outside of Meade's army.

The first day at Gettysburg passed with the Confederates hammering inward. On the second day Lee hurled powerful thrusts against both ends of Meade's line, hoping to break through and basket the federal force. A hellish din filled the air, more than 150,000 men in a small space two or three miles across firing until they had to use oversized bullets for their heated rifles and powder charges blew up as they were being rammed down smoking cannon barrels. The Confederates under the Texan J. B. Hood caught sight of a low eminence, Little Round Top, at the southern end of Meade's line and scrambled desperately to get to its summit to position cannon and blow out the entire Federal position.

Gouverneur Warren, Meade's chief of engineers, saw the importance of Little Round Top at the same time, snatched two brigades out of formation, led them to the top of the hill just before Hood's men could get there, and plunged into a nightmarish battle. Soon a New York regiment was on the scene, then more Federals, then a battery of artillery pulled

up by ropes. Hood poured in more men as soldiers fell on every side. They struggled hand to hand when the ammunition ran short, stabbing, clubbing, even throwing stones. Warren strode back and forth yelling over the din, his clothes torn by bullets, his ceremonial sword bloody. A cannonball tore off Hood's arm. Through the afternoon the struggle swayed back and forth; another Union corps came marching up the long road from Washington, D.C., to throw in reinforcements just in time. As the sun was setting, the Confederates were thrown back. The second day at Gettysburg was over.

That night Lee decided that Meade had weakened his center in order to reinforce his flanks and meet the attacks of the second day. Though his closest associate, James Longstreet, pleaded against the idea, Lee decided to charge Meade's center. He had a fresh body of troops, General George E. Pickett's Virginia division, 15,000 strong, and he resolved to hurl it through the Federal center, shatter the line, and win the war. By noon of the third day all the Confederate artillery was in position, and at 1 P.M. the cannonade, an earthshaking roar, began. After an hour of bombardment Pickett's division swung out from the trees, straightened up its lines, and began marching across the half-mile of intervening fields toward the Federal line's center.

Meade had been waiting for the attack. His own cannon bellowed out, and long lanes began to open up through Pickett's division, only to be quickly

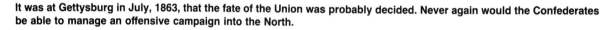

It was at Gettysburg in July, 1863, that the fate of the Union was probably decided. Never again would the Confederates be able to manage an offensive campaign into the North.

closed by men moving over from other files. A hail of rifle fire and cannister (huge buckshot fired from cannons) then began to shred the leading regiments, which broke into a trot, then into a run, the whole division screaming the rebel yell and racing directly into the inferno of smoke and rifle fire in front of them. Thousands were falling. Along the whole Union line from Little Round Top northward, the artillery was firing directly into the onrushing Confederates. Soon they reached the crest of the low roll of ground on which the Federals stood—its local name was Cemetery Ridge—and began hacking and bayoneting among the troops and guns there.

The line broke briefly, but then Federals from either side wheeled and charged into the Confederates. The high tide of the Confederacy broke, and the remnants of Pickett's division streamed back across the plain, thickly strewn with bodies and wounded men, to an ashen-faced Robert E. Lee, who was saying over and over, "It's all my fault . . . it's all my fault."

On the following day, July 4, 1863, when Lee turned southward again and a badly shaken Union army let him go, the Northern states celebrated wildly over the great victory. Then even more incredible news came in. General Ulysses Grant, who had early in the war recaptured western Tennessee from the Confederacy, had finally brought another long campaign to a successful conclusion. Having broken loose from his base of supplies and in swift marches and daring maneuvers backed the Confederates into the defenses of Vicksburg, where they had only the Mississippi River behind them, he had settled down to a month of siege and finally forced the surrender of 30,000 Confederate soldiers on the day of Meade's triumph.

The last Confederate stronghold on the Mississippi was taken; the Father of the Waters, as Lincoln said, "rolls unvexed to the sea." In early autumn 1863, Federal troops under Grant won the battle of Chattanooga, thus opening the prospect that the Union army would soon be able to strike into Georgia and Alabama, the very heart of the Confederacy.

The Last Chapter of the War Begins

More than a year of terribly hard and bloody fighting remained before the Confederacy would be defeated. One thing was by now clear: Neither side, to this point, could actually *destroy* the army on the other side. Modern armies were just too strong, too flexible, too well equipped, their commanders too successful in pulling back and disengaging before a total defeat eventuated. And as long as the Confederacy could put armies in the field that were reasonably well equipped and ready to fight, its defeat appeared impossible.

Even so, after Gettysburg and Vicksburg a deep (though not yet fatal) decay began to set in within the Confederacy's most vital resource: its morale, the readiness of its people to go on fighting. Now, after these great defeats, God seemed to be telling the South that He was *not* on their side. In the Confederacy's fall elections to Congress in 1863, two-thirds of the newly chosen representatives had opposed secession in 1861, showing an ominous swing in public opinion. Conscription and volunteering kept the Confederacy's army fairly close to full strength— the total was about 460,000—but only on paper. An enormous number of men were actually absent without leave; they were in fact deserters. The proportion was about 35 percent before Gettysburg; after that it rose to 40 percent. The prospects for victory were too discouraging, and tens of thousands of men simply left for their homes. "[F]ear and foreboding stealthily crept in to take over the corners of Confederate hearts and minds," note Richard Beringer and his colleagues, "left vacant as morale and will withered away." The South looked northward and saw the Union growing stronger and stronger, mobilizing immense resources. It was all deeply dismaying.

Nonetheless, the Confederacy endured for more than a year and a half after Gettysburg. Union armies, after all, had not gotten very far into the heartland of the Confederacy: the Carolinas, Alabama, Georgia, Mississippi, and Florida—and west of the Mississippi River, now in Northern hands, Arkansas and Texas were still Confederate. The worst fighting still lay ahead.

Grant Arrives in Supreme Command

As winter receded in early 1864, Abraham Lincoln appointed Ulysses S. Grant general in chief of all Union armies, east and west. For the first time Lincoln had a commander who was capable of conceiving of the entire war as one integrated campaign, in which the west was not a separate theater from the east, but one wing of a converging movement that, together with its eastern counterpart, would squeeze the Confederacy until the two came together and it died. This tactic is called "concentration in time": By forcing the South to fight two large Northern armies attacking at once, it was as if they had come together as one force on the same field.

Grant came eastward to direct the entire campaign from the headquarters of the Army of the Potomac—which, however, remained under the direct command of Meade—while William Tecumseh Sherman commanded the western army.

In May 1864 Grant swung the Army of the Potomac out of its camps and headed south toward Richmond with 100,000 men. It was his intention to fight, and fight, and fight again, never giving Lee and the Army of Northern Virginia any respite between battles, until he broke through the Confederacy's largest army, shattered it, and won the war. In early May the two armies locked in a terrible struggle, rocking back and forth through the confusion of the Wilderness. An area of second-growth timber and underbrush near Chancellorsville, it swallowed the armies, made organized maneuvering impossible, and

This two-day engagement, the Battle of the Wilderness, marked the beginning of General Grant's drive into Virginia, which eventually ended with Lee's surrender. Fought in a densely wooded area, the two-day battle cost the Union over 17,000 men. Many of the wounded on both sides died when the woods caught fire from exploding artillery rounds.

The Civil War 351

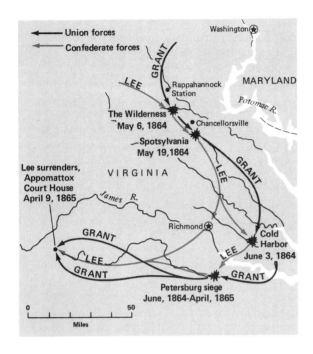

Appomattox, 1865

produced a horrible blind grappling in which everyone was shooting at everyone else. The dry woods caught fire from muzzle flashes, and the wounded expired in smoke and flames, crying for water. Reinforcements came in from both sides, and the noise of thousands of rifles filled the air with a deafening roar while enormous volleys poured out of the woods and smashed whole regiments and brigades.

Grant finally pulled back his army to the nearest crossroads, and as the long columns came out of the Wilderness he had them turn, not northward as they always had after an encounter with Lee, but southward again. Taking this step, Sherman later said, was "the supreme moment of [Grant's] life." The Confederates were astonished when they "discovered, after the contest in the Wilderness, that General Grant was not going to retire." In a few days there was another battle, at Spotsylvania Court House. Both sides suffered heavy losses, and once again Lee kept Grant from breaking through. Grant's army then continued marching steadily southward, Lee wheeling in front of him to stay between the Federals and Richmond. In early June the Army of the Potomac confronted the Confederate army near a sleepy crossroads tavern called Cold Harbor. The rebels

Sherman's Campaigns

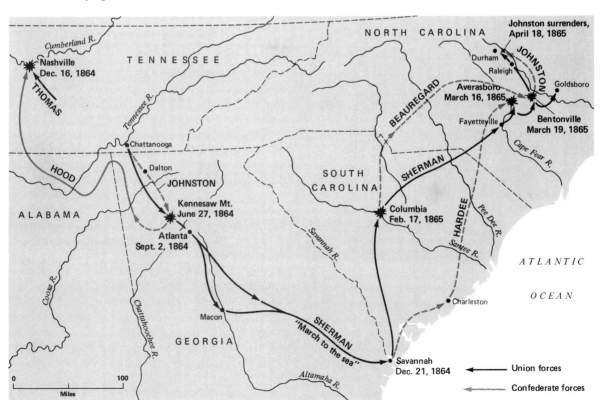

were well entrenched; only their black hats could be seen. Since the Chickahominy River was right behind them, Grant concluded that here was the place the war might be won, for the Confederates could not easily retreat.

This decision led to the most one-sided massacre in the war. As 40,000 Federal soldiers ran toward the Confederate trenches in the early light of June 1, 1864, they were clearly visible. Thousands of rifle barrels came over the trench parapets, and a deafening sound filled the air. The Federals bent forward as they charged, as if heading into a stiff gale, and fell like stones when shot. Whole companies died instantly. In fifteen minutes the attack was over. The Rebels lost almost no men at all; the Federals had 7,000 casualties. Grant never made a major frontal assault again.

From the beginning of the Wilderness battle to the end of Cold Harbor's ill-fated charge, the Federal army had suffered 55,000 casualties, a figure equal to the strength of Lee's entire army. But Grant could reinforce and rebuild; Lee could only await the next encounter. His men were now starving. "Hunger to starving men," a Confederate later wrote in remembrance of these months, "is wholly unrelated to the desire for food as that is commonly understood and felt. It is a great agony of the whole body and of the soul as well. It is unimaginable, all-pervading pain inflicted when the strength to endure pain is utterly gone. . . . It is a horror which, once suffered, leaves an impression that is never erased from the memory."

In mid-June Grant moved swiftly and covertly across the James River in an attempt to take Richmond from the rear. Surprised, Lee barely got enough men to Petersburg, an essential railroad junction south of Richmond, in time to keep Grant from taking the town. The Federals tried desperately to break through Lee's hastily assembled defenses, but failed. Then Grant pulled back, and both sides began digging trenches that eventually stretched for 50 miles in a great arc around Petersburg. For ten months the two armies fought the kind of trench warfare that the world was to know in World War I.

Sherman in the West

Meanwhile, General William Sherman was pushing forward the western wing of the unified assault against the Confederacy. In May 1864 he moved his army of some 100,000 men out of Chattanooga, Tennessee, and headed toward Atlanta, a city of great strategic importance because of its industry, size, and central location. Joseph E. Johnston, with a force half that of Sherman's, fought him off with great skill in a series of delaying actions, just as Lee was holding off Grant.

Sherman, however, fought a brilliant war of maneuver, relying almost entirely on turning movements to force Johnston out of his defensive positions, however skillfully they might be constructed, to retreat ever backward toward Atlanta. Sherman had, after all, twice as many men, and going around the end of Johnston's lines was relatively easy. Time and again Johnston would find large units of Sherman's army almost behind him, feeling for his lines of communication and forcing another withdrawal.

As Sherman approached Atlanta, President Jefferson Davis, losing patience with Johnston, abruptly removed him and put J. B. Hood, the one-armed veteran of Gettysburg, in command. A bold and courageous if not remarkably intelligent general, he rashly left his entrenchments for open battle, and he saw his army badly mauled. He then pulled back to defensive positions around Atlanta, and Sherman settled down to begin his siege in July 1864, a month after Grant had begun his at Petersburg.

Wartime Problems in the North

These were critical months in the North. Grant's horrifying casualties and his failure to defeat Lee produced dismay that was intensified when both he and Sherman bogged down in long sieges. The mood of spreading gloom had been long in preparation. Lincoln had many enemies, enthusiasm for the war had been dying off, and heated controversies had risen. A year before, in March 1863, the government had been forced to enact a conscription law because volunteering had fallen off badly. The first effort by the United States government to raise a military force by levying directly on the general population (rather than on the state governments), the act was badly drawn. "Conscription as practiced and enforced, evaded and obstructed, under this act," writes David Donald, "became one of the crying scandals of the war." It provided numerous exemptions and the opportunity of sending a substitute. The system produced only some 46,000 conscripts and 118,000 substitutes, constituting about 6 percent of the Union army.

It also produced enormous disorders. Provost

marshals hunted down evaders, troops had to be called out to enforce the law, secret societies resisted its enforcement, and enrollment officers were shot while carrying out their tasks. Draft "insurrections" had to be put down all over the North. The gravest occurred in New York City, where immigrant Irish workers, who competed with free blacks for unskilled jobs, were frightened that abolition would bring floods of Afro-Americans out of the South to Northern cities. When draftees' names were drawn on July 11, 1863, large sections of New York City exploded into rioting. Police were assaulted, buildings were burned, and blacks were hunted down unmercifully. Thousands were driven from the city, many of whom never came back. After five days army units arrived to stop the rioting, by which time there had been almost eighty deaths.

Those who sympathized with the South or deplored the war and wanted a compromise peace—called "Copperheads"—formed secret societies such as the Knights of the Golden Circle and the Sons of Liberty. Out of fear that they were in communication with the enemy and trying to bring on Northern defeat, the federal government launched programs against dissidents that stringently limited civil liberties. With doubtful constitutional legality, Lincoln suspended the habeas corpus privilege in 1861 (the right to have the government show cause before a judge why a prisoner is being detained without trial) and began to arrest and detain indefinitely large numbers of people suspected of antigovernment activity. (In March 1863 Congress passed a law authorizing the president to suspend habeas corpus.) In September 1862 Lincoln declared that anyone who discouraged enlistments, resisted the draft, or engaged in disloyal action was subject to martial law and trial by military courts. Almost 40,000 arrests appear to have been made during the war, most of them resulting in relatively brief periods of confinement.

Vallandigham: Copperhead Leader

In May 1863 a Democratic congressman from Ohio, Clement L. Vallandigham, was thrown in jail and tried by military court for advocating peace by negotiation. The case quickly became a national sensation, and Vallandigham's name became the rallying point for thousands of Lincoln's Copperhead opponents. Sentenced to imprisonment for the war's duration, he was subsequently released by Lincoln and banished

to the Confederacy. Soon he appeared in Canada issuing addresses to the American people. Secretly reentering the United States, he participated openly in the presidential campaign of 1864, and Lincoln made no further effort to disturb him.

Subsequent Supreme Court decisions declared that the trial of civilians by military court was unconstitutional. "Martial law," Justice David Davis declared in *Ex parte Milligan* (1866), "cannot arise from a *threatened* invasion. The necessity must be actual and present; the invasion real, such as effectually closes the courts and deposes the civil administration. . . . Martial rule can never exist where the courts are open, and in the proper and unobstructed exercise of their jurisdiction. It is . . . confined to the locality of actual war."

On top of these and other problems in the North there came a shocking Union defeat at Chancellorsville, Virginia, in the spring of 1863, followed by victories at Gettysburg and Vicksburg in July, tempered with the knowledge that Lee had been allowed to escape again. When the campaigning began once more in the spring of 1864, only to end in the sieges in June and July, the nation still had little over which to rejoice. In May there had even been a brief effort to find another Republican to nominate for the presidency in place of Lincoln, but little came of it. In June the party met in Baltimore, nominated the president for reelection, and chose Andrew Johnson of Tennessee as his running mate.

Lincoln's cause grew steadily grimmer as war ground on fruitlessly. Vallandigham was traversing the country calling for peace, and there were secret conversations with Confederates even by such individuals as Charles Francis Adams, the American minister in London. In July 1864 the Confederate cavalry commander Jubal Early intensified the spreading dismay by a spectacular raid in the North that for a time threatened the safety of the national capital. In these circumstances prominent Republicans talked of holding a new nominating convention and choosing someone besides Lincoln who would be a more "vigorous" president. "Mr. Lincoln is already beaten," wrote Horace Greeley to a friend. "He cannot be elected. And we must have another ticket to save us from utter overthrow."

The Democrats now tried to carry water on both shoulders. To meet the growing cry for peace, they had Vallandigham write the platform for their presidential campaign, which demanded halting hostilities "to the end that at the earliest possible moment peace may be restored on the basis of a Federal Union of the States." To satisfy those who wanted a president apparently more skilled in military matters than Lincoln, they chose George B. McClellan as their presidential nominee. He was not only a professional military man who had a wide following, he was also a known opponent of emancipation. All political observers pointed to a Democratic victory. Indeed, the president himself expected it, recording in a private memorandum in August that "this morning . . . it seems exceedingly probable that this Administration will not be re-elected."

Military Breakthrough

Then military events transformed everything. Sherman broke through Hood's defenses and took Atlanta on the first of September in one of the most exciting and climactic moments of the war. The months of frustration were ended, a great victory had been won,

and from then on the Union cause rolled steadily forward. In the new atmosphere Abraham Lincoln was reelected in November by a majority of more than 400,000 votes over McClellan and a landslide in the electoral college, 212 to 21.

General Sherman now began demonstrating how far he had veered from the traditional dictum that warfare should involve professional troops only. A civil war could not be won, Sherman believed, unless the people's morale and their warmaking capacity were destroyed. Jefferson Davis was reassuring Georgians that the Confederacy would overwhelm Sherman now that he was deep within their borders, as Napoleon had been overwhelmed in the depths of Russia. Sherman resolved to prove him wrong. "If the north can march an army right through the south," he telegraphed Grant, "it is proof positive that the north can prevail in this contest, leaving only open the question of its willingness to use that power. . . . Even without a battle, the results, oper-

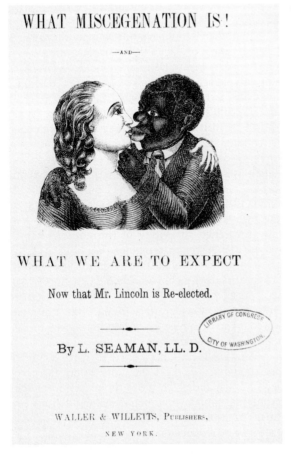

The political caricature was one method used by racists to arouse public sentiment against blacks.

ating upon the minds of sensible men, would produce fruits more than compensating for the expense, trouble, and risk."

So once more he broke loose from his base, burning Atlanta first and then beginning a long, slow march to the sea, over 200 miles away. Spreading out his troops to cover a swath 60 miles wide through the countryside, he instructed them to burn and destroy everything in their path with any conceivable value to the South's war effort. Railroads were torn up, their rails heated and twisted around poles. Bridges were destroyed, workshops leveled, public buildings burned, and all livestock and food (save, in most cases, what was needed for local subsistence) were slaughtered or taken away.

Many soldiers went far beyond Shermans' directives in their looting and pillaging, making that general's name ever after a byword in the South for barbaric cruelty. For all their plundering, however, the soldiers were careful not to injure civilians, and rape was practically unheard of. A Georgia newspaper described the scene: "Dead horses, cows, sheep, hogs, chickens, corn, wheat, cotton, books, paper, broken vehicles, coffeemills, and fragments of nearly every species of property that adorned the beautiful farms of [the countryside] strew the wayside, monuments of the meanness, rapacity, and hypocrisy of those who boast they are not robbers and do not interfere with private property."

By December Sherman was in Savannah. In February 1865 he began marching through South and North Carolina, dealing out the same waste and destruction. In that same month a peace conference was held on a Union ship lying at Hampton Roads in the estuary of the James River. Lincoln spoke for the North, giving as his terms the reunification of North and South, the ending of slavery, a complete cessation of all hostilities, and the disbanding of Confederate armies. Alexander Stephens, speaking for the Confederacy, communicated its unwillingness to accept this "unconditional submission."

The War Ends

But the end was not far away. The fall of Atlanta, and Sherman's subsequent march right through the Confederacy to the sea, had not only broken the stalemate but had also broken Confederate morale. The Confederacy's armies ceased launching any more attacks on Northern forces. They were simply wait-

ing, in remote encampments, or hunkered in the trenches around Petersburg, for the "Yanks" to attack. At the same time, Union armies, enthused in spirit—victories always do this for fighting forces—grew more aggressive. Grant kept lengthening his trenches before Petersburg, feeling for the end of Lee's position. When General Sherman's forces joined him, after their victorious campaign through the Carolinas, Grant finally was able to turn the flank of Lee's army, advancing around the end of the trench line.

Now everything was fluid again. On April 1, 1865, Grant won the battle of Five Forks in Lee's rear, the last important struggle of the war. Lee was forced to vacate the Petersburg trenches and begin his withdrawal. In France, Baron Jomini, now an old man who was paying careful attention to the American fighting, remarked on the "brilliant victory . . . obtained by General Grant." With a much-reduced army Lee fled westward, hoping to reach the mountains and join Confederate forces still existing in North Carolina under General Johnston. But Grant moved swiftly, getting his army out in front of Lee's exhausted and starving soldiers. He halted the Confederates at Appomattox Court House by the simple expedient of displaying his overwhelming force.

On April 9, 1865, Lee recognized the inevitable and, to stop further useless bloodshed, asked for peace terms. Grant had already been personally instructed by Lincoln to be magnanimous, and his terms were generous: Lee's men had only to lay down their arms and give their word that they would fight no more against the government of the United States of America. Grant allowed them to keep their private horses or mules "to work their little farms." Almost 30,000 men, the whole of Lee's army, surrendered. An army had finally been actually defeated and disbanded, not simply driven from the field of battle to fight again.

Similar proceedings elsewhere in the South wherever there were military units completed the ending of the Civil War over the next few weeks. Jefferson Davis breathed fire to the end and even talked stoutly of continuing resistance after Lee's surrender, but Joseph E. Johnston bluntly informed him that his men would not fight any more. On the tenth of May, near the border of Florida, Davis was captured. He was imprisoned for almost two years, released, and allowed to live quietly in Mississippi, writing his memoirs. Fourteen years after the defeat of the Confederacy he died at his estate, Beauvoir, near Biloxi, Mississippi.

Why the South Laid down Its Arms

The war, however, had actually come to an end long before Appomattox. The Confederacy's armies were melting away even before the year 1864 was out. As 1865 opened, less than half the soldiers on their rolls were actually with their units. Hundreds of thousands of Confederate soldiers had gone home, even though most of the Confederacy was still free of Union troops. There had, in fact, been little change in the amount of Confederate territory held permanently by the Union army since the fall of Vicksburg in July 1863; Sherman's marches were simply enormous raids. The Confederacy could still adequately supply its armies. And yet long before Appomattox, its soldiers, convinced that defeat was coming, were voting with their feet, and going home to care for their often-destitute families.

White Southerners seem to have concluded at last that God was telling them something. A devoutly religious people, they believed implicitly that God ordained all things, and surely if defeat was their portion, it meant that God was saying that fighting for slavery had been wrong from the beginning. As Dolly Burge, a Georgia planter's wife, put it, "If the South was right, God would give it victory; if slavery was wrong, 'I trust that He will show it unto us.'"

Guerrilla War: The Significance of Its Absence

When the end finally arrived, a most revealing thing occurred: The soldiers of the South did not scatter and begin the kind of guerrilla warfare against the victorious government that so often follows civil wars. Fighting and dying endlessly for a desperately desired nationhood, no matter what it might cost, has driven many peoples in the history of the world to struggle on and on as guerrillas. However, in the American South, national independence was simply not that fervently wished for. Southern men were certainly courageous enough to have fought on; of that, there was abundant evidence in the fighting just concluded. But after Appomattox Lee himself directly discouraged the idea of beginning a guerrilla war against the North, when one of his generals

suggested it, and so too did General Johnston. As Richard Beringer and his colleagues note,

> Few southerners wished to continue the fight. Slavery was gone, state rights appeared to be gone, soul-searing casualty lists indicated the loss of many young men, and God seemed to be against them. "O, God," prayed one Confederate in the summer of 1864, "wilt thou not interpose Thy strong arm to stop the bloody strife?" . . . The armies had not yet surrendered, but the people were beaten.

A Confederate congressman wrote, "Our people *are* subjugated—they are crushed in spirit—they have not the heart to do anything but meet together and recount their losses and suffering."

If a guerrilla war had been begun, then there would indeed have been the kind of bloody, savage, "uncivilized" war spread widely over many states that in fact the North and the South had not fought. As long as it was army against army, such killing as occurred fell within the bounds of what people believed to be honorable conduct. There were irregular bodies of men here and there, as in Missouri, who during the war had carried on a violent informal battle with the people of the other side, but that was widely frowned upon.

The armies rarely fired on each other's sentries, for example; the rules of war that both sides adopted forbade it. There was to be no "wanton" violence, the authorities decreed. When in 1863 Confederate troops fired on some of Sherman's troops while they were bathing, their commander immediately ordered that the firing cease. The Confederacy even ordained that land mines would not be used, for nothing would be gained save killing someone, and killing was only justified when part of some large movement of the armies. And now, with Lee's surrender, instead of hiving off to a mountain fastness in the South's interior to begin a guerrilla war, the Confederate soldiers simply laid down their arms and went home.

Lincoln's Last Days

Two of Lincoln's tasks were behind him by the time of his second inauguration in March 1865: saving the Union, which only awaited the last victories, and ending slavery. That institution was clearly "in the course of ultimate extinction," to use the phrase Lincoln had uttered so many times before his election in 1860. Now the problem before him was reconstructing the Union. He had already made his views known as to procedures (to be discussed in the next chapter); now he made his views known as to the spirit in which reconstruction was to be carried through. No utterance reveals more the inner character of Abraham Lincoln than his Second Inaugural Address. He spoke unreservedly in the language of intense religious feeling, calling for a peace of reconciliation.

> One-eighth of the whole population [he said] were colored slaves, not distributed generally over the Union, but localized in the Southern part of it. These slaves constituted a peculiar and powerful interest. All knew that this interest was, somehow, the cause of the war. To strengthen, perpetuate, and extend this interest was the object for which the insurgents would rend the Union, even by war; while the Government claimed no right to do more than to restrict the territorial enlargement of it. Neither party expected for the war the magnitude or the duration which it has already attained. Neither expected that the cause of the conflict might cease with, or even before, the conflict itself should cease. Each looked for an easier triumph, and a result less fundamental and astounding. Both read the same Bible, and pray to the same God; and each invokes His aid against the other. It may seem strange that any men should dare to ask a just God's assistance in wringing their bread from the sweat of other men's faces; but let us judge not, that we be not judged. The prayers of both could not be answered—that of neither has been answered fully. The Almighty has His own purposes. "Woe unto the world because of offenses! for it must needs be that offenses come; but woe to that man by whom the offense cometh."
>
> If we shall suppose that American slavery is one of those offenses, which, in the providence of God, must needs come, but which, having continued through His appointed time, He now wills to remove, and that He gives to both North and South this terrible war, as the woe due to those by whom the offense came, shall we discern therein any departure from those divine attributes which the believers in a living God always ascribe to Him? Fondly do we hope—fervently do we pray—that this mighty scourge of war may speedily pass away. Yet, if God wills that it continue until all the wealth piled by the bondsman's two hundred and fifty years of unrequited toil shall be sunk, and until every drop of blood drawn with the lash shall be paid with another drawn with the sword, as was said three thousand years ago, so still it must be said, "The judgments of the Lord are true and righteous altogether."
>
> With malice toward none; with charity for all; with firmness in the right, as God gives us to see the right, let us strive on to finish the work we are in; to bind up the nation's wounds, to care for him who shall have borne the battle, and for his widow, and his orphan—to do all which may achieve and cherish a just and lasting peace among ourselves, and with all nations.

On April 14, 1865—Good Friday—the Union flag was hoisted at Fort Sumter in Charleston harbor by the officer who had been driven from it four years before, Robert J. Anderson, now wearing general's stars. In Washington, Lincoln was in one of his rare moods of contentment and happiness. His son Robert was home safely from the fighting at Petersburg, the war was winding up rapidly, Congress was not in session (always a relief to presidents), and there were encouraging prospects that soon he would have the Southern states back in the Union and the nation reconstructed. At a cabinet meeting that morning, he promptly rejected the notion of a "hard" peace. "No one need expect me to take any part in hanging or killing these men, even the worst of them. Frighten them out of the country, open the gates, let down the bars, scare them off. Shoo!" he cried in his countryman's way, throwing up his large hands as if clearing a barnyard.

That evening he and his wife drove to Ford's Theater to see a play. Sometime after 10 P.M. a young actor in his twenties named John Wilkes Booth stepped up behind Abraham Lincoln where he sat in his chair, and shot him in the back of the head. Leaping to the stage, Booth shouted "*Sic semper tyrannis*," the motto of Virginia, and dashed out of the theater. Twelve days later, after a hectic chase in which he reportedly wondered why no one praised him for what he had done, he was cornered in a barn that was burning down around him and shot dead.

BIBLIOGRAPHY

I have benefited greatly in this edition from the powerful new revisionist study by Richard E. Beringer, Herman Hattaway, Archer Jones, and William N. Still, Jr., *Why the South Lost the Civil War* (1986). This chapter has also drawn on: Allan Nevins's *The War for the Union*, four vols. (1959–72); Bruce Catton's numerous volumes on the war, especially *A Stillness at Appomattox* (1953); Fletcher Pratt, *A Short History of the Civil War* (1966);

James C. Randall and David Donald, *The Civil War and Reconstruction* (1969); Alan Barker, *The Civil War in America* (1961); Stephen B. Oates, *With Malice toward None: The Life of Abraham Lincoln* (1977); the general analysis in Chapter VIII, Robert Kelley, *The Cultural Pattern in American Politics: The First Century* (1969); George M. Fredrickson, *The Inner Civil War: Northern Intellectuals and the Crisis of the Union* (1965); Philip S. Paludan, "The American Civil War Considered as a Crisis in Law and Order," *The American Historical Review* (1972); Grady McWhiney and Perry D. Jamieson, *Attack and Die: Civil War Military Tactics and the Southern Heritage* (1982); T. Harry Williams, *Lincoln and His Generals* (1952); William S. McFeely's Pulitzer Prize-winning *Grant: A Biography* (1981); E. B. Long, ed., *Personal Memoirs of U.S. Grant* (1952, 1982); a powerful novel, winner of the Pulitzer Prize, Michael Shaara's *The Killer Angels*; and Stephen Crane's classic *The Red Badge of Courage* (1895); Stephen W. Sears, *Landscape Turned Red: The Battle of Antietam* (1983); C. Vann Woodward, ed., *Mary Chesnut's Civil War* (1981); E. Merton Coulter, *The Confederate States of America, 1861–1865* (1950); T. B. Alexander and Richard E. Beringer, *The Anatomy of the Confederate Congress: A Study of the Influences of Members' Characteristics on Legislative Voting Behavior, 1861–1865* (1972); Carl N. Degler, *The Other South: Southern Dissenters in the Nineteenth Century* (1974); Emory Thomas, *The Confederacy as a Revolutionary Experience* (1971); Bertram Wyatt-Brown, *Southern Honor: Ethics & Behavior in the Old South* (1982); James McPherson, *The Struggle for Equality: Abolitionists and the Negro in the Civil War and Reconstruction* (1964); Bray Hammond, *Sovereignty and an Empty Purse: Banks and Politics in the Civil War* (1970); Leonard P. Curry, *Blueprint for Modern America: Legislation of the First Civil War Congress* (1968); Allan C. Bogue, *The Earnest Men: Republicans of the Civil War Senate* (1981); Laurence R. Veysey, *The Emergence of the American University* (1965); Adrian Cook, *The Armies of the Streets: The New York Draft Riots of 1863* (1974).

Students will find the following rich reading, as well: The extraordinary Time-Life Books, Inc., multivolume series, *The Civil War* (1983–); the new "standard work," superbly written, James M. McPherson's *Ordeal by Fire: The Civil War and Reconstruction* (1982); an intriguing piece of psychohistory, George B. Forgie's prize-winning *Patricide in the House Divided: A Psychological Interpretation of Lincoln and His Age* (1979); James H. Moorhead's probing look into the Yankee mind, *American Apocalypse: Yankee Protestants and the Civil War 1860–1869* (1978); a sophisticated political analysis, Eric Foner's *Politics and Ideology in the Age of the Civil War* (1980); a London *Times* correspondent's view, William Howard Russell's *My Diary North and South*, edited by Fletcher Pratt (1954); Shelby Foote's beautifully written multivolume history, still in process, *The Civil War: A Narrative* (1958–); C. C. Buel and Robert U. Johnson, eds., *Battles and Leaders of the Civil War*, 2 vols. (1956); Douglas S. Freeman's *Lee: A Biography*, four vols. (1934–35); Frank E. Vandiver, *Mighty Stonewall* (1957); Bell I. Wiley, *The Life of Johnny Reb* (1943) and *The Life of Billy Yank* (1952); V. C. Jones, *The Civil War at Sea*, 3 vols. (1960–62); Margaret Leech, *Reveille in Washington, 1860–1865* (1941). For the Civil War as an international event, see Harold Hyman, ed., *Heard 'Round the World: The Impact Abroad of the Civil War* (1969), and for its crucial influence upon American constitutional law, read Harold M. Hyman and William M. Wiecek, *Equal Justice under Law: Constitutional Development 1835–1875*, New American Nation Series (1982), and Philip S. Paludan, *A Covenant with Death: The Constitution, Law, and Equality in the Civil War Era* (1975).

20

Reconstruction

TIME LINE

1863 President Lincoln's Reconstruction plan issued

1864 Lincoln vetoes Wade-Davis bill; black leaders form Equal Rights League

1865 Andrew Johnson becomes seventeenth president of the United States; Johnson attempts Reconstruction of the Union; Southern white governments formed; Freedmen's Bureau established; Thirteenth Amendment abolishes slavery; Ku Klux Klan formed

1866 Johnson vetoes Freedmen's Bureau extension; civil-rights bill; congressional elections establish large Republican majority

1867 First Reconstruction Act launches Radical Reconstruction; the French withdraw from Mexico; Alaska purchased

1868 Impeachment trial of President Johnson; Fourteenth Amendment guarantees civil rights and extends citizenship to all persons born or naturalized in the United States; Ulysses S. Grant elected eighteenth president of the United States; Burlingame Treaty with China

1870s Terrorism against blacks in the South; flourishing of Darwinism and ideas of racial inferiority

1870 Fifteenth Amendment forbids denial of vote on racial grounds

1871 *Alabama* claims controversy settled with Great Britain

1876 Rutherford B. Hayes elected nineteenth president of the United States; end of Reconstruction

CHARLES SUMNER

Among the Republicans, the party of anti-Southernism, the most prominent Radical was Charles Sumner of Massachusetts. Tall, lordly, learned, and eloquent, Sumner was as passionate in his hatreds as he was in his affections. Because of his Senate speeches before the Civil War, he was reviled in the South as a "serpent," a "filthy reptile," and a "leper." Yankee to the bone, in love with English ways and culture, he shared aristocratic England's view that much of American life was lawless, crude, narrow, and ignorant, and that slavery was America's greatest disgrace. In his youth Sumner was a disciple of the saintly Unitarian leader William Ellery Channing, and he took up all of Channing's causes: hostility to war, the inhumanity of the prisons, illiteracy and ignorance among the masses—and slavery.

After the passage of the Kansas-Nebraska Act, Sumner attacked the South with a slashing, caustic vituperation that made even his Republican colleagues

wince, although the Northern masses were delighted with their champion and the New York *Times* lauded his "matchless eloquence and power." The May 1856 attack upon him at his Senate seat by Preston Brooks was one of the great flash points that drove South and North apart in unforgiving anger. Recovered and back in his Senate seat in 1859, he took up again his unending attack upon the "Barbarism of Slavery." During the secession crisis he stood fast against any compromises, and after war began he announced that the seceded states had abdicated all constitutional standing, and could be dealt with as conquered territory. Thus, their internal social arrangements could—and must—be totally transformed to blot out Southern barbarism.

One simple faith moved Sumner: that all people are created equal. During the Civil War, he prodded Lincoln unceasingly to free the slaves; nothing else would justify the holocaust. Afterward, he helped lead those Radical Republicans who wanted to secure economic and social as well as political and civil equality for blacks. All this sprang from his firm Yankee belief that governments exist not just to keep order and otherwise stand aside passively, but to be powerful instruments in reform, and in creating the conditions for a confident, prosperous, and sophisticated civilization. Alone among the intellectuals of his day, he chose an active career in the grubby, malodorous, and undignified world of politics in order to achieve his goals. In the crucial Reconstruction years, history and Charles Sumner came together in a rare fusion of vision and reality. Never able to get all that he wanted for black people, he nonetheless left a legacy for the future in the great civil rights constitutional amendments of those years, forged in an atmosphere of ideas that he had done much to create.

PART ONE:
RECONSTRUCTION: FIRST PHASE

The War Comes to an End

On Sunday, the ninth of April, 1865, Robert E. Lee and Ulysses S. Grant took their seats in Appomattox Court House, signed the articles of capitulation, and the civil war in America was over. The human cost had been appalling: 618,000 men had died, and another 400,000 had been wounded, which in the 1860s usually meant that they had sustained a lasting mutilation. Now that the fighting was over, a million and a half men still under arms could begin making their way homeward. The great North American republic was not going to be split into two (or perhaps more) nations: the Union had been restored. And to 4 million black Americans, a new life in freedom had come. Millions of white Americans, North and South, looked upon this fact with vast relief. Their United States of America was no longer shamed before the world by the crime of being a slave country. A historic victory for human liberty had been won.

Five days later, on Good Friday, the fourteenth of April, Abraham Lincoln was shot dead. Horror swept through the nation; rage seized the Union army, still encamped in the South. For a time it looked like the war against the South would erupt again, this time to exact a terrible revenge. Then it became clear that the assassination was the work of a tiny group of conspirators; the Confederacy itself had not, in its expiring death agonies, reached out to kill the president, and the anger subsided into grief. Stunned Northerners tried to absorb the fact of Lincoln's death. Mourners filed by his casket in the Capitol rotunda and massed silently by the railroad tracks to watch his funeral train take its slow way home to Springfield, Illinois. Black people grieved with a special poignance, for to them Lincoln was the Great Emancipator.

The Triumphant Ideology: Republicanism

The American people ended the Civil War with a profound sense that they had confirmed, as Abraham Lincoln had believed they had to, the ideology of republicanism. (It is important to keep in mind a crucial distinction: that between the Republican party, founded in 1854, and republicanism as the national ideology, born almost a hundred years before in the era of the American Revolution. Both Republicans and Democrats described themselves as, and were, "republicans," as distinct from "monarchists," or believers in monarchical institutions.)

Republicanism, the national creed, the justification for the United States of America since its founding in the 1780s, had been a precarious faith until the victory of the North in the Civil War. The world at large was still a world of monarchies and—with exceptions in western Europe—feudalism, and ever since the Revolution it had scoffed at the Americans and their republican experiment. The "people," it had been said over and over again, could not govern themselves. Put them in any sort of great crisis and they will prove too weak, selfish, shortsighted, ignorant, and self-indulgent to meet its challenges. All peoples needed established monarchies, titled aristocracies, and the wise rule of the educated and the wealthy to give them law and order, stability, true morality, and strong government.

In an agony of suffering and death, however, the great republic in North America had saved itself. It had demonstrated that a country could be founded in a democratic system of mass voting and mass political parties and still muster the iron will needed to subdue a massive challenge to the very principle of rule by the majority; of democratic law, order, and constitutional government. The Civil War was seen as a cleansing of the nation's many sins of self-indulgence, as well as a divine punishment for the crime of having allowed slavery to exist. After April 14, 1865, Lincoln himself became the martyr, the Christ-like figure whose death sealed the great purge.

Millions of Americans ended the Civil War, therefore, in a special state of mind. Now, it was said, they were ready to enter a fresh new era of glorious national achievement. The Civil War, then, had been a second American Revolution; it had been the confirming of American nationhood and the republican ideal. The nation that "We the people" had ordained in the Constitution was strong enough to survive. The republican idea would not simply endure; it was triumphant.

Nationalism Supreme

During the war the nationalist republicanism of the Republican party and of Yankee America had won out. (See the Overview of Chapter 26 for an explanation of the four modes of republicanism: the Democrats' libertarian and egalitarian republicanism; the Republicans' moralistic and nationalistic republicanism.) The Republican party had finally secured enactment in Washington of what amounted to the program called for so long before by Alexander Hamilton and by Henry Clay in his "American System": a strong protective tariff to encourage the growth of American industry; lavish federal aid for internal improvements that would speed transport and tie the economy together (railroads, and river and harbor improvements); a national system of currency and banking, controlled by private interests; a network of nationally endowed (via federal land grants) state universities to produce the educated elite to direct the new economy; and a homestead law to encourage rapid development of resources by giving the nationally owned public lands free to bona fide farmers. Thus, federal power was vastly expanded, and constitutional and economic nationalism firmly established.

The Meaning of Freedom

What did the ending of slavery mean to the former slaves? Some were alarmed, but most felt great joy. Now, one freedman is quoted in Leon Litwack's *Been in the Storm So Long* (1979) to have said, "I won't wake up some mornin' ter fin' dat my mammy or some ob de rest of my family am done sold." Separated families searched eagerly for each other. And the whipping was over! "Everybody went wild. . . . We was free. Just like that, we was free." There was a great burst of singing: "purty soon ev'ybody fo' miles around was singin' freedom songs." Some ran into the woods by themselves, saying over and over, "I'se free, I'se free!" A Virginia black man of advanced years went to the barn, leaped wildly from straw stack to straw stack, and "screamed and screamed!"

The war had been a strange experience for the slaves, watching the white men go off to the fighting and then feigning sorrow (or, in many cases, expressing it sincerely) when they were brought back dead or mutilated. Millions of blacks in the South remained slaves right up to the end of the fighting; in many parts of the South owners would not free their bonds-

men until officially notified by Union troops that they had to. However, in reality by midway in the Civil War slavery in the seceded states had already begun widely to disintegrate. Thousands were taken away by the Confederate government itself to labor for the military. Then as the Union forces speared deeper and deeper into the Confederacy, a kind of chaos broke out on the plantations that were in the vicinity of the advancing Northern armies. Many slaves refused to be slaves any more when Union forces drew near; they now demanded wages for their labor. Multitudes simply fled, heading behind the Union lines. "They flock to me, old and young," General William T. Sherman wrote during his army's March to the Sea through Georgia; "they pray and shout and mix up my name with Moses . . . as well as 'Abram Linkom', the Great Messiah of 'Dis jubilee'." (In the Border States, where as we have seen Lincoln's Emancipation Proclamation could not apply, tens of thousands of slaves won freedom by enlisting in the Union army; in Kentucky, 60 percent of all eligible black men took this route out of slavery.)

Tremendously gratifying to the freedmen was the knowledge that whatever they earned thereafter would be theirs to keep. A former Arkansas slave earned his first dollar working on the railroad, and "felt like the richest man in the world!" Most felt an immediate compulsion to leave their plantations, to get out from under white domination. Thousands drifted around the countryside; many tried to get by in the cities.

However, the former slaves soon learned that freedom had come to them in a tragically qualified condition. Southern whites of all sorts, whether Whig Unionists or unrepentant secessionists, agreed in being absolutely determined to do everything in their power, legal and illegal, to maintain *white superiority*. If the blacks were no longer slaves, they were going to be kept as much as possible under unquestioned white control; that is, in a kind of permanent second-class caste status. There would be *no voting by blacks, no equality in the courtroom, no publicly supported schooling*—the three things that black people and their leaders asked for most of all, over and over again.

Building a Class Relationship to Replace that of Slavery

And there would be *no economic freedom* for blacks, as it was known in the North. What the South now had before it was in fact an enormously complicated task. Some way or other, the former slaves had to be transformed into a free labor force; certainly, this was what they were determined to be. But where the black workers on plantations had before been slaves, and therefore totally under the orders of the masters in everything they did for no compensation whatever, beyond the food and clothing needed to remain alive and able to work, now they were to be employees who were due a wage for their labor. This they would now give only during specified hours, after which they would be presumably on their own.

That is, what now had to be evolved was a *class* relationship between people who formerly had been in the relationship of slaves and masters. What did this mean, in practice? In the Northern states, one of the central ideas that was proudly believed to lie at the very center of American life as the distinctive quality of Yankee civilization was the "free labor" ideology. America, it was said, was different from Europe precisely in its being built around the ideal of the *free laborer*: the classic American who as an independent citizen was not bound to a village to work for a great landowner or nobleman, or locked into a particular occupation. Rather, as a free and autonomous (independent, self-contained, self-governing) person he (rarely she) was free to move about from place to place in search of the best wage for his labor. Furthermore, he could take up whatever occupation or profession best suited his individual gifts of intelligence and character. "The career open to talents": This old Scottish phrasing of the social ideal was widely popular in America. As leaders like Abraham Lincoln said over and over, it was the highest boast of the people of the United States of America that it was in their country that the free labor ideal was most fully realizable and actually lived, by the common people. If someone were willing simply to work hard, it was said among Northerners, that person could get ahead in the race of life.

Southern whites, however, could never accept the concept of blacks as free laborers. Blacks were not going to be allowed to "get ahead" as they saw fit, to move about freely from place to place looking for the best job. They were certainly to be discouraged from moving to the cities and taking up city jobs. Most black people, everyone agreed (even the occupying Union army), must be kept on the land, as a subservient labor force entirely under the control of the landowners. How else, it was asked, could the cotton on which the South still desperately relied be planted, tended, and harvested? It was still a crop that required intensive hand labor, in the form of care given to each individual plant.

The Dream Destroyed: 40 Acres and a Mule

Thus, with Union army support local Southern white authorities tried hard to halt the black migration to the towns and cities. Blacks were also denied the opportunity of becoming landowners themselves, and by this means taking on that other classic American economic role: the *free and independent farmer*. For a time there was talk among northern Radical Republicans of taking land from the rebel plantation owners and breaking it up into 40-acre farms (with a provided mule) for the blacks; the freedmen were swept by excited rumors that this would take place, and black spokespersons themselves often said that nothing less was due to them. Had not their labor in fact created the plantations? After a brief flurry in this direction, however, the new president, Andrew Johnson, put a stop to it, ordering that all land be restored to the prewar owners.

Eventually, most black people found themselves forced to return to a farm somewhere and go to work again for the white-man boss, though this time for wages. However, working out a fair contract was extremely difficult. To the whites it was not just a class relationship, economic in nature, that they had with the blacks; it was a racial relationship, and this heated everything to fever pitch. The whites hated the demeaning (to them) task of having to bargain with former slaves, with people they regarded with contempt as quasi-animals. They put extremely stringent conditions in the work contracts, requiring that the blacks be again, in effect, slaves. They were often made to promise absolute obedience to the employer; they were whipped for being "uppity"; they had to agree to work from dawn to dusk; their "wages" were usually not to be paid until the crop was in, months in the future (few employers, in fact, had ready cash), and too often the black laborers would then be summarily fired, without any payment at all. As Southern local government got going again in the immediate postwar period, laws called Black Codes were passed giving total authority to employers and closing many occupations to blacks.

Violence against Blacks

Very soon the former slaves learned what it meant not to be worth anything in dollars to anyone, for now the white population, especially the part of it that was poor and with whom relations had always been bad, could maim, stab, torture, burn, and kill black people with no master to answer to. Violence in the prewar South had been primarily between whites; now it became white attacking black. In March 1865 Congress had created the Freedmen's Bureau to help freed slaves through the transition years. Many of its agents did all they could to protect black people from exploitive white employers, anti-black court systems, and violence, but no federal agency could ward off from 4 million black people the anger that 9 millions of white Southerners felt toward them for their "ingratitude" and "insolence" (anything manifesting an independent spirit was so described). The white South simply could not conceive of blacks in any other relation to whites than they had been in before—economically, socially, politically, or legally. Every change in white-black relations would be stiffly resisted. A phenomenon known formerly only in the North made its appearance in the South: the race riot. By 1867, whites and blacks had fought each other in bloody battles in the streets of Charleston, Norfolk, Richmond, Atlanta, Memphis, and New Orleans. There were hundreds of deaths and thousands of wounded.

"In some areas," writes historian Eric Foner, "violence against blacks reached staggering proportions in the immediate aftermath of the war. In Louisiana, reported a visitor . . . in 1865, 'they govern . . . by the pistol and the rifle.' " In places like Texas, where the Union army and the Freedmen's Bureau had little effective authority, "blacks, according to a Bureau official, 'are frequently beaten unmercifully, and shot down like wild beasts, without any provocation.' " After some obscure argument with local freedmen, whites near Pine Bluff, Arkansas, invaded a black settlement; on the next morning a visitor found "a sight that apald [sic] me 24 Negro men, woman and children were hanging to trees all round the Cabbins."

Violence was directed at anything that embodied the black desire for advancement, self-expression, and equal voice: black schools, black churches, black political gatherings. If whites were not treated by blacks with the same deference required of them in slave times, they were often bitterly charged with being insubordinate and shot. They were particularly in danger if they tried to behave like free and independent workers. Freed slaves, writes Foner, "were assaulted and murdered for attempting to leave plantations, disputing contract settlements, not laboring in the manner desired by their employers, attempting to buy or rent land, and resisting whippings."

As the courts were entirely controlled by whites, and sheriffs generally did not arrest whites for violence against blacks, no one was punished for these crimes. Nothing was more disheartening to blacks, in fact, than their total inability to receive anything like justice in the courts of the Southern states, even to bring suit or testify or sit on juries. "The idea of a *nigger* having the power of bringing a *white man* before a tribunal!" said one Georgian. "The Southern people ain't going to stand for that."

At the core of this ghastly scene lay a tragic paranoid delusion: Rumors frequently raced around among whites that the blacks in their locale were organizing for an insurrection, taking vengeance on their oppressors, which in fact they only rarely attempted. Once again, as in slave times, the most inhuman acts against blacks on the part of bullying, violence-prone whites, which in a less afflicted society would be widely condemned, were condoned by the white community at large on the (mistaken) ground that they were justified to protect that community against black assault.

The Black Family

The black family, surprisingly strong even in slavery, now clasped legality about itself. Thousands of "married" slave couples went to town to be legally wed; no master could ever sell man and wife and children apart again. Black women in striking numbers manifested their concept of freedom by doing as white women did: They withdrew from field work and devoted themselves to home, children, and kitchen. To the men, this was often a matter of pride, to be insisted upon. Henceforth, black women's role was like the Adam's-rib status of colonial white women: performing tasks that supplemented those of the black men in an agricultural household. They raised garden crops for the kitchen, prepared food, and earned income by doing washing for nearby white homes or serving as wet nurses.

Meanwhile, in the fields the black laborers, by common account, refused to work at the pace demanded in slavery times. A great slowdown occurred, much complained of by white employers. Per capita, the black work effort was down one-third by 1870, according to estimates.

The Dilemma of Reconstruction

What did the North intend to do about all this? At first, nothing at all. The Northern states greeted the end of the war with great relief and thanksgiving. In public celebrations of the event Northern leaders widely insisted that, as Abraham Lincoln had said, the task now was to bind up the nation's wounds, resume normal North-South relations, and be merciful toward the courageous and defeated enemy. As to the freedmen, even the famous black leader Frederick Douglass (the Martin Luther King, Jr., of his era), himself an escaped former slave who for many years before the war had labored for the cause of abolition, said, "Do nothing. . . . Give him a chance to stand on his own legs! Let him alone!" Governmental assistance, it was warned, would cause former slaves to remain dependent on the whites.

We must remember that the American Civil War ended in a peculiar way (as civil wars usually end)—that is, there was no peace treaty, in which terms of settlement were worked out. After all, the very existence of the Confederacy had been officially held to be illegitimate, and therefore its fall meant simply that it would dissolve and the South would be "back" in the Union. In the American fashion of local self-government, it was presumed that the states of the South would henceforth govern themselves as they had before, to include their race relations.

Clearly, however, someone had to do something to get those state governments up and running again, and this posed the inescapable question: By what process—and under what conditions? A hint had come late in December 1863, when Abraham Lincoln had issued a presidential proclamation offering pardon to any Southern white who would swear loyalty to the United States Constitution. A former Whig, he seems to have put his hopes for the future in former Whigs in the South, most of whom had joined the Democratic party when Whiggery dissolved. He knew that they had essentially Northern principles, drawn from the New England leadership of the Whig party, and he hoped to build new state governments in the South on such men. If a number of voters equal to one-tenth of those who cast ballots in the election of 1860 took such an oath, Lincoln stated,

then they could form a loyal state government and, after abolishing slavery, secure presidential recognition as being back in the Union. As to the blacks in the South, Lincoln clearly relied upon the former Whig leadership to meet their needs in a principled and just fashion, but without expecting or calling for the vote and the right to hold political office to be given to blacks.

In April 1865 when Lincoln was assassinated, Vice President Andrew Johnson assumed office. All eyes turned to see what manner of man was the new chief executive. Few liked him personally, for he was rigid and quarrelsome, but many respected his courage, personal strength, and vigorous administrative talents. From his early twenties he had won a long succession of political victories, serving in both houses of the Tennessee legislature, and as governor, congressman, and United States senator. A Jacksonian Democrat, he had blamed the Southern aristocracy for bringing on the Civil War. For this reason, Southern blacks reassured themselves that Johnson would be their friend. The only Southern senator to remain in Congress after his state seceded, he became the military governor of Tennesseee in 1862 and was chosen to be Lincoln's vice-president in 1864.

Conflicting Definitions of Reconstruction

President Johnson now had the enormous task of reknitting the Union, certainly one of the most gigantic public-policy tasks in American history. How did he define the situation? For one thing, he refused to use the word "Reconstruction." That term had been used for a number of years by a small group of Republican party activists in the North, often in the news, who were called "Radicals" (many had been abolitionists, or at least strong antislavery people, before the war). They had always believed that Southern civilization was so backward, so founded in ignorance, brutality, and sloth, so given to undemocratic, elitist, rule-from-above government, that it must be "reconstructed." Only in this way could the South be brought into the mainstream of true American republicanism.

Most important, Radicals believed, only in this way would the newly freed slave be guaranteed just treatment. "Radicalism when Lincoln died," writes Eric Foner, "was defined above all by an insistence upon black suffrage as the sine qua non of Reconstruction." High Republican leaders like Senator Charles

Sumner of Massachusetts would say that the Southern states had in fact left the Union when they seceded (the theory of "state suicide"), and that, therefore, Congress could treat them as conquered territories and force them, before readmission as states, to give the vote to black Southerners.

President Johnson entirely (and angrily) disagreed. He rejected the Radical theory of state suicide; he insisted again and again that his purpose was only to bring about "reunion"; and he would have no talk of "reconstructing" the South. Most of all, Johnson was determined to leave race relations in the South in the hands of its white people. "White men alone," he said in 1865, "must manage the South." He was, after all, a Southerner; he had been a slave owner, and he condemned out of hand all ideas of racial equality. Black people, he believed, were inferior beings who needed white supervision, and must remain in an inferior position. Johnson urged caution in giving black people the vote, for universal suffrage, he said, "would breed a war of races." He insisted over and over again that decisions on who should be able to vote must be left to the individual states. Southern whites soon came to regard the president, therefore, as on their side, for he stood between them and black suffrage.

Johnson Brings about "Reunion"

Johnson had a great opportunity before him. When he became president, Congress was not in session, and it would not be for another eight months, reconvening in December 1865. He could move ahead on his own, therefore, and bring about "reunion" before that body, and its irritating Radical Republican members, could even convene its next session. Always a decisive, energetic man, Johnson now pressed ahead briskly to get the Southern states in operation on his own authority as president. First, he accepted Reconstruction as complete in the four states that had already begun the process under Lincoln (Louisiana, Virginia, Tennessee, and Arkansas), and then he initiated proceedings in the other seven states. Appointing provisional state governors, he authorized them to register voters, who would then proceed to elect a full state government.

Who could vote? Any white male could vote who would take a loyalty oath, aside from some excluded groups. (At first Johnson made a great to-do about excluding the upper classes, who as a Jacksonian Democrat he had blamed for starting the war,

but then he quickly granted them pardons, upon individual application to him personally.) And when state legislatures were in operation, what steps did he require them to take before he would recognize them as fully restored states? They were few and simple. The president asked only that the revived states declare secession null and void from the beginning; repudiate any Confederate war debts (that is, Johnson did not want the new governments to pay off the debts of the rebel governments; anyone who had lent them money would simply have to lose it); and ratify the Thirteenth Amendment, which had terminated slavery in all of the United States, not just in the area covered by Lincoln's Emancipation Proclamation.

The Southern Reaction

At first the South was apathetic and submissive, expecting the North to make many demands for social change as its terms for readmission to the Union, and was apparently ready to make those changes. But since Johnson demanded so little and actually urged the Southern states, by many things that he said or implied, to pay little attention to Northern opinion, they soon began to show much of their old-time prideful independence, to mounting irritation in the North. They refused to ratify the Thirteenth Amendment (as in Mississippi), or quibbled about repudiating the Confederate debts (as in South Carolina), or only "repealed" their secession ordinances. Southerners elected to their constitutional conventions and new state governments the very men who had led them into secession and war. They even sent ex-Confederate generals, colonels, and congressmen (including the former vice-president of the Confederacy, Alexander Stephens) to Washington to be their elected representatives.

Worse yet, the reconstructed state governments enacted highly restrictive Black Codes. Marriages between Afro-Americans were finally recognized as legal, and blacks were allowed to own property and to sue and be sued. But black children could be bound out as apprentices; the terms of black labor contracts were specified, including hours and wages; and servants were prohibited from leaving their employers' premises without permission. If a black man tried to be other than an agricultural laborer, he had to get a license from a white judge. He could not enter any mechanical trade without going through a closely disciplined apprenticeship. Vagrancy laws made any

A view of the ruins of Charleston, South Carolina, following the bombardment of Union forces under General Sherman.

black person who wandered about, engaged in "disreputable occupations," or acted in a "disorderly manner" subject to arrest, after which he could be hired out to a white employer to serve his sentence. Blacks were not allowed to testify in court unless the case involved other blacks. Segregation in schools and public facilities was commonly decreed. Sometimes blacks could own only rural property, sometimes only urban. Most important, they could not bear arms or vote in elections.

The Earthquake Shift in the Northern Mind

These were historic events, for they produced an historic earthquake in the Northern mind and thus a new national context. We have seen that most people in the North, at war's end, were eager simply to welcome the South back into the Union. But not the *old* South that beat its black people, put Yankee-haters in office, and acted in a prideful and unrepentant manner. The Black Codes were enormously offensive to Northern values, especially to those of the Republicans. Clearly, the Black Codes' intent was effectively to make slaves again of the South's black people, and just as clearly, they violated every tenet of the "free labor" ideology in which Northerners took so much pride. Thus, almost alone, the Black Codes destroyed Johnsonian Reconstruction, for they not only angered Northerners but they also made

Northerners think again about Reconstruction. Their conclusion: Perhaps the Radical Republicans, to this point a distrusted minority, were right after all. Particularly bitter was the realization that the new Southern statutes were enforced by a police and court system in which blacks had utterly no voice at all.

And yet there was a strange paradox at work. The North in general was no more in favor of black equality than it had ever been. In recognition of blacks' fighting record during the war, some of the worst antiblack laws in the North were repealed after 1860, but only 7 percent of the 225,000 Afro-Americans in the Northern states were allowed the vote, it being granted to them in five New England states. Blacks were segregated in public facilities, schools, prisons, hospitals, churches, and even cemeteries. Many states still had laws against the immigration of free blacks, and everywhere there were obstacles to equal employment, equal housing, and equal rights. Both political parties insisted that they were for the white man.

On the other hand, many Northerners grieved for the condition of the Southern black population. They heard stories of killings, the peonage of the Black Codes, callousness, cruelty, and lynchings. By the end of 1865, when Congress was about to reassemble, there was a great deal of talk about doing something to promote black equality in some form. Fundamentally, this was what the term *Reconstruction* actually meant when it came into general use around 1862: some real and meaningful reconstruction of

Southern society and politics in order to give blacks a better life. To believe in this, as we have seen, was what it meant to be a Radical Republican.

If the goal of Radical Reconstruction was equality for blacks, what was meant by *equality*? How, in short, were the Republicans defining the issue? Almost unanimously Republicans believed that this meant at least *equality before the law*—in other words, civil rights. Black people should not be subject to legal restrictions that did not apply to whites. They should be able to testify in court, sit on juries, have the same punishments as whites for the same crimes, and not be told some things were crimes for them and not for whites. They should be able to be free laborers or free farmers. That is, they must be free to move about the countryside as they wished, take up any occupation, and give up one job for another. They must be able to own land wherever they wished, not be imprisoned for debts and hired out, and not be subject to apprenticeship laws that limited their freedom. Special curfew laws and vagrancy statutes were to be condemned.

Radical Republicans also insisted that there should be *equality in politics and government*: the right to vote, campaign on public issues, run for and hold office, and serve in government posts. A few of the more extreme Radical Republicans believed that black Americans should be granted *social equality*: in social relationships and in schooling, housing, and public accommodations. An even smaller number of Radicals joined with some of the black leaders in calling for *economic equality*. This meant providing skills and education, and, most revolutionary of all, confiscating rebel-owned plantations to give land to freed black people and make them truly independent, truly able to "get ahead."

The Freedmen's Bureau

The Freedmen's Bureau, an organization within the War Department, sent hundreds of local agents into every Southern locale to aid refugees and freedmen. It provided emergency food and housing and built more than forty hospitals. Searching out vacant lands (in some cases, in confiscated estates), it helped to settle some 30,000 people on the land. President Johnson severely cut back on this part of the bureau's work, however, by insisting that all land taken from the rebels be restored after they were pardoned. The bureau found jobs for thousands of blacks, then supervised hundreds of thousands of labor contracts to secure equitable treatment by white employers. It set up its own court system, under military law, to mediate disputes between employers and freedmen and preside over cases in criminal and civil law where one or both parties were black.

Its most lasting achievement was the building of thousands of schools—4,300 by the bureau's termination in 1872—to which hundreds of thousands of freedmen and their families flocked eagerly, usually to have instruction by a "teacher lady" from the Northern states. Southern whites hated the Freedmen's Bureau "more for what it stood for," as the historian George Bentley has written, "than for what it had done. . . . To most of them it was virtually a foreign government forced upon them and supported by an army of occupation. They resented its very existence, regardless of what it might do, for it had power over them and it was beyond their control."

The Crisis Begins

Congress was deeply troubled by the new context when it assembled in December 1865. Every Confederate state save Texas had completed Johnson's Reconstruction procedure, and a large group of elected representatives awaited admission to Congress. To Northern congressmen, the fact that many of these representatives had been Confederate leaders seemed bold and mocking. Indeed, "an uneasy conviction had spread throughout most of the North," Eric McKitrick has written, "that somehow the South had never really surrendered after all. . . . These feelings were neither focused nor organized; but they were pervasive, they seemed to ooze from everywhere and they invaded the repose of weary men who would have given much to be rid of them." It stuck in Northern throats to think of readmitting Southern representatives as though nothing had happened, particularly when alarming news about the oppression of black people was coming out of the South.

There was another consideration. For many years Republicans had labored fruitlessly (as Whigs) to shape a new kind of American nation. The Civil War had given them their opportunity, and they had swiftly passed the measures needed to open the new era. The Republicans were launched upon the building of a nation with a vigorously growing industrial economy fertilized and energized by the federal government working in close collaboration with the nation's leading entrepreneurs. With the emergence of efficiency and organization throughout the business world during the war and the creation of a strong federal government, the United States seemed about to become a strong and unified *nation* in place of the loose aggregation of separate states that had existed before.

It was too much to ask of human nature that the Republican majority should so quickly readmit the Southerners. They would bring in such a massive infusion of Democratic votes that, together with the Northern Democrats in Congress, they would form a majority. They might be able to enact a federal Black Code, or force the federal government to pay off the Confederate debt. They would certainly dismantle the economic system the Republicans had built up—the tariffs, bounties, banks, and other aids to business. Whatever happened, Republicans were determined not to go back to the old states' rights, decentralized, Southern-oriented regime that had dominated the nation since Jackson's day.

A joint committee on Reconstruction was formed with members from both houses of Congress, Thaddeus Stevens emerging as its central figure. Southern representatives were refused admission to Congress until that body decided that their states were actually back in the Union. Then a long investigation of Johnson's Reconstruction program was launched by the joint committee. In February 1866 the Republicans enacted a bill extending indefinitely the life of the Freedmen's Bureau (it was due to expire in June 1868). The bill provided that anyone "who should, by reason of state or local law, or regulation, custom, or prejudice, cause any other person to be deprived of any civil right was to be liable to punishment by one year's imprisonment or one thousand dollars' fine or both."

Johnson Strikes Back

President Johnson sent a ringing veto of the Freedmen's Bureau bill back to Congress in a step that polarized the politics of the whole postwar period. He condemned the Freedmen's Bureau as a monstrous intrusion on states' rights, condemned the use of military courts in peacetime as a violation of Southern civil rights, and scoffed at the notion that freedmen needed help. Three days later he publicly attacked Thaddeus Stevens, the leading Radical Republican in the House, and Charles Sumner in the Senate, as wild revolutionaries who were trying to take over the national government and inciting others to assassinate him.

Shortly thereafter a moderate Republican senator from Illinois, Lyman Trumball, secured passage of a civil rights bill to which, he thought, he had secured Johnson's approval. It established for the first time the status of "citizen of the United States" (formerly citizenship had been within a given state) and provided that the federal government could intervene within a state to ensure that citizens "of every race and color," save Indians not taxed, were given the same legal rights as white people.

Once again Johnson struck back with a veto. In his message he scorned a measure that would denominate as "United States citizens" the Chinese on the West Coast, the Indians who were taxed, and "the people called gypsies, as well as the entire race designated as blacks, people of color, Negroes, mulattoes, and persons of African blood."

Johnson's vetoes so outraged the moderates that they were driven over to join forces with the Radicals. His first veto had been upheld; his second one was overridden. From that point on, a strong and determined moderate and Radical Republican group in Congress, led by Sumner and Stevens, pushed vigorously ahead to take over Reconstruction, sweep away everything Johnson had done, and, eventually, come

Thaddeus Stevens (1792–1868), an adamant abolitionist, was dissatisfied with the Reconstruction policies of President Andrew Johnson and eventually led the impeachment forces against him.

within a single vote of impeaching the president himself.

The Fourteenth Amendment

The joint committee on Reconstruction began drafting a constitutional amendment that would place the principle of *equality before the law* beyond any future tampering—or so they believed. The measure drawn up did not by any means meet Thaddeus Stevens's demands. He urged the adoption of a simple but powerful statement: that all laws, state and national, should apply equally to all persons. "This was the true Radical argument," writes W. R. Brock. "It recognized that private prejudice could not be legislated out of existence, but maintained that discrimination could be prohibited in every activity touched by the law." There would always be discrimination in homes or private relations, "but they would have outlawed discrimination at the polls, in public places, on public transport, and in education."

The Republican majority, however, would not go this far with the Radicals. It was insisted that certain things were "privileges," not rights. The amendment should not apply, moderates said, to voting, or segregation in schools and public facilities. Its only reference to voting was to provide that a state's representation would be reduced in proportion to the number of its citizens denied the vote (this has never been applied). The amendment worked a powerful change, however, by making everyone born or naturalized in the American nation a citizen of the United States and forbidding all efforts by states to interfere with each citizen's fundamental civil rights. By conscious design, the amendment was broadened to make equal civil rights national in scope, protecting the rights of "any person" and not just those of blacks. (In the mid-1900s, its sweeping and powerful phrases would be enormously important weapons in social reform and in giving legitimacy to the aspirations of minority groups.)

Amendment XIV, The Constitution of the United States (ratified July 28, 1868). Section I. All persons born or naturalized in the United States, and subject to the jurisdiction thereof, are citizens of the United States and of the State wherein they reside. No State shall make or enforce any law which shall abridge the privileges or immunities of citizens of the United States; nor shall any State deprive any person of life, liberty, or property, without due process of law; nor deny to any person within its jurisdiction the equal protection of the laws. . . . Section 5. The Congress shall have power to enforce, by appropriate legislation, the provisions of this article.

The proposed amendment was adopted by both houses of Congress in June 1866 and sent on to the states. Johnson protested and recommended against ratification. The Southern states defeated this first attempt at ratification, for all the former states of the Confederacy, save Tennessee (where ratification was highly equivocal), rejected it, plus Kentucky and Delaware. This drove even deeper into the Northern mind the belief that the Southern states, as reconstructed by President Johnson, were arrogant and unregenerate. In the congressional elections held in the autumn of 1866, the South's refusal to accept equality before the law became the major issue.

Just as grave in the opinion of Northerners were race riots in Memphis and New Orleans in May and June 1866, in which policemen and whites murdered scores of blacks, shooting and knifing indiscriminately to "kill every damn nigger" they could find. No prosecutions were launched, and Johnson blamed it all on Northern Radicals. Then he made an intemperate "swing around the circle" in August and September, speaking in many Northern cities. This in itself was shockingly indiscreet. In the nineteenth century, presidents simply did not do this. They did not even campaign when they were presidential candidates. To do so would be demeaning—and Johnson was demeaned. Furthermore, he lost his temper, bandied words with hostile crowds, and destroyed whatever credibility he had left. The Republicans won a landslide victory, gaining a two-thirds majority in both houses of Congress.

PART TWO:
RECONSTRUCTION: SECOND PHASE

Congressional Reconstruction

Now the triumphant Radical Republicans could try to begin, two years after the end of the Civil War, a genuine *reconstruction* of Southern life, for with a two-thirds majority (which on race-relations questions held firm) they could override Johnson's objections. They undertook this task as leaders of a victorious Yankee culture at its most self-confident. "It is intended," said Thaddeus Stevens of Pennsylvania, New England-born and educated, "to revolutionize . . . Southern institutions, habits, and manners."

The Radical Republican journal *The Nation* defined the issue with clarity and force:

> We boast of having gone beyond others in social and political science, but we have at last come to a place where the claim is to be most solemnly tested. . . . Over and over again, in every form but one, have we set forth the principle of human equality before the law. We have boasted of our land as the free home of all races. We have insulted other nations with the vehemence of our declamation. And now we are brought face to face with a question that will test it all. . . . Is the negro a man? Say what we will, this is the real issue in the controversy respecting him.

As they assembled in Congress, three things, Republicans believed, must be achieved: The existing state governments in the South must be in effect rendered null and void; those who had been active rebels should not be allowed to play an active role in governing the South; and "the negroes should vote." Under the Constitution, where would Congress find the power to do these things? First, the "state suicide" theory was accepted: that the states had in fact seceded and were no more than conquered provinces with which Congress could deal as it saw fit. And then right there in Article IV, Section 4 of the Constitution, ignored until now, were powerful words: "The United States shall guarantee to every State in this Union a Republican Form of Government, and shall protect each of them against . . . domestic violence." When Congress quickly passed the First Reconstruction Act, enacted over Johnson's veto on March 2, 1867, it therefore stated that "no legal State governments or adequate protection for life or property now exist in the rebel States . . . and it is necessary that peace and good order should be enforced in said States until loyal and republican State governments can be legally established."

Under the Reconstruction Act, the ten states unreconstructed (Tennessee, having ratified the Fourteenth Amendment, was readmitted in July 1866) were grouped into five military districts, each under a federal military commander whose powers were superior to those of the state governments. The states were to call elections for the writing of new state constitutions, all male citizens "of whatever race, color, or previous condition" being enfranchised to vote except for those whites who had been federal officials and later supported the rebellion. The new constitutions were to guarantee black suffrage. After ratification, and after the new state governments had ratified the Fourteenth Amendment and that amendment had become part of the federal Constitution (as it did in July 1868), the states were entitled to be represented in Congress, though readmission would still require congressional enactment in each case.

The Question of Motive

Was Radical Reconstruction designed to help black people or to help the Republican party? For many years historians took the latter view. Hungry for the graft and corruption that officeholding allowed, and eager to maintain their protective tariffs and land bounties—so this version ran—greedy and vindictive Republicans incited Southern blacks to an "unnatural" hatred of whites, gave them the vote, then enrolled them in the Republican party to keep themselves in power. (This assessment was exactly that of Democrats when these events were going on.) In recent years historians have accepted that many Republicans sincerely wanted to help black people; that others simply wanted to make the blacks happy where they were, so they would not flood the Northern states; and that the desire to keep their own party in power, when that was the dominating motive, was not so discreditable as it has been depicted.

The Republicans, after all, had a different vision of what America should be. They had been frustrated by what they regarded as a "Southern conspiracy" in the antebellum years, and now they aimed at protecting the possibility that their Yankee, nationalist republican goal for the nation might be realized. It is clear, however, that Republican concern to help black people was limited. Thaddeus Stevens tried to get his colleagues to establish an economic foundation for black equality by allowing the confiscation of rebel estates and the redistribution of land. He was turned down. And there were no efforts to ensure social equality for black people. The dominant Republican view was that, given the vote and equality before the law, black persons were then to rise by their own initiative.

From our perspective, then, Radical Reconstruction could be thought of as not very radical at all. However, in the context of the time, it was an astonishing effort. "Alone among the nations that abolished slavery in the nineteenth century," Eric Foner remarks, "the United States, within a few years of emancipation, clothed its former slaves with citizenship rights equal to those of whites." Indeed, to deny the appellation "radical" to a reform that in reality it would take more than a century for the country to get close to actually realizing—to the extent that the United States has yet realized equal citizenship for all of its people—seems an over-particular use of the term. The enfranchisement of the Southern black people, said North Carolina's governor,

President Andrew Johnson, although personally unpopular, was nonetheless admired for his courage and vigorous administrative talents.

was simply a revolution, for as *The Nation* magazine observed, "It touches every portion of the social fabric, from foundation to apex."

Filled with its sense of epochal power, Congress also turned to put the implementing of this legislation—and therefore the presidency itself—under its direct control. It enacted legislation requiring the president to give orders to the army (which would put the laws into effect) only through its general-in-chief, who was Ulysses S. Grant. Then, fearing that Johnson might remove the secretary of war, Edwin Stanton (who, like Grant, was sympathetic to Radical goals), Congress passed the Tenure of Office Act, which took away the president's authority to remove cabinet members without the Senate's consent.

Another enactment limited the Supreme Court's authority so as to keep it from ruling on the legality of any Reconstruction legislation. Subsequent Reconstruction acts elaborated the powers of the military commanders so that any state official who should "hinder, delay, prevent or obstruct the due and proper administration" of the Reconstruction acts could be removed.

In August 1867 President Johnson tried to remove Secretary of War Stanton, primarily for failure to accept the president's directions but also in order to test the constitutionality of the Tenure of Office Act. In January 1868 the Senate refused to accept Stanton's suspension or to recognize another man whom Johnson had appointed in his place. In late February the House impeached the president for violating the Tenure of Office Act and a host of other vaguely worded "high crimes and misdemeanors." For more than two months, until the middle of May, a dramatic trial proceeded before the Senate. (The president was represented by legal counsel and spared the indignity of being present.) When the votes were taken, conviction fell one vote shy of the necessary two-thirds majority because seven Republicans—at great cost to their political careers—concluded that no case had been made. A public outcry arose against them as traitors to the nation.

Black Reconstruction

Meanwhile, "black Reconstruction" was under way in the South. The first thing to be said of the freed slaves was that the fears that had apparently driven South Carolina and the rest of the South into secession in 1860/61 were without foundation. The freedmen did *not* immediately rise in bloody violence against their former masters, dealing out the massacre and rapine that had hysterically been warned against for generations. The horrors of Santo Domingo and Haiti did not reenact themselves. Few more striking instances in history exist of a mass delusion leading millions of people into a needless, disastrous war. Race war did not break out when the freedmen were given the vote. Indeed, violent assaults against the white community and its institutions were not ever to be mounted by black Americans in the South, either in the Reconstruction years or in later generations. The massacring was instead to be in the other direction. When black Americans did in fact join in destructive outbreaks, it was to be almost a century later, and in Northern cities.

Some 700,000 black men were enfranchised in the Southern states as a result of the Radical Reconstruction program. In every state except Virginia, Republicans took control. In June 1868 six states were readmitted to the Union: Arkansas, North and South Carolina, Florida, Alabama, and Louisiana. The rest were readmitted in early 1870. Republican regimes did not last long: one year in Georgia, two in North Carolina, four in Texas, six in Alabama, Arkansas, and Mississippi, and nine in Florida, Louisiana, and South Carolina. When Republicans lost out, the Southern "Redeemers," who aimed at reestablishing white control, took over.

The years of Radical Reconstruction have traditionally been described as a carnival of corruption that left the South crippled by enormous debts. Hordes of ignorant and greedy blacks were pictured as taking over the legislatures, rolling drunkenly in the aisles and shouting approval for huge appropriations that went into the pockets of their carpetbagger leaders (Northerners come South to fish in troubled waters) or those of the scalawags (Southern whites who joined the plunder).

This picture is now largely discredited. There was corruption, some of it spectacular, but corruption was a national phenomenon in these years. Nothing in the South compared, for example, with the luxuriant graft then going on in New York City under "Boss" William M. Tweed. In only one state, South Carolina, was there a black majority in the legislature, and there only in the lower house. No blacks were elected governor; few were judges; and only seventeen served in Congress. Those who held official positions served admirably in most cases. Blacks were not vindictive, and often supported appeals that disenfranchised whites be given the vote and allowed to hold office. There were no attempts to overturn social relationships. Indeed, Reconstruction governments did little for the black person specifically. Heavy expenditures were made because the South had to be rebuilt after the war and because emancipation doubled the civil population. Millions of blacks formerly given nothing by state governments now were citizens needing services in schools, courts, and welfare agencies.

Reconstruction Reforms

The Reconstruction governments enacted major reforms. They gave the South its first system of public schools. Manhood suffrage free of property qualifications was enacted, and imprisonment for debts was terminated. Homestead laws guaranteed poor men a minimum amount of property safe from attachment for debts. Popular election of county officials replaced the former oligarchical system of appointment. Salaries were provided to public officials so that someone other than a rich planter could serve. The number of crimes punishable by death was reduced. Taxes were rearranged so as to bear on plantation owners rather than just on landless individuals.

The thousands of Northerners who came south after the Civil War, the "carpetbaggers," were not the depraved and dissolute adventurers they have been described to be. Many brought needed capital and entrepreneurial skills; others were serious reformers who sought to democratize the South and teach the poor—white and black. The "scalawags" (Southern whites who joined the Republican party, who briefly amounted to perhaps a quarter of the white population) were often former Whigs, or new men from poor counties, with little reputation in government. They were angry at the "bombastic, high falutin, aristocratic fools" who had dragged the South into a disastrous war, and who had been "driving negroes and poor helpless white people until they think they can control the world of mankind." They liked Republican policies of economic development, for they promised jobs where at present there was poverty, and called for social reforms.

Indeed, the "other South" still survived strong and healthy. The Whig party had died in the South in the 1850s, when the entire region swung to the Democratic party, but former Whigs bulked large in the Confederate congresses. It must be understood that within what had been the borders of the Confederacy, 49 percent of those casting ballots in the 1860

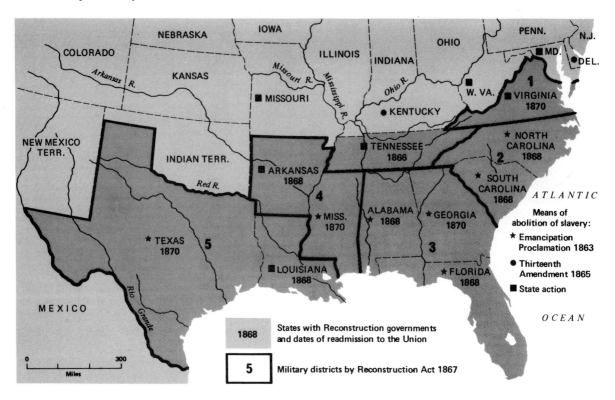

Reconstruction of the South, 1865–1877

presidential election had voted either for Bell or Douglas, thus indicating that they did not favor secession. Thousands of white Southerners served in the Union army during the war, forming almost ninety regiments. Appalachia was a hotbed of Unionism. And the white South's return so easily to the Union after the war can be understood only by taking into account that its fundamental loyalty to that Union was always strong, being overborne only in hysterical circumstances by fear of what never occurred—a black uprising.

Economic Reconstruction in the South

Radical Republicans wanted not only to reconstruct the blacks but also to reconstruct Southern white society. Yankees had said for many years that if slavery were only eliminated, then Southern whites would stop being lazy, thriftless people who shunned physical labor, and would start taking up the hard-working ways of Yankees. Now, Radical Republicans urged

Southern whites to take the road to industrialization and urbanization—and were delighted with the response. The business community of the South, composed largely of ex-Whigs who had always been irritated at the languid, unprogressive rule of the plantation owners, "burst into effusions of assent and hosannas of delivery." Thousands in the South had always admired Northern ways and had tried vainly to take their section in Yankee directions.

Virginia Conservatives—who took that name in politics to distinguish themselves from both the Democrats and the Republicans—worked to regenerate Virginia's economy along Northern capitalist lines. The task they took on was admittedly great. The war had left widespread devastation. To break out of the depressed conditions they were in, state governments eagerly pushed the building of railroads in the South. Project was piled on project with feverish haste, and almost every state invested huge sums in private companies. The railroad system was rebuilt, and a good deal of mileage added. New industries were encouraged by state grants of funds and tax privileges. Immigration was encouraged, and this produced a heavy influx of white settlement and Northern capital. Textile mills appeared in the Carolinas and in Georgia. The Richmond ironworks were rebuilt, and flourished more than ever. Northern Alabama's iron and coal resources were opened, and the city of Birmingham, soon to be the Pittsburgh of the South, made its appearance. A movement of population to the cities occurred, since textile mills and other urban industries offered jobs (to whites only).

Almost nine of ten black Southerners lived in the countryside. Here, sharecropping became the basis of the new postslavery farm economy. Produced primarily by the black man's determination to gain at least a semblance of independence, and not to work in gangs, as in slave times, sharecropping allowed black farmers to till rented farms without white supervision. The former plantations, where everyone, black and white, lived in a tightly clustered grouping of cabins and the "Big House," now were divided into many small units to which the former slaves scattered, there to live on their own in cabins of their construction.

White landlords provided not only the land, but seed, fertilizer, tools, food, and advice—necessities since very few ex-slaves had even minimal skills, and all lacked managerial experience and capital. In return, sharecropping farmers delivered half to two-thirds of their crop to the landowner. A halfway house in which most black farmers would remain suspended, sharecropping at least produced more income for them than they had gotten under slavery, and it removed the indignity of gang labor and immediate white management. Many were able to accumulate savings: By 1910, almost one-third of the land tilled by black farmers was owned by them.

For many black sharecroppers, something resembling peonage developed. (*Peons*, such as those who existed in Mexico in the nineteenth century, are held on their land in compulsory servitude to a master for the working out of a debt.) To buy supplies in local white-owned stores, blacks had to contract annual loans, which, if not paid off by the crop receipts, forced them to stay where they were to keep making payments. However, black farmers still retained considerable mobility. Furthermore, the productivity of the sharecropping system was considerable. The Southern cotton crop had dropped from 5.3 million bales annually before the war to 2.0 million in 1865, but it was back to 3.0 million bales by 1870 and 5.7 million bales by 1880. Other crops surged also, tobacco production rising rapidly, rice and sugar more slowly.

Unfortunately, the world demand for cotton began falling off. The slow market for cotton, together with falling prices, caused Southern per capita income to drop from 72 percent of the national average in 1860 to only 51 percent in 1880, where it remained until the twentieth century. Widespread soil exhaustion made Southern farm problems even worse. The postwar South, shattered by the war and wedded to a one-crop system suffering from sluggish demand, remained poor while the North boomed.

The Question of Segregation

The cities of the South had been thought of as white man's country before the war, though the black population in Southern cities ranged from 20 percent in Atlanta to slightly over 50 percent in Montgomery, Alabama. After 1865, city whites complained angrily that they were being inundated by footloose blacks fleeing the plantations, and in fact by 1870 almost all the South's leading cities had populations that were half white and half black.

What was to be done with these people? whites asked. Must they be schooled when young, taken care of in hospitals when ill, cared for in old-folks' homes when elderly, just like the whites? Would they live scattered about, as had the prewar black population that served as household help to white people? What kind of jobs would they be allowed to hold? Surely, it was said, no jobs currently assigned to white workers? How about crime and punishment, the police, the courts? One response is familiar: With regard to criminal justice, jobs, housing, and such public facilities as streetcars, hotels, and restaurants, the principle quickly laid down was *segregation*. But concerning public services, such as hospitals, schools, almshouses, asylums, and institutions for the physically handicapped, the response is not so familiar: It was *exclusion*. The cities were poor, it was hard for them to perform services even for their white citizens, and they simply refused to take on this great load—previously borne by masters—suddenly descending upon them with the ending of slavery.

The Freedmen's Bureau moved in to fill the gap at first, providing needed services for black people by building schools and erecting hospitals. Meanwhile, urban whites kept reiterating that black people belonged in the countryside, that town life was unhealthy for them. Clinics set up by Southern cities for indigent people limited their services to whites. After Radical Reconstruction began, Republican city administrations started providing facilities for black people and opening existing institutions to them for the first time—but on a segregated basis. This, in short, was to be the answer: It seemed to officials of the Freedmen's Bureau and to Radical Republicans that the great goal they should struggle for had to be to end the system of total exclusion.

The simple provision of services was regarded as a victory. That they were on a segregated basis seemed, until many more years were to pass, a relatively small price to pay. At least there was equal access, which, Republicans presumed, would involve equal, if separate, facilities. Equal but segregated access was at best a partial victory, for many facilities remained open only to whites, especially after the ending of Radical Reconstruction.

The very idea that there should be publicly supported schools was one of the great achievements won by Radical Republicans in the South. Both whites and blacks benefited from this campaign. However, from the beginning schooling was provided on a strictly segregated basis. City blacks got much better schooling than Southern blacks who lived on farms, which had much to do with stimulating black people to move to the city. The best blacks could hope for in the Reconstruction years after educational reform was put in place was for separate but equal treatment—a hope that in future years, after Southern white Redeemers took control of local government, was to be seriously frustrated. Separate eventually meant unequal. Richmond, Virginia, in 1890 spent roughly ten dollars apiece for the schooling of both black and white children, but in Montgomery the figures were approximately $5.50 and $3.50. Black schools were old and crowded; white schools were new and, for the times, reasonably well equipped. When high schools were built, they were usually only for white children, and salaries for black and white teachers were wide apart.

Grant's Administration

Meanwhile, national politics continued to make headlines and absorb the country's voters. The readmission of the first group of reconstructed Southern states in June 1868 was in time for them to vote in the presidential election of that year. Horatio Seymour, Democratic governor of New York during the Civil War and a strong opponent of racial equality, ran on the Democratic ticket. The Republicans chose the military hero Ulysses S. Grant, whose victory was materially aided by Republican votes in the electoral college won in the Republican-controlled Southern states.

Thus began an eight-year administration that has little to commend it to history save distasteful scandals. Grant was unqualified for the presidency, and he chose many subordinates who subsequently made free use of their opportunities. He allowed two noted stock market manipulators, Jay Gould and James Fisk, to be intimate with him until their activities in rigging the stock market became too blatant. Companies received monopoly contracts from the New York Customs House and made hundreds of thousands of dollars in graft. During Grant's administration the massive speculations of the Crédit Mobilier, the company formed to construct the Union Pacific Railroad, came to light. Congressmen were caught profiting from the scheme, and the scandal reached upward to involve Vice-President Schuyler Colfax. Secretary of the Treasury William Richardson was found aiding an arrangement whereby hundreds of railroads were forced to pay delinquent taxes, half of which, to the amount of hundreds of thousands of dollars, went to a henchman—and then, perhaps, to Richardson himself.

These activities were mirrored at every level of American government. In city councils, in boards of supervisors, in state legislatures—wherever profitable deals could be made, grafters were there, and compliant legislators assisted them. Much of the history of the period, wherever it is touched, consists of little but damaged reputations. Ice-house franchises, street-construction contracts, railroad land grants, bank subsidies, tax rebates, purchased jurors, judges, and sheriffs—the list is endless.

All this produced a new and consuming national concern that went far to dwarf everything else in the minds of many voters. No obsession was more central to the Democrats than the problem of corruption in the economy and in government. They believed it to be simply inherent in the way that Republicans ruled. Handing out land grants, protective tariffs, bank charters, immunities from taxation, railroad contracts, and every other kind of profitable privilege inevitably produced corruption. It was the very means, they insisted, by which the Republicans rooted themselves in power—buying up supporters by creating vested interests.

Many Republicans shared these worries. After all, for generations republicanism had been criticized in Europe as certain to lead to widespread dishonesty and graft as "the people," unchecked, took over power. It was not long before Republicans of traditional Yankee views were disillusioned with the Grant regime. It seemed cheap, opportunist, low in tone, and greedy. Grant was not interested in civil service reform, as they had assumed, and the spoils system flourished. Well-educated "independent" Republicans, such as E. L. Godkin of *The Nation* and Charles Francis Adams, broke away from the "regulars" of the Republican party in 1872 and resolved to run their own candidate for the presidency in place of Grant, who was nominated for a second term. Calling themselves Liberal Republicans, they chose Horace Greeley, editor of the New York *Tribune*, to oppose Grant. The Democrats swung in with them, nominating Greeley as their presidential candidate as well.

The result was a disastrous campaign. An eager and aggressive candidate who condemned Grant's policies, Greeley also championed such unpopular causes as women's rights, labor unions, vegetarianism, and social reform movements such as Fourierism, a form of communalism. He was ridiculed as a crank, and Grant secured a massive 750,000-vote majority. Exhausted, brokenhearted, and grieved by the recent death of his wife, Greeley died three weeks after the election.

Foreign Affairs: Seward and Fish

Two gifted secretaries of state, William Seward and Hamilton Fish, directed the nation's foreign relations with notable success during the administrations of Andrew Johnson and Ulysses Grant, respectively. Seward dealt successfully with a bold adventure that Napoleon III of France undertook in Mexico while the United States was involved in the Civil War. The French emperor installed an Austrian nobleman, Maximilian, on the Mexican "throne" in 1864. But as soon as the Civil War ended, Seward placed troops on the Mexican border and informed Napoleon that the United States would never recognize Maximilian's regime. By patient diplomacy he got the French to withdraw all their troops in 1867. Maximilian, who foolishly refused to leave with them, was executed by the Mexicans.

Seward also responded eagerly to a Russian offer to sell Alaska. He agreed to purchase it for $7.2 million and, in the face of much amused comment about Seward's Ice Box, secured the Senate's ratification of the treaty in April 1867. Looking to the Far East, Seward sent a gifted diplomatist, Anson Burlin-

game, to China to open that country to American trade. Hoping to fend off European partitioning of China, the United States formally recognized China's territorial integrity and promised no interference in Chinese affairs. In return, by the Burlingame Treaty (1868) American citizens were accorded the right of travel and residence in China and the right of freely exercising their religion there. This opened the way for an extensive involvement of American missionaries and traders in Chinese life over the next several generations.

The most explosive issue in Seward's hands after the war was the negotiation of claims against Great Britain arising from the activities during the Civil War of a group of Confederate commerce raiders—the *Alabama* chief among them—that the British had allowed to be built in their shipyards and taken to sea. These raiders sank or captured many Union merchant ships, causing huge losses to Northern merchants. The issue was still unsettled when Grant entered office. Hamilton Fish transferred the negotiations from London to Washington.

A joint high commission composed equally of Britons and Americans began discussions of the *Alabama* and other outstanding issues in Washington in 1871. A long dispute over who owned the San Juan Islands between the northern coast of the state of Washington and Vancouver Island, the British or the U.S., was referred to the German emperor for settlement (he decided they belonged to the United States). The Americans secured extensive privileges to fish in Canadian waters, and Canadian seamen were allowed to fish as far south as Delaware Bay. The *Alabama* claims were referred to a tribunal of arbitration in Geneva, with the result that the United States received $15.5 million, all "indirect" claims being ignored. A counterclaim arising from attacks on Canada by Irish-Americans in the Fenian organization, who sought in this way to free Ireland from British rule, gave almost $2 million to the British. The crowning achievement of Grant's administration, the complete restoration of good relations with Great Britain, was thus successfully completed.

The Fifteenth Amendment

After Grant's first election in 1868, the Republicans took up once more the problem of the black man in the South. They moved carefully, for the Northern states were still hostile to black enfranchisement. This had been shown in the first local elections held after passage of the First Reconstruction Act in March 1867. In state after state, the Democrats won handily on antiblack suffrage platforms. The journal *Independent* cynically remarked that "it ought to bring a blush to every white cheek in the loyal North to reflect that the political equality of American citizens is likely to be sooner achieved in Mississippi than in Illinois—sooner on the plantation of Jefferson Davis than around the grave of Abraham Lincoln!" In Ohio a proposal to establish black suffrage went down by 40,000 votes in the autumn.

Southerners had good reason to scoff, therefore, at the stated goals of Radical Republicanism. What hypocrisy it was, they said, for Republicans to protest moral sincerity! Northerners clearly had no interest in the black man. All they wanted was to get his votes behind the Republican ticket to keep the party in power in Washington. The charge of hypocrisy was the stock reply of Southern whites to everything the Republicans attempted. An editor in Raleigh, North Carolina, ridiculed Republicans in 1867 when members of their party voted two to one in the Pennsylvania legislature against giving the vote to black men. "This is a direct confession, by Northern Radicals, that they refuse to grant in Pennsylvania the '*justice*' they would enforce on the South. . . . And this is Radical meanness and hypocrisy—this their love for the negro." Even the Republican platform of 1868 perpetuated the dual standard, insisting that "every consideration of public safety, of gratitude, and of suffrage in all the loyal [i.e., Northern] States properly belongs to the people of those States."

When congressional Republicans decided after Grant's election to aid black suffrage, they had to move with care. Moderates and conservatives, not Radicals, dominated the writing of the Fifteenth Amendment. Even Wendell Phillips, a dyed-in-the-wool reformer since his days as a leading abolitionist, urged his followers, "For the first time in our lives we beseech them to be a little more politicians and a little less reformers." Radicals wanted a positive national guarantee that the vote would be permanently granted to blacks; moderates wanted only a negative statement that would deny taking the vote away simply on the ground of race or previous condition of servitude. As Oliver P. Morton put the matter, the intent was not to nationalize suffrage, but to leave it in state hands subject only to this one federal limitation. He went on to add, "They may, perhaps, require property or educational tests." Even a clause that would prohibit denial of officeholding on the ground of race was rejected.

Passed by Congress in February 1869, the Fifteenth Amendment went to the states and was ratified in March 1870 (Virginia, Mississippi, and Georgia were required to ratify as conditions of readmission, and they did so in early 1870). *Then, and only then, did black Americans finally secure the vote in the Northern states.*

Did Women Now Have the Vote?

The great constitutional reforms of the Reconstruction era had been undertaken with black Americans in mind, but to that small group of Americans who were both female and women's rights activists, the Fourteenth and Fifteenth Amendments opened up quite another possibility: the vote for women. They were, after all, citizens of the United States, and the Fourteenth Amendment stated that "no State shall make or enforce any law which shall abridge the privileges or immunities of citizens of the United States." Did not laws restricting the vote to men do just that?

Susan B. Anthony now led the way. A strong-hearted feminist in her fifties who for many years had been attacking head-on the ideology of "woman's place," in 1869 she had joined with Elizabeth Cady Stanton to found the National Woman Suffrage Association. In 1872, on the ground of her Fourteenth Amendment rights, she tried to register and vote in Rochester, New York. Arrested and convicted of breaking the law, she refused thereafter to pay the $100 fine levied. In a later case, *Minor* v. *Happerset* (1875), the United States Supreme Court ruled unanimously that suffrage was not part and parcel of citizenship, and that the states were within their constitutional powers in limiting the vote to men. "If the law is wrong," the Court said, "it ought to be changed; but the power for that is not with us."

The Fifteenth Amendment, however, had introduced a striking new idea. For the first time in American history, the federal Constitution had been changed to put a restriction on what the states could do in withholding the vote from groups of citizens. Why not use that device, with its power over every election in every state, to outlaw suffrage restriction on the ground of sex? In 1878 Senator Aaron Sargent of California introduced into Congress a proposed constitutional amendment which stated: "The right of citizens of the United States to vote shall not be denied or abridged by the United States or by any State on account of sex." Forty-two years later that proposal, in that exact language, would become the Nineteenth Amendment, but for the present, it got nowhere.

Counter-Reconstruction

The Reconstruction Acts were hated by most white Southerners, and they worked angrily to throw them off. Georgia may be taken as typical. First, in 1867, federally appointed officials registered not only 102,411 whites, but 98,507 blacks as voters, which mightily offended tens of thousands of whites. "I think most of the gentlemen felt as I did," a Georgia planter wrote, "that the negroes voting at all was such a wicked farce that it only deserved our contempt." Then a Republican party was created in Georgia that organized a coalition of blacks and whites. The latter were Unionists who had opposed secession and war, former Whigs, common men angry at the planters, and people who liked Yankee ideas of building railroads and turning the state's economy in industrial directions.

Initially victorious over the Democrats, the Republicans in Georgia wrote a new state constitution that guaranteed citizenship, equal protection of the law, and the vote to blacks. It also, for the first time in Georgia, called for the building of public schools. They were to be free, and, most striking, open to all children, white or black. Then a Republican state governor and a Republican-dominated legislature were elected. After it ratified the Fourteenth Amendment, Georgia was readmitted to the Union.

Democrats gathered in state convention to condemn all of this as literally "a crime." White Republicans were denounced as traitors to the South. Any white man voting their ticket, it was said, "should be driven from the white race, as Lucifer was driven from Heaven into a social Hell." (Remember that there would be no secret ballot in America for many years, so that a man's vote could be observed.) As for the new constitution, it was a "nigger-New England" production.

The Republicans launched an ambitious program of reform. As historian Numan V. Bartley writes in *The Creation of Modern Georgia* (1983), they

> endeavored to create a more dynamic social system based on equality before the law, to elevate the labor force through public education, to encourage railroad and industrial development with public aid, and to centralize and expand the authority of the governor's office. They demonstrated a serious commitment to black rights and strove to protect the interests of small property holders.

In the presidential election of 1868 the Democrats, fully revived by now, launched a hot blast of antiblack oratory. Demanding *home rule* (the end of federally dominated Reconstruction) and white supremacy, they began actively harassing both white and black Republicans. By this time a white terrorist organization, the Ku Klux Klan, was in full operation. Created in 1866, it had multiplied rapidly throughout the South through local "dens," which began indiscriminately shooting, hanging, whipping, torturing, burning, and drowning blacks, carpetbaggers, and scalawags. (Federal efforts to put down such violence, through "force bills" and federal troops, had little effect.) During the 1868 presidential campaign in Georgia, the Freedman's Bureau reported 142 "outrages" against blacks: 31 murders, 48 attempted murders, and 63 beatings—probably only a fraction of the total. Even more common, and certainly effective, was direct economic intimidation of black voters by their white planter employers. Meanwhile, murders of Republican white men, and attacks from ambush, occurred. It took real courage to be an active Republican, white or black, in the state of Georgia.

The Democrats swept Georgia in the presidential election of 1868. In many counties, no Republican votes were reported at all. In consequence, Congress in 1869 reimposed military rule and once more took over direct control of Georgia's state government. However, local government and law enforcement remained entirely in antiblack, anti-Republican hands, and the reign of terror went on.

Most Georgia whites were simply adamant that black people were not to be accepted on a basis of equality. Though by no means all Democrats were terrorists, they simply did not regard the Republican party as a legitimate opposition. Republicans, to them, were nothing but "damn Southern traitors." Thus, violence was condoned as a justified form of guerrilla warfare. Accepting the situation reluctantly, in 1870 the federal government readmitted Georgia to the Union. In subsequent state elections the Democrats took full control, and the Reconstruction experiment in Georgia was over.

The North's Reaction

What was the North to do? The only appropriate response, if it genuinely wished to reestablish interracial government in such states, was to renew Radical

Reconstruction. Huge sums of money must be spent for troops, the South must be flooded with agents of a revived Freedmen's Bureau, and military courts, where juries were not required, would have to be used extensively. In effect, the North would have to reopen the whole case of the white versus the black South.

It was a solution Northerners could not bring themselves to undertake. Their will, their sense of crusading—such as it had been—was dying. The North was ready to let the Southern black man and woman fend for themselves. Indeed, the passage of the Fifteenth Amendment in 1870 had seemed to most Northerners to close the account. Thereafter, blacks were to be on their own, like every other American—or so Northern whites conceived the situation to be.

Save in especially violent, white supremacist states like Mississippi, black voting was not wiped out in the South, once Democrats were back in control. In most of the South blacks continued for another twenty years to vote by the hundreds of thousands, schools were provided by white-dominated governments, a modicum of civil rights were guaranteed, and blacks even held office and sat on juries. It was not even necessary, in most cases, for Democrats to resort to violence in order to win elections; they had only to turn out and vote. Thousands of white Southerners in the old Whig regions—in North Carolina and throughout Appalachia—continued voting Republican until well into the twentieth century. The two-party system disappeared slowly and reluctantly in the South.

"Scientific" Racism

Northern commitment to racial equality had been, in the best of circumstances, only marginal. Indeed, in the Northern educated classes, where a moral concern for the welfare of black Americans had been strongest, a new climate of opinion was forming. Science and rationalism were flooding in. Charles Darwin's *The Origin of Species* (1859) acquired enormous popularity. It described nature as a system in which "natural selection" doomed the less prolific and reproductive species to extinction. Count Arthur Gobineau's *Essay on the Inequality of Races* (translated 1860) classified humankind into many separate races (French, German, Welsh, Irish, etc.), each supposedly carrying irremovable characteristics in its bloodstream.

Blending races always produced, he said, offspring that took on the characteristics of the "lower" race. One alleged quality of "lower" peoples was their passionate sexuality, which made them breed prolifically, whereas the more intelligent races had few children. Many educated Northerners of British (Anglo-Saxon) origin took from such "science" a grim lesson—that Darwinian concepts applied to human society too; that an attitude of "Social Darwinism" was the correct one to take. Certainly, they believed, the Anglo-Saxon race stood in grave peril. Though alleged to be intelligent and gifted, it could be overwhelmed by swarming inferior races if it did not take steps to guard its superior position. Genteel Northerners recoiled in distaste from the grimy, illiterate, strange-looking immigrants who with their huge families were crowding into the northeastern ports. Alarmed, Anglo-Saxon Northerners began to feel a new sympathy for their counterparts in the South who detested blacks.

Another line of reasoning emerged in this setting. Black people were not the equal of whites—this was accepted. But, according to the evolution thesis, they might *potentially* be equal sometime in the future. Social Darwinian concepts of natural selection and survival of the fittest seemed for such people to point toward long-range improvement. However, such progress would certainly be very long range indeed (so this line of thought ran). In the present circumstances, blacks were not ready for the full responsibilities of the ballot, of the professions, of social leadership.

A new paternalist attitude emerged among Southern whites: The task for enlightened white leadership lay in taking the vote away from blacks (as essential to making government honest and efficient, it was said, as eliminating "boss rule" in the corrupt politics of Northern cities), and then beginning slowly and carefully to train them for eventual full citizenship. This would call for schools that offered instruction in practical, humble arts rather than schools that offered the liberal arts, the traditional training for future elites. It would call for complete social and sexual segregation while generations of educational effort had its slow effect. By this means social conflict would be ended, for each race would have its separate sphere.

Many whites were influenced by the British social scientist Herbert Spencer's early book *First Principles* (1862), which was widely read in America. It was Spencer who derived from Darwin's theories the concept of survival of the fittest. Though he later made a place for education, in *First Principles* he held that the "social order is fixed by laws of nature precisely analogous to those of the physical order." Therefore, "the most that man can do . . . by this ignorance and conceit is to mar the operation of social laws." In short, people should leave social problems entirely alone. Avoid public-health measures, so that diseases will sweep away the unfit. Avoid even the building of lighthouses, for dangerous reefs will kill off the unfit seamen. Let the "laws of nature" operate.

In the election of 1876 Democrats attacked Republicans for forcing blacks to vote the Republican ticket.

Strong government is a curse, for it will always be misinformed and will make mistakes, thus disorganizing nature's wise plans.

The lessons were plain. What people thought to be science seemed to demonstrate conclusively that the black race was not equal to the white. Whatever took place without government interference was best, even though it might seem oppressive. All things must be looked at coolly, dispassionately, rationally. Moral arguments were irrelevant because they were "unscientific." Let the Southern whites have their way, for that was best for the Anglo-Saxon race. Government intervention would in any case be harmful.

The Election of 1876

The stage was now set for the official termination of Reconstruction. Only three states were still Republican in the South: South Carolina, Louisiana, and Florida, their governments shored up by federal troops. In the presidential election of 1876 the Republicans turned to a completely honest man whose public reputation was blameless, Rutherford B. Hayes, a former general in the Union army who was presently governor of Ohio. The Democrats turned to the wizened little man who was governor of New York, Samuel J. Tilden. He had led in destroying the Tweed Ring, which had taken millions from the government of New York City, and the Canal Ring, which had taken similarly huge sums from the state-run Erie Canal. Known to be "sound" on the racial equality question—he described black men as "an element of disease and death" in the body politic, to be expelled when possible—he had the priceless political advantage of being known also as a successful battler against corruption.

"It is not necessary for me to attempt to paint the state of political corruption to which we have been reduced," the reformer Henry George said in California as he called for Tilden's election. "It is the dark background to our national [centennial] rejoicing, the skeleton which has stood by us at the feast. Our Fourth of July orators do not proclaim

it; our newspapers do not announce it; we hardly whisper it to one another, but we all know, for we all feel, that beneath all our centennial rejoicing there exists in the public mind to-day a greater doubt of the success of Republican institutions than has existed before within the memory of our oldest man."

Tilden got a popular vote majority of about 250,000 in the election of 1876, but the presidency went to Rutherford B. Hayes. When it appeared that Tilden was one electoral vote shy of election if he did not get the three states in the South still in Republican hands, those states were "delivered" to Hayes. Congress was thrown into turmoil. Should it accept the disputed Republican votes from these states, or agree with the Democrats that the returns were fraudulent? Weeks of public and private negotiation took place in an atmosphere of near hysteria, many in the South and North warning of direct military action if the "steal" were successful. Not until early March 1877 was the Compromise of 1877 reached. The South agreed to allow Florida, Louisiana, and South Carolina to be counted in the Republican column as long as all federal troops were withdrawn from the South.

This was the "public" agreement. Some Southerners may have also thought that the South would actually get more economic aid from the Republicans than from the Northern Democrats. Samuel J. Tilden was too good a Jeffersonian not to practice what he preached—that no government aid should be given to private business. As governor in New York he had slashed all spending on internal improvements— canals, roads, and bridges. The South desperately needed its ports, rivers, bridges, and railroads rebuilt; it had not been able to get nearly enough done on its own; and the Republicans were clearly more friendly to providing federal aid to such enterprises than were the Democrats. They had constructed internal improvements all over the Northern states; perhaps they would do the same in the South if given the presidency once again. "The jobbers and monopolists of the North," said the disgruntled Montgomery Blair, "made common cause with the Southern oligarchy." Enough Southern votes in Congress were given to Hayes's cause to allow him to become president. Reconstruction was over.

BIBLIOGRAPHY

The Reconstruction era, like the Civil War, has stimulated the writing of hundreds of works of history, and they continue to roll off the press. I have been much guided, in rewriting the chapter for the fifth edition, by Eric Foner's major new book, *Reconstruction: America's Unfinished Revolution, 1863–1877*, the latest volume in Harper & Row's

New American Nation Series (1988). James M. McPherson has in recent years brought out two powerful studies, *Ordeal by Fire: The Civil War and Reconstruction* (1982), and *Battle Cry of Freedom: The Civil War Era* (1988). Equally important are: Michael Les Benedict, *A Compromise of Principle: Congressional Republicans and Reconstruction, 1863–1869* (1974); William Gillette, *Retreat from Reconstruction, 1869–1879* (1979); and Michael Perman, *Reunion without Compromise: The South and Reconstruction, 1865–1868* (1973). We have a new view of Ulysses Grant's presidency in William S. McFeely's award-winning *Grant: A Biography* (1981), cited for the previous chapter.

Special studies that I have relied on particularly have been: Paul C. Nagel, *This Sacred Trust: American Nationality 1798–1898* (1971); Walter Nugent, *Structures of American Social History* (1981); David Herbert Donald, *Charles Sumner and the Rights of Man* (1970); Eric L. McKitrick, *Andrew Johnson and Reconstruction* (1960); Numan V. Bartley, *The Creation of Modern Georgia* (1983); Jack P. Maddex, Jr., *The Virginia Conservatives, 1867–1879: A Study in Reconstruction Politics* (1970); Carl Degler, *The Other South: Southern Dissenters in the Nineteenth Century* (1974); Howard Rabinowitz, *Race Relations in the Urban South* (1978); Leon Litwack, *Been in the Storm So Long: The Aftermath of Slavery* (1979); Robert P. Sharkey, *Money, Class, and Party: An Economic Study of Civil War and Reconstruction* (1959); W. Elliot Brownlee, *Dynamics of Ascent: A History of the American Economy* (1978); James

M. McPherson, *The Struggle for Equality: Abolitionists and the Negro in the Civil War and Reconstruction* (1964); Herbert G. Gutman, *The Black Family in Slavery and Freedom 1750–1925* (1976); Herman Belz, *Reconstructing the Union: Theory and Policy during the Civil War* (1969); Anne Firor Scott and Andrew MacKay Scott, *One Half the People: The Fight for Woman Suffrage* (1982); Robert Bannister, *Social Darwinism: Science and Myth in Anglo-American Social Thought* (1979); William Gillette, *The Right to Vote: Politics and the Passage of the Fifteenth Amendment* (1965); C. Vann Woodward, *Reunion and Reaction: The Compromise of 1877 and the End of Reconstruction* (1966), as modified by Keith Ian Polakoff, *The Politics of Inertia: The Election of 1876 and the End of Reconstruction*; C. Vann Woodward, *American Counterpoint: Slavery and Racism in the North-South Dialogue* (1971); John Hope Franklin, *Reconstruction: After the Civil War* (1961); Kenneth M. Stampp, *The Era of Reconstruction, 1865–1877* (1965); LaWanda Cox and John H. Cox, *Politics, Principle, and Prejudice, 1865–1866* (1963); William R. Brock, *An American Crisis: Congress and Reconstruction, 1865–1867* (1963); Felice A. Bonadio, *North of Reconstruction: Ohio Politics, 1865–1879* (1970); James Mohr, *The Radical Republicans and Reform in New York during Reconstruction* (1973). See also Robert Kelley, *The Cultural Pattern in American Politics: The First Century* (1979), and *The Transatlantic Persuasion: The Liberal-Democratic Mind in the Age of Gladstone* (1969).

The Declaration of Independence

When in the Course of human events, it becomes necessary for one people to dissolve the political bands which have connected them with another, and to assume among the Powers of the earth, the separate and equal station to which the Laws of Nature and of Nature's God entitle them, a decent respect to the opinions of mankind requires that they should declare the causes which impel them to the separation.

We hold these truths to be self-evident, that all men are created equal, that they are endowed by their Creator with certain unalienable Rights, that among these are Life, Liberty and the pursuit of Happiness. That to secure these rights, Governments are instituted among Men, deriving their just powers from the consent of the governed, That whenever any Form of Government becomes destructive of these ends, it is the Right of the people to alter or to abolish it, and to institute new Government, laying its foundation on such principles and organizing its powers in such form, as to them shall seem most likely to effect their Safety and Happiness. Prudence, indeed, will dictate that Governments long established should not be changed for light and transient causes; and accordingly all experience hath shown, that mankind are more disposed to suffer, while evils are sufferable, than to right themselves by abolishing the forms to which they are accustomed. But when a long train of abuses and usurpations, pursuing invariably the same Object evinces a design to reduce them under absolute Despotism, it is their right, it is their duty, to throw off such Government, and to provide new Guards for their future security.—Such has been the patient sufferance of these Colonies; and such is now the necessity which constrains them to alter their former Systems of Government. The history of the present King of Great Britain is a history of repeated injuries and usurpations, all having in direct object the establishment of an absolute Tyranny over these States. To prove this, let Facts be summitted to a candid world.

He has refused his Assent to Laws, the most wholesome and necessary for the public good.

He has forbidden his Governors to pass Laws of immediate and pressing importance, unless suspended in their operation till his Assent should be obtained; and when so suspended, he has utterly neglected to attend to them.

He has refused to pass other Laws for the accommodation of large districts of people, unless those people would relinquish the right of Representation in the Legislature, a right inestimable to them and formidable to tyrants only.

He has called together legislative bodies at places unusual, uncomfortable, and distant from the depository of their public Records, for the sole purpose of fatiguing them into compliance with his measures.

He has dissolved Representative Houses repeatedly, for opposing with manly firmness his invasions on the rights of the people.

He has refused for a long time, after such dissolutions, to cause others to be elected; whereby the Legislative Powers, incapable of Annihilation, have returned to the People at large for their exercise; the State remaining in the mean time exposed to all the dangers of invasion from without, and convulsions within.

He has endeavoured to prevent the population of these States; for that purpose obstructing the Laws of Naturalization of Foreigners; refusing to pass others to encourage their migration hither, and raising the conditions of new Appropriations of Lands.

He has obstructed the Administration of Justice, by refusing his Assent to Laws for establishing Judiciary powers.

He has made Judges dependent on his Will alone, for the tenure of their offices, and the amount and payment of their salaries.

He has erected a multitude of New Offices, and sent hither swarms of Officers to harass our People, and eat out their substance.

He has kept among us in time of peace, Standing Armies without the Consent of our legislature.

He has affected to render the Military independent of and superior to the Civil power.

He has combined with others

to subject us to a jurisdiction foreign to our constitution, and unacknowledged by our laws; giving his Assent to their acts of pretended Legislation:

For quartering large bodies of armed troops among us:

For protecting them, by a mock Trial, from punishment for any Murders which they should commit on the Inhabitants of these States:

For cutting off our Trade with all parts of the world:

For imposing taxes on us without our Consent:

For depriving us in many cases, of the benefits of Trial by Jury:

For transporting us beyond Seas to be tried for pretended offences:

For abolishing the free System of English Laws in a neighbouring Province, establishing therein an Arbitrary government, and enlarging its Boundaries so as to render it at once an example and fit instrument for introducing the same absolute rule into these Colonies:

For taking away our Charters, abolishing our most valuable Laws, and altering fundamentally the Forms of our Governments:

For suspending our own Legislature, and declaring themselves invested with Power to legislate for us in all cases whatsoever.

He has abdicated Government here, by declaring us out of his Protection and waging War against us.

He has plundered our seas, ravaged our Coasts, burnt our towns, and destroyed the lives of our people.

56 signers

He is at this time transporting large Armies of foreign Mercenaries to compleat the works of death, desolation and tyranny, already begun with circumstances of Cruelty & perfidy scarcely paralleled in the most barbarous ages, and totally unworthy of the Head of a civilized nation.

He has constrained our fellow Citizens taken Captive on the high Seas to bear Arms against their Country, to become the executioners of their friends and Brethren, or to fall themselves by their Hands.

He has excited domestic insurrections amongst us, and has endeavoured to bring on the inhabitants of our frontiers, the merciless Indian Savages, whose known rule of warfare, is an undistinguished destruction of all ages, sexes and conditions.

In every stage of these Oppressions We have Petitioned for Redress in the most humble terms: Our repeated Petitions have been answered only by repeated injury. A Prince, whose character is thus marked by every act which may define a Tyrant, is unfit to be the ruler of a free people.

Nor have We been wanting in attention to our British brethren. We have warned them from time to time of attempts by their legislature to extend an unwarrantable jurisdiction over us. We have reminded them of the circumstances of our emigration and settlement here. We have appealed to their native justice and magnanimity, and we have conjured them by the ties of our common kindred to disavow these usurpations, which, would inevitably interrupt our connections and correspondence. They too have been deaf to the voice of justice and of consanguinity. We must, therefore, acquiesce in the necessity, which denounces our Separation, and hold them, as we hold the rest of mankind, Enemies in War, in Peace Friends.

We, therefore, the Representatives of the United States of America, in General Congress, Assembled, appealing to the Supreme Judge of the world for the rectitude of our intentions, do, in the Name, and by Authority of the good People of these Colonies, solemnly publish and declare, That these United Colonies are, and of Right ought to be Free and Independent States; that they are Absolved from all Allegiance to the British Crown, and that all political connection between them and the State of Great Britain, is and ought to be totally dissolved; and that as Free and Independent States, they have full Power to levy War, conclude Peace, contract Alliances, establish Commerce, and to do all other Acts and Things which Independent States may of right do. And for the support of this Declaration, with a firm reliance on the protection of divine Providence, we mutually pledge to each other our Lives, our Fortunes and our sacred Honor.

The Constitution of the United States

We the people of the United States, in order to form a more perfect Union, establish Justice, insure domestic Tranquility, provide for the common defense, promote the general Welfare, and secure the Blessings of Liberty to ourselves and our Posterity, do ordain and establish this CONSTITUTION for the United States of America.

ARTICLE I

Section 1. All legislative powers herein granted shall be vested in a Congress of the United States, which shall consist of a Senate and House of Representatives.

Section 2. The House of Representatives shall be composed of Members chosen every second Year by the People of the several States, and the Electors in each State shall have the Qualifications requisite for Electors of the most numerous Branch of the State Legislature.

No Person shall be a Representative who shall not have attained to the Age of twenty-five Years, and been seven Years a Citizen of the United States, and who shall not, when elected, be an Inhabitant of that State in which he shall be chosen.

Representatives and direct Taxes shall be apportioned among the several States which may be included within this Union, according to their respective Numbers, which shall be determined by adding to the whole Number of Free Persons, including those bound to Service for a Term of Years, and excluding Indians not taxed, three fifths of all other Persons. The actual Enumeration shall be made within three Years after the first Meeting of the Congress of the United States, and within every subsequent Term of ten Years, in such Manner as they shall by Law direct. The Number of Representatives shall not exceed one for every thirty Thousand, but each State shall have at Least one Representative; and until such enumeration shall be made, the State of New Hampshire shall be entitled to chuse three, Massachusetts, eight, Rhode Island and Providence Plantations one, Connecticut five, New York six, New Jersey four, Pennsylvania eight, Delaware one, Maryland six, Virginia ten, North Carolina five, South Carolina five, and Georgia three.

When vacancies happen in the Representation from any State, the Executive Authority thereof shall issue Writs of Election to fill such Vacancies.

The House of Representatives shall chuse their Speaker and other Officers; and shall have the sole Power of Impeachment.

Section 3. The Senate of the United States shall be composed of two Senators from each State, chosen by the Legislature thereof, for six Years; and each Senator shall have one Vote.

Immediately after they shall be assembled in Consequence of the first Election, they shall be divided as equally as may be into three Classes. The Seats of the Senators of the first Class shall be vacated at the Expiration of the second Year, of the second Class at the Expiration of the fourth Year, and of the third Class at the Expiration of the sixth Year, so that one-third may be chosen every second Year; and if Vacancies happen by Resignation, or otherwise during the Recess of the Legislature of any State, the Executive therefore may make temporary Appointments until the next Meeting of the Legislature, which shall then fill such Vacancies.

No Person shall be a Senator who shall not have attained to the Age of thirty Years, and been nine Years a Citizen of the United States, and who shall not, when elected, be an Inhabitant of that State in which he shall be chosen.

The Vice President of the United States shall be President of the Senate, but shall have no vote, unless they be equally divided.

The Senate shall choose their Officers, and also a President pro tempore, in the absence of the Vice President, or when he shall exercise the Office of President of the United States.

The Senate shall have the sole Power to try all Impeachments. When sitting for that purpose, they shall be on Oath or Affirmation. When the President of the United States is tried, the Chief Justice shall preside: And no person shall be convicted without the Concurrence of two thirds of the Members present.

Judgment in Cases of Impeachment shall not extend further than to removal from Office, and disqualification to hold and enjoy any Office of honor, Trust, or Profit under the United States: but the Party convicted shall nevertheless be liable and subject to Indictment, Trial, Judgment, and Punishment, according to Law.

Section 4. The Times, Places and Manner of holding Elections for Senators and Representatives, shall be prescribed in each State by the Legislature thereof; but the Congress may at any time by Law make or alter such Regulations, except as to the Places of Chusing Senators.

The Congress shall assemble at least once in every Year, and such Meeting shall be on the first Monday in December, unless they shall by Law appoint a different Day.

Section 5. Each House shall be the judge of the Elections, Returns and Qualifications of its own Members, and a Majority of each shall constitute a Quorum to do Business; but a smaller number may adjourn from day to day, and may be authorized to compel the Attendance of absent Members, in such Manner, and under such Penalties, as each House may provide.

Each House may determine the Rules of its Proceedings, punish its Members for disorderly Behaviour, and, with the Concurrence of two thirds, expel a Member.

Each House shall keep a Journal of its Proceedings, and from time to time publish the same, excepting such Parts as may in their Judgment require Secrecy; and the Yeas and Nays of the Members of either House on any question shall, at the Desire of one fifth of those Present, be entered on the Journal.

Neither House, during the Session of Congress, shall, without the Consent of the other, adjourn for more than three days, nor to any other Place than that in which the two Houses shall be sitting.

Section 6. The Senators and Representatives shall receive a Compensation for their Services, to be as-

certained by Law, and paid out of the Treasury of the United States. They shall in all Cases, except Treason, Felony, and Breach of the Peace, be privileged from Arrest during their Attendance at the Session of their respective Houses, and in going to and returning from the same; and for any Speech or Debate in either House, they shall not be questioned in any other Place.

No Senator or Representative shall, during the Time for which he was elected, be appointed to any civil Office under the Authority of the United States which shall have been created, or the Emoluments whereof shall have been increased during such time; and no Person holding any Office under the United States shall be a Member of either House during his Continuance in Office.

Section 7. All Bills for raising Revenue shall originate in the House of Representatives; but the Senate may propose or concur with Amendments as on other Bills.

Every Bill which shall have passed the House of Representatives and the Senate, shall, before it become a Law, be presented to the President of the United States; If he approve he shall sign it, but if not he shall return it, with his Objections, to that House in which it shall have originated, who shall enter the Objections at large on their Journal, and proceed to reconsider it. If after such Reconsideration two thirds of that House shall agree to pass the Bill, it shall be sent, together with the Objections, to the other House, by which it shall likewise be reconsidered, and if approved by two thirds of that House, it shall become a Law. But in all such Cases the Votes of both Houses shall be determined by Yeas and Nays, and the Names of the Persons voting for and against the Bill shall be entered on the Journal of each House respectively. If any Bill shall not be returned by the President within ten Days (Sundays excepted) after it shall have been presented to him, the Same shall be a Law, in like Manner as if he had signed it, unless the Congress by their Adjournment prevent its Return, in which Case it shall not be a Law.

Every Order, Resolution, or Vote to which the Concurrence of the

State and House of Representatives may be necessary (except on a question of Adjournment) shall be presented to the President of the United States; and before the Same shall take Effect, shall be approved by him, or being disapproved by him, shall be repassed by two thirds of the Senate and House of Representatives, according to the Rules and Limitations prescribed in the Case of a Bill.

Section 8. The Congress shall have Power To lay and collect Taxes, Duties, Imposts and Excises, to pay the Debts and provide for the common Defense and general Welfare of the United States; but all Duties, Imposts and Excises shall be uniform throughout the United States;

To borrow money on the credit of the United States;

To regulate Commerce with foreign Nations, and among the several States, and with the Indian Tribes;

To establish an uniform Rule of Naturalization, and uniform Laws on the subject of Bankruptcies throughout the United States;

To coin Money, regulate the Value thereof, and of foreign Coin, and fix the Standard of Weights and Measures;

To provide for the Punishment of counterfeiting the Securities and current Coin of the United States;

To Establish Post Offices and post Roads;

To promote the Progress of Science and useful Arts, by securing for limited Times to Authors and Inventors the exclusive Right to their respective Writings and Discoveries;

To constitute Tribunals inferior to the Supreme Court;

To define and punish Piracies and Felonies committed on the high Seas, and Offenses against the Law of Nations;

To declare War, grant Letters of Marque and Reprisal, and make Rules concerning Captures on Land and Water;

To raise and support Armies, but no Appropriation of Money to that Use shall be for a longer Term than two Years;

To provide and maintain a Navy;

To make Rules for the Government and Regulation of the land and naval forces;

To provide for calling forth the Militia to execute the Laws of the Union, suppress Insurrections and repel Invasions;

To provide for organizing, arming, and disciplining the Militia, and for governing such Part of them as may be employed in the Service of the United States, reserving to the States respectively, the Appointment of the Officers, and the Authority of training the Militia according to the discipline prescribed by Congress;

To exercise exclusive Legislation in all Cases whatsoever, over such District (not exceeding ten Miles square) as may, by Cession of particular States, and the acceptance of Congress, become the Seat of Government of the United States, and to exercise like Authority over all Places purchased by the Consent of the Legislature of the State in which the Same shall be, for the Erection of Forts, Magazines, Arsenals, dock-Yards, and other needful Buildings;—And

To make all Laws which shall be necessary and proper for carrying into Execution the foregoing Powers, and all other Powers vested by this Constitution in the Government of the United States, or in any Department or Officer thereof.

Section 9. The Migration or Importation of such Persons as any of the States now existing shall think proper to admit, shall not be prohibited by the Congress prior to the Year one thousand eight hundred and eight, but a tax on duty may be imposed on such Importation, not exceeding ten dollars for each Person.

The privilege of the Writ of Habeas Corpus shall not be suspended, unless when in Cases of Rebellion or Invasion the public Safety may require it.

No Bill of Attainder or ex post facto Law shall be passed.

No Capitation, or other direct, Tax shall be laid unless in Proportion to the Census or Enumeration herein before directed to be taken.

No Tax or Duty shall be laid on Articles exported from any State.

No Preference shall be given by any Regulation of Revenue to the Ports of one State over those of another: nor shall Vessels bound to, or from, one State, be obliged to enter, clear, or pay Duties in another.

No Money shall be drawn from the Treasury, but in Consequence of Appropriations made by Law; and a regular Statement and Account of the Receipts and Expenditures of all public Money shall be published from time to time.

No title of Nobility shall be granted by the United States: And no Person holding any Office of Profit or Trust under them, shall, without the Consent of the Congress, accept of any present, Emolument, Office, or Title, of any kind whatever, from any King, Prince or foreign State.

Section 10. No State shall enter into any Treaty Alliance, or Confederation; grant Letters of Marque and Reprisal; coin Money; emit Bills of Credit; make any Thing but gold and silver Coin a Tender in Payment of Debts; pass any Bill of Attainder, ex post facto Law, or Law impairing the Obligation of Contracts, or grant any Title of Nobility.

No State shall, without the Consent of the Congress, lay any Imposts or Duties on Imports or Exports, except what may be absolutely necessary for exercising its inspection Laws: and the net Produce of all Duties and Imposts, laid by any State on Imports or Exports, shall be for the Use of the Treasury of the United States; and all such Laws shall be subject to the Revision and Control of the Congress.

No State shall, without the Consent of Congress, lay any duty of Tonnage, keep Troops, or Ships of War in time of Peace, enter into any Agreement or Compact with another State, or with a foreign Power, or engage in War, unless actually invaded, or in such imminent Danger as will not admit of delay.

ARTICLE II

Section 1. The executive Power shall be vested in a President of the United States of America. He shall hold his Office during the Term of four Years, and, together with the Vice President, chosen for the same term, be elected, as follows:

Each State shall appoint, in such Manner as the Legislature thereof may direct, a Number of Electors, equal to the whole Number of Senators and Representatives to which the State may be entitled in the Congress: but no Senator or Representative, or Person holding an Office of Trust or Profit under the United States, shall be appointed an Elector.

The Electors shall meet in their respective States, and vote by Ballot for two Persons, of whom one at least shall not be an Inhabitant of the same State with themselves. And they shall make a list of all the Persons voted for, and of the Number of Votes for each; which List they shall sign and certify, and transmit sealed to the Seat of the Government of the United States, directed to the President of the Senate. The President of the Senate shall, in the Presence of the Senate and House of Representatives, open all the Certificates, and the Votes shall then be counted. The Person having the greatest Number of Votes shall be the President, if such Number be a Majority of the whole Number of Electors appointed; and if there be more than one who have such Majority, and have an equal Number of Votes, then the House of Representatives shall immediately chuse by Ballot one of them for President; and if no Person have a Majority, then from the five highest on the List the said House shall in like Manner chuse the President. But in chusing the President, the Votes shall be taken by States, the Representation from each State having one Vote; a quorum for this Purpose shall consist of a Member or Members from two thirds of the States, and a Majority of all the States shall be necessary to a Choice. In every Case, after the Choice of the President, the Person having the greatest Number of Votes of the Electors shall be the Vice President. But if there should remain two or more who have equal votes, the Senate shall chuse from them by Ballot the Vice President.

The Congress may determine the Time of chusing the Electors, and the Day on which they shall give their Votes; which Day shall be the same throughout the United States.

No person except a natural-born

citizen, or a Citizen of the United States, at the time of the Adoption of this Constitution, shall be eligible to the Office of President; neither shall any Person be eligible to that Office who shall not have attained to the Age of thirty-five Years, and been fourteen years a Resident within the United States.

In case of the Removal of the President from Office, or of his Death, Resignation or Inability to discharge the Powers and Duties of the said Office, the same shall devolve on the Vice President, and the Congress may by Law provide for the Case of Removal, Death, Resignation, or Inability, both of the President and Vice President, declaring what Officer shall then act as President, and such Officer shall act accordingly, until the Disability be removed, or a President shall be elected.

The President shall, at stated Times, receive for his Services a Compensation, which shall neither be increased nor diminished during the Period for which he shall have been elected, and he shall not receive within that Period any other Emolument from the United States, or any of them.

Before he enters on the Execution of his Office, he shall take the following Oath or Affirmation: "I do solemnly swear (or affirm) that I will faithfully execute the Office of President of the United States, and will, to the best of my Ability, preserve, protect, and defend the Constitution of the United States."

Section 2. The President shall be Commander in Chief of the Army and Navy of the United States, and of the Militia of the several States, when called into the actual Service of the United States; he may require the Opinion, in writing, of the principal Officer in each of the Executive Departments, upon any subject relating to the Duties of their respective Offices, and he shall have Power to Grant Reprieves and Pardons for Offenses against the United States, except in Cases of Impeachment.

He shall have Power, by and with the Advice and Consent of the Senate, to make Treaties, provided two thirds of the Senators present concur; and he shall nominate, and by and with the Advice and Consent of the Senate, shall appoint Ambassadors, other public Ministers and Consuls, Judges of the supreme Court, and all other Officers of the United States, whose Appointments are not herein otherwise provided for, and which shall be established by Law: but the Congress may by Law vest the Appointment of such inferior Officers, as they think proper, in the President alone, in the Courts of Law, or in the Heads of Departments.

The President shall have Power to fill up all Vacancies that may happen during the Recess of the Senate, by granting Commissions which shall expire at the end of their next Session.

Section 3. He shall from time to time give to the Congress Information of the State of the Union, and recommend to their Consideration such Measures as he shall judge necessary and expedient; he may, on extraordinary occasions, convene both Houses, or either of them, and in Case of Disagreement between them, with respect to the Time of Adjournment, he may adjourn them to such Time as he shall think proper; he shall receive Ambassadors and other public Ministers; he shall take Care that the Laws be faithfully executed, and shall Commission all the Officers of the United States.

Section 4. The President, Vice President and all civil Officers of the United States, shall be removed from Office on Impeachment for, and Conviction of, Treason, Bribery, or other high Crimes and Misdemeanors.

ARTICLE III

Section 1. The judicial Power of the United States, shall be vested in one supreme Court, and in such inferior Courts as the Congress may from time to time ordain and establish. The Judges, both of the supreme and inferior Courts shall hold their Offices during good Behaviour, and shall, at stated Times, receive for their Services, a Compensation, which shall not be diminished during their Continuance in Office.

Section 2. The judicial Power shall extend to all Cases, in Law and Equity, arising under this Constitution, the Laws of the United States, and Treaties made, or which shall be made, under their Authority;—to all Cases affecting Ambassadors, other public Ministers and Consuls;—to all Cases of admiralty and maritime Jurisdiction;—to Controversies to which the United States shall be a Party;— to Controversies between two or more States;—between a State and Citizens of another State;—between Citizens of different States;—between Citizens of the same State claiming Lands under Grants of different States, and between a State, or the Citizens thereof, and foreign States, Citizens or Subjects.

In all Cases affecting Ambassadors, other public Ministers and Consuls, and those in which a State shall be a Party, the supreme Court shall have original Jurisdiction. In all the other Cases before mentioned, the supreme Court shall have appellate Jurisdiction, both as to Law and Fact, with such Exceptions, and under such Regulations as the Congress shall make.

The trial of all Crimes, except in Cases of Impeachment, shall be by Jury; and such Trial shall be held in the State where the said Crimes shall have been committed; but when not committed within any State, the Trial shall be at such Place or Places as the Congress may by Law have directed.

Section 3. Treason against the United States, shall consist only in levying War against them, or in adhering to their Enemies, giving them Aid and Comfort. No Person shall be convicted of Treason unless on the Testimony of two Witnesses to the same overt Act, or on Confession in open Court.

The Congress shall have Power to declare the Punishment of Treason, but no Attainder of Treason shall work Corruption of Blood, or Forfeiture except during the Life of the Person attained.

ARTICLE IV

Section 1. Full Faith and Credit shall be given in each State to the public Acts, Records, and judicial Proceedings of every other State. And the Congress may by general Laws prescribe the Manner in which such Acts, Records and Proceedings shall be proved, and the Effect thereof.

Section 2. The Citizens of each State shall be entitled to all Privileges and Immunities of Citizens in the several States.

A Person charged in any State with Treason, Felony, or other Crime, who shall flee from Justice, and be found in another State, shall on demand of the executive Authority of the State from which he fled, be delivered up, to be removed to the State having Jurisdiction of the crime.

No Person held to Service or Labour in one State, under the Laws thereof, escaping into another, shall, in Consequence of any Law or Regulation therein, be discharged from such Service or Labour, but shall be delivered up on Claim of the Party to whom such Service or Labour may be due.

Section 3. New States may be admitted by Congress into this Union; but no new State shall be formed or erected within the Jurisdiction of any other State; nor any State be formed by the Junction of two or more States, or parts of States, without the Consent of the Legislatures of the States concerned as well as of the Congress.

The Congress shall have Power to dispose of and make all needful Rules and Regulations respecting the Territory or other Property belonging to the United States; and nothing in this Constitution shall be so construed as to Prejudice any Claims of the United States, or of any particular State.

Section 4. The United States shall guarantee to every State in this Union a Republican Form of Government, and shall protect each of them against Invasion; and on Application of the Legislature, or of the Executive (when the Legislature cannot be convened) against domestic Violence.

ARTICLE V

The Congress, whenever two thirds of both Houses shall deem it necessary, shall propose Amendments to this Constitution, or, on the Application of the Legislatures of two thirds of the several States, shall call a Convention for proposing Amendments, which, in either Case, shall be valid to all Intents and Purposes, as part of this Constitution, when ratified by the Legislatures of three fourths of the several States, or by Conventions in three fourths thereof, as the one or the other Mode of Ratification may be proposed by the Congress; Provided that no Amendment which may be made prior to the Year One thousand eight hundred and eight shall in any Manner affect the first and fourth Clauses in the Ninth Section of the first Article; and that no State, without its Consent, shall be deprived of its equal Suffrage in the Senate.

ARTICLE VI

All Debts contracted and Engagements entered into, before the Adoption of this Constitution, shall be as valid against the United States under this Constitution, as under the Confederation.

This Constitution, and the Laws of the United States which shall be made in Pursuance thereof: and all Treaties made, or which shall be made, under the Authority of the United States, shall be the supreme Law of the Land; and the Judges in every State shall be bound thereby, any Thing in the Constitution or laws of any State to the Contrary notwithstanding.

The Senators and Representatives before mentioned, and the Members of the several State Legislatures, and all executive and judicial Officers, both of the United States and of the several States, shall be bound by Oath or Affirmation to support this Constitution; but no religious Test shall ever be required as a qualification to any Office or public Trust under the United States.

ARTICLE VII

The Ratification of the Conventions of nine states shall be sufficient for the Establishment of this Constitution between the States so ratifying the same.

Done in Convention by the Unanimous Consent of the States present the Seventeenth Day of September in the Year of our Lord one thousand seven hundred and Eighty seven and of the Independence of the United States of America the Twelfth. In Witness whereof We have hereunto subscribed our Names.

Articles in Addition to, and Amendment of, the Constitution of the United States of America, Proposed by Congress, and Ratified by the Legislatures of the Several States, Pursuant to the Fifth Article of the Original Constitution.

AMENDMENT I [1791]

Congress shall make no law respecting an establishment of religion, or prohibiting the free exercise thereof; or abridging the freedom of speech, or of the press; or the right of the people peaceably to assemble, and to petition the Government for a redress of grievances.

AMENDMENT II [1791]

A well regulated Militia, being necessary to the security of a free State, the right of the people to keep and bear Arms, shall not be infringed.

AMENDMENT III [1791]

No Soldier shall, in time of peace, be quartered in any house, without the consent of the Owner, nor in time of war, but in a manner to be prescribed by law.

AMENDMENT IV [1791]

The right of the people to be secure in their persons, houses, papers, and effects, against unreasonable searches and seizures, shall not be violated, and no Warrants shall issue, but upon probable cause, supported by Oath or affirmation, and particularly describing the place to be searched, and the persons or things to be seized.

AMENDMENT V [1791]

No person shall be held to answer for a capital or otherwise infamous crime, unless on a presentment or indictment of a Grand Jury, except in cases arising in the land or naval forces, or in the Militia, when in actual service in time of War or public danger; nor shall any person be subject for the same offence to be twice put in jeopardy of life or limb; nor shall be compelled in any criminal case to be a witness against himself, nor be deprived of life, liberty, or property, without due process of law; nor shall private property be taken for public use, without just compensation.

AMENDMENT VI [1791]

In all criminal prosecutions, the accused shall enjoy the right to a speedy and public trial, by an impartial jury of the State and district wherein the crime shall have been committed, which district shall have been previously ascertained by law, and to be informed of the nature and cause of the accusation, to be confronted with the witnesses against him; to have compulsory process for obtaining witnesses in his favor, and to have the Assistance of Counsel for his defence.

AMENDMENT VII [1791]

In Suits at common law, where the value in controversy shall exceed twenty dollars, the right of trial by jury shall be preserved, and no fact tried by jury, shall be otherwise reexamined in any Court of the United States, than according to the rules of the common law.

AMENDMENT VIII [1791]

Excessive bail shall not be required, nor excessive fines imposed, nor cruel and unusual punishments inflicted.

AMENDMENT IX [1791]

The enumeration in the Constitution, of certain rights, shall not be construed to deny or disparage others retained by the people.

AMENDMENT X [1791]

The powers not delegated to the United States by the Constitution, nor prohibited by it to the States, are reserved to the States respectively, or to the people.

AMENDMENT XI [1798]

The Judicial power of the United States shall not be construed to extend to any suit in law or equity, commenced or prosecuted against one of the United States by Citizens of another State, or by Citizens or Subjects of any Foreign State.

AMENDMENT XII [1804]

The Electors shall meet in their respective States and vote by ballot for President and Vice-President, one of whom, at least, shall not be an inhabitant of the same state with themselves; they shall name in their ballots the person voted for as President, and in distinct ballots the person voted for as Vice-President, and they shall make distinct lists of all persons voted for as President, and all persons voted for as Vice-President, and of the number of votes for each, which lists they shall sign and certify, and transmit sealed to the seat of the government of the United States, directed to the President of the Senate;—The President of the Senate shall, in the presence of the Senate and House of Representatives, open all the certificates and the votes shall then be counted;—The person having the greatest number of votes for President, shall be the President, if such number be a majority of the whole number of Electors appointed; and if no person have such majority, then from the persons having the highest numbers not exceeding three on the list of those voted for as President, the House of Representatives shall choose immediately, by ballot, the President. But in choosing the President, the votes shall be taken by states, the representation from each state having one vote; a quorum for this purpose shall consist of a member or members from two-thirds of the states, and a majority of all the states shall be necessary to a choice. And if the House of Representatives shall not choose a President whenever the right of choice shall devolve upon them, before the fourth day of March next following, then the Vice-President shall act as President, as in the case of the death or other constitutional disability of the President.—The person having the greatest number of votes as Vice-President, shall be the Vice-President, if such number be a majority of the whole number of Electors appointed, and if no person have a majority, then from the two highest numbers on the list, the Senate shall choose the Vice-President; a quorum for the purpose shall consist of two-thirds of the whole number of Senators, and a majority of the whole number shall be necessary to a choice. But no person constitutionally ineligible to the office of the President shall be eligible to that of Vice-President of the United States.

AMENDMENT XIII [1865]

Section 1. Neither slavery nor involuntary servitude, except as a punishment for crime whereof the party shall have been duly convicted, shall exist within the United States, or any place subject to their jurisdiction.

Section 2. Congress shall have the power to enforce this article by appropriate legislation.

AMENDMENT XIV [1868]

Section 1. All persons born or naturalized in the United States, and subject to the jurisdiction thereof, are citizens of the United States and of the State wherein they reside. No state shall make or enforce any law which shall abridge the privileges or immunities of citizens of the United States; nor shall any State deprive any person of life, liberty, or property, without due process of law; nor deny to any person within its jurisdiction the equal protection of the laws.

Section 2. Representatives shall be apportioned among the several States according to their respective numbers, counting the whole number of persons in each State, excluding Indians not taxed. But when the right to vote at any election for the choice of electors for President and Vice President of the United States, Representatives in Congress, the Executive and Judicial officers of a State, or the members of the Legislature thereof, is denied to any of the male inhabitants of such State, being twenty-one years of age, and citizens of the United States, or in any way abridged, except for participation in rebellion, or other crime, the basis of representation therein shall be reduced in the proportion which the number of such male citizens shall bear to the whole number of male citizens twenty-one years of age in such State.

Section 3. No person shall be a Senator or Representative in Congress, or elector of President and Vice President, or hold any office, civil or military, under the United States, or under any State, who, having previously taken an oath, as a member of Congress, or as an officer of the United States, or as a member of any State legislature, or as an executive or judicial officer of any State, to support the Constitution of the United States, shall have engaged in insurrection or rebellion against the same, or given aid or comfort to the enemies thereof. But Congress may by a vote of two-thirds of each House, remove such disability.

Section 4. The validity of the public debt of the United States, authorized by law, including debts incurred for payment of pensions and bounties for services in suppressing insurrection or rebellion, shall not be questioned. But neither the United States nor any State shall assume or pay any debt or obligation incurred in aid of insurrection or rebellion against the United States, or any claim for the loss or emancipation of any slave; but all such debts, obligations, and claims shall be held illegal and void.

Section 5. The Congress shall have power to enforce, by appropriate legislation, the provisions of this article.

AMENDMENT XV [1870]

Section 1. The right of citizens of the United States to vote shall not be denied or abridged by the United States or by any State on account of race, color, or previous condition of servitude—

Section 2. The Congress shall have the power to enforce this article by appropriate legislation.

AMENDMENT XVI [1913]

The Congress shall have power to lay and collect taxes on incomes, from whatever source derived, without apportionment among the several States, and without regard to any census or enumeration.

AMENDMENT XVII [1913]

The Senate of the United States shall be composed of two Senators from each State, elected by the people thereof, for six years; and each Senator shall have one vote. The electors in each State shall have the qualifications requisite for electors of the most numerous branch of the State legislatures.

When vacancies happen in the representation of any State in the Senate, the executive authority of such State shall issue writs of election to fill such vacancies: *Provided,* That the legislature of any State may empower the executive thereof to make temporary appointments until the people fill the vacancies by election as the legislature may direct.

This amendment shall not be so construed as to affect the election or term of any Senator chosen before it becomes valid as part of the Constitution.

AMENDMENT XVIII [1919]

Section 1. After one year from the ratification of this article the manufacture, sale, or transportation of intoxicating liquors within, the importation thereof into, or the exportation thereof from the United States and all territory subject to the jurisdiction thereof for beverage purposes is hereby prohibited.

Section 2. The Congress and the several States shall have concurrent power to enforce this article by appropriate legislation.

Section 3. This article shall be inoperative unless it shall have been ratified as an amendment to the Constitution by the legislatures of the several States, as provided in the Constitution, within seven years from the date of the submission hereof to the States by the Congress.

AMENDMENT XIX [1920]

The right of citizens of the United States to vote shall not be denied or abridged by the United States or by any State on account of sex.

Congress shall have power to enforce this article by appropriate legislation.

AMENDMENT XX [1933]

Section 1. The terms of the President and Vice President shall end at noon on the 20th day of January, and the terms of Senators and Representatives at noon on the 3rd day of January, of the years in which such terms would have ended if this article had not been ratified; and the terms of their successors shall then begin.

Section 2. The Congress shall assemble at least once in every year, and such meeting shall begin at noon on the 3rd day of January, unless they shall by law appoint a different day.

Section 3. If, at the time fixed for the beginning of the term of the President, the President elect shall have died, the Vice-President elect shall become President. If a President shall not have been chosen before the time fixed for the beginning of his term, or if the President elect shall have failed to qualify, then the Vice President elect shall act as President until a President shall have qualified; and the Congress may by law provide for the case wherein neither a President elect nor a Vice President elect shall have qualified, declaring who shall then act as President, or the manner in which one who is to act shall be selected, and such person shall act accordingly until a President or Vice President shall have qualified.

Section 4. The Congress may by law provide for the case of the death of any of the persons from whom the House of Representatives may choose a President whenever the right of choice shall have devolved upon them, and for the case of the death of any of the persons from whom the Senate may choose a Vice President whenever the right of choice shall have devolved upon them.

Section 5. Sections 1 and 2 shall take effect on the 15th day of October following the ratification of this article.

Section 6. This article shall be inoperative unless it shall have been ratified as an amendment to the Constitution by the legislatures of three-fourths of the several States within seven years from the date of its submission.

AMENDMENT XXI [1933]

Section 1. The eighteenth article of amendment to the Constitution of the United States is hereby repealed.

Section 2. The transportation or importation into any State, Territory, or possession of the United States for delivery or use therein of intoxicating liquors, in violation of the laws thereof, is hereby prohibited.

Section 3. This article shall be inoperative unless it shall have been ratified as an amendment to the Constitution by conventions in the several States, as provided in the Constitution, within seven years from the date of the submission hereof to the States by the Congress.

AMENDMENT XXII [1951]

Section 1. No person shall be elected to the office of the President more than twice, and no person who

has held the office of President, or acted as President, for more than two years of a term to which some other person was elected President shall be elected to the office of President more than once.

But this Article shall not apply to any person holding the office of President when this Article was proposed by the Congress, and shall not prevent any person who may be holding the office of President, or acting as President, during the term within which this Article becomes operative from holding the office of President or acting as President during the remainder of such term.

AMENDMENT XXIII [1961]

Section 1. The District constituting the seat of Government of the United States shall appoint in such manner as the Congress may direct:

A number of electors of President and Vice President equal to the whole number of Senators and Representatives in Congress to which the District would be entitled if it were a State, but in no event more than the least populous State; they shall be in addition to those appointed by the States, but they shall be considered, for the purposes of the election of President and Vice President, to be electors appointed by a State; and they shall meet in the District and perform such duties as provided by the twelfth article of amendment.

Section 2. The Congress shall have power to enforce this article by appropriate legislation.

AMENDMENT XXIV [1964]

Section 1. The right of citizens of the United States to vote in any primary or other election for President or Vice President, for electors for President or Vice President, or for Senator or Representative in Congress, shall not be denied or abridged by the United States or any State by reason of failure to pay any poll tax or other tax.

Section 2. The Congress shall have power to enforce this article by appropriate legislation.

AMENDMENT XXV [1967]

Section 1. In case of the removal of the President from office or his death or resignation, the Vice President shall become President.

Section 2. Whenever there is a vacancy in the office of the Vice President, the President shall nominate a Vice President who shall take the office upon confirmation by a majority vote of both houses of Congress.

Section 3. Whenever the President transmits to the President pro tempore of the Senate and the Speaker of the House of Representatives his written declaration that he is unable to discharge the powers and duties of his office, and until he transmits to them a written declaration to the contrary, such powers and duties shall be discharged by the Vice President as Acting President.

Section 4. Whenever the Vice President and a majority of either the principal officers of the executive departments, or of such other body as Congress may by law provide, transmit to the President pro tempore of the Senate and the Speaker of the House of Representatives their written declaration that the President is unable to discharge the powers and duties of his office, the Vice President shall immediately assume the powers and duties of the office as Acting President.

Thereafter, when the President transmits to the President pro tempore of the Senate and the Speaker of the House of Representatives his written declaration that no inability exists, he shall resume the powers and duties of his office unless the Vice President and a majority of either the principal officers of the executive departments, or of such other body as Congress may by law provide, transmit within four days to the President pro tempore of the Senate and the Speaker of the House of Representatives their written declaration that the President is unable to discharge the powers and duties of his office. Thereupon Congress shall decide the issue, assembling within forty-eight hours for that purpose if not in session. If the Congress, within 21 days after receipt of the latter written declaration, or, if Congress is not in session, within 21 days after Congress is required to assemble, determines by two-thirds vote of both houses that the President is unable to discharge the powers and duties of his office, the Vice President shall continue to discharge the same as Acting President; otherwise, the President shall resume the powers and duties of his office.

AMENDMENT XXVI [1971]

Section 1. The right of citizens of the United States, who are 18 years of age or older, to vote shall not be denied or abridged by the United States or any State on account of age.

Section 2. The Congress shall have the power to enforce this article by appropriate legislation.

Presidential Elections

Year	Candidates	Party	Popular vote	Electoral vote
1789	**George Washington**			69
	John Adams			34
	Others			35
1792	**George Washington**			132
	John Adams			77
	George Clinton			50
	Others			5
1796	**John Adams**	Federalist		71
	Thomas Jefferson	Republican		68
	Thomas Pinckney	Federalist		59
	Aaron Burr	Republican		30
	Others			48
1800	**Thomas Jefferson**	Republican		73
	Aaron Burr	Republican		73
	John Adams	Federalist		65
	Charles C. Pinckney	Federalist		64
1804	**Thomas Jefferson**	Republican		162
	Charles C. Pinckney	Federalist		14
1808	**James Madison**	Republican		122
	Charles C. Pinckney	Federalist		47
	George Clinton	Independent-Republican		6
1812	**James Madison**	Republican		128
	DeWitt Clinton	Federalist		89
1816	**James Monroe**	Republican		183
	Rufus King	Federalist		34
1820	**James Monroe**	Democratic-Republican		231
	John Quincy Adams	Independent-Republican		1
1824	**John Quincy Adams**	Republican	108,740	84 (elected by the House of Representatives)
	Andrew Jackson	Republican	153,544	99
	Henry Clay	Republican	47,136	37
	William H. Crawford	Republican	46,618	41

Year	Candidates	Party	Popular vote	Electoral vote
1828	**Andrew Jackson**	Democratic	647,286	178
	John Quincy Adams	National Republican	508,064	83
1832	**Andrew Jackson**	Democratic	688,000	219
	Henry Clay	National Republican	530,000	49
	William Wirt	Anti-Masonic	255,000	7
	John Floyd	National Republican		11
1836	**Martin Van Buren**	Democratic	762,678	170
	William H. Harrison	Whig	549,000	73
	Hugh L. White	Whig	146,000	26
	Daniel Webster	Whig	41,000	14
1840	**William H. Harrison**	Whig	1,275,017	234
	Martin Van Buren	Democratic	1,128,702	60
1844	**James K. Polk**	Democratic	1,337,243	170
	Henry Clay	Whig	1,299,068	105
	James G. Birney	Liberty	62,300	
1848	**Zachary Taylor**	Whig	1,360,101	163
	Lewis Cass	Democratic	1,220,544	127
	Martin Van Buren	Free-Soil	291,263	
1852	**Franklin Pierce**	Democratic	1,601,274	254
	Winfield Scott	Whig	1,386,580	42
1856	**James Buchanan**	Democratic	1,838,169	174
	John C. Frémont	Republican	1,335,264	114
	Millard Fillmore	American	874,534	8
1860	**Abraham Lincoln**	Republican	1,866,452	180
	Stephen A. Douglas	Democratic	1,375,157	12
	John C. Breckinridge	Democratic	847,953	72
	John Bell	Constitutional Union	592,631	39
1864	**Abraham Lincoln**	Republican	2,213,665	212
	George B. McClellan	Democratic	1,805,237	21
1868	**Ulysses S. Grant**	Republican	3,012,833	214
	Horatio Seymour	Democratic	2,703,249	80
1872	**Ulysses S. Grant**	Republican	3,596,745	286
	Horace Greeley	Democratic	2,843,446	66
1876	**Rutherford B. Hayes**	Republican	4,036,572	185
	Samuel J. Tilden	Democratic	4,284,020	184
1880	**James A. Garfield**	Republican	4,449,053	214
	Winfield S. Hancock	Democratic	4,442,032	155
	James B. Weaver	Greenback-Labor	308,578	
1884	**Grover Cleveland**	Democratic	4,874,986	219
	James G. Blaine	Republican	4,851,981	182
	Benjamin F. Butler	Greenback-Labor	175,370	
1888	**Benjamin Harrison**	Republican	5,444,337	233
	Grover Cleveland	Democratic	5,540,050	168
1892	**Grover Cleveland**	Democratic	5,554,414	277
	Benjamin Harrison	Republican	5,190,802	145
	James B. Weaver	People's	1,027,329	22

Year	Candidates	Party	Popular vote	Electoral vote
1896	**William McKinley**	Republican	7,104,779	271
	William J. Bryan	Democratic; Populist	6,502,925	176
1900	**William McKinley**	Republican	7,219,530	292
	William J. Bryan	Democratic; Populist	6,356,734	155
1904	**Theodore Roosevelt**	Republican	7,628,834	336
	Alton B. Parker	Democratic	5,084,401	140
	Eugene V. Debs	Socialist	402,460	
1908	**William H. Taft**	Republican	7,679,006	321
	William J. Bryan	Democratic	6,409,106	162
	Eugene V. Debs	Socialist	420,820	
1912	**Woodrow Wilson**	Democratic	6,293,454	435
	Theodore Roosevelt	Progressive	4,119,538	88
	William H. Taft	Republican	3,484,980	8
	Eugene V. Debs	Socialist	897,011	
1916	**Woodrow Wilson**	Democratic	9,129,606	277
	Charles E. Hughes	Republican	8,538,221	254
1920	**Warren G. Harding**	Republican	16,152,200	404
	James M. Cox	Democratic	9,147,353	127
	Eugene V. Debs	Socialist	919,799	
1924	**Calvin Coolidge**	Republican	15,725,016	382
	John W. Davis	Democratic	8,385,586	136
	Robert M. LaFollette	Progressive	4,822,856	13
1928	**Herbert C. Hoover**	Republican	21,392,190	444
	Alfred E. Smith	Democratic	15,016,443	87
1932	**Franklin D. Roosevelt**	Democratic	22,809,638	472
	Herbert C. Hoover	Republican	15,758,901	59
	Norman Thomas	Socialist	881,951	
1936	**Franklin D. Roosevelt**	Democratic	27,751,612	523
	Alfred M. Landon	Republican	16,618,913	8
	William Lemke	Union	891,858	
1940	**Franklin D. Roosevelt**	Democratic	27,243,466	449
	Wendell L. Willkie	Republican	22,304,755	82
1944	**Franklin D. Roosevelt**	Democratic	25,602,505	432
	Thomas E. Dewey	Republican	22,006,278	99
1948	**Harry S. Truman**	Democratic	24,105,812	303
	Thomas E. Dewey	Republican	21,970,065	189
	J. Strom Thurmond	States' Rights	1,169,063	39
	Henry A. Wallace	Progressive	1,157,172	
1952	**Dwight D. Eisenhower**	Republican	33,936,234	442
	Adlai E. Stevenson	Democratic	27,314,992	89
1956	**Dwight D. Eisenhower**	Republican	35,590,472	457
	Adlai E. Stevenson	Democratic	26,022,752	73
1960	**John F. Kennedy**	Democratic	34,227,096	303
	Richard M. Nixon	Republican	34,108,546	219
1964	**Lyndon B. Johnson**	Democratic	43,126,233	486
	Barry M. Goldwater	Republican	27,174,989	53

Year	Candidates	Party	Popular vote	Electoral vote
1968	**Richard M. Nixon**	Republican	31,783,783	301
	Hubert H. Humphrey	Democratic	31,271,839	191
	George C. Wallace	Amer. Independent	9,899,557	46
1972	**Richard M. Nixon**	Republican	47,168,963	520
	George S. McGovern	Democratic	29,169,615	17
	John Hospers	Republican (noncandidate)		1
1976	**Jimmy Carter**	Democratic	40,827,292	297
	Gerald R. Ford	Republican	39,146,157	240
	Ronald Reagan	Republican (noncandidate)		1
1980	**Ronald Reagan**	Republican	43,899,248	489
	Jimmy Carter	Democratic	35,481,435	49
	John Anderson	Independent	5,719,437	
1984	**Ronald Reagan**	Republican	53,428,357	525
	Walter Mondale	Democratic	36,930,923	13
1988	**George Bush**	Republican	47,946,422	426
	Michael Dukakis	Democratic	41,016,429	112

Date of Statehood

Delaware	December 7, 1787	Michigan	January 16, 1837
Pennsylvania	December 12, 1787	Florida	March 3, 1845
New Jersey	December 18, 1787	Texas	December 29, 1845
Georgia	January 2, 1788	Iowa	December 28, 1846
Connecticut	January 9, 1788	Wisconsin	May 29, 1848
Massachusetts	February 6, 1788	California	September 9, 1850
Maryland	April 28, 1788	Minnesota	May 11, 1858
South Carolina	May 23, 1788	Oregon	February 14, 1859
New Hampshire	June 21, 1788	Kansas	January 29, 1861
Virginia	June 25, 1788	West Virginia	June 19, 1863
New York	July 26, 1788	Nevada	October 31, 1864
North Carolina	November 21, 1789	Nebraska	March 1, 1867
Rhode Island	May 29, 1790	Colorado	August 1, 1876
Vermont	March 4, 1791	North Dakota	November 2, 1889
Kentucky	June 1, 1792	South Dakota	November 2, 1889
Tennessee	June 1, 1796	Montana	November 8, 1889
Ohio	March 1, 1803	Washington	November 11, 1889
Louisiana	April 30, 1812	Idaho	July 3, 1890
Indiana	December 11, 1816	Wyoming	July 10, 1890
Mississippi	December 10, 1817	Utah	January 4, 1896
Illinois	December 3, 1818	Oklahoma	November 16, 1907
Alabama	December 14, 1819	New Mexico	January 6, 1912
Maine	March 15, 1820	Arizona	February 14, 1912
Missouri	August 10, 1821	Alaska	January 3, 1959
Arkansas	June 15, 1836	Hawaii	August 21, 1959

Population
of the United States

1790	3,929,214	1890	62,947,714
1800	5,308,483	1900	75,994,575
1810	7,239,881	1910	91,972,266
1820	9,638,453	1920	105,710,620
1830	12,860,453	1930	122,775,046
1840	17,063,353	1940	131,669,275
1850	23,191,876	1950	150,697,361
1860	31,443,321	1960	178,464,236
1870	39,818,449	1970	203,302,031
1880	50,155,783	1980	226,545,805
		1990	249,657,000 (est.)

Territorial Expansion

Louisiana Purchase	1803	The Philippines	1898–1946
Florida	1819	Puerto Rico	1899
Texas	1845	Guam	1899
Oregon	1846	American Samoa	1900
Mexican Cession	1848	Canal Zone	1904
Gadsden Purchase	1853	U.S. Virgin Islands	1917
Alaska	1867	Pacific Islands Trust	
Hawaii	1898	Territory	1947

Photo Acknowledgments

CHAPTER 1

Page 2, New York Public Library; page 5, Courtesy Library of Congress; page 7, New York Public Library; page 13, Courtesy Library of Congress; page 15, Courtesy Library of Congress; page 18, New York Public Library Picture Collection.

CHAPTER 2

Page 23, New York Public Library; page 26, Courtesy Library of Congress; page 30, Courtesy Library of Congress; page 33, Courtesy Library of Congress.

CHAPTER 3

Page 36, New York Public Library; page 39, Rare Book Division, The New York Public Library, Astor, Lenox, and Tilden Foundations; page 43, Courtesy Library of Congress; page 45, Courtesy Library of Congress; page 47, Courtesy Library of Congress.

CHAPTER 4

Page 51, New York Public Library; page 54, Courtesy Library of Congress; page 57, Quaker Collection, Haverford College Library; page 58, Quaker Collection, Haverford College Library; page 63, Courtesy Library of Congress.

CHAPTER 5

Page 67, New York Public Library; page 68, Courtesy of the New York Historical Society, New York City; page 80, Courtesy Library of Congress; page 84, Yale University Art Gallery, bequest of Eugene Phelps Edwards.

CHAPTER 6

Page 88, New York Public Library; page 90, Courtesy Library of Congress; page 100, Courtesy Library of Congress; page 101, Courtesy Library of Congress; page 107, Anne K. Brown Military Collection, Brown University Library.

CHAPTER 7

Page 111, New York Public Library; page 113, Courtesy Library of Congress; page 120, Courtesy Library of Congress; page 123 (top), Courtesy Library of Congress; page 123 (bottom), Courtesy Library of Congress.

CHAPTER 8

Page 128, Courtesy of The New York Historical Society, New York City; page 129, Courtesy Library of Congress; page 131, Courtesy Library of Congress; page 138, Yale University Art Gallery, gift of T. Dwight Partridge.

CHAPTER 9

Page 144, Field Museum of Natural History; page 146, Courtesy of The New York Historical Society, New York City; page 149, Courtesy Library of Congress; page 151, Courtesy Library of Congress; page 155, Courtesy Library of Congress.

CHAPTER 10

Page 161, The Bettmann Archive, Inc.; page 164, The Bettmann Archive, Inc.; page 165, Carpenter Center for Visual Arts, Harvard University; page 167, Courtesy Library of Congress; page 173, Courtesy Library of Congress.

CHAPTER 11

Page 180, New York Public Library; page 183, Courtesy Library of Congress; page 185, Courtesy Library of Congress; page 194, Courtesy Library of Congress.

CHAPTER 12

Page 197, painting by Joseph Kyle, Collection of Mrs. Alan Valentine, Smithsonian Institution; page 198, Courtesy Library of Congress; page 200, Courtesy Library of Congress; page 203, Collection of the New York Public Library, Astor, Lenox, and Tilden Foundations; page 204, Courtesy Library of Congress; page 207, The Granger Collection, N.Y.

CHAPTER 13

Page 220, New York Public Library; page 223, Courtesy of The New York Historical Society, New York City; page 226, Courtesy Library of Congress; page 237, George Eastman House.

CHAPTER 14

Page 241, New York Public Library; page 246, Courtesy Library of Congress; page 248, George Eastman House; page 254, The Bettmann Archive, Inc.; page 258, Courtesy Library of Congress.

CHAPTER 15

Page 264, Courtesy Library of Congress; page 268, Courtesy Library of Congress; page 271, Courtesy Library of Congress; page 273, Courtesy Library of Congress; page 277, Courtesy Library of Congress.

CHAPTER 16

Page 281, New York Public Library; page 283, Courtesy Library of Congress, page 285, State Historical Society of Wisconsin; page 294, Courtesy Library of Congress.

CHAPTER 17

Page 300, Courtesy Library of Congress; page 303, The Bettmann Archive, Inc.; page 305, Prints Division, The New York Public Library, Astor, Lenox, and Tilden Foundations; page 306, Kansas State Historical Society, Topeka; page 313, Prints Division, The New York Public Library, Astor, Lenox, and Tilden Foundations.

CHAPTER 18

Page 317, New York Public Library; page 320, Lloyd Ostendorf Collection; page 323, Boston Athenaeum; page 324, The Bettmann Archive, Inc.; page 329, Courtesy Library of Congress.

CHAPTER 19

Page 335, Courtesy Library of Congress; page 343, Valentine Museum, Richmond, Virginia; page 348, Courtesy Library of Congress; page 350, Courtesy Library of Congress; page 354, Courtesy Library of Congress.

CHAPTER 20

Page 360, New York Public Library; page 367, Courtesy Library of Congress; page 369, Courtesy Library of Congress; page 372, Courtesy Library of Congress; page 381, Culver Pictures.

Index